THE HISTORY OF THE BRITISH COAL INDUSTRY

Volume 2

1700–1830: THE INDUSTRIAL REVOLUTION

THE HISTORY OF
THE BRITISH COAL
INDUSTRY

Volume 2

1700–1830: The Industrial Revolution

by
MICHAEL W. FLINN
with the assistance of
DAVID STOKER

CLARENDON PRESS · OXFORD
1984

Oxford University Press, Walton Street, Oxford OX2 6DP

London Glasgow New York Toronto
Delhi Bombay Calcutta Madras Karachi
Kuala Lumpur Singapore Hong Kong Tokyo
Nairobi Dar es Salaam Cape Town
Melbourne Auckland
and associated companies in
Beirut Berlin Ibadan Mexico City Nicosia

Oxford is a trade mark of Oxford University Press

Published in the United States
by Oxford University Press, New York

British Library Cataloguing in Publication Data
Flinn, M. W.
    The history of the British coal industry.
    Vol. 2: 1700–1830
    1. Coal mines and mining—Great Britain—History
    I. Title
    338.2'724'0941   HD9551.5
    ISBN 0-19-828283-4

Library of Congress Cataloging in Publication Data
Flinn, Michael W. (Michael Walter), 1917–
    The history of the British coal industry.
    Bibliography: v. 2, p.
    Includes index.
    Contents: —v. 2. 1700–1830, the Industrial
    Revolution.
    1. Coal trade—Great Britain—History. 2. Coal
    mines and mining—Great Britain—History. I. Stoker,
    David S. II. Title.
    HD9551.5.F58 1983   338.2'724'0841   83-4194
    ISBN 0-19-828283-4 (v. 2)

Typeset by Joshua Associates, Oxford
Printed in Great Britain
at the University Press, Oxford

Foreword

By Lord Ezra

No comprehensive history of coal-mining in Britain has hitherto been written, despite the pre-eminence of the industry in the British economy and the wealth of records it has left: the sheer scale of such a task was daunting. This gap has been increasingly felt, notwithstanding the large number of books and articles which have been published covering particular aspects of the industry in recent years.

I was, therefore, very happy to be able as Chairman of the National Coal Board to help to initiate in 1975 the *History of the British Coal Industry*, of which this volume is the first to be published. It is the second in the chronological span of five volumes covering the industry from its early beginnings right up to the very recent past. In it Professor Flinn charts eloquently and skilfully the growth of the coal-mining industry in the eighteenth and early nineteenth centuries, and sets a high standard which I am confident the later volumes will maintain. I am delighted to welcome this first fruit of such a major undertaking and look forward eagerly to reading the other four volumes.

December 1982.

Acknowledgements

Even a very brief perusal of the footnotes to the text of this book will reveal that it is heavily based on the manuscript records of colliery undertakings of the eighteenth and early nineteenth centuries. Because coal-mining was widely distributed throughout Britain in this period, these sources for the history of the industry are similarly widely dispersed, and a first requirement for the preparation of this book was to locate and study these archives in scores of libraries, record offices, and estate muniment rooms around the country. To make this possible, at the start of this project the National Coal Board appointed Dr David Stoker as research assistant. His time was wholly occupied with this field of research and it will readily be appreciated therefore that his contribution to this book has been substantial. In addition to making available to me in scrupulously presented form the fruits of our sifting of a huge number of manuscript collections, Dr Stoker has also contributed to this volume with advice on numerous aspects of the interpretation of this material, and by the detailed criticism of early drafts of the book. I would like to take this opportunity to thank him for his invaluable collaboration at all stages in the book's preparation.

Both Dr Stoker and I were assisted with much courtesy and kindness by innumerable archivists and librarians, and it is a great pleasure to be able now formally to thank them all. At the risk of making individious distinctions I would like in particular to thank Mr R. Williams and Miss Margaret Norwell of the North of England Institute of Mining and Mechanical Engineers at Neville Hall, Newcastle upon Tyne. The latter's knowledge of the collections of both manuscripts and printed books in the Institute's library guided both of us in the course of a great many visits. Several manuscript collections elsewhere were made available to us by the kindness of their owners, and I would like to thank their Graces the Dukes of Beaufort and Norfolk, the Earl of Crawford and Balcarres, the Earl of Egremont, and Lord Lambton for graciously giving permission to consult their muniments and make use of material from them.

At all stages of my work, from the earliest plans to the final draft, I have benefited from the guidance of the Board's general adviser for this project, Professor Peter Mathias, assistance I acknowledge with pleasure and gratitude. Other colleagues in the Board's history project have also helped considerably by comments on drafts, or collaboration in the compilation of some of the statistical tables, and I would like to thank particularly Professor Roy Church, Dr John Hatcher, Dr John Kanefsky, and Dr Stephen Roberts. I am extremely grateful, too, to Mr Brian Brown and his colleagues in the Photographic Unit of the Board's North-east Area Headquarters for much beautiful and skilled work in the preparation of the photographs of contemporary prints from which the book's illustrations have been selected. The typing of the final draft was undertaken by Mrs A. Merryweather, Mrs P. Owen, and Mrs A. Tudor, and I am most grateful to them for their patience, skill, and accuracy.

M. W. F.

The Publishers deeply regret to announce the sudden death of Professor Flinn on 29 September 1983. He had completed all the work on the proofs and index of this book before he died.

Contents

Maps

Illustrations

(Between pages 266 and 267)

Tables

References to Sources in Footnotes

Manuscript sources. A list of collections used and the location of the record offices in which they are housed are given in the appropriate section of the bibliography. Abbreviations of record offices are given in 'Abbreviations in notes and bibliography'. In the footnotes the abbreviation of a record office is followed normally by the name of the collection, its reference number (where one has been allocated), and a page or folio number where relevant: thus, 'NuRO Delaval ZDE 310/42', meaning the Delaval manuscripts in the Northumberland County Record Office numbered ZDE in their catalogue, document 310, folio 42. In the manuscript collection of the North of England Institute of Mining and Mechanical Engineers in Newcastle-upon-Tyne the name of the collection is followed by two or three numbers for shelf (in the basement room where all the manuscript collections are housed on consecutively numbered shelves) and volume number on that shelf, with a page or folio number where relevant: thus, 'NEI Brandling 47/12/261', meaning the Brandling collection on shelf 47, volume number 12, folio 261. The Buddle collection, however, is housed separately at the North of England Institute, and is numbered by volume, without shelf numbers. Some volumes in the Buddle collection are divided into parts, and references of these cite the part in roman capitals after the volume number.

Printed books and articles. Works listed in the bibliography are cited in notes by author's name and date of publication only, followed by page references where relevant. For other works a full reference is given in the notes.

Unpublished theses. The full references for all theses used are set out in the thesis section of the bibliography. They are cited in notes by author's name only (followed by the word 'thesis' to indicate the section of the bibliography in which the full references may be found) with date and page numbers where relevant.

Parliamentary papers. References in notes to the principal parliamentary papers used have abbreviated titles which may be easily identified with the full references in the appropriate section of the bibliography. 'Select Committee' is abbreviated as *SC* and Royal Commission as *RC*. References to other papers are given in full in the notes.

Abbreviations in Notes and Bibliography

AA	*Archaeologia Aeliana*
BL	British Library
BPL	Birmingham Public Library
BRO	Bristol City Record Office
CJ	*Commons' Journal*
ClRO	Clwyd County Record Office
CLSG	County Library of South Glamorgan
CoRO	Coventry Record Office
CuRO	Cumbria County Record Office
DeRO	Derbyshire County Record Office
DUJ	*Durham University Journal*
DuRO	Durham County Record Office
EH	*Economic History* (Supplement to *Economic Journal*)
EHR	*Economic History Review*
GPL	Gateshead Public Library
GRO	Gloucestershire County Record Office
HMC	*Historical Manuscripts Commission*
IA	*Industrial Archaeology*
IAR	*Industrial Archaeology Review*
IRSH	*International Review of Social History*
JEH	*Journal of Economic History*
JRL	John Rylands Library, University of Manchester
KM	Kirkcaldy Museum
LCA	Leeds City Archives Department
LEA	Lambton Estate Archives
LaRO	Lancashire County Record Office
NCL	Newcastle City Library
NCRO	Nottingham City Record Office
NEI	North of England Institute of Mining and Mechanical Engineers
NH	*Northern History*
NLS	National Library of Scotland
NLW	National Library of Wales
NoRO	Nottinghamshire County Record Office
NUL	Nottingham University Library
NuRO	Northumberland County Record Office
PP	*Parliamentary Papers*
SCL	Sheffield City Library
ScRO	Scottish Record Office
ShRO	Shropshire County Record Office
SoRO	Somerset County Record Office
StRO	Staffordshire County Record Office

TC & WAAS	*Transactions of the Cumberland and Westmorland Antiquarian and Archaeological Society*
TH	*Transport History*
THSL & C	*Transactions of the Historic Society of Lancashire and Cheshire*
TL & CAS	*Transactions of the Lancashire and Cheshire Antiquarian Society*
TIME	*Transactions of the Institute of Mining Engineers*
TNEIME	*Transactions of the North of England Institute of Mining Engineers*
TNS	*Transactions of the Newcomen Society*
TWRO	Tyne and Wear County Record Office
UBHJ	*University of Birmingham Historical Journal*
UCNW	Library of the University College of North Wales
VCH	*Victoria County Histories*
WaRO	Warwickshire County Record Office
WiRO	Wigan Record Office
WMDL	Wakefield Metropolitan District Library

MAP 1

MIDLANDS, WALES AND SOUTH OF ENGLAND

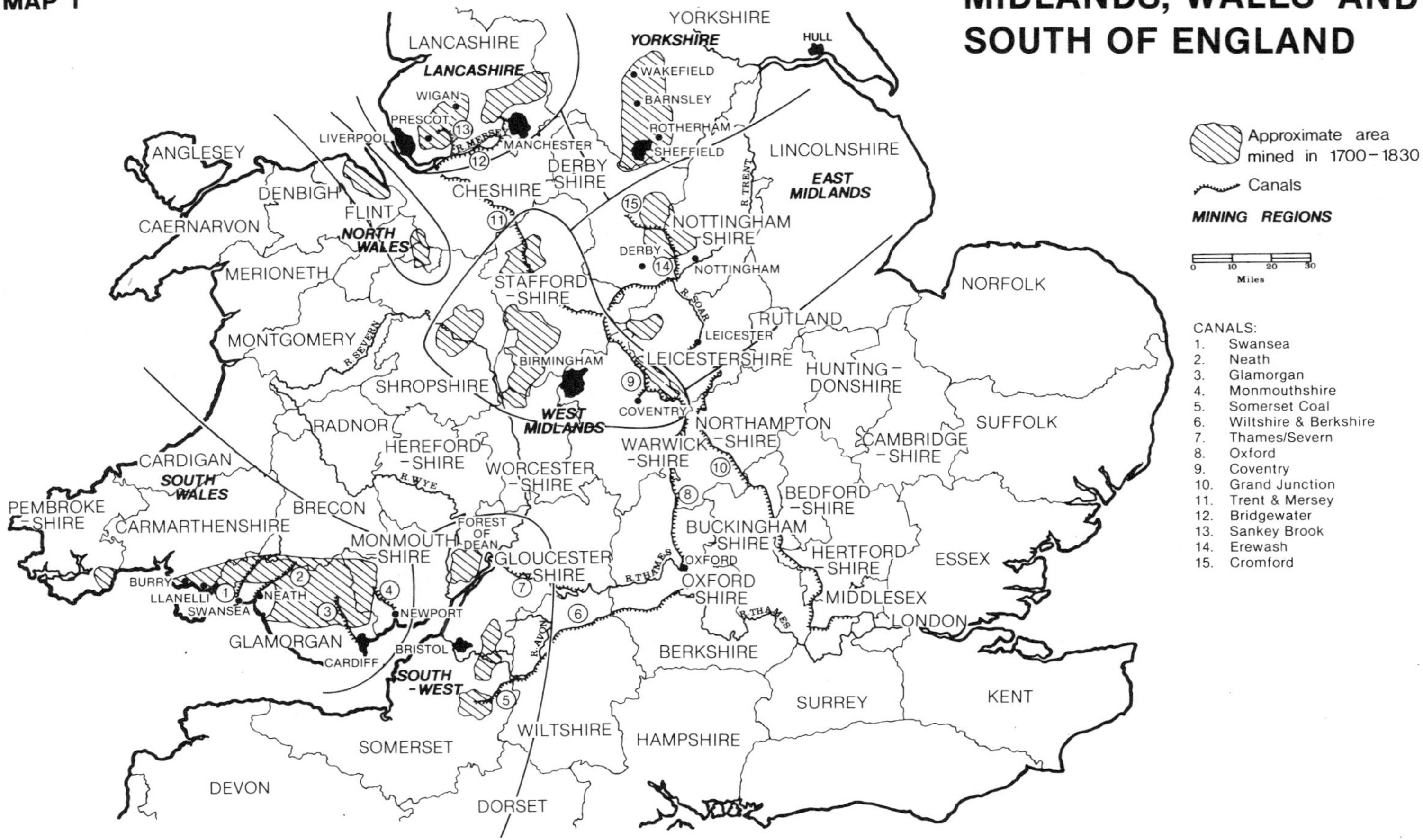
Approximate area mined in 1700–1830
Canals
MINING REGIONS
0 10 20 30
Miles
CANALS:
1. Swansea
2. Neath
3. Glamorgan
4. Monmouthshire
5. Somerset Coal
6. Wiltshire & Berkshire
7. Thames/Severn
8. Oxford
9. Coventry
10. Grand Junction
11. Trent & Mersey
12. Bridgewater
13. Sankey Brook
14. Erewash
15. Cromford
YORKSHIRE
YORKSHIRE
HULL
WAKEFIELD
BARNSLEY
ROTHERHAM
SHEFFIELD
LANCASHIRE
LANCASHIRE
WIGAN
PRESCOT
LIVERPOOL
R. MERSEY
MANCHESTER
LINCOLNSHIRE
EAST MIDLANDS
R. TRENT
ANGLESEY
DENBIGH
FLINT
CHESHIRE
DERBY -SHIRE
CAERNARVON
NORTH WALES
NOTTINGHAM -SHIRE
DERBY
NOTTINGHAM
MERIONETH
STAFFORD -SHIRE
R. SOAR
NORFOLK
RUTLAND
LEICESTER
MONTGOMERY
R. SEVERN
BIRMINGHAM
LEICESTERSHIRE
HUNTING -DONSHIRE
SHROPSHIRE
COVENTRY
WEST MIDLANDS
NORTHAMPTON -SHIRE
SUFFOLK
RADNOR
HEREFORD -SHIRE
WORCESTER -SHIRE
WARWICK -SHIRE
CAMBRIDGE -SHIRE
CARDIGAN
SOUTH WALES
R. WYE
BEDFORD -SHIRE
PEMBROKE -SHIRE
BRECON
CARMARTHENSHIRE
FOREST OF DEAN
BUCKINGHAM -SHIRE
MONMOUTH -SHIRE
GLOUCESTER -SHIRE
HERTFORD -SHIRE
ESSEX
OXFORD
R. THAMES
OXFORD -SHIRE
BURRY
LLANELLI
SWANSEA
NEATH
NEWPORT
MIDDLESEX
LONDON
GLAMORGAN
CARDIFF
BRISTOL
R. AVON
BERKSHIRE
SOUTH -WEST
SURREY
KENT
WILTSHIRE
HAMPSHIRE
SOMERSET
DEVON
DORSET

MAP 2

NORTH OF ENGLAND

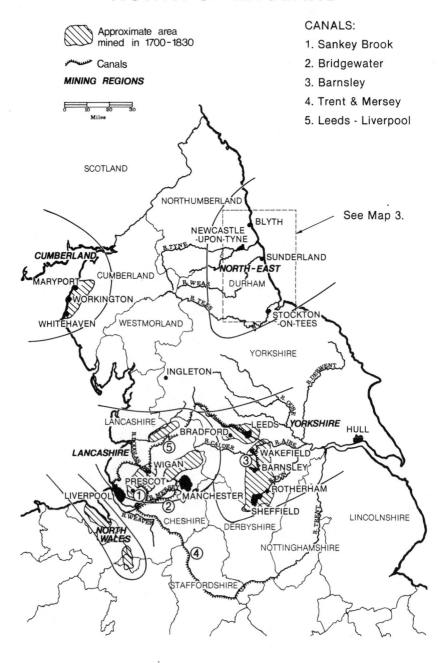

Approximate area mined in 1700–1830

Canals

MINING REGIONS

0   10   20   30
Miles

CANALS:

1. Sankey Brook
2. Bridgewater
3. Barnsley
4. Trent & Mersey
5. Leeds - Liverpool

SCOTLAND

NORTHUMBERLAND

BLYTH

See Map 3.

NEWCASTLE
-UPON-TYNE

R. TYNE

SUNDERLAND

CUMBERLAND

NORTH-EAST

MARYPORT

CUMBERLAND

R. WEAR

DURHAM

WORKINGTON

R. TEES

WHITEHAVEN

WESTMORLAND

STOCKTON
-ON-TEES

YORKSHIRE

INGLETON

R. DERWENT

R. OUSE

LANCASHIRE

BRADFORD

LEEDS **YORKSHIRE**

HULL

R. CALDER

LANCASHIRE

⑤

WAKEFIELD

WIGAN

③ BARNSLEY

R. AIRE

PRESCOT

ROTHERHAM

LIVERPOOL

① ② MANCHESTER

SHEFFIELD

R. WEAVER

CHESHIRE

DERBYSHIRE

LINCOLNSHIRE

R. TRENT

**NORTH
WALES**

④

NOTTINGHAMSHIRE

STAFFORDSHIRE

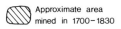

THE NORTH-EAST

MAP 3

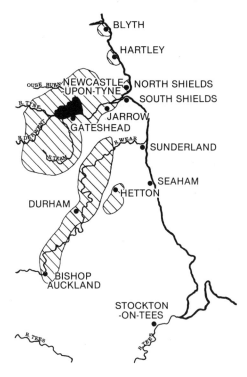

Approximate area
mined in 1700–1830

Miles
0 1 2 3 4 5

BLYTH

HARTLEY

OUSE BURN NEWCASTLE-UPON-TYNE NORTH SHIELDS

SOUTH SHIELDS

R. TYNE

JARROW

R. DERWENT

GATESHEAD

R. WEAR

SUNDERLAND

R. TEAM

SEAHAM

HETTON

DURHAM

BISHOP
AUCKLAND

STOCKTON
-ON-TEES

R. TEES

R. TEES

SCOTLAND

MAP 4

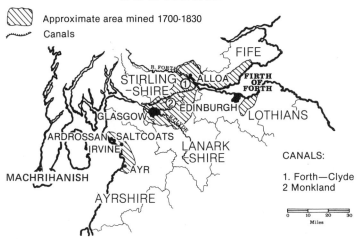

Approximate area mined 1700-1830

Canals

FIFE

R. FORTH

STIRLING
-SHIRE

ALLOA

FIRTH
OF
FORTH

EDINBURGH

LOTHIANS

GLASGOW

R. CLYDE

ARDROSSAN SALTCOATS

IRVINE

LANARK
-SHIRE

AYR

MACHRIHANISH

AYRSHIRE

CANALS:

1. Forth—Clyde
2 Monkland

Miles
0 10 20 30

Chapter 1

The Development of Coal-Mining, 1700–1830

At the opening of the eighteenth century most of the coal mined in Britain was used for domestic heating. Since the population of Britain at that time was little more than one-tenth of its late twentieth-century level, and since the use of coal for this purpose was heavily confined to town-dwellers, the demand was accordingly small. Though the technical problems of using coal rather than wood as a fuel had already been solved in a number of industries, these were mostly minor industries and their total consumption of coal scarcely rivalled that of the domestic consumers. The technical problems of smelting non-ferrous metals with coal had been solved by the end of the seventeenth century; but though coal could be used in the manufacture of iron goods from bar iron, as yet technical barriers prevented its use in the actual making of iron. Coal was also used to boil sea-water and brine in salt-making, in the manufacture of dye-stuffs, lime, bricks, and glass, and in the drying of malt. But the list of industrial uses for coal was still short: power in industry was drawn mainly from horses and moving water, though extensive use was made of wind-power in flour-milling, for example, and even in mining itself.

To these constraints on the demand for coal were added severe limitations on its supply. Mining, as the preceding volume in this series shows, was already in the early eighteenth century an old-established industry, and the most easily accessible seams had long been worked out. Though small quantities of coal were still being taken from shallow workings in some inland areas, a high proportion of the output in the major exporting coalfields was already coming from mines deep enough to raise acute technical problems of drainage and ventilation. Until these could be solved the only possibility of raising, or even of maintaining, production levels was the lateral extension of coalfields, but this recourse in its turn ran into problems of rising overland transport costs. The latter, indeed, already constituted one of the major restrictions on coal supply. The bulk and weight of coal were so high in relation to its value that freight charges quickly became disproportionate to pithead costs and drove the delivered price of coal beyond the reach of many potential consumers. Water transport, of course, was immensely cheaper than overland carriage, but only a small proportion of potential domestic and industrial consumers were accessible by the coastal and river navigations of the early eighteenth century, while many rich coal seams were so remote from the nearest navigable water as to be unavailable, for all practical purposes, so long as overland freight costs remained so high.

During the period after 1700 many of these constraints on both demand and supply were swept away, and by 1830 coal was being used for almost all the purposes it is used for today except in the generation of electricity. Within the opening two decades of the eighteenth century the two most vital breakthroughs had been achieved. Abraham Darby demonstrated the possibility of using coal, converted first into coke, as a substitute for charcoal in the smelting of iron. Later in the century the invention of potting and puddling made possible the use of coal in the conversion of pig iron, for which there were only limited uses in industry, to bar iron, the principal raw material for the making of iron wares. Thomas Newcomen contrived a practical form of utilization of steam-power using coal as the fuel. Restricted at first to pumping, steam-power was adapted in the last quarter of the eighteenth century to rotary motion, in which form it could drive machinery of all kinds. Later still, in the early years of the nineteenth century, the development of high-pressure steam-engines led to the evolution of the steam-locomotive and the marine-engine, and the modern railway and steamship were born. With the invention of methods of extracting tar and gas from coal in the last decades of the eighteenth century the gamut of principal modern coal usages was spanned.

Several of these new coal-consuming industrial processes had feedbacks that benefited the mining industry itself. Newcomen's steam-pump indeed found its principal employment at first in the drainage of coal-mines, and when steam-power was later adapted to rotary motion its earliest uses included the winding of coal and its surface haulage by locomotives. Few of these developments would have been possible without the great expansion in the manufacture of iron made practicable by the conversion during the eighteenth century to coke-smelting and -forging. Though the problems of drainage and ventilation of mines raised by the need to tap ever deeper seams could never be said to have been fully solved before 1830, if only because the persistent extension of both depth and scale of underground working progressively intensified the problems, technology advanced fast enough to permit most of these challenges to be met and to allow the industry to respond to rising demand. While these technological responses liberated the British mining industry from many of its earlier constraints, of no less importance were the developments of water, road, and rail transport that made possible great increases in the economically viable distances for the inland carriage of coal. Without these, freight charges would effectively have strangled the development made possible by other technical improvements.

Technology, therefore, whether in the mines themselves, in consuming or potentially consuming industries, or in the transportation of coal, broke down the barriers that had formerly restricted output at the same time as it stimulated expansion by creating major new sources of demand. That so much technological effort and inventiveness was directed towards both supply of, and demand for, coal has been traditionally attributed to the long history of both coal-mining and its industrial utilization before 1700. On the demand side, experience gained during the previous century in the design of reverberatory furnaces, the choice of refractories, in boiler-making and the manufacture of iron plates as well as in coke-making, provided an essential and invaluable foundation for the new technologies of the eighteenth century. In the mines themselves, the long experience on the one hand of the problems of depth and on the other of the surface movement of coal created, by the late seventeenth century, a body of technicians who were already masters of an impressive technology and who, under the persistent pressure of growing demand, demonstrated the ingenuity and resourcefulness that allowed the speedy adaptation and adoption of new techniques. The names of many of those responsible for these advances in mining technology have rarely reached the pages of the more general textbooks of eighteenth- and early nineteenth-century industrial history. They were practical craftsmen, working exclusively in the extraordinarily isolated world of the coal-mining industry and seldom feeling the need to publicize their achievements to wider horizons.

This absence of publicity for the achievements of British mining technology—Harris has pointed out that there were no published works in English of importance in this field between 'J.C.'s' *The Compleat Collier* of 1708 and John Curr's *The Coal Viewer* of 1797—has hitherto tended to mislead historians into assuming that, in contrast, for example, to the textile, iron, and engineering industries in the eighteenth century, there were few technological innovations of significance in coal-mining. Later chapters in this book demonstrate the falsity of this view. Some of the key inventions of the eighteenth and early nineteenth centuries were directly stimulated by the technical problems of coal extraction and transport, while throughout the period the industry's technicians showed an avidity for new, cost-saving technologies that was not exceeded by those of any other industry.

Nor was the fact that in the case of the coal industry many of the new methods were expensive of capital a major barrier. The very nature of the industry threw it into the hands of the major landowners, one of the very few groups in British society able to respond in the eighteenth and early nineteenth centuries to repeated calls for what were, by the standards of the day, unprecedentedly large investments. Their ability to do so was enhanced in this period by other financially rewarding developments in agriculture that probably pushed their incomes up faster than those of most other groups at that time; but it was no less important that, unlike landowning aristocracies elsewhere, they were not inhibited by any distaste for direct involvement in industrial ventures. In the mining industry dukes vied with marquises and baronets in the quest for mining profits, and when their own resources proved unequal to the voracious demands of the industry for more, and yet more, capital, they unhesitatingly sought partnerships with mercantile, industrial, and banking interests.

From the point of view of industrial development Britain's good fortune in the eighteenth and early nineteenth centuries was to possess huge reserves of coal not only well distributed over most of the country, but also of the variety of qualities required for the new energy and industrial uses. Most, though by no means all, of these resources were already being exploited at the opening of the eighteenth century. In some coalfields the sheer depth of economically viable seams, or the extremely gassy nature of the coal itself, discouraged the investment necessary to exploit them; in others the distance between workable seams and potential consumers, in combination with lack of access to water transport, hindered development. As technical advances in mining itself, however, as well as in coal transport and in coal-consuming industries, shifted the parameters of development, it was to be expected that the conditions surrounding the exploitation of individual coalfields would vary. Thus the history of mining in any one coalfield, as in the whole British economy, must be studied as an interplay between the changing pattern of demand and the response of mining technology. In this process of interaction the distribution of production between the coalfields already working at the opening of the eighteenth century must inevitably be shifted substantially. A similar redistribution must also have occurred within coalfields as local developments created new patterns of consumption.

In the remainder of this chapter these shifting regional and national patterns will be examined briefly in the context of the geological conditions in individual coalfields. In the remaining chapters this kind of broad overview must give way to a more detailed scrutiny of particular developments in technology, management, capitalization, marketing, and the organization of mining labour. A short conclusion returns once again to some of the broader issues raised by the role of an expanding industry within an economy also undergoing rapid transformation in its other sectors.

i. *The regional development of the industry*

For the purposes of this history, the coal-producing areas of Britain have been grouped into ten mining regions, as follows: Scotland, Cumberland, Lancashire, North Wales, South Wales, the South-west, the West Midlands, the East Midlands, Yorkshire, and the North-east. Within some of these regions there were several clearly separated coalfields. In the following survey of the broad growth of the mining industry during the period 1700 to 1830 the development of each mining region will be examined separately before turning to the aggregate picture.

In Scotland, with only two unimportant exceptions, the coal seams worked in the eighteenth and early nineteenth centuries were all located in the central belt. The exceptions were at Machrihanish in Kintyre, and at Brora in Sutherland, the latter developed by the Marquis of Stafford from 1812 as part of his grandiose scheme for converting the crofters into industrial workers.[1] In the central lowlands three main areas of the coalfield were exploited. Ayrshire coal was initially mined near the coast north of Ayr at Saltcoats, Stevenston, and Irvine. The development of waggonways and railways in the early nineteenth century led to some exploitation of mines further inland. A second mining area stretched from Lanarkshire south of the Clyde in a north-easterly belt through Renfrewshire, Dunbartonshire, Stirlingshire, Clackmannan, and West Lothian into west and central Fife. Mines were well distributed throughout this area where there were many workable seams. At Bo'ness on the south shore of the Firth of Forth there were, for example, eight seams with a total thickness of thirty feet, and further north in Fife twelve with a total of forty-six feet. Domestic demand in Glasgow and the miscellaneous industries of the upper Clyde provided markets for the mines of the western end of this area already in the early eighteenth century, while those at the eastern end had access to coastal shipping on both shores of the Firth of Forth. From

[1] E. Richards, *The Leviathan of Wealth* (London, 1973), 176–7.

the mid-eighteenth century the rise of coke iron-making, first at Carron on the south shore of the Firth of Forth, and later inland in Lanarkshire and Ayrshire, led to the growing importance of the southern part of this region. The third area, actually linked by dipping seams under the Firth of Forth to the Fife coalfield, lay in Midlothian and East Lothian to the south and east of Edinburgh. It was a small, intensively worked area. Apart from the rise of demand for iron-making, which led to increased output in the inland area from north Ayrshire through Lanarkshire to upper Forthside, the growth of output before 1830 in the Scottish coalfield was not accompanied by any radical geographical shift of coal production from one part of the coalfield to another.

The Scottish coalfields provided a variety of coals. Some of the splint coal produced in West Lothian was of such a high quality that it was able to compete successfully in small quantities in London for domestic heating against the high-grade coals of the North-east. In the early nineteenth century it was found possible to smelt iron ore, produced from the same mines, with splint coal raw, not coked—a valuable competitive saving. Saltpans on both the Ayrshire coast and on the Firth of Forth provided a valuable outlet for the poorer small coal. In general the Scottish coal seams were severely warped and fractured, making mining conditions difficult and expensive. 'The coal in Scotland', wrote Charles Beaumont in 1789, 'lies in a very different manner to that in England; the metals and minerals being in a state of confusion, unknown to the south of the island. . . . The minerals and metals are found and worked in all directions from the horizontal to near the perpendicular.'[2]

Mining on the north-west Cumberland coast was in its infancy at the opening of the eighteenth century. There had, it is true, been a very small trade in coal throughout most of the seventeenth century, but this seems to have been confined to the southern end of the coalfield. The workable Cumberland coalfield stretched along the Solway Firth coast from just south of Whitehaven to terminate in the north at Aspatria fault. There were some outcrops inland, but the seams dipped in general westwards beyond the coast. The exposed coalfield measured about sixteen miles from south-west to north-east by about four and a half miles wide. Five seams were workable, of which the most valuable, called at Whitehaven the Main Bank, contained eight different qualities of coal in bands up to three and a half feet in thickness. The first major steps in the development of the coalfield were taken by Sir John Lowther (d. 1706), who added to the land

    [2] Beaumont 1789, 7. This survey of the Scottish mining region is based mainly on Jars 1774-81, I, 265-82; and Duckham 1970, chap. 1.

owned by his family around Whitehaven by purchases of more coal-bearing land in the same area during the second half of the seventeenth century. By the end of the seventeenth century his major Whitehaven colliery was producing 20,000 tons a year and a successful trade to Dublin had been established. These enterprises were developed even more strenuously by Sir John's successor, Sir James, who took over the estate in 1706 (though formally inheriting only in 1725). The Whitehaven mines were divided into two complexes known as the Howgill colliery on the south-west side of the port, and the Whingill colliery to the north-east. With the aid of a noted family of viewers, the Speddings, the Lowthers expanded their colliery enterprises steadily throughout the eighteenth century, largely on the basis of the Irish trade. The Lowther output of 20,000 tons at the beginning of the eighteenth century reached 100,000 tons about 1740 and 200,000 tons by 1781, after which output stabilized until 1830, in spite of the opening of major new pits in the early years of the nineteenth century.

To the north of Whitehaven mining was largely in the hands of three families, the Christians, the Curwens, and the Senhouses, and the interests of the first two were amalgamated by a marriage in 1782. At Harrington a Curwen colliery was opened in 1783, and by 1804 was shipping 41,000 tons through Workington. The Curwen colliery at Workington itself was started in 1771, and had similarly achieved an output of 41,000 tons by 1816. A small colliery at Clifton was worked by a Newcastle owner between the late seventeenth and late eighteenth centuries, and another, possibly the furthest inland of the Cumberland collieries, at Greysouthen, seven miles from Workington, produced 21,000 tons in 1816. In the extreme north of this coalfield the Christians successfully opened a major colliery at Broughton in 1755 under lease from the Earl of Egremont, and produced 40,000 tons per year by 1777. This, and the neighbouring small Birkby colliery, shipped coal through Maryport, as did Ellenborough colliery, won by the Senhouses in the 1720s.

The principal growth of the Cumberland coalfield was during the first eighty years of the eighteenth century. It remained heavily dependent on Irish, particularly Dublin, demand, and, in the face of competition from other west coast coalfields, this market seems not to have allowed much growth in Cumberland between 1780 and 1830. The decline of demand from salt-making is unlikely to have been fully compensated by the construction of some small ironworks. Gabriel Jars estimated the output of the whole coalfield in the mid-1760s at 360,000 tons, and though there were important developments at Workington and Harrington after that date, the growth of production cannot have been very great after 1780.[3]

Further south the Lancashire coalfield, which spilled over in the south-east into north Cheshire, was worked quite extensively in the early eighteenth century by a large number of small mines. The whole coalfield was situated south of the River Ribble, and two main areas—one small and one large—may be distinguished. There were a number of small mines scattered over an area of central Lancashire from Darwen through Whalley and Burnley to near Colne, but the principal mining area of Lancashire lay south of a line from Chorley to Rochdale. This south Lancashire coalfield reached at its south-western tip to within a few miles of Liverpool and stretched in an arc through Wigan to the Irwell valley. Beyond Manchester it thinned out to continue to Stockport and near Macclesfield, though the quality of the coal remained high. The Arley Mine seam, for example, was reckoned to be the equal of Wallsend, the most famous of the north-east coals. It yielded a large quantity of gas and its slack made good coke. Cannel, formed from the spores of plants rather than from the woody tissues, was fairly common in the south-western portion of the coalfield, but in workable seams only in the neighbourhood of Wigan. It was soft and light, with a high gas content and burned brightly, giving off much heat. Elsewhere there were good house and steam coals. But in all parts the seams were thin and often of great inclination. There were many faults, some having throws of up to 3,000 feet.

There had been a long history of mining in Lancashire already by the opening of the eighteenth century, and the economic buoyancy of the Merseyside region from the last years of the seventeenth century onwards ensured steady expansion. The coalfield suffered from one major handicap: at no point did it border the coast or a major river. In the early eighteenth century, therefore, its output was limited by the small demands of the local landsale and the high cost of even short overland hauls to the major urban consuming centres of Manchester and Liverpool. It was this limitation that delayed the development of the many small, scattered mines around Rochdale. From early in the eighteenth century, however, the coalfield was the scene of major turnpike and waterway developments discussed in chapter 6 below, and by the 1760s the south-west sector of the coalfield was well enough served by cheap water transport in all the economically important directions to be able to respond to the

[3] This survey of the Cumberland mining region is based mainly on Jars 1774-81, I, 238-49; Fletcher 1876-7; Moore 1893-4, 616-32; *VCH Cumberland*, II, 348-83; Nef 1932, I, 70-2; Hughes 1965, 133-84; Wood 1971, 199-253; and Beckett 1981, chap. 3.

steady growth of demand. The chronology of expanding demand, however, had an uneven geographical impact. At first the pull of Liverpool and the industries of lower Merseyside and north Cheshire led to the disproportionately fast development of the extreme south-western sector in the St. Helens and Prescot area; later, with the rapid growth of cotton manufacture on the Preston–Manchester axis across the east of the coalfield, demand in that area began to redress the balance and allow the development of mines in inland areas hitherto undeveloped on account of the absence of demand.

Thanks to recent work we are now well informed about the growth of production in the south-western area of the coalfield. Langton believes that from an output of about 28,000 tons in the 1690s—marginally greater than the Cumberland output of the same period—there was a three-fold expansion of production in this part of the coalfield during the following fifty years, with an almost similar expansion in the next half-century. Without further estimates for the early nineteenth century or any comprehensive estimates for the eastern section of the coalfield, it is not possible to trace the growth of the output of the coalfield as a whole up to 1830 with any degree of confidence. But the progress of both population and industrialization in the area served by the eastern section suggests that continuing growth on the scale indicated for the south-west by Langton must certainly have occurred there too.[4]

The small North Wales mining region lay in two divisions: the northern section, almost wholly in Flintshire, stretched from Point of Ayr in the north to Hawarden, a few miles west of Chester, in the south. The seams, which included some cannel, much favoured for lime-burning, were heavily fractured and faulted, but this had allowed a certain amount of outcropping that ensured an early start to mining in this coalfield. A few miles to the south, and separated from the northern section by the great Bala fault, there was a further concentration of mines in a small area around the town of Wrexham. With the draining of the Malldraeth marsh in south-west Anglesey after 1811 small-scale mining developed there, too. An important difference between the Flintshire and Wrexham divisions of the coal-field was that the northern division had access to the sea on the Dee estuary, while the Wrexham area was landlocked. Both were areas of well-established mines at the opening of the eighteenth century. The slow silting-up of the Dee estuary, however, during the eighteenth century gradually shifted the balance of output away from the Hawarden area in favour of the more northerly mines with access

[4] This survey of the Lancashire mining region is based mainly on *VCH Lancashire*, II, 356–9; Wadsworth 1949; Anderson 1975; and Langton 1979.

to the coast at Bagillt and Mostyn. Though the Flintshire coalfield never succeeded in the Irish trade on the scale of Cumberland, the development of local industries, particularly after 1750, ensured it a steadily growing landsale. In the Wrexham area, however, growth was negligible until the establishment of iron-making in the area. While Bersham, near Wrexham, was the location of one of the earliest coke furnaces in the 1720s, the real expansion of iron-smelting here, and consequently of the mining attached to it, was after 1800. In 1828 there were forty-one pits on the 500-acre Brymbo Hall estate near Wrexham, and by 1830 it is probable that coal output in the Wrexham area slightly exceeded that of the northern half of the coalfield.[5]

The South Wales mining region is geographically much more extensive than that of North Wales, but in the period before 1830 mining was confined mainly to only two parts of it. In the Gower area around Swansea and Neath, where the coalfield borders the sea, the industry was already well established at the beginning of the eighteenth century, and continued to develop there. But the southern fringe of the coalfield turns inland to the east of Port Talbot and though the greatest reserves of coal were in the eastern section of the coalfield, at no point does this section reach within ten miles of the coast. In the absence, therefore, of major new land-sale industrial markets, the coal of the eastern valleys of this coal-field was destined to remain virtually unworked until the second half of the eighteenth century, while the mines of the smaller belt of coal from Llanelli to Neath prospered throughout the period.

In the western section of the coalfield the Upper Coal Series was so extensively faulted as to be difficult and expensive to work, and initially it was the Pennant Series that was more extensively worked in the coastal area between Llanelli and Neath. In particular there were numerous mines around Morriston and Llansamlet on the neck of the Gower peninsula to the north and north-west of Swansea. The heavy faulting, however, was not always seen as a disadvantage in an area of relatively small-scale mining. Edward Martin of Morris-ton, a leading expert on mining in the Swansea area, observed in 1806 that

contrary to what is generally supposed, a very obvious advantage arises from these slips [faults]. By throwing the strata of coal up and down in various ways they are spread over the face of the coalfield and the slips throw more and more of them up so near the surface of the ground as to be within our reach than could otherwise be got were the strata to keep the same dip without any inter-ruption or break.

[5] This survey of the North Wales mining region is based mainly on Dodd 1929, 199–210; and 1951, 189–203; Rawson 1941, 112–29; Lerry 1946; and Gruffydd thesis 1981.

The Lower Coal Series, however, were the richest in this area, but they outcropped in the Tawe and Neath valleys and although some small workings were opened up in the upper Tawe valley in the 1750s, the exploitation of these inland areas had to await the coming of canals towards the end of the eighteenth century. The two lower series produced a wide range of useful coals—bituminous coal used for coking, gas, and domestic heating; steam coal (earlier called 'coking coal', the name 'steam coal' not apparently being used before 1832); and anthracite, often known here as 'stone coal', used for malting and heating. The name 'culm' was commonly given in this coalfield to the small coal of stone coal or anthracite or semi-anthracite, and of the steam coal.

This section of the coalfield developed during the eighteenth and early nineteenth centuries on the strength of three principal outlets. There was a steady trade to Ireland, mainly to the southern ports; there was an equally steady trade supplying fuel for the steam-pumps that drained the Cornish copper mines, to which was added some trade to the ports of Somerset, north Devon, and north Cornwall; and there was a growing landsale to the industries of the coalfield itself, the principal consumers among which were the smelters of the Cornish copper carried by the cross-channel colliers as a return cargo. Much of the growth of these latter trades was accommodated from the late eighteenth century by the expansion of mining inland up the Tawe valley as far as Ystalyfera and the Neath valley as far as Aberpergwm, an expansion made possible by the sanctioning of the Neath canal in 1791 and of the Swansea canal in 1794.

At the eastern end of the region the beginning of large-scale mining waited for two developments—the beginnings of coke iron-making in the 1750s and 1760s mainly in the upper reaches of the valleys that lead down to Newport; and the opening of the Glamorganshire and Monmouthshire canals in 1790 and 1792 respectively. The location of the ironworks was determined, given that coal was plentiful over a fairly wide area, primarily by the siting of the iron-mines, and these were so far from the coast that initially no serious consideration seems to have been given to the possibility of exporting coal. The two canals were constructed for the purpose of carrying the finished iron to port, and it was only when this facility was available that coal also began to flow from the upper valleys. Perhaps more significant in view of subsequent developments in the second half of the nineteenth century was the fact that the Glamorganshire Canal passed the mouth of the Rhondda valleys at Treforest, and it was to this junction that in 1809 Walter Coffin built a tramroad to the first important Rhondda mine to open up the most westerly of the great valleys of the eastern section of the coalfield. The first coal was exported from Cardiff and Newport in 1797. But the markets served by seasale from the eastern mines were not among the faster-growing ones, and a high proportion of the coal mined in the eastern section continued to feed the iron furnaces. In 1828, when the combined seasale from Cardiff and Newport amounted to 455,000 tons, the ironworks of the upper valleys probably consumed over 1.5 million tons.

Thus in the whole region taken together the growth during the eighteenth century was steady rather than dramatic, deriving mainly from the growth of copper-smelting in the Swansea area and the coastal and Irish trades, with the rise of iron-making in the upper eastern valleys contributing in the latter part of the century. The first thirty years of the nineteenth century, in contrast, probably witnessed almost a three-fold rise in output which mainly reflected the enormous expansion of iron-making.[6]

The mining region designated 'South-west' consisted of three separate divisions. The Forest of Dean coalfield occupied the area between the River Wye and the Severn estuary mainly within the triangle bounded by Coleford, Cinderford, and Lydney, the last place serving as the principal water outlet for the coalfield. Across the Severn there was the Kingswood coalfield, a rather scattered area running in a belt from Brislington, south-east of Bristol, to Yate to the north-east. Thirdly, there was the Somerset coalfield centred on a small area around Radstock and Midsomer Norton, some ten miles south-west of Bath.

The Forest of Dean coalfield was an oval-shaped basin surrounded by belts of carboniferous limestone and millstone grit. The Cannop fault belt, a feature of the predominantly north–south faulting, divided the main basin in the east from the Worcester basin in the west. The Forest was unique among British coalfields in being located in a Royal Forest. Technically this meant that the prime economic consideration in the management of the area was the supply of timber, but the existence of both iron and coal in the Forest had tended to allow mining to take precedence over forestry. Coal had been mined since the Middle Ages, and though there is widespread evidence of iron-making in Roman times, the modern charcoal industry originated only in the early seventeenth century. Mining was regulated by a Mine Law Court and carried on by 'free miners'. The rights of free mining could be exercised only by those

---

[6] This survey of the South Wales mining region is based mainly on John 1943, 93–102, and 1950, chaps. 1 and 4; Walker thesis 1947, 144–72 and Appendices; Lewis 1959, chaps. 2 and 3; Thomas thesis 1974, 39–46; and Symons 1979.

born in the Hundred of St. Briavels, and a claim to a 'gale'—mining rights within a radius of one hundred yards of a strike—had to be registered at the Mine Law Court. Under these conditions, coal-mining tended to be monopolized by individual families working on an extremely small scale. Free miners worked in small teams or 'companies'. In 1788, 442 miners worked ninety-nine mines in sixty-six companies. The average mine at this period produced little more than twenty tons of coal per week.

Until the late eighteenth century, therefore, the Forest of Dean was a very small producer of coal. In the early decades of the nineteenth century, under pressure of wider market opportunities opened up by the construction of tramways and rising industrial demand, the pattern of organization began to change. The Crown, influenced by the need to increase the supply of shipbuilding timber during the French wars, began to tighten its hitherto lax administration of the Forest, diminishing the value of the varied perquisites of free mining. Free miners began to show a willingness to enter partnerships with 'foreigners' as a means of 'colouring' the mining activities of incomers with the capital necessary for larger-scale working. The Crown did not oppose the leasing or sale of gales by free miners to foreigners, and in 1835 the Forest Commissioners were able to report that 'by the greater outlay of capital which has taken place under the new system, the custom of working by partners and apprentices has been nearly abolished and has been succeeded by the working of the mines by hired labour.'[7] By 1841 foreigners controlled 55 per cent of the capacity of the Forest coalfield. The influx of capital allowed mining to move from the rim of the basin where the free miners had tapped the seams by drifts towards the centre of the basin where the greater depth called for vertical shafts and steam-drainage. Output rose from less than 100,000 tons a year in the late eighteenth century to 300,000 tons by the 1840s.[8]

The Somerset coal seams were mined in the eighteenth century in a small area in the north-east of the county around Radstock and Midsomer Norton. This area in turn was divided into two by the east–west Farmborough fault zone. In the northern part, around Paulton, the coal was exposed, and it was in this area that most mining took place in the first half of the eighteenth century. In the southern, or Radstock basin, the coal measures were concealed between Triassic and Jurassic overlays. Apart, therefore, from

---

[7] *Fourth Report of Dean Forest Commissioners*, PP 1835 XXXVI, 8–9, quoted by Davis thesis 1959, 45.

[8] This survey of the Forest of Dean coalfield is based mainly on Hart 1953 and 1971; Davis thesis 1959, 17–19, 62–73; and Fisher 1978.

occasional exposed patches, the workable seams here tended to be fairly deep, and were often severely faulted and steeply dipping. Somerset mining moved on to a new scale in the 1750s when local landowners and capitalists took leases on Duchy of Cornwall land around Midsomer Norton and Radstock. Steam drainage was introduced. There was further expansion when the Somerset Coal Canal and its associated waggonways came into use in the first decade of the nineteenth century. The isolation of the coalfield from the sea and from major industrial centres, however, confined this coalfield to landsale markets, while the severe conditions of faulting and dip kept costs high. Between them, therefore, both supply and demand factors tended to limit the expansion of this coalfield before the coming of the railways.

Because the Gloucestershire or Bristol coalfield was entirely exposed it could be worked by shallow bell-pits for sale in nearby Bristol. Thus in the Kingswood area in the late seventeenth century there were said to be seventy mines worked by 123 miners in all. The thinness of seams at the southern extremity of this coalfield led to the abandonment of working there by the end of the eighteenth century, and larger-scale development took place in the Kingswood area to the east of Bristol, where the Duke of Beaufort's Two Mile Hill pit was said to have reached a depth of 640 feet in 1779, and in the northern end of this elongated coalfield to the north-east of Bristol around Yate, Tortworth, and Pucklechurch.[9]

In the Midlands, coal was mined in no less than seven counties, and the geography of the industry is complex. For convenience the area has been divided into two mining regions, but several separate coalfields may be distinguished. The East Midlands mining region embraced all the mines in the counties of Nottinghamshire and Derbyshire, and the quite detached coalfield in the western part of the county of Leicestershire. In north Derbyshire, in the neighbourhood of Chesterfield, the coalfield is contiguous with the south Yorkshire coalfield, but the latter has been allocated to a separate mining region. The West Midlands mining region is even more diffuse. Mining took place in east Warwickshire, in both north and south Staffordshire (the latter coalfield embracing the Dudley enclave of Worcestershire), and in Shropshire.

Though the Warwickshire coalfield covers about eighty square miles in the triangle between Tamworth, Nuneaton, and Coventry, before 1830 coal was mined only along the western rim in a narrow belt running from Tamworth in the north to near Coventry in the

[9] This survey of the Somerset and Bristol coalfields is based mainly on *VCH Gloucestershire*, II, 236; Bulley 1953 and 1955; Davis thesis 1959, 6–13, 28–34, 55–60; and Clew 1970.

south. This belt was rarely more than one mile from east to west and in most places mining was concentrated in a strip a few hundred yards wide. The reason for this was the extremely sharp dip of the principal seams from the outcrop—mostly thirty degrees or more towards the south-west, so that at a few hundred yards from the outcrop even the highest seam lay beyond the depths accessible to the drainage and ventilation technologies of the eighteenth century. To complicate matters further, the coal measures here were overlain by the heavily water-bearing Lower Keuper Sandstone which presented unusually severe drainage problems. Though the coalfield's limits on three sides were set by major faults, within these bounds there were few faults. Although the coal made acceptable house fuel, because it was non-caking it cut the coalfield out of the growing market for coke later in the eighteenth century.

In the early eighteenth century the principal concentration of pits was at the southern end of the mining strip in the area near Bedworth. Although this was at that time the nearest coalfield to London, the area was not well served by navigable rivers, and the cost of overland carriage to London was absolutely prohibitive. Markets were initially restricted, in consequence, largely to the nearby city of Coventry. This coalfield, therefore, stood to gain much from the development of canals in the later eighteenth century, and it is hardly surprising that the Warwickshire coalowners were particularly active in the promotion of turnpike roads and canals. As these were developed broadly in the second half of the eighteenth century the increase as well as the changed orientation of demand encouraged development of first the central section of the coalfield around Atherstone, and later, but not until the 1820s, of the northern section towards Tamworth.[10]

In Staffordshire there were three distinct mining areas—south Staffordshire or the Black Country, Cannock Chase, and north Staffordshire. The first two of these areas were divided from each other by the Bentley faults running east–west near Wolverhampton and Walsall. South of these faults in the Black Country the principal source of coal was the tremendous Ten-Yard Coal. This was not so much a single seam thirty feet thick as a series of closely juxtaposed seams in which three groups of seams, known as the Top, Middle, and Bottom Coals, provided a variety of coals for all purposes. Towards the Bentley faults in the north these seams became more distinctly separated. The 'Thick Coal', as these seams were sometimes called, was rarely more than 400 feet below the surface and presented

[10] This survey of the Warwickshire coalfield is based mainly on *VCH Warwickshire*, II, 217-24; Mitcheson 1950; White theses 1969 and 1973; Grant thesis 1977.

the heaviest concentration in the country of coal at shallow depths. There is ample evidence of extensive exploitation throughout the period but no estimates of output, and it is probable that extreme disintegration of landholding in the area inhibited large-scale development. Clearly the coalfield supplied the numerous metal-workers of Birmingham and the Black Country with fuel. With the coming of canals in the last quarter of the eighteenth century, its markets, hitherto limited to a narrowly restricted landsale area, were much extended, and by the early nineteenth century coalowners in Leicestershire and Warwickshire were complaining of Black Country competition. Further expansion took place with the growth of a local coke iron industry from the 1780s. Thus it is likely that the fastest growth in south Staffordshire occurred during the last quarter of the eighteenth century, though fast growth certainly continued through the early decades of the nineteenth.

The Bentley faults threw the coal on the Cannock Chase side down by up to 350 feet, and the seams splayed out further. Further north the seams dipped beneath a Triassic rock overlay, and even in the exposed part of the field glacial drift impeded development. The coal here did not coke well, and a coke iron industry never replaced the lingering charcoal iron industry. For all these reasons the Cannock Chase field did not develop in this period on a scale comparable with that of its neighbour to the south. Further north still, in north Staffordshire, coal was worked in four areas, but one of these, in the Potteries, dominated. Here, in spite of much faulting and steep dips, there was great thickness of workable coal: the seams in the Potteries were said to have the greatest thickness of workable seams in Britain. While this field benefited from the development of the pottery industry after the middle of the eighteenth century, the major stimulus came from the opening of the Trent and Mersey canal in 1777.

Taken together, the three mining areas in Staffordshire contributed notably to the expansion of the British mining industry in the late eighteenth and early nineteenth centuries. Output at the beginning of the eighteenth century is likely to have been small and to have grown only slowly during the first half of the eighteenth century. With the stimulus of canal construction and the growth of the coke iron industry in the second half of the century, however, the relative importance of this coalfield grew, and by 1830 it was among the two or three largest in the country.[11]

The West Midlands mining region was completed by the Shropshire

[11] This survey of the Staffordshire coalfield is based mainly on VCH Staffordshire, II, 68-107; Court 1938, 149-69; Raybould 1968 and 1973, chap. 6.

coalfield. Though this coalfield extended some twenty-five miles from Wellington and Newport in the north to the Wyre Forest and Clee Hills in the south, it was nowhere more than four or five miles wide and barely one mile wide at Bridgnorth. Apart from an area of concentrated working astride the Severn at Coalbrookdale, mining was scattered and on a small scale. The principal section of this coalfield benefited from the early development of the coke iron industry at the Coalbrookdale works, though even here the fastest growth occurred during the second half of the eighteenth century. When the Shropshire iron industry failed to maintain its relative share of British iron output in the early nineteenth century in the face of the advance of the Staffordshire and South Wales producers, Shropshire coal output, too, began to lose ground relatively.[12]

In the Leicestershire coalfield of the East Midlands mining region working was concentrated in a relatively small area in the north-west of the county. Mining on a moderate scale was already established at the beginning of the eighteenth century in the neighbourhood of Measham, Coleorton, Swannington, and Lount. As in other Midland areas the absence of water navigation until later in the eighteenth century restricted sales to limited landsale markets. By the 1780s the best coal had been worked out in the Measham and Oakthorpe area. There was some expansion both to the north and south of Ashby-de-la-Zouch in the early decades of the nineteenth century in response to the creation of waterways and railways. Thus until the late eighteenth century coal production in Leicestershire was mainly concentrated in the Coleorton and Swannington area a few miles to the east of Ashby, but as a result of transport development around the turn of the century the centre of gravity shifted a few miles westwards.

The main producing area in the East Midlands, however, was further north in Nottinghamshire and Derbyshire. Once again, the isolation of this area from water transport in the early eighteenth century inhibited development and urban consumption tended to draw production to the neighbourhood of the towns, particularly Derby and Nottingham. The opening of the Erewash canal in 1779 proved to be a major stimulus.[13]

To the north of Chesterfield the Derbyshire coalfield merged with that of Yorkshire. Here, in the eighteenth century, mining was mainly concentrated in two areas: in south Yorkshire in the triangle

[12] This survey of the Shropshire coalfield is based mainly on Brown 1963-5 and 1976; Trinder 1973; and Goodwin thesis 1978.
[13] This survey of the East Midlands mining region is based mainly on *VCH Leicestershire*, II, 30-7; and C. P. Griffin 1978a.

formed by Barnsley, Rotherham, and Sheffield; and, in the West Riding, in the Leeds and Bradford area. There was, in addition, a small coalfield of shallow pits at Ingleton, worked by bell-pits throughout the eighteenth and early nineteenth centuries. In south Yorkshire the seams dip gently to the east, encouraging the earlier development on the western rim around Silkstone and in Sheffield itself. Seams were of a good thickness—particularly the 'Barnsley Thick' at between eight and nine feet thick near Hoyland and Elsecar —and provided a useful variety of coals. In south Yorkshire the lack of a water outlet in the early eighteenth century was to some extent made good by demand for coal from a vigorous metal-working industry, but the development of waterways—the Don navigation in 1733 and the Barnsley canal in 1793—broadened markets in the second half of the eighteenth century and even allowed this coalfield to compete with the North-east in the east-coast trade. More important, however, was the development of the coke iron industry after 1765 which led to a growing concentration of mining on the Sheffield–Rotherham axis. Further north the opening of the Aire-Calder navigation in 1699 encouraged the development of collieries within road transport distance of this route to markets in the East and North Ridings. This development was pushed further in the late eighteenth and early nineteenth centuries by the extension of river navigations and the construction of canals.[14]

Throughout the period 1700 to 1830, however, the British coal-mining industry was dominated by the north-east coalfield. This domination arose initially out of the ease of access in this area to seemingly inexhaustible supplies of high-quality house coal, to the coalfield's location astride two navigable rivers close to the sea, and, in spite of a long sea journey, to the lack of competition from any other coalfield on account of prohibitively long overland hauls in the principal market for house coal in London. Large-scale exploitation of this coalfield for the London market had started in the sixteenth century so that by the beginning of the eighteenth century the most easily won coal had already been worked out. But as coal in this coalfield became more difficult and expensive to mine in terms both of capital and current costs, the coalfield retained its supremacy by virtue of its ability to generate both the large-scale organization and the technology necessary to keep average costs at a level that continued to discourage competition from other coalfields in London. But the North-east was heavily dependent upon the east-coast trade

---

[14] This survey of the Yorkshire mining region is based mainly on Cox thesis 1960; A. Harris 1968, 313-18; Fletcher thesis 1973; Goodchild 1978, and 'The coal mining industry of the Lower Calder Valley, 1700–1860', typescript in WMDL, n.d.

and the London market in particular, and as other sources of demand developed during the eighteenth and early nineteenth centuries, the North-east, in spite of steady growth, slowly sacrificed something of its former dominant share of the national market.

The north-east coalfield extends on the east coast from the River Coquet in Northumberland to Hartlepool in County Durham. It stretches forty-eight miles from north to south, and at its widest point is twenty-four miles wide. At the opening of the eighteenth century the coals mined were in the Upper Coal Group, principally the High Main Seam which varied from two to eleven feet in thickness. It was mostly of a useful thickness of five to eight feet and was easily worked at shallow or moderate depths starting from the outcrops. Below the High Main were other workable seams—the Brockwell, the Main, and the Low Main. The general dip is very gradually eastwards, which encouraged early mining up-river rather than nearer the sea. This geological fact was of considerable importance to the development of the coalfield since it threw much of the early mining above Newcastle which had grown up at the lowest bridge point some ten miles from the mouth of the River Tyne. First, this allowed the mercantile groups in Newcastle to exercise a total control over the trade down-river; and, second, it required the use of river vessels, the keels, to transport the coal down-river to the sea-going colliers at Shields which were too large and unwieldy to penetrate sufficiently far up the river to load directly. The control of the river passage, a mere ten to fifteen miles, and of access to it, was thus central to the organization of this coal trade.

Within the workable area on Tyneside the seams formed a shallow basin round the rim of which they outcropped south of the source of the River Team on the high ground in the Pontop and Tanfield area. The faults in this coalfield run mainly east–north-east to west-south-west. The most important of these, the Ninety Fathom Dyke, with a throw to the north of anything from 250 to 1,000 feet, ran across the north of Newcastle to the Tyne near Lemington. For a long time this set the northern limit to mining on Tyneside. The Butterknowle fault, with a downthrow to the south, set the southern limit across central Durham. To the east of a line running south from South Shields, west of Sunderland, then in an arc embracing Houghton-le-Spring and Hetton towards the southern limits of the coalfield in County Durham, the coalfield is overlain with a thick covering of magnesian limestone. North of the Ninety Fathom Dyke coal was obtainable at workable depths at first only near the coast at Hartley and at one or two small landsale collieries inland. Not until the early nineteenth century had drainage and ventilation techniques advanced sufficiently to permit mines to be driven down to the High Main Seam immediately to the north of the Ninety Fathom Dyke where mining was still close enough to the Tyne to make seasale possible.

The Tyneside section of the coalfield was thus an area that can be sharply delineated. Within the coalfield its northern boundary until the nineteenth century was set by the Ninety Fathom Dyke fault. On its western and south-western boundary the high land (up to 1,000 feet above sea level) of the watershed between the Team and the Derwent set the limit to the waggonway carriage of coal down to the Tyne. To the south and east the boundary was made by the watershed between the Team and the Wear, and finally by the magnesian limestone overlay. The watersheds were effective bounds because the horse-power of waggonways could only cope with the downhill draught of full coal waggons. Not until the introduction of inclined planes operated by stationary steam-engines in the early nineteenth century could these bounds be transcended.

To the south of the Tyneside section was the area served by the River Wear, a smaller and more winding river. Sunderland, at its mouth, was on the magnesian limestone overlay, but keel transport was possible as far up-river as Lambton at the east of Chester-le-Street. This mining area was not extensive, however, being limited by the watersheds on either side of the Wear, the limit of navigability on the Wear, and the western edge of the magnesian limestone overlay.

Until the late eighteenth century it was assumed that the area of magnesian limestone was barren of coal, and in any case the depth of the bottom of the overlay lay beyond the range of current drainage technology. As early as 1772 borings had been made through the overlay and by 1793 it had been penetrated to depths of 396 feet and 505 feet respectively. These had reached the Three Quarters and Five Quarters seams but not the valuable Lower Main and Hutton seams which here were a great deal lower. Early in the nineteenth century, however, the geologist and surveyor, William Smith, already experienced in the Somerset coalfield, persuaded Colonel Braddyll, a major landowner on the magnesian limestone, to undertake exploratory borings.[15] Coal, at considerable but by then workable depth, was discovered, and an important new area of mining in east Durham south of Sunderland opened up rapidly during the 1820s.

The existence of workable coal in west Durham in a fairly broad area to the south-west of the City of Durham around Bishop Auckland

[15] Sill thesis 1974, 67; A. G. Davis, 'William Smith, civil engineer, geologist (1769-1839)', *TNS*, 23 (1942-3), 97.

was well known, but until the early nineteenth century its remoteness from navigable water, urban markets not served more economically from other sources, and concentrations of coal-using industries, had tended to confine mining here to small landsale collieries. Only with the introduction of steam-railways in the late 1820s was this area given an effective link with wider markets that proved a key to more rapid expansion.

In the early eighteenth century the north-east coalfield produced mainly house coal for the London and other east-coast markets. Coal for this market had to be 'great' coal, but the neat, large pieces called for could be produced only together with much 'small' coal. Small coal could be used in the boilers that fired the steam pumps and winding engines of the collieries themselves, and in the saltpans that were an important secondary industry of the coalfield. But these outlets for small coal were restricted and much of it was inevitably unsaleable waste, stowed underground where possible, but otherwise brought expensively to the surface, screened out, then burnt, used for road-mending, or dumped. Until the development of railways and steamships after 1830 there was relatively little use for the steam coals later to be an important product of the deep coalfield north of the Ninety Fathom Dyke. Up to 1830 the immediate Tyne valley continued to be the main source of the high-grade house coal, and the term 'Wallsend' coal, though strictly applicable only to the coal from this huge colliery on the north bank of the Tyne east of Newcastle, came to be commonly applied to all the high-grade house coals of Tyneside. The south-west Durham district produced excellent coking coal which ultimately became the foundation of the Tees-side (Cleveland) iron industry of the nineteenth century. East Durham and upper Tyneside produced good gas coals. Thus the north-east coalfield, originally noted primarily for its house coal, was able, as it grew geographically in the later eighteenth and early nineteenth centuries, to meet the growing demand for a wide range of coals.

The geographical configuration of the Tyne and Wear valleys combined with the lie of seams underground, with current technological limitations, and with the limited range of demand, to concentrate mining in the North-east at the opening of the eighteenth century in a rather restricted area of the upper Tyne, west of Newcastle and Gateshead, and astride the rivers Derwent and Team, tributaries of the Tyne from the south. Here the steeply rising valley sides allowed for the natural drainage of moderately shallow mines. But the depths to which natural drainage was possible were virtually worked out even in this area by the early eighteenth century and drainage by horse-power was of limited utility only. The geographical drift of mining in the early decades of the eighteenth century, therefore, was in a southerly and south-westerly direction towards the high ground of the Tanfield–Pontop area. For the plentiful seams of this area to be worked an effective system of waggonways was essential, since the further parts of the area were up to ten miles from the Tyne. But the configuration of this hilly country is such that these waggonways were inevitably channelled into the Derwent valley, a bottleneck in which wayleaves could be controlled relatively easily by a small number of landowners.

The adoption of steam-pumping, surprisingly a rather slow process in the North-east, began to change this situation towards the middle of the eighteenth century. Though problems of effective drainage were often acute, calling for multiple pumping-engines at some pits, the greater depths made possible by the Newcomen steam-pump allowed mines to be developed further down-river. Elswick, barely beyond the City walls to the west on the north bank, was won by steam-pumping around 1720. But as late as 1750 mining was still heavily concentrated in the area south of the Tyne between the rivers Derwent and Team, with only four out of thirty-one working sea-sale collieries north of the river. Under pressure to continue mining close to the river, and with the ability to work at greater depths, mining was pushed below the High Main Seam to the seams below. The Main Seam was worked from the second quarter of the eighteenth century at Jesmond, Heaton, and Byker. Particularly after 1750, when demand from the east-coast shipping trade began to accelerate, major new pits began to be sunk in the immediate environs of the City of Newcastle, particularly to the north and east of the city. While this geographical shift was occurring the older mines close to the river west of Newcastle were being abandoned and new waggonways were being built in and around the Derwent valley in an effort to maintain freedom of outlet for the mines in the Pontop area.

In the sustained, rapid expansion after the mid 1780s this eastwards drift was combined with a centrifugal pressure that reflected both the growth of demand and the working-out of up-river areas close to the river. This period saw the creation of some of the greatest and deepest of Tyneside collieries—Walker, Wallsend, Bigges Main, and Percy Main on the north bank, Hebburn and Jarrow on the south. The greater depths made possible by improved pumping machinery at last encouraged attempts to reach the coveted High Main coal north of the Ninety Fathom Dyke at Kenton, Coxlodge, Fawdon, and Gosforth. By the 1820s, with the growth in demand for steam coal, there were the beginnings of development in Northumberland, well north of Newcastle.

On Wearside, although there was steady expansion of output from the middle of the eighteenth century, mining for the seasale trade remained confined to a relatively small area to the east of Chester-le-Street, though small landsale collieries were scattered over a much wider area. For most of the eighteenth century the Main and Five Quarter seams in this area provided moderately good house coal, but when, towards the end of the century, the High Main coal on Tyneside was becoming exhausted, the Hutton seam was tapped on Wearside and this provided excellent house coal. This area was transformed, however, when the magnesian limestone overlay was penetrated around 1820 and a major new mining area opened around Hetton to the south of Houghton-le-Spring. This southwards push was accompanied by the creation of a new coal-exporting port at Seaham Harbour. Hetton colliery itself opened in 1822 and quickly became the largest colliery in the country. It was followed during the later 1820s by Elemore, Houghton, North Hetton, and Pittington collieries in the immediate area. While these developments were proceeding during the 1820s attempts were also being made to convert the landsale area of south-west Durham into a seasale area. Though the link, via the Stockton and Darlington railway and its connections, was created by 1825, the development of Stockton-on-Tees as a coal-exporting port and of the Bishop Auckland area as a seasale area was really a feature of the 1830s.[16]

ii. *The growth of output*

The foregoing survey has been conducted largely in non-quantitative terms. Any assessment of the industry's growth during the period from 1700 to 1830, however, must, sooner or later, attempt some estimate of output. Though statistics of colliery output that have come to light are extremely random, there are sufficient to confirm the very reasonable supposition, taking into account the advances in mining technology surveyed in chapters three and four below, that average colliery output grew steadily during the period. These figures are listed in Table 1.1, from which it is clear that, although the general trend of colliery output was upwards, there were, already in the first two-thirds of the eighteenth century, collieries whose outputs would have classed them as major enterprises even in the early nineteenth

[16] This survey of the north-east mining region is based mainly on Smailes 1935, 201–6; Raistrick 1936–7, 140–1; Hall 1862, 41–8; Mott 1962, 338–9, 1964–5, 4–5; and Cromar thesis 1977.

Table 1.1. *Output of selected collieries, 1700–1830*

Colliery	Mining Region	Year(s)	Annual average output (tons)	Source
Griff	W. Mids.	1701–2	10,710	White thesis 1969, 131
Griff	W. Mids.	1705	16,291	White thesis 1969, 131
3 collieries	Lancs.	1718–56	1,047	Langton 1980, 88
Measham	E. Mids.	1721–6	4,092	C. P. Griffin thesis 1969, 185
Swannington	E. Mids.	1724–7	5,866	C. P. Griffin thesis 1969, 185
Broughton	Cumb.	1756–61	8,492	CuRO Leconfield D/Lec/65/7
Greysouthen	Cumb.	1762–72	791	CuRO Leconfield D/Lec/65/7
Lount	E. Mids.	1763–76	3,771	C. P. Griffin thesis 1969, 185
Broughton	Cumb.	1763–93	35,384	CuRO Leconfield D/Lec/65/7, 12
Saltcoats	Scot.	1770–98	c.13,000	Duckham 1973, 22
Worsley	Lancs.	1773–9	41,565	LaRO Bridgewater NCBw/6/1–2
Griff	W. Mids.	1777–80	9,521	Bunker thesis 1952, 61–2
Worsley	Lancs.	1780–9	52,927	LaRO Bridgewater NCBw/6/1–2
Griff	W. Mids.	1782–1805	22,600	Grant thesis 1977, 217
Hawkesbury	W. Mids.	1785–94	29,600	Grant thesis 1977, 217
Worsley	Lancs.	1790–9	75,376	LaRO Bridgewater NCBw/6/1–2
Broughton	Cumb.	1793–1807	41,436	CuRO Leconfield D/Lec/65/12
Worsley	Lancs.	1800–10	86,797	LaRO Bridgewater NCBw/6/1–2
24 collieries	NE	1804	98,933	DuRO Joint Coal Owners' Association 263/not numbered
Hawarden	N. Wales	1811	c.70,000	Dodd 1929, 210
Northop	N. Wales	1811	c.25,000	Dodd 1929, 210
Greysouthen	Cumb.	1818–29	5,792	CuRO Leconfield D/Lec/127
Hetton	NE	1829	402,138	NEI Forster 49/8/189

Note on sources: The figure of twenty-four north-east collieries in 1804 is an unweighted mean. It is calculated by adding 79.2 per cent to the seasale, as estimated for 1800 in Table 1.6.

century. Such a colliery was the Lowthers' Howgill colliery at White-haven in Cumberland, though this colliery was probably a good example of the way in which a high output was related to the number of pits being worked at any one time. The wide range of outputs shown in Table 1.1 is probably an indication that it was not necessarily the larger undertakings whose records have survived, though it is unlikely that the very smallest collieries produced the kind of records that are still extant today. For this reason it should not be assumed that, apart from the figure from the group of major north-east collieries in 1804, the figures in Table 1.1 represent 'average' collieries: they are no more than random examples. In particular, the output of Hetton colliery was certainly not typical for the late 1820s: it was probably the largest colliery in the country at that time.

While national output rose, therefore, partly in consequence of an increase of the average colliery output, it is more likely to have grown by the multiplication of collieries. There were no national statistics of production until 1854, and many of the contemporary estimates were either wild guesses, or were built up from information such as quantities of coal carried on this or that river or canal that are extremely difficult to relate to particular mining regions. Contemporary estimates and those of earlier historians of the industry have been surveyed by Pollard,[17] and no useful purpose would be served by reviewing these once again here. Those engaged in the industry were not, on the whole, interested in statistics of regional or national production, and even national figures in the industry, like John Buddle junior, the great north-east viewer, never, so far as can be traced, committed themselves to estimates of total production. The data that are all that the historian has to guide him are those produced by coalowners' associations in the process of their regulation of the quantity of coal put on the market, customs statistics of the coastal and export trades in coal subject to taxes, figures derived from the receipts from tolls of canal and river navigation companies, and the output of, or consumption of coal by, coal-using industries. All of these can offer no more than guides to the growth of some sections of the trades in coal. Coalowners' associations were interested either in particular markets or can be shown not to have embraced all producers in a coalfield or region. Though there was probably little direct smuggling of coal, customs statistics probably took no account of over-weight shipments, and relate, of course, only to the proportion of coal produced that was marketed by sea; and some estuarine trades were exempted from the duties on coal carried coastwise. Statistics derived from inland waterway accounts are random: for some waterways there are long and apparently accurate series, for other major waterways like the Rivers Trent and Severn, virtually none. The problems of estimating consumption of coal-using industries are reviewed in chapter seven below. For some industries reasonable estimates may be made, but for other important coal-consuming industries like lime-burning or brick-making there are few data on which to build.

When all these problems have been reviewed there remains a large number of series, random figures, and estimates, which, after account is taken of their varying degrees of reliability, provide at least a basis for estimates of production. These, then, form the basis of Tables 1.2 and 1.3. These tables have been built up region by region, and, within some of the more complex regions, coalfield by coalfield. In clarification of the estimates, Table 1.4 sets out the estimates for

[17] Pollard 1980, 212–20.

Table 1.2. *Estimated output of coal, 1700–1830, by mining regions*
(000s of tons)

Mining region	1700	1750	1775	1800	1815	1830
Scotland	450	715	1,000	2,000	2,500	3,000
Cumberland	25	350	450	500	520	560
Lancashire	80	350	900	1,400	2,800	4,000
North Wales	25	80	110	150	350	600
South Wales	80	140	650	1,700	2,750	4,400
South-west	150	180	250	445	610	800
East Midlands	75	140	250	750	1,400	1,700
West Midlands	510	820	1,400	2,550	3,990	5,600
Yorkshire	300	500	850	1,100	1,950	2,800
North-east	1,290	1,955	2,990	4,450	5,395	6,915
Total (tons)	2,985	5,230	8,850	15,045	22,265	30,375
(tonnes)	3,033	5,314	8,992	15,286	22,621	30,861
Annual compounded rate of growth (%)		1.13	2.13	2.15	2.65	2.09

Note on sources: For the North-east mining region see the appendix to this chapter and Table 1.6. For other mining regions, the figures are estimates based on the sources for each region indicated in the notes to this chapter. In forming these estimates attention has been paid to Pollard's estimates (1980, Table 14), to the population of the areas served by the component coalfields of each region, to likely industrial consumption in each region, and to colliery consumption, miners' allowances, and waste. The figures for 1700 and 1830 have further been co-ordinated with estimates made by the authors of the preceding and succeeding volumes in this history.

Table 1.3. *Estimated output of coal, 1700–1830, by mining regions,*
as percentage of total output

Mining regions	1700	1750	1775	1800	1815	1830
Scotland	15.1	13.7	11.3	13.3	11.2	9.9
Cumberland	0.8	6.7	5.1	3.3	2.3	1.8
Lancashire	2.7	6.7	10.2	9.3	12.6	13.2
North Wales	0.8	1.5	1.2	1.0	1.6	2.0
South Wales	2.7	2.7	7.3	11.3	12.3	14.5
South-west	5.0	3.4	2.8	3.0	2.7	2.6
East Midlands	2.5	2.7	2.8	5.0	6.3	5.6
West Midlands	17.1	15.7	15.9	16.9	18.0	18.4
Yorkshire	10.1	9.5	9.6	7.3	8.8	9.2
North-east	43.2	37.4	33.8	29.6	24.2	22.8

Source: Table 1.2.

Table 1.4. *Estimated output of coal, 1700–1830, in component coalfields of selected mining regions*
(000s of tons)

Mining region	1700	1750	1775	1800	1815	1830
South Wales						
Western section (Swansea area)	70	100	250	500	850	1,150
Eastern section (East Glamorgan and Monmouthshire)	10	40	400	1,200	1,900	3,250
Total	80	140	650	1,700	2,750	4,400
South-west						
Forest of Dean	60	70	80	95	130	200
Somerset	50	60	95	210	280	350
Gloucestershire (Bristol)	40	50	75	140	200	250
Total	150	180	250	445	610	800
West Midlands						
Staffordshire	170	280	580	1,500	2,850	4,200
Warwickshire	40	40	70	150	150	180
Shropshire	300	500	750	900	990	1,220
Total	510	820	1,400	2,550	3,990	5,600
East Midlands						
Leicestershire	25	40	50	100	250	275
Derby/Notts.	50	100	200	650	1,150	1,425
Total	75	140	250	750	1,400	1,700

Sources: See note to Table 1.2.

output in the component coalfields of some of the mining regions. The estimates in these tables reveal that the growth of British coal production between 1700 and 1830 was more than tenfold. By the nature of an extractive industry in an economy that already, even in the early eighteenth century, showed many elements of maturity, growth rates were unlikely to vary dramatically from one sub-period to another. Table 1.2 none the less reveals that the industry's growth accelerated steadily up to 1815, and though the rate of growth declined after that date, the decline was small, the rate of growth continuing to be high. Other industries may have achieved faster rates of growth for short periods, but none sustained such significant rates for so long a period. Though there were obvious constraints in a deep-mining industry on sudden spurts of growth, there is little doubt that in the coal industry, too, concealed within the medium-length intervals employed in Table 1.2 there were short periods of faster growth of output.

An output of just over 2.9 million tons in 1700 implies a per capita consumption over the whole British population at that date of slightly more than 9 cwt. The growth of production by mid century, in a period of negligible population growth involved, therefore, a substantial rise in per capita consumption to about 16 cwt. Coal production continued to rise faster than population, so that by 1800, consumption per head had risen to over 27 cwt, and by 1830 to over 37 cwt. By this time per capita consumption was not far short of the 1980/1 levels of about 43 cwt.

At the opening of the eighteenth century almost half of British coal production came from the North-east, and the production of that mining region exceeded that of the next three largest regions put together. In 1830 the North-east was still the largest producer of the ten mining regions by a significant margin, but its share of total production had been reduced to less than one-quarter. Though the North-east's output was still more in 1830 than that of all the other British coalfields put together a mere fifty-five years earlier, the decline in its relative importance was due more to the very rapid change in the economic environment of other coalfields than to any inability of the North-east to sustain growth. In 1830 the North-east was still the acknowledged leader in technology, in the skill of its miners, and in the expertise of its managers. If its supremacy was being challenged it was largely because of the voracious demand for coal of the coke iron industry in the pre-hot blast era which was behind the rapid growth of mining in South Wales, Staffordshire, and Yorkshire since 1775. But the shifts in the pattern of demand, and, above all, the transformation of the transportation of coal in the second half of the eighteenth century and the early decades of the nineteenth had brought several of the other mining regions to a posi-tion nearer to equality with the North-east. At the beginning of the eighteenth century only Scotland and the West Midlands exceeded one-third of the output of the North-east: in 1830 five of the mining regions produced more than one-third of the North-east's output and one, the West Midlands, raised more than two-thirds of it. In order to raise coal production more than tenfold between 1700 and 1830 it had been necessary to redistribute coal production much more widely.

Not all the mining regions were able to match the fast national growth rate. Though the Scottish coalfields, for example, broadly maintained their relative position during the eighteenth century, they were unable to match the national growth rate in the early decades of the nineteenth. Much the same was true of the smaller Cumberland coalfield where growth from small beginnings was fast for the first three-quarters of the eighteenth century, but slow thereafter. The steady but undramatic growth in the South-west reflected both the smaller quantities of coal workable at competitive prices and the failure of the region to develop either large urban centres or any of the new coal-consuming industries. Certainly the growth between 1750 and 1830 had established a pattern for the future and demonstrated which mining regions had been able, and were likely to continue to be able, to meet the new demands of the nineteenth century: these were clearly Scotland, Lancashire, South Wales, both Midland regions, Yorkshire, and the North-east. It would have been a far-seeing expert who could have foreseen this pattern of development even in 1750.

It will be apparent from the foregoing that in spite of the growth of output during the eighteenth and early nineteenth centuries no new mining region was opened up: those that contributed to the industry's output in 1830 were already producing in 1700. Within mining regions, too, there was surprisingly little extension of mining areas. There was, as we have seen, some significant drift of centres of gravity in the North-east, but the more substantial exploitation of a new area occurred with the opening-up of the eastern sector of the South Wales coalfield in the second half of the eighteenth century. For the rest, expansion was achieved by more intensive development of existing areas in combination with deeper mining, and some centripetal expansion as dipping seams were followed outwards, and deeper pits pursued faulted seams. Distribution of production within coalfields was necessarily shifted in some degree, but the national map of mining location in 1830 was surprisingly little altered from that of 1700.

Appendix. The output of coal in the North-east

The basis of calculation of coal output in the North-east must be the series of coastwise shipments that are brought together in Table 7.3, since they undoubtedly record accurately and fairly completely a major part of the output of the north-east collieries. The coastwise shipments, however, exclude the following other elements in colliery output:

1. Exports to Ireland and to foreign and colonial markets
2. Overweight sales
3. Small coal waste
4. Local industrial and domestic consumption ('landsale')
5. Consumption by pumping and winding engines, ventilating furnaces, and smithies at the collieries themselves
6. Coal allowances for mineworkers.

Some allowance must be made for each of these items, and is made in Table 1.6 in the form of percentage additions to the known coastwise figures, estimated as follows:

1. *Exports.* Every attempt has been made to be sure that the figures used in Table 7.3 are for coastwise shipments only, so that exports must be taken separately into account. As Table 7.8 shows, the data for this item are seriously incomplete, and estimates must be made for years for which there are no sources.

2. *Overweight sales.* Shipments of coal from the North-east were normally measured by the keel, and there was a statutory procedure for ensuring standard loading of the keels (see p. 167 below). In spite of these precautions, however, there was general agreement that overloaded keels were the rule rather than the exception: colliery proprietors gave over-measure as an allowance against the breakage of 'great' coals and losses in transit, as a bribe or sweetener to ensure rapid collection and good handling to keep the reputation of their coal in the market, or simply as a disguised way of reducing the price to effect a sale. The standard keel-load was eight chaldrons, but there is ample evidence to indicate that nine chaldrons, if not more, were commonly loaded. Statements about overloading, however, tend to estimate maximum rather than average overloading, and it would probably be wise to assume a figure appreciably less than the 12.5 per cent indicated by the one-chaldron-to-eight figure. A rather arbitrary 9.5 per cent has been adopted as a constant addition to seasales throughout the period, except for 1830, by which time it has been assumed that loading by spout and drop would have tended to reduce overweight sales marginally.

3. *Small coal 'waste'.* This is perhaps the most difficult of all the additional elements to estimate. A substantial proportion of small coal was necessarily produced with the more valuable great coal. Some was not brought to the surface but was stacked underground as filling for the goafs. Only small coal brought to the surface is

accounted as part of the colliery output. Small coal, Buddle stated in 1830, amounted to anything between one-tenth and nine-tenths of coal cut, though it averaged about one-third.[1] The following proportions of small coal to total output have been noted from viewers' reports:

		%
Gateshead Park	1784	11.0
Jarrow	1813	14.3
Wallsend	1815	15.0
Walker	1817	25.0
Gateshead Park	1819	20.0
Backworth	1819	41.0
Jarrow	1819–22	31.0
Jarrow	1829	28.0

It would be a simple matter to settle on a standard average addition to seasale for small coal were it not for the fact that some of the small coal found sales, albeit at prices much lower than those for great coal; but an account of output does not need to take account of prices. Some of the small coal that collieries were able to dispose of, however, falls into some of the other categories of non-seasale coal. Following the establishment of differential export duties for great and small coal in 1816,[2] for example, increasing quantities of small coal were exported. By 1821 small coal accounted for 58.8 per cent of total overseas exports from north-east ports,[3] and a statement of 1825 indicated that this had led to a reduction of the waste of small coal at the pitheads.[4] Virtually all coal consumed by the collieries themselves was small coal, while the same was true of some of the landsale. An estimate for the disposal of the coal produced at Heaton colliery in 1823 illustrates well the role of small coal. In addition to 60,000 chaldrons of vendible seacoal selling at 28s. 6d. per chaldron, there was also produced 4,000 chaldrons of 'nut small coals' for seasale at 10s. per chaldron, 3,000 chaldrons of small coal for landsale to glasshouses at 3s. per chaldron, and 1,000 chaldrons of small coals sold at the pithead at 5s. per chaldron.[5]

The problem, then, is as much that of determining what proportion of small coal was disposed of as of what proportion of coal brought to the surface it accounted for. Line 9 in Table 1.6 aims to exclude all small coal taken into account under other headings, and

[1] NEI Buddle 14/200–1.   [2] 56 Geo. III, c. 127.   [3] *PP* 1821 (373) XVII. 83.
[4] NuRO Joint Coal Owners' Association 263, Minute book 1825–6, unnumbered enclosure.
[5] NEI Buddle 51/37.

relates therefore exclusively to waste. In 1830 Buddle estimated that between one-tenth and one-fifth of all coal brought to the surface was waste.[6] In Table 1.6 allowance has been made for the increasing outlet for small coal in exports and colliery consumption, offset by the decline in its consumption in salt-making. The figures appear to be high because they are related in this table to the seasale vend not to the total output.

4. *Landsale*. Possibly the largest of the elements unaccounted for and the most difficult to estimate. Two categories of landsale must be considered—(*a*) landsale by collieries not sharing in the seasale 'vend'; and (*b*) landsale by collieries sharing the seasale 'vend'.

(*a*) The only useful information on the otherwise extremely elusive north-east exclusively landsale collieries is Bailey's 1810 list for County Durham. As Pollard shows, this indicates that, for County Durham alone, they added 11.0 per cent to the seasales of the seasale collieries. We have no option but to assume a similar proportion for Northumberland.[7]

The remaining items must be considered together, because colliery accounts and viewers' reports are unfortunately inconsistent in their presentation of information in these areas. The data collected in Table 1.5 reveal something of both the scale of distribution under these headings and the problems of interpretation. Very few of the accounts that are sufficiently explicit to allow them to be included in this table take all the items into account, yet it is improbable that any colliery failed to distribute some of its output under each of the headings. Some accounts treat landsale as merely pithead sales, and add separate categories of 'river sales' and 'sales to glasshouses'. All these categories, however, are clearly non-seasale, and have been counted as landsale. Various items are grouped under 'colliery consumption': 'machine engines' (winding-engines), 'main engines' (pumping-engines), 'air tubes', 'pit fires', and 'underground furnaces' (for ventilating courses), and consumption by the colliery smithies. Even when distinguishing landsales from seasales, few accounts seem to think miners' allowances worth mentioning, though they clearly contributed a sufficiently significant proportion of total output to merit being taken into account.

The figures in Table 1.5 are sufficiently diverse to present formidable problems of striking means. For the landsale from seasale collieries a constant addition of 23 per cent has been adopted, as being very close to the mean of the figures in Table 1.5 as well as

[6] *SC Lords Coal Trade* 1830, 39.
[7] Bailey 1810, 12–26; Pollard 1980, 221–2.

to the figure for the immediate post-1830 period (to be published in volume 3 of this history and estimated by a quite different method from superior data). With the steady adoption of steam-pumping and winding, and convection ventilation during the eighteenth and early nineteenth centuries, increasing proportions of colliery output had to be assigned to these purposes. The figures in Table 1.5 are by no means chronologically consistent in this way since collieries clearly varied substantially from one to another in the use they made of steam-power. The graduated levels adopted in Table 1.6, however, reflect the general levels of those in Table 1.5, and aim to offer a realistic recognition of the growing colliery consumption of coal over the whole period. The figure of 5.2 per cent for miners' allowances is biased marginally upwards from those in Table 1.5 to allow for the firmer findings for the immediate post-1830 period.

The total percentage addition to the seasale for 1700 agrees fairly well with an estimate made by Simpson in 1930-1[8] using a survey in the Buddle papers[9] that listed Tyne collieries with their outputs in *scores* per day. This suggests their actual gross outputs since their seasales would normally be measured in *chaldrons*. A score (of corves) ranged from $4\frac{1}{2}$ to $5\frac{1}{2}$ tons, and, assuming 265 days worked in the year, the total output of the collieries listed amounted to around 900,000 tons at a time when the Newcastle coastwise trade has been estimated at 515,000 tons.

These estimates differ somewhat from these recently published by Pollard principally because he took no account of the Blyth trade or of overweight, but also because of some lack of clarity about exactly what items were accounted for in his non-seasale residue. For this, of course, the inconsistencies of the contemporary sources are to blame.

[8] T. V. Simpson, 'Old mining records and plans', *TIME* 81 (1930-1), 76-7.
[9] NEI Buddle 14/212.

Table 1.5. *Distribution of non-seasale deliveries of coal from north-east seasale collieries, 1784–1823*
(Deliveries as percentages of seasales)

Colliery	Date	Land- and river-sale	Colliery consumption	Miners' allowances	Source
Gateshead Park	1784	16.1	12.9	–	NEI Watson 8/11/15
Benwell	1789	26.9	14.1	–	NEI Watson 8/11/120
Spanish Closes and Heaton	1792–1802	1.8	6.1	2.6	NEI Buddle 14/409
Benwell	1799–1806	18.1	9.0	2.9	NEI Buddle 14/4
New Washington	1801	2.1	–	–	NEI Buddle 6/314
Sheriff Hill	1804	15.0	20.0		NEI Watson 8/8/196
Rainton and Herrington Mill	1805		6.3		NEI Buddle 8/127
Benwell	1810–13	66.5	–	–	NEI Watson 9/3/n.p.
Collingwood Main	1811	–	11.2	4.0	NEI Buddle 3/235
Murton[1]	1811	–	12.0	20.8[2]	NEI Buddle 3/269
Jarrow	1821	1.0	–	–	NEI Buddle 36/III/192
Hetton	1823	13.3	–	–	NuRO Wilson (Forest Hall) ZWI 3/338–40

Notes: 1. Non-vend sales are percentages of a combined total of seasale and landsale.
2. Includes waste.

Table 1.6. *Estimate of coal output of North-east mining region, 1700–1830, showing additions to seasales*

Category of output	1700	1750	1775	1800	1815	1830
1. Coastwise (000s of tons)	700	999	1,492	2,332	2,838	3,660
2. Exports (000s of tons)	50	120	200	150	150	340
3. Total seasale (000s of tons)	750	1,119	1,692	2,482	2,988	4,000
4. Landsale from seasale collieries (% of seasale)	23.0	23.0	23.0	23.0	23.0	23.0
5. Landsale collieries (% of seasale)	11.0	11.0	11.0	11.0	11.0	11.0
6. Colliery consumption (% of seasale)	3.0	6.0	8.0	11.0	13.0	14.0
7. Miners' allowances (% of seasale)	5.2	5.2	5.2	5.2	5.2	5.2
8. Over-measure (% of seasale)	9.5	9.5	9.5	9.5	9.5	8.5
9. Small coal (waste) (% of seasale)	20.0	20.0	20.0	19.5	18.8	17.8
10. Total percentage addition	71.7	74.7	76.7	79.2	80.5	79.5
11. Production represented by lines 4-9 (000s of tons)	538	836	1,298	1,966	2,405	2,915
12. Total production of (000s of tons)	1,288	1,955	2,990	4,448	5,393	6,915

Note on sources: Line 1: Table 7.3. In the absence of data for Sunderland and Blyth for 1700 the figure for that year is an estimate. Line 2: Table 7.8, with estimates for 1700, 1750, and 1775. Lines 4-9: see text of appendix.

Chapter 2

The Ownership and Management of Collieries

i. *Ownership*

British mining law determined broadly that the right to mine coal lay with the owner of the surface. Mostly this left the question of coal ownership in no doubt, but where the coal lay under common or copyhold land the question of mining rights was often uncertain. At Sedgeley in the Black Country copyholders could mine coal but not sell it or lease it, but in Staffordshire a kind of compromise generally seems to have been reached between landowners and copyholders: either could veto mining by the other. In Somerset in the late seventeenth century copyholders were apparently unable to prevent the owner from entering and mining.[1] In South Wales the position was more complicated. The value of mining rights became more apparent towards the middle of the eighteenth century, and it was generally tenants or occupiers who realized this before absentee landowners did. As a correspondent of Lord Mansel's put it in 1723: 'It is not ye value of the herbage that puts the gentlemen on the metal but a vein of coal, that is under it.' When the penny dropped, long-dead manorial prerogatives were exhumed and mineral rights reasserted in respect of copyhold and common land. The Duke of Beaufort, who actually owned relatively little land in Glamorgan, was nevertheless lord of the manor of ten manors in the coal-bearing lands of west Glamorgan as well as being paramount lord of the whole of Gower. The Marquess of Bute, similarly, owned not only the minerals beneath his freehold land, but, as lord of almost all the manors of east Glamorgan, those beneath the commons. By the mid-eighteenth century the local gentry of the western sector of the South Wales coalfield were no longer prepared to defer to the upper aristocracy at the expense of profitable exploitation of what they believed to be their own mineral rights, and, in a long-running battle of pamphlets, meetings, lawsuits, and clandestine mining, eventually established the invalidity of the Duke's claimed prerogatives.[2] In the eastern sector the landowning aristocrats were even slower to realize that they were sitting on valuable properties. 'When I first

[1] *VCH Staffordshire*, II, 94–5; *VCH Somerset*, II, 381–2.
[2] NLW Badminton 1910; Davies thesis 1969, 492; and see Martin 1978; and Osborne 1978.

went [in 1823] to investigate the very extensive mineral property of your lordship in South Wales', wrote Robert Bald to the Marquess of Bute in 1845, 'your lordship, your agents and your men of business had not the vestige of any mineral plans, records or sections of strata. . . . Your men of business and agents . . . previous to my report had not the least conception of the great value of these minerals.'[3] Here, however, the Marquess was ultimately more successful in asserting his claim to the rights, perhaps because it was mainly a case in the east, unlike in the west, of common, not copyhold land, and partly because those interested in the coal were almost universally 'foreign' iron companies, not local tenants.

The concentration, for geological reasons, of mines in relatively compact areas allowed a few fortunate landowners, often owning large tracts of land, to acquire control over many mines in a coalfield. Thus in Scotland, great landowners like the Duke of Buccleuch, with land in the Lothian coalfield, and the Duke of Hamilton, with estates in Lanarkshire and West Lothian, found themselves the owners of many mines, while, on a smaller scale, the Cunninghames of Auchenharvie and the Earls of Rothes developed mines on their estates in Ayrshire and Fife respectively. In Cumberland, almost all the mines were concentrated in the lands of a handful of estate owners—the Whitehaven mines on Lowther land, the Workington mines on the Curwen estate, and those round Maryport on the land of the Senhouses. In Lancashire there was a greater diffusion of ownership of both land and mines, but in coal-bearing areas major landowners like the Earl of Crawford and Balcarres and the Duke of Bridgewater drew a significant proportion of their incomes from mining. 'The basis of our fortunes', wrote the former to his son in 1822, 'is our coal and cannel mines. Colliers we are and colliers we must ever remain.'[4] In Yorkshire the Wentworth estate of the Fitzwilliams around Barnsley operated four collieries in 1795 and six in 1828, while the Fentons owned several mines in the neighbourhood of Leeds, and the Duke of Norfolk several in the Sheffield area. Lord Ferrers developed mines on his land in Leicestershire, Jacob Mogg on his estate in Somerset, and the Lords Dudley on theirs in the Black Country. In the North-east a small group of fortunate landowners —the Duke of Northumberland, the Earl of Scarbrough and the Lambton, Bowes, Liddell, Wortley, Clavering, Vane-Tempest, and Brandling families—drew huge incomes throughout the eighteenth and early nineteenth centuries from the development of mining on their estates.

[3] Robert Bald to Marquess of Bute, 4 Dec. 1845, quoted in Davies thesis 1969, 492.
[4] Sixth Earl to his son, 19 Jan. 1822, JRL Crawford and Balcarres 23/14/10.

Few landowners in any coalfield failed to take financial advantage of coal under their land where and whenever it was accessible by current mining techniques. Some landowners, finding that the exploitation of the mineral resources of their own land could be profitable, used some of the profits to buy more coal-bearing land. Between 1813 and 1822, for example, John Lambton, already in possession of some of the richest coal-bearing land on Wearside, bought further land at Newbottle, Witton Gilbert, and Nesham. Both Sir John and Sir James Lowther persistently sought to acquire more coal-bearing land in Cumberland during the first half of the eighteenth century, not without some success, while the Marquis of Londonderry leased additional coal-bearing land from the Dean and Chapter of Durham Cathedral at Pittington in County Durham in 1825.[5]

Several owners possessed a considerable number of collieries. The Church, in the persons of the Bishop of Durham, who owned eight seasale collieries, and the Dean and Chapter of the Cathedral, who owned six, held between them almost one-quarter of all the major seasale collieries in the North-east in the late 1820s, all of which they leased out. Both also owned some of the smaller landsale collieries: in 1810 the Bishop owned eleven and the Dean and Chapter three.[6] They were followed in the late 1820s by the Duke of Northumberland with six collieries, and he, too, did not work any directly. The landowning partnership of the Grand Allies owned, either individually or collectively, five collieries. The remaining Tyne owners held no more than one colliery each in 1828, though on the Wear the Lambtons owned three collieries and John Davison two.

Some landowners developed the mines on their land themselves through agents and managers, while others chose to remain rentiers and to leave the business of mining to others. The proportion who worked their own mines varied from coalfield to coalfield, and, within coalfields, from one period to another. It is probably correct that at some point during the nineteenth century landowners withdrew increasingly from active participation in mining to become rentiers, but there is little evidence of a trend in this direction before 1830. The position is clearest in the North-east. There, in the late 1820s, it was said that only five collieries out of forty-one on Tyneside were being worked by their owners, and four out of seventeen on Wearside. This statement, however, is something of an oversimplification. Some coalowners leased mines from other owners or entered into partnerships with others to lease mines; and some lessees

[5] 'List of estates and land bought for J. S. Lambton, 1813-1822', LEA not numbered; Beckett 1981, 19-25; Hiskey thesis 1978, 137-8.
[6] Bailey 1810, 12-14.

sub-let. Thus, according to a survey of 1828, the Brandlings, owners and operators of Gosforth colliery, also leased Heworth and Manor Wallsend collieries from the Dean and Chapter and shared in the lease of Coxlodge colliery. On Wearside, the Lambtons leased Cocken colliery from Ralph Carr, Lumley colliery from the Earl of Scarbrough, and Murton colliery from the Dean and Chapter in addition to working major collieries on their own land. The Marquis of Londonderry, who had acquired the Vane-Tempest interests by marriage, similarly added to these vast coal resources by leasing the Mill and North Pittington collieries from John Davison and the Dean and Chapter respectively.[7] In Yorkshire the Earl Fitzwilliam, already an important coalowner, leased further mines in the 1820s from neighbouring landowners when he was confident that he had an agent capable of managing them.[8] Though it is not possible in all cases to identify coal landowners with certainty, at least sixteen out of the forty-one Tyneside seasale collieries in 1828 were worked by landowners, and eleven out of the seventeen Wearside collieries. The 1828 list, however, relates solely to the greater seasale collieries and takes no account of the numerous smaller landsale collieries. It shows only twenty-one separate owners on Tyneside, yet a statement of 1822 spoke of between fifty and sixty owners.[9] The difference must be accounted for by the owners of the lesser landsale collieries.

In the first half of the eighteenth century it was not uncommon for the smaller collieries to be leased by working miners either in partnership or acting singly in an entrepreneurial capacity. This system operated in the small mines of the Derbyshire–Nottinghamshire border in the opening years of the eighteenth century. Goosewardsham colliery in Somerset, too, was leased in this way in 1708 to two colliers, Simon Dando and George Carter.[10] But as the century progressed and the scale of working and cost of equipment increased, mining operations quickly began to outgrow the resources of small groups of working colliers. For this reason from early in the century most of the collieries worked by non-landowners were leased by partnerships of men with greater financial resources than could be commanded by working miners. Where the partners can be identified, they were usually landowners, urban merchants, local bankers, or other professional men. Govan colliery in Lanarkshire was leased by two Glasgow merchants towards the end of the eighteenth century,

[7] NEI Buddle 25/III/1–15. There is another copy of this list in DuRO NCB First Deposit NCB/I/JB/2418.

[8] Fletcher thesis 1973, 21.   [9] NEI Bell 15/13/594.

[10] Hardy 1955–6, 147; Bulley 1955, 18.

while between 1785 and 1791 Halbeath colliery in Fife was leased by a partnership consisting of an Edinburgh lawyer, a white lead-maker from Newcastle and a third partner of unknown occupation from Durham. Smallcombe colliery in Somerset was operated by a partnership of twelve in 1797, while Stevenston colliery in Ayrshire was leased in 1719 by a partnership of thirteen shipmasters.[11] Darnall colliery in south Yorkshire in 1760 was operated by a partnership consisting of a local landowner and two Sheffield merchants, and the Duke of Norfolk's Sheffield colliery in 1820 was leased to a group of partners including a landowner, a merchant, a cutler, and a collier, the last two of whom were to act as managers. When it reopened in 1790 Baddesley colliery in Warwickshire was leased by a partnership of Banbury coal merchants. This 'Banbury Company' evidently proposed to supply their own town with coal along the Oxford Canal which had been open as far as Banbury since 1778. Garesfield colliery in the North-east was leased in 1823 by a partnership of six whose interest was divided into 96ths: three partners held eighty-seven shares between them, while two held only single shares. All were landowners in the region.[12] In the North-east colliery viewers appeared increasingly during the second half of the eighteenth century as members of partnerships operating mines. William Brown was probably the first, in the 1750s, to turn to mining investment in partnership with the banker, Matthew Bell, but others followed his example later. The names of several viewers, including that of John Buddle, may be identified among the partners leasing mines in the late 1820s.

The best known of the partnerships of coalowners was certainly the Grand Allies. There are two aspects of this partnership, and only one is relevant here. It was, primarily, a group of coalowners associating together for the purpose of restricting output and raising the price. As such it had much in common with other associations of owners, though for a time it was more successful than most. But, as a means towards these monopolistic ends, it also functioned as a partnership bringing together capital from a number of coalowners for the purpose of joint-stock mining. It emerged by stages between 1710 and 1726. In 1718 Sir Henry Liddell joined with William Cotesworth in a lease of Heaton colliery, and in 1722 the Liddells were joined by the Wortleys in the lease of other collieries. In a separate agreement of 1724 George Bowes and Lady Clavering entered a partnership to lease Collierly colliery, adding Ewhurst

[11] Payne 1961, 75; Payne forthcoming, 4; Bulley 1955, 25; Whatley 1977, 70.
[12] Hopkinson 1976, 13; Fletcher thesis 1973, 22; Grant thesis 1977, 225; NEI Buddle 19/no pagination.

colliery in the following year. Finally, in 1726, the Liddells, the Wortleys, George Bowes, William Cotesworth, and William Ord signed the 'Grand Alliance', taking over the lease of three Clavering collieries in the same year. In 1734 the Grand Allies took further leases of St. Anthony's and East Kenton collieries, and ten years later began the winning of Longbenton colliery. By 1750 they controlled, either by ownership or lease, sixteen of the twenty-seven seasale collieries south of the Tyne. Many other leases were taken and way-leaves rented for the sole purpose of denying them to competitors.

The geographical shift of mining on Tyneside described in chapter 1 began to deprive the Grand Allies of some of their monopolistic power during the third quarter of the century, but the family nature of the alliance gave it a degree of permanence and allowed the same families to remain active in the industry as a coalowning and leasing partnership right through to the early decades of the nineteenth century. Though the Grand Allies no longer dominated the seasale trade in coal as they had done in the second quarter of the eighteenth century, they remained important as owners and lessees in the industry. The 1828 list shows them owning five Tyne collieries and, either individually or in partnership, leasing seven others. By then some new families had joined the partnership—the Brandlings, the Russells of Brancepeth, and the Bells of Wolsington; but though the Liddells had now become Lords Ravensworth, and the Bowes the Lords Strathmore, the same families still formed the core of the partnership. The alliance had been cemented frequently during the century of its existence by inter-marriages between the families.[13]

There were two other groups of mining enterprises, however, that do not fit into any of the categories of ownership so far examined. First, the great expansion of the eastern sector of the South Wales coalfield was undertaken almost entirely by iron companies, and the operation of these mines was certainly integrated closely into the structure of these companies. The experience of the Coalbrookdale and Butterley iron companies shows that this was also true of some of the mining investment in Shropshire and Derbyshire, while, to some extent, the same must have been true of some of the Black Country development. In south Yorkshire and Cumberland many mines were leased to ironmasters after 1770. How far this inter-industry integration was carried in other related industries is less easily ascertained, but there was at least some linking of ownership between coal-mining and the copper and salt industries.

The second group of mines lying outside the general pattern of

[13] For sources of the history of the Grand Allies, see chapter 8, n. 5; and Anon., 'The Grand Allies'. 1890.

ownership was in the Forest of Dean in Gloucestershire. The Forest of Dean was a royal forest and mining there had been a prerogative of those born in the Hundred of St. Briavels since the Middle Ages. The Forest was administered by the Surveyor General of Woods in London through the Constable of the Castle of St. Briavels and his team of Deputy Gavellers. The 'free miners' had only to stake a claim to a 'gale' in the Mine Law Court to be free to mine for coal in an area initially of one hundred yards radius from the strike. This protected area was steadily increased during the late seventeenth and early eighteenth centuries until in 1754 it embraced a radius of one thousand yards. In practice the entry of free miners was tightly regulated by the Mine Law Court who made it difficult for all but sons of free miners to secure entitlement to gales. The Crown remained the owner of the land and drew a royalty of one-fifth share of the produce of mining. The combination of seams relatively near the surface, the limitation of working to relatively short distances from a shaft or drift opening, and the restriction of access to gales ensured that individual undertakings would be on the smallest of scales. In 1788, 99 mines were worked by 442 free miners and boys producing between them 1,816 tons of coal per week or about 90,000 tons per year. Miners worked in 'companies', normally of four 'verns' or partners.

Towards the end of the eighteenth century a range of economic pressures began to disturb this age-old pattern of working. The need to go deeper for workable seams in the very restricted coalfield area led first to the introduction of steam pumping—the first steam-engine in the Forest being recorded in 1777—and then, in the early years of the nineteenth century, to the construction of waggonways to give this hitherto landlocked coalfield access to water transport on the Wye and the Severn. The much enhanced demand for capital forced the free miners to begin to admit 'foreigners' by the 'colouring' of gales, a development that was not opposed by the Crown. Gradually during the early decades of the nineteenth century a small number of larger capitalist undertakings emerged to capture a growing proportion of Dean output. These were family firms and partnerships that drew their labour force from wage-earners as in all other coalfields. Small-scale free mining continued to exist side by side with the new large-scale businesses, but accounted for a diminishing proportion of the total production.[14]

[14] This account of the organization of mining in the Forest of Dean is based on Hart 1953 and 1971; *VCH Gloucestershire*, II, 230; Davis thesis 1959, 42-7, 62-73; and Fisher 1978.

ii. *The mining lease*

If mining was to be carried on by other than the immediate land-owner, some binding legal agreement between the operator and the owner was essential; and, given the expensive character of mining operations, the only satisfactory arrangement for the operator was an agreement for a period long enough to justify investment on the scale necessary to bring coal to the surface at all, and one that secured him against increases in the rent once coal had been brought to the surface. Thus the lease, securing mining rights to a capitalist for a period of years at a prearranged money payment, came to be the basis of all relationships between owners and operators.

While the lease gave the lessee rights to mine coal for a fixed period of years, the life of a colliery was uncertain. It follows that some leases were for green-field sites while others were for fully won and working mines. In the former case some investment, possibly substantial, would be necessary before coal could be got and sold; shafts must be sunk and levels driven, drainage and winding gear must be erected. It was normal for investment to be undertaken by the lessee, and it was his need to be assured of rights for a period long enough to allow him the possibility of securing an adequate return on his investment that required longer rather than shorter terms for leases to run. Where an established colliery was leased the calls on new investment might be very variable, ranging from massive re-equipment to an almost costless takeover of a fully equipped concern.

Rents under leases were calculated in a wide variety of ways. At the Fentons' Basingthorpe colliery in Yorkshire in 1762, for example, the rent was calculated at £40. 10s. per year for each hewer employed, though it was more common at that time in Yorkshire for the rent to be payable per acre mined. This was the method used on the Ogston estate in the 1740s where £42 per acre was levied annually, on the Wortley estate near Barnsley in 1717 where the rent was £25 per acre per year, and on Walter Fawkes's estate at Hawksworth near Leeds in 1814 when the annual rent was fixed at £60 per acre. It was also general in Staffordshire during the eighteenth century.[15] The rent at Griff colliery in Warwickshire in the early eighteenth century was fixed per pit.[16] Generally, however, one or both of two methods was used: a fixed sum per annum irrespective of the quantity of the coal mined; or an annual rent per unit of coal taken. Rents that did not vary with the quantity of coal mined were

[15] Hopkinson 1976, 21; SCL Wharncliffe Wh.M. 114/19; LCA 1546/64–5; *VCH Staffordshire*, II, 97.
[16] White thesis 1969, 45.

evident in Yorkshire at the Duke of Norfolk's Sheffield colliery during the 1780s, at the Low Moor colliery on the Stanhope estate in 1806, and at the Brandlings' Middleton colliery between 1813 and 1822. Similar fixed rents were found in Warwickshire at Griff colliery in 1730, and in Derbyshire at Burlow colliery in 1763 and at Newbold in 1788.[17]

Since coal resources workable by the available technology of the day were always limited, it was in the interest of the landlord to prevent lessees from heavy working at fixed rents that would exhaust his reserves prematurely. Restrictions on the extent of mining under fixed-rent leases were not common, but they were imposed on occasion. In the last years of the seventeenth century, for example, the lease of the Duke of Norfolk's Sheffield Park colliery allowed for the use of no more than ten getters at any one time, and Peter Browne's lease of a colliery at Stavely Westwood in 1700 from the Duke of Devonshire restricted him to two shafts at any one time, not to employ more than the usual number of hewers per shaft, and not to make use of any methods by which 'the said mines may be sooner wrought out or rendered the less beneficial'. Similarly, in a lease of mines at Newbold, Derbyshire, in 1788, the landowner reserved the right to increase the fixed rent in the event of new techniques of mining, making it possible to reach deeper seams. An 1820 lease of the Duke of Norfolk's Sheffield colliery included a condition that an investment of £18,000 was to be made by the lessees on new winnings.[18]

The most practical way of protecting the landowner, however, was to fix a rent that was proportional to the quantity of coal removed. This was done in South Wales, for example, on the estates of the Duke of Beaufort in the late eighteenth century and on those of William Williams in the early nineteenth century, and in Derbyshire in the mines worked by the Butterley Company.[19] More commonly a simple fraction of the pithead value of coal sold was used as the basis for calculation. In North Wales the rent was fixed at one-fifth of the proceeds of sales at a colliery on Lord Uxbridge's land in Anglesey in 1811, but at Sandycott and Mancott collieries on the Glynne estate in the 1740s one-eighth was levied on Main coal and one-seventh on other coal, though these rates had been standardized at one-eighth by 1792-3. In Cannock Chase, Staffordshire, a rent

[17] SCL Arundel Castle S196; SCL Spencer Stanhope 60579; LCA Middleton Colliery MC34; WaRO Newdigate of Arbury CR136/C618; Daniels and Ashton 1929-30, 124-5; Hardy 1955-6, 153.

[18] Hopkinson 1976, 8, 20; Hardy 1955-6, 153.

[19] NLW John Lloyd 76; NLW Aberpergwm 99; P. Riden, *The Butterley Company* (Chesterfield, 1973), 52.

of one-eighth was paid at Hazel Slade colliery in 1818, and in Somerset the Crown took one-eighth of the value of coal produced at Wetton near Midsomer Norton in 1765.[20] This system seems to have been most widespread in Scotland where one-eighth was paid at Lord Dunmore's mines in 1779–80, one-fifth at the Duke of Buccleuch's Sheriffhall colliery between 1810 and 1822, reduced to one-sixth after 1822, and one-seventh at Doura colliery in Ayrshire.[21] On the other hand, in a dispute at the Cunninghames' Ardeers colliery in Ayrshire in 1800, it was argued that in view of the low profitability 'a reasonable lordship' would be one-tenth, while at Leslie in Fife in 1773 it was said that 'the usual terms I have been witness to are to pay a fourth part of gross output for level free coall near the sea or city that affords constant sale or a good price, one fifth for levell free coalls that have not the above advantages, one seventh for coalls wrought by a water engine and one tenth when wrought by a fire engine, where the tacksmen of the two last are at the charge and risque of erecting the machinery and filling the works.'[22] At the end of the day, however, the most persuasive argument for the determination of royalty levels may have been the one propounded by the Marquess of Bute in a letter to his mineral agent about the rent to be set for a colliery to be leased to the Gadlys Iron Company: 'The royalty rent should be regulated according to their want of coal as well as by its quantity and their facilities of getting it.'[23]

Rents, however, could rarely be determined in isolation since one party to a lease was the lessee whose interest in it was his prospective profit. The relationship between levels of rents and profits had to take account of the virtual certainty of rents and the gamble of profits. When Sir Henry Vane-Tempest leased East Rainton colliery in Durham from the Dean and Chapter of Durham Cathedral in 1803, Buddle estimated that, with profit estimated at 2s. per chaldron, a rent of one-third of that amount, i.e. 8d. per chaldron, would be fair.[24] A similar proportion had been recommended sixty years earlier when calculating the rent of Carden colliery in Fife.[25]

In the North-east, where long experience of negotiation between landowner and mine operator had brought the mining lease to a high pitch of sophistication, a combination of fixed and proportional rents was most common. The practice of leasing collieries in order

[20] UCNW Plas Newydd III 4652; Rawson 1941, 120; NLW Glynne of Hawarden 3610–13; StRO Anglesey D603 M/2; SoRO Samborne DD/SA58.

[21] ShRO Forester SRO1224/173; ScRO Buccleuch GD224/986/3; ScRO Court of Session C596/638/1268.

[22] Mr. Weemyss to unknown recipient, 1 Feb. 1773, ScRO Balfour of Balbirnie 315.

[23] Marquess of Bute to E. P. Richards, 20 Jan. 1834, quoted by Davies thesis 1969, 508.

[24] NEI Buddle 8/81.   [25] ScRO Leven and Melville GD26/V/344/1.

to close them down to restrict output led landowners to demand a
'certain rent' to be paid annually whether or not coal was produced:
but, to safeguard themselves against over-rapid exploitation of their
reserves, a second rent proportional to output, known as the 'tentale' rent, since it was normally calculated per ten of coal raised,
was charged. (For the 'ten', see Appendix B.) An example of this was
the lease signed, after protracted negotiations, for Backworth colliery
on Tyneside in 1817. A certain rent of £1,000 per year was to be
paid, with an additional tentale rent of £1 per ten for all coal over
1,000 tens produced (about 46,000 tons).[26] Not surprisingly, when
John Buddle visited the Forest of Dean to make a general report, he
recommended a similar dual method for that coalfield.[27] The method
was also used in one of the few Cumberland collieries to be leased.
At Greysouthen colliery the lessee in the 1760s and 1770s paid a
certain yearly rent of £10 plus 4d. per ton, and in the 1820s a certain
rent of £8 plus 7½d. per ton.[28] Having regard to the considerable
difference in price between the large seasale coal and the almost
unsaleable small coal generated in the production of large coal,
lessees in the North-east sought to defend their interests by insisting
that the variable rents in leases be paid only on coal taken away from
the pits. Much small coal, of course, was left underground, but much,
too, was necessarily brought to the surface. To reduce payment to
the owners, this was then screened out.[29] At north-east landsale
collieries in the early nineteenth century certain rents ranged from
£20 to £1,000 and tentale rents up to 1s. per chaldron, which Buddle
estimated to amount to between one-tenth and one-sixth of the
selling price.[30]

It was usual in the eighteenth century to refer to both certain and
tentale payments as 'rents', but in the nineteenth century the latter
came increasingly to be termed 'royalties'. The distinction between
rents and royalties was no doubt a useful one at the time, but, as
royalties became increasingly important as colliery sizes grew, that
expression came to represent the whole price paid by the lessee to
the landowner.

Rents or royalties, however, were only a part of the payments that
passed between lessees and coalowners. The life of a colliery might
quite frequently extend beyond the period of an initial lease and
once its probable future profitability had been demonstrated by a
period of viable operation landlords were well placed to increase

---

[26] NEI Buddle 46a/60.
[27] 'Report on Forest of Dean' (n.d. probably 1832), NEI Buddle 51/302-3.
[28] CuRO Leconfield D/Lec/127.   [29] Holmes 1816, 70.
[30] DuRO NCB First Deposit NCB/I/JB/608.

share of the profits. They did this conventionally by exacting a fine for the renewal of a lease, and when the probable profitability of a colliery permitted it was possible for a landowner's revenue from fines to swell to become a significant proportion of his whole revenue from mines. Where, as in the North-east in the late eighteenth and early nineteenth centuries, leases were usually for twenty-one years, landowners often took advantage of the possibility of benefiting within that period from the proven profitability of a mine by building into the initial lease provision for renewal every seven years, allowing for the levying of a fine on the occasion of the renewals. With what were called 'filling-up' renewals, the expired term was added to the end of a lease to allow, on payment of renewal fines, for 'leap-frogging' extensions. The Select Committee on Church Leases explained in 1838 that 'a rent—usually nominal —was reserved, and a fine, from which the lessor's revenue in fact came, was payable at each time of renewal.'[31] But the Select Committee may have been inclined to exaggerate the nominal character of rents. When Wallsend colliery on north Tyneside was first leased by the Dean and Chapter of Durham Cathedral in 1778 the certain (as distinct from the tentale) rent was £200. In 1781 this was raised to £500. 10s., but the Dean and Chapter's revenue was increased by 'overworkings' (a form of tentale rent for production above a fixed quantity). After 1795 payments for overworkings were never less than £1,000 per year and after 1821 they rose to over £3,000. Renewal fines were payable over and above these rents.[32] Thanks to the good fortune of owning land in the areas of the coalfield that were developing fastest in the early nineteenth century, the Dean and Chapter were able to expand their revenue from fines substantially in this period—from an annual average of £4,782 per year in the quinquennium 1771-5 to one of £10,541 in the first quinquennium of the nineteenth century, and to one of £23,522 by the late 1820s. The Bishops of Durham, whose lands were concentrated principally in the older, dying parts of the coalfield around Gateshead and Whickham, were less well placed to benefit from the expansion of production, increasing their revenue from fines only from an annual average of £5,661 at the beginning of the nineteenth century to £8,992 by the late 1820s.[33]

Renewal fines were initially calculated as a purchase of the tentale rent, but, evidently observing the widening gap in the early nineteenth century between profits and tentale rents, the Dean and Chapter decided to recoup some of this difference by transferring the fines to

[31] SC Church Leases 1838, viii. [32] Hughes thesis 1963, 414.
[33] Hughes thesis 1963, 414-15.

a purchase on profits rather than rents. In the negotiations for the septennial renewal of the Vane-Tempest lease on Rainton colliery from the Dean and Chapter in 1819–20, this switch, 'both novel and unfair', in the agent's estimation, and tending 'to damp that spirit of enterprise . . . which constitutes the very essence of mining', was deeply resented, though it could not be resisted.[34]

The interests of landowners and lessees competed, too, in the length of leases. Mining investment was a long-term business and lessees had to be allowed time to bring their investments to fruition. The initial sinking of a major pit could take up to four years in the late eighteenth and early nineteenth centuries, and there was a considerable element of uncertainty about the difficulties to be encountered in the course of sinking. 'The real expenses to be incurred in establishing a colliery', wrote the Marquis of Anglesey's agent in 1815, '. . . cannot be exactly ascertained till it is done. Much depends on the quantity of water there may be to contend with, as also a variety of circumstances.'[35] Accordingly leases of less than twenty years were exceptional. Indeed, among the many leases in all coalfields in the eighteenth and early nineteenth centuries that have come to light in the archives, none were for less than twenty-one years, though this was probably the most favourite period. A number of leases were for thirty, thirty-one, and forty, forty-one, and forty-two years, but over that period only ninety-nine years was used at all frequently. In the North-east, as we have seen, use was made of a kind of 'running' twenty-one year leases renewable every seven years by the process of 'filling-up'. The very long leases relate mostly to the first half of the eighteenth century, and in the early nineteenth century twenty-one to thirty-one year leases were fairly general. There is no discernible trend in the length of leases over time except possibly for the discarding of the very long leases.[36]

While the provisions of leases were legally binding, there developed an understanding that under certain circumstances, they were renegotiable. In 1818, for example, the Marquis of Anglesey allowed a deduction of £20 from the agreed royalties towards a trial boring to prove the existence of coal at the projected Hazel Slade colliery on Cannock Chase in Staffordshire. Three years earlier the lessees of Jarrow colliery had appealed to the owner for a reduction of the tentale rent on account of difficult working conditions: after an

[34] Hiskey thesis 1978, 133–4.
[35] W. W. Bailey to Marquis of Anglesey, 6 Oct. 1815, StRO Anglesey D603/M/3/1/1.
[36] NLW John Lloyd 76; NEI Buddle 51/302; A. R. Griffin thesis 1969, 82; Beastall 1975, 14, 24, 35; Cromar 1978, 196–7, 206; Rawson 1941, 120.

inspection by four independent viewers a reduction from 34s. per ten to 25s. was accepted.[37]

Experience gained during the eighteenth and early nineteenth centuries was gradually teaching both landowners and lessees to use the provisions of the lease to safeguard their interests both in the short and the long run. The tendency was, accordingly, for leases to become more complex documents. As a historian of the Bute estate in South Wales expressed it, by the late 1820s mineral leases on the estate had become 'vast indentures specifying in detail the rights and obligations of landlord and tenant'.[38]

iii. *Colliery management*

The unit of organization in coal-mining during the eighteenth and early nineteenth centuries was commonly the colliery. When studied closely, however, the precise nature of a 'colliery' loses some of the simple clarity it appears to hold at first sight. First, it was a unit of organization rather than of mining. That is to say, a colliery might consist of more than one mining unit. The mining unit in this period might consist either of a pit, giving access vertically downwards to a series of roads leading to the coal faces, or of a drift (or 'day-level', as it was called in Cumberland and Scotland) leading horizontally or sloping from the face of a hillside to the workings. In some areas, notably in the Swansea and Neath valleys of west Glamorgan, coal was reached by a combination of drift and pit, the initial access being gained by a drift, but lower seams being approached by vertical pits from the drifts underground. When Charles Hatchett visited the Duke of Norfolk's Sheffield Park colliery in 1796 he found the workings approached through a drift though the coal was wound to the surface up a shaft.[39]

As is explained more fully in chapter four, as the scale of mining progressed during the eighteenth century it was quickly learned that a single ingress to the workings could not suffice to clear the air within the mine of the dangerous gases released from coal seams, and a second, and sometimes additional, entry to the workings created to allow through movement of air. Since the creation of access, whether by drift or by pit, was in itself expensive of capital, the maximum use of the access so gained was made by working outwards from the pit or drift bottom in as many directions as were consistent with the needs of drainage, transport, and the continuity of seams. The same entry to the coal could be, and was, employed to give

---

[37] StRO Anglesey D603 M/2; NEI Buddle 36/II/86.
[38] Davies thesis 1969, 508.   [39] Raistrick 1967, 70.

access to several seams. Thus at Hendreforgan colliery in the upper Swansea valley in 1818 three seams were worked—the Five Foot or Great Vein at 105 feet, the Milford 201 feet below that, and a three-foot seam a further 105 feet below the Milford.[40] In the North-east in the early nineteenth century it was common for several seams to be tapped from a single shaft so that the coals from the various seams could be mixed for sale in order to dispose of the poorer qualities with the better.[41]

As coal was taken out mining was necessarily pushed further and further from the drift or pit bottom. While various forms of underground haulage for coal from the working faces to the pit bottom were devised, there came a point at which the cost of hauling coal along the underground roads exceeded the cost of sinking a new pit. Where, as in Lancashire, seams were not far below the surface and the cost of sinking pits therefore not great, it paid to sink new pits fairly frequently—the 'Lancashire system'. Winding gear and drainage machinery were easily transplanted, too, and the disused shaft could be filled with waste just as worked-out roads and faces were used for stowing waste underground. In eighteenth-century Lancashire new pits were sunk when underground haulage exceeded about one hundred yards. A survey of seventeen Tyneside collieries of about the year 1700 showed that, even at that early date, only three had single pits, the remainder averaging just under three pits each, with the two largest having five each.[42] A 1773 map of the Duke of Norfolk's Sheffield Park colliery in south Yorkshire showed no less than eleven pits on average 130 yards apart.[43] Shaft lives in these circumstances were accordingly short: in south Yorkshire average life expectancy of a pit was four years, and in Lancashire three years was the normal life of a pit, and some pits had lives of little more than a year.[44] In this way collieries acquired a degree of mobility, their bounds being set only by the geographical limits to the mining rights held by the operator or by the workability of the seams being pursued underground. The same colliery might have operated for fifty years, but at the end of that period it was in a slightly different geographical area from the start of its life, and used a different set of shafts.

As mining was pushed to greater depths in the later eighteenth century, the economics of sinking forced a change of tactics. For the most part the greatly enhanced problems of ventilation still required at least two shafts, but the high cost of deep shafts called for their

---

[40] Thomas thesis 1974, 45. [41] Holmes 1816, 75.
[42] NEI Buddle 14/212. [43] Fletcher thesis 1973, 50.
[44] Fletcher thesis 1973, 50; Anderson 1975, 53-4.

utilization over much longer periods. This lengthening of shaft lives in turn led to considerable extension of underground roads and, in consequence, to the development of the technology of underground haulage. Where mining was already fairly deep at the opening of the eighteenth century, as in the North-east and Cumberland, this situation prevailed from the start of the period; but where, as in most other coalfields at the start of the century, mines were still comparatively shallow, this form of concentration emerged only later in the century or was delayed even into the early nineteenth century.

Further limitations on the access offered by a single pair of shafts, however, were posed by drainage and winding capabilities, and where, as in the North-east in the later eighteenth and early nineteenth centuries, seemingly unlimited quantities of coal were available within an area of acceptable underground haulage distances, additional sinkings might prove to be advantageous to increase the capacity of drainage and winding machinery. Multiple shafts became a feature of some of the very large collieries of the late eighteenth and early nineteenth centuries in the Tyne basin below the Newcastle bridge as well as in east Durham when the magnesian limestone overlay was pierced during the 1820s. Thus, in the early nineteenth century the several accesses to a major colliery like Wallsend on Tyneside were simply known as 'A', 'B', 'C' pit, etc. Each of these pits operated as entities, working their own distinctive seams and geographical areas underground, and served by their own pumping, winding, and ventilation machinery, but the pits were none the less worked together as part of a single organization and managerial unit —the colliery. The unity of such a grouping was effective underground as well as on the surface, since workings from separate pits were but parts of a single operation within a given geographical area, and might best be served by common systems of drainage and ventilation. Physically, therefore, pits in such a colliery might be linked underground, though they might remain separate sub-units for purposes of coal getting and employment.

For all these practical reasons collieries could vary substantially in their nature from coalfield to coalfield, as well as within coalfields, and certainly evolved in response to changing technology over time. A miner's loyalty was to his pit rather than to the larger entity of the colliery, and it is not without significance that in the world of miners' lore and speech the word 'pit' was almost invariably used to denote the workplace, whereas in the written records of mining that were the business of managers, viewers, and landowners, references are almost always to 'collieries'.

The planning of a colliery, which included decisions as to the order in which seams should be worked, the layout of roadways and ventilation courses underground, and the choice of working method, called for a very high level of knowledge of mining geology and technology. The day-to-day running of a colliery, however, within the framework dictated by these decisions, was of a very different order of management. Here the skills called for were supervisory and accounting: underground labour had to be allocated both in respect of tasks and skills and of location within the general geographical scheme of working; decisions and precautions had to be taken in the interests of safety; above all, control had to be exercised over the quantity of small coal sent up. Where piece-rates were involved, a system of tallies to identify coal sent to the surface with the workers, or groups of workers responsible for it must be instituted that not only worked but could be seen to work by the miners concerned. At the surface, pumping, winding, and ventilation machinery must be kept working with all that that implied in terms of labour supply, the supply and feeding of horses, and the maintenance of machinery by smiths and wrights. In the counting house attendance-records must be kept and wages paid; pithead sales of coal must be recorded and all cash transactions accounted for; coal sent from the colliery by waggonway must be recorded for accounting purposes. Finally, a detailed account of all costs and receipts must be kept for the information of the colliery owner or lessee.

The title and exact definition and allocation of these various routine managerial duties varied from coalfield to coalfield. Larger collieries required a managerial hierarchy, while in smaller collieries a single official might cope on his own. Only very rarely did owners directly manage their own mines. Robert Reid Cunninghame managed his own colliery at Saltcoats in Ayrshire up to his death in 1812, but it is not clear how far he delegated some duties, particularly those underground. Many collieries were merely one of many forms of economic activity associated with a landowner's estate, and the ultimate responsibility for the profitable running of the colliery lay with the landowner's agent who rarely concerned himself with the day-to-day running of the colliery. Again, depending upon the size of the colliery and the estate, the estate agent's degree of contact with day-to-day management might be close or remote. In the late eighteenth century, for example, Lord Dudley employed a separate mineral agent to supervise the mining activities on his mixed agricultural and industrial estate in the Black Country. The mineral agent's permanent salaried staff, which managed limestone quarries and iron mines as well as collieries, numbered thirty-three in 1804, and included a 'superintendent of the works', a travelling clerk, and two office clerks, a 'ganger of boats', and several bailiffs and weighing-machine keepers.[45] In south Yorkshire the Earl Fitzwilliam appointed John Deakin as Overlooker for all his collieries in 1797 in place of separate overlookers at each colliery.[46] When John Lambton came of age in 1813 he took back control of his mines from contractors and placed the actual management in the hands of a 'colliery board' consisting of the two resident viewers, the head viewer—John Buddle, a trusted family friend—and occasionally himself. This organization seems to have lasted for at least ten years.[47]

In Scotland the term manager, overseer, oversman, or grieve were variously used to designate officials employed in managerial capacities. A contract of 1709 between Sir John Clerk of Penicuik, owner of mines in Midlothian, and William Summervell and James Johnston, 'his Oversmen and Redsmen', required the latter to give receipts for all coal delivered to them from the miners, to maintain all underground roads to a height of five and a half feet and a width of three feet, to leave strong pillars to prevent surface subsidence, to maintain shafts and levels in good condition, to supervise necessary draining, to fine colliers 'who shall do any work amiss either contrary to the said Sir John his acts of Baron Court, contrary to Sir John or their express command', and so on through some twenty articles.[48] In 1715 the Duke of Hamilton engaged John Mann to oversee his Kinglass colliery in West Lothian and gave him powers to employ workers, to purchase equipment, and to sell the coal produced.[49] The directions of 1741 for the management of Clunie and Cadham collieries in Fife were clearly setting a grieve's qualifications very modestly when they required him to be 'a person of a good character who can write a tolerable hand of write and understand something of figures'.[50] An 1815 account of the Black Country spoke of 'ground bailiffs' who 'inspect for the proprietors' at salaries that suggested full-time on-site employment. In Lancashire mine managers were known either as supervisors or managers. The Blundells, principal mineowners in the Orrell coalfield of south-west Lancashire, employed Henry Ellam to manage their colliery in the 1780s at a salary of £50 per year. At the reopening of the Lanmorlais colliery in South Wales in the 1770s, the partners agreed that both the 'agent' and the 'auditor' should be shareholders. The agent was to receive

[45] Raybould 1973, 95, 182, 226–7.   [46] Mee 1975, 97.
[47] Hiskey thesis 1978, 85–6.
[48] ScRO Clerk of Penicuik GD18/995. There are similar 'instructions' of c.1700 for the grieve and an oversman.
[49] Nef 1932, I, 426.   [50] KM Rothes 40/82/1.

1s. 6d. for every weigh of coal shipped for himself and his clerks, and the auditor was to be remunerated by an allocation of two per cent of the profits. The partnership operating the Measham and Swannington collieries in Leicestershire in the 1720s appointed a 'general secretary' at a salary of £20. 16s. per annum, with an 'agent' at each colliery responsible for engaging and controlling the contractors and for selling the coal produced. The grieve at Strathore colliery in Fife about 1750 was paid 3s. 4d. per week, with a free house and coal.[51]

The larger collieries managed in this way also commonly found it necessary to employ a system of underground management. Those responsible for this work went by a variety of names—underground stewards, underlookers, overmen, or oversmen.

While it would not be difficult to compile a list of the routine duties that must have filled the working life of a mine manager in the eighteenth and early nineteenth centuries, there is a dearth of precise documentation on the subject. A memorandum of 1811 sets out nicely the general principles governing the manager's, Mr Tait's, duties at the Curwens' Broughton colliery in Cumberland:

Upon all occasions to consult with [Mr Johnson, the Curwens' estate agent], divise and be advised by him in the cheapest, most effectual and permanent means of carrying the works on to advantage and of all things to use the utmost energy and exertion to raise quantity, keeping in view at same time the safety of the works and its being carried on according to the tenure and nature of the case now subsisting between Ld. Egremont and Mr. Curwen. It is expected in general from Mr. Tait that he will be in some one or more of the pits daily and when not there to be about the coal works above ground, to see Mr. Johnson every evening at least and report to him any improvements or alterations he conceives necessary in order that they together may devise the means most proper for carrying it into effect.[52]

One fortunate survival, however, interestingly illuminates this corner of mining history. It is the daily journal of Henry Jackson, colliery manager of the Whitehaven collieries of the Lowther family, for the period January 1818 to July 1819. Two weeks taken at random from this journal indicate the nature of the duties required of a mine manager:

Monday 1 June 1818: underground checking workings, men and horses at Kell's pit.
Tuesday 2 June: checked staith, incline, and underground at Croft pit.
Wednesday 3 June: underground at Scalegill and checked Howgill Pit tops and Howgill staith.

[51] NuRO Society of Antiquaries ZAN M14 A9/8; Anderson 1975, 126; NLW Maybery 202; C. P. Griffin thesis 1969, 61; KM Rothes 40/82/8.
[52] Memorandum by William Swinburn, 4 Nov. 1811, CuRO Curwen D/Cu/6/25.

Thursday 4 June: Pit off work because of King's birthday except for Scalegill. Surveyed workings there.

Friday 5 June: checked staiths and waggonways.

Saturday 6 June: checked pit tops and went underground to measure haggers' yards.

Sunday 7 June: Rest.

Monday 7 December 1818: underground at Scalegill in the morning measuring. Checking pit tops in the afternoon.

Tuesday 8 December: at office filling in memorandum books, etc.

Wednesday 9 December: at office classing, checking and paying workers.

Thursday 10 December: underground at Kell's Pit surveying old workings.

Friday 11 December: checked staiths, pit yard and pit tops in the morning. Went underground at Croft Pit in the afternoon checking on work of haggers and blaskers.

Saturday 12 December: underground at Scalegill checking water, and later checking pit tops.

Sunday 13 December: Rest.

In other weeks Jackson's journal referred to 'night watching'—trying to catch coal thieves at the bank; surveying other parts of the Lowther estate which might have had nothing to do with coal; and spending an average of one day each week in the office catching up on paperwork. It emerges that Jackson spent a significant proportion of his time underground, and that 'showing the flag' in all parts of the collieries was as important as constant checking on equipment, machinery, and working practices to look to the safety of workers and the economical working of the mine.[53]

In the North Wales, West Midlands, and Yorkshire mining regions a rather different system of management was employed in many collieries which derived partly from the requirements of collective organization demanded by the longwall system, and partly from the short supply of educated men capable of assuming clerical and administrative tasks. Here the managerial responsibility was divided between the owner's or lessee's agent who looked after sales and accounting, while all aspects of labour management—engagement and allocation of workers, underground supervision, and payment—were handled by a sub-contractor known in Shropshire and Derbyshire as the charter-master, in North Wales as the 'chalter', and in Staffordshire and south Yorkshire as the 'butty'. Charter-masters, who often employed deputies or 'doggies' to supervise groups of workers underground, contracted with the owner's agent to raise a given quantity of coal at an agreed price. Contracts were normally of short duration to allow for fluctations in the market. The owner

[53] CuRO Lonsdale D/Lons/W/41.

supplied the basic fixed capital equipment—shaft, drainage, winding, and ventilation machinery—while the charter-master undertook to cut, haul, and wind the coal, prop roofs, fill the goafs, and to provide the movable equipment in the shape of horses, tubs, tools, and timber. In Shropshire charter-masters also drove the levels, which often called for reserves of capital for the payment of labour before coal could be won, while in Staffordshire the owners commonly added to this responsibility that of sinking the shafts. On the Earl of Dudley's estate in south Staffordshire, according to an account of 1815

all the pits are sunk, the ropes, engines, air-heads, railways, gateways and trollies are supplied or wrought at the expence of the Lord of the Manor. He also engages the coal loader who is paid 2d. per ton, and brakeman, whom they call an Engineer, and who has a guinea a week. The ground bailiffs inspect for the proprietors and have from 80 to 100£ a year. The *Butties*, who are also called charter masters, undertake the working of the collieries, and to pay the Lord of the Manor or his lessee, three shillings a ton for large coal, 2s. for lumps, and 14d. for slack. They find all underground labour, candles, tools, horses, fodder and wages. . . . The establishment belonging to the Butty above ground consists of a banksman 4s. a day, a bank lad to assist him 2s.; and a boy or woman to draw off the coals, with a horse to the canal 2s. a day.[54]

From as early as 1797 the agent on this estate had made use of a standardized and printed form of contract with the charter-masters.[55] At Griff colliery in Warwickshire in the early eighteenth century a diluted form of the charter-master system operated. The management here was firmly under the control of a senior bailiff advised by an independent expert, Henry Beighton. Hewing, putting, and other basic underground work was sub-contracted to 'companies' of miners led by experienced workers, but the employment and allocation of miners to companies remained in the employer's hands.[56] The charter-master's commitment to the owner was not, therefore, that of a salaried employee, but through the profit motive.[57]

'Contracting' was an extension of the charter-master or butty system. It normally involved the contractor (or contractors, since they were often partnerships) in a wider range of functions than those accepted by charter-masters, and was mostly regulated by formal contracts. The responsibilities of the contractors extended to providing the labour force for a colliery, extracting the coal, and either selling it and paying a rent or royalty for it, or delivering it

[54] MS volume 'On Dudley Coal Mines, 1815', NuRO Society of Antiquaries ZAN M14 A9/8.

[55] Raybould 1968, 534.   [56] White thesis 1969, 146–7.

[57] Based on Taylor 1960; Trinder 1973, 343–7; Richards 1974, 417; MS volume 'On Dudley Mines, 1815', NuRO Society of Antiquaries ZAN M14 A9/7–9; Rogers 1963, 122.

to the owner or lessee and receiving a piece-rate payment for it. In the North-east in the early nineteenth century it also involved, according to a report by four viewers on the Vane-Tempest collieries, 'placing in the hands of the contractor not only the seams of coal but the care, charge and management of the air and water-courses, etc. . . . with the whole of the live and dead stock.'[58] Such a contract was made in 1765 by 'Allen and Co.' to work the Duke of Leeds's Todwick Common colliery in Yorkshire: they were to drive levels, fill old pits, recover old pit-props, and get coal, with separate piece-rates of payment for each of these tasks.[59] Another, between Robert Smith and Lord Delaval in 1798, was for working a Northumberland pit for a term of twelve or fifteen years. Smith was to provide horses for underground haulage and to be paid for coal brought to the surface at a rate that increased with the depth of mining. There were safeguards to cover the working expenses of horses in the event of under-employment (presumably on account of slack sales), and it seems that in this case some fixed as well as circulating capital was provided by the contractor since there was a provision that 'at the end of the term, lessor to take the horses' Hay and Corn, as also what Machine may be then upon the colliery at a valuation'. This would none the less leave the owner or lessee with the provision of most of the fixed assets.[60] Taylor has shown that contracting of this kind was quite widespread in the North-east between roughly 1780 and 1815.[61] Clearly such an arrangement gave rise to problems of reponsibility for maintenance and the long-term planning of exploitation. A group of viewers consulted in 1814 by the Vane-Tempests advised the abandonment of this method of working. They pointed out that the collieries of Sir Ralph Milbanke, Sir Thomas Liddell, Mr Lambton, and others had all once been worked by contractors but had now been taken back into direct working. They believed that in the whole north-east coalfield this practice was 'entirely given up, having been found one of the most troublesome, expensive and, to the coal owners, unproductive ever resorted to'.[62]

iv. *Viewers*

The distinction between managers, who looked after the day-to-day running of collieries, and viewers, who advised on and directed larger issues of colliery design, construction, and development, was never

---

[58] 'Report on letting collieries to be worked by contract, 27 Oct. 1814', DuRO Londonderry D/Lo/B33, quoted in Hiskey thesis 1978, 82.
[59] Hopkinson 1976, 27.
[60] NuRO Delaval NRO1765/58.
[61] Taylor 1960, 220–30.
[62] DuRO Londonderry D/Lo/B33.

a clear one. Some managers developed skills and knowledge that created a demand for their expertise beyond merely the colliery of their principal employment. Some even, like William Brown in the North-east in the 1750s and 1760s, or Henry Ellam in Orrell, Lancashire, after 1788, turned to mine leasing and ownership themselves. William Dixon, while manager of Govan colliery, near Glasgow, was also a partner in the Calder Iron and Coal Works, and ultimately acquired the ownership of the Govan colliery.[63] Others developed a considerable element of freelance advising or supervising alongside a formal attachment to a single colliery. In the North-east the manager of one of the large seasale mines was generally called a 'viewer', though the expression was also applied to an expert whose entire livelihood was gained in the freelance sale of his services.

The expression 'viewer', most common in the North-east, but found elsewhere, derived from the verb 'to view', or survey, a colliery. But it is clear from the foregoing that viewers undertook a wide range of duties. The term 'viewer', however, is rarely met until the mid-eighteenth century, and it is likely that it emerged at the same time as the increasing scale of economic and technical problems of mining called into existence a new group of more highly and diversely skilled managers. By the late eighteenth century, however, there were consultant viewers, check viewers, resident viewers, head viewers, under-viewers, assistant viewers, and general viewers. No absolute distinction can be made between them and they were not mutually exclusive terms. Most major north-east collieries had both a resident and a consultant viewer. The consultant viewer was sometimes known as the check viewer, though this title was more commonly used to describe a consultant employed by the lessor to protect his interest. Each would be a salaried position, but the latter only attended part-time, usually one day a week. The resident viewer had the care and direction of the day-to-day running of the colliery while the consultant viewer gave him orders to be implemented. In such cases the consultant viewer was the head viewer. Sometimes the resident viewer was sufficiently accomplished for there to be no need of a consultant. Depending on the size of the colliery the head viewer might be assisted by one or more under-viewers. Such under-viewers were sometimes called assistant viewers, but the latter term was more usually attributed to those who were attached to a viewer rather than to a colliery. The most highly reputed viewers, often called general viewers, were surrounded by schools of apprentices and assistants. At the beginning of the nineteenth century there were three great schools in the North-east, headed by Buddle, Barnes, and Johnson.

[63] Payne 1961, 75.

There was great rivalry, even enmity, between them, and viewers who had taken their own place were still considered attached to the school of their 'master'. Apprentices would graduate to become assistants before finding an independent place of their own, usually on the recommendation of the general viewer.

Head viewers, whether resident or consultant, were a mixture of manager, engineer, surveyor, accountant, and agent. They were responsible for establishing the most efficient and effectual method of working collieries. They organized maintenance, repairs, and alterations, made surveys and plans, and were responsible for safety checks. They dealt with the paper work, ordering of materials, payment of bills, keeping of colliery records in diaries or memoranda books, dealt with correspondence often in the form of progress reports to the owners, and acted as negotiators for the owners in drawing up leases, wayleave agreements, and bonds. Their duties extended beyond the colliery. They were responsible for the waggon-ways and staithes, and, if they were agents as well, they would be involved in the sale of coal. Because the quality of coal determined its price, and the quality was partly determined by the methods of working imposed by the viewers, they had to take an interest in its sale by the fitters and in its reception on the London market.

A consultant viewer could, and usually did, hold the position at several collieries simultaneously. In addition to being consultant viewer to Lord Londonderry from the 1820s, John Buddle, for example, was head viewer and manager at Wallsend and Tanfield Moor. He was head viewer and part-owner at Benwell (1803–43), Heaton (1807–21), Sheriff Hill (1804–10), Backworth (1813–31), and Elswick (1804–43); and he was head viewer at Percy Main (1802–43), Hebburn (1803–13), Jarrow (1811–30), Cowpen (at least 1802–3), Walker (at least 1806–8), Washington, and the Lambton collieries (1806–19). He was agent for the Londonderry collieries (1819–43), and was check viewer for Ralph Riddell who was lessor of Kenton and Coxlodge collieries, and for the Revd John Collinson, the owner of Felling and lessor of Tyne Main collieries.

Most viewers deliberately arranged not to be fully occupied by such posts in order to leave time for freelance consultancies. The commissioning of individual reports, or views, was the basis of forward planning as opposed to routine supervision, and though by 1830 the emphasis had moved towards a more differentiated structure, there was never a clear division between consultant specialists and general management. Several owners commissioned views annually, but most views were the result of irregular, individual requests. Viewers provided expert opinion for forecasting. They would be employed to make estimates of the cost of winning and working, and to give their opinion on the likelihood of finding coal and of its possible extent. They were also commissioned to make reports or provide second opinions in response to specific difficulties or crises, often about foul air, creep, fires, or explosions. Viewers acted as valuers and also received commissions to function as arbitrators or referees. Valuations were made whenever an owner or part-owner wished to sell, or more commonly when an owner died and the value of his holding had to be estimated for his executors. Viewers would be used as arbitrators in disputes or negotiations between lessors and lessees, undertakers and owners, buyers and sellers, miners and owners, and the coalowners' committee and individual collieries. In 1778, for example, the Delaval estate agent sought advice about the appointment of a viewer to make a report on Bedlington colliery in Northumberland. He was recommended to appoint a Wear viewer on the ground that a Tyne viewer would be prejudiced against development of this colliery since any new working in this area would have to share in the Tyne seasale quota.[64]

Viewers were also engaged by coalowners who did not work their own mines but leased them to tenants. John Buddle senior, for example, was appointed viewer to the Bishop of Durham in 1792 and to the Dean and Chapter of Durham Cathedral in 1800. In this capacity he was largely concerned with advising on the terms of leases.[65] In 1810 the Duke of Northumberland's agents approached John Buddle junior for his opinion of a claim by the lessee of Shilbottle colliery for a reduction in rent: they suspected that the lessee had managed the colliery 'the better to answer his purpose of obtaining a reduction of rent'. After investigation Buddle reported that he thought the tenant's claim was fair and recommended a new level which would allow the tenant a reasonable profit.[66]

When submitting reports to employers viewers had to take account not merely of the facts of the situation, but also of the kind of advice they wanted to be given. In a covering letter of 1810 with a report on Fishwick Mains colliery Buddle explained to the lessee:

I have stated the prospect of finding coal in as favourable a point of view as *facts* would support me in doing, but if you would wish it appear in any other shape, I can easily alter the form without misrepresenting the facts, as I have stated nothing more than my *real opinion*. I however feel it necessary to state candidly to *yourself* that I scarcely think the prospect of finding coal so favourable (that is a workable seam) as to justify me in advising you to bore at your own expense to such a depth as would be necessary to set the question at

[64] NuRO Delaval ZDE 7/18/3.   [65] NEI Buddle 20/1 ; 15/no pagination.
[66] NEI Buddle 3/183–5.

rest, as I think the cost would be too great for an individual, unless the prospect of remuneration rested on safer ground.[67]

Any qualified viewer could be commissioned to make a report, but the reputation of the general viewers led to their attracting a disproportionate number of commissions. The prestige of the north-east viewers as the leading experts of the day meant that they received commissions from beyond their own coalfield. John Buddle senior reported in the 1780s on collieries in Yorkshire, and his son in the early nineteenth century on those of Cumberland, Lancashire, and Scotland, and in the 1830s on those in South Wales and the Forest of Dean.[68] In 1759 William Brown, Sir John Hussey Delaval's viewer at Hartley, and one of Lord Ravensworth's viewers went together to Newcastle-under-Lyme in Staffordshire to inspect an improved steam pumping engine by James Brindley. But Brindley was away erecting another engine in Coalbrookdale and they were obliged to return to the North-east having learned little.[69] Commissions were also received from abroad. Many of them—those that were the most straightforward or involved most travelling—were delegated to the assistants. Buddle sent an assistant to Portugal in 1825 to make a report for a group of English financiers considering investment, and another was sent to Russia in 1837 to report to Prince Lieven on coal exploration. In 1834 Buddle himself made a report, from information and plans sent to him, on Sydney colliery, Cape Breton Island, Nova Scotia, and in 1839 he sent out a viewer and six colliers to restore a colliery in Virginia. Other viewers also had foreign connections: in 1791 George Johnson sent one of his assistants to Poland to make a report on the likelihood of finding coal, and John Watson is reported to have won a colliery in Sweden.[70]

It is difficult to estimate the remuneration viewers received for their responsibilities and duties because evidence is patchy, because of the multiplicity of positions they held, and because fees that were related to output or profit could fluctuate alarmingly. When Thomas Stokoe was appointed viewer of all the collieries operated by the Grand Allies partnership in 1730 his salary was fixed at £40 per annum. The recommended salary for a newly appointed 'chief agent' (resident viewer) at Bedlington colliery in Northumberland in 1778 was £100 per year plus necessary travelling expenses. In 1758 John Watson accepted twenty guineas for acting as consultant viewer

---

[67] J. Buddle to Burnet Greive, 6 Oct. 1810, NEI Buddle 3/179.
[68] SCL Local Studies 27/47; NEI Buddle Atkinson 45/3/no pagination; NEI Buddle 19/102; JRL Crawford and Balcarres 23/6/202.
[69] W. Brown to Sir John Hussey Delaval, 9 Sept. 1759, NuRO Delaval ZDE 6/3/1.
[70] NEI Buddle Atkinson 45/3/no pagination; NEI Buddle 19/270.

(working one day a week) at a time when he normally charged twenty-five guineas.[71] In 1802 an account for a seven-page report on Broughton colliery in Cumberland by the Newcastle viewer, Sober Watkins, was queried by the owner who had commissioned it. Watkins's total bill of £339. 16s. 11d. included £63 for a surface survey of 3,182 acres, and £41. 15s. 8d. for several trips back to Newcastle. Watkins defended these charges on the grounds that 6d. per acre was the normal charge for ground surveys in Cumberland, and that it was usual for viewers to return to Newcastle from time to time to attend to their other affairs. This report had occupied him for twenty-five days and his assistant for thirty days.[72] In 1805 John Buddle junior earned £750, and in 1806 £1,200, in salaries as head viewer alone. This did not include his earnings from private practice: in 1807 he charged two guineas for a view, two guineas for a regular report, and one guinea for a consultation. By about 1830 he had a printed card on which was set out his whole scale of fees. Valuations were then charged in proportion to the value of the colliery, ranging from ten guineas for a colliery valued at between £5,000 and £10,000 to 100 guineas for one valued at over £150,000. Other inspections, consultations, estimates, and opinions were offered at fees ranging from one to five guineas, while time spent travelling was charged at two guineas a day.[73] George Hunter, a resident viewer at Penshaw colliery in County Durham where Buddle was agent, received a salary of £300 per year in 1828, though this was probably not very high for the period. Three years earlier he had turned down an offer of £550 to be resident viewer at the new Seghill colliery. Robert Bald, manager to the Earl of Mar and Kellie at his Alloa colliery on the Firth of Forth, received by an agreement of 1815 one-ninth of the profits of the undertaking with a minimum of £300 per annum and a maximum of £500. In the event, he earned the full £500 every year between 1815 and 1825 except in four years when his receipts fell only marginally below that figure.[74]

Viewers may also have been able to boost their earnings by other means. They seem to have supplied corving rods from Kent to collieries at a profit to themselves. Buddle wrote of the cost of them 'being one of the *secrets and mysteries* of the profession'. Leading viewers sometimes took a financial stake in collieries they were connected with. Buddle was part-owner of at least five collieries, but he always

---

[71] Grand Allies partnership minute book, 1727-38, NEI Grand Allies 18/volume not numbered; M. Newton to H. Flower, 9 Oct. 1778, NuRO Delaval ZDE 7/18/3; NuRO Delaval ZDE 6/1/8.

[72] CuRO Leconfield D/Lec/65/17, 19.

[73] NEI Buddle 15/185; DuRO NCB First Deposit NCB/I/JB/6, n.d. but probably 1830.

[74] ScRO Mar and Kellie GD124/17/587/6, 17.

took a minority share. He provided the bulk of the expertise, others the bulk of the capital. Before limited liability the personal financial involvement of an expert such as Buddle must have been reassuring. It is likely that capital would flow more easily into concerns he had a stake in, and that owners would encourage a financial involvement to get the most out of his services. Buddle also became involved in coal-related enterprises. He owned a steam flour-mill supplying flour to owners for sale at subsidized rates to the pitmen, and bought his own collier to trade from the newly built Seaham Harbour. He speculated in hay and oats, and was an agent between the Butterley Iron Company and the collieries in which it supplied machinery.[75]

Viewers in the period up to 1830 not only performed a wide range of functions but did so at several collieries simultaneously, as well as acting as freelance consultants. Such a system, at a time of increasing occupational specialization, was not without its critics. An anonymous writer, prompted by Buddle's death, suggested that 'what is call'd a head viewer, continues to obtain so many appointments that he can never be intimately acquainted with the minutiae of any concern he *pretends* to manage', a criticism which had been voiced as early as 1814.[76] There were, however, advantages to offset the self-evident truth of such allegations. A leading viewer was in a unique position: his knowledge of neighbouring collieries, of collieries working the same seam, as well as an awareness of developments elsewhere, could only improve his judgement. Buddle's employers could only benefit from his irresistible urge for 'a peep into the enemy's camp'.

John Buddle was sufficiently expert in many branches of engineering to be employed outside the industry. He was closely involved in the building of Seaham Harbour (1828–31), he advised on improvements to Blyth Harbour in 1837, and made a report on Warkworth Harbour in 1841. In 1808 he gave advice to the Thames Archway Company who were attempting to build a tunnel under the river between Rotherhithe and Limehouse. He reported on drainage in the Arkengarthdale lead-mines in Yorkshire in 1816, investigated mineral wells at Harrogate in 1837 and brine springs and salt-works in Staffordshire between 1839 and 1841, and in 1832 set out the line of the proposed Durham to South Shields railway. He dominated the coal industry of the North-east for most of the first half of the nineteenth century, not so much as an owner, but as an expert. He was a major witness before the Select Committees of 1830 and 1835 and the Commissions on the Combination Laws of 1825 and Children's

[75] NEI Buddle 23/45.
[76] J. Bedlington, *An Address to the Proprietors of Collieries*, 13 Sept. 1814, in bound scrapbook in NEI Bell 14/5/47.

Employment of 1842, and, when the leading coalowners decided in 1805 to formalize their 'Limitation of the Vend' as the Joint Northumberland and Durham Coal Owners' Association, he was the automatic choice as Secretary at a salary of £50 a year, raised in the following year to £100. He became a magistrate for the County of Northumberland and commanded the Wallsend Rifle Corps which he had founded in 1825. But in spite of being so obviously and necessarily an 'owners' man', he succeeded in retaining the confidence of the miners, surely as a result of his determination to improve safety in mines and his willingness to share the risks of the miners underground. He was actively interested, too, in founding schools in the villages of the collieries with which he was connected. A Unitarian, he also founded a chamber-music society in Newcastle. He never married. At his death in 1843 he was reputed to be worth over £150,000.[77]

In the circumstances of industrial management in the eighteenth century and of an expanding industry ever on the look-out for technological and managerial skills, it was to be expected that the viewers would originate in a wide range of occupations and social backgrounds. Some, like John Buddle senior, who died in 1806, started as miners, though he entered the viewing profession through school-teaching; but most went through some form of apprenticeship to other viewers, suggesting social origins at least in the artisan class. John Watson, for example, one of the best-known of the north-east viewers of the second half of the eighteenth century, was the son of a mariner and entered the profession by serving an apprenticeship as a viewer with his cousin, William Newton of Burnhopefield.[78] There was a long tradition of family succession in the profession. Three generations of the Smith family were viewers at the Lambton collieries in Durham in the second half of the eighteenth century: they were reputed to be the oldest family of viewers in the North-east and were celebrated mathematicians.[79] Robert Bald followed his father, Alexander Bald, as viewer at the Earl of Mar and Kellie's colliery at Alloa on the Firth of Forth, and became as famous in Scotland as did the younger John Buddle in the North-east. Benjamin Biram followed his father, Joshua Biram, as viewer to the Earl Fitzwilliam's Wentworth estate collieries in south Yorkshire in the 1820s. In Cumberland the Speddings formed almost a dynasty of viewers in the Lowther collieries from the early eighteenth century. John Buddle, the greatest of the north-east viewers, was assistant to his father at Wallsend colliery and took over from him on his death

[77] *DNB* under John Buddle; Hiskey thesis 1978; Welford and Hodgson 1913, 120.
[78] NEI Watson 8/4/1.   [79] NEI Bell 15/1/23.

in 1806. Other viewers entered the profession from the ownership of small collieries. William Brown, who was appointed viewer of Throckley colliery on the Northumberland side of the upper Tyne, had previously operated his own small landsale colliery in that area.[80] It was even possible—though how common it was is impossible to say—for miners to enter the ranks of viewers by way of deputyships and overmanships.

As technicians and managers, viewers stood between owners and miners. 'The management of large bodies of workmen is a subject of great importance', said one commentator of the 1830s. 'It is an art of great delicacy, which most people think very easy to be acquired, and yet which very few people ever thoroughly attain.'[81] Viewers mostly seem to have held the confidence of the miners, who respected their expertise and, in most cases, their willingness to share the risks of underground work. Both the miners and owners, for example, seem to have been willing to accept the arbitration of viewers in wage disputes. Thus in 1810, hewers in the Lambton collieries requested that a wage offer they found unacceptable be referred to the arbitration of two 'indifferent' viewers, one to be nominated by them, one by the owner. The owner accepted this, and the miners found the arbitration fair and abided by the viewers' decision.[82] In 1806, during a period of general inflation, the northeast owners agreed that every claim for an increased price for hewing be referred to the decision of two viewers, one nominated by themselves and one by the claimant. Similarly, in 1827, the Tyne owners ordered that a fair scale of wages be drawn up by a meeting of viewers and recommended it for general acceptance.[83]

A viewer's duties at the colliery meant that regular underground visits were essential. A resident viewer would be in the pits most days and a consultant viewer would go underground on almost every visit. Some of the greatest viewers, however, avoided the discomfort and danger of underground work whenever possible by sending their assistants down for all routine tasks. Three viewers—George Johnson, John Watson, and William Brown—were known to have given up underground visits altogether. This could not have helped their relationship with the miners. A deponent in a Chancery case declared that the pitmen, with their 'prejudices . . . will be more anxious to serve when the manager visits the pits and the workings . . . than they would or can reasonably be expected to be with a man who never

[80] NEI Bell 15/1/18.
[81] J. F. W. Johnston, *The Economy of a Coal-Field* (Durham, 1838), 70.
[82] NEI Buddle 34/II/62.
[83] NuRO Joint Coal Owners' Association 263, Minute Book 1805–15, 36, 2 Oct. 1806; Minute Book 1826–47, 7, 13 Mar. 1827.

enters a pit'. Buddle was well aware of such advantages and he had a reputation for being the first to go underground after an explosion. His personal presence not only gave his opinions greater weight with the miners, but must have improved the quality of his reports. It was important to be able to hear the noise of a creep, to see how coal fell, to feel the ventilation, and to see and smell the air.

This underground 'feel' was equally important in the training of viewers. Apprentices were taken on when they were approaching maturity, but there seems to have been a belief that experience should preferably be gained at an earlier age. Buddle said he was 'initiated into the mysteries of pit-work when not quite six years old'. He was one viewer with a reputation for not risking lives by cutting costs. But explosions could occur even with the most attentive and knowledgeable viewers. This responsibility lay heavily with some. After the 1812 disaster at Felling colliery the viewer, Straker, 'appears to have no confidence in anything he directs'. The blame was laid firmly at his door: 'there has seldom been an instance in the coal trade of popular prejudice running so high against any individual as it now serves to do against Straker. . . . He has been obliged to desert his house for 2 or 3 days.'[84]

The relationship with owners was more complex. Owners were, after all, the employers of viewers, and a viewer's responsibility lay principally to the owner. But viewers were professional men, with a loyalty to the standards of the profession reinforced by an overriding concern for the lives of the miners whose safety depended upon their judgement. As Buddle put it to one of his employers, Lord Londonderry: '*Advising* is the first branch of my duty, but *obeying* is the second, and I hope your Lordship will never find me pressing the former to the exclusion of the latter, when the sole responsibility is with your Lordship.'[85] On the other hand, he accepted the responsibility of putting his employer in full possession of the facts relevant to any judgement he might have to make. 'The more my employers know of their own affairs', he wrote to W. M. Pitt, of whose Tanfield Moor colliery he was viewer, 'and my manner of acting in them, the more comfortable and satisfactory it is to myself. I am therefore desirous . . . to establish a system of management and correspondence, which may keep you in regular communication with your affairs in this quarter—not to teaze you with trifling matters but to give you sufficient information in all material points.'[86]

Formally, the relationship between employers and viewers was regulated by contract or letter of appointment. The viewer appointed

[84] NEI Easton 17/7/134.   [85] Quoted in Hiskey thesis 1978, 117.
[86] NEI Buddle 22/86.

around 1800 to Sheriff Hill colliery was under contract to attend the colliery twice a week as well as 'upon any particular occasion when required and during an accident or misfortune'. On his regular visits he was to go down both pits and examine the state of the mine as well as of the workings.[87] The contract between the Duke of Norfolk and the consultant viewer appointed in 1813 to oversee operations in all the Duke's Yorkshire collieries stipulated:

> It is proposed to Mr. Wm. Locks to become the Surveyor of the Duke of Norfolk's Mines and Minerals from Mich[s]. 1813 and to continue the Plans and measurements thereof which are now in hand, and to make report on the State of all relating to such Mines and Minerals in his Grace's Estate in the West Riding of Yorkshire giving all time necessary for the business and at least twice a year giving a Week each time to the investigation, namely a Week in March and a Week in September each year but beginning by making a Complete Statement at present. The Salary, including all Expenses . . . and every item that might be brought in Charge, to be forty Guineas per Annum.[88]

Since so few colliery owners or tenants operated their own mines personally, salaried or feed managers were a universal feature of colliery operation throughout the period from 1700 to 1830; but it is abundantly clear that the character of these managers changed significantly during that period. The principal agents of this change were undoubtedly the increase in the scale of mines and the growing complexity of mining technology. The relatively small, shallow mines of the early eighteenth century rarely employed a sufficient labour force to call for a hierarchy of highly trained managerial staff, and the technology of simple wooden machinery activated by horse- or water-power was well within the grasp of most practical, mechanically minded men. A wide range of developments, however, not all of them technological, steadily altered the situation during the eighteenth and early nineteenth centuries to the point at which a supply of educated, specifically trained managers became essential to the growth of the industry. These developments included the evolution of the mining lease from a simple permission to extract coal in return for a fixed annual payment into a complex document regulating output, methods of working, and rates of extraction; the rise of combinations among producers that both created new forms of large-scale organization in the industry and, by regulating regional output, introduced a new 'political' element into colliery management; the evolution of new working methods; and a wide range of technological innovations—steam-pumping and -winding, ventilation, safety-lighting, and the use of railways both underground and on the

---

[87] ScRO Waldie-Griffith GDI/378/11, n.d. but probably c.1800.
[88] Fletcher thesis 1973, 15.

surface, at first horse-drawn, later powered by steam locomotives. All these developments are reviewed in succeeding chapters. The manager or viewer was expected not merely to be master of them all, but also to be abreast of new developments as they occurred or even to play a leading part in devising improved technologies.

It is not to be wondered at that while we are fairly well informed about the managers and viewers of the late eighteenth and early nineteenth centuries, we know relatively little about those of the early eighteenth century: they were not of the stature or importance to have left much mark on the records of the industry. As a key group, the managers began to emerge during the middle decades of the eighteenth century, and by the early decades of the nineteenth century they had come to be dominant figures in the industry— men powerful and influential in the community as well as in the industry by virtue of high technical skill and a magisterial range of competence. The subordinate managers of the early eighteenth century, had indeed evolved into a profession, albeit a profession as yet without formal, institutional status, yet already one with a recognized training and a secure social and economic position. As a step in the process of 'professionalization', a Colliery Viewers' Society had been formed at least by 1826. The best of the viewers were rightly very amply rewarded for their crucial contribution to the expansion and modernization of their industry. Their importance and success were not, of course, unique in the experience of British industry in this period: the emergence of a managerial class has been observed by historians of the iron, brewing, textile, and glass-making industries. But the diversity of skills called for in mining manage- ments—skills in the spheres of geology, mechanical engineering, labour relations, accounting, and the politics of big business— unquestionably placed the Buddles, the Speddings, the Birams, Curr, Bald, Watson, Johnson, and Brown in the forefront of the managerial revolution of the new industrial age.[89]

[89] This account of viewers draws heavily on Mathias Dunn, 'History of the viewers', MS in NEI Bell 15/1 ; Hiskey thesis 1978 ; DuRO NCB First Deposit NCB/I/JB/1844.

Chapter 3

Technology (1)

i. *Exploration, boring, and sinking*

The outcropping or 'bassetting' of coal solved two problems for the miner: it indicated where coal was to be found; and it gave easy access for mining. But by no means all coal seams in Britain crop out, and even those that do may run concealed for miles away from the 'basset'. By the end of the seventeenth century most fruitful outcrops of coal had been discovered and worked into the seam as far as drainage and hauling technology permitted; and if mining was to continue and expand it was clear that the mere tracing of seams from the outcrop was a far too limited expedient in the search for coal. The intelligent following of seams, it is true, had indicated the possibilities of hidden wealth, but it had also revealed that faults and changing angles of dip nullified expectations based on assumptions of the uninterrupted lateral extension of known seams.

At the beginning of the eighteenth century there was an almost total ignorance of geology. Apart from the absence of an understanding of the basic geological processes—the formation of rocks, the laying-down of strata, folding and weathering, glaciation and geomorphology, and the whole chronology of geological periodization—there was no adequate terminology, while cartographic techniques were inadequate for the accurate representation of geological data. In the early eighteenth century interest in earth science tended not to extend beyond a circle of 'gentlemen–amateurs'. Later in the century, however, agricultural and industrial developments stimulated a quest for a more systematic investigation of geology. The first steps towards the 'professionalization' of geological studies, as Porter has shown, were taken by surveyors connected with various branches of mining. But though learned societies in the fields of mineralogy and geology were founded in 1799 and 1807 respectively, the gentlemen–amateurs continued to dominate these studies at least until the formation of the Geological Survey in 1835.[1]

Practical mining had, none the less, made astonishing advances in tracing and gaining access to commercially workable seams long

[1] R. Porter, 'Gentlemen and geology: the emergence of a scientific career, 1660–1920', *Historical Journal* 21 (1978).

before mineral geology began to provide material guidance. Edward Martin published the first scientific study of coalfield geology in his 'Description of the Mineral Basin in the Counties of Glamorgan, Monmouth, Brecknock, Carmarthen and Pembroke' in 1806.[2] While he was at work, William Smith, 'the father of English geology', was acquiring a working knowledge of mining in the Somerset coalfield and developing his interest in geological mapping. In 1816 he published his *Delineation of Strata* which he followed by a long series of geological maps of counties. It was William Smith who surveyed the mineral properties of Colonel Braddyll in County Durham during the second decade of the nineteenth century and persuaded him that contrary to firmly held local belief, coal could be won from beneath the magnesian limestone.[3]

Throughout the eighteenth century, however, mining entrepreneurs were forced to rely on their own limited experience and the primitive folk-lore of mining geology. Sir John Clerk of Penicuik, for example, in his 'Dissertation' of 1740, advised that

All the Coal Seams in Great Britain running generally East and West with some few Variations, the best methods for discovering coal seams are, in my humble opinion these:

1[mo] To observe the Channels of all Rivers and Brooks running across these Strata from South to North, or which cross them obliquely, thus all the Coal Seams I have yet observed, whether lying flat or on Edge have Some where or other appeared in their Strikes or drifts. 2[do] To consider even Firths and Branches of the Sea, and all Rivers whatsoever which may run in a Line with these Strata, for by accidental Turns, Hitches, Ridges and Dykes they may be discovered, for instance most of all the Coal Seams in the Shires of Lothian, Fife, Stirling and Clackmannan, may be observed on the shoars of the Firth of Forth. 3[tio] To observe all the Gulphs or Slips of Hills and Eminencies, especially after great rains, for Such readily discover not only the Strata of Coal and Lymestone, but all the Veins of Metalls and Minerals which lye amongst them.[4]

This kind of simple, empirical observation, was still recommended in a guide of the 1830s.[5]

Surface observation and folk-lore, however, were poor foundations for an outlay of capital on a sinking, and already by the beginning of the eighteenth century, techniques of test boring had been developed. Boring was not only a means for ascertaining the

[2] *Philosophical Transactions of the Royal Society of London*, 1806, 342–7.
[3] For Smith see Mining Association of Great Britain 1926, 18–19; and A. G. Davies, 'William Smith, civil engineer, geologist (1769–1839)', *TNS*, 23 (1942–3).
[4] ScRO Clerk of Penicuik GD18/1069.
[5] Anon., *The History and Description of Fossil Fuel. The Collieries and Coal Trade of Great Britain* (London, 1835), 175.

existence of coal underground, but also for tracing the continuity of
a seam, for locating faults, and for determining the most advantageous
location for drainage shafts. Even if there was no immediate intention to mine coal, boring to discover the existence of underground
seams was an important determinant of land values in a mining
region. In the Orrell coalfield of south Lancashire land without coal
was worth £1 to £2 per acre in the mid-eighteenth century, but land
under which coal had been proved by boring sold for £70 to £80 per
acre.[6] For this reason some landowners were prepared to bore
speculatively. Joseph Pennington of Muncaster in Cumberland, for
example, who reinforced his local acquaintance with coal-mining by
marrying into the Lowther family, moved in the early years of the
eighteenth century to his estate at Warter in the East Riding of
Yorkshire. There he instituted a series of test borings for coal. The
search was supervised by the Revd Thomas Robinson, an amateur
geologist of Ousby, Cumberland, who employed a professional borer
from Cumberland. A four-inch seam of coal was apparently discovered in 1713, and colliers engaged and paid for three years on the
strength of this discovery; but commercial mining was never developed.
A more successful test boring was made in 1776–7 on the Duke of
Portland's land 'in the North part of the Estate near the Turnpike
Bar on the Chesterfield road' which found a seam five feet eight
inches thick at 210 feet down. Two other thinner seams were also
discovered nearby.[7]

The fullest accounts of the technique of boring come from the
early nineteenth century, but there is no reason to suppose that the
technique had changed much during the preceding century. The
boring rods were suspended by rope, pulley, and block from a timber
tripod. They were between four and nine feet in length and screwed
end-on one into the other. The boring bit or chisel of between two
and five inches in diameter was screwed to the lowest rod and a
brace-head with four arms for manual rotation fitted to the topmost
rod. Vertical pressure was exerted by the weight of the rods assisted
by the spring action of a freshly felled tree-trunk: two men worked
the vertical motion, using the tree-spring to raise and lower the
boring rods, and two others walked slowly round and round using
the brace-head to give a screwing motion to the rods. Two methods
were used to examine the nature of the 'wreck' or material loosened
by the chisel: either a shell-shaped scoop was lowered on the rods
in place of the chisel, or the cuttings were raised by a 'wimble' or
'sludger'——a hollow tube screwed to the lowest rod with a trap at

[6] Anderson 1975, 46.
[7] Neave 1973, 194–6; NCRO Portland DD3P/6/10.

the base to admit and then raise a section of the bore.[8] Boring by these methods could not be rapid. The need constantly to remove all the rods in order to replace the chisel by the scoop or wimble made the process tedious and slow. Attempts were made to improve the process by mechanization, but although a steam-powered boring-engine was invented by Richard Trevithick, which was said to have been used for boring through the magnesian limestone overlay in north-east Durham,[9] manual methods appear generally to have persisted. A boring at Houghton in County Durham in 1750 achieved only 123 feet in forty days.[10] In the 1820s James Ryan, an Irishman, invented a method of boring by which a solid core could be taken out section by section.[11] While a single bore might indicate the presence or absence of a coal seam underground, as did, for example, a trial boring to 489 feet in Somerset that led to the opening-up of mining in the Radstock area,[12] several bores were usually undertaken to ensure the continuity of a seam over a sufficiently wide area to justify investment in a sinking. Gabriel Jars was told in the North-east in the 1760s that a second bore was frequently necessary, and sometimes a third in an extract triangle to determine the inclination of the seam, because the drainage pit must be located at the lowest part of the area to be mined.[13]

Boring was a highly skilled craft invariably undertaken by specialized teams. As late as 1795 one firm, Messrs. Rawlings, was described as being 'the only respectable and professional borers in the north'.[14] A team consisted of a master-borer and four men who undertook boring by contract. Such a team proposed in May 1720 to bore for coal on Lord Molyneux's land at Sefton in Lancashire. 'They propose that they will undertake to find coal, his Lordship allowing them wages and if they find coal then his Lordship to allow them better gratuity and to allow them also Boring Nagers and Ropes and Utensils and to repair them.'[15] Gabriel Jars spoke of the master-borers of the North-east in the 1760s as experts in mining exploration: they knew the nature of seams in an area twenty miles around Newcastle to a depth of 600 feet. They undertook exploration and would ascertain whether seams were workable and at what depth. Their payment, which was, of course, the remuneration for

[8] Holmes 1816, 71–3; Anon., *History and Description of Fossil Fuel*, 176–9; Anderson 1967, 114–15; Anderson 1975, 47–9.

[9] Mining Association of Great Britain 1926, 27.

[10] Robertson 1970, 13.

[11] Article 'Mine' (supposed by R. Bald), *Edinburgh Encyclopedia* 1830, 330.

[12] Clew 1970, 13.

[13] Jars 1774–81, I, 185–6.

[14] NEI Buddle 26/1.

[15] LaRO Molyneux of Sefton DDM/4/3.

the whole team, was at the rate of 5s. per fathom of six feet for the first ten fathoms, 10s. for the next five fathoms, 15s. for the next five, and so on.[16] A team of borers from Northumberland led by Andrew Wake contracted to make a bore to test for a fault for the Ayrshire Coal Company in 1788–9. Payment in this case was on a time-rate basis, at 5s. per shift, and it took Wake and his team 288 shifts—nearly a year's work—to get down to the required depth of 378 feet.[17] A boring at Elsecar Old colliery in south Yorkshire, for which a bore of two and a quarter inches diameter was specified, was contracted in 1799 by John Bennard and Thomas Cooper at the rate of 2s. 6d. per yard for the first twelve yards, 5s. for the next twelve yards, and the remainder down to an existing drift at 7s. 6d. per yard.[18]

The existence of a workable seam underground having been established by boring, the next step was to gain access for working. Where workable seams lay very close to the surface and the scale of demand was small, the coal was commonly got by means of bell-pits or, very occasionally, by small open-cast workings. With this method a shaft was sunk to the seam and the coal taken out by working radially from the shaft bottom until the point at which the sides were in danger of falling in. This produced the bell-shaped pits that gave the method its name. Most bell-pits were circular, though some were occasionally oval, and rarely exceeded twenty feet in depth and a radius of sixteen to twenty feet at the base. When such a pit had been worked to its practical limit it was abandoned and another pit started nearby, the debris from the new pit being used to fill the old pit. Bell-pit working has been traced in Derbyshire, the Clyne valley of the western sector of the South Wales coalfield, and the Titterstone Clee Hill area of Shropshire in the eighteenth century, but it is probable that it was used in the smallest workings in most of the mining regions.[19]

For seams not accessible by bell-pits, or that it was desired to work on a larger scale—for the greater proportion of the coal mined in Britain in the eighteenth and early nineteenth centuries, that is to say—deeper mining was essential, and for this it was necessary to sink shafts deep enough to reach the seams to be worked and wide enough to allow for winding, pumping, and ventilation. The equipment used in sinking throughout the eighteenth and early nineteenth centuries was rudimentary, and it was a labour-intensive task that

[16] Jars 1774–81, I, 182–4.
[17] NEI Buddle 25/II/1–12.
[18] Fletcher thesis 1973, 47.
[19] A. R. Griffin 1969, 392–3; M. Williams 1958, 20; Goodwin thesis 1978, chap. 3.

involved outlay on wages for periods of several months, even years, before any returns could be obtained in the form of coal brought to the surface and sold. For this reason shafts were of no greater diameter than was absolutely necessary. But shafts served many purposes—as a means of access for the miners themselves, as passage-ways for winding coal in buckets, corves, or trucks to the surface and lowering the empty ones, as ventilation passages, and as channels for pumping machinery. As the technology of these various functions became more sophisticated, as mines became larger and the quantities of coal and water to be lifted to the surface through any one shaft increased, the need grew for shafts of ever-increasing diameters. In Lancashire, where shafts were shallow and close together, they were rarely more than seven and a half feet in diameter if circular, or seven and a half by five and a half feet if oval. In Somerset, where, probably because of marketing constraints, colliery outputs were seldom large but mines nevertheless deep, shafts were kept very narrow, rarely more than five feet in diameter before 1800 and as little as four and a half feet on occasion. Shafts in South Wales were rarely more than nine feet in diameter.[20] Where the strata were fairly dry, square shafts were used in Scotland: one of six feet square was constructed for a new winning at Bo'ness in West Lothian in 1741. Even smaller square shafts were employed for ventilation.[21] In the North-east, however, where technology was most advanced and the scale of the largest seasale collieries greater than in most other coal-fields, larger shafts were common much earlier. Gabriel Jars reported shafts to be circular and commonly twelve feet in diameter in the 1706s, while by 1830 shafts of up to fifteen feet in diameter were known.[22]

Sinking a shaft was fundamentally a matter of digging a hole— a pick-and-shovel job, to which was added the task of raising the spoil from the working bottom of the shaft. But in most situations it raised two technical problems that pushed sinking far beyond mere pick-and-shovel work. These were the problems of rock and water. Many shafts ran into rock strata before they reached the coal seams and penetrating these called for the use of explosives. There is no certainty when gunpowder was first used in mining in Britain, though it is clear that for a long time in coalmining it was used only in sinking and not for coal extraction. One authority believes that it was first used in British mining in the Cornish tin mines in 1689, and

[20] LaRO Molyneux of Sefton DDM/4/6; Bulley 1953, 76; *VCH Somerset*, II, 384; Roberts thesis 1953, 100.

[21] Duckham 1970, 55.

[22] Jars 1774–81, I, 268; *SC Accidents* 1835, Q.2137.

another in a Staffordshire copper-mine at Exton as early as the 1630s. There is, however, evidence of its use in sinking in Warwickshire in 1687, and in Somerset in 1719.[23] Sir Humphrey Mackworth was said to have used gunpowder to blast a level in his mines near Neath in 1710. A colliery at Burlow in Derbyshire was sunk in 1763. with the aid of gunpowder and another in the Orrell coalfield of Lancashire also in the 1760s.[24] However well founded this information may be, it is reasonably certain that gunpowder had come into use in the making of shafts and levels by the beginning of the eighteenth century. The real difficulty with its use was the lack of a safe method of ignition. Initially a fine train of powder was led from the charge to a piece of paper soaked with an explosive composition: the slow burning of the paper allowed the shot-firer to retire. There were obvious uncertainties and dangers attached to this procedure, but it was not until 1831 that the first safety fuse was invented by William Bickford.[25]

The second problem was more acute: sooner or later in the process of sinking water began to seep into the newly won shaft. This was, of course, simply one aspect of a wider technical problem, and the ways in which it was tackled are reviewed at some length in chapter 4. Suffice it to say here that some form of mechanical drainage was a normal element in the work and cost of sinking. Providing the rate of flow of water was within the capacity of the available pumping machinery, this was no more than a routine aspect of sinking. But there were many occasions when this problem got out of hand. 'This day at night at 11 o'clock', reported the sinkers at Houghton colliery in County Durham in 1750, 'Raised a great feeder of water which Feader is more than the Engin can manage by about 2 or 3 Hours in 24 Hours.'[26] The first attempt to win Wallsend colliery on the Tyne in 1778 ran into quicksands and the work had to be abandoned. Similarly the first attempt to reach the overlain coal at Hetton in east Durham after 1810 was defeated by large feeders of water from the yellow sands at the base of the magnesian limestone.[27] Most water was encountered during sinking to the first 250 to 300 feet: thereafter the strata were generally impervious.

The problem was met in Leicestershire, Warwickshire, and Yorkshire during the eighteenth century by what were called 'garlands'—

[23] Westwater 1965, 723; Galloway 1898, I, 227; Jackson 1903–4, 105; White thesis 1969, 59; Buller 1953, 67; VCH Somerset, II, 384.

[24] Roberts thesis 1953, 102; Daniels and Ashton 1929–30, 125; Anderson 1975, 55–6.

[25] Westwater 1965, 723–4; J. Taylor and P. F. Gay, British Coal Mining Explosives (London, 1958), 19.

[26] Robertson 1970, 10.

[27] Raistrick 1953–4, 23–4.

spiral water-courses formed round the perimeter of the shaft by clay, brick, or wooden channels that conducted the water clear of the shaft works to the sump from where it could be pumped clear.[28] Otherwise, some form of shaft lining was constructed. At first, in the North-east, a stone or brick lining was inserted as far as the first rock stratum; but this form of lining was rarely effective against substantial feeders of water, and something tougher was called for. 'I have seen a crater a hundred yards in diameter formed in this manner,' reported John Buddle in 1835. 'The whole surface within that circumference went down to the depth of several feet.'[29] The lining of the shaft with wood, called 'tubbing', seems to have been introduced first in the North-east about 1730. This was capable of holding back water at a pressure of 100 lb. per square inch. Wooden tubbing was widely used in Lancashire in the second half of the eighteenth century.[30] Alternatively, a wooden 'cribbing' was built into the shaft temporarily, to be replaced by a brick lining at a later stage. An account from Cumberland in 1756 sets out the value of wooden tubbing and cribbing very clearly. After describing the sub-division of oval shafts for ventilation purposes, the account continued:

These Pitts are also Cribb'd with Oak Timber let into the sides of the Pit, at every 3 or 4 foot distance from one another; and Deals also close joynted are nail'd to these Cribbs quite round the Pit, from Top to Bottom. This Cribbing and Lineing the Pits prevents the Water that is met with in sinking through little Bands of Coales and Cliffs of Stones from spreading into the Pit and falling down with great weight upon the sinkers. It also secures them from any loose pieces of Stone falling from the sides of the Pits, which before they reached the Bottom would acquire so great a Velocity that the Sinkers, being put up in so little room, could hardly escape being kill'd. By these means the sinkers are well secured and work with great Spirit; but the Expence of Timber and Deals is very great.[31]

The introduction of cast iron for tubbing has been attributed by one authority to John Buddle senior at Wallsend colliery in 1792, and by another to John Barnes at Walker colliery in 1795 or 1796.[32] Cast-iron tubbing at Percy Main in Northumberland was said to have been formed in 1796 of segments four feet by two feet fastened together by screwed bolts. Hetton colliery in north-east Durham was

[28] C. P. Griffin 1978a, 66; White 1969–70, 537.
[29] SC Accidents 1835, Q.2137.
[30] Anon., History and Description of Fossil Fuel 1835, 183; Anderson 1975, 52.
[31] CuRO Lonsdale D/Lons/L/Acc.629.
[32] Raistrick 1953–4, 23; Dunn 1844, 47; Anon., History and Description of Fossil Fuel 1835, 183; Hiskey thesis 1978, 67. The 1792 attribution to Buddle senior is the more probable.

finally won in 1820 with the aid of cast-iron tubbing, but its first use in Scotland was not until 1829 at Prestongrange colliery in East Lothian.[33] Expensive cast-iron tubbing became a common feature of the larger mines of the North-east in the early decades of the nineteenth century, though it was rarely necessary for more than a portion of a shaft. An account of the 1830s drawn from the experience of John Buddle referred to a sinking in which cast-iron tubbing was necessary for only six feet of the shaft. Once this distance was successfully passed and tubbed the shaft became dry; but the writer estimated that it cost £4,000 to sink these two yards. In another pit, however, Buddle was obliged to use 240 feet of tubbing. When Gosforth colliery, near Newcastle, was being won in 1824, the estimate allowed for thirty fathoms of tubbing in the large pit at £100 per fathom.[34]

Like boring, sinking was specialized team-work performed under contract, sometimes at a constant rate per yard sunk and sometimes at rates that increased with the depth of the shaft. By a contract of 1705, William Allen and four partners agreed to sink a shaft for the Hon. Charles Montague at Benwell at prices that started from 18s. per fathom for the first ten fathoms, and increased every ten fathoms until they reached 50s. per fathom below sixty fathoms. The contract contained clauses about pumping, shaft dimensions and lining, and provision of equipment.[35] The 144-feet shaft at Burlow in Derbyshire was sunk in 1763 by the contractor, Peter Booker, and his team at the constant rate of 10s. 6d. per yard, while at the Orrell colliery of Jonathan Blundell in Lancashire the standard sinking rate in the 1820s was 18s. per yard. A sinking agreement to make a new pit at Elsecar Old colliery on the Earl Fitzwilliam's Wentworth estate in south Yorkshire in 1799 contracted George and Humphrey Parkin and William Sellers to sink an oval pit seven feet by nine feet, 'the first sixteen yards at 16s. per yard, the second sixteen yards at 22s. per yard and the Remainder to the Coal at 28s. per yard'. By a further agreement of 1822 Joshua Biram on behalf of the Earl agreed with William Hague senior, William Hague junior, Joseph Jackson, George Glossop, and John Orgreaves for them to sink an engine pit at Park Gate colliery seventy-one feet deep at £1 per yard for the first twenty yards, two guineas per yard for the next twenty, and five guineas per yard for the remainder. The Earl was to provide each man with flannel for working clothing as well as tools and

---

[33] W. Green 1865–6, 214; Raistrick 1953–4, 24; Dunn 1844, 108.

[34] Transcribed volume of notes by David Jenkins for his 'History of Glamorganshire' (1839), NLW Miscellaneous 7885C/132; Anon., *History and Description of Fossil Fuel* 1835, 184: NEI Forster 49/9/102–3.

[35] DuRO NCB First Deposit NCB/I/X/3(12).

a horse gin with horses and drivers for lifting spoil and water. The sinkers were to work eight-hour shifts and pay for their own labourers. At twenty-two pits sunk on the Marquis of Anglesey's land in Staffordshire around 1830 the contract rates varied between £1 per yard and £1 8s., but these rates included bricking the shaft. In early eighteenth-century Leicestershire rates were normally between 5s. and 7s. per ell (forty-five inches) depending on the character of the strata, with substantially higher rates when hard rock was encountered.[36]

The depth of a shaft, particularly where it was for the 'engine' or pumping pit, normally represented the deepest part of a mine, though there were instances where levels inclined downwards even from the sump level. This was certainly the case with some of the Cumberland mines that followed the gently dipping seams under the sea, and was reported also at one or two collieries in the North-east. Needless to say, the depths of all pits in the eighteenth and early nineteenth centuries have not been recorded, but a great many have been, though it is likely that these relate to the deeper and larger collieries rather than to the shallower, smaller pits. Moreover, very little of the evidence relates to the first half of the eighteenth century, so that it is scarcely possible to trace accurately the increase of mining depths throughout the period 1700 to 1830.

In most of the coalfields of the eighteenth century mines were relatively shallow. Jars reported in 1765 that the deepest mines in north Staffordshire were no more than 120 feet, and that most were forty-eight to sixty feet deep.[37] Depths of up to 250 feet are recorded in the mid-eighteenth century in Scotland, Yorkshire, South Wales, Derbyshire, Lancashire, and Staffordshire. Even in these areas, however, the rise in demand and its geographical shifts obliged coal-owners to look for deeper coal in the late eighteenth and early nineteenth centuries. A pit of 600 feet at Bryn Coch in 1806 was believed to be the deepest in South Wales at that time, though a depth of 480 feet had already been passed in the Llansamlet pits in Gower during the 1770s. In Scotland, John Roebuck probably created the deepest pit for the time around 1760 with the 420 feet achieved at the School Yard Pit at Kinneil. The deepest Warwickshire pits in the eighteenth century were Hawkesbury sunk to 390 feet and Griff to 381 feet, but in 1820 a pit at Wyken was driven down to 734 feet. Three areas, however, were already notable in the mid-eighteenth century for deep mining—Cumberland, Somerset, and the North-east.

---

[36] Daniels and Ashton 1929, 125; Anderson 1967, 118; Fletcher thesis 1973, 52–3; StRO Anglesey D603/M/2; C. P. Griffin thesis 1969, 66.
[37] Jars 1774–81, I, 254.

The Saltom pit in Cumberland was first driven to 252 feet in 1729 and then pushed down further to 456 feet by 1731. One of the Whitehaven pits was 630 feet deep by the time of Sir John Clerk's visit in 1739 and was believed to be the deepest pit in England at that time. The King pit at the Whitehaven Howgill colliery was driven down to 993 feet in 1793, when it was almost certainly the deepest pit in the country. In Somerset a pit at Stratton Common was said to have penetrated to 420 feet in the 1690s, while at the Old Pit at Radstock one hundred years later coal was being brought from below 1,000 feet. A depth of more than 1,200 feet is reported to have been reached at Clandown in 1817. In the 1790s depths of 350 to 550 were fairly common in the Somerset coalfield, while a pit of 642 feet was reported in the Kingswood coalfield near Bristol in 1779.

There is a lack, unfortunately, of much information about the depths of pits in the North-east before the 1770s, by which time the deeper pits were just penetrating the 600 feet level. An estimate for sinking two pits at Walker colliery in 1713 allowed for a depth of 324 feet, while four pits at Byker in 1750 ranged from 396 feet to 468 feet. By the 1790s pits at Hebburn had passed the 750-feet mark and in the early years of the nineteenth century several pits at Lawson Main, Jarrow, St. Anthony's, Willington, and Howdon collieries had been driven below 800 feet. New pits at Gosforth and Jarrow in the 1820s were more than 1,000 feet, while the Monkwearmouth colliery, reaching for coal below the magnesian limestone, where sinking had begun in 1826, finally struck coal at 1,578 feet in 1834. These, of course, were all the deepest pits of their time, but a survey of 1828 shows that deep pits were the general rule rather than the exception in the North-east. This survey, while not stating pit depths for all collieries in the North-east, nevertheless does so for forty-nine of the principal, mainly seasale, collieries. The depths ranged from 120 feet to 1,080 feet, with an average of 543 feet.[38]

While there is less evidence about the smaller pits it is clear that small, shallow workings with a depth of not more than twenty feet, as well as the even shallower bell-pits, continued to be found in all coalfields. By the early nineteenth century they could have contributed no more than a very small proportion of the total output of coal. They may be likened to the domestic units of production in the textile and metal-working industries that continued to function alongside the new factories and large-scale units. By any standards,

[38] NEI Buddle 25/III/4–15. The other information about depths is drawn from too many sources to list. Most of the figures for the North-east, and some for other coalfields, come from Galloway 1898, I, *passim*.

on the other hand, the pits that produced the overwhelming proportion of coal mined by the early nineteenth century were deep
mines—deep enough, certainly, to raise all the problems, and call
for the techniques, of deep mining.

ii. *Methods of working*

When the shaft struck the seam to be worked, or reached the depth
calculated by the trial borings to give access to the seam, the sinkers
handed over to the owner or lessee. At this point a strategy for
extracting coal had to be worked out since the planning of the underground workings of a mine involved giving consideration to problems
of drainage, ventilation, underground haulage, and, above all, roof
support. In very few mines were the seams to be worked absolutely
horizontal: there was normally a dip in one direction. The dip would
dictate the flow of water underground, and drainage must work from
the lowest point of any working. If drainage was by natural flow
through sough or adit then all that was necessary was to arrange for
the adit to be driven from the lowest point of the working; but
drainage by mechanical pumping involved the use of a vertical shaft
and this required the shaft to be located at what was to be the lowest
point of the workings. Mining must normally be up-dip from the
sump at the foot of the drainage shaft. In collieries with multiple
shafts—and most of the larger collieries in the eighteenth and early
nineteenth centuries were obliged for purposes of ventilation to use
at least two shafts—the pumping or 'engine' pit was therefore
located at the lowest point of the area of working, while the winding
or 'coal' pit could be located nearer to what would be the central
point of the working area regardless of the depth of the seams
worked at that point.

It was from this 'coal' pit, the focus of working, that levels or
roads radiated to the working faces. The dimensions of levels
depended upon the thickness of the seams to be worked, but, with
the increasing use of horse-traction for underground haulage, they
were rarely less than six feet by four feet, and often more. For
reasons already considered, the length of levels varied fairly directly
with the depth of shafts. In the shallowest of bell-pit working, coal
was rarely taken more than a few yards from the pit bottom, and in
the relatively shallow pits of the Black Country, where, it was said
in 1815, 'shafts are sunk at a trifling expense', levels rarely exceeded
250 to 300 yards.[39] In areas of deep mining, in contrast, levels sometimes ran for long distances—over 600 yards at Timsbury and

[39] NuRO Society of Antiquaries ZAN M14 A9/7–8.

Camerton in Somerset by the 1820s, and one and a quarter to one and a half miles in south Yorkshire at the end of the eighteenth century. Felling colliery on Tyneside, working the Low Main seam at from 612 to 696 feet in 1812, ran for seventeen bords from east to west and twenty-five from north to south. As the pillars were twenty-six yards by eight yards, the workings, criss-crossed by roads, covered an area roughly 460 yards by 225 yards. The upcast and downcast pits, roughly at diagonally opposite corners of the workings, were 550 yards apart.[40] At Hetton colliery in Durham in the 1820s, probably the largest colliery of its day, the distance from the shaft to the north face workings was 700 yards, to the west face workings 1,200 yards, to the south face workings 600 yards, and to the east face workings 2,000 yards.[41] As far as possible roads were made level for ease of hauling.

In most collieries, however, the length of levels was determined, of course, not so much by the difficulty or cost of underground hauling as by the acreage of coal legally accessible to the operator. For this reason, highly fragmented land holdings at the northern end of the Warwickshire coalfield around Wilnecote prevented mining on all but the smallest of scales during the first half of the eighteenth century.[42] Many leases laid down a strict limit to the number of acres that might be worked, and it is worth bearing in mind that a shaft sunk in the centre of a square twenty-five-acre coal lease would permit levels driven to meet the sides of the square at right angles of no more than 175 yards. In the Black Country the area served by a pair of pits was often less than ten acres and rarely more than twenty.[43] In south-west Lancashire, where pits were shallow and frequently moved, a plan of 1760 showed no less than twenty-eight shafts in three fields with a total area of under twenty-nine acres. In such a situation levels must rarely have exceeded thirty or forty yards.[44] Where, as on Sir Richard Newdigate's land in the early eighteenth century, pits were no more than thirty yards apart, levels must have been even shorter.

The driving of levels was primarily to give access to the working area and, though some coal might be got in the process, as often as not the needs of hauling, drainage, and ventilation dictated a location and direction of a level that kept it clear of workable seams. In the numerous cases where the making of a level was merely a part

[40] Hodgson 1813, 6–7. A copy of this valuable pamphlet is in NuRO Forster ZFO/3.
[41] Bulley 1953, 68; Cox thesis 1960, 119; Raistrick 1967, 70; NuRO Wilson (Forest Hall) ZWI/4/437–45.
[42] Grant thesis 1977, 229.
[43] *VCH Staffordshire*, II, 86.
[44] Anderson 1967, 123.

of mine construction, driving was contracted out to specialized teams, as it was for boring and sinking. In Leicestershire in the early eighteenth century 'heading' or level driving, was contracted at rates varying from 6*d*. to 3*s*. 6*d*. per ell of forty-five inches. A level of seventy-two yards was constructed by a contractor at Burlow in Derbyshire in the 1760s at 6*s*. per yard.[45] At Houghton in Durham a contract was arranged in 1750 by which a group of partners was to receive 3*s*. 10*d*. per yard

to cut a Levell from the hitch to the Bore Hole or Sinking pitt . . . and in case it prove a hard bargain to have four shillings p yard. They are to work her with 9 men and to begin work at two o'clock in munday morning and to continue working to two o'clock on Saturday afternoon in Every week. The Men is to have paid them in the Bargain Seven shillings a week Each man. The Master to be at the expence of Sharping and Repairing the Gear.[46]

It was, of course, uneconomic to construct roadways of a larger cross-section than was absolutely necessary. Heights and widths were determined by the dimensions of the conveyance used for hauling. Where the motive power was human, the drawer or putter might be expected to work in a crouching or crawling position, so that a full human height was not called for; but when horses were more extensively used for underground haulage, a greater roof height was necessary. In late eighteenth-century Yorkshire the shallow seams around Bradford and Halifax were worked with roadways less than forty inches in height. At Sir John Clerk's Loanhead colliery in Midlothian, however, at the beginning of the eighteenth century, levels were ordered to be uniformly five and a half feet high by three feet broad.[47]

These main roads led from the shaft bottom to the working faces where the procedures for extracting coal were determined by the thickness of the seam and the character of the stratum forming the roof. Most usually extreme caution was exercised and a relatively small proportion only of the coal in any one seam extracted, leaving the rest to support the roof. By this method—the 'pillar and stall', 'bord and pillar', or 'short and narrow' method—coal was taken from passages—the bords or stalls—between pillars many yards square. This system was universally used in the North-east and in many other coalfields. Pillars were either square or rectangular. Those at George Humble's Houghton colliery in County Durham won in 1749–50 were sixteen and a half feet thick and in lengths

[45] C. P. Griffin thesis 1969, 67; Daniels and Ashton 1929, 126.
[46] Robertson 1970, 24.
[47] Machin 1958, 4; ScRO Clerk of Penicuik GD18/995/20.

varying from sixty to 120 feet. In Cumberland pillars in shallow pits were relatively small—twelve to fifteen feet square, and in deeper mines up to twenty by sixty-five feet.[48] The pillars found by Jars when he visited the North-east in 1765 were forty to forty-five feet square.[49] Generally speaking the deeper the mine the larger the size of pillar deemed necessary to support the greater weight of the roof. The size of the pillar was determined not only by the depth of the mine but by the firmness of the strata both above and below the seam being worked. With a soft underlying stratum the pressure per square foot on a small pillar could drive it into the ground, a process known as 'creep', thus reducing the height of ventilating or haulage roads. A similar phenomenon in the ceiling, known as 'crush' had the same effect. Pillars of this size allowed less than fifty per cent of the coal to be removed. Slightly smaller pillars, such as those left in the Barnsley district of south Yorkshire in the early eighteenth century, permitted up to two-thirds of the coal to be removed.[50]

The principal alternative to the pillar and stall method was the 'longwall' method, sometimes known from the areas in which it was already employed at the opening of the eighteenth century as the 'Lancashire system' or 'Shropshire system'. By this procedure a broad length of a seam was worked, all the coal being taken from it. Where the coal was removed the roof was initially supported by props, and as waste small coal was accumulated from the working it was stacked in the space cleared—the 'goaf' or 'gob'—so that in time the waste supported the roof and the props could be moved forward to support a more recently cleared area of roof. This system had the enormous advantage of allowing one hundred per cent of the coal to be removed, but it could be costly in other ways. The shifting of small coal into the goafs and the cutting and erection of props called for considerable extra labour underground. Furthermore the felling of large slabs of coal tended, with certain qualities of coal, to produce a very high proportion of unsaleable small coal. Finally, in spite of the packing of the goafs with waste, the longwall method frequently allowed the roof in the worked-out areas to settle. In deep mines this settlement might be taken up by the overlying strata, but in relatively shallow mines the result was often surface subsidence. The consequential damage to buildings could be expensive for the mine operator. Worse, it allowed overlying coal seams, whether

---

[48] Robertson 1970, 54; Wood 1971, 211.
[49] Jars 1774–81, I, 192.
[50] SC Lords Coal Trade 1830, 36; SC Accidents 1835, Qs.2107, 2111; Cox thesis 1960, 120.

workable ones or not, to break and release dangerous gas. It was this hazard that principally delayed the adoption of longwall working in the North-east and kept down extraction rates.[51]

As the cost of sinking and pumping, winding, and ventilating machinery grew in the later eighteenth and early nineteenth centuries, so the relative merit of the longwall system, with its one hundred per cent extraction rate, became more apparent. It was increasingly adopted where the conditions of gases and roof quality permitted. In most coalfields, however, coal was worked by some variant of either the bord and pillar or the longwall method, or the change was made from one system to the other. In Scotland the bord and pillar method, or 'room and stoop' as it was most commonly called, was generally used initially in mines whose scale exceeded that of small drifts from the outcrop. At depths of up to 150 feet rooms were up to fifteen feet wide and stoops six to ten feet square. When, by the early nineteenth century, depths of up to 480 feet were being worked, much larger stoops of up to forty feet square were left. With stoops this size over one-third of the coal was left unworked. Longwall working was introduced into Scotland after 1759 when the Carron iron company near Falkirk brought miners from Shropshire. From here the technique spread to neighbouring West Lothian mines. By the 1770s it had found its way into Lanarkshire, and was certainly employed at the Govan colliery opposite Glasgow in 1801. Its adoption, however, was gradual. As late as 1829, for example, Robert Bald found it necessary to recommend that the Redding colliery near Falkirk should switch to longwall working, 'the best and most profitable to be pursued'.[52]

In Cumberland, as in Scotland, small, shallow mines were worked by drift from the outcrop. The entrances to these mines were known as 'bear-mouths' or 'day-holes'. In the larger mines, however, vertical shafts became necessary, and the bord and pillar method of underground working was used exclusively until the nineteenth century. Here, too, the size of pillars tended to be increased as mines penetrated to greater depths. Jars, in 1765, found pillars only seven and a half feet square when there was a solid rock roof, but at Broughton Moor colliery in 1812 bords of fifteen feet width were driven between pillars of twenty-one feet by sixty-six feet.[53] The relatively shallow Lancashire coalfield encouraged the use of multiple shafts rather than extensive underground levels, and the shallowness of workings —many only between twenty and sixty feet deep—called only for

[51] *SC Accidents* 1835, Q.2111.
[52] Duckham 1970, 57–66; NLS NUM Scotland, Lanark Division, MS Dep. 227/158/16.
[53] Jars 1774–81, I, 240; Wood 1971, 211.

small pillars. Some eighteenth-century workings in Lancashire opened up subsequently in the twentieth century were found to have pillars only six to nine feet square. Longwall working seems to have been introduced into Lancashire in the larger mines that developed alongside the Sankey Navigation after 1757.

Pillar and stall working prevailed in the western sector of the South Wales coalfield where, for much of the eighteenth century, the steep-sided valleys allowed the seams to be approached by drifts rather than shafts, but in the Midlands widely varying conditions dictated the use of both pillar and stall and longwall. In the literature of mining, the longwall method is always said to have originated in Shropshire, but it was also used in the larger Derbyshire mines in the eighteenth century, where it was called the 'long bank' method, in Somerset and Leicestershire from quite early in the eighteenth century, and, from very early in the eighteenth century, at Sir Richard Newdigate's Griff colliery in Warwickshire, where it was taught to local miners by specialists brought from Shropshire.[54] In north Staffordshire, on the other hand, shallow bell-pits were employed right through to the late nineteenth century.

Further south, however, in the Black Country, the Ten Yard Coal presented quite different problems. The method of working was broadly pillar and stall, but the great height of the workings dictated the removal of the coal in layers starting from the base of the seam. We are fortunate in this case in having a good description of the method of working from the late eighteenth century:

The method of working the Ten Yard Coal in 1796 was nearly as follows: after making communication drifts from one shaft to another, each *Stall* or main opening is marked out by advancing into the solid mine of the lower division, called the benches or Humphries, a drift or cut eight yards in length and one in breadth which is widened by a succession of workmen, each taking in front of the coal from side to side of the original cut until it is eleven yards wide, when it receives the appellation of a *Stall*.

The next operation is getting the coal above the Humphries, which is effected by entering up, or cutting with the picks, a narrow slit from one stratum to another which brings down each from side to side of the stall.

But the business of entering up is attended with much labour and risk, for as it cannot be carried on with safety right forward, the workmen are obliged to leave here and there a piece of coal called a *Spur* until the entering up work is completed, when the spurs are carefully cut out and the block drops. But in taking down the first coals above the benches, the workmen are often obliged to leave a square pillar of that coal standing at the outside of the advanced work to

[54] White 1969–70, 536; *VCH Leicestershire*, II, 35.

prop the upper coal till they have entered up sufficiently to secure its fall, and
then the small pillar above-mentioned (by this time a good deal crushed) is cut
out with the picks: to this temporary pillar the workmen have given the denomination of *The Man of War*.

The Stalls before mentioned are carried on parallel to each other, and about
eighteen yards asunder, middle and middle, so that the pillar between each is
about eight yards in thickness and at every nineteen yards. As they advance a
cross opening of eleven yards wide is made from the one stall to the other; by
which means the pillars are all formed eight yards in length; and in this manner
all the stalls are carried on to their stated distance from the shaft in the lower
beds of the coal; for it is of much importance here to observe that only the
lower beds or about half the height of the whole seam is taken down as the
works advance.

The upper beds consisting of the roof, white coal, Tow coal, and brassils are
taken down as the workmen recede from the extremity towards the shaft,
leaving the roof behind them to fall into the space made by the Stalls and openings, which the miners here have thought proper to call '*The Gob*'.

If the works could be carried on in this manner without any further loss
than the square pillars of eight yards between every stall and cross opening
before mentioned the quantity of coal got would be a very large portion, not less
than 297/361 or about four fifths of the whole; but as this pillar is evidently too
weak, it is found necessary in many situations to leave pieces of whole mine
much stronger. The Benches are frequently left solid to prevent the bottom from
rising or as it is called here, '*blowing*': amd much of the top coal is frequently
lost in the *Gob*.

The black or small coal loosened by the Picks is deposited under foot—
upon the whole the size of the regular pillars and openings leads to no true
judgement of the quantity of coal got; and I have some reason to believe that
not more than one half of the seam, or about 22,500 tons of large coals are
wrought for sale out of one acre.[55]

The removal of so large a proportion of the coal, however, and,
indeed, the reference to the cleared space as the 'gob', had more in
common with longwall mining than pillar and stall working, and the
similarity with longwall was pressed further by the latter development of the removal of the 'man of war'. This was finally extracted,
as Buddle described in his evidence to the 1835 Select Committee on
Accidents in Mines, 'by driving transverse passages through it till it
stands on four thin legs'. The miners then chipped away at these
until they collapsed.[56] The ultimate collapse of the roof led to sub-
sidences on the surface which were massive on account of the great
thickness of the seam removed.

In Yorkshire the bord and pillar method of working gave way to
longwall working, or variants of it, during the second half of the

[55] NuRO Society of Antiquaries ZAN M14 A9/9–11.
[56] *SC Accidents* 1835, Q.2450.

eighteenth century. Longwall seems to have been adopted, for example, for working the Silkstone seam at the Duke of Norfolk's Sheffield Colliery in 1790, and for working the Barnsley seam there by 1814. Longwall was adopted only where the strata immediately above and below the coal were firm. A viewer's report on Attercliffe colliery, for example, recommended a return to bord and pillar working in 1789 on account of the softness of the roof arising from high seepage. But the methods most widely used in south Yorkshire in the late eighteenth and early nineteenth centuries were compromises between bord and pillar (known here as 'short and narrow') and longwall. The 'narrow bank' system, employed, for example, at Elsecar colliery in 1793, involved driving 'boardgates' at right angles from the levels up-dip towards the coutcrops. The coal between the boardgates was extracted in 'banks' eight or nine yards wide. A narrow pillar of coal one yard wide and the length of the bank was left, and these roof supports were supplemented by props in the cleared banks. The 'wide bank' system created banks in the same way up to eighty yards wide, leaving the boardgates protected by thick walls of coal which were later robbed to allow the roof to collapse in the goafs filled with waste. Charles Hatchett, who visited the Duke of Norfolk's Sheffield Park colliery in June 1796, described these methods as follows:

In the working places when they have removed a certain portion for twenty yards or more of the face of the seam of coal, they support the open part behind them with Punches or Props of timber which as they advance they remove and the incumbent strata gradually fall in and fill up the space. This can only be done when the Roof is brittle and not too strong. . . . When otherwise they can only cut away six or eight yards of coal and then leave eight yards as a support alternatively as at Newcastle.[57]

The home of the bord and pillar method, however, was the North-east. Indeed the bord and pillar method was often known as 'the Newcastle system'.[58] Here the great depth of working in the second half of the eighteenth century and the early nineteenth century called for great care in the support of the roof while the highly gaseous nature of the coal required the provision everywhere underground of through passages for the constant circulation of air. The nature of the seams in the North-east, too, was such that longwall working crushed so much of the great coal into small coal that it hardly paid to bring it to the surface.[59] Under pressure of the

[57] This account of mining methods in Yorkshire is based on Fletcher thesis 1973, 56–60; A. Raistrick (ed.), *The Hatchett Diary* (Truro, 1967), 70–2; Mee 1975, 25.
[58] NEI Buddle 21/171.   [59] Evidence of J. Buddle, *SC Accidents* 1835, Q.2112.

exhaustion of the more easily won coal, however, the bord and pillar system evolved in the North-east through three quite distinct phases. In the first, general until the 1760s, large pillars were left and barely fifty per cent of the coal was removed. At Houghton colliery, for example, in the process of winning in 1750, pillars were sixteen and a half feet wide and bords merely ten and a half feet wide, suggesting an even lower extraction rate.[60] Indeed, Buddle estimated that with this method it was only possible to extract up to forty-eight per cent of the coal in a seam, and forty per cent was a more usual rate.

But, as Raistrick has pointed out, 'it was clear that if pits were to win no more than ten or fifteen acres of coal with a bord and pillar system that left more than half the coal underground, the pits could not carry the expense of a steam engine and so coal could not be won.' John Buddle put it more precisely: 'Where a pit costs from £10,000 to £20,000 sinking, we cannot afford to sink a shaft every ten or twenty acres.'[61] To remain economically viable, the design of mines in the North-east had to change. From the mid-1760s pits began to take on a new character. They were obliged to penetrate into wider areas underground, and they had to raise their extraction rate. Thus, in the second phase beginning in the 1760s and continuing through the early decades of the nineteenth century the systematic 'robbing' of pillars was begun. This practice was said to have been introduced in 1795 by the viewer, Thomas Barnes, at Walker Colliery,[62] but Jars was reporting as early as 1765 that pillars of forty to forty-five feet were left to be removed when the mine was nearing the end of its life and when the pillars were the only coal remaining.[63] Barnes's practice, introduced first in the deeper collieries below the Tyne bridge at Newcastle like Bigge's Main and Wallsend, allowed one-quarter of the remaining coal to be removed by robbing one-half of alternate pillars.

It seems probable that what was begun in the middle of the eighteenth century as a final effort to win the last few tons from an old pit was developed by the end of the century into a carefully planned system of working. In mines newly won during this period a two-phase operation was sometimes envisaged from the start. A predetermined proportion of coal in each seam was extracted in the first phase, leaving strong pillars to be robbed in a second phase of operation. Such a plan was executed at Shilbottle colliery, according

[60] Robertson 1970, 54.
[61] Raistrick 1953–4, 22; SC Accidents 1835, Q.2012.
[62] W. Green 1865–6, 214; Dunn 1844, 27.
[63] Jars 1774–81, I, 192.

to a report of 1807.[64] Another report of 1810 reviewed two possible ways of working the coal at Washington New colliery in County Durham. The first was the old practice of leaving pillars just strong enough to support the roof, and the alternative was to leave stronger pillars initially, with the intention of coming back to rob them, a practice known as 'second working' that had the advantage of delaying the onset of creep. At Wallsend colliery in 1812 Buddle planned to take forty-five per cent of the seam at the first working and a further thirty per cent by pillar-robbing at the second working.[65] The size of the pillar left on the first working depended upon the depth: large pillars were needed for deeper working where the pressure of the roof was greater. Buddle estimated that this scheme of working allowed up to sixty-three-and-a-half per cent of the coal to be extracted. At first, alternate pillars were removed, and later even parts of the remaining pillars, by which means an extraction rate of up to eighty per cent could be achieved; but this practice led to creep and the consequential loss of the remaining coal. In favourable conditions of ventilation, however, it was judged on occasion to be practicable to remove the pillars entirely at the second working. This led, of course, to the roof falling in, though the great depth of the north-east mines by the late eighteenth and early nineteenth centuries generally prevented large-scale surface subsidence. The objections to allowing the roof to fall in, however, were first, that stacking space for unsaleable small coal was sacrificed, obliging it to be brought to the surface, and, second, that it fractured the next coal seams above the one just worked out, releasing gas and creating hazards. To avoid this eventuality, Buddle invented in the early years of the nineteenth century the technique of 'roof-bending'. This involved letting the roof down gradually by temporary props and making use of the creep. It avoided fracturing the higher seam.[66] The planned robbing of pillars was also practised in the lower Swansea valley of South Wales from the 1770s: in 1779, 500 weighs per acre were mined at the first working at Landore colliery, to be followed by a further 200 weighs at a second working by robbing the pillars.[67]

The third phase was introduced by Buddle in the early nineteenth century and was designed as much to meet the needs of ventilation as to increase the extraction rate. It was a kind of compromise between pillar and stall and longwall working that had something in

[64] Report on Shilbottle colliery, 28 Feb. 1807, NEI Buddle 21/171-2.

[65] NEI Buddle 3/148, and 33/III/327.

[66] This account of the second phase of pillar robbing and removal in the North-east is based on the evidence of John Buddle to SC Accidents 1835, Qs.2107, 2111, 2113; SC Lords Coal Trade 1830, 36-7.

[67] Roberts thesis 1953, 127.

common with the Yorkshire narrow and wide banks. It was called 'panel' working and involved dividing a pit into sub-districts divided from each other by thick barriers of coal and separately ventilated. Panels were from eight to twelve acres in area and were named after places or countries, while the surrounding solid walls of coal were left some forty to fifty yards in thickness, penetrated only by working roads and ventilation courses. As in longwall mining, the roofs of the panels were allowed to settle through creep when the coal had been taken out without disturbing the workings in other panels. Buddle's technique of roof-bending was applied to this method of extraction, in combination with carefully laid-out ventilation courses, and the use, after 1816, of the Davy lamp permitted very high rates of extraction.[68]

There was, therefore, a trend nationally away from pillar and stall mining towards the longwall method during the whole period from 1700 to 1830. True, longwall was not universally adopted: some regions, like South Wales, never turned to it before 1830, while other regions, notably Yorkshire and the North-east, evolved variants of it. The longwall method yielded certain clear economic advantages: its very high extraction rate, while not inherently raising the productivity of hewers, none the less saved some working costs by reducing the hauling distances underground and, by increasing the product of a pit, spread the capital costs of winning over a greater tonnage of coal. There were possibly some gains, too, from the greater degree of specialization of labour in working by the longwall method. The method, however, was not available to all coalfields, either on account of roof conditions or because the gaseous nature of the coal raised insuperable problems of ventilation. As we have seen, the variants of the longwall system adopted in the North-east in the early nineteenth century were viable only in conjunction with Buddle's sophisticated ventilation systems, while full advantage could be taken of their economies only after the adoption of the Davy safety lamp because of the greater generation of gas by longwall working. A further constraint was the availability of the relevant mining skills: miners used to working by pillar and stall could not easily adapt to the distinct skills of longwall working. Collieries that made the clear move from the one method to the other were often obliged to import miners skilled in the new method from other coalfields. Only where the change was made to a modified version of the longwall system was it practicable for miners to adapt their old skills to the new requirements.

[68] Article on 'Mine', *Edinburgh Encylopedia* 1830, XIV, 351; Anon., 'The Grand Allies', *Monthly Chronicle of North Country Lore and Legend*, 4 (1890), 171; SC Lords Coal Trade 1830, 36–7; SC Commons Coal Trade 1830, 273; Hiskey thesis 1978, 94.

iii. *Cutting and hauling*

Whatever the plan of a pit and the method of working, the actual cutting of the coal was also invariably done by handwork throughout the eighteenth and early nineteenth centuries. There were, necessarily, significant differences in the methods of cutting coal between the pillar and stall and longwall approaches, but in both methods coal was brought down from the face by pick and wedge or crowbar. A hewer was allocated a working area by the overman: in pillar and stall mines it would be a complete stall, and in longwall a section of a face. In the North-east early in the eighteenth century lots were drawn by the hewers to decide where each man should work. This 'cavilling' was to ensure a fair distribution of the easy and difficult places to work in a pit.[69] In late eighteenth-century Scotland 'rooms' at Pencaitland colliery in Midlothian were changed every four weeks: any miner changing earlier was fined and two men were chosen every month to enforce these regulations.[70]

From the management point of view a major requirement was to produce as much large coal as possible and to minimize the production of small coal for which there was little or no sale. 'In all collierys', ran a report on the Ardeers colliery in Ayrshire of 1801, 'the greatest care is taken that the coal shall be kept as entire as possible, particularly where it does not coke, and to encourage or rather bribe the workmen a much greater price is given for the great rather than for the chows or small coal.'[71] Buddle instituted extra supervisory measures at Heaton colliery in 1810 to prevent the hewers from sending up too much small coal.[72] To bring the coal down in as large pieces as possible a series of vertical and horizontal cuts were made. This was called 'curving' or 'kirving'. The first vertical cut was made from top to bottom of the seam at the end of a bord, with further vertical cuts at appropriate distances along the face of the bord or longwall being worked. Each 'jud' between these cuts was then undercut, a particularly difficult task calling for considerable skill and athleticism on the part of the hewer. Finally, wedges were driven in at the top of the jud to bring down the coal thus cut on three sides. This careful method, designed to maximize the output of large coal, was not, however, always faithfully followed. 'The English collier', observed one writer of 1816, 'only curves the top of the block and down one side, which causes the uncurved side to shatter

[69] G.M.C., 'The Heaton colliery disaster, 3 May 1815', typescript dated 1969 in NEI Miscellaneous 63/ZC/53/4.
[70] ScRO Hamilton of Pencaitland RH15/119/16/7.
[71] ScRO Court of Session C596/638/2359–60.
[72] NEI Buddle 32/I/221.

considerably on being forced out by the wedge.' He had noticed that Scottish miners curved down both sides consequently producing less small, wasted coal.[73]

There seem to have been few departures from these basic methods of cutting throughout the eighteenth century, and few, apparently, in the early nineteenth. The laboriousness of the process and the arduous nature of the labour involved, however, were constant stimuli to mechanization. Gunpowder, already used in sinking and driving levels, was a temptation; but in addition to its obvious dangers where gases were present, it shattered the coal too much for practical commercial purposes. But its elimination of some of the hardest of the hewer's labour was not without appeal:

> I've bray'd for hours at woody coal,
> Wi' airms myest droppin' frae the shouther;
> But now they just pop in a hole,
> And flap her down at yence wi' pouther.[74]

Gunpowder was certainly used to bring coal down at the Lambton's Murton colliery between 1814 and 1819, as well as at Hebburn colliery in the early years of the nineteenth century: complaints from London about the poor quality of Hebburn coal led Buddle to stop its use for cutting.[75] It was also said in 1820 to be used in Shropshire to bring down coal 'if the roof is very bound'.[76] In the light of later developments, however, the 'kirving machine' invented by one Captain Blair in 1811 was more interesting. Nothing is known of this machine except that it was steam-powered. Apart from the dangers of steam-engines at the working face, the machine was impractical, as indeed almost any cutting machine would have been in bord and pillar working. John Watson, the viewer, estimated that about ninety machines would be needed per colliery, while two men were required to operate each machine which would have to be moved forward and repositioned every day.[77] Another coal-cutting machine—the 'iron man'—was said to have been devised by the ironmaster John Wilkinson in the late eighteenth century and to have been introduced into his collieries at Bradley and Broseley in Shropshire. It was designed to make vertical cuts on both sides of a jud after the bottom had been undercut, but the Shropshire miners were

---

[73] Holmes 1816, 224. This comment is taken almost verbatim from Beaumont 1789, 12.

[74] 'The Pitman's Pay', MS poem by Thomas Wilson, 1826–30, apparently referring to a period c. 45 years earlier. NuRO Society of Antiquaries M18/Part 2/31.

[75] DuRO NCB First Deposit NCB/I/JB/2079; J. Buddle to Joseph Devey, 25 Jan. 1807, NEI Buddle 15/192.

[76] Brown 1962, 16.

[77] J. Watson to J. de Penthieu, 26 Nov. 1811, NEI Watson 5/11/5.

said to have refused to set the supports necessary to work the machine.[78] Not surprisingly, the adoption of machine cutting had to wait until more practical equipment was forthcoming.

Generally speaking, the seams exploited in the eighteenth and early nineteenth centuries were of a thickness that made for relatively easy working. Gabriel Jars found the seams worked by the Carron Company near Falkirk in Scotland in the 1760s were four feet thick, and those worked near Workington in Cumberland ranging from two feet three inches, the thinnest worked in the whole country, he said, to seven feet.[79] In thirty-six Tyneside collieries surveyed in 1828, the thinnest seams worked were of two feet six inches at Towneley Main and Elswick. At two other collieries seams of only three feet were worked, but in almost all collieries the seams worked were four feet thick or over: in twenty-one collieries seams of between five feet and six feet six inches were worked.[80] The Ten Yard coal in the Black Country of south Staffordshire was, of course, quite exceptional in the experience of British mining of the eighteenth and early nineteenth centuries. Though composed, as was explained in chapter one, of a number of separate, juxtaposed seams, it was worked as a single seam, and posed quite distinctive problems for working.

Coal cut even a few yards from the shaft bottom required to be carried thence to be wound to the surface, but coal cut up to a mile or more from the shaft bottom presented a major problem of underground transportation. Hauling—called in the eighteenth and early nineteenth centuries 'putting' (North-east), 'hurrying' (Yorkshire), 'trailing' (Cumberland), or 'hutching' (Forest of Dean)—was a major element in the costing of coal production. Some durable container was first needed which had then to be filled at the coal face, and some method of carrying or dragging it the full distance over the rough surface of underground roadways. At the beginning of the eighteenth century baskets called 'corves', or wooden boxes, sometimes called 'boarded corves' or in the Forest of Dean 'holds', were used almost universally for this purpose, though occasionally barrows were used, with or without planking for them to run on. A basket-type corf would load between three and six cwt. of coal. Most major collieries employed corvers or basket-makers to make them. Since corves had to withstand an enormous amount of heavy usage, a great deal of care was devoted to their design and manufacture.

[78] Brown 1963, 30.
[79] Jars 1774–81, I, 244, 266.
[80] NEI Buddle Atkinson 45/5/no pagination.

Corf rods are young hazels of four, five or six years growth, cost about 8*d*. a bundle containing fourscore Rods, the Ribs of the Baskets are made of the largest sort of these Rods round which the Small ones are Twisted. The scarcity of the Hazel Rods in this Country obliges us to have quantities of them from Lancashire and Millom, etc. brought by shipping that come from those Places in Ballast. The Boarded Corfs have their Feet and Posts of Alderwood which is not liable to splitt, the Barrs and Balks are made of Ash, the Boards for the sides, ends and bottoms of the Corfs are made of Barrel or Pipe Staves brought from Virginia, which being splitt out of clean grown Oak Timber, don't break like Boards that are sawn.'[81]

Corving rods were six feet long and as much as one and a quarter inches in diameter at the thick end. Though basket corves were still to be found in early nineteenth-century collieries they were steadily being replaced by the wooden box-type corves.[82]

Various methods were used to move the corves. Commonly in the early eighteenth century they were placed on wooden sledges or 'trams' which were then dragged along longitudinally laid planking.[83] This method was still being used in Lancashire in the last quarter of the eighteenth century where sleds with iron runners containing one and a half cwt. of coal were drawn by women or children with a belt and chain harness. In the larger collieries, however, the sheer inefficiency of human labour struggling against such a brake of friction led to the development of wheeled corves. Small iron wheels were fitted and greased, surprisingly, with pure Irish butter. At first, like the sledges, these ran on boards, but during the eighteenth century rails, in imitation of the surface waggonways, were used. Such an underground waggonway was sometimes called a 'rolley-way', the waggons themselves being the 'rolleys'. Wooden rails, as for the early surface waggonways, were used at first, and it is not possible to date the first use of such wooden rails underground. An underground waggonway using wooden wheels with iron bands running on flanged rails was said to have been installed at Sir Humphrey Mackworth's Neath colliery as early as 1698. Buddle dated the first use of wooden railways underground in the North-east to 1778. A view of Park Moor colliery near Gateshead in 1782 recommended the use of waggonways when coal had to be hauled more than 200 yards. Otherwise the use of barrows was advised. Wheeled corves running on wooden rails are known to have been used underground in the Duke of Norfolk's Sheffield collieries in 1776, a development that reduced the cost of hauling by sledge from

---

[81] Memorandum on the running of collieries, November 1756, CuRO Lonsdale D/Lons/ L/Acc.629.
[82] J. Buddle to Thomas Pix, 29 Apr. 1805, NEI Buddle 15/94.

$10\frac{1}{2}d$. per waggon to $6\frac{3}{4}d$.[84] The substitution of cast-iron for wooden rails seems to have been the innovation of John Curr, viewer to the Duke of Norfolk, between 1778 and 1787, but the fact that Curr himself gave them the name of 'Newcastle roads' and that he was himself born and brought up in Newcastle, suggests that, like so many other innovations in the industry at this period, they were first developed in the North-east. Curr's rails were strictly 'plate-ways', being flanged and carrying flangeless wheels. Iron rails were introduced into Shropshire in the mid-1790s, but were not adopted at the Curwen collieries in Cumberland until 1800. They were evidently adopted with enthusiasm in Whitehaven where there were said to be twenty miles of iron railway underground in the Lowther collieries by 1813.[85]

Whether sledges or wheeled waggons were used, the motive power was either human or horse: both were apparently used throughout the period up to 1830. Buddle found boys pulling hods (sledges) of two or three cwt. in the Forest of Dean in 1832, and a man-powered waggonway was used on the main road of the Moira colliery of Leciestershire until at least the end of the second decade of the nineteenth century.[86] When human power was used it was normally that of boys, but women 'bearers' were widely employed in eastern Scotland. In the North-east putters usually worked in pairs, a younger boy (the 'foal') assisting an older one (the 'heedsman'). But:

> The bits o' lads are badly used—
> The heedsman often run them blind—
> They're kick'd and cuff'd and bet and bruis'd
> And sometimes drop for want o' wind.

Not surprisingly the poet had a good word for innovations that reduced the sheer physical drudgery:

> God bless the man wi' peace and plenty
> That furst invented metal plates,
> Draw out his years to five times twenty
> Then slide him through the heevenly gates.[87]

Horses, of course, were capable of drawing heavier loads than humans and therefore of moving a greater quantity of coal to the

[83] Matthias Dunn, 'History of the viewers', MS in NEI Bell 15/1/7.

[84] Roberts thesis 1953, 130; J. Buddle to John Lambton, 9 Mar. 1807, NEI Buddle 15/261; GPL Cotesworth CK/9/78; R. A. Mott, *Sheffield Telegraph*, 23 Sept. 1933, cutting in SCL Local Studies 27/47; Report by J. Buddle senior on Sheffield Park colliery, 7 Apr. 1787, SCL Arundel Castle S215.

[85] B. Trinder, 'Early railways in East Shropshire', *Shropshire Newsletter*, 39 (1970); Wood 1971, 212; Mining Association of Great Britain 1926, 93.

[86] NEI Buddle 51/278; C. P. Griffin 1978a, 67.

[87] 'The Pitman's Pay', NuRO Society of Antiquaries M18/Part 2/21-7.

shaft bottom during the day or shift. And this capacity increased as
wooden waggonways were substituted for sledges, and, later, iron
rails for wooden rails. On Curr's cast-iron rails in Sheffield Park
colliery one horse could draw the equivalent of nine or ten corves.
When Charles Hatchett visited the colliery in 1796 he noticed that
'although each corf weighs about two-and-a-half cwt. and when
loaded contains between five and six cwt. of coals, one Horse is able
to draw without difficulty from ten to fourteen loaded corves at
each time, whereas before the Iron rail was used only two corves
could be drawn at once.' As the journey along the roadways of
Sheffield Park colliery were exceptionally long—one and a quarter to
one and a half miles—each horse and its guiding boy changed every
260 yards at staging points called 'pass byes' which were the only
places where the roadway was widened to permit passing.[88]

The economics of substituting horses for human traction underground were, however, complicated. Boys' wages were low, while
horses were expensive in terms both of capital and running costs.
The relationship between the two is well exemplified by a Newcastle
song:

> I had a little galloway
> His name was Little Chance
> He used to make the full uns fly
> And make the tyum uns dance.

An accident underground killed the galloway and injured the lad, its
driver:

> The boss he called the owerman in
> The happening to relate
> And when he heard that Chance was dead
> It made him twist his face.
> 'I know the lad was badly hurt,
> He was a stretcher case,
> But galloways like Little Chance
> Are harder to replace.'[89]

A good galloway for underground work might cost around £15 and
have a working life of little more than a dozen or fifteen years.
Perhaps more costly, though difficult to estimate, was the construction of roadways of dimensions suitable for horses rather than
humans or the enlarging of low-ceilinged passages to make horse
traction possible. And while a boy might be hired for a very few

[88] Curr 1797, 9; Raistrick 1967, 70-1.
[89] M. Dawney (ed.), *Doon the Wagon Way: Mining Songs from the North East* (London,
1973).

shillings a week, a horse cost many times more in feed, not to mention the labour of the boys looking after them. At Hebburn colliery on Tyneside in 1810, however, when the cost of horse-feed was high from wartime inflation, Buddle calculated that it cost 5s. 1½d. per day to keep a horse while its driver's wage was 1s. 2¼d. This figure is closely borne out by the claim that at Workington, Cumberland, in 1814 horses cost 30s. per week to feed. Horses had to be fed whether they worked or not, and Buddle estimated that underground horses worked between 260 and 273 days a year.[90]

There was, therefore, a steady progression during the eighteenth and early nineteenth centuries from sledges drawn by man-power, through wooden 'rolley ways', to iron-railed tramways drawn by horses. The chronology differed substantially from coalfield to coalfield. In many mines more than one kind of haulage was used simultaneously, boys drawing coal on sledges from the face to the main roadway where the corves were transferred to horse-drawn waggons on a wooden or iron railway.[91] It is certain, however, that by the early decades of the nineteenth century, horses were very widely used underground for haulage and that the industry in all parts of the country must have employed many thousands of horses for this purpose. As early as 1774, the Delavals' Hartley colliery in Northumberland employed thirty-one horses underground, while the Jarrow and Temple Main collieries on Tyneside in 1809 employed seventy-nine.[92] In mines entered by drifts, as in some instances in Cumberland, horses could be led in and out daily, permitting them to graze in the open, but, as in the majority of instances, in mines entered by shafts, horses, once sent down, stayed down for life. In pointing out this situation in the North-east in the 1760s, Jars also observed that the driest places underground were chosen for their stables.[93]

If, in the main, the horse-drawn tramway was the principal method of underground haulage in the early nineteenth century, in exceptional circumstances other techniques were available. Horse-drawn tramways were, in any case, restricted to level, or nearly level, roadways, and it was not invariable possible to provide these. At Whitehaven, for example, in the 1760s, four-wheeled waggons built up higher at the back than at the front were drawn up the incline of a drift by ropes pulled by a horse-operated whim-gin on the surface.[94] In Shropshire, Warwickshire, and Lancashire

[90] NEI Buddle 40/30; Wood 1971, 217; NEI Buddle 3/65, and 40/30.
[91] Jars 1774–81, I, 192.
[92] NuRO Delaval ZDE 7/7/4; NEI Watson 8/15/14.
[93] Jars 1774–81, I, 192.   [94] Jars 1774–81, I, 242–3.

underground canals were used for bringing coal from the face to the
open. A map of 1788 showed a quite complex system of underground canals in the Donnington and Wrockwardine Wood area on
the north side of the Severn Gorge. These canals were examined in
1791 by Samborne Palmer on behalf of a group of Somerset coalowners. At Brierley Hill he found coal from the face being lowered
down a 168-feet shaft inside the mine to barges on an underground
canal which then carried the coal direct to the ironworks at Coalbrookdale. When Griff colliery in Warwickshire was reconstructed
in the 1770s an old drainage channel underground was cleaned out
and adapted for use as a canal for underground haulage.[95]

The most dramatic use of underground canals for haulage, of
course, was at the Duke of Bridgewater's Worsley colliery in the
second half of the eighteenth century. This mine is known to have
been drained by a sough as early as 1737–8, but it was not until the
third Duke inherited and came of age that this sough was extended
to become one of the most famous canals in history. In 1759 the
Duke, prompted and advised by his agent, John Gilbert, with James
Brindley as consultant engineer, undertook the construction of a
canal from the mine at Worsley to the centre of Manchester. In the
course of designing and constructing this canal, Gilbert conceived the
idea of following the original sough back into the mines as an extension of the surface canal to enable coal to be loaded directly from
the face on to barges, and then carried by water directly from the
face to the quay in Manchester. A number of seams were worked in
the Worsley colliery, and, as these dipped fairly regularly, the canal,
as it drove horizontally into the hillside, cut conveniently through
the succession of seams. The main canal was ultimately driven four
miles from the surface, but at quite an early stage in its history the
decision was taken to construct a second underground canal 168 feet
below the main canal. This canal was connected to the main canal
by vertical shafts up which containers of coal from the lower canal
were wound by horse gin to the main canal. Later, a third canal was
added 249 feet below the main canal, and connected in the same
way. A higher level canal was finally constructed 105 feet above the
level of the main canal which in this instance was linked in 1795 to
the main canal by an underground inclined plane. The underground
canals were ten feet wide and provided a depth of water of three
and a half feet to four feet with eight feet headroom. The tunnels
were brick-lined throughout. There were frequent 'wides' or lay-byes
for passing. Barges were man-hauled and operated in trains. Coal cut

[95] I. J. Brown, 'Coal mining's history in Shropshire', *Shropshire Magazine*, 13 (1962),
16; Doughty 1978, 19; White 1973, 6.

at the face was first dragged by belt and chain in baskets of about two cwt., and loaded into boxes carried in the barges. The boxes were then lifted up the shafts to be loaded without emptying on to barges on the main canal. By the time the scheme was completed there was an astonishing total length of underground canals of forty-six miles.[96]

iv. *Winding*

Finally, the coal carried by these varied means to the shaft bottom had to be wound to the surface, no light task when shafts were several hundred feet deep. At all times the corf, box, or waggon used for underground haulage was not unloaded but wound directly up the shaft: this minimized labour at the shaft bottom, confining it merely to a 'hooker' whose job it was to attach the container to the rope and to release the empty containers when they returned. The motive power for winding during the first two-thirds of the eighteenth century was horse-power. The horse-gin or 'whim-gin' was a feature of almost every mine in this period. It consisted of a large wooden drum arranged for horizontal revolving. Crossbars on its shaft allowed one or more horses, tramping round a circular path to turn the drum and thus wind or unwind the rope to which the coal containers were hooked over pulleys placed immediately above the shaft. A variant of this type of horse-gin placed the winding drum on a horizontal axle immediately over the shaft and transmitted the horse-power through a large wooden-toothed gear-wheel. The former type was preferred since it allowed the horse-track and the winding drum to be moved well clear of the shaft top, thus facilitating the unhooking of the corves or waggons as they came to the surface. This type was generally used in the North-east, though the cog and pinion drive seems to have been more general in Scotland and Cumberland. Such a gin at the Lowther collieries was described by Sir John Clerk of Penicuik, the Scottish coalowner who visited Whitehaven in 1739. Here coal was wound by horses working eight-hour shifts in pairs: 'they go at a full Trot and the driver sits on the arm to which the Horses are fastened. The arm is twenty-four feet in length from the central stoop where it is fixed. The Barrel on which the roap rolls is eighteen feet in diameter.'[97] At Walker colliery on Tyneside in 1765 Jars described its 'unique' horse-gin. Its large wheel was made of cast-iron segments and two horses were harnessed to each of the

---

[96] This account of canal haulage at Worsley colliery is based on Malet 1977, 41, 78–92; and Mullineux 1961.

[97] ScRO Clerk of Penicuik GD18/2115/5.

four drawing arms: this allowed a corf to be raised from 600 feet in two minutes. At Landore in South Wales twelve horses working in relays were able to raise eighty tons of coal from 300 feet each twenty-four hours.[98]

As collieries increased in depth and size from the middle decades of the eighteenth century, the limitations of horse-gins began to threaten to become a serious bottleneck. Even with round-the-clock winding such as Sir John Clerk reported from Whitehaven in 1739, a single horse-gin was unlikely to be able to raise much more than one hundred tons a day, which restricted colliery output to around 25,000 tons per year. Multiple shafts and whim-gins were in part an answer to this problem, but the high capital and operating cost of horses was a stimulus in the search for alternative sources of winding-power. Water-power was one possible alternative. Winding by means of a common water-wheel was observed by Charles Hatchett on his visit to south Yorkshire in 1796 at both Sheffield Park and Attercliffe collieries. It was also reported at Bryncoch in South Wales in 1767. At the reconstructed Griff colliery, Warwickshire, in the 1770s Smeaton designed a thirty-six-foot diameter water-wheel for winding simultaneously from two pits. At the George pit at Whitehaven in 1787 winding was by a two-way water-wheel fed by water from the pumping-engine. A document of 1798 lists no fewer than ten of the major north-east collieries, including Wallsend, Walker, Felling, and Bigges Main, winding by means of water-wheels.[99] In South Wales where the hilly country allowed the use of adits to lead water away from shaft bottoms, a device known as 'the balance' was quite widely used in the second half of the eighteenth century. This made use of the gravity of water-filled tubs as counter-weights to draw up loaded coal corves. As the water was released from the tubs at the shaft bottom it flowed away down an adit and the weight of the empty corf returned the empty water-tub to the surface.[1] An ingenious variant on the balance was devised by John Buddle senior in 1780. Recognizing that an adequate flow of water to activate a surface water-wheel for winding was rarely available in England, but that many collieries were plagued by feeders running into the shaft through strata well below the surface, he designed a balance in which the counterweight tub was filled from an underground feeder and the difference in heights to be travelled by the corf and the counterweight controlled by winding their ropes

[98] Jars 1774–81, I, 194; Roberts thesis 1953, 137.

[99] Raistrick 1967, 70; Roberts thesis 1953, 138; Grant thesis 1977, 205; Fletcher 1876–7, 291; VCH·Cumberland, II, 355; BPL Boulton and Watt 26.

[1] John 1950, 144; Roberts thesis 1953, 139.

on a large and a small drum respectively on the same axle. The filling and emptying of the tub was managed by valves controlled manually from the surface.[2]

But the knowledge of the potential power of steam, already, as is more fully described in the next chapter, in the mid-eighteenth century widely used in mining for drainage, indicated where the ultimate solution to the problem of winding might lie. Given the extraordinary ingenuity of the mining engineers of the eighteenth century it could only be a matter of time before attempts would be made to harness steam-power to winding. The problem of steam-power at this time, however, lay in the reciprocal motion of the early Newcomen engine. The see-saw motion of the beam was well suited to the operation of pumps, but winding called for some form of rotary motion, and it is well known that until the inventions of Pickard and Watt in the early 1780s, the transition from reciprocal to rotary motion had not been achieved.

It is clear, however, that various attempts to translate the reciprocal motion of the Newcomen engine to the rotary drive of a winding drum were made before the 1780s. The earliest such engine of which definite record exists was at the Delavals' colliery at Hartley on the Northumberland coast. Here, in 1763, Joseph Oxley built a Newcomen engine with a sixty-inch cylinder for winding, and a second in 1765. It is not known how the reciprocal motion of these engines was translated into rotary motion for winding, but they appear not to have worked very well. The miners distrusted them and would not use them for descending and ascending the pit. They were said to raise a corf every minute, but when Gabriel Jars visited Hartley in 1765 they were not working. In 1768 James Watt visited Hartley to inspect one of the engines and found it working sluggishly and irregularly which he attributed to the absence of a fly-wheel.[3] There is, however, a less well-documented possibility of the adaptation of a Newcomen engine for winding at Longbenton colliery at Newcastle from 1747. This is said to have drawn coal from 351 feet and is illustrated on a map of 1749 which shows three Newcomen engines at Longbenton—two pumping water over water-wheels from which ropes led to pulleys over the shaft, and the single engine standing immediately beside a horse-less horse-gin. There is, unfortunately, again no indication as to how the reciprocal motion was translated into rotary motion.[4] Another Newcomen engine was

[2] NEI Bell 14/3/396–400.
[3] 'A journey through Leicester, Nottinghamshire, Yorkshire, Cumberland, Westmorland, Lancashire, Derbyshire', unsigned and undated MS (probably c.1770), CoRO Official Records, Diaries, 18; Jars 1774–81, I, 207; Foster thesis 1948, 32.
[4] NEI Watson 20/9; Louis 1931–2, 527–8.

said to have operated a winding-gin at Walker colliery on Tyneside
in 1758, while an engraving of Black Boy colliery near Bishop
Auckland in County Durham of 1774 shows a winding gear driven,
apparently directly, by a steam-engine.[5]

The improvement in the efficiency of the steam-engine by Watt's
invention of the separate condensing cylinder in 1769 did nothing to
solve the problem of rotary motion, and it is likely that desultory
attempts to adapt engines of both old and new design to winding
continued to be made on the coalfields. When, however, Pickard
patented his crank in 1780 and Watt his sun and planet motion for
rotary motion in 1781, the way was open for the general adaptation
for both Newcomen-type and Boulton and Watt engines for colliery
winding. Within twenty years steam-winding became very general in
British coal-mining. Boulton and Watt winding-engines were installed
at Whitehaven in 1788, 1789, and 1793, at Baglan colliery in South
Wales in 1793, and winding engines of unknown make at Elsecar
New colliery in south Yorkshire in 1796 and at Radstock Old pit in
Somerset in 1800.[6]

Until the Pickard patent lapsed in 1791 it is probable that all
Boulton and Watt rotary engines used the sun and planet motion,
though thereafter the simpler crank motion became general. Since
the Watt design was pirated frequently before the expiry of his
patent in 1800 there is little doubt that Pickard's crank was, too;
and with the continuance of the manufacture of Newcomen-type
engines throughout the eighteenth century, and the evolution during
the later decades of the century and into the nineteenth century of
other designs, already by the 1790s mineowners had a wide range of
choice of types of winding engines. By 1800 it is estimated that at
least 130 steam winding-engines had been installed in British
collieries. All but twelve of these had been installed in the 1790s,
so that there is little difficulty in establishing 1790 as the effective
beginning of steam-winding generally in Britain. Forty-three of these
engines were of Boulton and Watt design, whether licensed or pirated,
fifty-two of basically Newcomen design, and thirty-seven of other
types.[7] The relative lack of popularity of the Boulton and Watt
engines, in spite of their advantages over Newcomen-type engines
of considerable fuel economy, is not easy to explain. Certainly the
premium payable under the patent until 1800 was a disincentive
as were the higher capital and maintenance costs, but a document

[5] Louis 1931–2, 529; comment by A. M. Headley in *TNEIME*, 83 (1931–2), 108–9.
[6] Fletcher 1876–7, 292; Wood 1971, 214–5; Roberts thesis 1953, 140; Mee 1975, 25; Bulley 1953, 78.
[7] I am indebted to Dr J. Kanefsky for this information.

of 1798 indicates that Boulton and Watt engines were more than twice as expensive in winding rope, calculated at a rate per ton of coal raised per hundred fathoms of shaft depth.[8] Small steam-engines used for winding were called 'whimseys' and were very widely used in the early nineteenth century. When travelling in the Black Country in 1821, Joshua Field, a London engineer, recounted:

> We stopt at several works and coalpits and we were amused with the small engines used for drawing the coal and oar from the pits; they are almost all on one plan except a few of the newest. They are atmospheric engines having a condenser and air pump and denominated bastard engines. The general appellation of engines used for this purpose is a Whimsey. They are managed very well by boys who in drawing the coal have constantly to stop, start and reverse them which they do very expertly. Hundreds of these engines are to be seen working in all directions out of doors, few have any more engine house than a small shelter for the boy underneath the beam center. When a pit is out they seldom move the Whimsey but leave it in a ruinous state, and we are informed that above a hundred are to be met with in Staffordshire alone.[9]

By the early years of the nineteenth century winding-engines were usually run at 250 feet per minute, though Curr knew of engines in Staffordshire that ran at 500 feet per minute. Winding at these speeds made a great impression on young boys during their first descents:

> They popp'd us in a jiffy down
> Through smoke and styth and sellin' heat,
> And often spinnin' roun' and roun'
> Just like a geuss upon a speet.[10]

In the early eighteenth century hemp rope was exclusively used in winding. It was strong, flexible, and fairly durable. The winding rope used by the Butterley Company in Derbyshire at the end of the eighteenth century was generally about two inches in diameter and was purchased from a Newcastle supplier. But hemp rope was expensive, and tended to twist to some degree under tension, so that corves, or miners who simply put a leg through a loop of rope to ascend or descend, spun round in the shaft. Unless replaced in good time, sooner or later ropes snapped, with danger to workers at the shaft bottom as corves fell down the shaft, or loss of life if miners were using the rope. An invention by John Curr, viewer to the Duke of Norfolk in Sheffield, in 1798 solved the problem of spinning. His

[8] BPL Boulton and Watt 26.
[9] J. W. Hall 1925–6, 12–14.
[10] J. Curr to J. Buddle, 26 May 1803, DuRO NCB First Deposit NCB/I/JB/360; 'The Pitman's Pay', NuRO Society of Antiquaries ZAN M18/Part 2/13.

flat rope was made by stitching together two or more ropes with hemp or linen thread, or with brass or iron wire. The flat rope was wound on itself on the drum, thus reducing the speed of winding as the corf neared the bottom of the shaft. The use of Curr's flat ropes spread slowly but steadily to other coalfields. Their adoption at Lawwood colliery near Barnsley, for example, at no great distance from Curr's base, was not reported until 1823, though they were in fairly wide use in Staffordshire by that time.[11]

A further development of the late eighteenth century contributed to the disappearance of common hemp rope in winding—the iron chain. Single-link chains were first used towards the end of the eighteenth century, but were not favoured by miners because of the dangers of a single link breaking. Flat winding chains, however, linking two or more chains side by side in imitation of Curr's flat rope, were developed in the Black Country, the home of chain-making, around 1800, and it is said that their use spread quickly to other coalfields. They were in use at Landore colliery near Swansea already by 1805. The credit for the invention of winding chains, however, has been given to Gilbert Gilpin of Coalport, near Shifnal in Shropshire. An account of 1807 described the grooved pulleys and winding drums he used to ensure smooth winding. Chains were both cheaper and much more durable than ropes. The cost of providing winding chain for a pit 240 feet deep for a period of three years and four months was calculated in 1807 to have been £43 11s., compared with £171 17s. for ropes. In 1814 Gilpin claimed that 'upwards of 8,000 yards of pit chain made by him are now in use in the mines of the Lilleshall Company'.[12]

From quite early in the eighteenth century shaft tubbing had been lined so that corves being wound up or down could slide smoothly against the sides of the shaft.[13] There remained, however, hazards arising from corves catching each other and spilling coal as they passed in mid-shaft. Once again the resourceful John Curr in Sheffield tackled this problem with the introduction in 1788 of guide-rails to ensure the smooth, uninterrupted movement of loaded and empty corves in the shaft. These 'conductors' were used in conjunction with 'tipplers' at the surface for the mechanical unhooking of the full corves and their replacement by empty corves. Curr's system offered

[11] SCL Local Studies 27/47; H. W. Dickinson, 'A condensed history of rope-making', *TNS* 23 (1942–3), 78; Mott 1969–70, 6; Bland 1930–1, 121–2; Mee 1975, 123; J. W. Hall 1925–6.

[12] CuRO Lonsdale D/Lons/W/Collieries and the Coal Trade/38/4; Lones 1930–1, 45; I. J. Brown, 'When Shropshire led the way in safe winding from the pits', *Shropshire Magazine* 14 (1962), 37–42.

[13] Jars 1774–81, I, 191.

two economic advantages: by eliminating the continual twisting and and untwisting of the ropes it reduced wear on it and prolonged its life; and by permitting the carriage of coal all the way from the hewer to the bank in a single corf it reduced breakage and increased the proportion of round coal to small brought to the surface. There is very little evidence of the spread of Curr's guide rails. A visitor from Somerset reported their use in other Yorkshire collieries in 1794, but it seems that neither guide rails nor flat ropes were used in South Wales before 1832.[14]

Winding, then, was substantially transformed between 1700 and 1830. At the opening of the eighteenth century the horse-gin draw- ing coal by a single hemp rope was almost universal. With the increase of pit depths during the eighteenth century this method became increasingly hazardous and expensive. Various substitutions of mechanical for horse-power were tried, ending with the rapid development from about 1790 of steam-winding. By 1830, though no doubt some horse-gins might still be found working some of the smaller mines, steam-winding was almost universal. And to match this important advance in mechanization, various forms of flat rope or chains, working, in some mines at least, with shaft guide rails, replaced the single, hemp rope with its spinning load of corf or miners. The wire rope, of course, was not invented until the mid- 1830s.

The substitution of steam- for horse-power in winding, which, as we have seen, was a major technological development of the period after 1790, probably reduced the number of horses employed for this purpose, though it should be borne in mind that for every larger colliery that turned to steam-winding in this period there were other smaller ones starting up that still found it economic to use horse- power. But the increase in the use of horses for underground haulage may have gone some way to offset this diminution. It may safely be assumed that in all but the very smallest undertakings some horses were employed in collieries throughout the period from 1700 to 1830. A valuation of 1813 for Cowthorn Hill colliery in the Bristol coalfield showed that eleven horses were employed at what was clearly a relatively small colliery, while at the larger Hartley colliery in Northumberland in 1774, thirty-one horses were employed under- ground and thirty-eight on the surface, and seventy in 1803, includ- ing fifty-two Galloways for underground haulage.[15] The most comprehensive accounts of the employment of horses in collieries

[14] Curr 1789; Raistrick 1967, 70; Mott 1969–70, 6; Bulley 1953, 77; Roberts thesis 1953, 141.
[15] BRO Haynes 14381/B/7; NuRO Delaval ZDE 7/7/4; and Delaval (Hastings) 650/G1/3.

comes, however, from the Lowther mines in Cumberland towards the end of the eighteenth century. There, at the Howgill and Scalegill collieries in 1787, a total of 183 horses were employed—seventy-two for underground haulage, eighty-seven working the gins, sixteen for miscellaneous jobbing and carting, and eight sick or lame. In 1799 a census of horses in all the Lowther collieries gave for every horse its name, age, cost, from whom, and when, bought, and where it was currently employed and kept. The ages of the 159 horses listed ranged from six to twenty-five years. Some of the very oldest were described as 'very bad' or 'wore out'.[16]

Few problems exercised the minds of north-east viewers so much as that of 'small' coal. Whatever the methods of cutting and hauling employed, the production of small coal alongside the desirable round in substantial proportions was unavoidable, but for the first three-quarters of the eighteenth century the coal brought to the surface was sent unsorted to the consumer. Under pressure from competition, however, particularly in the North-east for the London market, and encouraged by the growing tendency of leases to calculate rent on the basis of coal sold rather than coal brought to the surface, in the 1770s efforts began to be made to supply 'round' coal unmixed with 'small' coal. Screening appears to have been introduced in the North-east about this time, and there is evidence of its use in south Yorkshire by 1785 and in Cumberland by the late 1780s.[17] The 'mischievous practice' of screening—a 'sacrifice of men and materials'—was said to have been employed first by William Brown at Willington colliery in the North-east as early as 1760 but there is no evidence of its general use until about 1770 when it was adopted by the older up-river collieries on the Tyne in the hope of producing a commodity that would compete more effectively against the cheaper coals of the newer, down-river collieries.[18] The screens used consisted of longitudinal bars set on a slope with the gaps between them adjusted to the size of coal it was desired to screen out. In 1816 the government was persuaded to make a small concession on the export duty, allowing a reduction for small coal which was in demand for sugar-refining and other industrial processes in some overseas markets. This led to double screening, the normal small coal being first passed through a half-inch screen, this being the lower limit of the size of coals acceptable for domestic consumers. What passed through this was then passed over a three-eighths of an inch screen, this being the upper limit of the size of coals qualifying for the reduced export duty.

[16] CuRO Lonsdale D/Lons/W/Collieries and the Coal Trade/31, 32.
[17] *SC Commons Coal Trade* 1830, 280; SCL Arundel Castle S212; NEI Bell 14/2/510.
[18] W. Green 1865–6, 205; Sykes thesis 1928, 48; Edington 1813, 57.

Screening could be done underground or on the surface. Underground screening called for space, both for the screens and for stowing the screened, useless small coal, and, except with longwall working, this was not always available. On the other hand, surface screening involved wastage of labour and fuel in hauling and winding a largely unsaleable product. Screening was done underground at Hebburn colliery and some pits of Wallsend colliery on Tyneside in 1813, but at G pit at Wallsend colliery in 1815 there was not space for screens underground though some separation of round from small was done by raking. Backworth colliery on Tyneside screened out twenty per cent underground in 1819 and a further twenty per cent at the surface.[19] A survey of thirty-three Tyneside collieries in 1828 showed all but one screening either below or above ground. Eight did some screening underground, but these also put their coal through a second screening on the surface. Some collieries took out as little as ten per cent of the coal hewn, others a great deal more. Walker and Benwell collieries, for example, screened out forty per cent on the surface, and Percy Main one-quarter underground and a further quarter on the surface. The unweighted mean of the coal screened out in all these collieries was 26.4 per cent, almost all of which was taken out on the surface.[20] A similar list of 1818 for Durham collieries in the Bishop Auckland area showed that they screened out 25.5 per cent on average.[21] There is a dearth of information about screening in other coalfields. It was reported not to be practised at all in South Wales in 1805, but to be the usual practice in south-west Lancashire and North Wales for the Irish trade. At the Duke of Hamilton's Bo'ness colliery on the Firth of Forth around 1800 small coal ('culm') was separated underground from medium coal ('chews') by 'brandered' shovels with bars one inch apart.[22]

To screen out over one-quarter of coal produced underground and carried to the surface so laboriously and expensively would appear at first sight to have been extremely uneconomic. It did, however, contribute to raising the price of the large coal sold, and there were some possibilities of disposing of the quantities screened out. Small coal was used in the colliery engines themselves and often in the miners' personal allowance. There were also, as we have seen, some export markets for small coal, while industrial developments (examined in chapter seven below) added new sources of demand for it. By the late 1820s it was possible to claim that 'small coal is of

[19] NEI Buddle 40/256; 33/IV/114; 33/IV/236; and 46a/156-7.
[20] NEI Buddle Atkinson 45/5/no pagination.
[21] NEI Buddle 6/268-71.
[22] CuRO Lonsdale D/Lons/W/Collieries and the Coal Trade/38/22, 24, 26, 30; ScRO Court of Session CS96/638/1789.

more value now than it was formerly'. The Lambton collieries in Durham found small coal 'in great request for gas manufacture in this country and for sugar refineries at Hamburg'.[23] Double screening, which first separated the small coal from the large coal and then took out the dust and very small fragments from the saleable small coal, and the act of 1816 which reduced the export duty on small coal, contributed to this development as well as the rise of new consuming industries. By the early nineteenth century 'slating'— the picking out by hand of stones and slates—was also commonly undertaken. This could only be done efficiently during daylight, and Buddle regretted on more than one occasion the limitation on production this requirement imposed during the winter months.[24]

It becomes very difficult, therefore, to estimate the proportion of small coal that was actually wasted. Not all small coal produced was waste, though clearly the proportion stowed underground was. Of the small coal brought to the surface and screened away from the large coal a use, sometimes even a commercial market, was found for much of it. But when allowance is made for small coal exported, sold for local industrial consumption, consumed in colliery steam-engines, or allowed to miners, there still remained normally a surplus which could only be burned on the surface, used for road-making or waggonway ballast, or stacked in heaps or bings. This residue was an expensive waste, and it is not surprising that every effort was made to reduce it either by not creating it in the process of getting coal or by finding some sale for it by secondary screening.

[23] LEA MP10.
[24] J. Buddle to Joseph Devey, 14 Jan. 1807, NEI Buddle 15/177; and ibid. 25 Jan. 1807, NEI Buddle 15/192.

Chapter 4

Technology (2)

Even in the early eighteenth century few mines were shallow enough to avoid problems arising from the underground accumulation of gas and water. Coal seams themselves generated dangerous gases, and water inevitably and speedily found its way into mines. Surface water could run into and down shafts. 'There is no colliery whatsoever', commented a Derbyshire mineowner in 1739, 'but the ground will break and let in the Land-Flood, in some measure, after great rains.'[1] About one-third of the rainfall in Britain, it seems, is estimated to percolate through the surface soil to the strata below, and Anderson has estimated that in the Orrell coalfield of south-west Lancashire this amounted to approximately 1,250 tons of water seeping through every acre each year.[2] The principal difficulty, therefore, arose from underground water movements—springs, feeders, or seepage—that were often directed by permeable or impermeable strata into shafts and workings. On occasion veritable underground rivers would be tapped in the course of sinking or working which could drown a pit in a matter of hours. In many instances these inflows of water never dried up so that only round-the-clock pumping could keep the workings dry.

Tubbing—at first wooden, and later cast iron, as described in chapter three above—kept water out of shafts, but, from one source or another, water accumulated at the lowest point of a pit. Deep pits necessarily involved raising the water to the surface up a perpendicular shaft, so that it was essential when planning a colliery to site the drainage pit at what would be the lowest point of working. At this point a sump or 'dib-hole' would be dug to receive the regular flow of water from which it could then be most conveniently raised to the surface. Where it was necessary to follow a seam down-dip, drainage channels might have to be cut to allow excess water to flow into a dib-hole created in an extension of the shaft.

[1] NCRO Edge LLE 42/10.
[2] 'Memorandum made by J. Buddle (senior) and (?) Stephenson, 17 Apr. 1789, NEI Bell 46/14/no pagination; Anderson 1975, 171. Both Buddle and Anderson agree on the proportion of one-third.

i. *Drainage*

Virtually every mine, then, apart from the merest outcrop scratch-ings, had to face up to the need for systematic drainage as a routine aspect of working. It goes without saying that the deeper the pit and the more extensive the network of levels underground, the larger the quantity of water to be removed daily. Broadly, there could only be two solutions to the problem: either to arrange for the water to be run out of the mine by gravity, or to lift the water mechanically to the surface. The first alternative was clearly the most attractive since it did not involve continuous expenditure on the operation of machinery—gravity did the work. It was possible, for example, to drain most of the early mines that exploited the High Main seam on the high ground to the south and south-west of Newcastle by adit. Similarly the shallow workings—averaging fifty to sixty feet, the deepest being 120 feet—in north Staffordshire around Newcastle-under-Lyme in the 1760s were all drained by adit.[3] The driving of adits was an essential preliminary to large-scale developments in the Whitehaven pits of the Lowther family. A 400-yard adit was first driven in the Howgill area in 1700 which was later extended to 1,400 yards to lay dry a wide area for working. The Whingill area at White-haven was subsequently opened up in the second decade of the century by a one and a half mile adit from Bransty Beck. Soughs were commonly used for drainage in the Orrell coalfield (south-west Lancashire). At Worsley, in south-east Lancashire, a drainage sough is known to have existed in 1737 and the underground canal system (see p. 98 above) that was extensively developed there after 1759 for haulage purposes was initially excavated as a drainage canal.[4] Soughs or adits were small in cross-section, in south-west Lancashire rarely more than four feet high or wide, and often narrower. Sir John Clerk II of Penicuik in Scotland, in his 'Dissertation' of 1740, recommended five and a half feet by two feet as the most suitable dimensions for adits or 'day-levels', as they were most commonly called in Scotland.[5] The narrower they could be made, the less likelihood there was of roof falls which could block the passage of water and be expensive to clear.

But the possibilities for employing soughs or adits were necessarily extremely limited since they required the existence, within a reason-able distance, of naturally drained land the surface of which was lower than that of the pit sump. Only mining in hilly districts could

[3] Raistrick 1936-7, 141; Mott 1964-5, 4; Jars 1774-81, I, 254-5.
[4] Moore 1893-4, 620, 622; Anderson 1975, 71; Mullineux 1961, 153; Malet 1977, 28.
[5] ScRO Clerk of Penicuik GD18/1069.

possibly meet these requirements, and it is clear that even in hilly areas not many hundreds of feet of depth would put a pit sump below the point at which it could be run out by driving a sough horizontally to an adjacent valley. At lesser depths this method was possible, however, and some coalfields—notably the North-east, Cumberland, Derbyshire, South Wales, and Somerset—were in sufficiently hilly country.

Horizontal drainage adits or soughs were, accordingly, a regular feature of early mining. The initial cost of a long adit, however, might be high. A Derbyshire coalowner claimed in 1739, possibly with some exaggeration, that he and his partners had laid out 'near 20,000 *l* expence in making soughs and other expensive work to drain and work their collieries'. More realistically, a proposed sough 900 yards long on Barnsley Moor in south Yorkshire in 1716 was estimated to cost £1,000. Later in the century an adit at Timsbury in Somerset constructed in 1791–2 cost £1,200.[6] There was a readiness, therefore, to lay out considerable sums in driving adits, often for long distances, and serving several pits. A sough in Warwickshire running west of Blackwell and Teversal commenced in 1703 was extended gradually until in 1774 it ran for a total length of five miles and had its roof supported by a single line of pit props. Because its cost was shared between several owners it clearly drained a number of pits. In Fife, where adits were known as 'day-levels', the mean length of twenty-seven known adits was one and a quarter miles. Fordell colliery in that county was drained by one of three and a half miles in length with a further two miles of branches draining six pits in all.[7] Though adits involved no direct operating costs, they could, nevertheless, be costly to maintain since they were easily blocked either by roof falls or by debris carried down after heavy flows.

Adits continued to serve mines in some areas right through into the nineteenth century. One eighteenth-century adit in the Orrell coalfield of south-west Lancashire was still draining a colliery in the late 1970s.[8] But the limits of the method were severe: in flatter country, like much of the east and west Midlands, or even in hillier country with mines of greater depth, the technique was not available. In these cases, of growing frequency during the eighteenth century as mines penetrated to greater depths, the second alternative of lifting the water mechanically up the shaft had to be resorted to. The switch from the one alternative to the other was a major decision

[6] NCRO Edge LLE 42/10; Hopkinson 1976, 26; Bulley 1953, 70.
[7] C. P. Griffin thesis 1969, 295; A. R. Griffin 1971, 23; Wilson 1978, 3.
[8] Anderson 1975, 74.

in any mine operation, since the mechanical lifting of water involved the continuous expenditure of energy, and hence operating costs. Mechanical drainage necessarily raised production costs, sometimes substantially.

Water could be lifted perpendicularly either in buckets, which might be either single buckets hooked on to a rope, or a succession of buckets on a continuous chain, or by rag and chain pumps, both common in the early eighteenth century. Three sources of power were available to raise the buckets or turn the continuous chains. There was some use of wind-power. George Mowbray, for example, the owner of Double Dykes colliery in the North-east is known to have employed a 'wind engine' for draining in 1738, as was the Prescot Hall colliery in south-west Lancashire in the 1730s. Windmills for mine drainage were quite common in the early eighteenth century in the Scottish coalfield of Fife.[9] Clearly, however, given the erratic nature of wind, this was viable only where small quantities of water accumulated that could be moved by no more than a few hours of pumping a day. 'J.C.', writing in 1708, had little use for wind-powered drainage: 'As for Wind-Mills', he wrote, 'or Ginns that go by Wind, 'tis sure the wind blows not to purpose at all times.' 'It follows', he went on, 'we must have a method whereby to draw this water when we please.' This view was echoed from Scotland in 1740 by Sir John Clerk of Penicuik, though he was obliged to add that a 'want of wind' was something 'which one wou'd not readily suspect in a Country like Scotland'.[10]

To a limited extent the control desired by J.C. could be achieved by water-power, the oldest, most reliable, and most widely used source of energy in early eighteenth-century industry. But water-power depended upon the availability of an adequate flow of water at the requisite elevation and sufficiently close to the pit-head to be brought easily by a leet. The sheer improbability of this solution ruled out this alternative in many, if not most, mining situations. 'There is not', admitted J.C., 'that conveniency of water every where.'[11] Where adequate running water was available, however, it was utilized for drainage. Lumley colliery in Durham had main pumps worked by a water-wheel already in the late seventeenth century. Pumping at Winstanley in south-west Lancashire in the mid-eighteenth century was by water-wheel, as were new pits in near-by Orrell in 1740 and 1763. In Scotland by the middle decades of the eighteenth century water-wheels of up to thirty feet in diameter

[9] Hughes 1949, 31; Langton 1979, 113; Duckham 1970, 77–8.
[10] 'J.C.' 1708, 29; Duckham 1968b, 222.
[11] J. C. 1708, 28–9.

were harnessed to mine pumps, some through a reciprocating motion so that they could operate rod pumps.[12] Great ingenuity was displayed in bringing water to the pit-head for this purpose. The most remarkable example is certainly James Brindley's drainage engineering at Wet Earth colliery in the Irwell valley of south-east Lancashire. The drainage problems of this colliery, sunk in 1747, arose from its location close to the river Irwell. Water flowed in from the river through fissures and subterranean cracks in the sandstone walls of the gorge through which the river ran at this point. Brindley, already some years before his engagement with the Duke of Bridgewater experienced in problems of mining engineering in the north Staffordshire coalfield, was engaged by the owner, John Edensor Heathcote, in 1752 to advise on drainage. He decided in favour of the use of water-power to operate pumps, but was obliged by the low elevation of the colliery close to the river in the gorge to draw the feeder that was to supply the water-wheel from one mile up-river on the opposite bank. Half-way along its course the feeder passed under the river by means of an inverted syphon thirty-two feet below its surface level. The feeder was led the whole distance in a tunnel seven and a half feet in cross-section and brick-lined where it passed through shale to a twenty-two foot diameter water-wheel housed at the pit-head in an underground chamber. This elaborate and expensive drainage system raised 158 gallons of water a minute and operated for over half a century.[13]

In spite, however, of ingenuity of this kind, mechanical drainage in the vast majority of instances obliged resort to the third source of energy—horse-power. Probably the greatest proportion of water taken from coal-mines at the beginning of the eighteenth century was drawn to the surface by horse-power. Horses turned 'gins' that either raised buckets of water singly or turned a continuous chain of buckets. Horses were expensive items of capital equipment with fairly high depreciation costs—their working lives of little more than a dozen years were appreciably less than those of most other items of machinery or equipment. Twenty-eight 'gin horses' were estimated to cost the Lambton pit at Lumley a total of £336 in 1775.[14] Since they could only work effectively in spells of a few hours out of each twenty-four, multiple teams were needed for shift working when pumping needed, as was so often the case, to be kept up round the clock. They were expensive to feed; and they called for additional man-power to handle them. A horse-powered pump at Orrell in

[12] Matthias Dunn, 'History of the viewers', MS in NEI Bell 13/1/6; Bankes 1939, 47; Anderson 1975, 80–1; Duckham 1970, 80.
[13] Banks and Schofield 1968.   [14] Beastall 1975, 26.

south-west Lancashire in the late 1750s required four horses with
two men to operate it, and cost £12 12s. per month to run.[15] But the
limitations of alternative technologies for colliery drainage obliged
most mine operators to assume this element in their costs. Before
Brindley's dramatic hydraulic scheme of 1752 at West Earth colliery,
water was raised by horse-gin in 'kibbles'—five foot diameter, five
foot deep buckets holding about 600 gallons of water and weighing
three tons gross, raised one at a time by a pair of pony teams. The
whole cycle of filling the kibble, raising it the 160 feet of the shaft,
emptying it, and returning it to the pit-bottom, occupied at least
six minutes, or a rate of about 100 gallons per minute.[16] In the
Lowther collieries at Whitehaven in the 1760s water was taken out
using horses to draw tubs of water on underground waggonways up
the slope of drifts to the surface. In the Saltom pit, which followed
the downward sloping seam over a mile under the sea, water was
drawn from the deepest part of the workings to the foot of the shaft
by the sea's edge in tubs up an inclined plane operated by a horse-
gin at the shaft bottom.[17]

Gravity, wind, water- and horse-power, then, were capable of
only a very modest contribution to the drainage of mines. If drainage technology were to stand still at the point reached at the beginning of the eighteenth century, mining in Britain could scarcely have
expanded and must probably have begun to show diminishing
returns. At depths of between ninety and 150 feet the influx of
water almost invariably created problems insoluble by the technology of the day, so that when seams of lesser depths were exhausted
mining must cease. Most British coal-reserves, of course, lay at
greater depths. There was a future for mining in Britain only if some
more efficient drainage techniques became available.

The solution to the problem lay in steam-power. There is a long
and interesting pre-history of the crucial inventions of Thomas
Savery and Thomas Newcomen that has still not been fully un-
ravelled, but for practical purposes the relevance of steam-power for
coal-mining begins with the patenting by Thomas Savery in 1698
of his atmospheric pump. Though the potentialities of steam-power
had been recognized for some time, Savery was the first to devise
a practical method of harnessing the power of atmospheric pressure
to raise water. His machine, the only moving parts of which were
a few valves, first created a partial vacuum by driving out the air in
a chamber with an injection of steam. The steam was then condensed

[15] Anderson 1975, 82.
[16] Banks and Schofield 1968, 97.
[17] Jars 1774–81, I, 241–3.

by means of a jet of cold water, and the resultant partial vacuum was filled with water forced upwards into the chamber by the normal pressure of atmosphere upon the surface of the water reservoir. The injection of the steam at pressure was also used to force water upwards. A repetition of the cycle of steam injection, condensing, and atmospheric pressure achieved a regular but intermittent raising of water. Atmospheric pressure, of course, was incapable of drawing water to a greater height than thirty-two feet, and to be of practical use in mine drainage two or more Savery pumps would have had to be installed in series.

In 1699 Savery secured an act of Parliament extending the fourteen years of the original patent by twenty-one years to 1733. In the event, the Savery pump was so restricted in its practical applications that it was little used. One or two were installed for pumping urban water supplies, but only one, at Willingworth colliery in Staffordshire, built in 1706, is known to have actually been used for the drainage of coal-mines.[18] Savery pumps seem to have found their greatest use during the last quarter of the eighteenth century for returning water to mill-ponds to keep water-wheels turning. The limited heights to which they were capable of raising water tended to confine them to this task. Apart from other shortcomings the use by the Savery pump of high pressure steam was beyond the technical competence of the day: the success of the Newcomen pump was due in part to its restriction to the use of atmospheric pressure which kept it within the limits of early eighteenth-century capability.

The Savery pump was important in the history of mining technology for two reasons: first, the principle of atmospheric pressure it embodied was the basis of the first really successful machine-pump; and, second, Savery's long-lived patent provided the cover for this later development. The successful invention was, of course, that of Thomas Newcomen, a Dartmouth ironmonger. It is assumed that Newcomen's metal-working business brought him into contact with the tin- and copper-miners of Cornwall so that he would be familiar with the problems of mine drainage. It is possible, too, though it has not been established beyond doubt, that Newcomen made the acquaintance of Savery when the latter made occasional visits to the naval dockyards of the South-west in his capacity as Treasurer of the Sick and Wounded Commission.[19] It is not known when Newcomen put together his first working steam-pump, but the first to be installed in a coal-mine was in Staffordshire in 1712. Newcomen's pump employed Savery's principle of the use of atmospheric pressure on

---

[18] I am indebted to Dr J. Kanefsky for this information.
[19] Rolt and Allen 1977, 38.

a partial vacuum created by condensing steam in a chamber, but used this power to draw down a piston in a cylinder. The piston was attached to one end of a beam which, rocking on its fulcrum, activated a rod pump from its other end. The essential components of a Newcomen pump, therefore, were a boiler, a condensing cylinder with piston, a rocker beam, and a rod pump, together with valve gear to admit steam and water at the correct phases of the cycle, and the housing necessary to support the rocker beam. The early Newcomen engines were capable of about eight to twelve strokes a minute. By linking a series of pumps to the rocker beam vertically one above the other they could raise water from depths of many hundreds of feet.

The Newcomen pump was clumsy, and uneconomic in its use of fuel. The limitations of early eighteenth-century engineering—the combination of wood and metal parts, and ill-fitting pistons resulting from roughly bored cylinders—maximized friction. But it worked, and was considerably cheaper per gallon of water raised than the old methods of horse-gins. The Newcomen engine also made possible the raising of water in quantities and from depths quite unthinkable by the technologies it began to replace. Its adoption from 1712 removed two major barriers to mining development. First, it reduced drainage costs quite substantially where, as in most deeper pits, drainage hitherto had been carried out by horse-power. The cost of horse drainage lay in the capital cost of the large number of horses required for shift-work, and in the running costs of their feed, and the wages of the men required to look after them. It was claimed, for example, that one Newcomen engine at Griff colliery in Warwickshire costing £150 per year to operate in fuel, maintenance, and labour, replaced horse-pumping by a team of fifty horses costing £900 per year in feed and labour. This statement, however, was made in 1744, by which time three engines had been installed at Griff.[20] Second, it made possible the drainage of pits to depths greater than had been practicable by previous drainage techniques: it became practicable to exploit seams of coal hitherto effectively inaccessible.

It goes without saying that, once developed, the Newcomen pump, commonly known in the mining industry as the 'fire engine'—'one of the Noblest Inventions of this or the last age'[21]—was not immediately and extensively adopted. There were various brakes on the process of adoption. It was a relatively expensive item of capital equipment; there were, initially at least, relatively few engineers with the skill, knowledge, and competence to manufacture the parts,

[20] Grant thesis 1977, 170.
[21] 'A Dissertation on Coal', ScRO Clerk of Penicuik GD18/1069/24.

above all the cylinder, and erect the engine; and, from the start, the use of the engine was governed by patent rights.

Though the Savery and Newcomen engines shared in common their use of atmospheric pressure, there is little doubt that they were sufficiently differentiated for it to have been possible for Newcomen to have taken out a separate patent had he so wished. Yet he chose to make an agreement with Savery to allow his engines to be subject to Savery's patent rights. While it may seem odd that Newcomen should have been willing to share the potentially substantial rewards of his successful and valuable invention with the inventor of a device of so little practical use, there were nevertheless good reasons behind his decision. It is extremely unlikely that Newcomen would have been granted a patent for more than fourteen years. An independent application from him would certainly have been vigorously opposed by Savery, while the known uselessness of Savery's pump would have stood in the way of any similar extension of an initial period had he secured his own patent. Agreement with Savery gave Newcomen control over his invention until 1733, far longer than he could have obtained from a separate patent.

The agreement between Savery and Newcomen, possibly reached as early as 1705, was of far-reaching importance to the mining industry.[22] Savery died in 1715, and, in return for payment of outstanding debts and an annuity for life, his widow granted all rights in the patent to a body known as the Proprietors of the Invention for raising Water by Fire.[23] The Proprietors included Newcomen until his death in 1718, but throughout their existence until the expiry of the extended patent in 1733 they were dominated by their secretary, John Meres. He it was who negotiated agreements for all engines erected under licence. When it is considered that licences to erect engines were commonly sold for royalties of up to £350 per annum, and that probably up to one hundred engines were erected during the period of the patent, it can be seen that, with an annual income in the region of £20,000 in its last years, the Proprietors' eighteen years must have brought them a reward for their initial small investment running well into six figures. Well might a pamphleteer have written in 1720:

> Why must my stupid Fancy e'er admire
> The way of raising water up by Fire?
> That cursed Engine pump'd my Pockets dry,
> And left no Fire to warm my fingers by.[24]

[22] Rolt and Allen 1977, 38–40.   [23] Alan Smith 1977–8.
[24] Quoted by Rolt and Allen 1977, 70.

The first engines were certainly built by Newcomen himself, with or without the help of his capable assistant, John Calley, but even before his death in 1718 the need for engineers capable of supervising the erection of engines was apparent. Some time must elapse before a sufficient number of engineers skilled in this new branch of engineering could be trained. The partnership leasing Stevenston colliery in Ayrshire arranged for the purchase of an engine in 1719, but the engine could not be erected until 1720 because Meres could not persuade any of his skilled erectors to go to work in 'wet and slavish' Scotland. In Cumberland, the Lowthers were afraid that Stevenston would entice their engine-builder, Peter Walker, to go north to work for them. Walker did, in fact, go to Stevenston, but he returned to Whitehaven with the Scottish engine still only half-built.[25] A small group of engine-builders, however, emerged fairly quickly. These included Samuel, the second son of John Calley, who was still working with steam-engines in 1745, and an enterprising Swedish engineer, Marten Triewald, who, after working for several years in England, returned to Sweden where he also built Newcomen engines and wrote one of the earliest descriptions of the engine.

Undoubtedly the most important of the early engine-builders, however, not least because he was also a Proprietor, was Stonier Parrott.[26] Parrott worked in a partnership with his father, Richard Parrott, a Staffordshire landowner, and his father's neighbour, George Sparrow. Stonier Parrott, however, an energetic, though ultimately unsuccessful entreprenuer, was the active partner and made arrangements between 1714 and his bankruptcy in 1732 for the construction of at least fourteen engines. Parrott and his partners aimed to create a monopoly within a monopoly by becoming the sole agents for the negotiation of licences with the Proprietors. In this they were unsuccessful, if only because it was impossible for Parrott to travel around the coalfields fast enough to negotiate with all mineowners interested in installing Newcomen engines. Nor was the partnership entirely straightforward in its dealings. Sparrow, who quarrelled fiercely with his partners, was not above dealing behind their backs, while the disposition of a limited supply of cylinders kept some customers waiting a long time. The negotiations between the Proprietors and William Cotesworth and his 'Grand Allies' partners are well documented:[27] starting in 1715, Cotesworth and his partners were still without an engine in 1724, though others had been erected in the North-east long before. Parrott employed as his assistant engineer Henry Beighton. Born near Griff colliery in Warwickshire, Beighton was a real engineer

[25] Whatley 1977, 70–2.   [26] Rowlands 1968–9.   [27] Hughes 1949.

who did most of his work in the North-east. In 1717 he built engines at Oxclose and Washington Fell collieries. He made scientific calculations about the engine and devised improved valve gears. After the expiry of the patent in 1733 engine-building became open to competition, and specialist engine-builders emerged in the principal coal-fields. Anderson notes three Lancashire suppliers by the 1780s, and there were others in Derbyshire and Denbighshire.[28]

The major technical problems in the erection of engines were the construction of boilers, and the casting and boring of cylinders. It seems, for example, that in 1719 there was literally only one smith in the whole country capable of making boilers.[29] Fortunately, the technique of making salt-pans was relevant to the fabrication of boilers and was available in the North-east. Nearby, too, was the Crowley firm, one of the country's prime suppliers of iron plates. Cylinders were initially made of brass, but their high cost encouraged the development of cast-iron cylinders. Brass cylinders might cost up to five times as much as iron ones of similar size. The first known iron cylinder was made in 1718, and from 1722 the Coalbrookdale Company in Shropshire, which pioneered the smelting of iron with coke, undertook the production of cast-iron cyclinders. With the aid of a new boring mill erected in 1734, which reduced the costly breakages of boring bars, they were for several decades virtually the sole suppliers of cast-iron cyclinders. Their records have been an invaluable source of information about the spread of the Newcomen engine.[30]

In the face of all these problems, the spread of the Newcomen engine was remarkably rapid. The first engine may have been installed in a Cornish tin-mine even before 1710, but the evidence for this is exiguous in the extreme.[31] The erection of the first engine in a coal-mine in 1712, however, is better substantiated, though there remains some dispute as to its exact location. Most of the available indirect evidence favours the Coneygree Park colliery near Tipton in the Black Country, but the alternative possibility of a mine on the outskirts of Wolverhampton cannot yet be entirely ruled out.[32] The development of the engine after 1712 is now well documented, at least until the expiry of the patent in 1733. The earliest engines were well scattered—one at Griff in Warwickshire in 1714 where the Parrotts and Beighton would certainly have familiarized themselves

[28] Anderson 1957, 155.

[29] Rowlands 1968-9, 53-4.

[30] Rogers 1976, 11; Allen 1969-70, 170; A. Raistrick, *Dynasty of Ironfounders* (London, 1953), 128-38; Rolt and Allen 1977, 108.

[31] Rolt and Allen 1977, 45.

[32] Rolt and Allen 1977, 46-54; Allen 1964-5, 59; Henderson 1947-9.

with it, one at Hawarden in Flintshire in 1714–15, one at Austhorpe near Leeds also in 1714–15, one at Whitehaven, and another at Broseley in Shropshire in 1715. The first in the North-east was at Tanfield Lea in 1715,[33] and in the following four years seven more were erected on Tyneside. By the end of 1719 at least twenty engines had been installed in British coal-mines, while during the 1720s a further forty-two were built, widely scattered round the British coalfield. Of the installations during the 1720s only seven were in the North-east, though a further seven were known to have been completed there by the end of 1731. Several collieries installed more than one engine. Wyken colliery in Warwickshire had put up three already by 1722, while at Heaton colliery in the North-east four were known to have been erected between 1729 and 1731. By the time of the expiry of Savery's patent in 1733 and with it the ending of the Proprietors' ability to impose their handsome levy on steam-pumping operations throughout Britain, that is to say over a period of twenty-one years, seventy-eight Newcomen steam-pumps are believed to have been installed in British collieries. They were divided between the coalfields as shown in Table 4.1. The predominance of the West Midlands region in the steam-pump building activity of the period up to 1733 is far in excess of the coalfield's share of British coal output at that time. Within the coalfield, the Warwickshire area predominated: sixteen of the early pumps were erected there, compared with eleven in Staffordshire and the Black Country, and five in Shropshire. In the Black Country there is little doubt that the possibility of gaining easy access to the thirty-foot seam was a prime incentive to the initiation of steam-pumping, while in Warwickshire the relatively high number of engines is to be explained by the over-lying of the coal measures by heavily water-bearing strata and the steep dip of the seams worked which quickly necessitated deep mining. Both Staffordshire and Warwickshire, of course, were the home grounds of the Parrott partnership, the most vigorous sales-men of the new invention.

Though the North-east was the second most important mining region for steam-pump construction, in relation to output it was clearly lagging behind other regions. It has been suggested that this lag was due to the unsatisfactory experience of Ridley with an early Coalbrookdale cast-iron cylinder in 1731 which confirmed the north-eastern preference for brass cylinders; but this seems unlikely, not only because Ridley was at odds with many of the principal coalowners

[33] The Tanfield Leigh engine is clearly shown on a map dated October 1715 in NEI Watson 34/25.

Table 4.1. *Distribution of Newcomen
pumping engines at coal-mines,
1712–1733*

Mining region	Number of engines
Scotland	7
Cumberland	1
Lancashire	1
North Wales	4
South Wales	2
South-west	—
West Midlands	32
East Midlands	3
Yorkshire	2
North-east	26
Total	78

Source: I am indebted to Dr J. W. Kanefsky
and Dr J. A. Robey for this information which
is drawn from their computer-based listing of
eighteenth-century steam-engines at coal-mines.

of the North-east, but also because the lag was apparent long before
1731. More likely the greater cost and smaller size of brass cylinders,
which called for the more costly employment of multiple engines,
are said to have inhibited the more rapid adoption of steam-pumping
in the North-east. Of the twenty-two iron cylinders known to have
been cast at Coalbrookdale by 1733, only one was ordered from the
North-east. As late as 1752 there were still several brassfounders at
work in the North-east making cylinder castings for engines.[34]

The expiry of the patent in 1733 removed a major inhibition to
steam-pump installation. Rents of up to £350 per annum were a
substantial element in the costing of any early eighteenth-century
colliery, and with only an initial capital cost and normal running
costs to consider after 1733, steam-pumping became a much more
attractive proposition. Table 4.2 shows the distribution of
Newcomen engines erected between the expiry of the patent in
1733 and the installation of the first Boulton and Watt engine for
the drainage of a coal-mine in 1776. It is probably not unreasonable
to assume that by the 1770s a steam-pump was a normal feature
of all but the smallest and shallowest collieries in Britain. Since

[34] Rolt and Allen 1977, 61–7.

Table 4.2. *Distribution of Newcomen pumping engines at coal-mines,*
1734–1775

Mining region	1734–9	1740–9	1750–9	1760–9	1770–5	Total
Scotland	1	1	0	20	12	34
Cumberland	2	1	0	3	0	6
Lancashire	0	3	3	7	6	19
North Wales	2	1	0	4	0	7
South Wales	0	0	3	6	1	10
South-west	2	8	8	13	2	33
West Midlands	5	6	9	2	12	34
East Midlands	3	1	1	8	6	19
Yorkshire	2	4	4	2	14	26
North-east	6	24	22	75	6	133
Total	23	49	50	140	59	321

Source: See Table 4.1.

multiple pits were a common feature of collieries in many coalfields, multiple steam-pumps were frequent, and were often moved from pit to pit as old pits became exhausted and new ones were sunk. Byker colliery on Tyneside built its ninth engine in 1761, and Long Benton its seventh in 1765. At Newbiggin (Tynemouth Moor) four were built together in 1769, no doubt draining separate pits. Newcomen pumps had limited lives, of course, just as any machine must eventually wear out, and the number of engines known to have been erected over a given period should not be equated with those actually in operation at the end of that period. Engines were abandoned, sold second-hand to other collieries, or left idle through the stoppage of a colliery for reasons other than flooding. But the slow speed of operation of the Newcomen engine reduced wear and tear and, with careful attention, an engine could give very long service. The Newcomen steam-pump installed at Elsecar colliery, Yorkshire, in 1795 was still operating in 1923.[35] William Brown, viewer of Throckley colliery, compiled a list of steam-pumps 'all on the Newcomen principle' 'at work drawing water' in 1769. It showed ninety-nine engines at work, including six at Byker, four at Tynemouth Moor, and four at his own Throckley colliery. Most of the engines in the list were in the North-east, but six were in Cumberland, one in Nottingham, and three is Scotland. His count of eighty-nine for the North-east was not, however, comprehensive.[36] A considerably

[35] A. K. Clayton, 'The Newcomen-type engine at Elsecar, West Riding', *TNS*, 35 (1962–3).
[36] NEI Bell 15/1, copied into Matthias Dunn's MS 'History of the viewers', 14.

greater number of engines had been erected at one time or another between the first in 1715 and the time of Brown's survey.

As steam-pumps became more numerous they also increased in size and pumping capacity. The early engines of the 1710s mostly had cylinders with diameters in the range sixteen inches to twenty-four inches. After 1720 cylinder size grew steadily: from an average of twenty-six inches during the 1720s it rose to an average of forty-seven inches in the 1750s to culminate in the monster eighty-two inches diameter cylinder of the 1812 Newcomen engine at the William Pit at Whitehaven. The larger cylinders could not be supplied with steam by single boilers, and from the middle of the eighteenth century multiple boilers became common. The increase in size was accompanied by growing sophistication and consequential greater efficiency and reliability in operation. The many engineers who worked on Newcomen engines during the eighteenth century included James Brindley, the noted canal engineer, who patented an improvement of sufficient importance to send two north-east viewers down to Newcastle-under-Lyme in 1759 to find out whether it would be of interest to them,[37] and William Brown, perhaps the most famous of the mid-eighteenth-century viewers, who supervised the erection of no less than twenty-two engines in the North-east between 1756 and 1776, as well as three in Scotland. He appreciated the importance of an adequate steam supply, for which he recommended multiple boilers. He provided the engine he built at Benwell in 1762 with three boilers and a larger engine at Walker in the following year with four.[38] Of the various engineers who also contributed to the detailed improvement of engine design the best known was John Smeaton. He made a scientific study of the engine and contributed a number of improvements to boiler and cylinder design, the injection nozzle, and the regulator. Engines of Smeaton type, called 'Pentrich engines' were also built by the Derbyshire engineer, F. Thompson, of Ashover.[39]

Rather less is known about the actual water-pumps operated by steam power than about the steam-engines themselves. It seems that rod-operated pumps were introduced in place of bucket-pumps in the early years of the eighteenth century immediately prior to the discovery of steam-power itself. An early pioneer of these pumps was the great hydraulics engineer, George Sorocold.[40] The maximum

[37] W. Brown to Sir John Delaval, 9 Sept. 1759, NuRO Delaval 6/3/1.

[38] Rolt and Allen 1977, 107–8, quoting Matthias Dunn 1844.

[39] A. Stowers, 'The development of the atmospheric steam engine after Newcomen's death in 1729', TNS, 35 (1962–3); W. T. Anderson, 'Notes on an old colliery pumping engine (1791)', TIME, 52 (1916–17).

[40] F. Williamson, 'George Sorocold of Derby. A pioneer of water supply', Derby Archaeological Society Journal, 57, n.s. 10 (1936).

lift obtained by a single rod-pump was 135 feet, often less in practice, so that to raise water through greater heights a series of such
pumps, lifting water into staging cisterns, was needed. At these
depths the weight of the rods themselves became an important element in the functioning and design of engines. The pump pipes
themselves were at first universally of wood, preferably elm or oak.
A trunk of thirteen to fourteen inches diameter or above was neces-
ary, allowing a bore of six inches. In the 1720s, however, the Coalbrookdale Company was employing a technique of casting iron
pipes, and from this time these began to take the place of the less
durable and efficient wooden pipes.[41]

In 1769, as is well known, James Watt patented his improved
steam-pump, the principal feature of which was the separate condenser. The addition of the separate condenser enormously improved
the efficiency of the engine, reducing its fuel consumption accordingly.
Like Savery, Watt and his partner, Matthew Boulton, patented the
new invention, and, like him, too, secured an act of Parliament
extending the patent's life. From 1769 to 1800 Boulton and Watt
were able to exact a levy on their improved steam-pump similar to
that exacted by the Proprietors of the Savery/Newcomen patent
between 1715 and 1733. Their royalty was normally estimated at
one-third of the cost of the fuel saved by replacing a Newcomen
engine with a Boulton and Watt engine of similar capacity. Though
in tons of coal per annum this saving might appear to be fairly substantial, in terms of the pithead price of the relatively inferior coal
fed into the Newcomen boilers, the saving might not be very great.

That the mining industry investigated the newly available technology carefully and scrutinized costings thoroughly is well illustrated
by the following memorandum of the late 1770s:

We hear from Coventrey that a few days ago a trial was made between a Fire
Engine at Hawkesberry Colliery near that town, viz. 1 of the old Construction,
and 1 of the new improved Engines. The result was as follows. The new Engine
raised 99.711 cubic feet of water 130 yards perpendicular Height in the space of
48 Hours and Consumed 4 tons 16 cwt. of coal. The old Engine raised in the
same space of Time to the same height only 84.124 Cubic feet of water and
consumed 17 tons 18 cwt. of coal. The superiority of the new Engine errected
by Messrs. Bolton and Watt must therefore greatly promote the mining interest
of this kingdom since the proprietors of mines may save by the new improvement a sum equal to two thirds of that usually expended in fuel and likewise
may have such Engines errected on the terms of the Old Construction. The
Ingenuity and utility of the Contrivances of Messrs. Bolton and Watt respecting
the fire Engine in certain situations and confessed by all able and Experienced

[41] A. Raistrick, *Dynasty of Ironfounders* (London, 1953), 129–39.

mechanitians; but how they will apply as heighly advantageous to the Coal-mining interest in the Circle of Newcastle may deserve examination.

Now if the Engine at Hawkesburry upon the old construction raised only 84.124 cubic feet of water with 17 tons 8 cwt. of coals while the new one raised 99.711 cubic feet of water it will follow by proportion that the old Engine to raise 99.711 cubic feet of water would consume 26 tons 12 cwt 1 qtr 26 lbs. But the new Engine only consumed 4.16.0.0. Saved by the new Engine in doing the same work 15.6.1.26. But if $\frac{1}{3}$ of these savings be annually paid to the patentees according to there proposals it will be the same expence to the prorietors as if so much more was burnt by the Engine and which will be 5.5.1.27 to which is added the Coals burnt by the Engine 4.16.0.0. — 10.1.1.27 Expence on Acct. of fuel to the proprietor in raising 99.711 cubic feet of water 130 yards perpendicular which is som more than $\frac{1}{3}$ the Expence of the Old Engine at Hawkesburry.

As many Gentlemen in your own Neighbourhood tho' greatley interested in Coal mines may not be acquainted with what hath been already don in the Circle of Newcastle previous to the production of Messrs. Boulton Watt it seams necessary on this occasion that it be fully stated that the Gentlemen interested in the Coal trade may clearly see how in this respect there intrest will lay.

In July 1772 an experiment was tried upon an Engine at Longbenton Colliery constructed as then commonly in use and esteemed the best in that part of the countrey which was 62 inches cylinder. The result of which was that it raised at the rate of 122.708 Cube Feet of water in 48 Hours to the perpendicular Height of 122 yards and consumed 23 tons 1 cwt 1 qtr 15 lbs which is less than the Hawkesburry old Engine by 13 cwt 11 lbs of Coals in 48 Hours. This trial was made previous to the Errection of a new Engine at the same colliery for which Mr. Smeaton was then engaged to give the design which was to be also of 52 Inches Cylinder upon Newcommon principle (now called the old Construction) but with improvements of his own which experiment was expressly made that it might be clearley seen in what degree Mr. Smeaton proposed improvements would in reallity take place.

The plan was then Delivered and the errection of the new Engine was proceeded with the same year but not being Immediately wanted the work was chiefley don in the year 1773 and the new Engine was started in February 1774 and in may following a trial was made thereof similar to the former the result of which was that the new Engine raised at the rate of 206.569 cube feet of water in 48 Hours to a perpendicular height of 98 yards 2 feet with 15 tons 13 cwt 1qtr (page torn) lbs Coals which being arithmetically reduced to 99.711 Cubic feet at 130 yards will amount to 10 tons 1 cwt 19 lbs which is little more than half the Coals used by the Old Engine at Longbenton a little less than $\frac{1}{2}$ used at Hawkesburry Old Engine and sum more then double of the Coals used by Hawkburry new Engine. But the expence maintenance of the Hawkburry new Engine to the proprietor being as before stated 10 tons 1 cwt 1 qtr 27 lbs And that of Longbenton new Engine 10.1.0.19 — 0.0.1.8

NB What is here stated of the experiments at Longbenton is exclusive of each engine drawing its Injection water. The Coals were to both as the engines commonly work with Viz. Small such as when sold are used by the Salt pans and Bougt at the rate of 2d per Fodder.[42]

Thus the incentive to prefer a Boulton and Watt engine to one of 'the common construction' was seldom great before the end of the eighteenth century so long as it was required for pithead operation. Though Boulton and Watt steam-pumps began, therefore, to be installed in coal-mines from the 1770s and became economically more attractive to mine operators during the 1790s as the expiry of the extended patent approached, Newcomen engines remained popular and continued to be installed until well into the nineteenth century. When John Farey surveyed Derbyshire in the early years of the nineteenth century he 'met with no pumping engine on Boulton and Watt's principle at a coal-pit; the old atmospheric engines, well-contrived and executed, being thought to answer better in such situations'.[43] Even before the expiry of the Boulton and Watt patent in 1800 a number of engine-builders began fitting Newcomen engines with condensing cylinders in what must have been infringements of the Boulton and Watt patent. These so-called 'bastard' engines became very common in the early nineteenth century, particularly in the Black Country, though one is recorded at Radstock in Somerset as early as 1782.[44]

Boulton and Watt engines, however, were not merely cheaper to operate, an advantage over those of 'the old construction' that became more effective after the expiry of the patent in 1800, they were also more efficient in lifting water from the greatest depths, and accordingly made steady progress in ousting the Newcomen engines. The first Boulton and Watt engine known to be put to work in the drainage of coal-mines was at Bloomfield colliery in the Black Country in 1776, while in the North-east Byker introduced one in 1778. A report of 1798 indicated at least eight Boulton and Watt engines at work there, though two of these were rotative engines used for winding.[45]

It was originally thought that, during the period of Boulton and Watt's patent—1769–1800—that firm enjoyed a monopoly of the manufacture and supply of steam-pumps, so that their output, ascertainable fairly accurately from their copious records, accounted for the whole British production. More recent writers have shown

[42] NuRO 1765 Delaval (Additional), n.d. but post-1778.

[43] F. Nixon, 'The early steam engine in Derbyshire', TNS, 31 (1957–9), quoting J. Farey, General View of the Agriculture and Minerals of Derbyshire (London, 1807).

[44] Bulley 1953, 73.

[45] BPL Boulton and Watt 26. Another rough list of 1797 in the same box cited three Boulton and Watt pumping-engines in the North-east and ten winding-engines.

how far from the truth this is.[46] Newcomen engines continued to be made and installed in large numbers, while Boulton and Watt engines were pirated and a number of 'cross-breed' engines were devised and manufactured. Kanefsky and Robey estimated that nearly 1,500 steam-engines of all kinds were manufactured during the last twenty years of the eighteenth century, 373 of these being employed in the coal industry. Because an increasing proportion of these were winding-engines and some were used for both winding and pumping, it becomes impossible to trace the chronology of steam-pumping in the last decades of the eighteenth century with any precision. Kanefsky and Robey have definitely traced 828 new steam-engines of all makes erected in British coal-mines by the year 1800, though they believe that the true total may lie between 950 and 1,000. They were used for both pumping and winding, though it would probably not be unreasonable to assume that the majority at that date were still used for pumping. They were divided between the mining regions in the proportions shown in Table 4.3.

Table 4.3. *Distribution of steam pumping engines (all types) erected in British coal-mines up to 1800*

Mining region	percentage of total
Scotland	17.0
Cumberland	3.3
Lancashire	7.2
North Wales	1.4
South Wales	2.2
South-west	5.5
West Midlands	22.7
East Midlands	4.8
Yorkshire	8.1
North-east	26.6

Source: See Table 4.1.

The freeing of manufacture after 1800 led to increasing employment of steam-engines for pumping as well as to greater diversification of types of engine. In the absence of comprehensive estimates of numbers and powers of steam-engines in the early nineteenth century[47] we

[46] J. R. Harris 1967; Musson and Robinson 1959; Kanefsky and Robey 1980.
[47] von Tunzelmann 1978, 110–13 has estimated the total steam horse-power ultilized in the industry in the first half of the nineteenth century; Kanefsky thesis 1979, chap. 4.

can say little more than that, for workings on any scale and at depths exceeding 100 feet, steam-pumping by Newcomen or Boulton and Watt engines, or derivatives of them, was the rule.

ii. *Ventilation*

With the aid of the steam-pump the battle against water was very largely won during the eighteenth and early nineteenth centuries. The problems created by gases, however, were more intractable. In the shallower seams not only was it not too difficult to arrange for some circulation of air to move the gases away, but some of the gases were also able to escape naturally through fissures or the porosity of the covering strata. It was generally considered that pits of up to 180 feet deep raised few serious problems of ventilation, but that at greater depths positive action was required to rid the workings of these gases. The progressive increase of depths during the eighteenth and early nineteenth centuries greatly increased the problems of ventilation. Blowers of gas once released might supply gas for years on end and sources opened up by underground working tended to accumulate dangerously towards the roof of workings or remain undisturbed but undispersed in disused parts of mines.

The nature of the gases encountered in coal-mining was first examined systematically by Robert Plot, the Staffordshire naturalist, towards the end of the seventeenth century.[48] He classified them into seven categories, but his criteria would certainly not be acceptable today. There was a desire to understand how the gases behaved, though it is doubtful whether there was available in the eighteenth and early nineteenth centuries a sufficient understanding of their chemistry to provide any practical advice to the miners who had to deal with them. In 1733, for example, Sir James Lowther sent bladders filled with gas from his pits in Cumberland to the Royal Society in London for examination, and Sir John Clerk of Penicuik filled several pages of his 'dissertation' of 1740 with not very scientific or helpful descriptions of 'foggy' and 'poisonous' airs and 'bituminous exhalations'.[49]

For practical purposes, however, there were principally two gases that were dangerous to miners. They were known as 'firedamp', a methane gas, and 'chokedamp'. The former was the most common and certainly, when mixed in the air of workings with coal-dust, the most dangerous. It was easily ignited and caused explosions.

---

[48] Robert Plot, *The Natural History of Staffordshire* (Oxford, 1686), 133–4; *VCH Staffordshire*, II, 92.
[49] Hardwick and O'Shea 1915–16, 556; ScRO Clerk of Penicuik GD18/1069/28–30.

The quantity as well as the nature of the gases varied considerably from coalfield to coalfield. In Cumberland and the North-east the continuous generation of gas underground quickly led to highly dangerous build-ups of concentrations unless regularly dispersed. Speaking of the Bensham seam at Wallsend colliery, Buddle once said that 'I had nothing to do but set a candle, and then could set a thousand fissures on fire; the whole face of the working was a gas-pipe from every pore of the coal.'[50] In some instances the gases were piped to the surface and flared off there. In 1765 Gabriel Jars was told that Sir John Lowther had offered to illuminate the main streets of Whitehaven by gas piped from his mines.[51] This interesting proposal, antedating William Murdoch's better-known experiments with coal-gas lighting by more than thirty years, was unfortunately not taken up. In the Black Country gas escaping from old or current workings was often to be seen burning as jets from the ground.

So far as the lives of miners were concerned, in the eighteenth and nineteenth centuries firedamp was a major hazard, but choke-damp suffocated miners and could kill if those affected were not immediately removed to the fresh air. A description of 1816 vividly depicted the horrors of underground explosions and distinguished between the effects of the two types of gas.

. . . enveloping the unhappy miners in quick burning fire,—awful and horrible as this situation is, 'tis but the prelude to what is still more dreadful—the equition suddenly attains its height, a momentous silence ensues, and an immense volume of highly rarified air is produced, this naturally seeks the direct course to the pit which has the ascending current of air for the ventilation of the colliery, acquires incalculable velocity and force, with the noise of the loudest thunder and sweeps before it into horrible ruin and destruction the unhappy miners, with the horses, carriages and working implements, and dashes, mangles and buries them in one common ruin amid the rubbish and timbers carried along this fiery desolating tempest.

Those who escaped this blast by finding a place of safety were still, however, in danger.

Their inevitable fate is at hand, and the return of the after draught of pestilential air, arising from the exploded gas soon envelops them, they feel it insufferable, suffocating heat, a few exhalations unerves their active limbs, the knees bend down, and reclining upon their Mother Earth the heavy sleep of death soon overpowers their frame and they sleep to wake no more.[52]

At about the same time as this statement was made, Buddle expressed the view that only about one-quarter of the fatalities caused by

[50] SC Accidents 1835, Q.2095.   [51] Jars 1774–81, I, 248.
[52] I. R. Bald to James Russell, 16 Nov. 1816, ScRO NCB Scottish Division CB10/14, 4–7.

explosions of firedamp resulted from the blast itself; the remaining three-quarters of the deaths were due to suffocation from the gases generated in the explosion.[53]

Certain gases, then, were dangerous to miners in themselves, but others were dangerous only if ignited. Since some form of lighting underground, however, was a prerequisite of working, the risks of ignition were necessarily omnipresent. Until 1815 virtually the only form of lighting available for underground working was candles, and their naked flames posed the greatest single hazard to the lives of miners in this period. Though this danger was recognized, it was accepted primarily because there were at the time no practical alternatives. During the second quarter of the eighteenth century, and possibly as early as 1730, the steel-mill was invented and introduced first in Cumberland, it is said, by Carlisle Spedding, colliery-steward to the Lowthers. Its use was adopted in the North-east, it was believed, in 1763 following a serious explosion at Fatfield colliery. In this device a continuous light was produced from a flint held against the surface of a small circular grindstone which was rotated at a high speed through gears from a handle. It was un-economic since it absorbed the labour of one worker to operate it and the light it gave off was poor. It was said that one worker could provide sufficient light for six or seven other workers, though Buddle claimed that they were tiring to operate so that two men had to be employed to take turn and turn about with them.[54] It was widely believed to be safer than a candle, though there were few grounds for this belief and explosions following its use were known. The most Buddle would say of the steel-mill was that 'it is in a degree less dangerous than the naked light'.[55] He did, however, bring steel-mills back into Hebburn colliery in 1812 during a period when gas concentrations were high. Though they continued in use here and there into the early nineteenth century they failed to displace the candle as the principal form of underground illumination, and did not survive the coming of safety-lamps after 1815.[56]

By the early eighteenth century miners had learned to read the symptoms of gas presence by the colour of the flames of their candles. Firedamp turned the flame blue, while a severe accumulation would extinguish it. The same applied to the sparks from steel-mills, and the boys who operated them were trained to keep a constant watch on the colour of the sparks. But these warnings

[53] Buddle 1814, 12.
[54] Beckett 1981, 71–2; Dunn 1844, 23; SC Lords Coal Trade 1830, 33.
[55] SC Commons Coal Trade 1830, 273.
[56] SC Accidents 1835, Q. 2073.; NEI Buddle 40/202.

were not entirely reliable, and disaster often struck without any warning symptoms being observed.

By the end of the eighteenth century and the early years of the nineteenth, however, with the increase in scale and depth of pits, especially in the North-east, disasters caused by explosions underground reached a scale which began, even at that period, to cause anxiety if not to the acquiescent miners themselves, or to their employers, at least to humanitarians in the mining areas. Disasters involving severe loss of life had become now monthly rather than annual occurrences. There were two possible solutions to the problem: either to rid the mines of the dangerous gases by efficient draughts of air, or to devise a form of lighting that would not ignite the gases. Both solutions were ultimately sought since they were not really alternatives. Chokedamp could kill without ignition just as firedamp could explode with ignition, so that efficient ventilation was as important as safe lighting. As a last resort, seams known to be extremely gassy could be sealed off, or never worked. This last was the case, for example, with the uppermost seam in the Cumberland field at Workington in the mid-eighteenth century.[57]

Given the depth of mines in the early eighteenth century and the distance of underground faces from shaft bottoms, the efficient circulation of air in mines proved extremely difficult with the limited technical resources of the period. But the need to circulate fresh air and to drive out the gases was generally recognized, and efforts, often expensive efforts, were made to achieve this. The prime physical principle utilized in this endeavour was the convection current imparted to air by heat: a fire placed in a vertical shaft caused the air in the shaft to rise. A complete circuit of air was essential for this principle to be adapted to the successful ventilation of mines. In districts such as Lancashire and Cumberland where sough drainage was usual, the problem of ventilation was somewhat eased since the sough itself provided a through channel for fresh air entering a single shaft. In this situation the flow of water along the sough also helped to create a movement of the air. Pits drained by soughs were, of course, generally shallow and less encumbered by severe concentrations of gas. Already by the beginning of the eighteenth century, however, it was becoming usual, in all except the very smallest of mines, to provide two shafts to an underground working, one a downcast shaft to admit fresh air, and the other an upcast shaft to draw out the dangerous gases. The upcast shaft was normally also the working shaft for winding and pumping (the 'engine' shaft). If the small scale of operations made two shafts too

[57] Jars 1774–81, I, 247.

expensive a luxury, a single shaft was divided vertically down the centre by bratticing to create the two divisions for ventilation. This was the practice, for example, in the deep Lowther pits in Cumberland in the mid-eighteenth century, though this 'short cut' was believed to increase the risks of explosion.[58] Buddle admitted that the catastrophe that killed fifty-two miners at Wallsend in 1821 was due to an initial explosion that wrecked the bottom thirty fathoms of bratticing, blocking the shaft; this interruption to the course of ventilation led to the second, fatal explosion.[59] Circulation of air was achieved by placing a fire either suspended in a brazier at the top of the shaft, or in a hearth at the foot of the shaft, and the updraught was assisted by the tall chimney at the pithead that is a feature of so many prints of eighteenth- and early nineteenth-century coal-mines.[60]

Simple ventilation schemes of this kind suffered from various inefficiencies and risks. It was even possible, as happened at Lawsons colliery in the North-east in the 1820s, for an accumulation of gas in a faultily ventilated shaft to be ignited by lightning.[61] Blazing fires at shaft bottoms ran a real risk of igniting the gases before they had dispersed sufficiently to become harmless, and if, in response to this danger, they were placed as far as possible from the openings to levels, they became less effective. In shafts with wooden bratticing there was a danger of the fire drying out the wood and setting light to it. As Buddle admitted, 'we have had some horrible accidents from the shaft brattices catching fire.'[62] To avoid this the woodwork was sometimes deluged with water to keep it cool. One way of reducing the risk of an explosion of gases in the working shaft was to place the fire in a separate, shallow shaft a few yards away from the upcast shaft, and to draw the gases by pipe out of the shaft into this secondary shaft.[63] The extremely gassy Lowther pits at Whitehaven used an ignited jet of gas at the shaft bottom drawn by pipe from the workings to augment the updraught. A similar principle was invoked in the North-east in the early nineteenth century as steam haulage-engines were installed underground and their waste heat directed to boost the ventilating current in the upcast shaft.[64]

But the principal difficulty lay in the problem of getting the fresh air to circulate into both the current workings and the worked-out

[58] Holmes 1816, 165; 'Memoranda on the running of collieries, Nov 1756', CuRO Lonsdale D/Lons/L/Acc. 629. For the employment of such methods in South Wales, see NLW 788C, 132; in Derbyshire/Nottinghamshire, see A. R. Griffin thesis 1969, I, 11.

[59] SC Accidents 1835, Qs.2122–6.

[60] Ventilation methods of this kind are described in Hinsley 1969–70, 26–7.

[61] SC Accidents 1835, Qs.2198–2202.   [62] SC Accidents 1835, Q.2127.

[63] This method is described in Sir John Clerk's 'Dissertation on coal' (1740), in ScRO Clerk of Penicuik GD18/1069, 32.

[64] VCH Cumberland, II, 356; Hinsley 1969–70, 30.

stalls where dangerous concentrations easily built up. The currently worked face was, of course, continously moving forward in a dead end creating pockets of gas inaccessible to the circulating air in precisely the areas where working men were therefore most at risk. Consideration of this problem evoked important technical advances from two of the greatest viewers of this period. About 1760, James Spedding, son of Carlisle Spedding, both viewers of the Whitehaven collieries of the Lowther family, devised a system of air circulation known as 'coursing the air'.[65] This was no more than an extension of the traditional ventilation methods, but involved directing a maximum draught through all parts of the workings by a route determined by trap-doors and deliberate blocking of passages. The route could be changed easily to keep the draught directed into current workings and diverted if necessary to clear out accumulations in old workings. It had the effect, according to Buddle, 'of forming, generally speaking, every passage of the workings into an air-pipe'. But it also tended, in his view, to concentrate the gases, so that there was a risk of explosion at the furnace that set the air and gases in motion. This danger created a need for a 'waterfall' to be available to quench the furnace at very short notice.[66]

The Revd John Hodgson described the ventilation system in one such mine—Felling colliery on Tyneside in 1812:

Stoppings and *trap-doors* . . . are placed to divert the current of atmospheric air through proper channels. The stoppings are made of bricks and lime; and in this colliery, were strengthened on each side with a wall of stone. The trap-doors are made of wood: each of them is attended by a boy about seven, eight or ten years old; and they are seldom used but in the avenues leading from the working shaft to the workings. . . .

In all large collieries the air is accelerated through the workings, by placing a large fire, sometimes at the bottom, and sometimes at the top of the up-cast shaft, which in these cases is covered over and connected with a *furnace tube* or chimney, by an arched gallery of brick from 40 to 60 feet in length. In this colliery the furnace was about six feet from the bottom of the tube.

The first *course of the air*, after descending the John Pit, was under the arch, up the inner narrow board and the stable board, to the trap-door at the head of the narrow boards; then down the board next south to the stable board; and so afterwards up two boards and down other two, till it traversed the newly formed *sheth* or set or workings, branching from the southernmost part of the double-headways on the east: from thence it passed over the two arches up the outer board of the narrow boards, to the most westerly sheth of boards, and after fanning them, found its way down the crane board, along the drift to the

---

[65] Moore 1893–4, 624; Buddle's evidence to SC *Accidents* 1835, Q.1999.
[66] SC *Accidents* 1835, Q.1999.

William Pit, through which it ascended into the furnace, and thence, charged with noxious vapours, into the open air.[67]

In 1816 Holmes calculated that a mine extending 500 yards square would require ventilation courses stretching eighteen miles to clear every passageway.[68] By the 1830s Buddle was claiming that he knew of collieries in which air was circulated round underground courses as long as thirty miles before being finally drawn to the surface. Inevitably these extremely long courses resulted in some loss of efficiency, and about 1810, by a practice known as 'splitting the courses', or 'double' or 'compound' ventilation, Buddle found a way at Wallsend colliery of shortening the courses while still ventilating all parts of a large mine. He first multiplied the number of shafts, a costly expedient only practicable in a colliery having access to high-quality coal over a wide area. The main current of air was split at the bottom of each of the downcast shafts and directed into separate divisions of the underground workings. He simultaneously improved the efficiency of the draught by installing the furnaces at the foot of the upcast shafts but removed the danger of their igniting the out-flowing gases by directing the gases themselves round a bypassing 'dumb' drift.[69]

Variations of these simple expedients for introducing fresh air to drive out dangerous gases underground were evolved in all coalfields. In south Staffordshire, where the sheer height of the Ten-Yard seam created particular problems for the accumulation of gases in the high roof, a system of driving separate 'air-heads' or 'air-headings' parallel to the 'gait-road' or working level to facilitate air circulation was devised about 1808 by James Ryan. By linking the gait-roads and the air-heads frequently with connecting 'thirlings' it was possible to bring the circulation to current workings as they advanced. Ryan, who was awarded a gold medal and one hundred guineas by the Royal Society of Arts in 1816 for his work on mine ventilation, had 'no hesitation in affirming, from many years experience in Mining, that I could readily, and at comparatively a small expence, entirely clear the Mines of Great Britain of that destructive air to which such multitudes of your poor countrymen have fallen the unfortunate victims.' Ryan's scheme, however skilfully and efficiently it channelled the ventilation courses through and out of the pits, was still dependent on the limited draught set up by a convection furnace, and

[67] Hodgson 1813, 7–9.

[68] Holmes 1816, 82.

[69] T. E. Forster, 'Historical notes on Wallsend colliery', *TNEIME*, 15 (1897–8), 92; Hiskey thesis 1978, 67, 93.

though it was adopted in the Dudley and other collieries in the Black Country, was, after inspection by Buddle and other north-east experts in 1815, condemned by them as useless. This condemnation, in its turn, may have been inspired at least partly by inter-regional jealousy, and by a refusal by men of the North-east to accept that other mining regions were capable of technological leadership.[70]

Sir John Clerk of Penicuik described some mechanical ventilation systems employing water- and wind-power to activate bellows in his 'Dissertation' of 1740, but did not indicate whether in his travels to the North of England during the few years previously he had ever seen such machinery used.[71] Bellows, probably worked by man-power, were, however, used underground in some Lancashire collieries, particularly in the highly gassy cannel mines, in the early part of the eighteenth century. Giant bellows powered by falling water pumped air into the Worsley colliery of the Duke of Bridgewater from the 1760s.[72] In 1758 it was said that one Keane Fitzgerald invented a method of converting the reciprocating motion of the steam-pump into rotary motion to operate two rotary mine ventilators at Walker colliery on Tyneside. Since this machine attracted no notice— certainly not from Jars only a few years later—it must be assumed that it was not a success and was not imitated. Another mechanical ventilator known as 'White's Air Machine' was installed at Griff colliery, Warwickshire, in 1791. Though it was not reported as failing, it likewise attracted no comment or imitators.[73] By the early decades of the nineteenth century, however, the extension of the use of steam-power for drainage and winding suggested the possibility of employing it also for ventilation. In 1807 Buddle attempted to augment the draught of the ventilation plant at Hebburn colliery by the use of a steam-jet, and then turned to the reciprocating motion of the Newcomen engine which he adapted to operate bellows to draw the gases by suction out of a shaft. For this purpose a piston five feet square and with an eight-foot stroke was used, said to be capable of drawing out 6,000 cubic feet of waste air per minute. A mechanical fan-ventilator was tried unsuccessfully at the Union pit in Workington, Cumberland, in 1814.[74] The real breakthrough to modern ventilation, however, came only at the very end of the

---

[70] VCH Staffordshire, II, 92; MS volume 'On Dudley coal mines, 1815', in NuRO Society of Antiquaries ZAN M14 A9; Dunn 1844, 32; Holmes 1816, 87–92; The Appeal of James Ryan, Director of Mines, to Proprietors of Collieries and Men of Humanity (Birmingham, 1817).

[71] ScRO Clerk of Penicuik GD18/1069, 32.

[72] Langton 1979, 109, 191; Malet 1977, 87.

[73] Louis 1931–2, 529; Grant thesis 1977, 208.

[74] VCH Durham, II, 345; Hinsley 1969–70, 31; VCH Cumberland, II, 356.

period covered by this book: the first successful steam-driven fan was installed horizontally at the top of the shaft of a colliery near Paisley in 1827.[75]

By 1830 mine ventilation by air circulation had come a long way since 1700. The problems created by deeper mining with its concomitant more extensive underground working had focused the attention of viewers and managers on the need somehow or other to secure a vigorous circulation of air over long distances and through tortuous courses underground. Much was achieved with the application of intelligence, effort, and ingenuity, but progress was bound to be severely restricted until the development of mechanical ventilation: fires, no matter how well placed, could never create an adequate updraught, and could, if less than properly sited, constitute a danger in themselves. The movement of air depended on the strict supervision of the stoppings and the operation of trap-doors. Straker, the viewer at the Brandlings' Felling colliery, took the view that three-quarters of pit explosions resulted from the dislocation of the air courses through the throwing-down of stoppings.[76] Clarifying this point in 1813, Buddle explained that the seventy-five per cent of the lives lost in explosions through suffocation after the explosion could be saved if the ventilation current could be reactivated immediately after the explosion. To achieve this the 'stoppings' had to be reinstated immediately, and he proposed a system of emergency stoppings with strong, blast-proof pillars that would fall into position by gravity. He quoted the example of an explosion at Percy Main in April 1813 in which the pillars of the stoppings held firm so that the ventilation course was immediately restored and no lives were lost through suffocation; 'but if the pillaring had been wanting', he explained, 'not an individual could have been rescued from its [chokedamp's] suffocating powers'.[77]

Up to 1830 it is probably fair to say that the increase in the scale of mines was proceeding faster than the ability of the engineers to ventilate them, with the consequence that mines were becoming no less dangerous, and possible more so. The continuing and probably growing toll of life in mines was a reflection of the fact that there were so few effective alternatives to convection ventilation. Even well-designed schemes tended to leave pockets of gas in roofs, old workings, as well as in currently worked stalls, and in too many mines the speed of generation of dangerous gases exceeded the capacity of ventilating systems to clear them. In some coalfields, particularly in South Wales and south Staffordshire, it was common practice throughout the period to employ 'firemen' whose task was

[75] Hinsley 1969–70, 32.   [76] NEI Forster 49/8/182.   [77] Buddle 1814, 14.

to explode pockets of gas before the main shift of workers came down. This was accomplished by complicated arrangements of poles, string, wire, and pulleys, which enabled the firemen to raise a lighted candle into a suspected pocket of gas from the relatively safe retreat of underground stables or holes in walls or floors where he could be protected from the blast by a stout wooden door.[78] Though this was unsatisfactory since the extent of a gas concentration was difficult to gauge and the explosion might damage equipment or cause roof falls, it was at least temporarily effective in clearing gas by combustion and making a working area relatively safe for a few hours.

iii. *Lighting*

So long, however, as ventilation systems were imperfect—and so unceasing was the generation of gases from coal seams that it was virtually impossible to devise and maintain completely efficient ventilation—there was bound to be a serious probability of explosion while lighting involved naked flames or the sparks of steel-mills, and ventilation called for the lighting of furnaces underground or in shafts. As late as 1814 Buddle was obliged to admit that 'the only method we are at present acquainted with for the prevention of accidents by fire is the thorough ventilation of the several passages and workings of the mine.'[79] It became apparent, therefore, that the other solution to the problem of explosions—the invention of a form of lighting that would not ignite gases—must be sought at the same time as improvements in ventilation continued to be pursued. There is no evidence of attempts to devise a safety-lamp before the second decade of the nineteenth century, and it is tempting to suppose that it was the substantial increase in fatalities from explosions in the North-east, where safety-lamps were first evolved, that first caused attention to be focused on the problem. Hair's under-registered mortality figures show how the deaths from mining accidents in the North-east rose from an annual average of 1.2 per 1,000 employed between 1795 and 1809, to 3.2 per 1,000 in 1810–14, and 4.4 in 1815–19.[80] The absence of adequate information for the estimation of comparable mortality rates for earlier periods may, however, conceal high rates before the end of the eighteenth century, and it might be unwise to assume that the scale of mortality in the second decade of the nineteenth century represented a new peak. In the event, however, it was a major disaster that precipitated the course of events that led to the invention of

[78] 'Collieries and the coal trade' (1805), CuRO Lonsdale D/Lons/W.
[79] Buddle 1814, 5.   [80] P. E. H. Hair 1968.

effective safety-lamps. An explosion at Brandling Main colliery, Felling, on south Tyneside on 25 May 1812 caused the deaths of ninety-two miners and proved to be the straw that broke the camel's back of local apathy among the employing class of the North-east. Feelings ran very high locally against the colliery's viewer, and the Revd John Hodgson, the incumbent of the parish of Jarrow and Heworth within which Felling colliery was situated, gave as much publicity to the accident as he could in a series of articles in the *Newcastle Courant* and elsewhere, 'contrary to the feelings of the coal owners'.[81] This publicity attracted the attention of other professional men, including the Bishop of Durham and other local clergy, and led to the formation in October 1813 of a Society for the Prevention of Accidents in Coal Mines. This Society necessarily included as patrons and committee members the principal landowners, mineowners, viewers, and clergy, but it is clear that the initiative and pressure for its formation came from professional interests outside the immediate circles of the industry.

Simultaneously with these events the first practical endeavours were being made to devise a safety-lamp. In late 1811 and early 1812 William Clanny, a Sunderland doctor, was experimenting with such a lamp. He recognized that the problem was to insulate the flame from the surrounding air at the same time as allowing a sufficient flow of air to keep the flame burning, and to embody these functions in a lamp strong enough to withstand the rough usage of mine working. After several failures he eventually devised a lamp which filtered both its air intake and outlet through water, for which hand-bellows and a separate operator were needed. He described this in a paper to the Royal Society on 20 May 1813.[82] The lamp was tested in Harrington Mill colliery but seems not to have found any general acceptance. It was suggested at the time that there was apathy and even some opposition to Clanny's lamp from viewers and owners.[83] Meanwhile, however, the Society for the Prevention of Accidents in Coal Mines started issuing reports, the first of which included a valuable survey of existing ventilation technology of Buddle,[84] and some of its members and some outsiders were continuing to give publicity to mining accidents as well as attempting to devise safety lamps.

In 1815, after several abortive attempts, and stimulated perhaps by an enormously high number of fatalities—there were 197 deaths

[81] NEI Easton 17/7/134; Galloway 1898, I, 422.
[82] Galloway 1898, I, 421.
[83] Holmes 1816, 177.
[84] Buddle 1814.

in north-eastern mines in that year[85]—the Society at last succeeded in getting in touch with Sir Humphry Davy, the famous scientist employed by the Royal Institution who had once been Lambton's tutor. By good fortune Davy was in Scotland at the time and agreed to visit the North-east on his way south. Arriving in Newcastle on 23 August, he met both Buddle and Clanny and had an opportunity to examine the latter's lamp. After several days of discussions he went off to London promising to put his mind to the problem, with which, so far as is known, he had not been previously acquainted. Clearly he set about his task promptly, experimenting with igniting firedamp in various situations. He kept the Society in the North-east informed about his progress in letters to the Revd John Hodgson during October. He quickly discovered that the gas had a relatively low inflammability and that it would not ignite through an aperture of less than one-eighth of an inch. The reason for this was the loss of heat in contact with the cooling surface. This led him to devise a lamp that was airtight except for small tubes of that guage to admit air. He made known his discovery initially to Hodgson in a letter dated 15 October.[86] This lamp, however, was only a stepping-stone on the way to his crowning achievement, the wire-gauze lamp. Embodying his discovery that firedamp could not be ignited through very small apertures, the new lamp's flame was now wholly surrounded by a metallic tissue 'permeable to light and air and impermeable to flame',[87] and the protective glass cylinder was dispensed with entirely. The wire-gauze lamp was announced to the Royal Society on 9 November 1815, and the first models arrived in the North-east in early January 1816. They were immediately tried out in Hebburn colliery by Hodgson, Buddle and Matthias Dunn to their complete satisfaction. Later in 1816 Davy added a small, but valuable, modification to the wire-gauze lamp. This was a tin reflector placed inside the gauze for its full height and round a portion of its circumference. Besides increasing the light on the working side of the lamp this also protected the flame from any fierce blower thus reducing the risk of explosion.[88]

While Davy was at work in London during the autumn of 1815, however, another experimenter, the great railway engineer, George Stephenson, was also grappling with the same problem. From his account, it seems that he started his experiments in August 1815 at almost exactly the same time as, and conceivably a few days before,

[85] NEI Buddle 8/11.
[86] Revd. J. Hodgson to John Buddle, n.d., NuRO 510.
[87] Sir H. Davy to J. G. Lambton, 29 Oct. 1816, LEA DP55/2.
[88] Sir H. Davy to J. G. Lambton, 9 Sept. 1816, LEA DP55/2.

Davy was introduced to the problem in Newcastle.[89] He did so in association with the young Nicholas Wood, an apprentice viewer, who forty years later wrote a first-hand account of the experiments. His first lamp, which admitted air through a tube adjustable up to half an inch diameter, was tested on 21 October and proved to be a failure because of its inability to sustain a full flame. A second lamp with multiple air inlets was tested at Killingworth on 4 November and, although an improvement on the first, was still not wholly satisfactory. Finally, in late November, Stephenson devised a third, improved lamp in which the air chamber and lamp glass were covered by a perforated plate that was clearly not far removed from Davy's wire-gauze. It was tried at Killingworth on 30 November and declared 'to be perfectly safe and burn extremely well'.[90]

Stephenson's and Davy's work therefore proceeded almost simultaneously, though Davy succeeded in announcing his most successful lamp three weeks ahead of Stephenson. Unhappily, however, the spate of experimentation and invention in the autumn of 1815 was followed immediately by recrimination and accusations of plagiarism. Davy, perhaps because he produced what was ultimately the most widely accepted lamp, was accused of taking over the ideas of both Stephenson and Clanny, though he later protested that 'I never heard a word of George Stevenson [sic] and his lamps till six weeks after my principle of security had been published', while Stephenson, in his turn, was alleged by Davy and others to have pirated Davy's ideas.[91] Stephenson, of course, actually demonstrated his perforated plate lamp in the North-east several weeks before Davy was able to show his wire-gauze lamp there. On the other hand, Davy's final version was publicly described in London as early as 9 November, at which time Stephenson was still apparently working with his earlier versions which either failed to burn properly or made use of air-inlet tubes too large for safety. Stephenson was emphatic that he had conceived his ideas of a safety-lamp before Davy visited the North-east in August and claimed that at no time was he ever even informed that Davy was working on a lamp. Since, however, he was still working on the imperfect 'tube' lamps into November, it is

---

[89] G. Stephenson to A. Tillcock, 13 Mar. 1817, NuRO Brandling ZBG 26/1.

[90] This description of the inventions of the lamps of Clanny, Davy, and Stephenson is based on an unsigned and undated memorandum (probably of 1817) in LEA DP55/2; N. Wood 1857–8; Galloway 1898, I, 420–39; Holmes 1816, 177–217; Rolt 1960, chap. 2; Hartley 1960, and 1966, chap. 9; A. R. Griffin 1978; and the supplementary documents cited.

[91] Sir H. Davy to J. G. Lambton, 29 Oct. 1816, LEA DP55/2; Sir H. Davy to unknown recipient, 3 Mar. 1818, NuRO 510; Holmes 1816, 204; and a poem by Tam Glen entitled 'Hocus Pocus, or the Juddle of the Lamp' (cutting from *The Visitor*, 1 Apr. 1816, in NEI Bell 14/5/223.)

unlikely that he conceived the crucial feature of the perforated plate any earlier than Davy hit upon the wire-gauze. Nicholas Wood, Stephenson's young collaborator, conceded that both Davy and Stephenson were 'original and separate discoverers of the principle'.[92] The verdict must surely be that although the two inventions were *effectively* made almost simultaneously and that it was the distance between London and Newcastle that allowed disputes about precedence to arise, Davy's successful idea actually emerged to the public about three weeks ahead of Stephenson's.

In the event, sides were taken in the Newcastle coal trade. The great coalowner, Charles Brandling, and members of the Grand Allies' consortium, Stephenson's employers, espoused his cause, while Davy was ardently and articulately supported by Buddle, Lambton, and many others. While it seems likely that Clanny's early lamp may have pointed Davy in what was ultimately the right direction, Davy's lamp was none the less clearly the product of empirical and genuinely original experimentation prompted by an understanding of scientific principles quite beyond Clanny's and probably Stephenson's capabilities. Stephenson, who must also have known something of Clanny's lamp before he started work, certainly worked quite independently of Davy and produced a very similar solution to the problem at much the same time in spite of his total lack of theoretical training. Davy consistently took the view that Stephenson's lamp did not reach minimum safety requirements. '*It is not a safe lamp*', he wrote to Lampton, 'for the apertures below are four times too large, and those above 20 times too large.' He referred to Stephenson's lamp derisively as 'his glass exploding machine' in spite of the fact that it seems to have been used widely with much success.[93] Matthias Dunn, who, with Buddle and Hodgson, had tested both lamps in Hebburn colliery in January 1816 pronounced that the Davy lamp 'unquestionably possesses many advantages over that of Stephenson, particularly from its being constructed without Glass which is one unsurmountable objection, besides its portability and cheapness'.[94] The Stephenson lamp, however, was said to be marginally safer than the Davy lamp, but gave only half as much light, a serious objection in view of complaints against the feebleness of the light even from the Davy lamp.[95] There is little doubt, however, that Davy's greater success with the wire-gauze lamp, his sponsorship by the prestigious Society for Preventing

[92] N. Wood 1857–8, 45.
[93] Sir H. Davy to J. G. Lambton, 29 Oct. 1816 (Davy's italics), LEA DP55/2.
[94] Memorandum dated 9 Jan. 1816, NEI Forster 49/3/72–4.
[95] A. R. Griffin 1978, 730.

Accidents in Coal Mines, and his status as a knight and official scientist to the Royal Institution helped him to receive the lion's share of acclamation. When the time came in 1816 for the issue of rewards, the 'coal trade' in Newcastle presented Davy with silver plate valued at £1,611 and Stephenson with one hundred guineas. In 1817, however, Stephenson's supporters organized a dinner to celebrate his achievement at which he was presented with a silver tankard and £1,000.[96]

The lamps by Davy and Stephenson were, of course, merely the beginning of a long story of the evolution of safety-lamps. In the fifteen years following their inventions there were improvements by George Upton and many others.[97] William Clanny, the first to enter the field of safety lamp design, later produced a more sophisticated model. It was a rather cumbersome 'steam-lamp' which involved a miniature water-boiler.[98] Each colliery district, each viewer, and no doubt each miner had views about which models best suited their needs and local conditions. There is, unfortunately, no way of assessing the speed with which safety-lamps were adopted either in each coalfield or in the industry as a whole. There are merely occasional indications of their use, as for example in Buddle's diary at Jarrow colliery where he indicated in 1817 that it would be necessary to employ one lampkeeper or 'Davy-keeper' on each shift in the East pit.[99] By the 1830s Buddle estimated that there were 1,000 to 1,500 Davy lamps in daily use in the collieries with which he was associated, and nearly 900 in the Londonderry pits alone. They were cheap, costing only 5 or 6s., and were manufactured locally.[1] Stephenson's 'Geordie' lamps, too, became popular, being exclusively used in the pits of the Grand Allies, though Stephenson had quickly discarded his perforated plate in favour of Davy's wire-gauze, a rather significant acknowledgement of the superiority of a key element in Davy's invention. Thereafter, the only effective difference between the lamps was the retention of the glass cylinder in the 'Geordie' lamps and the insertion of the tin reflector in the Davy lamp.

But there were clearly many collieries where there was less enthusiasm for the new lamps. The Sheffield Coal Company was still purchasing candles for its collieries at Sheffield Park and Attercliffe in

[96] 'List of plate presented to Sir Humphry Davy', and undated memorandum, NuRO 510; Rolt 1960, 31.
[97] SC Accidents 1835, vii–viii.
[98] NEI Forster 49/3/83.
[99] NEI Buddle 36/II/161; SC Accidents 1835, Q.2188.
[1] SC Accidents 1835, Q.223; SC Lords Coal Trade 1830, 33; SC Accidents 1835, Q.2217.

in 1830, while at Elsecar New colliery near Barnsley the eleven safety-lamps listed in an inventory of 1833 were used for inspection for gas rather than for normal working.[2] The early lamps gave a very poor working light, and miners were obviously under temptation to revert to candles.[3] 'I have a man at Morpeth House of Correction now for taking off the top of his Davy,' reported Buddle in 1830.[4] In September 1816, however, Davy issued a handbill purporting to measure the amount of light provided by different forms of pit lighting. It does not indicate what the unit of measurement was, but the results were as follows:[5]

Miner's candle	45.5
A lamp with a tin-plate reflector for diminishing the circulation of the air, and facing a blower	49
A single common lamp	39
A double copper wire lamp	25
A steel mill, unequal and uncertain, but at its greatest intensity. A steel mill is nearly twice as expensive as a wire gauze safety lamp.	25

In the course of working underground the mesh of the wire-gauze tended to clog with dust and reduce the illumination.[6] The lamp, too, was very fragile; the wire-gauze was easily pierced by a miner's pick or by falls from the face or roof. Miners tended to continue working with slightly damaged lamps though 'a very small opening even less than the twentieth part of an inch will make the surrounding gas explode'. Nor was the Davy lamp so reliable a guide for the miner to the strength of the ventilating current as was the flame of a candle.[7] It seems, too, that there were circumstances in which a Davy lamp could spark off an explosion: if a lamp was placed in a direct jet of gas from a blower, the flame could be blown against the gauze and effect ignition unless it were fitted with one of Davy's reflectors. In his evidence to the Select Committee on Accidents in Mines of 1835 George Upton was very emphatic that viewers and miners should be made aware of this hazard, though Davy himself

[2] Fletcher thesis 1973, 61.

[3] VCH Staffordshire, II, 92.

[4] SC Commons Coal Trade 1830, 273.

[5] Suggestions arising from Inspections of Wire Gauze Lamps in their Working State, in Mines, by H. Davy, 9 Sept. 1816, NEI Watson 5/26.

[6] Newspaper-cutting of letter from J. Buddle, 1 June 1816, NEI Bell 14/5/378.

[7] I. R. Bald to J. Russell, 16 Nov. 1816, ScRO NCB Scottish Division CB10/14, 19; SC Accidents 1835, Q.2072.

had always warned against the danger of using his lamp in a strong draught.[8] In south Staffordshire, where the Davy lamp was said to be used first in 1817, miners demanded extra pay to work with it, presumably because the poor light from it reduced their output and earnings.[9] 'The Davy lamp was a great safety invention,' wrote Hinsley, 'but it needed informed supervision.'[10] In 1819 the management at the Lowther collieries in Whitehaven issued a printed notice announcing fines for miners neglecting to use the safety-lamp: 'If any Hewer, or other Workman, employed in the Whitehaven Coal-Pits where any danger can exist from Fire Damp, shall neglect to approach his Work with the SAFETY LAMP, or shall use CANDLES in doing so, he shall (for every Offence) forfeit the Sum of Five Shillings. And when Orders are given to continue the Use of the Lamp, during the whole Time of Working, any person who shall remove the SAFETY CYCLINDER or use Candles in the Workings, shall also forfeit Five Shillings.'[11] Buddle, however, claimed in 1835 that he had only known of one explosion with the Davy lamp in twenty years experience of its use, possibly the one at the Lambton colliery in 1817 which Davy hoped 'will be the last'.[12] Another disaster, however, at Brandling's Gosforth colliery at Middleton, near Leeds, when twenty-four men and boys were killed, was attributed to an explosion set off by a red-hot Davy lamp, but the fact that this was a Brandling colliery must leave the attribution in some doubt.[13]

The principal consequence of the adoption of the safety-lamp, however, was the confidence it gave to owners and viewers to work in underground areas hitherto considered dangerous, and in consequence to press on with deeper and more extensive underground workings. 'Its [the safety-lamp's] importance in a national point of view', wrote Buddle to Davy in 1824, 'is enabling the miner to produce the coal to the community, which without its aid, *never could have seen the light of day.*' In 1830 he was prepared to say that 'almost all the collieries below the bridge on the Tyne would have been at this time extinct, but for the Safety lamp.' 'We are working mines', he also said in the same year, 'from having the advantage of the safety lamp, which we could not have possibly worked without

---

[8] *SC Accidents* 1835, Qs.3986–8; Hartley 1966, 116.

[9] Lones 1930–1, 45.

[10] Hinsley 1969–70, 29.

[11] *Regulations in the Whitehaven Collieries relative to the use of Sir Humphry Davy's Safety Lamp* (Whitehaven, 13 Nov. 1819), CuRO Lonsdale D/Lons/W Additional Records.

[12] *SC Accidents* 1835, Q.2224; Sir H. Davy to J. G. Lambton, 8 Sept. 1817, LEA DP55/2.

[13] Rolt 1960, 34.

it, and of course they are in a more dangerous situation, and the risk is increased in a very great degree.'[14] The miner himself saw the lamp, however, as an evil which allowed workers to be put in more dangerous situations. The extent to which this view was correct must, however, surely have been reflected in the statistics of fatal accidents. There was no immediate diminution in the annual number of fatalities which reached their peak, according to Hair's calculations, in the quinquennium 1815–19. But the Select Committee of 1835 noted none the less that while in the eighteen years previous to the invention of the safety-lamp there had been, according to its calculations, 447 fatalities in the North-east, in the eighteen years since the invention there had been 538.[15] The Committee was aware, of course, that there had in the meantime been a substantial increase of output and employment: Hair's index shows a sharp decline in the number of deaths per 1,000 employees after 1820 in spite of the continuing increase in the depth and scale of underground working, so that it is possible to argue that, in the North-east at least, after an initial period, the safety-lamp both made possible more extensive underground working and helped to reduce the cost of mining in terms of human lives. But it is worth remembering that the early safety-lamp was very imperfect and was used in conjunction with very inefficient ventilation systems. Mining continued, for this reason, to be a highly dangerous occupation: in the late 1820s an average of over twenty-five miners lost their lives in the North-east every year, most of them as a result of explosions.[16]

[14] J. Buddle to Sir H. Davy, 1 Jan. 1824, NuRO 510 (Buddle's italics); and see Hinsley 1969–70, 28; SC Commons Coal Trade 1830, 273; SC Lords Coal Trade 1830, 32.
[15] SC Accidents 1835, iv.
[16] P. E. H. Hair 1968, 551.

Chapter 5

The Transport of Coal

i. *Road and rail transport*

The business of producing coal was by no means completed when the coal was raised to the pithead and placed 'on the bank'. From the pithead it had to be transported to the consumer, and because the weight of coal was high in relation to its value throughout the eighteenth and early nineteenth centuries, transport charges added significantly to its pithead cost. Working from the valuation of commodities entering trade by the Inspector-General of Imports and Exports in 1754, Davis listed some thirty-two commodities according to their value per ton. At the head of the list was wrought silk at £3,920, while half-way down the list was sugar at £27 per ton: coal was at the bottom of the list at less than £1 per ton.[1] Yet much the same amount of carriage-space and draught-power was required for a ton of coal as for a ton of silk. Clearly the carriage of coal from the pithead to the consumer was a major element in the economics of coal consumption. It was customarily assumed, in the eighteenth century, that land carriage of coal doubled its pithead price in ten miles. By water, on the other hand, the productivity of both humans and animal labour was much higher: a river vessel might easily in the eighteenth century load twenty tons of coal, and a coastal collier fifteen times as much. It was assumed that coal could be carried twenty times as far by water as by land for the same unit cost.

The economics of coal distribution in the early eighteenth century thus very obviously dictated the use wherever possible of water rather than overland transport. Yet mines were where nature rather than the convenience of water transport determined, and consumers were not necessarily collected at locations suitable for delivery by water. For these reasons, and in spite of the heavy cost of road transport, a not insignificant proportion of coal produced in the early eighteenth century was carried from mine to consumer, or at least for a part of its journey, by road. Most of the coal mined at the Duke of Bridgewater's colliery at Worsley in south Lancashire, for example, was carried to Manchester by pack-horse in the years

[1] Davis 1962, 177.

before he built his famous canal.[2] Even where the greater part of the journey between mine and consumer could be arranged by water, there was initially the problem of carrying the coal from pithead to the nearest navigable water. This problem, for example, greeted Sir John Lowther in his plans to develop the mines on his land in west Cumberland in the opening years of the eighteenth century. He had no difficulty in deciding that the existing transport of coal by pack-horse was inefficient and turned instead to the use of carts. These, however, were not without their problems: neither humans nor packhorses were accustomed to these monsters. 'A cart being an uncommon thing here in those days struck such a terror into the poor country people who to save themselves were glad to gett up their coals at any ship they could where they would be sure to be free from the carts.' And since 'all carts are a plague to packhorses', Lowther's carts were ordered to load early in the morning or at night to 'leave the coast clear to all packhorses'.[3]

Sir John's mines were relatively close to the sea, however. Coal-fields more remote from the sea and the larger rivers were obliged to place more reliance on road transport. One historian of the Somerset coalfield, for example, believes that the landsale area there was somewhat greater than the ten to twelve miles radius often assumed to be the limit of overland coal carriage. Glastonbury was supplied from mines at Midsomer Norton (sixteen miles), and War-minster from Radstock (fifteen miles). In this area farmers buying coal brought their own carts to the pithead, but much coal distribu-tion was undertaken by small merchants and dealers living locally. The stock of a Bath coal-merchant in 1795 included a broad-wheeled waggon, two narrow-wheeled waggons, a cart, and five horses.[4] Measham colliery in Leicestershire in 1724 disposed of much of its coal by road transport, and although most of its customers were within ten miles, some were as far away as Burton-on-Trent (thirteen miles), Hinckley (fifteen miles), and Shenton (eighteen miles).[5] In the eighteenth century the rapidly growing town of Liverpool drew its entire coal supply by road from mines near Prescot seven miles away until the opening of the river Douglas navigation in 1740 made an alternative supply route available, and the desire to reduce the cost of the carriage of coal was the principal motive behind the creation of the Prescot–Liverpool turnpike of 1725. In these inland coalfields road improvement by turnpike trusts increased the sales of

[2] Clegg 1965, 91.

[3] 'Note book of John Spedding, 1703', 18; and 1705, no pagination, CuRO Lonsdale D/Lons/W/Collieries.

[4] Bulley 1953, 58–9.

[5] C. P. Griffin thesis 1969, 196.

coal by road. In Somerset in the 1750s and 1760s the extension of turnpike roads was warmly greeted by coalowners, while in Derbyshire the desire to expand the markets for coal was a major stimulus to road-building. The Turners, coalowners of Swanwick in the latter county, rebuilt the road from their colliery to Matlock at their own expense in the 1730s, and a desire to gain access to markets was said to have been the main purpose of roads from pits in north Derbyshire to Buxton and Sparrowpit.[6] The revival in the fortunes of the Warwickshire coalfield from the middle decades of the eighteenth century has been attributed to the increase in the market area brought about by the construction of turnpike roads. The principal mineowner in this coalfield in the 1760s, Sir Roger Newdigate, himself invested in the Coventry to Hinckley turnpike.[7] In South Wales coalowners were often the most enthusiastic promoters of turnpike trusts. The role of the coal trade in stimulating turnpike developments was often recognized in specially negotiated low tolls for coal.[8]

With or without the aid of improved roads, and in spite of transport costs high in relation to its pithead price, coal continued to be transported by road, even by pack-horse, in some areas until well into the nineteenth century. True, in these districts the radius supplied remained small and the scale of mining was accordingly severely circumscribed. In the Rochdale area of south Lancashire, for example, royalties were still being calculated per horse-load of coal in the late 1820s. Similarly, the isolated Ingleton coalfield in west Yorkshire continued into the nineteenth century to distribute its coal by cart and pack-horse over a wide area of north Lancashire and the Craven district of Yorkshire.[9]

But even with the improved roads offered by the turnpike trusts the constraints of the road carriage of coal were severe enough to encourage efforts to devise alternative means of transport. In the early 1790s, for example, carriage of coal in Somerset, where relatively soft road surfaces and steep gradients set limits to the productivity of draught horses, added seventy-five per cent to the pithead price in Bath.[10] One solution to these problems, devised first by Huntingdon Beaumont in the early years of the seventeenth century, was to create special ways for coal waggons with steady, slight gradients

---

[6] W. Albert, *The Turnpike Road System in England, 1663–1840* (Cambridge, 1972), 46; 'Plan of Proposed Somerset Coal Canal', 1793, SoRO Hylton; Bulley 1953, 54; Hopkinson 1976, 14.

[7] Grant thesis 1977, 183–4.

[8] Roberts thesis 1953, 147.

[9] Wadsworth 1949, 107; A. Harris 1968, 317–18.

[10] Bulley 1953, 51–4.

and wooden rails to reduce the friction of wheels. One horse on such a 'waggonway' could pull as much as two horses and two oxen together with a wain on a road.[11] Even allowing for the capital cost of laying down waggonways, the greatly enhanced productivity of horses reduced transport costs. An estimate for Tanfield Moor colliery of 1711 showed that transport to the river Tyne by road in wains allowed a profit of £1 17s. 6d. per ten, but that transport by waggonway would increase profit to £5 5s. 9d. per ten.[12] The wooden waggonways were particularly suitable for the short, mainly downhill journeys from mines to the nearest coastal or river navigation. Though first used at Woolaton, near Nottingham, as early as 1604, they were not rapidly taken up in other coalfields.[13] In the North-east, where the most extensive development of the waggonways eventually took place, and where the valleys of the rivers Tyne and Wear offered the most favourable situation for their use, the first enduring developments appeared only in the later seventeenth century. After his success in Nottinghamshire, however, Huntington Beaumont had laid down a waggonway for a mine he leased at Cowpen, near Blyth in Northumberland, in 1605, but this venture was not a success and the waggonway ceased to operate in 1614. The first lasting waggonway in the North-east that can be dated with certainty appears to have been the Crawcrook line on upper Tyneside which is known to have been in existence in 1663, though a line from Fawdon colliery may have been laid as early as 1656. These were followed by others from Ravensworth and Winlaton in the 1660s and 1670s. By the beginning of the eighteenth century waggonways had become a fairly common feature of mines in the North-east. They were by no means universal, however, even for the larger, seasale collieries. In 1726 Jesmond colliery, north of the Tyne, was believed to be employing more than 700 wains leading coal to staithes on the Ouseburn, while up-river Benwell and Fenham collieries used 6–700 carts to carry their coal down to Scotswood quay.[14] The first Wearside waggonway was constructed in the 1690s, the first in Yorkshire and Scotland in 1722, in Cumberland in the early 1730s, and in South Wales in 1740.

Waggonways with wooden rails had therefore already come into use by the early decades of the eighteenth century in most of the principal coalfields. At this stage their function was almost exclusively to carry coal from pitheads to the nearest water navigation

[11] NEI Buddle 14/288–9.

[12] Estimate, n.d. (but almost certainly 1711), GPL Cotesworth CK/12/20.

[13] R. S. Smith, 'Huntingdon Beaumont, adventurer in coal mines', *Renaissance and Modern Studies*, I (1957); and 'England's first rails: a reconsideration', ibid., 4 (1960).

[14] W. Green 1865–6, 203; Dunn 1844, 22.

on the first leg of its journey to the consumer. In Scotland, Cumberland, and South Wales this meant leading the coal down to the quayside at the coal ports, in the North-east to the staithes on the rivers Tyne and Wear, and in the inland coalfields of Lancashire, Yorkshire, the Midlands, and the Forest of Dean to the nearest river. There were, however, a small number of waggonways which led from collieries or from waterways serving collieries directly to consumers. Such a line, for example, was completed in 1819 from Pinxton on the Cromford canal in Nottinghamshire to the urban outlet of Mansfield, a line which carried almost a quarter of a million tons of coal in its first seven years of operation.[15] Given these limited, though crucial, functions, there was seldom any call in the eighteenth and early nineteenth centuries for waggonways of more than a few miles in length. Between 1724 and 1738 the average length of waggonways on Tyneside was said to have increased from three and a half miles to five miles, and by 1785 the most distant collieries from the river were said to be Bushblades, eleven miles away, and at Stanley, twelve miles away, both south of the Tanfield area.[16] An account of collieries in the North-east of 1828 lists sixty-two collieries almost all of which depended for their outlets on waggonways to the riverside staithes with lengths varying from a few hundred yards to ten miles. By this date the average Tyne waggonway had reverted to about three and a half miles, presumably on account of the substitution of down-river collieries for those on the high ground between the rivers Team and Derwent that had predominated during the first half of the eighteenth century. Wear waggonways in 1828 averaged four and three quarter miles.[17]

Since almost all coal waggonways led from a colliery to a river or harbour, they ran, by the nature of things, downhill, so that the loaded waggons could take advantage of gravity; but the horse still had to pull the empty waggon back up the hill, and if the most effective use was to be made of expensive horse-power, the gradient must be steady and not too great: one in Monmouthshire in the 1820s was carefully engineered to give a steady 1 in 100.[18] Curves, too, could not be too sharp: the Howgill colliery waggonway in Cumberland avoided them by the use of turntables.[19] These requirements called for the use of cuttings, embankments, bridges, and tunnels. An embankment at Tanfield in County Durham in the

[15] H. Green 1935–6, 67.

[16] NEI Forster 49/5/153; NEI Watson 8/8/239. The distances are probably exaggerated.

[17] DuRO NCB First Deposit NCB/I/JB/2418; and a similar list of the same date in NEI Buddle 25/III/4–15.

[18] CuRO Lonsdale D/Lons/W/38/19.

[19] Moore 1893–4, 625.

1720s was 100 feet high and 300 feet wide across the base. Bridges were commonly of wooden construction, but the larger ones were of stone. The Causey Arch built in 1725–6 carried a waggonway running north to the Tyne eighty feet above a ravine with a span of 105 feet—the earliest major railway arch. Tunnels were used to cut through the highest obstructions. The most remarkable of these was the two-mile tunnel ('the world's first underground railway') built in 1770 on the waggonway from Old Kenton colliery to the north bank of the Tyne west of Newcastle. In situations where steeper gradients could not be avoided, 'inclined planes' were employed. These were so arranged that the loaded waggons took advantage of gravity to pull the returning empty waggons up the incline by means of a rope and pulley. In Monmouthshire in the early nineteenth century many hillside collieries were connected to a main tramway by inclined planes, and Thomas Fenton's Rothwell Haigh colliery near Leeds was connected to the river Aire by an inclined plane in 1789.[20] One of the most ambitious, if not over-ambitious, waggonways, built to link Urpeth colliery near Chester-le-Street in Durham with the lower Tyne in 1809, was nine miles long and negotiated high ground in the course of its cross-country route by no less than three separate inclined planes all operated by means of stationary steam-engines. The different capacities of these engines and the horses taking over the waggons on the flatter ground between the inclined planes, variously capable of drawing three, four, five, six, or seven waggons at a time, involved frequent re-forming of trains. So long and compli-cated a journey proved uneconomic in the end and the partnership running the colliery soon went bankrupt.[21]

Rails were initially made of wood with a flat surface and right-angle edges which called for flanged wheels (the true 'waggonway'). The timbers from which the rails were constructed were carefully squared to about five to six inches by four to five inches and then fixed flat side up to wooden sleepers with wooden pegs. The gauge was normally about four feet, though some wider gauges were known.[22] Rails were usually made of beech, and sleepers of oak, though a longer-wearing 'double rail' superimposed a replaceable strip of beech on top of an oak rail.[23] But even the best wooden rails wore out quickly and had normally to be replaced within three years. To reduce both wear and friction the practice of laying wrought-iron plates on the surface of the wooden rails was begun,

[20] CuRO Lonsdale D/Lons/W/38/18; Goodchild 1978, 19.
[21] NEI Forster 49/13/1–4.
[22] Jars 1774–81, I, 200.
[23] NEI Buddle 24/46.

probably in the second decade of the eighteenth century. There is some evidence of their use both in Yorkshire and the North-east from the 1760s. Cast-iron rails were introduced in 1767 when the Coalbrookdale iron company in Shropshire was seeking to keep its furnaces in blast during a slack period. These rails, three to six feet long, wore out more slowly than wooden rails and reduced friction: they thus reduced maintenance costs and raised the productivity of draught horses. Buddle reckoned that a horse could 'do more work by 30 per cent on an iron way than on a wooden way; but frequently he will do 50 or even 100 per cent more'.[24] Their economic attraction increased with the rapid rise of timber prices during the Napoleonic War. But though an important advance on wooden rails, cast-iron rails tended to be brittle and to break under heavy weight, and after the invention by Henry Cort in the 1780s of the puddling and rolling processes it was natural that efforts should be made to replace cast-iron by wrought-iron rails. This was first achieved in the Cumberland coalfield in 1808, and the use of wrought-iron for this purpose seems to have spread steadily from that date. Some rails were constructed with L-shaped angle plates which supported flangeless wheels (properly called 'tramways'). Tramways, particularly as they were developed in the nineteenth century, were claimed to be more efficient, but waggonways using flanged wheels remained more common, certainly in the North-east. The Monmouthshire way of the 1820s was a tramway built to replace an older waggonway: it was claimed that one horse could pull four waggons each of two tons on the tramway against only two waggons on the waggonway.[25] Many of the Derbyshire lines, too, were tramways.

The appearance of the standard waggon is well known from many contemporary prints. Its four wheels, initially of wood, but from the 1750s increasingly of cast iron, were twenty-seven to forty-six inches in diameter. In the North-east it was designed to carry a standard load of one Newcastle chaldron (53 cwt.) which was made statutory following an act of 1815.[26] This compared very favourably with wains that carried only 17½ cwt., and carts 8¾ cwt. In other coalfields the capacity was generally slightly less. The waggons were equipped with brakes, on the lever of which the driver sometimes sat during the downhill journey to check the speed. Side-doors or hopper-bottoms were fitted for unloading.

Although tracks and waggons were usually owned by the colliery owner or lessee, waggoners were generally independent contractors

[24] NEI Buddle 15/261–3.
[25] CuRO Lonsdale D/Lons/W/38/19.
[26] 55 Geo. III, c. 118; NuRO Joint Coal Owners' Association 263, Minute Book 1820, 24.

who provided their own horses and worked for a piece-rate. All the waggon horses at the Lowther Howgill colliery at Whitehaven in 1787, for example, were supplied by farmers who were tenants on the Lowther estate, an arrangement that also operated on Lord Scarbrough's Lumley estate and elsewhere in the North-east.[27] The virtue of this arrangement was that it was flexible: tenants could 'lead' as a part-time occupation and thus be paid only when there was a call for their labour, whereas full-time waggoners would have become a standing overhead cost. To ensure an ample supply of horses for haulage, landlords in the South Wales coalfield inserted a clause into farmers' leases requiring them to provide horses for coal transport at the usual rates.[28] In mining areas a horse was therefore an asset the value of which could run to between six and twelve months' income for a tenant. In this circumstance it was a valuable piece of property that needed to be safeguarded. The waggoners of Pontop colliery formed a mutual insurance society in 1827— a friendly society called the Pontop Colliery Waggon Horse Collection—in which benefits were payable in respect of the illness, accident to, or death of horses rather than humans.[29]

After James Watt adapted steam-power to rotary motion in 1781, it was only a matter of time before a steam-locomotive would be evolved capable of taking over from the horse on the waggonways. Initially the use of atmospheric pressure by eighteenth-century steam-engines, whether of Newcomen or Watt design, required such large boilers and cylinders that their adaptation to mobility on the waggonways seemed to be out of the question. The weight and bulk of these engines made them unfit for waggonway use. In 1804, however, making use of steam at higher than atmospheric pressure, Richard Trevithick demonstrated a working locomotive in South Wales. But while his locomotive drew an impressive train of coal waggons, it was so heavy that it occasionally broke the cast-iron rails it ran on, and this was to be the fate of a number of imitators.[30] In the first year of Trevithick's success, Christopher Blackett, owner of Wylam colliery in Northumberland, ordered a locomotive of Trevithick type to be built in Gateshead. Though completed in 1805, this locomotive never ran at Wylam: Blackett's heart apparently sank when he saw the bulk of the locomotive and realized that it would instantly have smashed through the rails of the Wylam waggonway.

[27] CuRO Lonsdale D/Lons/W/31; Beastall 1975, 24; W. Green 1865-6, 215.
[28] Roberts thesis 1953, 146.
[29] NuRO Armstrong 725 F/65.
[30] G. F. Westcott, *The British Railway Locomotive, 1803–1853* (London, 1958), 3.

The breakthrough to practical locomotive design for colliery use was achieved almost simultaneously in several coalfields. At Charles Brandling's Gosforth colliery at Middleton near Leeds John Blenkinsop successfully operated a locomotive from June 1812 to pull loaded coal waggons along a waggonway to Hunslet staith on the river Aire. Writing from Middleton in January 1813, he spoke of 'the complete success of my Patent Steam Carriage which is daily at work at this place and is performing the work of sixteen horses and eight men', though two months later he told his correspondent that he hoped that by April of that year 'I will be able to inform you when the Middleton Road will be finished.' Presumably the Middleton locomotive was running in 1812 and early 1813 on only a portion of the whole projected line. This locomotive relied for traction on a cog wheel engaging in a rack placed alongside one of the rails, in spite of Trevithick's demonstration in 1804 that the weight of a locomotive provided sufficient friction to grip the rails. A locomotive was tried at one of the Lowther's Whitehaven collieries in 1812, but the rails would not stand its weight. Other locomotives, presumably of similar design and also relying on cog and rack drive, were installed in 1813 at Orrell colliery in Lancashire,[31] and on a line from Coxlodge and Fawdon collieries in Northumberland. Blenkinsop's correspondence unfortunately leaves some doubt as to the exact nature of the engines he was operating and recommending in 1813. Though all were quite clearly of rack and cog design, the cost of the Coxlodge and Fawdon engine included a royalty payment in respect of Trevithick's patent, while proposals made to three other prospective buyers in 1813 and 1814 all referred explicitly to royalty payments to Blenkinsop himself.[32] Blenkinsop's contribution to locomotive design may have consisted in little more than the cog and rack transmission.

While Blenkinsop was establishing in this way his claim to have produced and demonstrated successfully the first steam-powered railway, in Northumberland several engineers were working their way a little more hesitatingly towards a similar end. William and Edward Chapman, William Hedley, and George Stephenson were all experimenting with locomotive design and construction in 1812, 1813, and 1814. The Chapman experiments in 1812–13 were rather costly failures, while a first, four-wheeled version of Hedley's *Wylam Dilly* of 1813 proved too heavy for its cast-iron plate rails. In addition

[31] Moore 1893–4, 632; J. H. M. Bankes and J. R. Harris, 'The first Lancashire locomotive', *Journal of Transport History*, 5 (1961–2).

[32] The information in this paragraph is drawn from estimates and copy letters in a Report Book of John Blenkinsop, 1809–1829', 17–78, in LCA 1546 (photocopy in NuRO 962).

to the excessive weight of these early locomotives, their inventors had also failed to solve the problem of the generation of an adequate supply of steam to keep the engine in motion. Boilers with a single flue failed to provide a sufficient heating surface, and even Trevithick's brilliant device of turning the cylinder's exhaust flue into the boiler flue's chimney to create a powerful draught on the boiler fire, imitated by Stephenson with his *Blucher* of 1814, did not provide the complete answer. Stephenson continued his experiments, finding some success by increasing the diameter of the boiler flue. The ultimate solution of multiple boiler tubes was not found until after 1830.[33]

Both Hedley and Stephenson employed smooth rails, finding that the weight of their engines provided sufficient friction to grip the rails and pull a train of waggons without slipping, thus enabling them to dispense with Blenkinsop's rather expensive racks. Because of the weight of the early locomotives the success of their development was dependent also upon the parallel improvement of the rails on which they were to run. The Killingworth waggonway, for example, the scene of some of the most important experiments in locomotive traction, was using wooden rails with a metal strip surface when Stephenson began his experiments. By 1818 it had changed to cast-iron edge rails, finally switching to wrought-iron rails in 1820.[34]

As a result of these developments, from 1815 locomotives were steadily replacing horses for waggonway haulage in most coalfields. Their quick success was undoubtedly due to their economic advantage over horse-power. A calculation by Charles Brandling at the time of the adoption of Blenkinsop's locomotive at Middleton in 1813 showed that the annual cost of coal carriage by horse-drawn waggons to Hunslet staith was £2,900, and of locomotive operation £830. The calculation did not take account of capital costs in either case though it might be supposed that the forty horses to be replaced would have cost at least as much as the three locomotives planned. The saving was reckoned to be the difference between 1s. 5½d. per chaldron for horse power, and 6¼d. for steam traction.[35] The Blenkinsop-type engine at Orrell, Lancashire, was estimated to save £500 per year compared with horse traction.[36] A detailed estimate by Blenkinsop of 1813 for the projected conversion to steam traction of the waggonway from the Coxlodge and Fawdon collieries showed the cost of horse traction over the five and a half miles as 3s. 1¾d. per

[33] Rolt 1960, 41–57.
[34] D. Johnson, 'The Black Roads', *Northern Architect*, Sept. 1965, 546.
[35] Rimmer 1955, 45.
[36] Anderson 1975, 117.

chaldron, but with steam traction, employing five locomotives, a mere 5¾d. per chaldron. The capital cost of adapting the waggon-way, including the purchase of rack rails and seven locomotives would have been £6,247, but this could be more than offset by the proceeds of the sale of seventy-seven horses and some materials from the present track, leaving a net capital gain of £1,911 10s. It seems that steam-power was adopted at least experimentally on this line, since John Watson, the viewer at Kenton, which shared the use of the Coxlodge and Fawdon line, writing to the Duke of Portland's agent in October 1813, spoke about the operation of one engine on the line. There were similar calculations of 1813 for Lockwood's colliery in Morriston, near Swansea, showing a saving of eighty-eight per cent compared with the use of horses, and for a Lancashire colliery, with similar savings. The principal saving in the use of steam-locomotion in place of horse-power lay in the ratios between fuel, feed, and labour inputs, and power output: the fuel for an engine cost about the same as the feed for one horse, but while a horse led by one waggonman pulled a single waggon loaded with from two to four tons of coal, an engine with a crew of one or two men would draw up to twenty waggons at a time. 'The engine', wrote John Watson enthusiastically in 1813 about the Blenkinsop model on the Coxlodge and Fawdon line, 'is capable of drawing 16 Twenty four Boll wagons each journey which we compute will weigh with the Coals therein 64 Tons.'[37]

Most waggonways, particularly those outside the North-east, were owned and exclusively used by the owners of the collieries they served. This sometimes involved ownership being shared between partners in a colliery undertaking. The Derwent Haugh waggonway, for example, valued in 1789 at £1,902. 5s. 3½d., was shared in units of twenty-fifths between six partners.[38] Some, however, were shared, by negotiated agreements between adjacent collieries, while others were 'public' waggonways made available by their owners for any user at a freight rate per unit of coal carried. An example of the former, which was common in the North-east, was the Flatworth colliery waggonway on north Tyneside east of Newcastle for the use of which the owners of Murton colliery agreed in 1804 to pay a freight of 3s. 3d. per ten mile,[39] and of the latter a line down to Lydney on the Severn from the Forest of Dean where the fragmented nature of 'free mining' virtually excluded working on a scale large

[37] Report Book of John Blenkinsop, 18–19, 66–78, LCA 1546. (Watson's letter is also in NEI Watson 5/10/32a); NEI Watson 9/13/no pagination.
[38] NEI Bell 46/19/no pagination.
[39] NEI Buddle 14/96.

enough to encourage investment in waggonways by individual operators.[40] A similar public railway of two and a half miles was laid out on Wakefield Outwood in west Yorkshire, a large common, by enclosure commissioners in 1793–6 to prevent excessive wear on roads by the carriage of coal to wharves on the river Calder. A group of local lawyers and merchants put up the capital and a standard freight rate was laid down by the commissioners.[41] The Royal Commission of 1871 listed seven Forest of Dean railways, authorized by acts of Parliament between 1802 and 1815, on which coal was carried.[42] In the North-east, the scale of investment and the concentration of many large collieries in small areas obliged mine-owners to share the use of waggonways to a much greater extent than elsewhere.

With their engineering works, rails, waggons, horses, and, later, locomotives, waggonways added a considerable capital item to the cost of mining. The Grand Allies' forty-two miles of waggonways on Tyneside in 1739 was said to have involved a capital outlay of £50,000, or £1,190 per mile.[43] The round figure may involve some exaggeration. In 1791 Hugh Seton estimated a capital cost of about £837 per mile for a proposed waggonway in Midlothian, and in the 1770s the Lumley (Wearside) waggonway was costed at 4s. 6¼d. per yard, or £398 per mile.[44] In the later eighteenth century costs of around £750 per mile were more common, but in 1810 an estimate for a waggonway at Murton colliery in the North-east put the capital cost at £1,203 per mile, while in 1819 the ten miles of the Pinxton to Mansfield waggonway cost £22,800 or £2,280 per mile.[45] An estimate of 1830 put the cost of a new thousand-yard waggonway to Craw-crook colliery on south Tyneside at a rate of £2,825 per mile.

Operating costs, too, though lower than road transport costs would have been, were nevertheless a significant addition to the pit-head price of coal. The 1813 estimate of the five and a half mile line built in 1811 from Coxlodge and Fawdon collieries illustrates vividly the elements that went into the cost of operating a waggon-way. To carry a total of 60,000 chaldrons a year from the two collieries eighty-one horses were needed. This led to the following annual operating costs:

[40] 'Report on Forest of Dean by J. Buddle' (n.d. but probably 1832), NEI Buddle 51/279.

[41] Goodchild 1977, 1.

[42] RC Coal 1871, 32; A. I. Brown, 'The Bullo Pill tramroad railway', Local History Bulletin (Gloucestershire County Council), 44 (1981).

[43] NEI Buddle 14/353. Another account of the same year gave a total of 48½ miles (DuRO Strathmore D/St/176).

[44] Duckham 1970, 215; Beastall 1975, 27.

[45] H. Green 1935–6, 67; Hopkinson 1976, 29; DuRO NCB First Deposit NCB/I/JB/1918.

	£	s.	d.
Food for the above horses at £50 each per annum	4050	0	0
Trapping for 81 horses at 3 gns. per annum	255	3	0
Farriers wages, drugs, and shoeing for the above at 1s. each per week	210	12	0
Decay of horses at 8 at £45 each	360	0	0
Greasing and ballasting the road 5½ miles at £150 per mile	825	0	0
Waggonmens wages for leading 60,000 chaldrons at 1/0d. per chaldron	3000	0	0
Eight horsekeepers wages at 18s. per week or per annum	374	8	0
House rent and fire coal for 81 waggonmen and 8 horsekeepers at 2/6 per week each or per annum	578	10	0
	9653	13	0
Deduct for manure bred by 81 horses	200	0	0
	9453	13	0

which is at the rate of 3s. 1¾d. a chaldron.[46]

This was the equivalent of roughly 2½d. per ton/mile. In 1813 Coxlodge coal was selling FOB Newcastle at about 20s. per chaldron, so that the waggonway operating costs represented about sixteen per cent of the price paid by the shipmaster in Newcastle. This estimate, however, made no allowance for the cost of waggonway maintenance and a calculation of about the same period showed that this could amount to £310 per mile per year, which would add £1,705 to the annual cost of the Coxlodge and Fawdon line.[47] The costs of a substantially longer haul by stationary engines and locomotives from Stanley colliery, south-west of Gateshead, to Jarrow, a distance of about fifteen miles, were set out in a statement of 1822. This railway was originally constructed in 1804 for horse operation assisted by stationary steam-engines on inclined planes. Some time before 1822 locomotives had replaced horses as the principal motive power.[48] In this case the waggonway operated by the colliery only covered part of the journey to the staith, the second stage of the journey being made over an existing line for which a rent was paid to another colliery. The statement may be summarized as follows:

[46] 'Report Book of John Blenkinsop', 18–19, 66–78, LCA 1546.
[47] NEI Johnson 12/1–4 (n.d. but probably 1814–21).
[48] NEI Forster 44/13/1–4.

	£	s.	d.
Wear and tear of ropes, rollers, etc.	1,360	0	0
— do — locomotives, including coal	120	0	0
— do — stationary engines	600	0	0
Wages of 14 men	582	0	0
Wages of 6 waggonway wrights	249	0	0
Wear and tear of 100 waggons	500	0	0
Wages of 4 wrights and smiths	166	8	0
Interest on capital at 10%	2,236	8	0
Eight wayleave rents	1,100	0	0
Ground damage, say	60	0	0
To Mount Moor colliery for carriage on to Jarrow	1,547	15	11
	8,521	11	11

For an assumed 30,000 chaldrons per year, this equalled 5s. 8d. per chaldron, or about 1.7d. per ton/mile.[49] This was only an estimate, and possibly based on an optimistically large quantity to be carried. It was even more optimistic than the $2\frac{1}{2}d$. per ton/mile estimated for the Coxlodge and Fawdon line. The reality was a little different. Actual costs on waggonways from six Lambton collieries in 1828 ranged from 3.3d. per ton/mile to 12.3d.[50] In spite, however, of these substantial additions to pithead prices, where waggonways replaced existing road transport they effectively lowered the delivered price of coal. The Pinxton to Mansfield waggonway of 1819, for example, reduced the price of coal in Mansfield from between 10s. and 13s. per ton to between 8s. and 8s. 6d. per ton.[51]

Waggonways of all kinds, whether with horse- or steam-traction, as well as roads and tracks used for the overland carriage of coal, were confronted by one major problem—access to land. In the eighteenth century private Acts of Parliament gave the constructors of a public utility like a turnpike road or a canal rights of compulsory purchase of land on the principle that the benefits to the public of this use of the land overrode even the almost sacrosanct rights of private ownership. In the event, however, most turnpike trusts or canal companies preferred to negotiate 'free' agreements for the purchase of land though the powers of compulsory purchase resting in the background may have contributed to a landowner's decision to sell. But the beginnings of the waggonways predated the era of private legislation for these purposes, and in the eighteenth century

[49] NEI Buddle 22/129.
[50] 'Estimate of working costs at Lambton pits, 1828', LEA unnumbered.
[51] H. Green 1935–6, 67.

the intention of most operators to keep them for private use would probably have excluded them anyway from the scope of such a procedure. Builders of waggonways were obliged, therefore, to negotiate with the landowner for the purchase or rent of the land they required. Riparian ownership was equally important since access to a river or harbour and 'staith room' was also a necessity. As a bargaining counter to persuade landowners to concede wayleaves it was sometimes advisable for mine operators to agree to give the landowner's tenants the economic advantage of the right to lead the coal on the proposed waggonway. This was conceded at Stella colliery on Tyneside, for example, in the opening years of the eighteenth century, 'where ye Rytoners have ye sole leading of ye Grand Lease coals, and att an established price before they would grant any way leave'.[52]

In coalfields where mines were few and scattered, access for waggonways probably created few serious problems, but where, as in the North-east, collieries were many and closely concentrated, and land was held by owners with experience in the economics of coal-mining, then access for 'wayleaves', as the right to cross another's land was called, could be the subject of bitter bargaining. It was not unknown for an owner to refuse a wayleave outright, if this meant denying an advantage to a competitor. Sir John Lawson, for example, who owned coal-bearing land at Cramlington some eight or nine miles north of Newcastle investigated the possibility in 1786 of mining: to transport his coal over such a distance to the Tyne would involve paying so many wayleave rents as to remove all profit, while he was advised that to carry his coal the shorter distance to the east coast ports of Blyth or Hartley would involve crossing the lands of Lords Ridley and Delaval, who, as coalowners themselves, would be unlikely to grant him wayleave at all.[53] In the mid-eighteenth century a mine operator in South Wales called Morris wrote to the Duke of Beaufort to complain that the Duke's steward had refused wayleave which prevented him from carrying away coal from mines on Treboth common.[54] A similar complaint was made in 1782 by the owner of Kinnaird colliery on the south shore of the Firth of Forth against Dundas of Carronhall and the Carron Company for closing roads through their estate at Quarole to prevent him from leading his coal to Carronshore. Not until 1786 was an agreement made to permit the coalowner, for a rent of 4d. per chalder, to have a wayleave.[55] There were also 'negative wayleaves', which were

[52] Henry Liddell to Sir John Clavering, 4 Jan. 1711, GPL Cotesworth CK/12/17.
[53] NEI Watson 8/4/157.
[54] NWL Badminton 2149 (n.d. but probably c.1750).
[55] ScRO Carlops and Abbotskerse GD65/238, 247.

defined as 'paying a certain rent to the owners of the ground to prevent any person coming through it but those they think fit, or giving money down for not letting others pass'.[56]

The control of wayleaves was thus a powerful weapon in the hands of a group of coalowners anxious to create a restrictive or monopolistic agreement. Control of access to the riverside staithes was effectively control over entry to the coal shipping trade, leaving the coalowner with access only to the small landsale trade. The partners to the early eighteenth-century Tyneside 'regulation' were accused in 1711 of preventing other collieries from working by the denial of wayleaves,[57] and this weapon was most vigorously and ruthlessly used by the partnership called the 'Grand Allies' during the second quarter of the eighteenth century. Controlling much of the land to the immediate south of the river Tyne up-river from Gateshead, this partnership was well placed to regulate the carriage of coal from the areas on either side of the river Derwent that were being most vigorously exploited at that period. It embarked quite deliberately on a policy of land purchase and leasing with a view to consolidating its control over its competitors' carriage of coal to the river. In 1739 the viewer, Thomas Slaker, estimated that most of the fifty to sixty Tyne collieries not being worked at that time were prevented from operating because of denial of wayleaves, and it was believed in London that agreements to deny wayleaves were responsible for pushing up the price of coal at Newcastle.[58] W. Loraine admitted in a letter to John Lambton of 1822 that he had bought an estate in County Durham at a price that 'is about £3,000 more than its intrinsic value as an estate, but its situation, as a stop to Lord Stewart [later the Marquis of Londonderry], should he buy Nesham's colliery, make it in my opinion, an object well worth the sacrifice.'[59] It is doubtful whether Lambton would have applauded Loraine's acumen at this moment since John Buddle was just then negotiating a rather complex agreement between him and Lord Stewart about mutual wayleaves over each other's adjoining estates.[60] This agreement, between two major, neighbouring coalowners noted for their intense economic and political rivalry, was itself testimony to the immense importance of wayleaves. In the long history of north-east mining, too many landowners had found that the ownership of coal-bearing land was not in itself sufficient: access to river or sea was as essential.

[56] NEI Buddle 14/286.
[57] GPL Cotesworth CK/3/63.
[58] NEI Buddle 14/352 and 14/270; Cromar 1978, 196–207.
[59] W. Loraine to J. G. Lambton, 31 Jan. 1822, LEA MP11/5.
[60] Lord Stewart to J. G. Lambton, 5 Feb. 1822, enclosing draft of agreement dated 31 Jan. 1822, LEA MP11/1.

Lambton and Lord Londonderry were further involved in complex wayleave politics two years later. William Russell, another member of the small group of major Wearside coalowners, had applied to both landowners for wayleave for his Newton coal across their estates to the Penshaw staith on the Wear; in return he offered to withdraw his support from the Stockton to Darlington railway scheme and refuse that company permission to cross his land. The outcome of this proposal is not known, but both Lambton and Lord Londonderry were hostile to the idea of a rival outlet on the Tees for Durham coal.[61]

In spite of all these restrictive practices, a large number of waggon-ways, as we have seen, were nevertheless built on secured wayleaves. While it may have been in the interests of some coalowning land-lords to use the denial of wayleaves as a means of restricting competition, it was equally in the interests of others to extract as large a levy as the local competitive circumstances of the trade would stand from coal passing over their land. To maximize the wayleave rent it was obviously desirable to relate the rent to the quantity of coal carried, and though this was done, it was not, according to Buddle in 1821, the usual practice.[62] Fixed rents were more common. Whatever the method of calculation, wayleaves were often a quite substantial elements in costs. Wayleave rent from the Bucksnook colliery high up in the Pontop area of Durham amounted to £42 15s. for the year 1718, a figure which should be related to the rent for the colliery itself of £37.[63] Burdon Moor colliery in 1723 paid William Cotesworth a wayleave rent of £208 12s. 6d. for the passage of 834 tens at 5d. per ten, and Lumley colliery in the 1770s paid £300 per annum to carry an annual output of 20,000 chaldrons across Tempest land.[64] The waggonway on which Blenkinsop's locomotive ran from Middleton colliery near Leeds paid around £400 per year for wayleaves rent out of total annual running costs of about £20–£25,000 between 1816 and 1821.[65] Estimates of two possible routes for waggonways to the coast from Hetton colliery in 1811 involved wayleave rents of £1,855 for one and £2,352 for the other.[66] A typical wayleave agreement was one granted for Fawdon colliery by 1799:

conditions on which Mrs and Mr Montague are willing to grant libery of way-leaves, etc. from Fawdon colliery.

[61] J. Buddle to W. Russell, 1 Sept. 1824, NEI Buddle Atkinson 47/37/42.
[62] J. Buddle to G. Ainsley, 20 Feb. 1821, DuRO NCB First Deposit NCB/I/JB/1990.
[63] GPL Cotesworth CK/5/25.
[64] SCL Wharncliffe Wh.M.115/7.
[65] LCA Middleton Colliery MC34.
[66] DuRO Londonderry D/Lo/E601 (1).

For Liberty of Wayleave and Staith Room £500 per Annum for 800 Tens of Coals; and 10s. 6d. per Ten for all Coals led above that Quantity.
For Interest of Money laid out in the original Erection for the Staith £50 per Annum.
For each Pitman's house 25s. 0d. per Annum.
All damage to Ground to be paid for agreeable to the Custom of the Country.
The Staith and Pitmen's houses to be given up on having Six Months Notice: Mrs and Mr Montague giving Assurance of Staith Room on some other Part of the River Tyne on the Denton Estate.[67]

The technical and legal problems once solved, then, ways were found in the eighteenth and early nineteenth centuries to carry coal in great and growing quantities to the nearest water navigation whence it could be more cheaply transported onwards on the longer section of its journey to the consumer. Without the waggonways the coal industry could not have expanded to meet the growing demand of the period since even the improved roads of the eighteenth and early nineteenth centuries could not easily have withstood the constant battering of the incessant traffic of heavy coal wains. The waggonways of the North-east permitted the lateral movement away from the rivers in search of mines from which coal could still be got at depths manageable by the drainage and ventilation technologies of the time. The exhaustion or drowning of the pits nearer the rivers in the early eighteenth century must, in the absence of waggonways, have led to remorselessly rising marginal costs. It is perhaps worth remembering, however, that though steam locomotives were clearly bringing the coal industry into a new age during the last fifteen years before 1830, they did little to relax the grip of water transport on the distribution of coal: before 1830 steam-railways, like their horse-drawn predecessors, restricted themselves to carrying coal to the nearest water navigation. They did not supersede water for some years after 1830.[68]

ii. River transport

Once 'doon the waggonway', the coal had to be transferred to river-going vessels. River banks were necessarily above water level, and in the tidal reaches of rivers, as on the stretches of the rivers Tyne and Wear where coal was brought by waggonway, the banks might be substantially above the level at low tide. There was a problem,

[67] Agreement dated 17 Apr. 1799, NEI Buddle 14/242.
[68] This account of wooden waggonways is based, apart from the sources cited, on Tomlinson 1914, 4–19; Lee 1948–9 and 1951; Jackman 1962, 461–74; Mott 1964–5 and 1969–70, Lewis 1970.

therefore, of negotiating differences in height, while, in order to give the waggons, their horses and waggoners a quick turn-round, some facilities for stocking coal at the riverside, were necessary. On the Tyne stocks of coal had to be kept at the riverside as well as at the pithead during the period in winter when coastal shipping was laid up.[69] It was not desirable to keep large stocks at the riverside: they were, as Buddle senior wrote in 1793, 'often flooded . . . and become very little better than rubbish'.[70] To meet these various needs the 'staith' was evolved. A staith was a riverside quay which served as a waggonway terminus with a chute to guide coal emptied from a waggon either from its side-door or floor hopper into the hold of the keel moored below. It was a heavy wooden construction and generally roofed over, large enough to allow storage space to cope with the irregular movements of both waggons and river craft. Tyne staithes were built to accommodate up to six keels at a time.[71] The staithes at Whitehaven in 1815, which, of course, were harbour, not riverside, staithes, could stock up to 3,000 waggon loads (6,750 tons) of coal.[72] Those at Newport (Monmouthshire) were holding 17,000 tons at the time of a report of the late 1820s, but this was said to be an unusually large stock.[73] A staithman or 'offputter' looked after each staith: on the Earl of Scarbrough's staith at the Wearside terminus of his Lumley waggonway the responsibilities of the staith-man for checking and recording quantities unloaded and shipped were recognized in the early 1780s by a relatively high yearly wage of £40 with a free house.[74]

Though most familiar on the rivers of the North-east, staithes were a nation-wide feature since rivers and harbours in many parts of the country were used for coal shipment. Some rivers, above all the relatively short lower reaches of the Tyne and Wear, could be used in their natural state by small or medium-sized river vessels, but others called for extensive improvement before they could be used for this purpose. Virtually all rivers, large or small, that reached to within ten miles of a coalfield were pressed into service to get coal away to the coast for onward shipment by coastal navigation, or to consumers nearer to hand either up- or down-river. The larger rivers like the Severn, the Thames, the Trent, and the Ouse were already accessible for coal traffic by the beginning of the eighteenth century,

[69] Matthias Dunn, 'History of the Viewers', 17, MS in NEI Bell 13/1.

[70] J. Buddle to W. Emm, 1 Mar. 1793, NEI Buddle 20/6.

[71] NEI Buddle 14/312.

[72] 'Notebook containing replies to Mr. Lyson's queries on the Whitehaven collieries, 1815', CuRO Lonsdale/Colliery Reports not yet listed.

[73] CuRO Lonsdale D/Lons/W/38/22.

[74] Beastall 1975, 36.

though civil engineering during the eighteenth century substantially extended the navigable limits of these rivers and also made some of their tributaries available for coal traffic. Other lesser rivers were opened to coal transportation only as a result of extensive improvement brought about by local promoters acting under the authority of private acts of Parliament.

The principal method of improving the navigation of a river— making the waterway open to freight vessels at all times of the year —was to create a greater depth of water by means of a weir. In a lowland river a weir could add a few feet of depth for several miles up-river, but it involved the construction of a lock to enable vessels to bypass it. Otherwise dredging was employed, though sometimes new cuts were made across meanders to achieve improved natural dredging by speeding the flow. Finally, since sails were an unreliable and uncertain method of propulsion on the winding British rivers, the construction of a tow-path for horse or man hauling, or 'haling', of boats, was often essential. Smaller rivers that were 'improved' in these ways during the eighteenth century to make them available for coal transportation included the Douglas (Lancashire), the Weaver (Cheshire), the Soar (Leicestershire), and the Don (Yorkshire). Many other smaller rivers carried coal during the eighteenth century, but their improvement was initiated as much for the benefit of other trades as for the coal trade. The improvement of the river Don, for example, running through south Yorkshire to join the Ouse just below its junction with the Aire, was initiated by a private Act of 1726. By 1733 the river had been made navigable as far upstream as Aldwark, and to Tinsley, a mere three miles from the centre of Sheffield, by 1751. By 1732, a local historian of the industry has claimed, south Yorkshire coal was competing effectively with Durham coal in the Humber estuary and its several tributary valleys. The navigation proved to be an important stimulus to the development of the industry in the Don valley from the middle of the century, above all in the area immediately around the terminus at Tinsley. By 1722 an estimated 80–90,000 tons of coal a year were passing down the river.[75]

The Don, of course, served the iron, steel, and cutlery industries of south Yorkshire as much as it aided the mining industry. The Douglas navigation of Lancashire, on the other hand, was almost exclusively a coal navigation. At the opening of the eighteenth century the south-west Lancashire coalfield was not approachable by any water navigation, and, since waggonways developed here only slowly, was at first entirely dependent upon road transport to

[75] Hopkinson 1976, 10–13; Willan 1936, 33–4, 75–7.

get its coal to Wigan, Liverpool, and the Mersey estuary. The river Douglas flows north-westwards from Wigan to enter the sea in the Ribble estuary, and apart from the Sankey Brook which connected the southern part of the coalfield with the Mersey estuary, but which proved initially too small for practical 'improvement', the Douglas was the only water penetrating the coalfield capable of improvement to the point of navigability. An act for its improvement was secured in 1720, but it was not until 1733 that a start was made on the necessary engineering works, and 1742 before the full length of sixteen miles to Wigan was completed with eight locks and a fall of seventy-two feet. In spite of the limited availability of markets once the coal entered the sea at the Ribble estuary, and the handicap of the additional surcharge of the duty on coastwise shipments, a steady and useful down-river trade developed.[76]

Compared with the trade on the rivers Tyne and Wear, however, the quantities of coal carried on these smaller rivers serving the inland coalfields were of minor significance. For most of the eighteenth century every ton of coal shipped down the east coast to London and other destinations had first to be carried down these north-eastern rivers before being transshipped on to the larger vessels capable of making what could be the rough voyage southwards. These coastal vessels were incapable of sailing more than a very short distance up-river and were obliged to load at Shields and Sunderland at the mouths of the rivers. On the Tyne, however, the highest staithes were fourteen miles up-river from Shields, and on the Wear nine miles from Sunderland. The lighters that carried coal on these two rivers from the staithes to Shields and Sunderland were the keels. Keels were also used at Hartley on the Northumberland coast before Sir John Hussey Delaval built the new harbour there in 1764, and at Inverkeithing on the Firth of Forth, where the harbour was too small to accommodate the number of vessels that came to load the coal from Halbeath colliery so that keels had to be used as lighters to take it to vessels anchored further out in the Firth.[77]

On the Tyne a keel was a fairly standardized vessel: it was forty to forty-two feet long, with a beam of nineteen feet. Wear keels were marginally longer, squarer, and of lesser draught than Tyne keels. Tyne keels were worked by three men and a boy; Wear keels by one man and a boy. In the Tyne keels both bow and stern were decked with a forecastle at the bow and a small cabin or 'huddock' at the stern. The hold amidships was flanked by narrow platforms used for working the boat. A single mast carried a square sail to allow

[76] Langton 1979, 161–5; Anderson 1975, 27–39; Willan 1936, 70–1, 128.
[77] Payne forthcoming.

advantage to be taken of a following wind, but provision had to be made for unshipping the mast when passing under the Tyne bridge in Newcastle. Normally the keels were propelled by oars, taking advantage of tides in both directions. The large main oar over the port side was worked by two men (the 'bullies') and a boy (the 'pee-dee'), and the keel was kept on course by the skipper, working the 'swape' or shorter stern oar in rhythm with the main oar. In shallow waters 'puoys'—eighteen-feet-long punt-poles—were used, the keelman walking the length of the side-platforms pushing with bare feet. This process of 'settin' was done, according to Heslop, 'with the smartness of a drill exercise, the movements timed and in unison.' Some time in the early nineteenth century, but probably nearer to 1830 than 1800, keels began to adopt an improved sailing rig with a fore-and-aft rig instead of a square rig, and a rudder. Though this still had to allow for lowering the mast to pass under the Tyne bridge, it reduced the labour of sculling by allowing the keel to sail closer to the wind and to tack.[78] A round voyage of a keel from one of the uppermost Tyne staithes took fourteen hours, since the keel's crew also shovelled its cargo into the collier and then waited for the return tide to assist them back up-river again.

Both Tyne and Wear keels loaded eight Newcastle chaldrons or just over twenty-one tons. Since, however, the colliers bought the coal by the keel, there was a constant tendency, under the pressure of persuading the collier's master to buy, to give overweight, so that keels commonly carried more than eight chaldrons. It was said that keels were, in fact, capable of carrying up to fourteen chaldrons but that they were dangerously unseaworthy with such a load. The overloading of keels, however, was a major issue on the rivers throughout the eighteenth century. To counter this practice various legislative attempts were made to measure and enforce maximum keel cargoes. Acts of 1677 and 1694 had required the marking of keels and had appointed commissioners to enforce it,[79] but the abuse continued throughout the eighteenth century. In 1769, in evidence to a parliamentary committee, Thomas Port asserted that over-measure was general and usually amounted to an extra two chaldrons over the statutory eight.[80] An elaborate system of marking both stern and bow with nails to produce a 'Plimsoll-line' type of marking by

[78] This account of the Tyne keel is based largely on a very scholarly account in a manuscript article 'Keels and keelmen' by R. Oliver Heslop (n.d. but probably c.1900) in NEI Miscellaneous 60/ZA/3a. Metcalf 1937, 4, however, suggests that the fore-and-aft rig began to appear as early as the late eighteenth century. Wear keels are described in Miller thesis 1978, Appendix A, and their detailed dimensions set out in NEI Buddle 30/75.

[79] 29 Car. II, c.8; 6 and 7 Wm. III, c.10; Nef 1932, II, 252.

[80] TWRO Tyne Keelmen 394/29/25.

chaldrons up to nine chaldrons and allowing for both salt and fresh water was proposed in 1771,[81] but there was no further legislation until 1815 when an act reordered the marking of boats and gave the commissioners power to confiscate overloaded keels. But a broadsheet of 1819 issued by the keelmen spoke of 'the overmeasure which has been carried in Keels beyond the Eight chaldrons in each Keel', as though this were still normal practice.[82]

In spite of the increase in the coastwise coal trade from the North-east during the eighteenth and early nineteenth centuries there does not appear to have been a very great increase in the number of keels on the Tyne. Though their numbers were estimated at 400 at the beginning of the eighteenth century, an account of the period 1709–19, more convincing on account of its origin and precision, counted 338.[83] The committee operating an early eighteenth-century 'regulation' agreed in 1710 to employ only 260 keels on the river in the following year, but it is doubtful whether this committee controlled more than a proportion of the whole trade.[84] Although Gabriel Jars repeated the common estimate of 400 Tyne keels again in 1765, another estimate of 1772 allowed only 450 keels for both rivers.[85] During the 1790s an annual average of 338 keels worked on the Tyne, and 452 on the Wear, and a general statistical account of the north-east coal trade of 1828 estimated 300 Tyne keels and 200 Wear keels.[86]

Though these estimates mostly lack precision, it is likely that the number of keels on the Tyne reached a peak of nearly 400 in the late eighteenth century. Their number probably declined thereafter as colliers began to load directly from staithes below the Tyne bridge at Newcastle, and, from 1812, on the lower Wear. At these staithes coal was discharged from waggonway waggons down 'spouts' directly into the holds of the waiting colliers. There were no fundamental differences between the spouts and the common method of loading keels, but the saving gained by eliminating the keels was obvious. Why had the Tyne and Wear colliers not loaded directly earlier? Spouts had been used at Hartley from the opening of the new deep-water harbour there in 1764. There do not appear to have been any

[81] NEI Watson 8/10/122–3.
[82] 55 Geo.III, c.118; NuRO Joint Coal Owners' Association 263, Minute Book 1820, 24; TWRO Tyne Keelmen 394/42, dated 20 Oct. 1819.
[83] Heslop MS article, NEI Miscellaneous 60/ZA/3a; NEI Bell 15/1/7; GPL Cotesworth CK/3/15.
[84] GPL Cotesworth CK/3/11.
[85] Jars 1774–81, I, 207; NEI Watson 5/26/40.
[86] First SC Coal Trade 1800, 631; NuRO Wilson (Forest Hall) ZWI/5/177. There is also an estimate of 570 coal keels on the Wear for 1809 by Robert Surtees, quoted in Miller thesis 1978, 348.

improvements to the navigation of the river Tyne so long as it remained the responsibility of the Corporation of Newcastle until the 1850s. For a brief period at each high tide it was always possible for colliers to make their way some distance up-river, though it would clearly not be worth their while to do so if indirect loading via keels was still necessary. The upper limit of navigation on the Tyne for sea-going colliers was the winding course and hazardous navigation of the river as it approached Newcastle rather than the Tyne bridge itself, though the adoption of steam tugs on the Tyne from 1818 enabled the colliers to reach higher staithes more easily at all states of the tide.[87] Nor is there any reason to suppose that the opposition to such a change by the keelmen would have been any more effective at some earlier period than it was when they struck against it during the first quarter of the nineteenth century.

The explanation of the timing of this development almost certainly lies in the chronology of mining development on Tyneside. Until towards the end of the eighteenth century a high proportion of the coastwise coal exports from the Tyne originated in collieries served by staithes above the bridge or not far below it. As these collieries gradually became exhausted after 1775 there was a pronounced shift down-river. The big, new collieries of the years 1775–1810 sent their coal to staithes on the lower reaches of the river more easily accessible to colliers. As the advantages of direct loading became apparent, waggonways were constructed in north-easterly and south-easterly directions instead of due north and south by the shortest route to the river. In 1822, for example, a line of eleven and a half miles was planned from Stanley, south-west of Gateshead, to the lower Tyne at Jarrow, to be operated by stationary engines and locomotives.[88] More importantly, the eastwards, down-river drift shifted the centre of gravity of Tyneside mining away from the hilly area of steep-sided valleys south-west of Newcastle and Gateshead where the lie of the land sharply restricted the possible routes of waggonways and so threw them into the grip of the controllers of wayleaves, to the flatter land nearer the coast, where the nature of the territory, by allowing a freer choice of waggonway routes, prevented the monopolistic control of wayleaves by any one small group.[89]

It goes without saying that the keelmen resisted this move to take away their livelihoods, and they organized strikes against them from as early as 1770. In 1815 the Wear keelmen attacked the recently

[87] Dunn 1844, 51.
[88] C. E. Mountford, *The Bowes Railway formerly the Pontop and Jarrow Railway* (Industrial Railway Society and Tyne and Wear Industrial Monuments Trust, 1976).
[89] Cromar 1979, 54.

constructed 'spout' staith at Sunderland, setting fire to the wood-work and causing damage to the tune of £6,000.[90] There were particularly bitter strikes on Tyneside in 1809, 1819, and 1822, the last persisting for ten weeks—the 'long stop'—and although the keelmen offered a compromise of allowing the colliers to load up to the equivalent of six keels by spout, the rest to come from keels, they won no concessions.[91] 'It is obvious', commented the *Newcastle Courant* in 1819, 'that this is to ask the coalowner or shipowner to substitute an expensive manual labour for a cheap machinery which is already erected and in operation: a demand wholly incompatible with all the acknowledged principles of freedom in trade.'[92] The position of the keelmen was exacerbated by the development during the second decade of the nineteenth century of 'drops', a mechanism for lowering whole waggonway waggons directly into the holds of colliers and unloading them by dropping a hinged flap. By reducing the height of the fall of the coal this minimized breakage which tended to lower its selling price. Drops were invented in 1800 by William Chapman of Newcastle, but it was ten years before the first was erected at Wallsend. By 1828, of forty-one seasale collieries on the Tyne only ten delivered to keels: all the remainder loaded directly to the colliers. Nine out of seventeen Wear seasale collieries, on the other hand, still did so, and a further five used both keels and spouts.[93] In the 1820s Buddle made use of drops on the Wear to effect a further improvement in the handling of Lord Londonderry's coal. He fitted keels with 'tubs' which were loaded directly from the waggons at the drops, and could then be transferred by crane directly into the colliers at Sunderland. This eliminated the 'casting' of coal from keel to collier, lowered costs by as much as 2s. per chaldron, but further reduced the work for keel-men.[94]

The keelmen began seriously to experience a fate similar to that of the handloom weavers. Under the remorseless pressure of advancing technology their numbers dwindled. At their peak in the late eighteenth century those on the Tyne probably numbered about 1,600. After the failure of the 1822 strike keels no longer carried the boy as part of the crew. In 1822 it was estimated that there were 900 keelmen representing probably 300 keels, of which two-thirds were now above the bridge. By 1827 these numbers were

[90] T. H. Hair 1844, 41.
[91] Rowe 1969, 112–25.
[92] 2 Oct. 1819, quoted in McCord 1967, 95.
[93] NuRO Wilson (Forest Hall) ZWI/4/381–2; Rowe 1969, 112; NEI Buddle 25/4–15; Skempton 1973–4.
[94] Hiskey thesis 1978, 124–6.

said to be reduced to 850, of whom all but 150 were above the bridge.[95]

Until the end of the eighteenth century, however, virtually all north-east coal for the coastal and export trades was carried between staith and collier by keel, and in 1830, in spite of the changes brought by spouts and drops, most staithes on the Wear and all those on the Tyne above the bridge continued to use the keels. No coal at all was carried out of the region by road or railway. Coastal navigation therefore played an indispensable role in linking the coal-field to its principal markets. In 1830 John Buddle estimated that one-quarter of the country's consumption of coal was carried to the consumers by coastal navigation.[96] One hundred and thirty years earlier the proportion was probably higher.

iii. Coastal transport

A traffic amounting, as Table 7.3 below shows, to around three and a half million tons in 1830 and possibly rather less than one million tons at the beginning of the eighteenth century called for the employment of a considerable shipping fleet. The vessels that carried the coal were not, however, specialized. Many looked for general cargoes when the coal trade was slack, and so were of all the types found in commercial shipping at the time—brigs, barques, schooners, or sloops; but when engaged in the coal trade they were generally referred to as 'colliers'. The colliers of the eighteenth and early nineteenth centuries were large by the standards of coastal, and even ocean-going, vessels of the day. It is by no means easy to assess the average size of vessels employed in the coastal trade. Hausman believes that it was unusual for a collier to leave New-castle without a full cargo,[97] a claim that is generally supported by a collier master's statement of 1739 that was modified only by the proviso that less than full ladings were taken on the first and last voyages of each year, probably because at the extremes of the season weather would be at its worst.[98] The average cargoes of colliers leaving Newcastle in years for which there are statements were as follows:[99]

[95] Rowe 1969, 123–5.
[96] NEI Buddle Atkinson 45/5/16.
[97] Hausman 1977a, 464.
[98] NEI Buddle 14/367.
[99] GPL Cotesworth CK/3/71; TWRO Tyne Keelmen 394/28; NEI Bell 14/8/41–3. These figures relate to the weight of cargoes carried. The registered tonnage of vessels was calcu-lated in quite a different way (see Davis 1962, 7). In 1828, for example, 862 ships registered at Newcastle averaged 216 registered tons, and 588 at Sunderland 161 registered tons.

1712	(10 ships)	336 tons
1765	(26 ships)	320 tons
1828	(109 ships)	316 tons

On the other hand, a return of collier arrivals at London for the years 1811–19 showed an average cargo of only 211 tons, and for 1826–30 one of 291 tons per ship.[1] The disparity between the sizes of cargoes leaving Newcastle and those arriving in London may, of course, be explained by part-unloading at intermediate harbours, by corrupt practices in the Port of London, or by the arrival of smaller ships from ports other than Newcastle. Since there were few changes in shipbuilding technology between 1700 and 1830 that were likely to affect the size of ships, an average capacity of 300–30 tons for a collier throughout the period may reasonably be assumed. This implies over 10,000 voyages a year to carry the east coast traffic in 1830, and around 3,000 in the early eighteenth century. This rough estimate is broadly borne out by such quantitative evidence as is available. In 1775, 4,343 coal shipments cleared from Newcastle, and between 1815 and 1819 an annual average of 5,506. The entire coal import of London required an annual average of 6,407 shipments between 1820 and 1827.[2] Since in the 1820s London imports accounted for rather more than half of the whole east-coast traffic, an estimate of rather more than 10,000 voyages per year may not be far off the mark for this period.

It is difficult to estimate how many vessels were needed to make this number of voyages. Not all that participated in the trade did so exclusively, of course. Some took part in the overseas trade in coal, while others found occasional general cargoes. The *Molly and Jenny*, for example, built in 1752, made thirteen voyages from Newcastle during 1752 and 1753, six to London and the remainder to Hamburg, Amsterdam, Norway, and the Baltic.[3] Although the coal trade of the east coast was on the whole fairly steady, even quite minor annual fluctuations of so large an employer of shipping must leave vessels unemployed from time to time and so provide them with an opportunity or even a need to find alternative cargoes. The fall in London imports, for example, from 651,000 tons in 1737 to 585,000 in the following year would have called for about 200 fewer sailings, while the more substantial fall from 1826 to 1827 would similarly have reduced the demand for sailings by nearly 500.

[1] 'A brief compendium of the natural, political and commercial history of coal', n.d. but probably 1840s, DuRO NCB First Deposit NCB/I/X/154; newspaper-cutting in LEA MP12/4; pamphlet n.d. but probably 1819, in NEI Watson 5/26.

[2] NEI Watson 8/11/108; pamphlet n.d. but probably 1819, in NEI Watson 5/26; PP 1828 (469) XIX.462.

[3] NuRO Carr-Ellison ZCE 10/14/315–23.

But trade fluctuations were not the only disruptions to the trade. In wartime—and in the seventy-six years between 1739 and 1815 there were forty-five years of war—there were the twin hazards of enemy privateers and the press-gang.[4] It is hard to know which was the more to be feared. In May 1779, for example, French privateers got among the collier fleet soon after it had left the Tyne and several of the ships were attacked, captured, and immediately ransomed, and in September the American privateer, *Paul Jones*, interfered with the trade.[5] Convoying was the only defence, but it was delaying and expensive. 'Privateers so much invest the coast', wrote Delaval's agent from Hartley in 1779, 'that the collier vessels do all incline to go in fleets and not otherwise, which practices greatly hurts the trade of this port.'[6] In the same year Sir John Hussey Delaval's agent reported to him that the press had been so active at Hartley and Blyth that 'there are none left to sale the ships', and eleven years later, though there was no war, he announced that as a result of the press shipping was again stopped and coal prices were accordingly rising in London.[7] When the French war was resumed in 1803 after the short-lived Peace of Amiens the whole coal trade of the North-east was brought almost to a stop by the press-gang, which took some keelmen and prevented others from working for fear of being taken.[8] Between the outbreak of war in 1793 and November 1800 no less than 2,781 seamen were impressed for the navy at the ports of Newcastle and Sunderland alone, and a further 1,597 'volunteered' for service. Such levies must have raised real problems for manning the keels and colliers, and it is not surprising to find the shipmasters of Workington in Cumberland agreeing in 1770:

that if any seamen shall be imprest into His Majesties service from on board any ship having a legal protection whilst they are employed in the duty of the said ship, at our joint expence, in proportion to the burthen of our respective ships, to use all lawful means for the recovery of the said seamen by bringing actions or otherwise as may be best advised.[9]

But the most constant hazard in the trade was the weather. The North Sea was notorious for high and unpredictable winds. In May 1782 miners at the Delaval pits were put on short time because no

---

[4] N. McCord, 'The impress service in N.E.England during the Napoleonic War', *Mariner's Mirror*, 54 (1968).
[5] NuRO Delaval ZDE 4/4/13; Beastall 1975, 32.
[6] NuRO Delaval ZDE 4/4/13.
[7] NuRO Delaval ZDE 3/7/24, and 4/4/16.
[8] J. Buddle to M. Russell, 11 May 1803, NEI Buddle 15/12.
[9] *Second SC Coal Trade* 1800, 41; CuRO Curwen D/Cu/6/120.

ship had been able to sail for six weeks owing to adverse winds.[10] Colliers were wise not to attempt to sail in bad weather since, heavily laden as they were, a sudden storm catching them before they could retreat to the shelter of one of the east-coast harbours or the lee of a headland could be disastrous. In 1800 it was reported that sixty-nine out of seventy-one vessels taking coal from the North-east to London were wrecked, while twenty-four years later Buddle commented on a report that one hundred colliers had been sunk or wrecked in an October gale.[11] Moller has traced through the Port Books the number of colliers lost at sea between the North-east and the Thames in six random years in the first half of the eighteenth century. No less than seventy-one colliers were lost in the two years 1703 and 1710, though these represented slightly less than one per cent of sailings in those years: forty-six of these were lost in 1703, no doubt most of them in the terrible North Sea storm of November 1703. After the first decade of the century, the route seems to have become noticeably safer and losses averaged only four a year, or 0.1 per cent of sailings.[12]

With these risks, shipping naturally tended to try to avoid the worst of the weather in mid-winter. Attempts were made from time to time to impose a close season for shipping during the winter. Whitby shipowners approached the Newcastle shipowners in 1717 proposing that 'no ships begin to Load Coales before ye 10th day of March', while in 1784 it emerged that it was not possible for colliers to obtain marine insurance 'for the three winter months and need more money to get them to sea'.[13] There is no evidence to indicate that these efforts were wholly successful, and plenty to show that sailings continued through the calendar, though winter sailings were always fewer than those in summer. Though the evidence is sparse, it is possible that, in response to market conditions in London— demand for coal for domestic heating was, after all, at its peak in mid winter—the sailing season was progressively stretched during the eighteenth century.[14] In 1813 London's imports during January and December amounted to eighty-nine per cent of the two-monthly average for the whole year.[15] Sailings in 1776 from Seaton Sluice in Northumberland showed the following monthly pattern:

[10] NuRO Delaval ZDE 4/4/65.

[11] NEI Miscellaneous 63/ZC/53/4; G. B. Hodgson, *Wreck Register for the North-east Coast* (*Sheilds Gazette*, 1904); NEI Buddle 22/187.

[12] Moller thesis 1933, 708.

[13] GPL Cotesworth CP/1/6; J. Crooks to Sir John Hussey Delaval, 21 May 1784, NuRO Delaval ZDE 4/5/45.

[14] Hausman 1977a, 464 n. 13.

[15] NuRO Joint Coal Owners' Association 263, Minute Book 1805–15, 243.

January	7
February	8
March	3
April	9
May	8
June	10
July	15
August	14
September	9
October	9
November	6
December	10

In 1807, however, a similar schedule showed no sailings in the four weeks ending 21 January, and only three in the preceding four weeks.[16] Even in 1826 Lambton's fitter was reporting to him on 26 February that the ships that had been laid up (presumably in Sunderland) were only then fitting out for the recommencement of the coastal trade.[17] Mid-winter sailing, always risky, was encouraged by the high prices obtainable for household coal in London, and some skippers could apparently always be found who were willing to accept the risks for the sake of the higher profit. In 1817 a monthly division of the annual vend was formally agreed by a committee of principal coalowners, as follows:[18]

	percentage of annual vend
January	5.0
February	5.0
March	6.0
April	7.5
May	8.5
June	9.0
July	9.5
August	10.5
September	10.5
October	10.0
November	9.5
December	9.0

An important determinant of the number of possible voyages in a year was, of course, the turn-round time at each port. Here it was not so much the loading or unloading time that was the principal

[16] NuRO Delaval ZDE 18/3/1, 7.
[17] W. Loraine to J. G. Lambton, 26 Feb. 1826, LEA MP11/1.
[18] NuRO Joint Coal Owners' Association 263, Minute Book 1817, 14.

factor (though from time to time the interplay of the various groups in the pool of London contending for the monopolistic domination of the trade introduced delays into the turn-round in London), as the need to wait for a favourable wind to permit the safe crossing of the awkward bar at the mouth of the Tyne and to proceed southwards, or to negotiate the long narrow channel of the Thames out of London. The introduction of steam-vessels at the very end of the period covered by this book contributed to cutting down these wasteful delays and to the more efficient use of capital and labour on the coastal routes. A Sunderland fitter who had been in the trade for fifty years knew of many occasions when contrary winds and high seas had trapped colliers in port for four to six weeks, but his partner was able to report in 1827 that during the three years during which steam boats had been employed in the Wear trade the longest he had known them to be held in the harbour was five days.[19] Harbour improvement could assist turn-round by making a harbour safer and easier to approach and leave in less than perfect weather conditions. The construction of the new harbour at Seaton Sluice in 1764 made it possible for colliers to make ten voyages each year compared with only seven before.[20] Sunderland harbour, initially so difficult of access that fitters found shipmasters reluctant to take on coal there, was successively improved during the eighteenth century so that by 1817 it was said to be preferred to the Tyne ports.[21]

Referring to the days of sailing vessels in the eighteenth century, Hausman reckoned that the speediest round-trip from Newcastle to London and back again occupied one month, so that, allowing for the close season for sailings during the worst months of the winter, the maximum possible number of voyages of any one collier could make would be eight or nine. The average, however, he estimated was just over four.[22] His conclusions are generally supported by evidence from the Delaval trade at Seaton Sluice. Here, in 1776, twenty-one colliers took part in the trade. Their sailings during that year ranged from one to nine, with a mean of 5.1. They do, however, seem to fall into two groups—those that participated regularly, and probably exclusively, in the trade (nine ships made six or more voyages, seven making eight or nine), and those that traded casually (eight made three or fewer voyages), though many of the latter may well have loaded at Newcastle or Sunderland as well. In the

[19] W. Spence to J. Buddle, 13 Sept. 1827, DuRO NCB First Deposit NCB/I/JB/1350.
[20] J. Crooks to Sir John Hussey Delaval, 21 Nov. 1781, NuRO Delaval ZDE 4/4/53; Foster thesis 1948, 10–11.
[21] A. W. Skempton, 'The engineers of Sunderland harbour, 1718–1817', Industrial Archaeological Review, 1975.
[22] Hausman 1977a, 464.

latter event the average number of voyages made by each collier would rise above 5.1.[23] In 1800, however, Thomas Richmond, master of a collier with twenty-eight years' experience in the trade, asserted that smaller vessels usually made between eight and eleven voyages a year though larger ones rarely achieved more than seven.[24]

When all these contingencies are taken into account, the problem of assessing the number of vessels in the coastal trade are apparent. Colliers were registered in many ports—Stockton, Whitby, Scarborough, King's Lynn, and Ipswich, as well as in Newcastle, Sunderland, and London—and not all, as we have seen, confined themselves exclusively to the coal trade. The best contemporary estimates all relate to the 1820s, though since ships' sizes are unlikely to have changed greatly over the preceding century and a quarter it is easy to make proportionate estimates for earlier periods. An estimate of 1824 by Buddle showed 1,400 ships employed in the east-coast trade, 800 of them trading from the Tyne, 538 from the Wear, and 62 from the Blyth area, while another of 1828 by R. W. Brandling suggested that the whole coastal coal trade round Britain employed a total of 1,360 ships.[25] There was, however, a categorical statement, also of 1828, that there were registered at the Custom House of Newcastle 862 ships, and at Sunderland 588, making a total for these two ports alone of 1,450, though this total could have included vessels other than colliers.[26] We should clearly not be far wrong if we assume that by the 1820s the coal trade round all British coasts employed in the region of 1,750 vessels fully and permanently: this would imply an employment of perhaps 500 in the early eighteenth century. In fact, a statement of 1703 estimated 600 ships working from Newcastle alone, though the tendency for such 'round-figure' estimates supplied by the trade at this period would be towards exaggeration.[27]

Like most other ships in the eighteenth and early nineteenth centuries, colliers were mostly owned in shares, primarily to divide the risks. Evidence concerning the capital cost is sparse, though a list of 109 ships insured in the Coal Trade Association in South Shields for 1828 shows a range of values from £600 to £4,500 with an average of £1,714.[28] Although many of the ships were registered at north-east ports, and a few in London, their origin and ownership

[23] NuRO Delaval ZDE 18/3/1.
[24] *First SC Coal Trade* 1800, 562.
[25] NEI Buddle Atkinson 45/5/no pagination; Memorandum by R. W. Brandling, 16, NEI Buddle Atkinson 45/5.
[26] NuRO Wilson (Forest Hall) ZWI 5/177.
[27] NEI Watson 5/26/40.
[28] NEI Bell 14/8/41-3.

was much more scattered, and most east coast ports of any size participated in the trade in this way. The same scattering also prevailed in the Bristol Channel and Firth of Forth ports. This dispersion of registration allowed some geographical spread of ownership, widening the base for the supply of capital. The number and value of colliers in the 1820s implies a total investment in the region of £3 million. The ship's master normally had a stake in the ownership, and many owners of part-shares, some of whom had shares in several colliers, turned out to be coalowners, fitters, or merchants in the London coal trade. Lord Scarbrough, for example, owner of the Lumley pits in the early eighteenth century, possessed part-shares in five colliers in 1727. The fitters he employed also had shares in the same vessels.[29]

However many shared in the ownership of a collier, the master always retained the Grand Bill of Sale which effectively conferred on him the management of the ship. A surprising but important feature of the east-coast coal trade was that the masters, on behalf of their fellow-owners, normally acquired ownership of the coal they carried: they were middle-men and not mere freighters. Masters negotiated with fitters in Newcastle or Sunderland for the purchase of a cargo, the loading of which was then arranged by the fitters; they were responsible for all payments incidental to the voyage— port dues at the port of departure, seamen's wages, victualling, and taxes and dues in London or at any other port visited en route— and ultimately for the sale of the coal in London; and were under obligation to render written accounts of all transactions once a year to their co-owners. Similar functions were also performed by masters in the Firth of Forth coastal trade.[30]

In making all these arrangements the master had to have the profit of the voyage—and hence the ultimate return on the capital invested—very much in mind. Providing the ship successfully completed the voyage, profit seems to have been fairly regular. A statement of 1821 shows that shipowners normally assumed a 'rate of freight' (gross profit?) ranging from 9s. 6d. to 11s. 8d. per Newcastle chaldron for standard coals, but over 40s. for the highest grade coals in January and February sailings.[31] In the 1820s Buddle was prepared to estimate that on average shipowners could expect to receive a return on their capital of eight per cent annually,[32] and Hausman has cited careful calculations of profitability for the early

[29] Beastall 1975, 21.
[30] ScRO Mar and Kellie GD124/17/581–2.
[31] NuRO Joint Coal Owners' Association 263, Minute Book 1821–3, 89.
[32] NEI Watson 5/26/42.

eighteenth century showing that colliers costing £1,400 and making eight voyages each would show profits in 1729 ranging from one per cent to twenty-four per cent. Similar calculations for 1738 show returns ranging from four per cent to eighteen per cent. Hausman has reworked these eighteenth-century calculations and suggests that, after allowing for interest on capital, depreciation (at five per cent per annum) and insurance, a net profit of twelve per cent was obtainable.[33] These are hypothetical calculations based on data supplied by participants in a controversy about profitability, and would probably not cover the whole range of experience.

The only detailed east-coast colliers' accounts that have been traced suggest profits at the lower rather than the higher end of these ranges. The *Thomas and Francis* plied regularly in the 1730s between New-castle and London. With a capacity of 168 Newcastle chaldrons (445 tons) she was manned by a master, mate, carpenter, cook, eight sea-men, and three boys. In fifty-seven voyages between March 1734 and October 1740 her accounts show an average profit of 5.7 per cent over costs.[34] The *Molly and Jenny* which mixed voyages from New-castle to London with longer trips to the continent in 1752 and 1753 made a total of only £127 15s. net profit on six London voyages: even allowing for the fact that other trading voyages were also made in these years, and assuming that these profits are net of all expenses, they could hardly be regarded as attractive returns on a newly launched ship costing £1,637.[35] Sixty years later the *Eleanor*, sailing between Blyth and London, seemed to fare no better. Four voyages in 1812 produced a total loss of £44 7s. 4d., and four more in the following year one of £32 14s. 8d. Yet when this vessel varied the routine of east-coast voyages by going to St. Petersburg and Sweden to take on hemp and iron, it made a profit of £304 7s. 4d. on a single voyage.[36] On the west coast, however, the accounts of a collier trading regularly between Workington and Dublin have survived and show more profitable operation. These are for the *Unity*, bought in April 1760 for £510. Her normal cargo was about forty-five waggons, or just over 100 tons. She made six voyages between May and October 1760, ten voyages in 1761, seven in 1762, and one in 1763 for which there are accounts. In the full year 1761 (the accounts for two voyages in 1762 are missing) profits amounted to £202, which looks like a very satisfactory return for one year on an investment of only £510.[37]

[33] Hausman 1977a, 467–72.
[34] DuRO Strathmore D/St/v1475, v1482.
[35] NuRO Carr-Ellison ZCE 10/14/315–23.
[36] NuRO Ridley (Blagdon) ZRI 23/7; and see also Humble 1975.
[37] Broughton colliery account book, 1760–3, CuRO Senhouse D/Sen/Colliery/not numbered.

A principal element in the cost of shipping was, of course, the wages of seamen. Crews varied in proportion to the size of the ship. Six hundred colliers in 1703 were estimated to employ a total of 4,500 men and boys—an average of between seven and eight per ship.[38] By 1824 the estimated 1,400 vessels in the east-coast trade were said to have employed 14,000 men, though another estimate of the same decade assumed an average crew of eleven to each ship.[39] Official figures for colliers arriving in London in the years 1826 and 1827, however, which are precise if not accurate, show an average crew of only 8.7 for each of the 13,349 arrivals in the Port of London in those years.[40]

Important though the coastal trade was in the distribution of coal,[41] it was restricted by its very nature to serving the country's periphery. Markets in the interior of the country were still, up to the middle of the eighteenth century, dependent upon their proximity to the navigable portion of a river, a requirement which, in spite of the great advances in river navigation during the eighteenth century, still left large numbers of potential consumers virtually inaccessible to coal supplies. More seriously, the limitations of river and coastal navigation isolated a number of coalfields from potential consumers by a belt of territory devoid of water transport and too broad to be crossed economically by road transport. In the circumstances of the first half of the eighteenth century certain coalfields—notably those of Lancashire, Yorkshire, Somerset, the East and West Midlands, together with the more inland parts of the Scottish and South Wales coalfields—were confined to markets accessible by road transport only.

iv. Canal transport

The developments of river navigation of the first half of the eighteenth century, however, were suggestive. Most of the techniques of river engineering were transferable to 'deadwater' navigations, and when the possibilities of the extension of river navigation were very largely exhausted by the middle of the eighteenth century, the move to add more mileage to the water navigation network by adding canals to rivers was a natural and obvious development. It was initially, of course, a matter of economics. A canal involved creating a waterway where none had hitherto existed, a proceeding necessarily more

---

[38] NEI Watson 5/26/40.

[39] NEI Buddle Atkinson 45/5/no pagination, and 'Memorandum by R. W. Brandling', 12.

[40] PP 1828 (469) XIX.462.

[41] Apart from the particular sources and authorities cited, this account of the coastal trade in coal is based mainly on Westerfield 1915, 229-32; Willan 1938, 55-69; Davis 1962, 60-6, 91-4; and Finch 1973.

expensive than the mere improvement of an existing waterway; and it had to be demonstrated that the carriage of coal would both meet the interest on a large outlay of capital and undercut existing road or waggonway freight charges. William Brown, the north-east viewer, believed that canals were an attractive proposition. Writing to the Earl of Darlington in 1773 about the transport of coal from a colliery near Staindrop he argued that 'such a canal will not cost half the expence of a waggonway and when once made needs no repair and the expence of conveyance by water is not $\frac{1}{4}$th the expence by waggons.'[42] It was clear to the industrialists of the mid and late eighteenth century that though canals might well serve the needs of many industries and even of agriculture, the initial test of their viability must be the carriage of coal. 'Every canal', asserted the greatest of the canal-builders, the third Duke of Bridgewater, in a much-quoted, if inelegant, aphorism, 'must have coals at the heel of it.'[43] And the earliest canals were, indeed, coal navigations.

The first such canals connected Griff colliery in Warwickshire to a nearby tramway: they were constructed before 1711, and were referred to as 'boatways'.[44] The Griff example seems not to have been followed for almost half a century, but, when it came, the first public imitator was an instructive example, since it served a coal-field which, though largely separated from its principal potential markets by a belt of countryside devoid of navigable rivers, was not nearly as isolated as were some coalfields. At its nearest points the coalfield of south-west Lancashire was a mere nine miles from the centre of Liverpool and ten miles from the navigable lower reaches of the river Mersey from which the Weaver navigation of 1721 led to the salt-producing centres of north Cheshire. And, as we have seen, as early as the 1730s, improvement of the river Douglas had provided an outlet by water transport for the northern collieries of the coalfield. Yet in 1755 a group of Liverpool merchants and industrialists were sufficiently concerned by the high cost of coal carriage to Liverpool by the turnpike constructed principally for this purpose only in 1725 that they set in motion the steps to promote a canal known, from the stream it replaced, as the Sankey Brook Navigation. Completed in 1757, this canal speedily developed a sub-stantial trade in coal from the St. Helens area of the coalfield to domestic and industrial consumers in Liverpool and Merseyside as well as to the salt-makers along the Weaver navigation. Household coal, which before the construction of the navigation had cost

---

[42] W. Brown to Earl of Darlington, 24 Jan. 1773, NEI Watson 8/10/158.
[43] Malet 1977.
[44] Ardayfio thesis 1974, 67.

$5\frac{1}{2}d$. per cwt. in Liverpool, was being offered at $4\frac{1}{2}d$. by 1759.[45]

The importance of the Sankey Brook Navigation lay not merely in the fact that it was the first public coal canal in Britain but also in the shortness of the land-carriage distances it replaced: where a sufficiently large trade was involved, it paid to substitute water-transport for land carriage over even quite short distances. Nor was the Navigation without impact on the development of the coalfield itself. The reduction in the delivered price of coal from the St. Helens area of the coalfield, coinciding as it did with the growth of various coal-consuming industries in south Lancashire, Merseyside, and north Cheshire, stimulated production in that part of the coal-field. The St. Helens or southern part of the coalfield, which in 1740 is estimated to have produced only 8,000 tons, or just over ten per cent of the total output of the south-west Lancashire coalfield, produced 115,000 tons in 1760, fifty-eight per cent of the coalfield's total production. Conversely, the south-western section of the coal-field, hitherto enjoying, by virtue of its proximity along the turnpike to Liverpool, a virtual monopoly of the domestic and industrial market in coal there, scarcely increased its output at all between 1740 and 1760, and suffered a decline in its share of the coalfield's total output from sixty-four per cent to twenty-eight per cent.[46]

The Sankey Brook Navigation was the brainchild principally of Liverpool coal consumers. Further east in the Lancashire coalfield a major coalowner, the third Duke of Bridgewater, saw a canal as the means of exploiting the market for his coal. His mines near Worsley were a mere six miles from the centre of their main urban market in Manchester; but this distance was sufficient to bring the delivered cost of coal in Manchester up to between $5\frac{1}{2}d$. and $7d$. per cwt. When the Duke, encouraged by his visionary agent, John Gilbert, decided to petition Parliament for powers to construct a canal from Worsley to Manchester in 1758, he took the bold step of committing himself to sell coal on his quayside in central Manchester at no more than $4d$. per cwt. for a period of forty years. The Duke secured his act in 1759, and by 1763 was selling coal from the canal in Manchester, though it was the following year before he completed his central Manchester terminus.

In one unusual sense, the Worsley canal was merely an extension of an existing waterway. Looking round for a solution to one of a canal-builder's major problems—a supply of water for the summit level—John Gilbert hit on the idea of linking the new canal to the

[45] T. C. Barker and J. R. Harris, *A Merseyside Town in the Industrial Revolution. St. Helens, 1750–1900* (Liverpool, 1954), 11–23, 28.

[46] Langton 1979, 154.

drainage sough of the Worsley mines, thus allowing it to be fed by innumerable springs within the mines. During the 1730s and 1740s the Duke's father had developed drainage soughs in these mines and may well have been the first mineowner to employ water transport for underground haulage: it is known that boats were being used to bring coal from the face to the mouth of the sough as early as 1743. From the early 1760s, therefore, coal was carried directly from the face underground to the quayside in Manchester.[47]

After his success with the short Worsley canal, the Duke extended his navigation westwards into central Lancashire, and south of the Mersey to the navigable estuary at Runcorn. In the forty years after 1760 the successful examples of Sankey and Worsley were imitated in all coalfields except those of the North-east and Cumberland where proximity to existing coastal or river navigation made the development of canals unnecessary. At the western end of the South Wales coalfield the Swansea Valley canal of 1798 made possible the exploitation of mines seventeen miles from sea carriage in the upper Tawe valley. A number of shorter canals were also built in the Swansea district to facilitate the transport of coal to the quayside. Some of these, like one of three and a half miles from Llanwern colliery at Llansamlet to the Neath river completed in 1790 with Telford's assistance, were privately owned and used exclusively by individual collieries.[48] In Somerset, where mining in hilly country was restricted by an overland carriage of between ten and fifteen miles to markets in the towns of the Avon valley, the Somerset Coal Canal was authorized in 1794 and opened in 1805. Although the southern branch of this canal presented technical problems that were never solved, the northern branch leading from mines in the area of High Littleton and Dunkerton to the Avon at Monkton Combe, was very successful, and by the late 1820s was carrying over 100,000 tons of coal a year.[49] In Gloucestershire the Stroudwater canal, linking the Stroud cloth-making district with the tidal reach of the river Severn, was begun in 1782 in order to bring Forest of Dean or South Wales coal for the growing woollen industry.[50] In Scotland, the Monkland canal, opened in 1792, was constructed to bring coal from Lanarkshire to Glasgow, and although some of the pits at Stevenston in Ayrshire were only two and a half miles from the harbour at Saltcoats, a short canal was built in 1772 to reduce transport costs.[51] In Shropshire coal canals were built as feeders

[47] Malet 1977, 27–62; Mullineux 1961, 152–5.
[48] Roberts thesis 1953, 150.
[49] K. R. Clew, *The Somerset Coal Canal and Railways* (Newton Abbot, 1970).
[50] M. Handford, *The Stroudwater Canal* (Gloucester, 1979).
[51] Duckham 1970, 220–2.

to the river Severn, and since in the area of the coalfield the river flows through a steep-sided gorge, the final link between these canals and the river had to be made by inclined planes.[52]

It is hardly surprising that the most extensive developments of canals for coal traffic were in the inland coalfields of the East Midlands, the West Midlands, and Yorkshire. In each of these areas there was a foundation of a river navigation network on which to build, and during the last forty years of the eighteenth century a very elaborate system of canals was constructed linking and extending the navigable portions of the rivers Aire, Calder, Don, Ouse, Trent, Derwent, and Soar. Some of the most heavily used canals in the whole country served mines in Nottinghamshire and Derbyshire.[53]

Many canals, therefore, were constructed in the late eighteenth century solely or principally for the carriage of coal. But the mining industry also took advantage of canals built initially to serve other industries. In this way the Glamorgan and Monmouthshire canals of 1790 and 1792 respectively, built primarily to carry iron down to the coast from the great new ironworks of Merthyr Tydvil and the Afon valley, were the means of giving the hitherto unexploited seams of the upper South Wales valleys access to markets along and across the Severn and its estuary. Similarly, the Leeds–Liverpool canal, built between 1777 and 1780 and designed to give the manufacturing districts of the West Riding of Yorkshire access to Liverpool, also gave the northern parts of the Lancashire coalfield cheaper access to Liverpool.[54] Even the Kennet and Avon, and Wiltshire and Berkshire canals, meandering through intensely rural areas and seemingly remote from potential coal traffic, were utilized by Somerset mineowners to extend the markets for their coal eastwards. In 1824 the Kennet and Avon canal carried over 200,000 tons of coal, though it is not clear how much of this was coal from the North-east entering the canal at its eastern end via Reading and London, or south-west coal entering from its western end of the Avon.[55] Similarly, the Trent and Mersey canal proved to be a valuable stimulus to mines in north Staffordshire after its completion in 1777,[56] while the Grand Junction and Coventry canals gave Leicestershire and Warwickshire mines access to London and allowed them to threaten there, for the first time in the history of the coal trade, the pre-eminence of the coal exports of the North-east.[57]

[52] Trinder 1973, 126–34.
[53] Hopkinson 1976.
[54] Joseph Dawson to W. S. Stanhope, 28 Mar. 1826, SCL Spencer Stanhope 60579.
[55] Davis thesis 1959, 58, and Appendix Table A.1.
[56] VCH Staffordshire, II, 77–9.
[57] VCH Leicestershire, II, 37.

It was rarely possible for a canal, other than a short, private one, to serve all collieries in any area, if only because of the need of canals to follow contours as far as possible. Waggonways were therefore commonly constructed to link collieries to canals at their nearest points. The owner of collieries near the Sankey Brook Navigation advertised in Liverpool in 1757 that 'the Waggon Road and other conveniences are fixed in such a manner that Flatts may be loaden in a few hours'.[58] A map of 1835 shows no fewer than thirty-one railways serving as feeders to the Erewash and Nottingham canals, while the making of the branch from the Coventry canal at Marston Bridge to Ashby-de-la-Zouch in Leicestershire between 1794 and 1805 was quickly followed by the construction of feeder waggon-ways from collieries at Heather, Normanton-le-Heath, Lount, and Staunton Harold.[59]

Any canal necessarily threatened to alter the existing market structure. The purpose of building one was generally to enlarge the market of an existing colliery or group of collieries, or to make it possible to allow new producers to compete in existing markets; and in either case some threat was posed to the interests of existing mineowners somewhere. Sometimes the proprietors of a projected new canal contrived to ensure some competitive advantage for themselves in the provisions of the private act of Parliament. Thus a clause was slipped into a supplementary act that authorized an extension of the Monmouthshire canal in 1797 exempting coals brought down that canal and shipped in the Bristol Channel eastwards of the Holmes from the coastwise duty, a privilege that gave coalowners along the canal an advantage over coalowners further west, and allowed Newport to capture most of the up-channel trade formerly enjoyed by Cardiff.[60] Somerset coalowners protested in 1817 against the exemption from the coastwise duty of Forest of Dean producers who were able to send their coal across the Severn and up the Stroudwater canal thus gaining an unfair advantage in Wiltshire and Berkshire over Somerset coal: this exemption had been given by the Commission of Treasury in an order of 1816 of which the Somerset coalowners had no knowledge.[61] The Stroudwater canal had already in 1786 affected the landsale of coal from the Mayshill colliery in the Bristol coalfield.[62] With many colliery districts jostling for urban

---

[58] J. R. Harris, 'Railways of the St. Helens Coalfield down to 1830: a note', *TH* 2 (1956), 175.

[59] H. Green 1935–6, 65–6; *VCH Leicestershire*, II, 37.

[60] Petition dated 16 Feb. 1803, CLSG Miscellaneous MS 4.778; *Report of the Select Committee on Petitions of the Coalowners in South Wales*, PP 1810 IV, 11–12.

[61] BL Add. MSS 38, 367, fo. 1.

[62] Lord Middleton to Thomas Smyth, 11 Nov. 1786, BRO Ashton Court AC/AS98.

and industrial markets, the delicate balance of markets and competitive advantage was most easily upset in the East and West Midlands.[63]
In 1785, for example, Warwickshire coalowners united in opposition to a proposal to make a connection between Coventry and
collieries at Wednesbury in Staffordshire. The core of the Warwickshire coalowners' objection was to a rate of $1d.$ per ton/mile for coal
to be carried on the new link between Birmingham and Fazeley in
contrast to a rate of $1\frac{1}{2}d.$ standard throughout the Coventry and
Oxford canal systems. This would have given the Staffordshire coalowners, with their better quality coals, an advantage in Coventry
over the nearer Warwickshire mines.[64]

The largest interest to be threatened by the new canals, however,
was that of the north-east suppliers in the London market, a
monopoly they had enjoyed, thanks to London's great overland
distance from the nearest mining area, ever since the beginnings of
the domestic use of coal, and the north-east coalowners scrutinized
carefully every canal act that could possibly jeopardize this
monopoly as it came before Parliament. The Oxford canal, for
example, of 1769, created a waterway from the Midlands coalfields
via the Thames to London, but the north-east owners managed to
secure the insertion of a clause into its act prohibiting the carriage
of coal beyond Oxford.[65] In 1793 the Grand Junction canal linked
London directly with several mining districts of the Midlands, and
it had certainly been the hope of the canal proprietors that they
would profit from the carriage of coal to the capital. But the north-
east coalowners saw to it that the act for this canal contained a
clause prohibiting the carriage of coal beyond the tunnel at Langley-
bury. In 1800 this prohibition was amended to allow a maximum of
50,000 tons a year to pass through to Paddington. Similarly, a clause
in the Wiltshire and Berkshire canal act prohibited the carriage of
coal further east than Reading. To make quite sure that Midland
and southern canals would not threaten the position of the north-
east producers in the London market, and to compensate for the
coastwise duty, an act of 1805 placed a duty of about 10s. per
London chaldron on all coal carried by canal into London.[66] The
Coventry canal of 1768 also opened the London market via the
Grand Junction to Leicestershire producers, and its threat to the
coalowners of the North-east in the London market led them to

---

[63] See, e.g., A. T. Patterson, 'The making of the Leicestershire canals, 1766–1814',
Transactions of the Leicestershire Archaeological Society, 27 (1951); Ardayfio thesis 1975;
and C. P. Griffin 1978b, 227–8.
[64] BL Add. MSS 38, 345, fo. 110; WaRO Newdigate (Additional) CR764/264.
[65] Grant thesis 1977, 186, n. 18.
[66] 33 Geo. III, c. 80; Grant thesis 1977, 194; 35 Geo. III, c. 52; 45 Geo. III, c. 128.

petition the House of Commons against the canal.[67] North-east coal-owners opposed the bill for the Paddington canal in 1806 because it would help to reduce the price of competing Midlands coal in central London. But the hopes of the Midlands coalowners and the fears of those of the North-east were never realized. The trade was not recorded until it became dutiable in 1805; but at its peak in 1809 it amounted only to 17,300 tons, compared with coastwise imports of almost one and a half million tons, and it fell away to little more than 2,500 tons annually in the late 1810s and 1820s.[68] At least, that is the official record. It was claimed in 1804, however, that 'from Staffordshire immense quantities are brought down the canals and smuggled into London where they can be bought and sold at a much cheaper rate than the sea coals, no duty being paid on them—they have now got to such a pitch of hardihood that they publicly advertise them.'[69] That was before the imposition of the duty on canal and river carriage of coal into London: after 1805 the incentive to smuggle coal into London was even greater.

It is not possible, of course, to assess precisely the effect of canal-building upon either the quantities of coal sold or the geographical distribution of its production, though there can be little doubt that in both these areas it was profound. In areas in which, before the coming of the canals, the distance from mining districts or from water-transport had effectively priced coal out of the market, coal now became a commodity that could be afforded; in other areas the reduction in the price of delivered coal raised the quantity demanded; and in yet others, above all in the eastern valleys of South Wales, it became economically feasible to develop mining areas hitherto unexploited on account of lack of access to any market. In some areas, above all in the East and West Midlands, the canals generated competition between coalfields that itself was responsible for lowering the price of coal.[70] In any case the canals should not be considered in isolation: they were basically extensions of river navigation networks, and many canals were primarily a means of passing coal on to the rivers. Many waggonways, similarly, particularly outside the North-east, were, in their turn, extensions of the canals. By the early decades of the nineteenth century almost all coal consumed in Britain was carried over some part of its journey from mine to consumer by waggonway and inland navigation: very little used the roads. In 1808 it was estimated, for example, that

[67] VCH Leicestershire, II, 37; CJ 1769, XXXII, 289.

[68] PP 1814–15 (239) X.365; and 1826–7 (495) XVIII.13. Slightly differing figures are given in NEI Forster 49/18/115.

[69] NuRO Delaval (Hastings) 650/H9.

[70] Ardayfio thesis 1974, 61.

more than 270,000 tons of coal were shipped from Derbyshire on the Cromford, Derby, and Erewash canals and by the Trent navigation, while a deputation of Wear coalowners estimated in 1816 that no less than five and a half million tons of coal were carried by inland navigation and railroads in the Yorkshire, East and West Midlands coalfields.[71] With rare exceptions, however, the canals did not fundamentally disrupt the regional market economy of the coal industry. Canals, as a historian of the south-west coalfield observed in respect of the markets for its products, 'never succeeded in making coal competitive in more distant markets'.[72] They may have shaken the local markets for individual coalfields into a new equilibrium and, at the most, redistributed some peripheral markets on the borders of neighbouring coalfields.

That the development of coal transportation has been examined here in some detail is a recognition of its importance to the expansion of the industry in the eighteenth and early nineteenth centuries. Many minor changes contributed to this development, as we have seen, as well as some major ones. Of the latter, four were of outstanding significance. First, the substitution of carts and wains for pack-horses in the road transport of coal which was, of course, already in progress at the opening of the eighteenth century. By raising the productivity of expensive horses it substantially reduced the delivered price of coal thus leading to increased demand. Though the proportion of all coal produced that was carried by road was much reduced during the period 1700 to 1830, road carriage was never completely supplanted by other forms of transport and was even substantially encouraged within this period by the construction of turnpike roads. Second, the widespread adoption of waggonways. Though an innovation of the seventeenth century, their general adoption was a feature of the eighteenth century. The third major development—the substitution of the steam-locomotive for horse-traction on waggonways—began only in the year 1812, but its value in reducing land transport costs and in making possible land carriage routes hitherto impracticable was so great and so quickly demonstrated that the steam-powered railway was widespread in British mining regions well before the public passenger railways, which have attracted so much more attention from historians, appeared on the scene. The coming of steam-locomotion initiated the decline in the enormous number of horses, a decline that was a major aspect of change in the mining industry of the nineteenth century. Finally, and probably most decisive of all as a stop-gap

---

[71] Wood 1950, 31; *RC Coal* 1871, 40.
[72] Davis thesis 1959, 60.

before the coming of the steam-railway, the creation between the 1750s and the first decade of the nineteenth century of the inland waterways by improved river navigations and canals, two indivisible aspects of the same development. The impact of these developments varied considerably from coalfield to coalfield. Their major role in some coalfields like South Wales, Lancashire, and the East and West Midlands contributed substantially to their changing importance relative to others like the North-east and Cumberland where canals had no part to play.

Chapter 6

Capital

i. *Capital requirements*

It is easy to assume that mining in a period as far back as the early eighteenth century made relatively few demands on capital: coal was all hand cut and mostly hauled by human-power underground; only in the largest pits was animal or simple wind- or water-driven machinery used to augment human-power; cutting equipment amounted to little more than hand tools; and for hauling beneath the surface the coal was loaded in corves on to small wooden sledges. For the small drift mines that characterized the Derbyshire, Bristol, and Forest of Dean coalfields in the early eighteenth century or in the bell-pits of Staffordshire and Shropshire, this type of equipment may well have sufficed; but already at that time mines in many of the British coalfields had developed to a scale and in ways that called for investment on an altogether larger scale. While it is clearly not possible to put a figure to it, a high proportion of the coal mined, even at the beginning of the eighteenth century was taken from moderately deep pits; and investment in mining increased more than proportionately to the depth of pits.

'What do you mean by the capital of that Colliery?', Francis Thompson, former manager of Washington colliery in County Durham was asked by the 1800 Select Committee. 'The sinking of pits', he replied, 'erecting fire engine, gins, laying waggon ways, waggons, and erecting a staith, and all other materials necessary for working the Colliery. I do not mean to include the expence of working the Colliery.'[1] Sinking itself, surprisingly, was not a particularly heavy expense, which is why it was common to sink new pits at no great distance from older ones to minimize the expense and technical problems of long-distance haulage underground. Even with the wider-bore pits of the early nineteenth century, sinking, though a specialized skill, called for little other than hand tools. The sinking costs for two pits each of 900 feet depth for the projected new colliery at Gosforth in Northumberland were estimated in 1824 to account for only six per cent of the whole winning cost.[2] But until

---

[1] *First SC Coal Trade* 1800, 542.
[2] NEI Forster 49/9/102–3.

the pit was sunk to the first workable seam and a start made with underground levels, no coal could be taken out and no sales effected to offset a growing capital expenditure. While a shallow pit could probably be sunk in a matter of weeks, the really deep pits of the early nineteenth century could take four years or more in construction—a long gestation period in which to forego all returns to investment.

Already in the eighteenth century pits were penetrating to depths sufficient to call for pumping to keep them dry as the sinkers advanced, and owners showed by their accounting that they accepted pumping costs incurred during sinking as a necessary item of capital expenditure. Pumping costs were divided between the cost of the machinery—small in the case of a horse-gin (though the capital cost of the number of horses necessary to work the shifts in continuous drainage should not be underestimated), substantial if a steam-pump was necessary; and the running costs of the pumping operation—labour to look after the horses or tend the steam engine, and feed for the horses or coal for the boilers. As the diameter and depth of shafts increased towards the end of the eighteenth century and into the nineteenth, tubbing became more generally essential, a fairly substantial addition to the cost of sinking. Tubbing and walling at the projected Gosforth Colliery of 1824, for example, were expected to amount to eleven and a half per cent of total costs, nearly twice as much as the actual sinking.[3]

But the shaft itself, and the levels that gave access to the workings were only the beginning of the investment necessary to create one of the larger mines of the later eighteenth or early nineteenth centuries. By then, at least two shafts were considered necessary for ventilation purposes. Rails had to be laid down underground for haulage to the shaft bottom from workings which might now, because it was no longer cheap to sink deep, tubbed shafts, be long distances away. Solidly constructed trap-doors had to be erected to direct the 'course' of the ventilation draught. Pumping and winding machinery had to be installed. From quite early in the eighteenth century steam-pumps were increasingly used for this purpose, and in the larger collieries sometimes more than one engine. Griff colliery in Warwickshire installed three between 1714 and 1725, Heaton on Tyneside six between 1729 and 1741, and Howgill in Cumberland five between 1717 and 1740. When they came in from the 1790s, steam winding-engines were an additional item of capital expenditure. Nor did the investment stop at the pit-head. Collieries that sold their entire output by landsale from the pit-head were necessarily small, and of those that looked for the wider and larger markets that

[3] NEI Forster 49/9/102–3.

only water carriage could give them very few indeed were located conveniently at the water-side. Waggonways were an essential element in the capital equipment of many collieries, and at over £1,000 per mile in the early nineteenth century they could easily be a major item of investment even before the cost of rolling stock was taken into account. An estimate for a waggonway of 1,000 yards to connect the new Crawcrook colliery on Tyneside to the 'public railway' in 1830 allowed, in addition to £1,605 for the track, £1,320 for sixty waggons, £700 for a new staith, £640 for eighteen waggon horses, and £900 for eighteen waggonmen's houses.[4] Throughout much of the period mineowners were obliged to erect housing, particularly if the mines were any distance from existing settlements.

An early example of a costing for a new winning was for a sinking at North Wood colliery in the North-east in 1753 to a depth of 252 feet. It came to £1,614, the major item being a fire-engine at £1,000. This project involved, as was usual at the time, sinking two shafts— an 'engine' pit for pumping and ventilation, and a 'coal' pit for winding.[5] A rather more detailed estimate exists for the creation of a new colliery at Tanfield Lea in the North-east in 1755. Three shafts of 360 feet were envisaged, one for the engine and two for coal. Total sinking costs, which included drainage costs during sinking for the three shafts, were expected to amount to £2,160. A fire-engine, which had to be installed in time to drain during the sinking and driving of levels, was costed at £1,200. 'Laying and levelling' two tracks of waggonway a distance of 2,178 yards with necessary bridges, presumably to a connecting line, since Tanfield is seven or eight miles from the Tyne staithes, would cost a further £748. To this layout of £4,107 on construction costs was added in this instance 'the purchase money' of £4,000, which can only indicate that land was being bought outright.[6] An estimate for a new pit at Lumley on the Wear in 1775 with an anticipated seasale production of 20,000 chaldrons (53,000 tons) amounted to £10,836. Construction was begun in 1775, and the first saleable coal was raised in January 1779. By the spring of 1780 it became apparent that the original pump was inadequate, and a new, larger one had to be ordered at £1,200. Inevitably actual outlay of capital exceeded the original optimistic estimate, and by 1783 it was found that total outlay for the new winning had amounted to £17,000.[7]

A detailed calculation by John Buddle of the 'stock' of Elswick

[4] DuRO NCB First Deposit NCB/I/JB/1918.
[5] NEI Forster 49/4/207.
[6] NEI Forster 49/4/171–2.
[7] Beastall 1975, 26–33.

colliery at 31 December 1809 covers all equipment and stocks at the colliery, but excludes the cost of sinking and driving levels, and totals £15,693. At the time of the valuation the colliery was completely won and 'in a situation to produce between 15,000 and 20,000 chaldrons of ship coals yearly', though Buddle believed that 'this quantity is much beyond what there is any reasonable prospect of obtaining.' In a return of 1815 Elswick is shown as employing 130 workers above and below ground, well below the Tyne seasale colliery average of 319 workers. It was therefore a relatively small colliery by north-east seasale standards. But Buddle noted that 'by the Colliery books it appears that the Total Sum advanced by the Proprietors up to the 31st December 1809' amounted to £20,426, to which he added a further £4,577 'owing to sundry tradesmen'. If we assume that these last debts were incurred in the purchase or creation of capital equipment, the total investment amounted to just over £25,000.[8]

There is little doubt that the decision to install a steam-pumping engine in an existing mine was a major one for any colliery owner in the eighteenth century. Steam-pumps always represented a significant element in total capital costs: five engines erected between 1729 and 1765 represented an average of 35.7 per cent of total capital costs for the creation of the pits they served. We have no more costings but may be set beside total investment until after 1800, but thirteen such costings between 1800 and 1824, when the engines erected were probably all, or mostly, Boulton and Watt engines, accounted for an average of 20.5 per cent of total investment. The average costs of eight Newcomen engines erected between 1725 and 1770 was £1,140, and of fifteen miscellaneous pumping-engines erected between 1790 and 1825 £2,034.[9]

The process of investment during the winning of a new pit is well illustrated by two detailed accounts at either end of the period covered by this volume. They reveal, incidentally, the immense growth in scale over the nearly one hundred years that separates them. The first relates to the 'new intended coal-works and Fire Engine' at Woolaton, Nottingham, in 1733 and 1734. Sinkers were paid both by the yard and by the day, and other workers were paid by the day for 'drawing water', apparently manually in buckets; but

---

[8] NEI Miscellaneous 63/ZC/48/1.

[9] These averages are drawn from either pre-sinking estimates or post-sinking accounts, and relate to the following collieries: Newbottle 1729, Griff 1729–30, North Wood 1753, Throckley 1753, Tanfield Lea 1755, Fenham and Benwell 1765, Murton 1800, Coxlodge 1804, East Kenton 1804, Gosforth 1806, Chapter Main 1809, Jarrow and Temple Main 1809, Aifreton 1811, Manor Wallsend 1814, Brereton Hayes 1816, Hetton 1820, Gosforth 1824, and one on Anglesey 1825.

within four months payments were being made for driving the gin horse, which indicates that a horse-gin for pumping had been erected. Lime, timber, candles, gunpowder, and ironwork were bought repeatedly in small quantities, and craftsmen of various kinds were being paid at daily rates. Most payments, however, were in shillings and pence only. After just over twelve months' work £632 had been paid out, but small quantities of saleable coal were already being taken out.[10] The second account of the 'Expences attending the sinking of the New Pit near Houghton' by John Lambton in east Durham illustrates a very similar process though on a very different scale. It covers six years—1823-8—in each of which the first item of expenditure is sinkers' wages. At the end of six years over £8,500 had been laid out in sinkers' wages, and much expenditure incurred on timber, 'cast metal cribs' (for tubbing), castings for pumping engines (two), ropes, bricks, candles, gunpowder, and nails, with substantial payments each year for the labour of smiths, wrights, masons, carters, slaters, and enginemen, and a recurring item for 'house rents'. The second year saw the highest outlay, and by the end of six years £38,276 had been spent solely on the mine, for there is no reference to the building of waggonways or houses.[11]

A mine constructed in this way was eventually, after a gestation period ranging from a few months to several years, ready for the hewers and putters to go down to work and send up coal. An investment had been made which, all other things being equal, was designed to increase total production; it was, in other words, net investment. But, even the most casual of glances at the financial records of collieries in this, or any other period, reveals that the initial investment was merely the beginning of an unending flow of capital. Two distinct areas of investment were called for merely to maintain output at a given level. The first of these is obvious enough—depreciation, the replacement of equipment due to normal wear and tear, and obsolescence. With much wooden machinery and the use of many horses with relatively short working lives, this was a routine matter in a colliery operation, but a capital-consuming one nevertheless. The second area, however, probably made greater demands on capital: new workings to replace exhausted ones called for new levels, deeper shafts, extended underground railways, more powerful pumping machinery. New technologies called for new equipment even in productive, profitable collieries: as soon as they became available, many collieries hastened to equip themselves with steam-pumps, underground railways, steam winding-engines, ventilation-courses, steam-locomotives, safety-lamps, and a host of other developments.

[10] NUL Middleton Mi Ac 133.   [11] LEA not numbered.

This 'running' investment may reasonably be differentiated from depreciation. It was, of course, an unavoidable element in investment in an extractive industry in which the problems of maintaining output went far beyond the mere maintenance and replacement of equipment. The endless sinking of new shafts in the 'Lancashire system', the cutting of new drainage soughs, the extension of existing shafts to lower seams, the driving of new levels, the installation of steam-pumps to preserve a mine from drowning, were all essential, if expensive, activities that had to be undertaken if the original investment was not to be written off prematurely. At Sheriffhall colliery in Scotland, between January 1721 and April 1722, £568 had to be spent for additional sinking and other efforts to trace the seam after it had been cut off by a dyke.[12] Running investment at Govan colliery, Glasgow, described by Payne as 'relatively low . . . and easily met from current revenue', none the less amounted to £882 in the two-year period 1804–5.[13] A valuation of Newbottle colliery on Wearside of 1815 allowed £10,483 for a 'new winning, and maintaining colliery capable of vending 60,000 chaldrons'.[14] At Alloa colliery on the Firth of Forth £17,000 was 'expended in new fittings and workings' in a twenty-four year period up to 1818,[15] while an estimate of 1829 put at £34,800 the amount that had been spent on machinery, waggonways, and new sinkings at Lord Londonderry's Rainton colliery in County Durham since 1820.[16] Merely to maintain a given level of output in a single colliery, and, by extension, in the industry as a whole, require a constant flow of running investment. The true level of gross fixed investment in the mining industry, in other words, may be gauged only by aggregating together the net investment, the running investment, and depreciation.

John Buddle set out the case for running investment very explicitly in a memorandum about the Lambton collieries of 1810 which raises so many issues illustrating the problem of maintaining output and profitability in mine operation in the long run that it is worth quoting at some length:

When a trade of any kind becomes less profitable than usual, it naturally occurs to those concerned in it, that there must be some cause for the same; and that an investigation is necessary to ascertain, at least, how much diminution is occasioned, even if it should not be attended with a more favourable result. This observation unfortunately applies to the Colliery Concerns of the Lambton Family, and the object of this Report, is, to endeavour to account for the

[12] ScRO Buccleuch GD224/52.   [13] Payne 1961, 87.
[14] NuRO Armstrong 725/F/17/120.
[15] ScRO Mar and Kellie GD24/17/581/14.
[16] DuRO Londonderry D/Lo/303, quoted in Hiskey thesis 1978, 129.

comparatively small Profits which the Lambton Collieries have produced for several years past.

When Lambton Collieries were in their most flourishing state, the supply of Coals was obtained from the High-main Coal Seam almost exclusively. This Seam, besides possessing the advantage of being at a moderate depth from the surface, was 6 feet thick, of superior quality and easy to work, as appears by the Colliery Books at that period. Besides combining all the above advantages, the sale of Coals from this Seam was almost unlimited, as there were not then so many rival Collieries in the Trade, and of course fewer competitors to contend with.

The facility with which the Coals from this Seam were obtained and sold, naturally occasioned its being wrought in large quantities, while the lower Seams were in a great measure untouched and neglected; and it does not appear ever to have been in the contemplation of the Parties that it was necessary to work a *due proportion* of the lower Seams jointly with the High-main, in order to render the Revenue to be derived from the Collieries more permanent; but, as was then too generally the case in the Coal Trade, they had preferred present profit to the future welfare of the concern.

This inordinate working of the High-main Coal continued until, with the exception of Pensher, it was nearly exhaused in all the Lambton Collieries. To supply the usual Vend of Coals from these Collieries, and to enable the late General and Mr Lambton to support the character of the first Coal Owner on the River Wear which they then held, the winning of the *Lower Seams* (Maudlin, Lowmain and the Hutton) became indispensable.

The winning of the lower Seams was accordingly carried into effect at Haraton Colliery and afterwards at the other Collieries successively, and the quantity of Coal wrought from them increased progressively as the High-main Seam became exhausted, till in the end nearly the whole Vend was supplied by them.

For some time after the whole Vend was supplied by the lower Seams, the want of the High-main, in point of profit, was not materially felt. . . . In course of time, however, as the workings became extended, the putting charge became serious, and the sinking of New Pits became still more expensive owing to the increased depth to the lower Seams and the difficulty of passing through the old workings of the High-main Seam, which in many places were filled with water. Besides the increased expence and difficulty of working the lower Seams, the Coals which they produced were not so saleable as the High Main Coals, and that preference which was necessary to enable the Lambton Collieries to obtain their accustomed Vend, could with difficulty be maintained, owing in a considerable degree to the supply of Coals of similar quality as well as High Main coals, which was furnished by other collieries on the River Wear.

The above considerations induced the Winning of New Pensher Colliery. This winning was undertaken with a view to obtain a further supply of High-main Coal; but owing to the great *dip* or inclination of the Seam, which makes it expensive to work, and, the coal not being of the best quality, that advantage, which was expected to result from the undertaking, particularly since the Rise Coal was wrought off, has not been realised.[17]

[17] NEI Buddle 3/193–207.

Buddle then went on to list in each of the ten years surveyed the items of capital expenditure required to modernize the Lambton collieries and sustain their level of production. In 1800 a large Boulton and Watt pumping-engine was bought to drain Murton colliery at a cost of £2,376. In the following year this cost a further £1,733 to erect. A new pit was also sunk at Murton at a cost of £594, new houses for pitmen were built for £1,475, new levels driven at a cost of £1,381, and a new waggonway laid down for £350. In 1801, apart from completing the installation of the new pumping-engine, more pitmen's houses were built at a cost of £369, the tower of D pit pumping-engine was enlarged for £759, and alterations were made to underground works at Penshaw colliery to the extent of £259. In the following year further work on the Murton pumping-engine pit and levels cost £1,918, widening a shaft at Harraton colliery cost £785, the construction of a 'coal machine and engine' (winding gear?) at Harraton cost £2,743, and another at Houghtongate cost £1,454, while that year's contribution to the housing of pitmen cost a further £364. So the pattern continued from year to year— new pits, drainage adits, pitmen's houses, new pumping-engines. Every year some sinking charges were incurred and some pitmen's housing built. It is not easy to differentiate in these accounts between what twentieth-century accounting procedures would allocate to current costs, to depreciation and to capital expenditure, but a rough separation of the three indicates that in each of the ten years from 1800 to 1809 an annual average of £4,470 was invested in the fixed assets of the estate's mines.

Another paper of 1827 further illustrates these problems at the Lambton's Newbottle colliery on Wearside. It summarized sums laid out during the preceding five years. Some items, such as £800 for 'repairing the colliery main pumping engine' and £600 for 'repairing the sump pit shaft' fall very clearly into the category of current costs. But £1,400 for 'preparing a new way for an inclined plane near the spouts', £3,000 for 'three new lowering machines at the spouts' (drops), and an unspecified sum on 'laying a waggonway to the Elizabeth Pit 1,430 yards and raising a considerable battery [embankment] for ditto' equally clearly involve the creation of new assets.[18] The Vane-Tempest accounts for 1814–15 similarly show £4,403 of 'extraordinary expenditure' which included the cost of sinking a new shaft, extending a waggonway and building a new stables and houses.[19]

Just as the range of investment in the winning and development

[18] LEA MP12/6.
[19] DuRO Londonderry D/Lo/B38.

of a colliery may be underestimated, so, too, can the calls on circulating capital in mining easily be overlooked. On the face of it, circulating capital may seem unimportant in an extractive industry, which, almost by definition, employs no raw materials and so does not need to keep stocks of them. Even the fuel consumed by pumping- and winding-engines can be assumed to be of very low cost and large stocks of it to be unnecessary from the very nature of the situation. But in the eighteenth and early nineteenth centuries much hauling, pumping, and winding was still done by horse-power. The raw material input of oats and hay was a significant item of running costs, and capital was invested in stocks of horse-feed. A valuation of the Jarrow and Temple Main collieries of 1809 showed stocks of oats and hay worth £1,147 out of a total valuation of all dead and live stock of just under £25,000. A Hebburn valuation of 1814 showed very similar figures.[20]

Circulating capital includes stocks of finished products as well as of raw materials, and most collieries kept stocks of coal 'on the bank' or at the staith. In the early nineteenth century valuations these were called 'resting coals', and could amount to quite substantial quantities. Stocks varied both seasonally and according to the state of trade. On more than one occasion proposals were voiced in the Newcastle seasale trade for the complete cessation of mining for a period while stocks at pitheads and on the staithes were reduced. Such an agreement was evidently made in the spring of 1729 between coalowners, shipmasters, and fitters in the North-east.[21] In January 1826 John Lambton had to make an additional £15,000 available to finance his mining operations during the three months of slack sales.[22] At Jarrow and Temple Main in 1809 'resting coals' were valued at over £5,000 out of the total valuation of around £25,000, at Hebburn in 1814 £1,500 on top of live stock valued at £8,000, at the Vane-Tempest collieries in Durham in 1814 nearly £10,000 on top of live and dead stock worth £42,708, and at the Haigh colliery in Lancashire of the Earl of Crawford and Balcarres the stock of cannel and coal at the pit-brow was assessed at £10,000 over and above machinery and implements valued at £26,000.[23] In Warwickshire, where, in the early eighteenth century, the scale of operation was smaller, coal stocks on the bank at Griff colliery were valued at £1,557 in 1727.[24] There are some other smaller items that should strictly be included

[20] NEI Watson 8/15/1–46; NEI Forster 49/9/102–3.
[21] G. Liddell to H. Ellison, 13 Feb. 1729, GPL Ellison A32/36.
[22] H. Stephenson to J. G. Lambton, 8 Jan. 1826, LEA MP12/not numbered.
[23] NEI Watson 8/15/45; NEI Buddle 41/31; DuRO Londonderry d/Lo/B38; LEA DP20; NEI Forster 49/8/189; NuRO Wilson (Forest Hall) 4/385–8; T. H. Hair 1844, 43–4; Kenwood thesis 1962, 83.   [24] Grant thesis 1977, 172.

under the head of 'circulating capital'—stocks of timber, iron, and tools, and what was described as 'waygoing crops'—either crops like hay on land beside waggonways or field crops on farmland integrated with colliery undertakings primarily for horse-feed purposes.

Finally there is the problem of trade credit and debts. We know that in some undertakings this could be a significant, if not substantial, element in circulating capital. The Earl of Crawford's Haigh colliery had outstanding debts owing to him of over £20,000 in 1822. At four Fitzwilliam south Yorkshire collieries in 1799 credit sales amounted to forty-seven per cent of total sales, and by 1820 at one of these to eighty-six per cent.[25] In the mining records at our disposal, however, there is generally very little information at all about debts, and some evidence that mineowners were very often net debtors rather than net creditors. Some may have had their cash flows financed by their employees, the balance of whose pay after the payment of subsistence money was sometimes held over for long periods; but many more may have needed quite large sums to finance loans to workers.

Circulating capital therefore consisted largely of two major items —stocks of horse-feed, and stocks of unsold coal at the bank. In three valuations of the period 1809–14 these two items average 18.5 per cent of the total valuations of dead and live stock, and must therefore be a smaller percentage of the total of fixed and circulating capital if sinking costs are added.[26] We are not likely to be very far from the truth if we allow ten per cent of total fixed capital for circulating capital. At so low a proportion, the mining industry was clearly unique among British industries in this period. In general, circulating capital represented a high, though, as time went on, diminishing proportion of total capital. In relatively few industries before 1830 did fixed capital exceed fifty per cent of total capital requirements and in some industries during the eighteenth century the proportion could sink as low as ten per cent.[27]

ii. *The scale of investment*

What, then, was the scale of investment in the British mining industry of the eighteenth and early nineteenth centuries? The extant records of the industry, many of which were created primarily for the purpose

[25] Smith thesis 1974, 67–8.

[26] Chapter Main colliery 1809 (NEI Watson 8/14/1-12); Jarrow and Temple Main collieries 1809 (NEI Watson 8/15/1-46); Hebburn colliery 1814 (NEI Buddle 41/31).

[27] S. Pollard, 'Fixed capital in the Industrial Revolution in Britain', *JEH* 24 (1964), 303–5.

of financial accounting, contain a great deal of material relating to investment, but it goes without saying that it is by no means easy to relate this to modern concepts of capitalization. So far as fixed investment is concerned there were several different types of accounts relevant to this problem. There are, for example, many volumes of viewers' books devoted largely to valuations of collieries. These were estimates of the worth of a set of assets in a mine to its owner based on current profits extended over the anticipated life of a colliery or over a number of years' purchase determined by an assumed rate of interest. Full as they are of detail, they turn out to be very little help in assessing the extent of the fixed capital of undertakings.

More relevant to the problem in hand were pre-start estimates for new mining projects. These were often quite careful and detailed, though experience generally showed that they under- rather than over-estimated costs. Less frequently there are post-sinking accounts of the actual cost of the creation of mines, and these, because of their detailed precision, are quite the most useful indicators of investment levels. It is these two types of account that have been used in the analysis that follows. Closely associated with them are the valuations made by viewers of what were called 'live' and 'dead' stock. 'Live' stock was what would be removable and saleable in the event of the closing down of operations, and was commonly assessed at current market, or, where relevant, second-hand prices. The category embraced steam-engines, waggonway rolling-stock, horses, timber, and ironware, rope, stocks of horse-feed, and coal on the bank or at the staith. 'Dead' stock, consisting of shafts and permanent buildings, was not removable and remained the property of the lessor.[28] These valuations have two defects in the present context: they never include costs of sinking and driving levels; and they are never explicit as to whether the valuations are at historic costs, replacement costs, or merely second-hand market values.

A figure of total fixed investment in a mine is more valuable if it can be related to a figure of the annual output of the mine, since only in this way will it be possible to form some assessment of the changing scale of investment over time. In only a small number of instances has it been possible to relate a reliable figure of total investment in a mine to its known or estimated output, and the details of these examples are set out in Table 6.1. Means for sub-periods are calculated in Table 6.2. The arithmetic of these tables is complicated by the fact that, for north-east collieries which provide the majority of the examples, the output was always expressed in terms

[28] Greenwell 1970, 84.

Table 6.1 *Fixed capital and output in selected collieries, 1730–1825*

Date	Colliery	Mining region	Fixed capital £	Estimated output	Corrected output (tons)	Fixed capital per ton £
1730	Griff	E. Mids.	1,992	12,000 stacks	18,000	0.11
1770s	Lanmorlais	S. Wales	4,200	3,000 weighs	24,000	0.18
1777–83	Lumley	NE	17,000	20,000 chs.	87,821	0.19
1788	25 Tyne collieries	NE	246,000	468,000 chs.	2,071,134	0.12
1789	Attercliffe	Yorks	10,535	18,000 loads	24,300	0.43
1803	Willington	NE	13,200	30,000 chs.	133,719	0.10
1804	Coxlodge	NE	25,000	20,000 chs.	89,358	0.28
1804	Hartley Main	NE	14,586	15,000 chs.	67,018	0.22
1806	Gosforth	NE	44,000	30,000 chs.	134,196	0.33
1808	All Tyne collieries	NE	883,000	619,125 chs.	2,772,751	0.32
1809	Elswick	NE	24,998	20,000 chs.	89,570	0.28
1811	Alfreton	W. Mids.	1,850	6,000 tons	6,000	0.31
1814	Jarrow	NE	35,449	30,000 chs.	134,752	0.26
1821	Crawcrook	NE	16,000	25,000 chs.	112,029	0.14
1822	Nesham Main	NE	22,567	40,000 chs.	178,928	0.13
1825	Seghill	NE	32,000	30,000 chs.	134,196	0.24
1825	Nr. Wrexham	N. Wales	15,000	40,000 tons	40,000	0.37

[See p. 202 for Notes on Sources]

Table 6.2 *Weighted average fixed capital/output ratios, 1730–1825*

Period	Number of collieries	Total fixed capital (£)	Total corrected output (tons)	Fixed capital per ton (£)
1730–89	28	369,192	2,225,255	0.13
1803–14	–	1,042,083	3,427,364	0.30
1821–5	4	83,567	465,153	0.18

Source: Table 6.1. Weighting by corrected output.

of the 'vend', and, as the discussion of this problem in the Appendix to Chapter 1 shows, this represented only the proportion of a mine's output that was sent for seasale. An appropriate adjustment, as indicated in the note on sources to Table 6.1, must therefore be made to arrive at the actual output.

The figures in the right-hand columns of these tables indicate, therefore, the fixed capital cost per additional ton of coal produced during the eighteenth and early nineteenth centuries. The rise and fall of these figures must, of course, reflect three main influences—the rise and fall of the general level of the prices relevant to mine-building before and after the peak of 1813, the rising real cost of extracting coal from ever-increasing depths, and changes in the

Note on sources (Table 6.1): The data are located as follows:

Griff 1730	WaRO Newdigate of Arbury CR136/B1771.
Lanmorlais 1770s	NLW Maybery.
Lumley 1775–83	Beastall 1975, 28–32.
25 Tyne collieries 1788	NEI Watson 8/11/110.
Attercliffe 1789	NEI Bell 46/14/no pagination.
Willington 1803	NEI Watson 8/8/302–4.
Coxlodge 1804	NEI Buddle 21/79–80.
Hartley Main 1804	NEI Watson 8/8/419.
Gosforth 1806	NEI Buddle 21/134–8.
All Tyne collieries 1808	NEI Buddle 23/44. Output = Tyne vend for 1808 corrected as per Appendix to Chapter 1.
Elswick 1809	NEI Miscellaneous 63 ZC/48/1.
Aifreton 1811	LCA 1546/54.
Jarrow 1814	NEI Buddle 36/I/13–14, 62–3.
Crawcrook 1821	DuRO NCB First Deposit NCB/I/JB/1970.
Nesham Main 1822	LEA MP12/6.
Seghill 1825	DuRO NCB First Deposit NCB/I/JB/572.
Nr. Wrexham 1825	NLW Chirk Castle F/11239.

Warwickshire stacks have been converted at the rate of 1.5 tons to the stack, and Swansea weighs at 8 tons to the weigh. An approximate percentage from Table 1.6, but omitting the allowance for landsale collieries, has been added to the vend figures for north-east collieries to raise seasale to total output.

productivity of capital. There is no possibility of accurately modifying the current costs in these tables by an index of mining investment costs, and because these costs may have moved in ways that differed significantly from the cost-of-living indices that are all that are otherwise available, there is probably little to be gained by attempting to modify them by one of these indices. A very rough comparison with the index of coal prices in Table 9.4, however, suggests that while the fixed capital costs of mining investment may have broadly kept pace with the rising price of coal during the second half of the eighteenth century, it may have fallen slightly by the same criterion during the deflation after 1813. The implication of these possibilities is that in real terms the capital cost of mining was falling throughout the period—in other words, that the marginal productivity of mining capital was rising.

Table 6.1 is also of interest in indicating the order of magnitude of fixed investment in mining enterprises at various dates during the eighteenth and early nineteenth centuries. Numerous other stock valuations, while not entered in the table on account of incompleteness, generally confirm these levels. The figures indicate that the larger mining enterprises generally called for what were, by the standards of the period, very large investments. The average insured value of 110 large cotton mills in 1795, for example, ran to only £6,960, and of fifty-five Scottish cotton mills of all sizes in the same year to £5,314,[29] while the fixed capital of seven miscellaneous non-ferrous metal undertakings between 1782 and 1832 averaged £4,933.[30] Individual firms, of course, owning many mills, furnaces, or processes in integrated undertakings, had much larger fixed capitals; and the same applied in mining. Thus the stock of the Lambton group of collieries was assessed in December 1825 at £187,000, and the family's mining agent believed that in the four and a half year period up to December 1826 a sum of not less than £140,000 had been put into 'new winnings and improvements'.[31] By 1835 Buddle estimated the value of all the working Lambton collieries, including the fixed and movable stock, at £384,381.[32] When the construction of Seaham harbour is taken into account, it is likely that investment in the neighbouring Londonderry mining undertakings would by 1830 have exceeded these figures. An account of 1815, no doubt exaggerated with the passage of time,

[29] S. D. Chapman, 'Fixed capital formation in the British cotton industry, 1770–1815', *EHR* 2nd ser. 23 (1970), 256–7, 262–3.

[30] Pollard, *JEH* 24, 304.

[31] 'Valuation of Stock, Dec 1825', LEA not numbered; W. Loraine to E. Ellice, 2 May 1827, LEA MP11/5.

[32] DuRO NCB First Deposit NCB/I/JB/2082.

estimated that between 1705 and 1755 Sir James Lowther had invested no less than £500,000 in his Whitehaven collieries.[33] These mining investments may be compared with the £166,000 of the Coalbrookdale Company in 1809 and the £160,000 of the Crawshays in 1813 in the iron industry (both these figures included some mining investment), the £272,000 in Marshalls in 1828 and the £397,000 in Gott and Wormalds by 1815 in the textile industry, and the £575,000 and £759,000 respectively in 1830 in Truman, Hanbury, and Buxtons, and Barclay Perkins respectively in brewing.[34]

Tables 6.1 and 6.2, however, relate only to initial fixed capital costs, and as we saw earlier, the mining industry was unique in calling for continuing creation of new fixed assets if the initial output was to be maintained. We are, unfortunately, far less well placed to assess the running investment needed to maintain output. The figure of £4,470 annual running investment in the Lambton collieries during the first ten years of the nineteenth century may have been unusually high in that it related to collieries that had been allowed to run down rather seriously in the preceding years, and it may also have involved some net investment. If, to err on the conservative side, we halve the figure, and relate it to the likely annual output of the Lambton collieries in 1810 of 388,000 tons, then the running investment necessary to maintain this level of production would be 0.58p per ton per year. For a national output of about nineteen million tons in 1810, this would have called for an annual running investment of about £110,000. At about this time, as Table 1.1 above indicates, output of British mines was increasing at about 360,000 tons each year. The estimates in Table 6.1 suggest that such a growth would call for an annual fixed investment of about £108,000. Added to the running investment needed merely to maintain output at a stationary level this suggests a total fixed investment around 1810 of about £220,000 per year. Table 6.3 extends the calculation on these lines to other periods, and compares the figures arrived at with Feinstein's recent estimate. There is a surprising measure of agreement about the order of magnitude of investment in mining in these estimates that have been arrived at in quite different ways.

The implication of these estimates is, as Feinstein has demonstrated, that investment in mining constituted a very small part of total fixed investment in Britain during the eighteenth and early nineteenth centuries. Feinstein estimated that gross domestic capital

[33] 'Notebook containing replies to Mr. Lyson's queries on the Whitehaven collieries, 1815', CuRO Lonsdale, Colliery Reports not yet listed.
[34] F. Crouzet, 'Capital formation in Great Britain during the Industrial Revolution', in F. Crouzet (ed.), *Capital Formation in the Industrial Revolution* (London, 1972), 199.

Table 6.3 *Estimates of annual fixed capital formation
in coal-mining at current prices, 1730-1820s*

| Feinstein | | New estimate | |
Period	£000s	Period	£000s
1760s	32	1730–89	44
1770s	16		
1780s	40		
1790s	96		
1800s	120	1803–14	220
1810s	256		
1820s	256	1821–25	232

Note on sources: C. H. Feinstein, 'Capital formation in Great Britain', in P. Mathias and M. M. Postan (eds.), *Cambridge Economic History of Europe*, VII Part I (Cambridge, 1978). His estimates are for 'mining and quarrying', and they have accordingly been reduced here by the 20 per cent of total that he estimates (for 1860) relate to non-coal mining and quarrying. His method is to estimate a figure of capital required to produce a ton of output for each decade starting in the relatively well-established early twentieth century and working backwards from them. This is then used as a capital/output ratio and multiplied by output, selecting the output years carefully to relate to years when capital was most fully employed. This produced a series of capital stock at current prices. The differences between points in the series may then easily be converted into annual capital formation figures.

New estimate: see text pp. 200–4 for method. The net fixed investment is derived from Table 6.2, and the annual increases of output indicated by Table 1.2. The estimate of running investment required to maintain output is calculated from the data discussed on pp. 197, 204, and the estimated actual production figures in Table 1.2.

formation in coal-mining never accounted for more than one per cent of gross national investment until 1810 and did not rise to two per cent of the total until the 1810s and 1820s. Mining investment, of course, was a higher proportion of industrial capital formation, possibly as much as four per cent in the second decade of the nineteenth century.[35] The implication of the capital/output ratios in the right-hand columns of Tables 6.1 and 6.2 is that the national output approaching thirty million tons in the late 1820s would require, at the capital/output ratios of the two examples for the year 1825, a total investment in the mining industry of about £6.0 million. Though the older collieries at this time would be producing at the lower capital costs of the earlier periods of their construction, these lower costs would have been offset to some extent by the higher capital costs of collieries constructed at the time of the high prices of the early years of the nineteenth century.

There are very few contemporary estimates of total investment in the mining industry of the late eighteenth and early nineteenth

[35] C. H. Feinstein, 'Capital formation in Great Britain', in P. Mathias and M. M. Postan (eds.), *The Cambridge Economic History of Europe*, VII, Part I (Cambridge, 1978), 42.

centuries with which to compare these new estimates, and in none of them is there any indication that the figure has been arrived at by anything other than informed guesswork. An estimate of twenty-five seasale collieries on the Tyne of 1788 showed a total capital 'sunk in winning' of £346,000. Tyne output at this time, after making allowance for landsale and other uses, may have been around twenty per cent of national output, indicating that, on the same basis, the national investment may then have amounted to perhaps £1.7 million.[36] Buddle estimated the 'capital employed on the River Tyne' in 1808 at £883,000 at a time when, at a rough estimate, the Tyne was producing possibly sixteen per cent of the national output, which implies by the same token a total investment for the whole country of about £5.5 million.[37] By 1828 he was prepared to estimate Tyne capital at £1.5 million and total north-east investment at £2.25,[38] and a statement of 1824, possibly a little exaggerated because it was made in a broadsheet extolling the north-east coal industry's contribution to the economy, assessed the capital in all north-east seasale collieries at more than £2 million.[39] If the north-east output is assumed to have been about twenty-three per cent of the whole national output at this time (see Table 1.3) and allowing for the contribution of the landsale collieries, this implies a total investment of just over £9 million; but the scale of capitalization in the North-east in the late 1820s is probably a poor guide to the scale in other coalfields. Deeper pits, more sophisticated drainage, winding and ventilation technology, and more extensive use of steam-railways on the surface is likely to have called for substantially higher investment per unit of output there than in other coalfields, and we are unlikely to be very wrong in accepting a level of total fixed capital in the British coal-mining industry in the late 1820s of around £6 million.

iii. *Sources of capital*

Because landowners, particularly the larger ones, are easily identifiable, there is little difficulty in determining the sources of the capital in the mines they worked or leased. Much of this capital may have stemmed from the ploughed-back profits of mining itself, like the £11,529 invested in 'the new railway to Sunderland' built by Lord Durham (Lambton) in 1830 which was specifically deducted

[36] NEI Watson 8/11/110.
[37] NEI Buddle 23/44.
[38] *SC Lords Coal Trade* 1830, 34, 52.
[39] NEI Buddle Atkinson 45/5/no pagination.

from the gross profit of the collieries of £44,318.[40] But it is equally possible that some of it was drawn from estate rents derived preponderantly from agriculture: estate accounts rarely distinguished before 1830 between the different sources of capital returned to the development of the estate. An estate was viewed, and operated, as an integrated concern. Thus, so far as a considerable proportion of the capital invested in coal-mining in this period is concerned, it can never be possible to distinguish between its ultimate origins in mining itself or in agriculture. Clearly one cannot rule out agricultural rents as a possible source of mining capital.

Though landowners broadened their bases by associating between themselves, only very rarely did they look for capital outside the very small circle of coalowning landowners. Fawdonfield colliery was worked in the 1720s by a partnership of seven individuals, most of whom may definitely be identified as local landowners and the remainder probably so. Shares were in sixty-fourths, the largest shareholder taking $\frac{16}{64}$ ths, and the smallest $\frac{3}{64}$ ths.[41] Most Somerset mines were worked by partnerships whose members were usually landowners, including the owner of the mine worked. Probably because of shortage of capital in an area of limited industrial resources, few Somerset partnerships were on a scale large enough to operate more than one or two collieries.[42] From time to time, however, and particularly in times of most rapid development, landowners needed to look beyond their own resources for capital, and it is this element in capital supply that is often more difficult to trace. Sir Roger Newdigate, for example, borrowed on mortgage the £20,000 necessary to reconstruct Griff colliery in Warwickshire in 1777 from the London banker, Robert Child. £12,000 of this loan was still outstanding in 1788.[43] Both John Lambton and the Marquis of Londonderry borrowed heavily in the 1820s from bankers and others, though loans of this kind were ultimately repaid and must be considered simply as means of anticipating revenue that would be used for investment. It is very likely that the anticipated revenues in these instances were the future gross profits of the mining enterprises themselves, so that the capital may be said to have been raised from ploughed-back anticipated profits. In 1824 Lambton had outstanding loans of over £40,000 borrowed from twelve lenders in round sums ranging from £450 to £10,000, and by 1827 owed no less than £250,000.[44]

[40] 'Report on Lambton collieries for 1830', LEA not numbered.
[41] GPL Cotesworth CK/6/10.   [42] Bulley 1955, 30.
[43] White thesis 1969, 86.
[44] LEA MP12/2; W. Loraine to J. G. Lambton, 2 May 1827, LEA MP11/5.

There is not a great deal of evidence that the rising country banks of the late eighteenth and early nineteenth centuries played much part in the provision of fixed capital for mining, and the relatively small role of circulating capital in the industry prevented them from assisting extensively in the form of industrial investment that was most congenial to them. In all his exceedingly thorough investigation of the records of the country banks in this period, Pressnell found little evidence of their investment in coal-mining. Gurney's of Norwich, oddly, invested 'in a colliery concern in Wales'; the North Wales Bank established in 1791 at Holywell, Flintshire, had coal-mining connections; and the Swansea and Carmarthen bank of Fendal, Jelf, and Company invested in a colliery at Abergwm in 1791. Only in the North-east do bankers appear to have played any significant part in mining investment, though even here it is unlikely that it was as significant as Cromar has claimed. Some of the partners of the Newcastle Bank founded in 1756 were closely associated with the coal industry: Ralph Carr was a grandson of one of the creators of the Grand Allies, William Cotesworth; Matthew Bell came from a family of Hostmen; and John Cookson was owner of salt and chemical works at South Shields. Probably more significant was the Sunderland bank of Russell, Allan, and Maling founded in 1787. William Russell was a very active figure in north-east mining, and there is some evidence of direct investment in the industry by this bank.[45] John Lambton borrowed heavily—up to £54,000 in 1826—from his London banker to finance his great expansion of the 1820s and was accordingly squeezed in the bank crisis of 1825-6.[46] So, too, did Lord Londonderry. A landowner borrowing for mining investment, however, borrowed *qua* landowner, and was able to offer his land as security. In general it is not easy to trace bank commitment to mining investment as distinct from the activities of individual banking partners. Banking investment is more likely to have been indirect, banking profits rather than bank deposits being converted into mining capital in the name of individual proprietors rather than in that of the bank.

Where capital was called for from beyond the immediate circle of landowners, their associates, and bankers, the vehicle was usually the partnership and, less commonly and only towards the end of the period up to 1830, the joint stock company. These forms of industrial organization, as we saw in chapter two, brought a wider range of investors into the business of mining. Partners in mining enterprises in the later eighteenth and early nineteenth centuries

[45] L. S. Pressnell, *Country Banking in the Industrial Revolution* (Oxford, 1956), 19, 23, 343; Cromar thesis 1977, 121–2.
[46] W. Loraine to J. G. Lambton, 15 Jan. 1826, LEA MP11/5.

included lawyers, clergymen, merchants, industrialists, bankers, and ships' captains as well as landowners and colliery managers and viewers. The investments of this very miscellaneous group of partners indicates the wide dispersal of sources of capital for an important and possibly growing sector of the industry.

As the scale of mining grew in the early decades of the nineteenth century the fixed capital sums required began to outgrow the resources of even wealthy merchants and landowners, and the 1820s saw the appearance, for the first time in mining history, of the mining company. Theoretically, company law since the Bubble Act of 1720 had declared illegal any joint stock of more than six partners without parliamentary approval. This restriction was not lifted until 1825, but the Hetton Coal Company, the largest of the pre-1830 mining companies, was already in existence in 1822, and some investment had taken place before that year. A letter of 1823 refers to 'the present comp.' in connection with Hetton colliery, and the 1828 list enumerates seventeen partners or shareholders.[47] The Hetton company was important not only because it was one of the most heavily capitalized companies before 1830, but also becuase it was the first undertaking to reach the seams of east Durham under the magnesian limestone overlay. This involved sinking to greater depths than ever before, and, since it was an entirely new area for mining, the opening up of a new system of railways to the coast. Several pits were sunk by the company, and the sum invested grew steadily in the company's early years. By 1828 the live and dead stock of the company, which did not include the cost of sinking and driving levels, was assessed at £108,892, to which should be added the cost of land purchased, colliers' houses, and a quay at Sunderland, amounting to £37,051.[48] But the Hetton Company was important, too, in that its huge capital came largely, if not entirely, from non-landowning sources. Its driving force came from Arthur Mowbray who left the service of Lord Stewart (later Marquis of Londonderry) to set up this venture. His fellow-shareholders (too numerous to be called partners) were of diverse origin, and much of his capital, in contrast to that of most of the rest of the north-east mines, came from outside the region. 'By dint of prowling round the Royal Exchange and Stock Market', wrote Lord Londonderry in 1828, Mowbray had 'completely got Hetton under weigh in London'.[49]

[47] Kenwood thesis 1962, 83; Lord Londonderry to John Lambton, 15 Dec. 1823, LEA MP12/20; NEI Buddle 25/III/13.
[48] DuRO NCB First Deposit NCB/I/JB/2047; DuRO Londonderry D/Lo/C150.
[49] Lord Londonderry to John Buddle, 13 Sept. 1828, NuRO NCB First Deposit NCB/I/JB/1516, quoted in Hiskey thesis 1978, 36.

The Lillieshall Company, formed to operate the Shropshire mines of the Marquis of Stafford in 1802, was no more than a device by which the Marquis raised capital by selling a half share of the enterprise to four local partners.[50]

Finally, the integration of mining with other industries provided, even early in the eighteenth century but increasingly into the early nineteenth century, an independent source of capital. In particular, the iron-making companies that went in for coalowning found their own sources of capital to do so. Since these iron companies accounted for almost twenty per cent of total coal consumption by 1830 and mostly provided their own coal supplies, this source of capital constituted an invaluable contribution to the capitalization of coal-mining by the early nineteenth century. Though the sources of capital for the iron industry were diverse, this sector of mining investment would contribute towards a shifting of the balance of capital sources in so far as landowners were, in general, far less prominent in iron industry investment than they were in mining investment. Outside the iron industry there was probably not much extensive integration with coal-mining, and where it existed, as, for example, with salt-making, the flow of investment may well have been in the opposite direction—from coal to the integrated concerns rather than from them to coal, as in the iron industry.

The structure of capital ownership in the coal industry of the eighteenth and early nineteenth centuries is therefore complex. Clearly the ownership of mining capital must not be confused with the ownership of coal-bearing land. In the mines that were owner-operated, the capital mostly came from landed sources which may have included the ploughed-back profits of previous mine-operation; but in the mines, probably the majority, that were worked on leases, the capital was put up by the lessees, and these were of varied origins. Some, as we have seen, were landowners, even landowners who were also working mines on their own land, but others were from diverse occupations. Lessees were necessarily possessed of some wealth, since they had either to buy shares in an existing mine or contribute to the capitalization of a new or developing venture. In an eighteenth- and early nineteenth-century context this meant that they were most likely to be industrialists, merchants, or bankers. The only clearly identifiable group outside these circles were the viewers whose skill and experience were not only assets in any mining enterprise, but had in a number of cases secured them rewards large enough to bring them into the investing class. In spite of the growing diversity of investors, however, it is clear that for most of the

[50] Richards 1974, 416.

eighteenth century much of the industry's capital undoubtedly came from ploughed-back profits. But while this source remained important, some at least of the capital that financed the great expansion of the late eighteenth and early nineteenth centuries was of more diverse origins. This is most obviously true in the mines that were developed in association with iron-making.

Chapter 7

Markets

Because, at the beginning of the eighteenth century, there were relatively few industrial uses for coal and none for energy purposes, almost half of the coal marketed was used for domestic heating. This imposed a restraint on the absolute scale of the demand for coal since the population of Britain at the beginning of the eighteenth century was only about six and a half million, the majority of whom probably had no effective access to coal supplies. Without new sources of demand, the growth of the market for coal would necessarily be limited to the rate of growth of the population living in areas with easy access to coal supplies. Since it was over 110 years before the British population doubled its 1700 level, the growth of demand from this source was unlikely to provide much stimulus to dramatic change in the industry. Necessarily, the substantial expansion of the industry during the eighteenth and early nineteenth centuries derived very largely from new industrial and energy uses.

i. Seasale: the coastwise and export trades

A survey of the markets for coal may best be begun by taking advantage of the fairly well-recorded coastal trades. Starting in the north, it seems unlikely that more than a small porportion of the output of Scottish mines entered the coastal trade in search of markets beyond the restricted radius of overland sale. The Ayrshire ports were not well placed for coastal markets. To the north the Clyde towns and industry were better served by local Lanarkshire suppliers, while the poor, peat-burning west coast north of the Clyde offered no possibilities whatsoever; to the south Galloway and the Solway Firth counties were more economically supplied from Cumberland. Shipments from the Ayrshire coast were accordingly confined almost entirely to exports to Ireland. On the east, both shores of the Firth of Forth were lined with mines, a fact which in itself tended to reduce the need for much coastal movement. All Scottish east-coast ports together imported 136,000 tons of Firth of Forth coal in 1800, a trade that increased only to 156,000 tons by 1815.[1] In spite of the repeal in 1793 of the duty on Scottish coal carried coastwise, the

[1] ScRO Mar and Kellie GD 124/17/580/2.

English share of the trade to Scottish east-coast ports increased from 19.5 per cent in 1800–2 to 29.3 per cent in 1813–15, and although all domestic coal consumed north of Dundee was said in 1818 to be English, largely from the Wear, Dundee itself was still taking between thirty and forty per cent of its coastwise imports from Scottish ports between 1812 and 1816.[2]

The important Cumberland coalfield also concentrated, like its Ayrshire competitor, and for similar reasons, on the export trade to Ireland, though from time to time the Lowthers explored the possibility of markets round the English coast. A calculation of 1712 suggests that they thought of trying to break into the Bristol Channel trade, and a specially commissioned study of the South Wales trade of 1805 shows that the Lowthers still fostered hopes of breaking into that market. But there is no evidence that they ever succeeded in doing so; nor did they ever succeed in getting more than isolated cargoes to London.[3] Further south, Lancashire coal found its way to the coast in the early eighteenth century mainly by means of overland carriage to Liverpool, but though some was sent from thence to Ireland, the Lancashire coast to the north offered only the smallest of markets, while the North Wales coast to the south and west was more economically served from the Dee estuary. From the late 1730s some Lancashire coal found its way to the coast on the Ribble estuary via the Douglas navigation, and after 1755 by the Sankey Brook navigation to the Mersey estuary at Runcorn; but the coastal trade from the Lancashire coalfield never assumed major importance. The Hawarden coalfield in Flintshire sent coal up the Dee estuary to Chester, but apart from exports to Ireland, this coalfield and its neighbours along the Flintshire coast had to make do with an exiguous demand along the North Wales coast.[4]

At the beginning of the eighteenth century coastwise shipments from South Wales were sent only from the ports at the western end of the coalfield—principally Swansea and Neath, with small quantities from South Burry and Porthcawl. The mines in the valleys of the eastern end of the coalfield had to wait until the construction of canals towards the end of the eighteenth century gave them access to the coast. The coastwise trade from the Gower district was very steady and grew persistently during the eighteenth century. Shipments in 1709–10 were above 25,000 tons per year, and grew to just

[2] 3 Geo. III c. 69; *PP* 1816 (473) XIV.495; ScRO Mar and Kellie GD124/17/581/2, and 585/5.

[3] CuRO Lonsdale D/Lons/W31; ibid. D/Lons/W 'Collieries and the Coal Trade'; *RC Coal* 1871, 14.

[4] A. S. Davies, 'The first steam engine in Wales and its Staffordshire owners, 1714', *TNS* 18 (1937–8); Moller thesis 1933, 425.

over 250,000 tons by the end of the century. In the early eighteenth
century the markets supplied were up the Severn valley as far as
Bewdley and Bridgnorth, Bristol, the Bristol Channel ports of Somerset, Devon and Cornwall, and round Land's End as far east as Exeter.
The steady development of steam-pumping in the Cornish coppermines created an invaluable market for the mines of the Swansea
district, a trade encouraged by the remission of the coastwise duties
in 1741.[5] There was a concentration of copper-smelting around
Swansea too, that ensured return cargoes of ore for the Swansea
colliers. By 1829 Cornwall imported over 162,000 tons of coal,
most, if not all, of which must have come from the Swansea district.[6]
After the construction of the Glamorgan and Monmouthshire canals
towards the end of the century had opened up the eastern sector
of the coalfield, shipments from Cardiff and Newport, which had
been on the smallest of scales earlier in the century, began to assume
importance. Newport, better placed for the trade of the upper Bristol
Channel than Cardiff, took the lion's share: coastwise exports of less
than 10,000 tons a year in 1798 grew rapidly thereafter—32,277
tons in 1800 to 148,019 tons in 1809. Most of the trade from
Cardiff and Newport in the early nineteenth century was up-channel
or directly cross-channel to Bristol, Gloucester, Chepstow, and Bridg-
water, only about one-fifth finding sales to the west.[7] The small scale
of the Forest of Dean industry during the eighteenth century left it
poorly placed to compete with its larger-scale neighbours further
west, but the organizational changes of the early nineteenth century
allowed it to begin to find markets by coastal and river navigation.
Some house coal was shipped from Lydney down the estuary to
Bristol, and other sales were found across and higher up the Severn
in Gloucester as well as up the Wye.[8]

   The Somerset coalfield, and those in the East and West Midlands,
Derbyshire, and Yorkshire, were all too far from coasts to be able to
enter into the coastwise trade. Only in the district immediately to
the South of the Humber were Yorkshire coals, making use of canals
and river navigations, able to compete with coal shipped coastwise
from the North-east. In the 1820s and early 1830s coalowners from
both the North-east and Derbyshire sent reporters to Boston, Wisbech, and other ports south of the Humber to study coal marketing
there. Thomas Croudace reported to John Lambton in the North-
east in 1822 that he was 'sorry to find that the collieries in the
N'borhood of Leeds, Barnsley and Sheffield are interfering very

[5] 14 Geo.II, c.41.   [6] D. T. Williams 1940, 194; CuRO Lonsdale D/Lons/W38.
[7] Jones thesis 1929, 208–9; CuRO Lonsdale D/Lons/W38.
[8] Davis thesis 1959, 47.

much with our trade to various coasting markets, Boston, Wisbech, etc. They are supplied by canals, free of duty and their trade is increasing considerably.' In 1831 Derbyshire coalowners received a report about sales of Derbyshire and Yorkshire coal in Lincoln, Boston, and many other Lincolnshire and Northamptonshire towns. The Yorkshire coals, in particular, were preferred by domestic consumers, brewers, and brick-makers for their superior quality.[9]

The coastal trades of Scotland, Wales, and the English west coast were, therefore, very local, few cargoes travelling more than fifty or sixty miles, and most appreciably less. In sharp contrast to this localization, however, almost all ports on the English south and east coasts were supplied from the north-east coalfield. Though figures are not available for the eighteenth century to assess precisely the share of the north-east ports in the whole British coastwise trade in coal, there can be little doubt that it predominated. Table 7.1, which sets out the position in 1816, show that in the early nineteenth

Table 7.1 *Coastwise shipments of coal, 1816*

Mining Region	Port (with creeks)	Coastwise shipments (000s of tons)	% share of total
North-east	Newcastle	1,708	
	Sunderland	961	
	Blyth	123	
		2,792	81.5
South Wales	Cardiff	7	
	Newport	172	
	Llanelli	31	
	Pembroke	29	
	Swansea	166	
		405	11.8
Cumberland	Whitehaven	23	0.7
Lancashire	Liverpool	34	1.0
Yorkshire	Hull	15	0.4
Scotland	various	157	4.6
		3,424	100.0

Source: PP 1818 (415) XIV.165.

[9] Thomas Croudace to J. G. Lambton, 22 May 1822, Lea MP11/1; Report by George Pickering and John Burton, 1831, DeRO Miller Mundy 517.

century, in spite of considerable growth in coastwise shipments from South Wales, the North-east still dominated the trade. The situation changed little by 1824 when a further return showed a total coastal trade of 4.1 million tons in a year when the north-east ports contributed 79.5 per cent of the total trade.[10]

The dominance of the north-east ports in the coasting trade was assured by the grip of the North-east on the London market. In 1830 London took ninety-six per cent of its coastwise coal imports from the north-east ports, and as yet very little coal entered London other than coastwise. The remaining few per cent of London's coastwise imports came, according to a return of 1811–13, from South Wales (Swansea, Pembroke, and Neath) and Scotland (Inverkeithing and Greenock). There had been small shipments, mostly very small, from South Wales, Scotland, Cumberland, and Hull in the mid-eighteenth century.[11] Table 7.2, which illustrates the growth of London's coal imports over the whole period from 1700 to 1830, shows a four-fold increase over those years, a rate of growth probably somewhat faster than that of London's population, indicating some rise in per capita consumption and possibly the expansion of the 're-export' trade up the Thames valley. This growth was clearly rather irregular, being concentrated largely in the periods 1715–30, 1760–75, and 1785 onwards. While there is little doubt that domestic heating was the prime source of demand in the London market, London's many industries—brewing, baking, brick-making, ship-building, metal-working and glass-making—together made up a significant share of the total. It was believed in Newcastle—'it is a well ascertained fact'—that between 1814 and 1819 gas manufacture and steam-engines alone added 185,000 tons to London's demand for coal.[12]

Table 7.2 shows, too, that, while London accounted for almost two-thirds of the coastwise shipments from north-east ports in the first half of the eighteenth century, this share diminished gradually during the second half, accounting for little more than half by the early decades of the nineteenth century. The importance of coastal markets outside London—a trade known in the North-east simply as 'the coast'[13]—has tended to be overlooked in the past. Table 7.3 sets out, so far as the available data permit, the coastwise shipments from north-east ports. Throughout the period 1700–1830 this trade was heavily confined to the two ports of Newcastle and

[10] *PP* 1825 (124) XX.363.
[11] *SC Coal Trade* 1836, 137–8; NEI Watson 8/9/329; *RC Coal* 1871, Comm.E. 15–22.
[12] NEI Watson 5/25/3.
[13] NEI Buddle 22/149.

Table 7.2 *Coastwise imports of coal into London from all*
British ports, 1700-1830

Period	Annual average (000s of tons)	Inter-quinquennial annual average rate of increase	London's share of North-east coastwise shipments
1700-4	445	—	n.d.
1705-9	458	0.6	n.d.
1710-14	479	0.9	n.d.
1715-19	549	2.6	n.d.
1720-4	597	1.7	63.7
1725-9	642	1.5	63.8
1730-4	616	−0.8	63.8
1735-9	643	0.9	n.d.
1740-4	643	0.0	n.d.
1745-9	636	−0.2	64.2
1750-4	677	1.3	60.2
1755-9	670	−0.2	60.5
1760-4	728	1.7	62.4
1765-9	817	2.5	60.5
1770-4	868	1.2	59.9
1775-9	865	−0.1	57.6
1780-4	896	0.7	60.4
1785-9	1,002	2.4	58.0
1790-4	1,061	1.2	57.0
1795-9	1,129	1.3	55.2
1800-4	1,234	1.9	54.8
1805-9	1,299	1.1	52.9
1810-14	1,435	2.1	53.0
1815-19	1,551	1.6	54.7
1820-4	1,704	3.1	53.7
1825-9	1,953	1.8	58.6
1830	2,079	—	n.d.

Note on source: This table is compiled from Table 7.3 and from the following series:

1700-10, 1713-1806	NuRO Joint Coal Owners' Association 263 Minute book 1805-15, 56-8.
1701-10, 1713-1806	Moller thesis 1933, 797-8.
1713-1806	NEI Buddle 14/205-7; also in NEI Bell 14/7/519-21.
1745-64	BL Add. MSS 38, 382, fo. 8.
1795-1808	NEI Watson 13/97/no pagination.
1795-1817	NEI Watson 5/9/10.
1800-26	NEI Buddle Atkinson 45/5/no pagination.
1806-8	NEI Watson 8/9/100.
1811-19	NEI Watson 5/26, pamphlet (no title) n.d. but probably 1820.
1822-8	*SC Lords Coal Trade* 1830, 139.
1826-30	*Account of Coal imported into London*, PP 1833 (25) XXXIII. 199.

Most of the above series agreed where they overlap, but not all do. Where they do not agree, the differences are mostly small, and are almost certainly to be explained by the use of different starting and ending dates for the year, although all the series use a full calendar year for each of the years covered. In compiling this table preference has been given to series that agree at points of overlap.

Table 7.3. *Coastwise shipments of coal from north-east ports, 1700–1830*
(annual averages, 000s of tons)

Period	Newcastle		Sunderland		Blyth		Total	Inter-period rate of increase (% per annum)
	000 tons	share of total	000 tons	share of total	000 tons	share of total		
1700–4	515		—		—		—	
1705–9	478		—		—			
1710–14	445¹		—		—		—	
1715–19	—		—		—		—	
1720–4	637²	71.2	(226)³	25.3	32⁷	3.5	895	
1725–9	680	71.1	(247)	25.8	29	3.1	956	1.4
1730–4	(697)	72.6	(232)	24.2	31	3.2	960	0.1
1735–9	(689)	66.4	(297)⁴	28.6	51	5.0	1,037	1.6
1740–4	(684)		—		38			
1745–9	(685)	66.5	(314)⁵	30.5	31	3.0	1,030	
1750–4	(742)	65.5	(342)	30.2	48	4.3	1,132	2.0
1755–9	(683)	61.6	(379)	34.2	46	4.2	1,108	−0.4
1760–4	(743)	63.3	(388)	33.1	42	3.6	1,173	1.2
1765–9	865	64.0	(428)	31.7	58	4.3	1,351	3.0
1770–4	886	60.8	(507)	34.8	65	4.4	1,458	1.6
1775–9	868	58.7	(519)	35.1	91	6.2	1,478	0.3
1780–4	930	62.3	(478)	32.0	85	5.7	1,493	0.2
1785–9	1,068	59.8	(620)	34.7	97	5.5	1,785	3.9
1790–4	1,104	59.6	648	35.0	100	5.4	1,852	0.7
1795–9	1,170	59.0	712	35.9	101	5.1	1,983	1.4
1800–4	1,362	60.5	770	34.2	118	5.3	2,250	2.7
1805–9	1,500	61.1	834	34.0	122	4.9	2,456	1.8
1810–14	1,659	60.8	917	33.6	153	5.6	2,729	2.2
1815–19	1,729	60.9	982	34.6	127	4.5	2,838	0.8
1820–4	1,870	58.9	1,161	36.6	144	4.5	3,175	2.4
1825–9	1,922	55.8	1,391⁶	40.4	132	3.8	3,445	1.8
1830	2,167				134			

Notes: ¹ 1710 only.   ² 1722–4 only.   ³ 1721–4 only.   ⁴ 1735–6 only.
⁵ 1748–9 only.   ⁶ 1825–8 only.   ⁷ 1722–4 only.

Notes on sources:
The principal difficulty arising out of the sources for this table is to distinguish the coastwise trade from total seasale. Many sources speak either of 'exports' or 'the vend', and these expressions have been taken to mean the sum of coastwise plus overseas exports. Some sources distinguish explicitly between the 'coastwise' and 'overseas' trades, and these have been used wherever they are available in the construction of this table. Unfortunately there are substantial gaps in the 'coastwise' series, and these have had to be filled by 'vend' or 'exports' series reduced by estimates of overseas exports. The following series (all originally in Newcastle chaldrons) have been used in the compilation of the table. Those marked 'C' relate explicitly to the coastwise trade, and those marked 'V' relate to 'Vend' or 'exports'.

Newcastle: 1700–10   C   Dendy 1901, 260.
1722–39   C   NEI Grand Allies, Partnership minute book 1727–38, 18/ volume not numbered/68.
1740–90   V   NEI Buddle 14/205–7; also in NuRO Joint Coal Owners' Association, Minute book 1805–15, 56–8.
1791–7   C   First SC Coal Trade 1800, 614.
1798–1821 C   NuRO Joint Coal Owners' Association, Minute book 1821–2, 140.

[*See opposite page for Notes on sources cont.*]

Sunderland. These, of course, were customs precincts, for, in the former case, the coastal shipments actually left from North or South Shields at the mouth of the Tyne. Small quantities also sailed regularly from Blyth, again a customs precinct which embraced Hartley, Seaton Sluice, and Cullercoats as well as Blyth: the greater part of Blyth's exports in fact emanated from the Delaval mines at Hartley. In the early decades of the nineteenth century efforts were made to open up new outlets less dependent upon the monopolizing tendencies of commercial operators on the rivers Tyne and Wear, or upon wayleave owners. As mining began to spread into the area of east Durham under the magnesian limestone covering in the years after the French Wars, the attractions of the coast south of Sunderland led to the establishment of Seaham by the Marquis of Londonderry in the 1820s. The development of longer railways with steam-locomotives also encouraged owners in west Durham to develop outlets on the Tees. In 1830 some 24,314 tons left Stockton-on-Tees, the beginnings of what was quickly to become an important trade. A return of 1827 showed that this trade was distributed to seventeen east coast ports from Aberdeen to Ramsgate, with London taking less than one-tenth.[14]

Though the figures in Table 7.3 involve a considerable element of

---

	1800–23	C	NEI Buddle 51/185–6.
	1821–30	C	Porter 1847, 278.
Sunderland:	1721–36, 1748–87	V	Miller thesis 1978, App. B.
	1788–99	C	*SC Coal Trade* 1800, 591–2.
	1800–23	C	NEI Buddle 51/185–6.
	1822–7	C	NEI Buddle Atkinson 45/5/no pagination.
Blyth:	1722–39	C	NEI Grand Allies, Partnership minute book, 1727–38, 18/volume not numbered/68.
	1725–1830	C	NEI Watson 8/19/insert.

Corrections to the 'vend' series for Newcastle 1740–90 and for Sunderland 1721–36 and 1747–87 have been made in the following way:

Newcastle 1740–90:   −9.5 per cent. (In 1730 the quantity of exports was 9.48 per cent of coastwise shipments, and in 1791–1800 they averaged 9.42 per cent (Moller thesis 1933, 717; and *SC Coal Trade* 1800, 614).)

Sunderland 1721–36:   a subtraction varying according to a linear interpolation based on known ratios of exports to coastwise of 15.0 per cent in 1710 and 21.2 per cent in 1730 (Moller thesis 1933, 717), and remaining constant at 21.2 per cent from 1731 to 1736.

1748–87:   −21 per cent. (In 1730 exports amounted to 21.2 per cent of coastwise shipments, and in 1791–3 they averaged 20.8 per cent. (Moller thesis 1933, 717; *SC Coal Trade* 1800, 614.)

Estimates derived in this way are shown in the table within brackets. A dash (−) indicates that no data are available.

[14] *SC Coal Trade* 1836, 137–8; DuRO NCB First Deposit NCB/I/JB/607.

estimation, they indicate a probable trebling of north-east coastwise
exports between the 1720s and the 1820s. Bearing in mind the high
share of London in this trade, it is hardly surprising that this growth
was concentrated in much the same periods—1725–35, the 1760s,
and after 1785—as was the London trade. Moller's study of the
early eighteenth-century port books gives some indication of the
distribution of the trade to 'the coast'. In 1710, out of 413,387 tons
shipped coastwise from Newcastle, 345,910 tons, or 83.7 per cent
of the total, were destined for London. King's Lynn, with ninety-
one shipments out of the total of 1,947 (approximately five per
cent) was the next most important destination, followed by Portsmouth, where the naval dockyard was probably the principal consumer, with seventy-three, Yarmouth with sixty-eight, Sandwich
with sixty-six, Wells (which must be Wells-next-the-Sea in Norfolk)
with sixty-three, Southampton with thirty-six, Rochester with thirty-
four, and Hull with twenty-nine. Almost every port on the east and
south coasts as far as Exeter received some cargoes of north-east coal.
While Newcastle's trade was therefore extremely wide, embracing
ports up to 600 miles away, it was nevertheless heavily concentrated
on London. Sunderland's trade, on the other hand, growing more
rapidly during the eighteenth century from smaller beginnings, was
more evenly distributed between London and 'the coast'. In 1710
London was the destination of only twenty-eight per cent of Sunderland's shipments, Yarmouth taking thirteen per cent, King's Lynn
eight per cent, Boston seven per cent and Whitby six per cent. By
1749, an even smaller share went to London—only eight per cent,
while Yarmouth took twenty-one per cent and Whitby eight per
cent. In the two years between October 1811 and October 1813,
London imported only 7.6 per cent of its total requirements from
Sunderland, as against 87.6 per cent from Newcastle, at a time when,
as Table 7.3 shows, Sunderland's total coastwise trade amounted to
more than half of Newcastle's.[15]

   Table 7.4 shows the distribution of English and Welsh coastwise
imports for the year 1829. With the exception of the coal-exporting
counties of Wales, the North-east, and the North-west, every coastal
county imported coal: coal-producing coastal counties like Yorkshire
and Somerset took small quantities only into areas not served by
their own mines. Gloucestershire, though technically a coastal
county, is omitted from this return presumably because its imports,
from Newport and the Forest of Dean, were exempted from the
coastwise duty.
   With relatively few economically worked sources of coal of her

   [15] NuRO Joint Coal Owners' Association 263, Minute Book 1805–15, 243.

Table 7.4. *English and Welsh counties into which coal was brought coastwise, 1829*

County	Coastwise imports (000s of tons)	Percentage share of total coastwise imports
London	2,057	52.5
Kent	233	5.9
Sussex	171	4.4
Hampshire	167	4.3
Dorset	64	1.6
Devon	273	7.0
Cornwall	163	4.1
Somerset	28	0.7
Anglesey	72	1.8
Yorkshire	34	0.9
Lincolnshire	32	0.8
Cambridgeshire	38	1.0
Norfolk	369	9.4
Suffolk	83	2.1
Essex	136	3.5
Total	3,920	100.0

Source: PP 1830 (301) XXVII.131.

own, Ireland was, throughout the eighteenth and early nineteenth centuries, a useful market for coalfields suitably placed for export from the Scottish, English, and Welsh west coasts. The areas that took advantage of this opportunity were principally Ayrshire, Cumberland, and the western section of the South Wales coalfield, though some south Lancashire and Flintshire exports also found their way to Ireland.[16] Given the low level of industrial development in Ireland at this period there can be little doubt that most of the coal exported from the British west coast was consumed for domestic heating in the principal towns of the Irish east and south coasts, though urban industries like brewing, sugar-boiling, and glass-making, particularly in Dublin, supplemented later by the linen industry of Ulster, added to the demand. Table 7.5 illustrates, from the available statistics, the growth of this trade.

During the eighteenth century the largest contribution to the trade was made by Cumberland. It was, indeed, a trade of the utmost importance to this coalfield, since apart from an exiguous landsale, it had very few other outlets. From the effective beginnings of

[16] Unerigg Colliery Book, 1762–3, CuRO Benson D/Ben/3540.

Table 7.5. *British coal exports to Ireland, 1700–1828*
(Annual totals or averages, 000s of tons)

Year or period	Quantity
1700	40
1730	86
1750	98
1770	174
1780	211
1790	333
1800	399
1804	506
1816–19	625
1820–4	660
1825–8	717

Note on sources: This table is compiled from the following sources:
  Scottish exports 1700–90: L. E. Cochran 'Scottish trade with Ireland in the 18th century' (unpublished paper presented to Economic History Conference, Loughborough 1981).
  Britain 1700–1800: L. M. Cullen, *Anglo-Irish Trade, 1660–1800* (Manchester, 1968), 79. Cullen's figures are drawn from the *Journals of the Irish House of Commons*, Vol. 14. (1700–year ending 25 December; 1720–50—years ending 25 March; 1770–1800—years ending 5 January).
  Britain 1804: CuRO Lonsdale D/Lons/W/Collieries and the Coal Trade, 29.
  Britain 1816–18: *PP* 1818 (415) XIV.165.
  Britain 1819–28: *RC Coal* 1871, Comm.E, 48.

large-scale mining in Cumberland at the end of the seventeenth century the Irish trade was the key to its development. Whitehaven exports to Ireland grew from 18,520 tons in 1710–11 to 25,209 tons in 1719–20, and to 49,968 tons in 1739–40; by the early years of the nineteenth century Whitehaven alone, supplied almost exclusively by the Lowther mines, was exporting an annual average for the years 1803–14 of 196,900 tons, probably about one-third of the entire Irish trade. To this should be added 29,250 tons (annual average for the years 1809–13) exported through Workington, Harrington, and Maryport. The Workington trade had, however, fallen substantially during the French Wars: from an annual average of 44,690 tons in 1800–7 the trade declined to 28,609 tons in 1808–16.[17] A high proportion of the Cumberland trade was with Dublin. In 1815 sixty-four per cent of all shipments from Whitehaven were to Dublin, followed by Belfast taking thirteen per cent, Strangford

[17] Moller thesis 1933, 790; 'Notebook containing replies to Mr Lyson's queries on the Whitehaven collieries, 1815', CuRO Lonsdale, Colliery reports not yet listed; CuRO Curwen D/Cu6/18.

taking eight per cent and Waterford six per cent: the remaining eight per cent of the shipments were divided between nine other east and south coast ports.[18] The great hold of Whitehaven on the Dublin trade was the achievement of Sir James Lowther in the first half of the eighteenth century. 'Neither the Welsh, who before him were in possession hereof', wrote Dr Brownrigg to Sir James's successor in 1765 in an effort to dissuade him from petitioning Parliament for a statutory monopoly of the trade, 'nor the Scotch at Ayr, Irwin [Irvine] and Saltcoats, who long strove hard to gain it, nor the Irish from Newry and Ballycastle, aided by £100,000 of the public money, could stand in competition with him therein.'[19] By 1816, a year for which a detailed statement of the Irish trade is available, the geographical division of the trade was as set out in Table 7.6, while Table 7.7 sets out in more detail, for the year 1814, the distribution of the trade between both British and Irish ports.

Table 7.6. *Origins of British coal exports to Ireland*
1816

Mining Region	(000s of tons)	Percentage share of total
Cumberland	224	36.5
Scotland	150	24.5
South Wales	126	20.6
Lancashire	73	11.9
North Wales	26	4.2
Others	14	2.3

Source: PP 1818 (415) XIV.165.

The Scottish trade was carried on almost entirely from the Ayrshire coast, initially from the ports of Saltcoats, Irvine, and Ardrossan, to which, in a £100,000 investment between 1808 and 1812, the Duke of Portland added Troon, connecting it to his mines near Kilmarnock by a waggonway. Not even the subsidizing of exports from the Clyde to Ireland in 1815 by the ephemeral combination of Glasgow and Monkland canal coalowners by means of a levy on the local trade succeeded in breaking the Ayrshire hold on the Scottish trade to Ireland.[20] Though Scotland provided 21.6 per cent of the trade in 1709, it failed to retain this share in the remainder of the

[18] CuRO Lonsdale D/Lons/W Miscellaneous colliery accounts.
[19] Dr Brownrigg to Sir James Lowther, 29 Aug. 1765, CuRO Lonsdale D/Lons/W/ Correspondence, Bundle 47.   [20] Hamilton 1930, 135.

Table 7.7. *Shipments of coal from specified British ports to specified Irish ports, 1814*
(number of ships)

From	Destination								
	Belfast	Cork	Dublin	Strangford	Waterford	Wexford	Wicklow	Others[1]	Total
Whitehaven	154	26	751	93	69	0	6	67	1,166
Irvine	286	46	374	29	3	0	0	238	1,042
Liverpool	5	46	147	11	56	89	71	318	743
Workington	214	0	267	30	1	0	1	185	698
Cardiff	1	294	6	0	20	4	0	140	465
Llanelli	4	83	81	0	51	16	5	143	383
Swansea	0	25	43	0	145	24	5	154	376
Ayr	34	62	78	9	7	0	0	129	319
Greenock and Glasgow	54	24	44	0	33	0	0	156	311
Chester	1	5	201	1	2	0	6	10	226
Neath	0	58	11	0	0	1	11	27	108
Others[2]	51	16	84	0	8	13	5	127	304
Total	804	685	2,087	173	395	147	110	1,694	6,141

Notes: [1] Includes Drogheda, Dundalk, Limerick, Londonderry, Newry, Youghall, Ballyraine, Larne, Newport and Westport, Sligo, Dingle, Galway, Killybegs, Kinsale, Ross, Coleraine, Carlingford.
[2] Includes Preston, Maryport, Parkgate, Harrington, Pembroke, Caernarvon, Newport, Newcastle, Saltcoats, Milford, Ilfracombe.

Source: CuRO Lonsdale D/Lons/W/Miscellaneous Colliery Accounts.

eighteenth century, only recovering it again in the early years of the nineteenth century.[21] Further south, some Lancashire coal was shipped to Ireland from Liverpool, but transport costs from the coalfield to Liverpool, even with the new waterways of the mid-eighteenth century, placed it at a disadvantage in competition with Cumberland.[22] Some small shipments were also made in the early decades of the eighteenth century from the Flintshire ports of Bagillt and Mostyn, but the trade had virtually ceased by 1740.[23] In South Wales the most westerly portion of the coalfield was naturally most advantageously placed for the Irish trade, and most of the trade passed though the port of Swansea. It grew steadily from small beginnings early in the eighteenth century to reach about 7,500 tons in 1719, 54,000 tons in 1803, and 209,000 tons in 1828.[24]

The third sea-borne market for coal in the eighteenth and early nineteenth centuries was the foreign trade. It was not to be expected that a commodity with a value so low in relation to its bulk should find extensive overseas markets in an age when few ships carried more than 300 tons: but lack of coal resources in some nearby countries ensured modest overseas markets throughout the period. Unfortunately there are few good statistics of the trade: Table 7.8 brings together such as there are relating to the export trade from north-east ports, and Table 7.9 presents a broken series of British coal exports from 1765 onwards. The two tables together establish that while the North-east, for obvious geographical reasons, took little part in the Irish trade, it accounted for a fairly high proportion of the foreign trade, at least for the brief period in the early nineteenth century when it is possible to distinguish the foreign trade from the Irish trade. This is confirmed by a return of 1830 which showed that 67.5 per cent of the exports to colonial and foreign countries in that year passed through north-eastern ports. A further 10.4 per cent was shipped from Liverpool.[25] Table 7.9 makes it clear that the foreign and colonial trade in coal was never of the first importance to the mining industry in the eighteenth and early nineteenth centuries. From less than three per cent of total production in the 1770s, the trade fell to less than two per cent by 1830. Wars were periodically damaging to the trade, and a heavy export duty was permanently injurious. The sharp growth in the trade after 1815

[21] Duckham 1970, 225–6.

[22] Langton 1979, 172.

[23] A. S. Davies, 'The first steam engine in Wales and its Staffordshire owners, 1714', *TNS* 18 (1937–8), 67; Dodd 1929, 199; Gruffydd thesis 1981, 183.

[24] D. T. Williams 1940, 198; 'Collieries and the Coal Trade', 11, CuRO Lonsdale D/Lons/W38; *RC Coal* 1871, 50.

[25] *PP* 1833 (25) XXXIII.199.

Table 7.8. *Overseas exports from north-east ports, 1700–1830*
(annual averages, 000s of tons)

Period	Newcastle	Sunderland	Blyth	Total
1700	33	24	n.d.	—
1710	27	27	n.d.	—
1715–19	n.d.	n.d.	n.d.	—
1722–4	49	n.d.	4	—
1725–9	46	n.d.	4	—
1730–4	57	50[1]	4	111
1735–9	51	72[2]	5	128
1790–4	108[3]	129	0	237
1795–9	111	15	0	126
1800–4	127	33[4]	0	160
1805–9	81	9	0	90
1810–14	56	10	0	66
1815–19	119	40	2	161
1820–4	128	41	4	173
1825–9	159	45[5]	4	208
1830	197	142	n.d.	c.310

Notes: [1] 1730 only.   [2] 1738–9 only.   [3] 1791–4 only.
[4] 1801–4 only.   [5] 1825–8 only.

Note on sources: This table is compiled from the following series, all in Newcastle chaldrons in the original:

Newcastle:	1700	unpublished paper by A. Dietz (Glasgow, n.d.)
	1710, 1730	Moller thesis 1933, 751–3.
	1722–6, 1722–39	NEI Grand Allies 18/volume not numbered (Partnership minute book 1727–38), 21, 68.
	1791–9	*First SC Coal Trade* 1800, 614.
	1798–1817	NuRO Ridley (Blagdon) ZRI 25/31.
	1798–1821	NuRO Joint Coal Owners' Association 263 Minute book 1822–3, 12.
	1801–30	Porter 1847, 278 (in tons).
	1802–5	NEI Bell 15/11/48.
	1802–21	NEI Watson 11/18/12.
	1806–8, 1810–12	NEI Watson 8/9/99.
	1822–4, 1822–6	NEI Buddle Atkinson 45/5/no pagination.
	1830	*PP* 1833 (25) XXXIII.199.
Sunderland:	1700	unpublished paper by A. Dietz (Glasgow, n.d.)
	1710, 1730	Moller thesis 1933, 758.
	1738–9	W. M. Hughes 1970, 229.
	1790–9, 1817–21	*PP* 1821 (373) XVII.83. This series has been moved forward one year for the years 1790–9 in this paper in error, as may be corrected from the *First SC Coal Trade* 1800, 614.
	1801–28	Porter 1847, 278 (in tons).
	1822–7	NEI Buddle Atkinson 45/5/no pagination.
	1830	*PP* 1833 (25) XXXIII.199.
Blyth:	1722–6, 1722–39	NEI Grand Allies 18/volume not numbered (Partnership minute book 1727–38), 21, 68.
	1725–1831	NEI Watson 8/19/insert.
	1798–1817	NuRO Ridley (Blagdon) ZRI 25/31.
	1798–1821	NuRO Joint Coal Owners' Association 263 Minute book 1822–3, 140.
	1812–21	NEI Watson 11/18/13.
	1822–4	NEI Buddle Atkinson 45/5/no pagination.

Table 7.9. *British exports of coal (Ireland, colonial, and foreign),*
1765-1830
(annual averages, 000s of tons)

Period	Total Ireland, colonial and foreign	Foreign and colonial only
1765-9	447	(270)
1770-4	414	(244)
1775-9	449	(240)
1780-4	414	(200)
1785-9	611	(280)
1790-4	684	(350)
1795-9	555	(150)
1800-4	596	(200)
1805-8	625	(120)
1816-19	n.d.	250
1820-4	932	265
1825-8	1,062	345
1830	n.d.	504

Note on sources: This table is compiled from the following series:
1765-1808   Schumpeter 1960, Tables VIII and IX.
1816-29   PP 1830-1 (267) X.331.
1819-28   RC Coal 1871, Appendix to Report of Comm.E, 48.
1830   PP 1833 (25) XXXIII.199.

No attempt has been made to adapt Schumpeter's figures for the period before 1765 (her series starts in 1697), because they have the appearance of being incomplete. For the whole period of her Table VIII (1697-1780), coal exports are shown in Winton (i.e. London) chaldrons, Newcastle chaldrons, and tons. This was the practice of the Customs department, which received returns in these different measures depending upon the group of ports from which the exports originated: they are not conversions one of the other, but must be aggregated to give total exports. (Parliamentary returns were still presented in this inconvenient form in the 1820s.) Until 1764, however, Schumpeter's Table VIII lists only exports in Winton chaldrons, and the absence of any figures in Newcastle chaldrons can only suggest that, for whatever reasons, exports from north-east ports are omitted from the table for this period. They start suddenly in 1765 at a level (annual average 1765-9 of 323,000 tons) which cannot indicate the beginnings of a new trade. (Moller has shown, from the Port Books, exports from Newcastle and Sunderland of 54,000 tons in 1710, and 114,000 tons in 1730 (thesis 1933, 716-17), and there is a complete series from 1722 onwards showing regular exports from Blyth (see Table 7.7).) The exports in Winton chaldrons in Schumpeter's Tables VIII and IX must relate principally to exports to Ireland from Cumberland and South Wales, while her series of 'Kennel', measured in tons, almost certainly relates to exports of Cannel coal from Lancashire.

There are two further problems arising out of the export statistics. First, for the purposes of trade statistics, Ireland was treated as a foreign country until some time after the Union of 1800: Schumpeter's series clearly include the Irish trade as 'overseas' until they end in 1808. The 1819-28 table is sub-divided into separate series for Ireland, the colonies, and foreign countries, and a comparison of the last two columns of this table shows that the 1816-29 series excludes Ireland. For the sake of continuity with the long Schumpeter series, in this table exports to Ireland have been included as 'overseas' for the years when these figures are available. Second, Schumpeter's tables relate to exports from English and Welsh ports only to 1791, and from British ports from 1792 to 1808. An estimate of Scottish overseas exports (including those to Ireland) derived by making linear interpolations based on an assumption of 10,000 tons in 1700 and an annual average of 73,572 in 1790-4 has been added to the Schumpeter series between 1765 and 1791. (T. C. Smout, *Scottish Trade on the Eve of Union, 1660-1707* (Edinburgh, 1963), 224-9; and *First SC Coal Trade 1800*, 615-21.

Exports to foreign and colonial destinations only from 1765 to 1808 have been estimated by deducting estimates of exports to Ireland derived from Table 7.5 from the 'total' exports. These estimates are shown in the table within brackets.

probably owed more to the reduction of the duty on small coal than to the restoration of trade with the ending of the French war.

While it is generally true, as Table 7.10 shows from the small amount of information available, that the bulk of coal exports were sent to countries immediately across the North Sea and the English Channel, small quantities found their way further afield, a distribution that had also prevailed during the first half of the eighteenth century. Some coal, for example, was shipped to Russia during the 1820s, and there were similar shipments amounting to between ten and twenty per cent of all sailings from Newcastle in the first half of the eighteenth century through the Sound to the Baltic.[26]

Table 7.10. *Distribution of coal export markets,*
1794–1830
(per cent of total exports)

Destination	From North-east 1794	From North-east 1826	From Great Britain 1830
Russia	0.4	4.5	5.3
Denmark	—	27.4	19.8
Germany	1.4	11.9	15.0
Holland	62.9	0.9	4.5
France	15.8	16.8	10.3
United States	3.9	2.0	6.3
Channel Islands	3.1	9.2	9.8
Colonies	—	10.1	15.5
Others	12.5	17.2	13.5

Sources: North-east 1794 and 1826: NEI Buddle Atkinson 45/5/no pagination.
Great Britain 1830: *PP* 1833 (25) XXXIII.119.

It is likely that these took advantage of low freights as return cargoes for the massive imports of Baltic timber. The coal exported to the Continent and the Baltic was mainly of low quality, and, as these trades were severely reduced during the French wars at the beginning of the nineteenth century, it was the collieries like Washington New colliery in County Durham that produced a high proportion of this type of coal that were disproportionately affected.[27] Small quantities, as Table 7.10 shows, were shipped to 'the Plantations', which after 1783 must mean the West Indies (nine per cent of total exports in 1830), and there is evidence in the early nineteenth

[26] Moller thesis 1933, 751–7.   [27] NEI Buddle 3/153.

century of shipments to Malta, Gibraltar, the East Indies, St. Helena, Brazil, Canada, Newfoundland.[28] The single colliery of Pitfirrane in Fife exported very widely in the early eighteenth century. Between 1714 and 1738 cargoes were sent to Dieppe, Lisbon, Rotterdam, Danzig, Bergen, Bilbao, Bordeaux, Ostend, Christiansand, Copenhagen, Amsterdam, Gothenburg, Hamburg, and Stavanger.[29]

Not all collieries, even in the principal exporting districts like the North-east and South Wales, shared in the export trade, but those that did seem to have made it a major part of their business. A list of north-east collieries for the years 1804–6 shows only ten out of thirty-one collieries vending coal overseas. Some, like Garesfield, Marley Hill, and Whitfield, sold more overseas than coastwise, but nearly all exporting collieries sold a significant proportion of their output abroad. Adair's Main colliery, for which a detailed breakdown of sales exists for the years 1804–7, sold 12.3 per cent of its total output overseas in these years.[30]

ii. *Landsale: domestic and industrial consumers*

At the opening of the eighteenth century the three divisions of the sea-borne trade together accounted for nearly forty per cent of all coal sales: by the 1820s the growth of new landsale markets had almost halved this share. The preponderant proportion of total consumption that was carried from pit to consumer either by inland navigation or surface transport, is, unfortunately, even less amenable to precise measurement than is the sea-borne trade. Not only do we have access to only random figures of canal and river traffic, but the consumption of coal by major industries like iron is often concealed by the vertical integration of mining and iron-making in single enterprises. In the north-east coalfield, too, better documented than other coalfields in respect of its sea-borne trade, there was little interest in recording the landsale. Corporate regulation of the trade from the Hostmen's Company in the seventeenth century through organizations like the Grand Allies in the eighteenth century and the Joint Coal Owners' Association of the early nineteenth century were concerned almost exclusively with control over the sea-borne trade —the Vend—and allowed owners complete freedom for their landsale. The often detailed statistical information prepared by these organizations related exclusively to collieries participating in the

[28] Returns for 1822–6 and 1828, NEI Buddle Atkinson 45/5/no pagination; *PP* 1833 (25) XXXIII.199.
[29] NLS Halkett of Pitfirrane 6482/59.
[30] NEI Watson 8/9/29; NEI Buddle 23/42.

sea-borne trade, and it is often difficult to trace even the existence of the landsale collieries. Yet they were very numerous. In 1810 Bailey listed thirty-four 'water sale' collieries in County Durham with 'vends' totalling three and a half million tons (substantially greater than the actual seasale from the county at that time), and thirty-five additional, 'landsale' collieries selling 390,000 tons. Most of the seasale collieries also enjoyed some landsale even where seasale was clearly the principal business. New Washington colliery in County Durham, for example, sold 1,100 tons landsale in the second half of 1801 compared with nearly 52,000 tons seasale. In the ten-year period 1792–1802 the Spanish Closes and Heaton collieries on Tyneside sold 1.6 per cent of their total output landsale. Another, Benwell, between 1799 and 1806 sold 14.3 per cent landsale, while a third, Adair's Main, sold as much coal locally by landsale in 1804–5 as it did by sea.[31] Clearly the landsale collieries, even in the North-east, the coalfield of large-scale mining, were much smaller than the seasale collieries. Without access to water transport and not competing, on geographical grounds, or because of denial of wayleaves, or because the owners were not powerful enough to break into the cartel controlling the Vend, in the sea-borne trade, they were forced to rest content with extremely local markets. But landsale collieries could acquire seasale status if economic circumstances changed in their favour. Wylam colliery, for example, the most westerly of north Tyneside mines, acquired an outlet to seasale in 1764 after a way-leave agreement with the Earl of Carlisle permitted the laying-down of a waggonway to the highest staithes at Lemington. As a consequence of the growing inability of mines in the south-west Tyne-side sector to maintain output, many mines in the north-west sector (north of the Tyne and west of the Ouseburn) switched from land-sale to seasale during the third quarter of the eighteenth century.[32]

Thus, even the coalfields, like those of the North-east, Cumberland, and South Wales, that concentrated on the sea-borne trade, found some local landsale for a proportion of their output. Other, mainly inland coalfields, were almost wholly dependent on the landsale. We get occasional glimpses of their sales through the statistics of canal and river traffic. The Lancashire coalfield, for example, sent probably 15,000 tons a year down the Douglas navigation by 1758, a trade that rose to 26,000 tons by 1773, while by the 1820s the Leeds–Liverpool canal was carrying 250,000 tons of coal each year.[33] By 1771 90,000 tons of coal were passing down the Sankey Brook

[31] NEI Buddle 12/93, 14/42, 14/409 and 23/42.
[32] Cromar 1979, 49–50.
[33] Langton 1979, 163–4; RC Coal 1871, 34.

navigation. In the south-east of the county the sale of coal from the Duke of Bridgewater's Worsley mine down his canal to Manchester rose from 17,000 tons in 1765 to 52,000 tons in 1782 and 102,000 tons in 1800. In South Wales the Swansea canal was carrying 50,000 tons a year in the early nineteenth century, and 120,000 tons by the 1820s. In the Midlands, the Cromford canal linking mines in south Derbyshire with the river Derwent was carrying nearly 290,000 tons a year in the late 1820s, while the Nottingham canal carried about 170,000 tons to the city of Nottingham, and the Erewash canal over 300,000 tons yearly.[34]

It is, of course, not possible to derive from inland navigation records a comprehensive account of the quantity of coal being distributed in any single year, and the historian must draw what conclusions he can from scraps of information to assess the ability of coal producers to reach consumers. Many of these scraps of information suggest that by the early nineteenth century, as a result of the development of road, waggonway, river, and canal transport in the preceding half century or more, there can have been relatively few areas of the country to which transport costs of coal were still so heavy as to be prohibitive. Such as still existed were likely to have been in highland areas of relatively sparse population, so that the proportion of the total population effectively without access to coal was by then probably extremely small. By the end of the eighteenth century many rural areas of Leicestershire and Warwickshire were drawing supplies from mines in that county and neighbouring Derbyshire and Nottinghamshire thanks to the recently constructed network of river and canal navigations. The Ellesmere canal, opened in 1806, allowed Denbighshire coal to be carried into Cheshire and Staffordshire. Rural districts of north Lancashire and the Craven district of Yorkshire were supplied by road from the isolated coalfield near Ingleton. In north Staffordshire, where mining development had been held back in the early eighteenth century through lack of good communications, the building of roads and canals after 1750 provided a major stimulus by allowing coal to be carried cheaply to the burgeoning iron and pottery industries as well as to the increasingly numerous domestic consumers.[35]

By the early nineteenth century it seems probable that most urban dwellers and many of those in rural areas heated their homes and cooked with coal, the supplies reaching them along the coasts, via every natural and artificial navigable waterway, and along many of the turnpike roads. Because of the key role of the new methods of transportation in the distribution of coal to these domestic consumers, many of them must have become coal consumers for the first time during the late eighteenth and early nineteenth centuries. Unfortunately we have only occasional glimpses of the extent of urban coal consumption. Kendal, in Westmorland, with a population of about 8,000, consumed 18,000 tons of coal annually around 1806. Edinburgh and Leith, with a population of 81,404 in 1801, were estimated to take about 200,000 tons of coal annually.[36] These figures, which, of course, include consumption for both domestic heating and urban industrial uses, suggest urban per capita coal consumption rates of two and a quarter to two and a half tons annually. Since in 1801 about twenty-five per cent of the British population lived in towns, and in 1831 possibly thirty per cent, this implies urban consumption of 5.5 million tons and ten million tons in 1801 and 1831 respectively.

Most of the new transport facilities, however, were provided initially to carry coal not to domestic consumers, but to industrial consumers, and there can be little doubt that rising industrial consumption of coal provided the fastest growing sector of demand for coal before 1830. Already by the early decades of the eighteenth century many major industries used coal as an essential fuel in their manufacturing processes. The technique of smelting copper with coal, for example, had been learned in the last years of the seventeenth century, and it is from this period, too, that the large-scale exploitation of the Cornish copper deposits dates, a development that owed much to the availability, from the early years of the eighteenth century, of the Newcomen steam-pump. Without its own supplies of coal, Cornwall turned to the nearest convenient source—the western end of the South Wales coalfield—across the Bristol Channel to fuel its pumping engines, and sent its ores back there for smelting, a link that was to prove a mainstay of the economies of both Cornwall and the coalfield around Swansea through the eighteenth century and into the nineteenth. 'The chief consumption of Swansea coals', ran an account of 1805, 'proceeds from copper works. There are 7 copper works on the River Tawe, all within 2 miles of Swansea. Each of these works has from 50 to 60 air furnaces smelting copper ore, and all this is smelted by Swansea coal.'[37] It has been claimed that in the mid-eighteenth century fifty per cent of British copper smelting was centred on Swansea, and by the end of the century

---

[36] JRL Crawford and Balcarres 23/6/334; Hassan 1972, 126.
[37] 'Collieries and the coal trade', CuRO Lonsdale D/Lons/W38/10.

ninety per cent. Box colliery near Llanelli, for which accounts survive for the years 1817–20, sent 37.5 per cent of its output in those years to the copper-smelters.[38] Copper-smelting was an important consumer in the North Wales coalfield, too, after 1750.[39] Outside Wales, copper-smelting was on a smaller scale and much more scattered. Some smelting was carried on at various times during the eighteenth century in south Lancashire, drawing ore from Cheshire and coal from Lancashire, in Staffordshire using local coal to smelt Cheshire ore, in Flintshire and Denbighshire using both local coal and ore, and in Bristol using Somerset and Gloucestershire coal to smelt Somerset ore. From the 1780s the Parys mine in Anglesey became the most important source of ore outside Cornwall, and this ore was carried for smelting near the coalfields of south Lancashire and Flintshire. From about 1,000 tons at the beginning of the eighteenth century the output of copper in Britain seems to have climbed to around 7,500 tons at the end of the century, and may have reached 15,000 tons by 1830. Using John's estimates of coal consumption in the smelting process, this suggests consumption by the whole industry of about 30,000 tons of coal in the early eighteenth century rising to 150,000 tons at the end of the century, and 225,000 tons by 1830.[40]

Another major coal-consuming industry similarly already using substantial quantities of coal at the beginning of the eighteenth century was salt-making. Salt was made in three principal ways in the eighteenth century. Sea-water was evaporated by boiling in large iron pans; brine, springing naturally from underground, was similarly evaporated by boiling; and rock-salt was mined underground, crushed, and mixed with water to make a brine which, in its turn, was then evaporated in the same way as was brine and sea-water. In the last case the cost of mining rock-salt was offset by the much higher salt content of the brine produced from the rock-salt as well as by the saving of transport costs gained by carrying the rock to the coal rather than the coal to the refinery as was necessary for reducing the natural brine. At the beginning of the eighteenth century sea-salt was manufactured principally on the north-east coast near Shields with north-east coal, and on the shores of the Firth of Forth where there was also a plentiful local supply of coal. Brine was found in

[38] Roberts thesis 1953, 16; NLW Neville, Druce & Co (Llanelli), Box colliery accounts.
[39] Rawson 1941, 127; Dodd 1929, 202.
[40] John 1950, 150. This brief survey of copper-smelting is based on J. R. Harris, *The Copper King* (Liverpool, 1964); and R. O. Roberts, 'The development and decline of the non-ferrous metal smelting industries in South Wales', *Transactions of the Honourable Society of Cymmrodorion* (1956), reprinted in W. E. Minchinton (ed.), *Industrial South Wales, 1750–1914* (London, 1969).

Cheshire, Staffordshire, and Worcestershire, though by the early eighteenth century the last two counties were of minor importance. Rock-salt was discovered in 1670 at Marbury in Cheshire near Northwich, the location of the principal brine industry.

It was clearly advantageous to carry the rock-salt, the mining of which began seriously in 1690, at least as far as the Mersey estuary, leaving only a relatively short overland carriage for the coal of the southern fringe of the Lancashire coalfield. This threat to the Cheshire brinemen, who were obliged to bring coal by an expensive, three-stage journey over land, water, and land again from Lancashire to the Northwich area, led to a prolonged struggle in which the power of the state to tax the processes differentially was invoked first by one side and then by the other. But rock-salt refineries were set up on the Mersey in the 1690s, and, though with varying fortunes, both rock- and brine-salt were exported in increasing quantities from Liverpool from that period. The needs of the Merseyside industry led to, and were fostered by, the construction, first, of the River Weaver navigation between 1721 and 1733, and, later, of the Sankey Brook navigation between 1754 and 1757, which, between them, provided a continuous water passage for the coal of Lancashire to the salt refineries of the Mersey and north Cheshire. In the first year of the Weaver navigation the brinemen consumed 9,000 tons of coal, all of which had first been carried by pack-horse and cart from the pits in Lancashire to the Mersey. The opening of the Sankey Brook navigation increased this trade, and by 1771 90,000 tons of coal passed down the navigation, much of it, certainly, for the salt-makers. In 1800 85,000 tons of Lancashire coal passed up the Weaver navigation to the salt refineries, a year in which 106,000 tons of salt were sent down the river. Production of rock- and brine-salt in the Merseyside area more than trebled between 1800 and 1840. Merseyside salt production may have been in the region of 350,000 tons a year by 1830, suggesting coal consumption of possibly 280,000 tons annually.[41]

In contrast to the Merseyside brine- and rock-salt industry, the sea-salt industry of Tyneside experienced a gradual decline during the eighteenth century, probably on account of the poorer quality

---

[41] This brief summary of the growth of the Merseyside salt industry is based on Barker 1951; W. H. Chaloner, 'Salt in Cheshire, 1600–1870', *Transactions of the Lancashire and Cheshire Antiquarian Society*, 71 (1961); and E. Hughes, *Studies in Administration and Finance, 1558–1825* (Manchester, 1934). Cheshire brine was reported to consume between 12 and 30 cwt. of coal per ton of salt, depending upon the salinity of the brine, and rock-salt rather less. In 1819 a national average of 13 cwt. for one ton of salt was assumed. (*Tables and Facts relative to the Coal Duties* (London, 1819), pamphlet in NuRO Ridley (Blagdon) ZRI 25/31, 5.)

of the product compared with that of its southern competitors and the falling transport costs of the Merseyside producers following the construction of the new waterways between 1721 and 1757. At its peak in the early years of the eighteenth century the Tyneside sea-salt industry produced about 12,500 tons yearly, an output probably roughly equal to that of the Merseyside producers. But decline became apparent during the 1720s; sales had halved by mid century, and became insignificant by the end of the century. In contrast to brine- and rock-salt which mostly required less than one ton of coal to make one ton of salt, sea-salt consumed between six and eight tons, a requirement which necessarily located the industry on coalfields by the sea. The Tyneside industry was able, at least until the development of new waterways on Merseyside, to remain competitive even in the face of such a high fuel/output ratio because the 'pan-coal' it consumed was the rejected small coal from pits producing primarily 'great coals' for the coastal trade. Thus the Shields salt-pans could be supplied with coal in the early eighteenth century at 2s. 6d. per ton at a time when, before the opening of the Weaver navigation, the Northwich brinemen were obliged to pay over 16s. The low-grade coal could be bought by the north-east salt-makers at half the cost of 'shipcoal', and without the salt industry much of this coal would probably not even have been brought to the surface. This important link between the two industries led, during the early decades of the eighteenth century while Tyneside salt-making was still important, to the gradual takeover of ownership of the salt-pans by north-east coalowners, primarily with a view to ensuring an outlet for their small coals. The Tyneside industry's coal consumption probably ran to rather less than 100,000 tons yearly at the beginning of the eighteenth century, and the salt-pans had ceased to be an effective market for coal by the early nineteeth century.[42]

Outside the North-east, sea-salt was manufactured on a commercial scale only in Scotland, in Cumberland, and on the Hampshire coast. In the last district the high cost of imported coal was offset partly by exposing the sea-water to a preliminary evaporation by solar heat in shallow depressions on the shore before letting it into the salt-pans. Two areas of Scotland met the requirements of sea-saltmaking by the existence of coalfields adjacent to the coast—Ayrshire and the Firth of Forth. Salt-making had been established at Saltcoats in Ayrshire by Robert Cunninghame, owner of coal-mines, towards the end of the seventeenth century, and this enterprise seems to have endured until at least 1830. Between 1771 and 1783 his Stevenston

---

[42] This survey of the Tyneside salt industry is based on J. Ellis, 'The decline and fall of the Tyneside salt industry, 1660–1790: a re-examination', *EHR*, 2nd ser. 33 (1980).

colliery supplied thirty-eight per cent of its output to salt works, and
the neighbouring Westfield colliery 19.3 per cent of its production
between 1783 and 1798.[43] There are, unfortunately, no statistics of
Scottish salt production and very few indicators even of the trends of
development in the industry during the eighteenth and early nineteenth centuries. Nef has estimated a coal consumption in Scottish
saltmaking of 150,000 tons a year at the end of the seventeenth
century, and Duckham, who suggests that this may somewhat overestimate the actual consumption and believes that there is unlikely
to have been much, if any, expansion of the industry before the
1790s, estimates annual consumption around 140,000 tons in the
dozen years following 1771. There may have been some growth in
the 1790s, but the repeal of all the salt duties in 1825, by removing
the differential that had until then protected Scottish producers
from the competition of cheaper English salt, initiated the final
decay of salt-making in Scotland.[44]

Clearly no more than the roughest of estimates of coal consumption by the whole British salt industry are possible. Rather more
than 250,000 tons may have been consumed at the beginning of the
eighteenth century, of which possibly ninety per cent was divided
roughly equally between Tyneside and Scotland. By the 1770s the
consumption was probably marginally less, the great growth of the
Merseyside industry making only a relatively small impact on total
coal consumption on account of its low coal consumption per unit
of output, and being probably more than offset by the decline of the
Tyneside industry. The continuing decline of the Tyneside industry
after the 1770s combined with the very slight growth of the Scottish
industry between the 1790s and the early 1820s were, however,
probably more than offset by the substantial growth on Merseyside,
so that by 1825 consumption by the whole industry may have risen
to around 400,000 tons. Thereafter the decline of Scottish output
was probably at least offset by the continuing rise of Merseyside
production.

Many other industries were already coal consumers at the opening
of the eighteenth century, and most of these experienced expansion
during the century, if only as a result of population growth. Some,
by moving from small-scale, possibly domestic, production to large-
scale, factory production, almost certainly increased their per capita
coal consumption in the process. In addition to the copper industry
already taken into account, other non-ferrous metal industries

[43] ScRO Court of Session C596/638/3/1912–16, 1924–8.
[44] This survey of salt-making in Scotland is based on Nef 1932, I, 207–8; Duckham
1970, 15–16, 26; and A. and N. Clow, *The Chemical Revolution* (London, 1952), chap. 2.

consumed coal in smelting, casting, and working. The Hawarden mines in Flintshire sent coal to local lead and brass works, for example, while lead-smelting and tin-plate manufacture also used coal in the early eighteenth century at the western end of the South Wales coalfield. Brass-founding at Bristol was served by the Forest of Dean.[45] The navy was a small, though steady, customer for the mines throughout the period as Beveridge's price series for the Portsmouth dockyard and elsewhere indicate. In 1810 the navy was said to have bought 27,200 tons of coal from the North-east for delivery at dockyards in the Thames and on the south coast where it was probably used principally in metal-work and tar-heating.[46] Tar-making itself was developed as a by-product industry of mining from the 1780s principally by Lord Dundonald. He took out a patent in 1782 and set up a distillery at Culross of the north shore of the Firth of Forth in the same year. His patent was extended in 1785 for a further twenty-one years, and the British Tar Company he founded began a steady business making tar in the vicinity of several iron-works where there was a ready market for the coke produced as a by-product. Another successful tar-making works was established in 1814, some time after the final expiry of Dundonald's patent, at Elsecar colliery on the Fitzwilliam estate in south Yorkshire.[47]

A further group of coal-consuming industry that experienced massive expansion during the eighteenth century as the result of the adoption of methods of large-scale production was the china and pottery manufacture. Though heavily concentrated in Staffordshire, and therefore providing a valuable additional source of demand for coal in the north Staffordshire coalfield, developments in the industry also created new markets for coal in Flintshire, where the Buckley pottery that had opened in 1737 was employing 230 workers by 1818, and in Derby, which provided an outlet for the Butterley Company from the 1790s.[48]

A further group of coal-consuming industries was associated with the building industry, and may be assumed to have grown at least in proportion to the expansion of that major industry in this great period of urban building. Glass-making, which had learned to use coal as its fuel in the early seventeenth century, was established by the opening of the eighteenth century on the coalfield in the

[45] Rawson 1941, 128; Dodd 1929, 202; Davis thesis 1959, 47; D. T. Williams 1940, 197; RC Coal 1871, 50.

[46] Beveridge 1939, 577-8, 591; NEI Buddle 14/151.

[47] A. and N. Clow, The Chemical Revolution (London, 1952), 389–423; Mee 1975, 66-70.

[48] J. Lindsay, 'The Butterley Company works, 1792–1816', Derbyshire Archaeological Journal, 85 (1965), 38.

North-east, while important new works were set up on the southern fringe of the Lancashire coalfield from the 1720s. Adair's Main colliery on Tyneside sold half of its annual output of about 32,000 tons to glass works. In 1823, when the Wear mines shipped a total of 1,276,736 tons, they also sold 59,898 tons of coal to the local glasshouses and lime-kilns. In south Yorkshire in the mid-eighteenth century owners of glassworks at Bolsterstone and Catcliffe operated their own coal-mines.[49] Brick-making, too, was a substantial consumer of coal. Widely dispersed throughout the country to minimize the carriage of a heavy, low-value commodity, the industry provided a landsale market on virtually every coalfield. It was an industry often integrated by landowners with their mining operations, as, for example, by Lord Ferrers at his Lount colliery in Leicestershire.[50] It is quite impossible to assess the consumption at any one point in time of these industries, but some idea of the growth of their consumption may be indicated by Shannon's index of brick production based on the returns of the brick excise duty. This roughly doubled between 1785 and 1830.[51] Lime was used in building, too, but its principal use was in agriculture. Its raw material, like brick-making, was widely available, but its consumption of coal tended to confine its location either on or very close to coalfields. Like the other industries supplying the building trade, it was useful to coalowners because it took up the small coal not otherwise easily saleable but produced unavoidably in the process of obtaining large coal for domestic buyers. There is evidence of lime-burning using coal in the Forest of Dean, South Wales, and Leicestershire.[52]

A final group of industries already consuming coal in the early eighteenth century was in the food and drink trades. Distilling, presumably gin-making, was among the London industries mentioned as coal consumers in the 1730s, as was baking in the 1790s.[53] Brewing, however, was probably the largest consumer in this group. It is known that coke was first used in the malting industry as early as 1640. In 1703, at a time when large-scale brewing was heavily concentrated in the metropolis, a return showed thirty-seven 'common brewers' holding stocks of coal. Their total stocks amounted only to 4,600 tons, and if, as seems likely, given the seasonal irregularity and uncertainty of coal deliveries to London at that time, they were holding stocks equal to about one month's consumption, their

[49] T. C. Barker, *Pilkington Brothers and the Glass Industry* (London, 1960), 36–54; NEI Buddle 23/42; DuRO NCB First Deposit NCB/I/JB/471/175; Hopkinson 1976, 12.
[50] C. P. Griffin thesis 1969, 27.
[51] H. A. Shannon, 'Bricks—a trade index, 1785–1849', *Economica* (1934).
[52] Davis thesis 1959, 70; Roberts thesis 1953, 18–19; C. P. Griffin thesis 1969, 27.
[53] NEI Buddle 14/117, 379.

annual consumption may have been just over 50,000 tons, possibly a little more than one-tenth of London's total consumption at that time, a proportion of which might well justify Mathias's belief that 'collectively they were . . . among the most important non-domestic users of coal in the land.' Coal was used in drying the malt. By the end of the seventeenth century, for example, there were seventy-six malt-houses in Derby, all using coke supplied from the Derbyshire coalfield. Derby malt, it seems, was widely used by brewers in Lancashire and Cheshire.[54] It was also used in heating the coppers, and towards the end of the eighteenth century, in the steam-pumps that became a feature of all the larger breweries. By 1830 thirty-six Boulton and Watt engines had been installed in breweries, most of them in London, and it is probable that engines by other makers were also used. Though large-scale brewing was heavily concentrated in London, the sheer cost of transporting the manufactured beer long distances inland enforced a wide distribution of brewing generally, and although both malt and brewed beer were subject to excises, the excise returns do not necessarily provide an entirely reliable guide to the growth of the industry. Since the returns of beer production show only a fifty per cent increase in production during the eighteenth century, followed by virtual stagnation during the early nineteenth century, they seem unlikely to reflect very accurately the actual trends in the industry.[55]

Virtually all these miscellaneous industrial uses for coal in the eighteenth and early nineteenth centuries involved no particularly intractable technical problems. Technical advances, however, were responsible for developments that created three major new markets for coal during the eighteenth century. In all these areas—iron-making, steam-power, and gas supply—the scale of the developments made possible by the technical advances was so great that by 1830 they constituted together a significant proportion of the total demand for coal. When the extension of steam-power to railways and steam shipping is taken into account, they ultimately provided the foundation of a major part of the nineteenth-century growth of the industry.

At the opening of the eighteenth century the several processes in the manufacture of iron and steel used nothing but wood, in the form of charcoal, as fuel. As is now well known, in or shortly after 1709 the Shropshire ironmaster, Abraham Darby, succeeded in

---

[54] W. H. Walton, 'Early use of coke in Derby', *Journal of the Derbyshire Archaeological and Natural History Society*, 7 (1933), 17.

[55] This brief survey of coal consumption in the brewing industry is based on P. Mathias, *The Brewing Industry in England, 1700–1830* (Cambridge, 1959).

smelting iron using coked coal as the fuel. Though the key to his success was his decision to coke the coal before using it in his blast furnace, a choice which undoubtedly owed much to his earlier experience in the manufacture of equipment for malt-making, there was also an element of luck in his achievement, since his local coals and iron ores turned out to be of just the right chemical composition in combination to produce a commercially viable metal when put together in the blast furnace. Other ironmasters elsewhere, using other coals and other ores, were at first unsuccessful in imitating him. Darby's coke-smelted iron could be used initially only for the fine castings that were an important branch of his business, and it was several decades before more than a handful of ironmasters elsewhere were able to follow his example. Indeed it was not until about 1749–50 that his son succeeded in producing a coke-smelted pig iron that was capable of conversion in the forge to usable bar iron. This second development, though dependent, of course, upon the earlier development of the first Abraham Darby, was of greater economic significance, since in the mid-eighteenth century the market for cast iron, the only use for coke-smelted iron in the first half of the century, accounted for probably less than ten per cent of the whole demand for iron. The costs of coke-smelting, too, compared with those of charcoal-smelting, as Hyde has shown, played an important role in the gradual substitution of coke for charcoal in iron smelting, and it was not until the mid-1750s that the economic advantage of coke-smelting was sufficiently clearly established for the process effectively to begin to displace charcoal-smelting. Coke-smelting substituted a fuel in almost limitless supply, the price of which was unlikely to be driven up by increasing demand, for one in strictly limited supply, the price of which was extremely sensitive to increases in demand. Once under way, however, the process of substitution was irresistible, and although the last charcoal furnace lingered on in Sussex until 1812, coke-smelting could be said to be virtually unchallenged by the late 1780s.

Smelting, however, is only the first stage in the process of making iron in any form other than cast iron. In the early eighteenth century a very high proportion of the pig iron from the blast furnaces was converted into bar iron in forges. Forging was a double process involving repeated heating, re-heating, and hammering in the 'finery' and 'chafery' forges to reduce the carbon and other impurities in high-carbon, hard, brittle pig iron in converting it into low-carbon, malleable bar iron. In both the forges, charcoal was used as the fuel, and the forging process almost trebled the cost of bar iron compared with that of pig iron. Thus the Darbys' success with coke-smelting was only part of the answer to the problem created by an inelastic supply of charcoal. As important, therefore, as the Darbys' discovery of coke-smelting were, first, as Hyde has shown, the evolution during the 1760s of potting, and, second, the invention by Henry Cort in 1783–4 of puddling. Though puddling quickly superseded potting, both processes allowed the substitution of coal for charcoal in the conversion of pig iron into bar iron, and allowed coal to be used either raw or as coke in all the processes of iron-making. To convert bar iron into steel, however, continued to require charcoal until Bessemer's invention of 1856.

The process of coking coal for smelting involved, of course, a considerable weight reduction, and until the invention of the hot blast by Neilson in 1828 coke-smelting consumed up to eight tons of coal for every ton of pig iron produced. Puddling further consumed between four and eight tons of coal per ton of bar iron converted, and coal was also consumed in the steam-engines that were rapidly substituted for water power after 1775 to drive the bellows of blast-furnaces. Table 7.11 sets out estimates of coal consumption by the iron industry up to 1830. The table starts only in 1750 because virtually no coal was consumed in the industry during the era of charcoal-smelting and -forging. It reveals at once that by 1830 the iron industry had become a major customer for coal, and a mainstay of the mining industry. The expansion of iron-making and of its demand for coal was particularly fast during the 1790s and the 1820s.

Not every coalfield benefited from this enormous expansion of demand, because the location of iron-making depended upon the immediate availability of both coal and iron ore, and, if possible, the limestone that was used as a flux in the furnaces. Further, the coal had to be good coking coal. Table 7.12 shows the fairly rapidly changing geographical distribution of pig-iron manufacture in Britain for the period following the general adoption of coke-smelting. Shropshire, not surprisingly on account of its pioneering role in the development of coke-smelting, took the largest share of production on the eve of the great expansion of puddling; but, like Scotland and Yorkshire/Derbyshire, it failed to retain its share of the expansion in the face of the rise of the Staffordshire and South Wales industries. By 1830 these two districts claimed three-quarters of the total make of pig iron. Though small quantities of iron were made in the North-east and Lancashire, these coalfields gained very little from the growth of iron-making, and the Cumberland, East Midlands, North Wales, and South-west coalfields benefited scarcely at all. Mott quotes an eighteenth-century writer to the effect that the

Table 7.11. Consumption of coal in iron-making, 1750–1830
(000s of tons of iron and coal)

Year	Smelting		Steam-blowing		Conversion to bar iron		Calcining	Total
	output of coke pig iron	consumption of coal	number of steam-blown furnaces in blast	consumption of coal	output of bar iron	consumption of coal	consumption of coal	total coal consumption
1750	2.6	21	—	—	—	—	—	21
1760	10.0	70	—	—	—	—	—	70
1780	36.5	195	43	58	5	13	12	278
1788	55.5	350	60	81	32	83	18	532
1805	258.0	1,497	173	234	100	750	84	2,565
1815	395.0	2,197	200	271	150	975	128	3,571
1820	400.0	2,164	215	291	200	1,100	130	3,685
1830	578.0	3,506	375	508	350	1,400	220	5,634

Note on sources: Pig and bar iron national and regional output figures, and the number of steam-blown furnaces in blast, from C. K. Hyde, *Technological Change and the British Iron Industry, 1700–1870* (Princeton, New Jersey, 1977), 67, 108, 113, 137; and A. Birch, *The Economic History of the British Iron and Steel Industry, 1784–1879* (London, 1967), 25, 46–7, 124–5, 128, 130–1. I am indebted to Professor Hyde for figures of coal consumption in the smelting, potting, and puddling processes. Apart from showing a general tendency to fall over time as furnace efficiency improved, there were substantial regional variations in the consumption of coal per ton of pig iron in smelting. In the estimates of this table separate consumption rates have been used from 1788 for the South Wales iron output where, thanks to high carbon coal, fuel efficiency was very great (Hyde's figures for South Wales are confirmed by a useful statement of 1827 concerning coke and coal consumption by ironworks in CLSG Miscellaneous MS 4.575); for Scotland, where, because the splint coal was mostly used raw in the furnace, fuel consumption was extremely high; and an average figure for the remaining iron-making districts. There are no good regional coke-iron output data before 1788, but the smallness of the total output allowed a single estimated national coal consumption figure to be used without fear of serious distortion of the total.

Steam-blowing engine consumption. Consumption varied with the nature of both coal and ore used from about one ton of coal per ton of pig iron smelted in Staffordshire around 1830 to half that quantity in Scotland. A national average of 15 cwt. per ton of pig iron has been assumed. I am grateful to Dr J. Kanefsky for this information.

Coal consumption in conversion of pig to bar. Professor Hyde's data for coal consumption in the potting process, which had been assumed to have been operating for 1780 and 1788 bar iron conversion, show an average of about 2.6 tons of coal per ton of bar iron. For puddling, which has been assumed to have been operating for the years from 1805, his data show coal consumption falling steadily from 7.5 tons per ton of bar iron in 1805 to 4.0 tons in 1830.

Calcining. Estimated to have consumed on average 6½ cwt. of coal per ton of pig iron produced.

Table 7.12. *Regional distribution of coke pig-iron production, 1788–1830*
(percentages of total)

| Year | West Midlands | | South Wales | Scotland | All |
	Shropshire	Staffordshire			other regions
1788	44.9	12.4	20.4	10.4	11.9
1806	21.3	18.8	28.3	9.0	22.6
1815	12.7	31.6	35.4	5.1	15.2
1830	10.8	31.2	40.9	5.8	11.3

Sources: C. K. Hyde, *Technological Change and the British Iron Industry, 1700–1870* (Princeton, New Jersey, 1977), 114, 123; A. Birch, *The Economic History of the British Iron and Steel Industry, 1784–1879* (London, 1967), 46, 130, 133; RC Coal 1871, 29–30.

north-east coals 'abound with sulphur and are improper to be used with iron', adding that being also strongly caking, they were also unsuitable for the hearth process of coke-making.[56] Most districts of the West Midlands coalfield shared in the growth, but in Scotland the Fife and Lothians district experienced no boost from iron-making, and the western sector of the South Wales coalfield, where the Pennant series of coal measures were often highly sulphurous, experienced relatively little of the enormous impetus imparted by the rise of iron-making in the valleys of the eastern sector.

The growth of demand for coal by the iron smelters came as something entirely new in Staffordshire and the eastern section of the South Wales coalfield where mining had hitherto been on a rather small scale. The relatively large scale of the demand created by the new iron works could not be easily assimilated into the existing structure of mining in these districts. Had large-scale iron-making developed in the North-east, or even in the Swansea area of South Wales, it might well have been possible for the existing coalowners to adapt their production to the new demand and to find the capital to do so. But this was hardly possible in Staffordshire and eastern South Wales, and in these districts the ironmasters were obliged to make their own provision for coal supplies.

All ironmasters, of course, recognized the desirability of securing their own independent supplies of coal in order not to be at the mercy of the coalowners at times of high demand. In the early years of the expansion of coke iron-making in Shropshire the Coalbrook-dale Company had shown the way in this development. The company seems at first to have bought its coal from small independent miners

[56] R. A. Mott, quoting J. A. Cramer, *Art of Essaying* (1741), in 'Abraham Darby (I and II) and the coal-iron industry', *TNS* 31 (1957–9), 63.

in the neighbourhood, but with the major expansion of coke-smelting following the construction of the Horsehay and Ketley works in the 1750s, it went in for direct mining, leasing pits in nearby Dawley, Lawley, Ketley, Wrockwardine Wood, and Donnington Wood. It was said, possibly with some exaggeration, to be employing at that time 3,000 men in mining who produced annually 700,000 tons of coal and 42,000 tons of iron ore.[57] John Wilkinson sank several pits on the Brymbo Hall estate near Wrexham on the North Wales coalfield after he had taken over the Bersham furnace in 1762. In south Yorkshire in 1810 mines on the Wentworth estate were supplying over half their output to ironworks on the estate.[58] In Scotland, similarly, the Carron Company, which had opted from its start in 1759 for coke-smelting, at first contracted with a local mine operator, Thomas Dundas, to take weekly deliveries from his Quarrole mine, but quickly arranged leases for mining coal themselves on the nearby land of James Bruce of Kinnaird and eventually from Dundas himself and other adjacent estates. But an account of Dunmore colliery showed that in 1779–81 the company was purchasing coal from outside as well.[59] Not far away the Shotts Iron Company of 1801 acquired its own mines by the outright purchase of coal-bearing land adjacent to its new blast-furnaces. Several iron companies in Ayrshire and Lanarkshire took leases of coal-mines from the 1790s onwards.[60] The Earl of Crawford and Balcarres established an iron-smelting and -processing works at Haigh near Wigan in 1788 to serve as an outlet for the coal mined on his estate. Perhaps partly because of difficulties arising from the nature of the coal, and partly also because of the doubtful competence of the managers employed, the venture was not very successful and was abandoned by 1815.[61]

But the major developments in direct mining by ironmasters came in the eastern valleys of the South Wales coalfield. Here, all the great ironworks, starting with the first coke furnaces at Hirwaun in 1756, and continuing with the development of the huge undertakings at Dowlais (1759), Plymouth (1763), Cyfarthfa (1765), where coal

[57] A. Raistrick, *Dynasty of Ironfounders* (London, 1953), 70; R. A. Mott, 'The Coalbrookdale Horsehay Works, Part I', *TNS* 31 (1957–9), 272; I. J. Brown, 'The mineral wealth of Coalbrookdale: Part I', *Bulletin of the Peak District Mines Historical Society*, 2 (1963–5), 260–1.

[58] Dodd 1929, 204; Mee 1975, 32.

[59] R. H. Campbell, *Carron Company* (Edinburgh and London, 1961), 32, 46–9; ShRO Forester SRO1224/173.

[60] A. Muir, *The Story of Shotts* (Edinburgh, n.d.), 2–3, 8; J. Butt, 'The Scottish iron and steel industry before the hot-blast', *Journal of the West of Scotland Iron and Steel Institute*, 73 (1965–6).

[61] A Birch, 'The Haigh ironworks, 1789–1856', *Bulletin of the John Rylands Library*, 35 (1953).

consumption was said in 1825 to be 700 tons a day (250,000 tons a year),[62] Sirhowy (1778), Penydarren (1784), and Blaenavon (1789) all made arrangements to lease mines in the neighbourhood of their furnaces, provided the capital for developing the mines, and managed the mines as an integrated part of their concerns. The Cyfarthfa works secured mining rights from the land owner, the Earl of Plymouth, in a lease of 1765, and the Hirwaun works from the Dowager Countess of Windsor.[63] Some of the iron companies produced coal in excess of their own needs and this was sent down the waggon-ways and canals to provide much of the exports from Cardiff and Newport.

Until the development of puddling from the 1790s the iron industry directly produced few finished goods. Puddling and rolling permitted the direct production of rails, plates, and girders, and after 1790 these products took an increasing proportion of the make of bar iron. But before then, and to a diminishing extent after then, bar iron was processed at slitting mills and forges into the wide range of small ironware that constituted the end-products of the industry —nails, tools, hoops, bands, hinges, locks, and horseshoes. Though there were a few large-scale manufacturers of this smith-ware in the eighteenth and early nineteenth centuries like the Crowleys of Tyne-side, and some concentrations of specialized branches like nail-making in the Black Country and the Firth of Forth, for the most part the industry was widely scattered throughout the country. All the processes involved the use of coal to heat the material to make it workable under the hammer. The Crowley works at Winlaton on the coalfield south of the Tyne used about 1,600 tons a year in the early years of the eighteenth century and the firm had other works at nearby Winlaton Mill and Swalwell.[64] It was works like these that accounted for some of the otherwise rather elusive landsale of collieries in the North-east.

If the growth of the iron industry provided the principal new source of demand for the produce of the mines, the gas industry, founded as the result of discoveries by William Murdoch and others in the 1790s, was to become scarcely less important. Before 1812, however, gas lighting was not employed on more than a small, domestic scale, gas being manufactured privately for use in a single building, as when, in 1805, Murdoch lit Phillips and Lee's cotton-mill in Salford with gas. The public use of gas for street and private

[62] CLSG Miscellaneous 4.575.
[63] Wilkins 1888, 66.
[64] M. W. Flinn, *Men of Iron. The Crowleys in the Early Iron Industry* (Edinburgh, 1962), 117–18.

house illumination from mains laid under streets began with the formation of the London Gas Light and Coke Company in 1812. Thereafter private companies for public gas supply were quickly formed in many towns, and contracts were signed with local authorities for street-lighting. By the late 1820s, following a great boom in the construction of gas works and mains between 1818 and 1826 there was gas lighting in most towns with populations of 10,000 or more.[65] In Scotland, for example, where there were good gas coals in Midlothian and West Lothian, gas-supply companies were founded in Glasgow in 1817, in Edinburgh in 1818, Paisley and Dundee in 1823, and Greenock in 1829.[66] There is, unhappily, no means of assessing the coal consumption of the gas industry in its early days. But even with only eighteen years of effective history behind it in 1830, the industry provided a market of growing importance in many districts of most coalfields, wherever there was coal suitable for gas-making. A witness to the Lords Select Committee of 1830 believed that the coming of gas lighting had increased per capita coal consumption since 'the general establishment of gas works' (probably no more than ten years) by eleven per cent.[67]

The last of the three major new industrial consumers of coal in the eighteenth and early nineteenth centuries was the steam-engine. At first, as we saw in chapter four, the steam-engine was used almost exclusively for mine drainage, though, with use in the non-ferrous metal mines as well as in coal-mining, the total number of engines was rather larger than that indicated in Tables 4.1 and 4.2. From about 1775 the use of steam-engines began to be extended to blast-furnace blowing, and from the 1780s to mine winding. With the adaptation of the engine by Watt in 1781 to rotary motion many new uses were found for it, above all in driving textile-machinery in mills. From the early years of the nineteenth century, steam-locomotion was developed, and a major new use for steam-power found. The most recent estimate of the number of steam-engines made in the eighteenth century shows just under 2,200 engines known to have been built before 1800, with a total of 2,500 being more probable. Of these, perhaps 1,500, with a total horse-power of 37,500, were still at work in 1800. At an average fuel consumption of 20 lb. per horse-power per hour, their coal consumption must

[65] Brownlie 1922-3, 57-9; M. E. Falkus, 'The British gas industry before 1850', EHR, 2nd ser. 20 (1967).

[66] Hassan 1977, 49-51.

[67] SC Lords Coal Trade 1830, 101. The witness's actual form of comparison was that annual coal consumption of nine chaldrons by every eight people had increased to ten chaldrons. It is clear that this increase related only to domestic consumption by urban consumers.

have been around 1,250,000 tons.[68] The sheer number of engines and the variety of makes and makers of them in the nineteenth century defy precise enumeration. Moreover the range of sizes of engines increased, and with that their consumption of coal. Von Tunzelmann, whose work offers the most useful guide to the use of steam-power in the early nineteenth century, has approached the problem through horse-power, while noting quite wide variations in coal consumption per unit of horse-power by different types of engines. At the end of the eighteenth century he estimates that a Newcomen-type reciprocating engine consumed on average twenty-five lb. of coal per horse-power per hour, Boulton and Watt-type reciprocating engines little more than half that at twelve and a half to fifteen lb., and Boulton and Watt-type rotative engines about twenty-two lb. By 1856 average consumption by all types of engine was down to twelve lb. per horse-power per hour. On this basis he is willing to accept that coal consumption by steam-engines of all kinds in 1800 amounted to about one-tenth of the country's coal consumption. If, as is possible, he has underestimated slightly the number of Newcomen-type engines still working in 1800, the figure may therefore be even higher, say in the region of 1.5 million tons, but this figure, of course, includes steam-engines used in both mining and iron-smelting. It is much more difficult to assess consumption by steam-engines in 1830. Kanefsky has estimated that total steam horse-power in 1830 was about 165,000, which at a slightly lower rate of fuel consumption than he estimated for 1800—say, 17–18 lb. per horse-power hour—implies a total fuel consumption of 4.6–4.9 million tons; of these about 1.3 million tons were consumed in collieries, and 0.7 million tons in ironworks engines including rolling mills, etc.[69]

The emergence of these new sources of demand, above all from gas and steam-power, made a very particular and valuable contribution to the economics of coal-mining. Steam-engines and gas retorts preferred small to large coal, but it was the hitherto largely unsaleable proportion of coal unavoidably produced in the process of getting the large coal demanded by domestic consumers that had formerly been one of the most acute problems faced by mine managements. Some small coal was necessarily produced in all mines, and though mines themselves consumed a proportion, and in most mining regions there was some sale for it to salt-pans or glass-houses, few collieries were able to dispose of more than a fraction of their

[68] Kanefsky and Robey 1980, 169; Kanefsky thesis 1979, 172–3, 277.
[69] G. N. von Tunzelmann, *Steam Power and British Industrialization to 1860* (Oxford, 1978), 110–13; Kanefsky thesis 1979, 172–3, 336.

small coal. Gas-lighting and steam-power thus contributed substantially to the economics of mining in the early nineteenth century by taking up a growing proportion of the small coal hitherto largely valueless.

iii. *The distribution of coal consumption*

Industrialists planning the use of steam-power naturally located their enterprises, if at all possible, on or near a coalfield to minimize the cost of transport of coal. But it was not to be expected that the growth of demand would affect each coalfield similarly. Indeed the shifting geographical pattern of the distribution of production revealed in Table 1.2 was determined more by the changing nature of demand reviewed in this chapter than by the impact of changing production technology. Thus the decline in relative importance of the North-east that emerges very clearly from Table 1.2 surely reflects the inability of the area to attract more than a few small ironworks, as well as the decline of its sea-salt industry in the face of competition from the more efficient brine- and rock-salt industries of Merseyside. On the other hand the ability of this coalfield to retain its primacy among British coalfields throughout the period covered by this volume was certainly a consequence of its continuing competitiveness for domestic heating, thanks to the large scale of its operations, in the markets served by the coastal trade. Above all, the North-east retained its hold on a London market still growing steadily into the nineteenth century. And an abundance of cheap coal attracted to the area, in an era of rapid industrialization, a wide variety of small- and medium-scale industrial enterprises. Markets for coal in the North-east were probably more diverse than has been allowed by those who have been willing to assume that the statistics of the 'Vend' represent the whole output of the coalfield. An undated estimate, probably of the period 1810–15, but deriving from a statement 'sworn before the commissioners' indicated that about 26,500 tons of Sunderland coal were used in 'potteries, lime-kilns, etc.',[70] while in the years 1804–7, Adair's Main colliery on Tyneside, for example, distributed its sale as follows:[71]

	per cent
Coastwise vend	45.7
Export	11.6
Glass-houses	21.7
Small coal	7.3
Landsale	13.8

[70] Holmes 1816, 234.   [71] NEI Buddle 23/42.

The Scottish coalfield marginally failed to retain its share of total output perhaps partly because Scotland's share of British population was falling, but mainly because Scotland, too, like the North-east of England, was unable to develop and retain its share of the newer iron industry, though this situation was to be sharply reversed as a result of Scotland's lead in developing the hot-blast process during the 1830s. Nor did the Scottish sea-salt industry long survive the repeal of the salt excise in 1825. Though, after some loss during the middle and later eighteenth century, Scotland's west-coast mines recovered their former share of the Irish trade, on the east coast Scottish mines were losing coastal trade to the English North-east. The Cumberland coalfield shared a similar experience. While it was successful in maintaining its position in the Irish trade, few other developments favoured it very much. Very little of the growth of the coastal trade came its way, and there were too few industrial developments in the North-west beyond a very little iron-making on the coalfield and the development of cotton factories in Carlisle to boost its sales very substantially in the late eighteenth and early nineteenth centuries. The period of fastest growth in Cumberland was certainly the first half of the eighteenth century when its buoyancy was attributable to the rise of the Irish trade: there was too little else in the North-west to sustain this early growth.

Further south, the Lancashire coalfield, with relatively few indigenous coal-using industries in the early eighteenth century, was heavily dependent on the development of water-transport to give it access to the potentially rich markets that surrounded it. With the construction of these waterways between 1740 and 1765 the coalfield benefited from the demand of the rising industries—salt-making, the urban demand of two of the most rapidly growing cities in the country, the growth of some minor industries—copper-smelting, glass-making, chemicals, and, above all, the rise of the factory production of cotton cloth in the south-eastern area of the coalfield after about 1790. The Lancashire coalfield developed, therefore, primarily in response to the landsale demand: its principal coastal outlets—Liverpool and the Ribble estuary—were not sufficiently well placed in relation either to the coalfield itself or to seasale markets for it to secure much of the increase of the Irish and coastal markets. Much the same influences determined the fortunes of the North Wales coalfield. Sales here were largely confined to local domestic and industrial landsale, and beyond some varied industrial developments in iron, copper, lead, and pottery, there were no great new sources of demand.

The South Wales coalfield, however, did benefit substantially from

some of the major developments. The non-ferrous metal industries, the supply to the steam-pumps of the Cornish coppermines, and other coastal and export trades concentrated and
sustained production at the western end of the coalfield for the
greater part of the eighteenth century. This sub-division of
the coalfield benefited to some extent from the expansion of the
late eighteenth and early nineteenth centuries in the copper and
iron industries, but the major element in the expansion of
mining in South Wales was unquestionably the establishment of
large-scale iron-making in the eastern valleys. By 1830 this trade
alone must have accounted for upwards of seventy-five per cent
of the coal output of South Wales. In contrast to this great new
source of demand, the south-west coalfield was scarcely able to
take advantage of many of the new industrial developments. With
a coastal trade confined throughout the period up to 1830 to
the upper Severn estuary, its markets remained restricted largely
to the local landsale, and, with few exceptions, this landsale area
was not the scene of many of the major new industrial developments of the period. True, the Stroudwater canal had been
opened in 1779 to give Forest of Dean coal access to the
factory woollen industry that was developing in the valleys
around Stroud, but apart from minor industries in Bristol, there
were few other significant new sources of demand.

The three major inland coalfields in Yorkshire and the East
and West Midlands, however, all profited substantially from the
new sources of demand, though the lion's share of the gain
accrued to the West Midlands primarily on account of the rise of
the Staffordshire iron industry. The Black Country, too, was the
location of a major concentration of metal-working, and this
probably rose to some degree in proportion to the growth of
iron-making. Though the developing industries of the East Midlands were diverse and not, on the whole, major consumers of
coal, mining in this and the West Midlands coalfields benefited
from the general flatness of the land which made possible the
creation during the last thirty years of the eighteenth century of
a network of canals. These carried coal cheaply and allowed the
collieries to supply coal for domestic heating and miscellaneous
industrial use to a wide area of relatively dense population.

It will have been apparent from the foregoing that there is a
far from adequate supply of quantitative information to enable
the historian to reconstruct with any precision the changing
pattern of distribution of coal production between the principal
groups of consumers. But if this task cannot be done with any

pretence of accuracy, it seems worthwhile nevertheless to attempt a rough estimate of this division, making use wherever possible of such data as are available and have been reviewed in this chapter. In Table 7.13, which presents these estimates, every effort has been made to avoid double counting, as, for example, could be involved by not observing the use of steam-engines in the iron industry. The particular breakdown employed is determined by the availability of statistical information. Though, as the Table's 'Note on sources' reveals, these figures cannot be used as anything more than the roughest of indicators, some of the trends revealed were of an order of magnitude that even substantial revision of the actual figures would not alter greatly. Up to 1775 the growth in the industry derived very generally from most of the traditional sources of demand. In the absence of the creation of new facilities for inland transport beyond the improvement of the navigability of some rivers, much of the increase in demand in this period was channelled into the coastal trade. Already, however, by 1775 consumption of coal by steam-power and in the iron industry were beginning to shift the traditional distribution of consumption. After 1775, and above all after 1800, the three new uses for coal in steam-power, iron- and gas-making accounted for a high proportion of the whole increase in the market for coal.

Table 7.13. *Distribution of coal consumption, 1700-1830*
(000s of tons, and percentages of total consumption)

Markets	1700		1750		1775		1800		1830	
	000s of tons	%	000s of tons	%	000s of tons	%	000s of tons	%	000s of tons	%
Exports										
1. Ireland	40	1.3	100	1.9	190	2.1	400	2.7	750	2.5
2. Foreign countries	100	3.4	300	5.7	230	2.6	100	0.7	500	1.6
Total	140	4.7	400	7.6	420	4.7	500	3.3	1,250	4.1
Major industries										
3. Iron	–	–	20	0.4	200	2.3	1,800	12.0	5,635	18.6
4. Copper	30	1.0	50	1.0	80	0.9	150	1.0	240	0.8
5. Salt	250	8.4	300	5.7	310	3.5	325	2.2	350	1.2
6. Gas	–	–	–	–	–	–	–	–	500	1.6
7. Others	890	29.8	1,700	32.5	3,160	35.7	5,315	35.3	7,250	23.9
Other consumers										
8. Collieries	55	1.8	130	2.5	250	2.8	560	3.7	1,500	4.9
9. Small coal (waste)	200	5.7	410	7.8	670	7.6	1,045	6.9	2,150	7.0
10. Domestic	1,420	47.6	2,220	42.5	3,760	42.5	5,350	35.5	11,500	37.9
Total	2,985		5,230		8,850		15,045		30,375	

Note on sources:

Line 1: based on Table 7.5.

Line 2: based on Table 7.8 and using Table 7.7 to make estimates for 1700 and 1750.

Line 3: from Table 7.10.

Lines 4–5: estimates based on sources cited in text above, pp. 232–6.

Line 6: based on estimate in Holland 1835 for coal consumed in gas-making for London in 1834 of 200,000 London chaldrons. Allowing for the re-sale of coke, and assuming that in 1830 London accounted for one-third of all gas produced in the country, a national consumption of 500,000 tons seems probable.

Line 7: these include glass, lime, bricks, brewing, distilling, non-ferrous metals other than copper, metal-working, chemicals, baking, and all industries other than those enumerated in lines 3–6 using steam-power (principally textiles). Since the consumption of most of these industries is quite incalculable, this line is certainly the least likely to be reliable, if only because it has been arrived at residually, by subtracting all other lines from the total. The total was estimated initially in Table 1.2, being built up from regional output estimates.

Line 8: colliery consumption includes coal used for steam-pumping and winding, ventilation furnaces, colliery smithies, and steam-railways. The 1830 percentage is based on several colliery accounts of the 1820s: earlier figures are reduced from this to allow for the progressive introduction of steam-pumping and winding and colliery railways.

Line 9: see Appendix to chapter 1 for a discussion of the problem of estimating waste in the North-east. A slightly lower national percentage has been assumed to make allowance for differences in mining methods, quantities of waste brought to the surface, and the varying ability of the different mining regions to sell their small coal. A small progressive increase has been made to the percentages before 1830 to allow for the growing market for small coal for steam-power.

Line 10: based on an assumption of one ton per head of population with access to domestic coal supplies. It has been assumed that, as a result of transport developments, this population increased progressively as a percentage of total population.

Chapter 8

The Organization of Coal Marketing

i. *The organization of coal suppliers*

Until industries like coke iron-making or those making intensive use of steam-power began the major shift in the distribution of coal consumption that took effect from the last decades of the eighteenth century, in many coalfields the principal markets for coal were off the coalfields—in some important instances remote from them. This distancing of consumer from producer necessarily interposed middlemen, while the relatively small number of major producers and of merchants buying for distribution to the ultimate consumers encouraged the development of oligopolistic conditions in the market, in which the power to control prices and the quantity of coal placed on the market was sought, and from time to time won, by first one group and then another. This situation was as true of the trade supplying London, the largest single supply route in the eighteenth and nineteenth centuries, as of other trades—the Irish trade from Cumberland and Ayrshire, the Firth of Forth trade, and the Bristol Channel trade. It would have been foreign to the nature of capitalist organization for any other pattern to emerge.

In these coastal trades, but above all in the east coast trade, the principal groups struggling for the dominance that aimed to channel the lion's share of the trades' profits into their own pockets were the coalowners, the shippers, and the merchants at the consumers' end of the supply lines. Other groups, like the shipping agents at the exporting ports, or those organizing the unloading of colliers at the importing ports, fought round the fringes of the main struggle and were occasionally enlisted as allies by one or other of the main contestants, but rarely achieved the role of principals.

While it is important for the purposes of the examination of the organization of coal marketing in this period to distinguish between these competing groups, it should not escape notice that their personnel was not always as differentiated as their functions. Some of the wilier participants in the struggle hedged their bets by keeping feet in more than one camp at the same time. Thus both London merchants and north-east coalowners became part-owners of colliers, while some north-east owners entered into partnerships with London merchants. In general, however, the groups acted independently in accordance with the demands of their distinctive interests.

In the North-east, where the homogeneity of the major seasale trade was imposed by the dominance of the London market, the congruence of interests inevitably pushed coal suppliers towards common action. But coalowners everywhere faced the same problems, and, in spite of what was often a fiercely competitive situation, stood to gain by common action. In addition to their relations with landowners, they faced on the one hand their markets, often tightly restricted both geographically and in terms of the types of consumer and quality of coal demanded, and the body of their workers on the other. Inevitably, wherever mining on any scale was carried on in a concentrated area, there was a tendency for mining enterprises to combine.

Even the relatively small-scale operators in Somerset managed to speak with a common voice from the 1790s to protest against increases in turnpike road tolls, to oppose the threat of duty-free privileges at all Severn ports, which would have opened their land-sale areas of Somerset and north Devon to cheaper South Wales coal, and to oppose a bill to build a tramway from the south Gloucester coalfield to the Avon at Bitton.[1] The Erewash coalmasters of Nottinghamshire formed a permanent association in 1798, as did those of the Black Country in 1816, those of the Firth of Forth and Lothians some time before 1772, and those of south Derbyshire some time before 1822. An association of South Wales owners clearly existed in 1823, when it sent a delegation to Newcastle to discuss a petition against the coastwise duty, but the variety of types of coal and the scattered nature of the markets seem to have discouraged any attempts at price control in this coalfield.[2] Several of these regional associations showed interest in price control, the regulation of output, and wage determination. In some cases it was simply a matter of members agreeing to keep the association informed about their output, the wages they paid, and the prices at which they sold, but there can have been little to be gained from reporting of this kind unless it was intended to lead to common action. The Forth proprietors in 1776, for example, in the course of formal meetings of which minutes were kept, agreed to continue a price control that had been instituted the previous year, as did the

[1] Bulley 1953, 58.

[2] Roberts thesis 1953, 213; P. Riden, *The Butterley Company, 1790–1830* (Chesterfield, 1973), 41; A. R. and C. P. Griffin 1973, 97–9; NLS Cadell of Grange 12/1; ScRO Mar and Kellie GD124/17/580/2; ScRO Clerk of Penicuik GD18/1119; DeRO Miller Mundy 517 Additional Deposit, not numbered; NuRO Joint Coal Owners' Association 263, Minute Book 1822–3, 73.

Somerset association in 1792, while the Erewash proprietors agreed in 1802 to negotiate as a body with canal companies for coal freight rates.[3]

Most was at stake, however, in the North-east. There the scale of operations, both in individual undertakings and in the coalfield as a whole, was appreciably larger than in other coalfields, and the high proportion of the output that was sent to London both exposed the trade to monopolizing tendencies at the London end of the trade and offered the most favourable conditions for the emergence of combinations. Even quite small variations in either costs or prices could make substantial differences to the total profits of coalowners. Not surprisingly some form of association existed in the coalfield for the greater part of the period from 1700 to 1830.

The Wear coalowners signed a seven-year price agreement in 1727,[4] for example, but three principal organizations dominated the coal trade of the North-east during the eighteenth and early nineteenth centuries—the Grand Alliance from 1726 until it began to lose power during the third quarter of the eighteenth century, the 'Limitation of the Vend' from 1771, and the Joint Durham and Northumberland Coal Owners' Association from 1805 until after 1830. The first and the last of these have left a mass of records which permits their activities to be traced in considerable detail.[5] The Grand Allies may be said to have come together in response to a situation in which the Company of Hostmen, formerly—in the seventeenth century—a fairly effective organization of monopolistic regulation, had become increasingly divorced from the actual owners and lessees of mines. As a result of the inability of the Tyne coal-masters to agree mutually on a price and output policy, a group of the more powerful coalowning families came together in the hopes of bringing under a single organization a sufficient proportion of the seasale output of the Tyne valley to be able to persuade, if not oblige, the remainder to follow suit. The first, tentative moves

[3] 'Minutes of meeting of River Forth Coal Proprietors, 10 Jan. 1776', NLS Cadell of Grange 12/1; Bulley 1953, 58; Riden, *Butterley Company*, 41.

[4] Beastall 1975, 20.

[5] The early records of the Grand Allies are to be found in the papers of William Cotesworth, the first secretary of the Allies until his death in 1726, in GPL; in the Grand Allies collection in NEI; in the Strathmore papers in DuRO: and in the Armstrong papers in NuRO. The minutes of the Joint Durham and Northumberland Coal Owners' Association from 1805, and other records, are in the NuRO. The bulk and interest of these papers has encouraged quite extensive use of them by Sweezy 1938, who, however, was unable to make use of the Cotesworth, Armstrong, Grand Allies, and Strathmore collections or of the Association's minutes before the volume starting in 1826; by Hughes 1952; and in the theses by Sykes 1928, Ellis 1975, and Cromar 1977. The following account of the Grand Allies and the Joint Coal Owners' Association is based, where not otherwise stated, on these works.

towards collaboration between some of the families that ultimately merged in the Grand Alliance took the form of the establishment of a 'Coal Office' in Newcastle in 1701. This seems to have been little more than an agreement between a group of proprietors and a few fitters to provide some security of marketing, and not to have been concerned with price or output regulation. It failed within two or three years, but was replaced in 1708 by a more formal 'regulation' which established a regular quota for sales and took some steps towards price and quality control. Attempts were made to coerce non-members by the denial of wayleaves, while London sales were guaranteed by the payments of a premium to dealers. William Cotesworth, not at that time an owner, was appointed secretary and sent to London to negotiate with the dealers there and give evidence on the north-eastern coalowners' behalf before a parliamentary enquiry.

The parliamentary committee before which Cotesworth gave evidence in 1710 was considering a bill to prohibit combinations among owners that tended to result in higher coal prices in London. Cotesworth succeeded in diverting its attention towards some monopolistic practices by the shipmasters and lightermen, and the act as it finally emerged in 1711,[6] while condemning combinations among coalowners, did so in terms that Cotesworth believed to be fairly innocuous. Indeed, after discreetly suspending their formal meetings during the first half of 1711, the Newcastle coalowners resumed their acitivites quite openly in July of that year. In 1711 the regulation had controlled only just under half of the North-east's seasale, though two-thirds of the Tyne sale, so that as well as the shipmasters, lightermen, and London merchants, the regulation had to contend with 'interlopers' on its doorstep. The combination of forces against it was too much, and in 1715 it broke up. It was, however, during this 'regulation's' existence that a crucial step was taken that was to alter significantly the environment of any future combination. In 1712, William Cotesworth, operating behind his brother-in-law's name, acquired the manors of Gateshead and Whickham, and transferred exclusive leases of wayleaves across this key access to the south bank of the Tyne to his partners in the regulation. It was this step that allowed Cotesworth to claim in 1720 that most of the coal mined in the Tyne valley was marketed 'by my Lycence or under my influence'.[7]

On 27 June 1726, Sidney Wortley, Edward Wortley, Thomas Ord, George Liddell, Sir Henry Liddell, George Bowes, and William Cotesworth signed the articles of agreement known as 'the Grand Alliance'. They 'have for their respective interests, benefitts and

[6] 9 Anne c.28.　　[7] Quoted by Ellis thesis 1975, 55.

advantages mutually agreed to join some of their collierys and to enter into a friendship and partnership for the purchasing or taking other collierys and for the winning and working of coles thereat and to exchange benefitts and kindnesses with each other upon a lasting foundation.'[8] This alliance, with remarkably little change in the constitution of the group of families comprising it certainly proved to be 'a lasting foundation'. It endured for well over a century, though its impact on the coal trade was greatest in the first quarter-century of its existence. Its foremost purpose was to create a union of principal coalowners so firm and powerful that other proprietors must join it in an effective regulation. To this end the original allies must have the harmonious base of mutual agreements over watercourses, wayleaves, and partnerships. They were spasmodically successful in their aim of forcing wider participation in 'regulations'. Agreements, each initially for three years, were signed in 1731, 1746, and 1773.[9]

It has been suggested that the Alliance was a response to the difficulties of profit-making in a trade that was broadly stagnating. It is unfortunate that the years 1711–21 inclusive are the only ones in the eighteenth century for which there are no surviving statistics of the Newcastle seasale. Yet such evidence as there is suggests quite solid growth of the trade during the first quarter of the century. In the quinquennium 1720–4 London's imports were sixteen per cent up on those of 1710–19, and twenty-one per cent up on those of 1700–9. It is true that London's trade grew only very slowly in the 1730s, '40s, and '50s, and during this period Newcastle's share of the North-east's seasale fell from 72.2 per cent to 61.7 per cent;[10] but this was after the formation of the Grand Alliance and could therefore have been a consequence rather than a cause of its formation.

In the near-stagnant market of the late 1720s, '30s, and '40s the policy of the Grand Allies was to secure as great a share of the market for themselves as possible. They pursued this aim by buying up collieries, wayleaves, and land essential for wayleaves, and taking leases, mainly in the area between the Derwent and Team rivers. In many instances these purchases and leases were for the purpose of restricting the output of competitors rather than for accumulating productive capacity in their own hands. Sir James Clavering, an opponent of the Grand Allies whose land and collieries in the Derwent valley were almost surrounded by those of the Alliance, asserted in 1738 that the Allies were currently paying £5,000 per

[8] GPL Cotesworth CK/13/26.
[9] DuRO NCB First Deposit, Miscellaneous, NCB/I/X/143–5.
[10] See Tables 7.2 and 7.3.

annum in dead rents for collieries they were not working. This was an exaggeration for the benefit of a parliamentary committee, for the real figure at that time, according to the internal records of the Alliance, was £2,565.[11]

The limitations of current drainage technology confined development in this period to the area immediately south of the Tyne. It was indeed possible to develop mines further south in the Pontop and Tanfield area, but successful working there depended upon wayleave access for waggonways to the Tyne, and the lie of the land obliged these waggonways to make use of the Derwent valley on their graded downhill journey to the staithes. Control over these vital wayleaves allowed the Grand Allies to force competitors either to cease mining or to spend the large sums of capital necessary to build new waggonways. By their ownership of the manors of Whickham and Gateshead they exercised control of access to the river frontage between the Team and the Derwent, and by the closure of the 'Old Western Way' waggonway in 1738 they forced owners of mines in the Tanfield area to spend about £10,000 constructing a 'New Western Way' down the western bank of the Derwent in 1740. In the short period between the closing of the old waggonway and the opening of the new the Grand Allies controlled the greater part of the Tyne output, and their near-monopoly was reflected in a very sharp rise in prices in 1739.[12] Of the nine new collieries opened on Tyneside between 1726 and 1750, the Grand Allies controlled eight. Their activities did not go unnoticed even as far away as London.

They pay annual consideration for letting their Mines lye unwrought. They rent a great Number of Staiths or Coal Wharfs, of which they make no use at all, save that of debarring others from coming there. Besides all this, they have got into their Possession, by one means or other, so large a share of all the Lands adjoining to the river Tyne, that they have almost totally debarred all other Persons from Access to them, especially on the South Side, where the best coals are. . . . Great numbers of these Wayleaves the Grand Allies have ingrossed into their own Hands, and pay dead Rents . . . not to use them, but to exclude everybody else.[13]

The faster growth of the seasale market after mid century combined with the growing capacity and efficiency of steam-pumps to encourage the development of mines north of the Tyne and east of the Team, outside the area so tightly controlled by the Grand Allies. But though their share of the whole seasale output of the North-east

[11] DuRO Strathmore D/St/248, 312, v1373.
[12] Cromar 1978, 204; and see Table 9.4.
[13] Anon., *Enquiry into the Reasons of the Advance in the Price of Coal this Seven Years Past* (1739), 13–14, quoted by Sykes thesis 1928, 36.

began to diminish during the third quarter of the eighteenth century, they still remained the major grouping of owners and lessees. The decline of their ability to dominate the whole trade, however, raised once again the possibility of a 'regulation' which could only operate effectively as a partnership of equals. In 1771 a new combination, known as the 'Limitation of the Vend', came into existence in the seasale trade of the North-east, in response, according to an early nineteenth-century commentator, to the initiation of the wasteful practice of screening by the up-river collieries on the Tyne.[14] On the other hand, combinations were always more probable in times of stagnating rather than of buoyant trade. Attempts to form a regulation in 1749 and 1750 failed,[15] and there does not seem to have been any form of joint regulation during the 1750s and 1760s when Newcastle's coastwise trade expanded steadily, while the cessation of growth in the 1770s quickly brought a regulatory combination.

No documentary evidence from the regulation of 1771 has come to light, but, as Francis Thompson, its self-avowed first secretary, reported to the 1800 Select Committee, when asked whether there was any formal agreement in 1771, 'That cannot be well known, being contrary to Act of Parliament.' He insisted, however, that this organization regulated both prices and vend.[16] It does not seem to have enjoyed a continuous existence until 1805 when it was known as the Joint Durham and Northumberland Coal Owners' Association. There were several years in each decade between 1771 and the 1830s when the regulation broke down. The regulation seems to have collapsed for the first time in 1780, and, in spite of efforts to re-form it, was not renewed until 1785. In 1784 Sir John Delaval's agent had written to him announcing the failure of attempts to form a Tyne coalowners' association. There was a further interval of competitive trading in 1795 and part of 1796.[17] A regulation seems to have existed in 1801 when James Kirton, the Shields shipping agent, wrote to his employer in London: 'I understand a Meeting took place at NCastle with the Coal Owners. . . . There Resolutions is not publicly known. It is thote by people in General thay dow not intend to lower the Coals. It is my Opinion and Others the principle of there Meeting was to regulate the Vends (That thay kept perfect Secret).'[18] It is very likely that it was the issue of extravagantly high binding payments (see chapter eleven below) that induced the

---

[14] Edington 1813, 57.
[15] William Brown to Carlisle Spedding, 13 Jan. 1749 and 30 Apr. 1750, NEI Brown 16/1/1, 4.
[16] *First SC Coal Trade* 1800, 541.
[17] NuRO Delaval 4/5/37; Cromar thesis 1978, 143–8.
[18] Ville 1981, 153.

founding of a formal coalowners' association in 1805. After the formal constitution of the 1805 association, annual meetings of all owners were held. A permanent office was established in Newcastle and John Buddle appointed secretary in 1806 with a salary of £100 per annum. The Association's routine work was financed by a levy on each chaldron vended by members.

One major issue of joint action between the coalowners of the North-east was, however, never fully resolved before 1830. 'It is clear to this meeting', ran a minute of a joint meeting of owners from both Tyne and Wear in 1819, 'that nothing but a limitation of the vend from both rivers can produce the effect of raising the price of coals in the London and coast markets.' A regulation on either river was valueless without the co-operation of the other. At times, it is clear, the two rivers did succeed in co-operating. At these times a joint committee co-ordinated the work of separate 'river' committees; but at other times the effect of the decisions of the Tyne committee, always the more cohesive body, was weakened by the refusal of the Wear owners to accept the inevitable domination of the larger group. The Wear owners refused, for example, to agree to a joint regulation in September 1823 on the basis of 750,000 chaldrons for the Tyne and 450,000 for the Wear, though they settled one month later for 775,000 for the Tyne and 484,000 for the Wear. Part of the difficulty lay in the inability of the Wear owners to agree among themselves. Wear owners were fewer in number than those of the Tyne and by the 1820s some produced more coal than any Tyne owner. In particular, jealousy between Lambton and Londonderry made common action on Wearside difficult. In 1825 Lord Lambton had refused to accept a lower proportion of the Wear vend than Lord Londonderry and at a general meeting of owners on both rivers in 1829 all agreed to a joint regulation except Lord Durham (Lambton): he objected to Tyne owners sitting in judgement on his claims for quotas. When a unanimous agreement was finally hammered out in June of that year the joint committee that was to determine the yearly vend was to give equal voting rights to the two rivers. The joint committee left the division of each river's quota to local committees with elaborate provisions for appeals by any one owner against the quotas allocated.

Theoretically the constitution of the Joint Association allowed for democratic management: each member colliery appointed one representative to attend the general meetings, and the general meetings elected the management committees. Practice was probably different. A letter from Buddle in 1808 reported that on the day prior to the general meeting of the Tyne owners the proprietors of the nine 'best

collieries' had met together and agreed to a reduction in output—
a regulation within a regulation.[19] Indeed, the extent to which the
Committee could be dominated by a single man should not be underestimated. From 1806 to 1831, John Buddle was secretary of the
Tyne Committee on which he also regularly represented Wallsend
and Jarrow collieries. As agent at one time or another to both the
Lambton and Londonderry groups of collieries he also occasionally
attended meetings of the Wear Committee. His immense reputation,
combined with the fact that he was the first spokesman for the north-
east industry on all parliamentary enquiries must have made it very
difficult to offer serious opposition to him on either committee.[20]

These constitutional problems serve to emphasize the central role
of the vend in any association of north-east owners. The prime,
though not the sole, purpose of these associations was the use of
monopoly power to maximize profits, and the means of raising
profits were to be the restriction of output, the elimination of price
competition, and the control, so far as possible, of labour costs.

In all discussions about the activities of any regulation or association, control over the quantity of coal put on the market was
assumed to be the most important objective. 'Nothing can better the
state of the Trade at large', it was asserted in 1820, 'both shipping
and Colly. interest, but restriction of quantity.'[21] The 'vend' was
always assumed to relate to the quantity of coal sold by sea. Landsales were never subjected to control and exports, too, were normally
exempted from the restriction of the vend.[22] Whether for one or
both rivers, and whether determined by the looser bodies that
organized the 'Limitation of the Vend' after 1771 or by the Joint
Association after 1805, the total vend was fixed by a central committee and represented its judgement of the quantity that the coastwise market would bear without forcing the price down. The division
of the total between the participating collieries was made in relation
to the 'basis'—a predetermined, assumed vend for each colliery that
fixed its proportion of the total and could be adjusted according to
the size of the actual vend in each year. The annual vend was then
further subdivided into fortnightly or monthly allocations. Collieries
were to submit certified monthly returns showing how their monthly
shipments corresponded with their monthly vend allocations. Short-
falls could be compensated for by cash payments or permission could

[19] John Buddle to William Russell, 6 Jan. 1808, NEI Buddle 15/250. The 'best collieries'
were sometimes called 'first-class' collieries, and seem to have been those with vends over
30,000 chaldrons.
[20] Hiskey thesis 1978, 189–90.
[21] 'Hints on Regulation', 1820, NuRO Forster ZFO/1.
[22] RC Coal 1871, 12.

be given for them to be made good in later months, though this had to be specifically sought. Excess shipments were subject to heavy fines. Monthly vends were determined at short notice to allow for the state of the market to be watched in the short run with great care. A meeting of the Tyne committee on 28 April 1821 acceded to a request from a deputation of shipowners asking for the May vend to be reduced by fifty chaldrons per thousand because of the decline in prices in London. Failure to agree about the subdivision of the vend between collieries led to open trade for periods in 1795-6, 1800-1, 1818-19, 1820, 1822, 1826, and 1829.[23] The 1820 break arose because of the intransigence of the owners of Fawdon and Pelaw Main collieries over their share of the vend, but the frequent failures of the 1820s were, at least so far as the Wear Committee was concerned, generally attributed to the emergence of the Hetton Company, a large, untraditional grouping of mainly non-landowners, 'a pack of madmen', as Lord Londonderry described them in 1825, 'with swords in their hands slashing about them on all sides, ruthless of consequences'.[24]

A corollary of regulating the vend and prices was the standardization of measures. The traditional flexibility of coal measures had always been the means by which individual shippers were able to circumvent a regulation. The loading of a keel with nine chaldrons instead of eight when colliers' cargoes were bought by the keel was a way of effectively reducing an authorized price by twelve and a half per cent while not appearing to do so. A statement of 1824 placed 'a strict attention to the statute measure' high in its list of priorities for the Association, while an article of an agreement of 1827 laid down 'that no colliery shall on any account exceed the Statute Measure per Cha.' A meeting in 1819 had recommended that the construction of waggonway waggons be altered so that they could hold their correct measures when filled 'strike-full' without being heaped, and to ensure that these orders were carried out in 1825 the Tyne Committee appointed an inspector who was to be paid sixty guineas for three and a half months' service, with an assistant at 30s. per week, to examine the filling of waggons and the loading of keels. Within one month the inspector had reported seven collieries for offences against these regulations. A threat to report offending collieries to the revenue officers is a useful reminder that over-measure deceived the official statistics as well as competitors.

---

[23] DuRO NCB First Deposit NCB/I/JB/2434; NEI Buddle 20/15; Hiskey thesis 1978, 186-7.

[24] Marquis of Londonderry to J. Buddle, 5 June 1825, DuRO Londonderry D/Lo/C142, quoted in Hiskey thesis 1978, 193.

The Joint Association of the early nineteenth century naturally assumed the role of the mouthpiece of the north-east industry, though it must be remembered that it never represented more than the seasale sector of the industry. So long as there was a tax on the coastal and export trades in coal, the North-east, with only a relatively small landsale, had a permanent interest in bringing pressure to bear on governments. In 1823 the Tyne committee of the Joint Association co-operated with the London-based Committee for the Repeal of the Duties on Coals in an approach to the government and voted money in support. In 1824 they produced a printed brochure which set out the case for repeal, or at least equalization, of the duties on the coastwise trade and was clearly intended for distribution to members of Parliament. There were frequent communications to the government on minor technicalities of measures and tax rates. It also emerges from a minute of 1828 that members of Parliament, particularly those like Sir Matthew White Ridley and Sir Henry Vane-Tempest, with a direct interest in the local industry, were 'retained' by the Association to maintain the fight against the duties. They were, of course, ultimately successful in 1831. Local members were also used as intermediaries to oppose in Parliament canal schemes that, by linking London and east coast areas with coalfields in the Midlands, might threaten to erode the North-east's markets.[25]

The Joint Coal Owners' Association brought together owners on the Tyne, the Wear, and Hartley and Blyth. In 1811 an attempt was made to create a local organization of owners in the area of Northumberland served by the port of Blyth and its creeks. It was to be tied to an agreement over wayleaves and dead-rents which demonstrated that the Grand Allies were not alone in these kinds of practices. Sir Matthew White Ridley and his partner, Mr Taylor Winship, bought a majority share in Cowpen colliery and, in order to leave this colliery a clear run of the Blyth trade, and in return for a wayleave across land of the Delavals who traded through Hartley, Sir Matthew agreed to close down his Plessey colliery for an annual compensation of £1,800. In the event, the joint agreement fell through, and in 1821 Cowpen colliery joined the Joint Association as a member of the Tyne committee.[26]

In Scotland, the Glasgow market presented some features that made it comparable with the London market and evoked, for short periods, a similar response from the local suppliers. Because of the

[25] *Statement of the Case of the Northern Coal Owners* (Newcastle, 1823), DuRO NCB First Deposit NCB/I/JB/2519.

[26] William Stobart to Sir Matthew White Ridley, 17 May 1813; and J. Buddle to Sir Matthew White Ridley, 20 Jan. 1823, NuRO Ridley (Blagdon) ZRI 35/5/1.

unsuitability of the upper Clyde for the navigation of colliers that might have brought coal from the Ayrshire coast, the Glasgow market was the virtual monopoly of suppliers within easy road-carriage distance of the city. Not surprisingly, in 1790 these coal-owners formed a combination to regulate the supply and fix the price. To achieve this they created jointly a selling company—the Glasgow Coal Company—which was to have the monopoly of sales in Glasgow, and which bought agreed quotas from the individual collieries in the combine for re-sale at predetermined prices in Glasgow. The same year, however, witnessed the opening of the Monkland canal linking the Airdrie and Coatbridge district with the Clyde below Glasgow, and the Glasgow Coal Company quickly found that it was being undersold by newly opened mines on the canal. The combination collapsed within a few years, but was re-formed in 1813. This time the agreement was to restrict output with a view to raising prices in Glasgow. Competition from the major canalside colliery at Faskine, however, kept prices down until, in the following year, the members of the combination collectively bought up their competitor. For a few years the strengthened combination succeeded in regulating the Glasgow market to its members' advantage, but deteriorating market conditions in 1817 broke it up as individual owners chafed at its restrictions.[27]

The north-east Association, its predecessors, and imitators never intended to pursue anything other than the interests of the owners and lessees. While they assumed, on occasion contrary to the reality of the law, that any combination or strike by their employees was illegal and ought to be broken up, if necessary with the use of the armed forces of the Crown, they never doubted the legality and appropriateness of their own combinations. The effect of the particularly powerful and effective north-eastern monopoly of seasale owners on the development of the industry is, however, not easily assessed. London consumers automatically attributed what they believed to be the artificially high level of coal prices to the combination of the north-eastern owners. The owners' intention, according to a minute of 1824, was 'to supply the *real natural* demand for coals without forcing them on the markets'. While this suggests that the owners were ignorant of the concept of a downward-sloping demand curve, it also hints that the maximization of output played at least some part beside price maintenance in the policies of the Association. Certainly in the 1820s, in the years when a limitation operated, a tight control of prices was intended. A memorandum of

[27] Hamilton 1930.

1820 insisted that a regulation automatically required 'the standard price of every description of coal to be fixed at the commencement of the Regn., and no alteration to take place without leave of the Comm.'[28] In 1824, with a restored regulation, the Tyne committee could assert 'that the principles on which the regulation was founded and unanimously agreed to, were the adherence to the established selling price of each colliery', though within four days of stating this principle, the same committee conceded a request from Buddle, as representative of Wallsend colliery, for a reduction in the price of Wallsend coals because they had 'fallen into disrepute at Market'. Certainly the number of lists of colliery prices among the records of the Joint Association indicates that, if the Association was not active in controlling prices at all times, it took steps to keep a close watch on pricing policies of members.

The object of most monopolies is to increase profits, and the regulations of the north-east coalowners were no exception. In an industry in which ploughed-back profits were such an essential element in the provision of capital, monopoly profits claimed some justification in safeguarding the future supply of capital. In his evidence to the 1830 Select Committee Buddle argued that cutthroat competition in a trade as rigidly structured as the east-coast coal trade would have kept profits at a level too low to permit the accumulation of capital without which the constant high level of investment, so essential to an extractive industry, could not have been sustained. He also expressed the view that, given permanent surplus capacity in the north-east industry, competitive trading would drive down prices to the point at which only the largest and most heavily capitalized undertakings could stay in business; and when the weakest had been driven into bankruptcy, the few powerful owners would the more easily control the trade thereafter to their own advantage. The regulations were justified in this way as protecting both smaller and larger producers in the North-east, as well, ultimately, as the consumers.[29] Buddle summed up his attitude to the owners' combination in a letter to Lord Londonderry of 1835.

The true spirit and principle of a regulation is that it should benefit *all* classes, and make the whole trade move harmoniously, and beneficially, as if it belonged to one joint stock company. How then can any individual possessed of common sense and a justly balanced mind think to pursue his own particular interest, to the prejudice of the Body? Has not this been tried again and again, by the

[28] NuRO Forster ZFO, 'Memorandum dated 2 June 1820'.
[29] SC *Lords Coal Trade* 1830, 69-70.

1. Diagram of Curr's design for pithead gear

2. Waggonway with keel and staith in background

J. Christie Lith.ᵗ Newcastle.

3. Pithead in North-east, early nineteenth century (showing corves, rolleys, and waggonway).

4. Diagram of a four-horse winding gin at a North-east pit

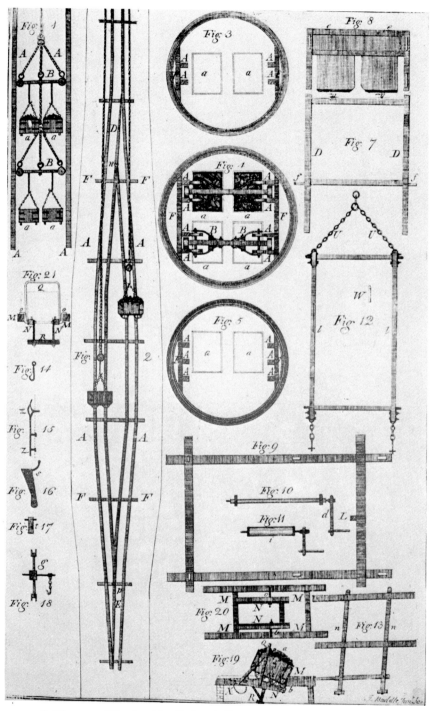

5. Diagrams of Curr's guide-rails for winding, 1789. The diagram is signed by
John Buddle junior, then aged sixteen.

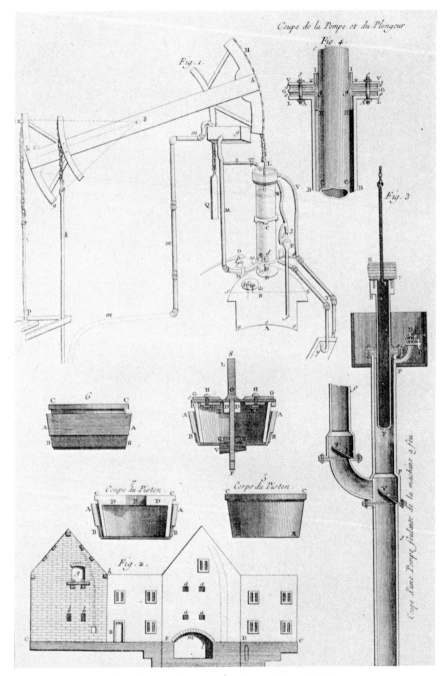

_6. Diagrams of steam-pumping machinery, 1773.

(a)

(b)

(c)

7. Sketches from a map of the Longbenton estate near Newcastle, 1749
  (a) Loaded waggon on horse-drawn waggonway
  (b) A pair of Newcomen pumping-engines
  (c) What appears to be steam-winding gear

8. Drop at Wallsend on the north bank of the Tyne.

powerful, the obstinate or the presumptious, in every class of the Trade, and has not the result been invariably the same—a *complete* failure?[30]

At first sight it might seem strange that there never emerged before 1830 a national organization of coalowners. There is, as we have seen, enough evidence to indicate that, at one period or another, almost every coalfield developed a coalowners' association, and there is little doubt that in the largest of the pre-1830 coalfields—the North-east—the association was enduring and moderately ineffective. Only a single instance has come to light of two regional associations —those of South Wales and the North-east in 1823—co-operating. The absence of national organization is surely to be explained in terms of the intense regionalization of the mining industry and its markets before 1830. Every coalfield was, it is true, threatened to some extent by its neighbours round the fringes of its markets: Somerset owners looked apprehensively over their shoulders at their South Wales competitors; Cumberland, Lancashire, North and South Wales jostled for preference in the Irish trade; Warwickshire owners were indignant at the invasion of their markets by Staffordshire coals benefitting from cheap canal freights; and the North-east bristled at the least hint of competition from the Midlands in the London market. But the greater part of the market for each coalfield remained largely inviolate from competition before 1830. In its analysis of coal markets in the 1820s, the 1830 Commons Select Committee was able confidently to draw a map dividing the country into twelve consuming areas, each distinctly supplied by particular coalfields. The reason for the absence of a national organization of coalowners surely lay in the absence of a national market. Before 1830 there was still very little inter-regional competition, but the development of railways after 1830 would quickly change this situation.

ii. *Middle-men in coal marketing*

When the coal trade from the North-east to London first began to assume importance during the sixteenth century, the trade was entirely in the hands of the major Newcastle merchants who had incorporated themselves in the Company of Hostmen. A charter of the City of Newcastle of 1600 conferred on the Hostmen control of the coal trade, though the legal basis of the monopoly of the trade which the Company claimed that this charter confirmed to them,

[30] J. Buddle to Marquis of Londonderry, 3 June 1835, DuRO Londonderry D/Lo/C142, quoted in Hiskey thesis 1978, 190.

and for which they paid the Crown not only an outright sum of £80 but a perpetual duty of 1s. per chaldron on all coal shipped from the port, was insecure. This is not the place to follow the fortunes of the Hostmen's Company since its importance lies in the sixteenth and seventeenth centuries rather than later. Suffice it to note that by the opening of the eighteenth century its role in the control of the coal trade of the North-east was already very much reduced. The coalowners in the immediate vicinity of the City of Newcastle who had formerly dominated the Company were, with the exhaustion of the riverside pits and the shift of mining to the areas, particularly in the south-west, further from the river, no longer the major coal-owners of the region. Many of the new owners were not free of the Company, while as time progressed Hostmen had become more and more middle-men in coal marketing than coalowners and controllers of the trade. While the monopoly of the Company, in so far as it was regarded at all in the eighteenth century, was preserved by the 'colouring' of the shipment of coal produced and marketed by non-Hostmen by the employment of Hostmen as shipping agents, the effective power in the coal trade passed into the hands of the major coalowners or lessees who were more often than not land-owners in the counties of Durham and Northumberland rather than citizens and merchants of the City of Newcastle.[31]

The shipping agents employed by the owners had been known from the seventeenth century as fitters. They remained members of the Hostmen's Company as a matter of form and convenience, but this membership ceased to be a matter of real significance during the eighteenth and nineteenth centuries. William Cotesworth defined a Tyne fitter in 1711 as 'an agent hired by the coalowner by the year and is the person yt transacts the bargaine of buying and selling between the master of the ship and the coalowner and has the direction of the keles or lighters yt takes the coales from the staithes or wharfes and carries them on board the ships.'[32] The management of the keels involved the employment of keelmen, and, though keel-men were paid effectively at piece-rates, that is to say by the keel loaded, taken down-river and unloaded into colliers, the normal practice in the North-east was for them to be engaged by bond to the fitter for a year at a time. The keelmen were therefore employees of specific fitters. The keels themselves were owned by the fitters and since they normally owned several keels, some capital was necessary to enter business as a fitter. In the early nineteenth century Tyne keels cost between £130 and £150 each, and Wear keels about

[31] For the history of the Hostmen's Company see Dendy 1901; Nef 1932, II, 119–33.
[32] GPL Cotesworth CK/3/60.

£90. An early eighteenth-century list named thirty-four fitters owning 338 keels. The largest number owned by a single fitter was twenty-two.[33] By the 1820s, when the keelmen were fighting their losing battle against the spouts and drops, the Tyne fitters had begun the practice of charging keel-rent to the keelmen.[34] The employment of keelmen also involved the additional employment of supervisors

to look after [the keelmen] and see that they take in their measure of coals at ye warfs, and after so taken in, to order ye same on board their respective ships. They are a set of men by no means to be trusted and without some one to look after them, they will never, or rarely, take in ye statute or King's measure . . . and that without being well look'd after, frequently imbezel and dispose of coals in their way down to Shields.[35]

On the Tyne it was not uncommon for fitters to take work from a number of coalowners, remaining independent agents, but on the Wear owners were more usually able to insist on the exclusive services of fitters who therefore tended to become their employees. On the Wear, too, though coalowners appear to have owned the keels, the fitters actually bought the coal from the owners and re-sold it to collier masters, taking the commercial risk of the trans-action. An agreement of 1727 between Wear coalowners and fitters reveals that coalowners and fitters both participated in the owner-ship of colliers, that owners had agreed not to sell coal to the fitters below a certain price while the fitters for their part agreed not to sell to masters under a certain price. The agreement also indicated that one of the principal coalowners, Lord Scarbrough, employed four fitters.[36] It is evident that this was a reciprocal agreement between equal parties. Similarly, in 1800 Sir Henry Vane-Tempest agreed with six fitters to deal exclusively with them for a period of one year.[37] It seems that Wear fitters were effectively merchants, making their living by buying and selling, though their independence was circum-scribed by their binding themselves to a single coalowner. On the Tyne, however, fitters drew their remuneration from a standing retaining fee per chaldron from the owners and/or a 'fittage' charge per chaldron said to compensate them for the management of the keels and their guarantee of bad debts.[38]

[33] NEI Buddle 14/113; NEI Watson 8/8/293; GPL Cotesworth CJ/3/15, n.d. but probably 1709–19.

[34] *Address to the Keelmen of the River Tyne*, 9 Oct. 1822, NEI Bell 15/13/590.

[35] 'Mr Mosley's remarks about keelmen', 1768, TWRO Tyne Keelmen 394/29.

[36] NEI Buddle Atkinson 45/5/no pagination; Beastall 1975, 20–1.

[37] NEI Buddle 8/1.

[38] NEI Buddle Atkinson 45/5/7; N. Clayton to J. Buddle, 8 Feb. 1823, DuRO NCB First Deposit NCB/I/JB/299.

By the early decades of the nineteenth century technical change, mainly in the form of the replacement of the keels by spouts and drops, began to erode the usefulness of fitters, and coalowners took over the management of the transfer of coal from staith to collier themselves. Collier masters acting for the shipowners, bought coal directly from coalowners at their own staithes and the coal was not put into keels or delivered from the spouts until a ship had been contracted to receive it.[39] Similar pressures were evidently at work on the Wear at about the same time, since John Lambton proposed in 1825 to dispense with the service of fitters. It is not known whether he acted on this proposal.[40]

While it was the normal practice for shipmasters, acting as agents for the owners, to negotiate directly with the fitters in the purchase of coal in the North-east, at least one larger shipowning firm found it advantageous to employ its own agent to look after its interests at the loading end and to negotiate with the fitters on behalf of its whole fleet rather than leave this to the masters. Michael Henley and Son owned over twenty vessels which they employed mainly but not exclusively in the east-coast coal trade, and chartered others for the same purpose. In 1799 they came to an arrangement with one of their former captains, James Kirton, to act as their permanent shipping agent in Shields. Kirton not only bought coal from fitters and allocated it to the Henleys' ships, he also bought, sold, and chartered ships on their behalf, arranged for repairs to ships, advised on the engagement of captains and crews, and provided a day-to-day intelligence service about market conditions in the North-east. His letters to his principals in London during the early years of the nineteenth century are an invaluable guide to the intricacies of the Newcastle coal-market.[41] There may have been other shipping agents in the North-east performing similar functions, but their activities have not so far come to light.

Very little is known, unfortunately, about the organization of the coal trade at ports outside the North-east, though it is clear that middle-men found some useful roles. In 1737, for example, Cumberland coalowners discovered a need for an agent to safeguard their interests at the Dublin end of their Irish trade. The 'pursers' and porters at Dublin were said to be defrauding the shipmasters in respect both of quantity and price, and the coalowners at Whitehaven

[39] Printed objections to the Sunderland Coal Trade bill, Apr. 1824, NEI Buddle Atkinson 45/5/no pagination.
[40] 'Reasons why the Fitters at Sunderland belonging to JGL sho'd not be done away', 1825, LEA MP11/1.
[41] Ville 1981. The Henley papers, including Kirton's correspondence, are now housed in the National Maritime Museum (NMM HNL/15).

and Workington set up a committee that appointed Thomas Bacon as their sole agent in Dublin to look after their interests. Bacon was to receive a salary of £150 per annum and to be assisted by twelve pursers each with £40 per annum. These salaries were met by a levy on coal shipped. It is not known how long this arrangement lasted, but a further similar set of appointments was made in 1755.[42]

The fortunate survival of a report of 1818 on the Alloa coal trade provides a valuable account of the evolution of the organization of the coal trade on the east coast of Scotland. Before the repeal of the Scottish coasting duty in 1793

the whole trade was carried on by the shipmasters, who loaded coals on their own account. They granted bills for the amount at a month's date; which bills were paid with uncommon regularity, and comparatively few bad debts were made. . . . [After 1793] coal merchants known by the name of Coal Brokers established themselves, and took the trade out of the hands of the shipmasters. They bought whole cargoes either from the Shipmasters at market or sent vessels to load at the Collieries. Along with the sale of Scotch coals they uniformly sold English coals; and the latter being decidedly a more profitable concern, they were more zealous to promote the sale of these coals than of Scotch.

The River Forth Coalmasters, finding that their sales was thus rapidly declining, owing to the Coal Brokers, had to step forward and establish Agents at the different Ports, such as Leith, Perth, Dundee, etc. etc. to sell their coals exclusively; and though sales have by this plan been greatly promoted, the whole state of the Trade has been rendered uncommonly intricate and heavy to carry on, owing to the sales being chiefly on credit, and in very small quantities; and so very inconvenient and perplexed have these agencies become, that they are now only carried on from absolute necessity, and will be carried on no longer than other arrangements can be made. A violent competition has thus been produced. The credit has been extended to three months, and the bad debts and returned bills are at least three times greater than they were formerly.[43]

In most trades round the coast, but above all in the trade between the North-east and London, the shipmaster, acting on behalf of the shipowners, acted technically as a principal. He bought coal independently at the exporting port and sold it freely at the importing port, paying his crew and taking his profit from the difference. In practice the master's role as an independent middle-man was much more circumscribed. Many of the part-owners of the ships on whose behalf he acted were coalowners or fitters themselves, and while he may have enjoyed some freedom of action, though within the very severe constraints of the market structure, to dispose of the cargo in London, there is so little evidence of real bargaining between

[42] CuRO Lonsdale D/Lons/W/Whitehaven 30; CuRO Curwen D/Cu/3/51.
[43] ScRO Mar and Kellie GD124/17/58/2–3.

fitter or owner and shipmaster in the North-east that it seems more likely that the reality of the trade was that the shipmaster acted as little more than an agent for the fitter or owner.

This arrangement probably prevailed in times when the trade was subject to 'regulation'. At other times the fierceness of competition led to more flexible arrangements. In particular it produced a form of organization known as 'freighting'. This simply meant the owner sending coal to London at his own risk instead of leaving the commercial risk of buying and re-selling to the shipmaster. At times when the market was so slack that shipmasters preferred to keep their ships idle rather than risk buying, owners chartered colliers at agreed freight rates per chaldron. In 1829 it was reported that shipowners were able to obtain 8s. per chaldron for freighting from Newcastle to London in summer and 10s. in winter.[44] Buddle believed that freighting was encouraged by the clerks in the fitting offices 'who being stimulated by the hopes of numerous *Foys* and *Snacks* got by freighting have the knack of persuading their masters that it is the best way to vend their coals'. He claimed that some clerks were able by these means to make £400 per annum over and above their salaries.[45] If Buddle was correct, the clerks' persuasion was only likely to be effective in particularly slack times. In a letter of 1830 Buddle explained that freighting occurred only when the price of coal in London was not high enough to induce shipmasters to take on coal in the North-east on their own account. The coalowners, on the other hand, were confronted with the choice between growing stocks of deteriorating coal and an absence of revenue on the one hand, and laying out money on freight for cargoes of coal that might well sell at a loss in London on the other. 'The consequence is', Buddle wrote later, 'that they seldom leave any profit almost, and sometimes sell to loss.'[46] So they did. In 1827 Buddle himself was obliged to report a loss of £1,666. 19s. 6d. by freighting from Hebburn colliery on Tyneside. Freighting was, indeed, 'a woeful practice, being injurious to the Trade at large as well as to the parties immediately concerned, and ought to be abolished. The only apology that can be offered in the present instance is, I believe, that *necessity has no law*.'[47]

Because freighting was regarded as an unmitigated evil in the trade it probably came only rarely to formal notice. The only statistical report that has come to hand relates to the first five months of 1807.

---

[44] NEI Buddle Atkinson 45/5/136.
[45] J. Buddle to W. Russell, 26 Jan. 1808, NEI Buddle 15/275.
[46] J. Buddle to W. M. Pitt, 20 June and 11 Dec. 1830, NEI Buddle 22/263, 268.
[47] NEI Buddle 41/146; J. Buddle to G. Silvertop, 31 Dec. 1806, NEI Buddle 15/170.

In that period Tyne collieries shipped in the normal way (at ship-masters' risk) 193,007 chaldrons. But stocks of coal on Tyneside at the beginning of June amounted to 101,760 chaldrons, and 27,402 chaldrons were 'vended by freighting' during this five-month period.[48] The Delavals' agent diagnosed the undesirable consequences of freighting very acutely as early as 1798. Freighting, he argued, would attract 'stranger' vessels to the port of Hartley, and this would encourage their regular shippers to demand the same treatment regularly or to leave the port. The buyers of coal in London, he pointed out, would sense the coalowners' desperation and immediately reduce their offering prices. He believed that even in slack times it was wiser to stick to the usual method of leaving the risk to the regular shipmasters, but to encourage them by offering over-weight.[49]

iii. *The organization of the London market*

Before entering a discussion of the organization of coal marketing in London some effort should be made to put the trade in perspective. Because London consumers were articulate and had easy access to Parliament, the London coal trade attracted a quite disproportionate amount of attention. Superficially the coal industry appears to have been the subject of a great deal of parliamentary concern during the eighteenth and early nineteenth centuries. A statement of the early nineteenth century claimed that during the eighteenth century over two hundred acts and orders had been passed regulating the industry, and this was probably not an exaggeration.[50] Yet closer examination reveals that, apart from questions of taxation, almost all this regulation was concerned with the London market. And this parliamentary interest has been closely reflected in the historiography of the industry: more scholarly attention has been focused on this aspect of the industry's history than on almost all other aspects put together. Yet the London market never accounted for more than a minor share of the nation's coal consumption: indeed, in spite of the importance accorded to it in discussions about coal marketing in the North-east, it never preponderated in sales from the coal-field, though it may have been the largest single outlet. Table 8.1 sets out the proportions of London consumption in British output and in that of the North-east. Even in the coastwise trade from the North-east, the share of the London market declined slowly from

[48] NEI Watson 13/97/no pagination.
[49] J. Bryers to Sir John Hussey Delaval, 26 Aug. 1798, NuRO Delaval ZDE 3/23/65.
[50] NEI Bell 14/2/509.

Table 8.1. *Shares of the London market in British and North-east output*

Output (000s of tons)	1700	1750	1800	1830
Great Britain	2,985	5,230	15,045	30,375
North-east	1,210	2,070	4,005	6,915
North-east coastwise shipments	700[1]	1,120	2,480	3,660
Imports (000s of tons)				
London	445	677	1,234	2,079
London's imports as percentage of:				
Great Britain output	14.9	12.9	8.2	6.8
North-east output	36.8	32.7	30.8	30.1
North-east coastwise shipments	63.6	60.4	49.8	56.8

Note: 1 Estimate.
Sources: Tables 1.2, 7.2, and 7.3.

just less than two-thirds at the opening of the eighteenth century to a little more than one-half by 1830.

With this reservation in mind let us turn now to the organization of coal marketing in London.[51] The occasional periods of freighting apart, the normal method of trading was for the shipmaster to arrive in the Thames seeking to sell his cargo to the highest bidder and hoping to cover the costs of the voyage and leave some profit for the shipowners. By the early eighteenth century the trade in which he participated had already well over a century of experience behind it. In consequence the market he confronted had already evolved a considerable degree of organization. The principal operations that gave rise to this sophisticated organization were, firstly, transferring the coal from the colliers moored in the river in the Pool of London to lighters and unloading the lighters to riverside wharves; and

[51] This account of the organization of the London import trade in coal is based, where not otherwise indicated, on HMC, *House of Lords, 1702–04*, 235–6; *SC Coal Trade* 1800; H. Humpherus, *History of the Origin and Progress of the Company of Watermen and Lightermen of the River Thames* (London, 3 vols., 1887–9); W. E. Hooper, *The London Coal Exchange* (London, 1907); Westerfield 1915, 232–9; Sykes thesis 1928, 21–30; Fraser-Stephens 1952; R. Smith 1961; Ellis thesis 1975, 88–92. Of these, R. Smith 1961 is unquestionably the most valuable.

secondly, the splitting of whole cargoes of coal into the small lots called for by individual consumers. The first of these operations created the group that owned the lighters; the second necessitated one group of merchants who bought big and sold small, and another that negotiated sales on behalf of owners and shipmasters.

The use of lighters for unloading was called for by the sheer impossibility of finding wharf space for the vast numbers of colliers unloading at any one point in time. As we saw in chapter five, there were over 6,000 arrivals in the port of London each year in the 1820s, and probably one-third of that number in the early years of the eighteenth century. Not only were these arrivals heavily concentrated in the eight or nine months between early spring and late autumn, but even within that period arrivals tended to be bunched on account of the vagaries of the winds in the North Sea, or, in wartime, because convoy sailing was adopted. It was not uncommon to see two or three hundred colliers standing in the river at once either unloading or waiting to be unloaded.[52]

In the absence of any mechanical unloading devices the coal had to be shovelled from the holds of the colliers into the lighters alongside and it was at this point in the handling of the coal that it was measured for taxation purposes by the *meters*. The actual shovelling was done by teams of sixteen coal-heavers, who threw the coal from platform to platform within the hold until it could finally be thrown into the measuring vat from which it was tipped over the side into the lighters. This primitive and highly labour-intensive method was not changed until the 1750s, when baskets were introduced. Gangs of nine filled the baskets and raised them by rope and pulley to deck level for emptying into the measuring vat. These workers were known as 'coal-whippers'. By 1769 it was estimated that one-third of London's coal was unloaded by whipping and the remainder by the coal-heavers. It is probable that whipping was general by the beginning of the nineteenth century.

Because of the irregular and often bunched arrivals of the colliers which led to occasional periods of high demand for labour, the supply of heavers and whippers was excessive, creating a situation ripe for their exploitation. Pay was by piece-rates for the gang and tended to fluctuate violently, being subject to demand which might vary from day to day and even from hour to hour. In 1756, for example, the highest rate paid was 3s. per 'score' (of London chaldrons—about 26½ tons) which was paid at the height of the shipping season for four days in September, and the lowest was 1s. per score paid on one day in February when there would be very little demand

[52] R. Smith 1961, 142, quoting *Gentleman's Magazine*, 1799.

for this kind of labour. These workers were heavily exploited by the undertakers who paid part of their wages in beer or foodstuffs. A series of acts of Parliament (of 1758, 1770, 1803, 1807, and 1831) endeavoured, without any real success, to curb these abuses. Coal-heaving and whipping was a low and unsatisfactory grade of work, and was relegated, as so often happens, largely to immigrant labour. In 1768 it was estimated that two-thirds of this labour force in London was Irish.[53]

At the opening of the eighteenth century the group of middle-men who had interposed themselves between the shipmasters and the coal retailers were known as *coal-brokers* or *crimps*. At this time they were a rather diverse group of men ranging from little more than gang-leaders of the heavers to relatively wealthy merchants. Along-side this wide-ranging group and by no means clearly differentiated from them in the early decades of the eighteenth century were the owners of the lighters that brought the coal from ship to shore. As capitalists rather than manual workers the owners of lighters had been able to incorporate themselves into a gild. The Company of Watermen and Lightermen controlled this trade in the late seven-teenth century. At this period when the coal, once brought ashore, was sold at Billingsgate, the Lightermen, with their control over the essential link between ship and shore, traded directly in coal. 'Where-as Billingsgate ought to be a free market . . .', complained the writer of a broadsheet of 1703, 'it is plain the same is now Restricted by a small number of Lightermen who are now the Sole Buyers, to whom all Consumers of Coal apply themselves.'[54] The House of Commons' Committee of 1729 discovered that ten lightermen con-trolled two-thirds of the whole trade. Though lightermen not free of the Company seem to have existed, the small group of leading members of the Company were able to exert pressure on shipmasters not to sell to the non-Company lightermen under threat of refusing ever to buy from them. In 1730, however, in response to revelations of the extent of the manipulation of the London market by the members of the Watermen's and Lightermen's Company, the City of London modified the Company's charter, destroying its monopolistic powers. Thus after 1730 the Lightermen, as the principal buyers of coal from shipmasters, appear to have given way to a group of un-incoporated merchants, though this development may have already been initiated even before 1730.

The undoing of the Lightermen was also assisted by an organiza-tion set up by the shipowners to protect themselves against the

---

[53] For the coal-heavers and whippers, see George 1929; Sykes thesis 1928, 23–5.
[54] Quoted by Sykes thesis 1928, 57.

Lightermen. In 1729, in order to present a collective front to the monopoly of the Lightermen, the shipowners set up an office at the Dog Tavern in Billingsgate. Here a register of arrivals was kept so that cargoes could be sold and colliers unloaded in strict rotation, and a small number of agents were employed to handle the sale of coal to the Lightermen. One of these agents was Benjamin Horne. The son of a Quaker glover of Arundel in Sussex, Horne had managed to set himself up as an independent coal factor as early as 1719, securing one of only three or four agencies at the Dog Tavern Office in 1729. He prospered in the coal trade, leaving £70,000 at his death in 1766, and the firm he founded ultimately became Charrington's, one of London's largest coal-traders.

This flexible and fairly undifferentiated market structure was neither sufficiently free from abuses to satisfy the coalowners, shipowners, and consumers nor produced any group strong enough to dominate the trade and defend itself against outraged consumers or other interested parties in Parliament or City. With the decline of the power of the Lightermen, however, around 1730, three quite distinct groups with specialized functions appeared to be emerging. First, the lesser crimps found themselves left only with the business of providing the gangs of heavers: they became known as *under-takers*, and, later in the eighteenth century, were normally dockside publicans or small shopkeepers. The term 'crimp' degenerated into little more than a pejorative. Second, in a direct response to the needs felt by north-east coalowners to retain agents in London to look after their individual interests, there emerged a group of *factors*. The name 'factor' seems to have come into use first about 1710, and the role of factor became clearly differentiated after about 1730. Third, were the *buyers*. Towards the end of the eighteenth century three classes of buyers had emerged. *First buyers* were the principal buyers: they negotiated the purchase from factors of not less than whole cargoes. Indeed, factors would negotiate only with first buyers. *Second buyers* were merchants who bought smaller quantities from first buyers for retailing mainly outside London, and *third buyers* were small London retailers who sold to consumers from small sheds.

By the end of the eighteenth century the interplay of interest in the London market, modified only slightly by the legislation of Parliament and the City, had produced a complex, but stable, form of organization. The coal *factors* emerged as little more than agents of the coalowners, performing a specific set of functions on commission. By 1788 it was apparent that all north-east coalowners retained the services of a factor in London, who was contacted by the shipmasters on their arrival in the Thames: it was common for information about arrival and cargoes to be sent by land from Gravesend or even further down-river to ensure the prompt action that would facilitate a quick turn-round. On receipt of this notification the factor had three main tasks to perform: to arrange with an undertaker for the manning of the necessary lighters; to complete the necessary paperwork in connection with the payment of state and City taxes, which involved arranging with the meter office for the attendance of coal-meters; and to negotiate the sale of the coal with a buyer. The emergence of a fairly clearly defined set of functions was marked by the foundation in 1772 of the Coal Factors Society, initially with twelve members. Factors normally worked on a commission which, at the end of the eighteenth century, stood at 10s. per cent, but some also acted as general financial agents for the coalowners while others, for an additional *del credere* commission, guaranteed payment by the buyers. Since factors normally accepted agencies from a number of coalowners they were never numerous. In 1800 there were said to be only fourteen of them, and although their small numbers gave rise to unease in the North-east, they remained about this figure well into the nineteenth century.

It was, however, the coal-buyers who dominated the trade. It was they who in 1769 took the trade away from Billingsgate to a new Coal Exchange. First buyers were more numerous than factors, there being an estimated forty to fifty around 1770, fifty-six or fifty-seven in 1785, and seventy to seventy-five by 1800. Since they bought whole cargoes, and could be involved in the purchase of many simultaneously, the trade called for a fairly large capital. It was estimated in the 1780s that the average capital employed by a first buyer was around £10,000. They did not expect to make much gain from mere buying and selling, but took their profits from their ownership and operation of lighters, and from a series of customary gratuities and premiums. The actual sales of the coal cargoes were negotiated between the factors and buyers on the Coal Exchange. Buyers re-sold coal to a range of different types of customers: to *loaders* who distributed coal by river beyond London, otherwise known as second buyers; to *dealers*, who retailed to householders; to *retailers*, who re-sold from small sheds by the bushel (the equivalent of today's hardware shops selling coal by the paper sack); and to industrial consumers. Thus the buyer was a wholesaler in coal. Shipmasters who tried to negotiate sales directly with buyers came up against a wall of refusal.

An essential link in the chain of the London trade was the measurement of the coal as it was unloaded. The measurement served for both tax purposes and the satisfaction of the buyers. The coal *meters* who performed this function were appointed by the City. The principal meter was assisted by about fifteen deputy coal meters, who in turn appointed assistant meters, or helpers to the deputy meters, of whom there were 106 in 1800 and 158 in 1824. It was the last of these that supervised the filling of the measuring vats on board the colliers. Meters were paid a fee per score of chalrons measured, but also received victualling during their period on board, a free vat of coal per collier unloaded, a gratuity, and any bribes the master might be disposed to offer for false measure. There is little doubt, however, that the real rewards of metering were drawn off by the deputy meters. Vacancies for these places were auctioned, and one sold for £4,430 in 1761.[55]

The whole complicated system of factors, buyers, undertakers, meters, and their clerks and deputies creaked with corruption. The buyers looked for a proportion of their gains in the profits of buying in bulk and re-sale in smaller lots, but, since stock-holding was an important part of their business, also looked to speculative gains from price movements. But they also sought to improve their margins by taking premiums from shipmasters and selling by undermeasure. 'The first buyer when selling to a consumer', testified a factor to the 1800 Select Committee, 'proposes to give him . . . 21 chaldrons, charging him only 20, but actually delivers him only $17\frac{1}{2}$.'[56] Factors mixed inferior coal with good, selling it all as 'best'. Meters accepted bribes to falsify measures. 'There is a species of fraud upon the consumers in London, of which you are probably aware', wrote Lord Lambton's agent in 1829, 'called "winning a long five"—i.e. bribing the meters to make 5 chaldrons out of 6—equal to 20 per cent.'[57] Not surprisingly the corruption and the high, fluctuating price of coal in London encouraged the production of schemes for the complete takeover of the market by the City and the maintenance of a stock of coal in London which could be used rather like the twentieth-century Exchange Equalization Account to stabilize the price and equilibrate supply and demand. Such a scheme was recommended in 1708, though nothing, of course, came of it.[58]

iv. *State regulation and the taxation of the coal trade*

The coastwise coal trade, and particularly that from the North-east to London, attracted the attention of the state for several reasons. As

---

[55] Sykes thesis 1928, 29, quoting *Gentleman's Magazine*, 1761, 187.
[56] SC *Coal Trade* 1800, 556.
[57] SC *Coal Trade* 1800, 552; W. Loraine to Lord Lambton, 23 Apr. 1829, LEA MP11/5.
[58] BL Add.MSS 28, 948, fos. 172, 174.

a coastwise trade the goods were necessarily channelled through ports where customs officers were already in position: the trade was potentially more taxable than were many overland trades where evasion would have been easier. The homogeneity of the product, and the absence, above all in a large city like London, of a substitute—the supply of firewood on a scale large enough to heat all London's homes was no longer practicable by the eighteenth century—which reduced its elasticity of demand, enhanced the trade's attractiveness to the tax collector. The many abuses against honest and open trading in London and the tendency towards monopolistic practices at both ends of the east-coast route constantly set one group in the trade against another and encouraged appeals by aggrieved parties to Parliament to curb the activities of opponents. Finally, the effect of any commercial practice aimed at enhancing the profits of one or other group in the trade would, if successful, be to raise the price to the ultimate consumer; but the London market brought together perhaps the most articulate and influential set of consumers in the country who invariably reacted vociferously to any sharp increase in coal prices. While consumers of the products of other industries might, in the general atmosphere of industrial *laissez-faire* that prevailed during the eighteenth and early nineteenth centuries, have no alternative but to cut down their consumption in the face of raised prices, the consequence of a consumers' revolt in the London coal trade was an appeal to Parliament to restore fair and open trading. A sharp increase in coal prices or the revelation of new forms of restrictive practice lay immediately behind the establishment of most of the many parliamentary committees that debated the coal trade throughout the eighteenth and early nineteenth centuries.

The result of all this concern was that while the production of coal remained, as did most other industries in this period, almost wholly free from government interference, the trade in coal attracted almost constant government attention and a range of heavy, almost punitive taxes. 'There are nearly 200 regulations and Acts of Parliament respecting the coal trade', exclaimed a report in the late 1830s, 'most of them utterly inconsistent with every just principle of political economy.'[59] By the time this claim was made some regulations had already been withdrawn and acts repealed, but it was not unreasonable to assert that this governmental activity might in no way be interpreted as a policy towards the coal trade: it was never more than a hotch-potch of expedients, sometimes contradictory and almost invariably either ineffective or damaging to the

[59] DuRO NCB First Deposit NCB/I/X/154.

industry, or both. Above all, the coastwise coal trade, by virtue of the high proportion of all British shipping that was involved in it, was the prime nursery of seamen in an era when Britain's defence was largely a matter of sea-power and when normal naval policy was to rely for the wartime manning of warships on the impressment of merchant seamen. There was a general and well-founded understanding right through to the final defeat of Napoleon that the coastwise coal trade was the backbone of naval defence; yet throughout the period government policy seemed set to strangle the trade.

There was, however, a body of legislation, much of it embodied in private acts for roads, canals, and enclosures, that could be said charitably to reflect a general determination by Parliament to foster the development of the industry, but which was in reality no more than a manifestation of Parliament's traditional willingness in this period to yield to articulate private interests providing that there was not too much evidence of an equally articulate opposition. Characteristic of this class of legislation were the enclosure acts of 1758 and 1767 relating to the manor of Wilnecote in Warwickshire, which specifically provided for land drainage and access for mining purposes, others of 1776 that gave Lord Dudley the control over land in Dudley and Kingswinford that he needed to develop coal-mining there, and the act of 1793 referred to in chapter five above for enclosing the common of Wakefield Outwood and constructing a public coal railway across it.[60]

But the greater proportion of the numerous acts of Parliament relating to the coal trade in the eighteenth and early nineteenth centuries was aimed at the abuses and monopolistic practices. Their aim could be said to be to reduce the price of coal to consumers by restoring conditions of free trade and perfect competition. These acts may be categorized as anti-combination and price regulatory, and Hausman has pointed out that while the former were heeded to the extent of enforcing a degree of covertness in the activities of would-be monopolizing groups, the latter seem not to have been enforced at all.[61]

Only in the sphere of taxation was government action decisive and enforced. All the seasale trades in coal were burdened, throughout the period up to 1830, by substantial taxes. These taxes had mostly been initiated during the seventeenth century, so that the history of their origins does not belong to this volume. There was, first, the 'King's Duty' on all coastwise traffic first levied in 1695 and 1698 and modified in 1710 and 1711. It was extremely complex, varying

---

[60] WaRO Paul of Tamworth CR153/87; Raybould 1968, 529.
[61] Hausman 1977b, 253.

in accordance with the kind of coal shipped, and after 1816 with the
size of coal shipped (a fiscal change which required the separate
screening of coal for export), whether shipment was in British or
foreign bottoms, and according to destination—the Isle of Man,
the Channel Islands, Ireland, the colonies, the United States, and
other foreign destinations all qualifying for different rates of tax.
The general level of rates varied, too, from time to time. There were
no less than twenty-eight acts of Parliament between 1703 and 1831
dealing with the coastwise duty. These duties were supplemented so
far as London imports were concerned by the 'Church Duty'. This
tax, originally levied in 1667 after the Great Fire, was intended to
assist in financing the rebuilding of St. Paul's cathedral and other
London churches. Its obvious convenience, ease of collection, and
relatively painless nature led to its successive extension, first of all
in 1710 to finance the construction of fifty new churches in the
London suburbs, and later to pay stipends for their ministers. In
addition to these general duties some supplementary taxes were
imposed on the main east-coast trade. The Duke of Richmond's duty
of 1s. per Newcastle chaldron was originally levied on coastwise
exports from Newcastle in 1677 to make a provision for the son of
Charles II's mistress, the Duchess of Portsmouth, and replaced the
tax of 1s. per chaldron granted freely by the Hostmen's Company
in 1600 in return for a grant of monopoly of the trade. In 1790 this
tax, then assessed to be worth £19,000 per year to its private bene-
ficiaries, was commuted by the government for a lump sum of
£633,333 worth of government bonds. The Orphans' Duty had been
originally levied in 1694 to rescue the City of London from insol-
vency arising from mismanagement of its orphans' fund. In 1767
this levy of 10d. per London chaldron was diverted to pay for a list
of public works starting with Blackfriars Bridge. The London trade
was further burdened with some City dues, and duties to meet the
cost of metage.

By a perversity of fiscal policy, the Irish and foreign trades were
less heavily taxed until 1770 than the home coastal trade. The
rationale of the tax on exports was explained, with characteristic
Mercantilist over-simplification, by the author of a pamphlet
offering advice to Elizabeth I in 1598. 'The greater Imposition you
shall please to lay upon [coals for export] . . .', he wrote, 'the fewer
wilbe transported and the prices continew the easier to your majesties subects.'[62] Early Stuart governments accordingly pushed the
export duty up to high levels, but in 1694 it was reduced to the

[62] Nef 1932, II, 219.

level that in some instances allowed foreigners to buy British coal more cheaply than British consumers.[63]

Together these taxes amounted to an enormous imposition on the sea-borne coal trades. In the absence of effective foreign competition, the coastwise trade may be said to have been able to bear this level of taxation, but the addition to the price for the consumer must have lowered the effective demand for the product. The damaging effect of the taxes was not lost on Adam Smith. 'In a country where the winters are so cold as in Great Britain', he wrote in the *Wealth of Nations* in 1776

fuel is, during that season, a necessary of life, not only for the purpose of dressing victuals, but for the comfortable subsistence of many different sorts of workmen who work within doors; and coals are the cheapest of all fuel. The price of fuel has so important an influence upon that of labour that all over Great Britain manufacturers have confined themselves principally to the coal countries; other parts of the country, on account of the high price of this necessary article, not being able to work so cheap. ... If a bounty could in any case be reasonable, it might perhaps be so upon the transportation of coals from those parts of the country in which they abound, to those in which they are wanted. But the legislature, instead of a bounty has imposed a tax of three shillings and threepence on a ton upon coal carried coastways, which upon most sorts of coal is more than sixty per cent. of the original price at the coalpit. Coals carried either by land or by inland navigation pay no duty. Where they are naturally cheap they are consumed duty free: where they are naturally dear, they are loaded with a heavy duty.[64]

Hausman estimates that the taxes added thirty per cent to the cost of coal to the London consumer, but a statement of 1730 showed that the 'King's Duty' on a cargo of coal costing £104 at the pithead at Newcastle amounted to £128. 7s., while other taxes and dues at Newcastle and London added a further £48. 3s. 4d.[65] A calculation of 1824 showed that the various taxes and dues on shipments from the Tyne payable at London amounted to 10s. 8d. per London chaldron, at a time when the average FOB selling price on the Tyne was 13s.[66] There can be no doubt at all that, having regard to the significant proportion of the coal industry's sales that was carried to its consumers by sea, the fiscal policies of eighteenth- and early nineteenth-century governments exercised a most powerful brake on the development of the industry. Certainly the specially high

[63] Bunning 1883.

[64] Adam Smith, *An Inquiry into the Nature and Causes of the Wealth of Nations* (ed. E. Cannan, London, 1904), II, 358.

[65] DuRO Strathmore D/St/176.

[66] *Statement of the Case of the Northern Coal Owners* (1824), broadsheet in DuRO NCB First Deposit NCB/I/JB/2519.

rates on London imports were believed to have acted as a disincentive to the location of coal-using industries in London. 'Those acquainted with the metropolis', wrote McCulloch in 1830, 'can hardly require to be told that the pressure of this most impolitic tax has already caused the desertion, to a great extent, of several manufacturers in its neighbourhood.'[67] But the sheer scale of the government's interest in the trade provided the most powerful argument for its continuance. In 1789 coal duties contributed £551,919 to the government's total revenue of £16.7 million, and in 1820 £1,026,733 to a revenue of £58.1 million. With yields like these from a single tax that cost a mere £15,000 a year to collect no government could afford to give way to the logic of free trade.[68]

Both the coal producers and traders, whose market was restricted by these taxes, and the consumers—or at least the more vocal section of those in London who were in a position to make their voices heard—objected frequently and vociferously to the taxes. Much of the voluminous pamphlet literature generated by the eighteenth-century coal trade was concerned with this problem. The Joint Durham and Northumberland Coal Owners' Association directed much of its energy, particularly during the 1820s, to a campaign for the reduction or removal of the duties, and in 1823 joined with South Wales coalowners in sending a delegation to parliament to urge abolition.[69] A Committee for the Repeal of the Duties of Coals carried Coastwise was established in London following meetings in London and Newcastle in February 1823 to co-ordinate the lobbying, to publicize its views, and to organize petitions from all coastal importing areas. It set out its case in a moderately phrased pamphlet in 1824 in which it stressed the inequality arising from the freedom of canal-borne coal from the coastwise duty.[70]

The objections were not merely to the heavy burden of the taxes generally, but to their unequal incidence. The City of London, for example, objected in 1830 to the London imports paying forty-eight per cent of all the government's revenue from coal taxes, a proportion which was substantially greater than the London imports' share of the total seasale of coal at that period.[71] There were, moreover,

[67] Quoted by Sweezy 1938, 162.

[68] *RC Coal* 1871, 24; *PP* 1823 (137) XIII.403; NEI Buddle Atkinson 45/5/18.

[69] NuRO Joint Coal Owners' Association 263, Minute Book 1822–3, 73–6.

[70] NuRO Joint Coal Owners' Association 263, Minute Book 1823–4, 10–11; BL Add. MSS 38, 293, fos. 8, 152; broadsheet issued by *Committee appointed to seek the Repeal of the Coast Duties on Coals* (London, 1823); NuRO Joint Coal Owners' Association 263, Minute Book 1822–3, 73–6; ibid., 1823–4, 10–11; *Statement of the Case of the Northern Coal Owners* (1824), in DuRO NCB First Deposit NCB/I/JB/2519.

[71] *Durham Chronicle*, 9 Oct. 1830, in scrapbook of newspaper cuttings, 1830, NEI Buddle 53.

exemptions from the duties that were more objectionable because of the competitive advantage they bestowed on particular producers or groups of producers. In the early years of the eighteenth century, for example, the Scottish government exempted from all duties coal produced on the Fife lands of the Halkett family, on account, it was said, of the difficulty of working thin and tortuous seams. Finally, in 1788, the British government paid the family the sum of £40,000 to redeem this grant.[72] The duty on coal shipped coastwise raised endless problems of the definition of 'coastwise', since at some point every estuary becomes a river and ceases to have a coastline. The Treasury accepted that the Holme islands off Weston-super-Mare separated coast from river in the Bristol Channel so that the Forest of Dean and the eastern section of South Wales enjoyed a substantial advantage in the Severn basin over competitors further west. The cross-Bristol Channel trade from Swansea to the Cornish coppermines was exempted from the coastwise duty in 1741, as was the trade from Scottish ports in 1793, concessions that could scarcely be expected to appeal to the sense of fairness of other coastal traders. For the government, the yield of the taxes was the unanswerable jusification for their retention. As late as November 1830 the Duke of Wellington was able to make a spirited reply to a letter from the Marquis of Londonderry supporting petitions for the abolition of the coastwise duties. 'I understand that the coal owners upon the Tyne and Wear', the Duke wrote, 'propose to lower the wages of the labourers in their service this winter, and I have been already applied to for the assistance of troops to preserve the lives of his Majesties subjects. The interest of debts is not paid, and troops are not supported without money, and money cannot be found to pay these demands without taxes.'[73]

Opposition to the taxes was renewed in 1829, and met this time with a growing willingness on the part of the government to listen to free trade arguments.[74] It led to the appointment of a Lords Select Committee in 1830 which recommended the abolition of all duties on coastwise shipments of coal. The recommendation was put into effect in an act of 1831. The export duty was also reduced in 1831 and again in 1834, but not abolished until 1845 (for exports in British shipping) and 1850 (for exports in foreign bottoms). Such growth, therefore, as occurred in the sea-borne coal trade during the whole period covered by this volume was achieved in spite of the crushing burden of heavy fixed duties.

[72] NLS Halkett of Pitfirrane 6482.
[73] Duke of Wellington to Marquis of Londonderry, 11 Nov. 1830, DuRO NCB First Deposit NCB/I/JB/1894.
[74] NuRO Joint Coal Owners' Association 263, Minute Book 1826–47, 53, 57–9, 67–8.

Chapter 9

The Economics of Mining

i. *Costs*

As in all industrial operations, the trading profits of enterprises in coal-mining were the differences between current costs and current revenue. Most of the current costs of operating a coal-mine are easily identifiable: they are the labour costs of cutting, hauling, and winding coal, plus those of drainage, ventilation, and necessary maintenance work both above and below ground. There is a grey area in the labour costs of preparatory underground work: the extension of existing levels and the opening of new bords were, it seems, normally entered as current production costs, while the creation and equipment of new levels, the deepening of existing shafts, or the sinking of new ventilation or winding shafts were 'extraordinary' expenses in the sense referred to in chapter six. But there were other aspects of cost accounting that raised problems. Not all coal brought to the surface was either saleable or sold, while estimates or calculations of profits, either in total or per unit of measure, tended to be made on the basis of prices received for the major part of the output that went for land or seasale. Coal consumed by the colliery itself was rarely charged back as a production cost, nor was the miners' coal allowance, or the waste that was either stacked or burned, but for which hewers may have been paid.

Where some kind of sub-contracting of the underground working was employed, the costing of coal-getting was a relatively simple matter, since the contractor undertook to deliver coal to the pithead at an agreed price per unit of measure. But where wage-labour directly engaged by the mineowner was employed, the costing of hewing and putting was extremely complicated. Even in the North-east, out of five collieries for which there are detailed hewing and putting rate agreements for 1812, only three (Coxlodge, Collingwood Main, and Cowpen) quoted rates per twenty-peck corf, while one (Backworth) quoted a rate per eighteen-peck corf, and another (Benwell) per sixteen-peck corf.[1] There were allowances for wet working, for working a seam split by a band of waste material (an allowance that varied according to the thickness of the band), for making headways,

[1] NuRO Joint Coal Owners' Association 263, Minute book 1805–15, 169.

for working narrow bords, and for putting various distances. Thus, coal produced in different parts of a colliery in conditions of varying difficulty, but which all sold at a uniform price, might show a wide range of actual costs. Further, while in the North-east there was a series of standard rates for coal produced and it was up to the management through its supervision and disciplinary measures to keep the proportion of small coal within acceptable limits, in other coalfields wage rates differentiated between great and small coals sent up to the surface. Such a differentiation operated, for example, at Harberlands colliery in Derbyshire in the late 1790s.[2]

Depending on the coalfield and the method of working underground, there were many other specialized costs to be taken into account. In longwall working waste had to be stacked in the goaf, and props had to be set in position. Ventilation needs created a distinct body of specialized labour involving furnacemen and boys operating the trap-doors that controlled and directed the underground air 'courses'. A costing for Collingwood Main colliery in the North-east for 1811 gives some indication of the enormous range of underground work that entered into the broad category of 'hewing and putting':

The average price of Hewing, etc. underground as taken from the Pit Bills, for 6 Months, appear to be per Score £0 12s. 3d. N.B. The above includes Hewing, Driving, Overmen and Deputies Wages, Drawing, Props, laying Barroways, Lampkeepers Wages, Cranemen . . . keeping Trap doors, Driving Headways, Holing Walls, Wet, Double and narrow working, Putting thro' Holes, Cutting Sumps and Leading Water, Building Stoppings. . . . Allowance given to the Men for the Band in the Seam and Coals stowed Underground.

To these underground labour costs were added 'Keeping Underground Horses including Gears', which amounted to 4s. 6d. per Score, or nearly thirty-seven per cent of the human labour costs, and the cost of materials consumed underground in the process of producing coal —oil and wicks for lamps, candles, props, and other timber for ventilation doors and stoppings, tools, nails, and smith-work— which added a further 2s 8½d. per score to underground costs.[3]

Where underground haulage was done by human labour, its cost was subsumed within the heading of the labour of putters. But as the use of horses drawing sledges or corves on underground waggonways increased towards the end of the eighteenth century, this element in production costs came more and more to consist of the cost of feeding horses and paying their drivers. An estimate of 1801 put the

[2] DeRO Sitwell 1000 Coal Box 4/9M, 11M.
[3] NEI Watson 8/9/196.

cost of keeping a horse underground for one year, exclusive of its capital cost, at £53. 11s., and drivers' wages, at 18d. per day for 270 working days, at £20. 5s.[4] When estimated per unit of coal hauled, however, account had to be taken of the need to keep additional horses in reserve in the event of accidents or heavy loads. In 1807 Buddle made a very careful check on the cost of keeping underground horses at Wallsend colliery. Out of a total cost of £49. 7s., feed accounted for £37. 7s., labour for £5. 4s., interest and depreciation £3. 15s., and shoeing, farriery, and trapping £3. 1s. 5d. An estimate of 1811 added twenty-two per cent to the basic costs of horse and driver to allow for 'helping horses' and drivers in the proportion of six to thirty, and 'spare horses for accidents' in the proportion of two to thirty.[5]

A detailed costing of 1801 for the Lambton collieries in Durham itemized costs for a vast range of jobs essential for the continuing operation of pits. In addition to hewing and putting (here done by horses), the calculation listed 'winning out headways', 'holing walls', 'drifting bords, burning bords and laying boards out wider', 'setting over hitches, setting over bulks, putting down sumps, double working, levels, wet working, etc.', 'setting through dykes and sinking stappels', 'boring and drifting against old works', 'keeping trap doors and shutting them at nights', 'hooking on the corves at the shaft', 'ditto at Crane and craneman's wages', 'building stoppings, labourage, bricks, lime, lead and attendance', 'keeping the underground fire lamp, coals included', 'laying, repairing, removing, upholding and greasing underground waggonway', 'overman's wages', 'deputies' wages and assistants', 'charterman's wages', 'taking up bottom coal to make horse height', 'repairing pit shafts', 'nails for all colliery purposes', 'oil and drivers' candles, lamp wick and lamp lighter', 'smithwork, shovel boards and corf bows included', 'subsistence to sick, lame and burnt pitmen', 'surgery', 'binding and retaining pitmen', 'consideration to pitmen for crossing the water', and 'leading water underground'. There are many items here for which one would like a fuller explanation. Of the total costs of 13s. 7¾d. per score, the basic operations of hewing and putting accounted for 8s. 6½d. or 62.6 per cent.[6]

Raising coal up the pit-shaft incurred a further range of costs. Until steam-winding came in towards the end of the eighteenth century, the principal cost of winding lay in the feed of the horses operating the winding-gins to which was added the cost of the wages

[4] NEI Johnson 5/6.
[5] NEI Buddle 24/39; NEI Johnson 5/113.
[6] 'Memoranda re the Lambton collieries, 1800–1810', NEI Buddle 13.

of the men or boys looking after the horses and the replacement of materials used in the winding process—primarily the rope. Though the object of the substitution of steam- for horse-winding was the reduction of costs, winding still remained a significant item of costs. An estimate of steam-winding costs for Walker colliery in the North-east in 1798 analysed in Table 9.1 illustrates the elements in the cost of the new process. The Boulton and Watt Engine for which the estimate was made was designed to raise about 120 tons of coal daily up a shaft of 660 feet.

Table 9.1. *Steam-winding costs, Walker colliery, 1798*

	Cost per year			Per cent of total
	£	s.	d.	
Engine man's wages	36	8	0	13.4
Oil, candles, tallow, and packing	15	12	0	5.7
Iron and smith work, timber and carpenter work, bricks, lime and mason work	18	4	0	6.7
Cast iron, brass, and copper work	19	10	0	7.2
Interest on capital of £1,500 being the expense of first erection	130	0	0	47.9
Coals: 130 chaldrons at 8s. per chaldron	52	0	0	19.1
Total	271	14	0	100.0

Source: BPL Boulton and Watt Box 26.

Drainage costs, an element in the cost of almost every mine, were very similar in composition to those of winding. Until the advent of steam-pumping it was a question largely of horse-feed and the labour of a small number of men or boys driving the horses, together with craftsmen's labour and materials for maintenance. Steam-pumping was adopted primarily, as we have seen, because it was more effective than horse-powered pumping; but it was also cheaper. Fuel, as was demonstrated by the example of the Walker winding-engine above, was a relatively small element in costs, while the labour requirements for both operation and maintenance were no greater than for horse-powered drainage. The saving was in horse-feed, which was offset only in part by interest on the relatively high capital cost of steam-power.

Getting coal out of the ground and to the surface, of course, was not the whole business of producing coal. Though in some cases the consumer took his coal away from the pithead himself, in the vast majority of instances the mineowner was obliged to undertake some part of the trouble and cost of transporting the coal to the consumer. The accounts of collieries in most mining regions show that surface transport was a routine element in production costs. In the North-east the coal was not sold by the mineowner until his fitter had loaded it on to the collier at Shields or Sunderland, and in this district waggonway, staith, and keel costs were an important element in production costs. An estimate of costs of 1806 for an annual vend of 30,000 chaldrons from Felling and Carr's Hill collieries showed working cost per chaldron 'to lay coals on the surface' of 10s. 10d., to which was added the 'expense of laying coals on board ship 7s. 2d., making a total cost of 18s. per chaldron'.[7] In Cumberland, South Yorkshire, and several other coalfields, similarly, waggonway costs were an unavoidable part of the cost of getting coal to the initial purchaser.

Like all other production processes the cost of waggonway carriage turns out to consist of far more than merely the basic labour costs and the feed of the horses. Even where there were no problems of competition from rivals, it was customary, as Buddle explained in a letter of 1821 to the Earl of Elgin, to pay twice the normal rent for land occupied by a waggonway.[8] An estimate of 1813 for the Cox-lodge and Fawdon collieries waggonway in Northumberland, when, because of war demand, the costs of horses and feed were exceptionally high, illustrates very well the range of elements in the costs of running and maintaining a waggonway. It includes horse-feed, wear and tear on equipment, permanent way maintenance, wages and rent for waggonmen, and depreciation. Horse-feed and drivers' wages account for just under three-quarters of the total costs. Another estimate of 1801 puts the cost of feeding a horse at £53. 11s. per year, and one of 1811, by which time the price of grain had risen further, at £70.[9] Another document of about the same period makes it clear that variations in the materials used in the construction of a waggonway as well as variations in the density of traffic could make quite significant differences in maintenance costs. A wholly

[7] NEI Watson 8/9/64.
[8] J. Buddle to Earl of Elgin, 31 Dec. 1821, NEI Buddle Atkinson 45/3/no pagination.
[9] NEI Johnson 5/6, 113.

wooden track carrying 4,000 tens of coal annually cost 2s. 2d. per ten/mile to maintain, but a metal running-plate superimposed on the wooden rail and with an 'ashed run' laid down to reduce sleeper wear reduced costs for the same amount of traffic to 1s. 11¼d. per ten/mile. A wholly wooden track carrying only 2,200 tens per year achieved lower total maintenance costs, but higher average costs per ten. The maintenance of wooden waggonways was largely a matter of replacing timber. The running rails themselves were replaced yearly, 'bottom rails' and sleepers every four years, to which was added the cost of ballast and labour.[10]

The distribution of all costs up to the point of delivery to the initial purchaser is illustrated in Table 9.2. This Table must be read with great caution. Almost every colliery whose accounts are analysed here employed different categories of expenditure, and took account of, or failed to take account of, different items in their accounts. Some of the data are drawn from estimates and others from actual accounts of a year's operations: it is not always possible to say with assurance whether a documentary statement is an estimate or an exact account. As will be seen, in no one case can items of expenditure be found to match all the categories into which, for the purposes of analysis, the costs have been divided. Fittage, for example, strictly applied only to north-east collieries. It represented all payments to fitters, including the cost of keel transport down-river and local taxes and dues, as well as the remuneration for the fitters themselves. The great variability of rent charges arises from the existence of both owner-operated and leased collieries, as well as from the fact that some collieries rented houses for their employees and farms for the supply of horse-feed. Some collieries simply did not bother to take taxes into account, though some taxes must have been chargeable to the enterprises. The taxes for which colliery enterprises were liable were poor rates, road assessments, land and window taxes, while some collieries also made voluntary contributions to the local poor fund or other charities. Similarly, some accounts ignored the question of the supervisory labour and salaried administrators. The worst confusions—and hence the greatest degree of unreliability in the table—arise out of surface craftsmen's wages and waggonway costs. In the former case all wages have sometimes been lumped together, making it impossible to differentiate between underground labour costs and the costs of surface craft labour like that of carpenters, masons, and smiths. Some accounts make no allowance for materials like timber and ironwork, yet the heavy expenditure in this category itemized in other accounts indicates

[10] 'Observations on Rail Roads', n.d., but probably 1814–21, NEI Johnson 12/1–4.

Table 9.2. *Distribution of mining costs, 1717–1830*
(percentages of total costs)

Colliery	Mining region	Date	Mining wages [1]	Craftsmen's wages and materials [2]	Administrative salaries	Pumping	Waggonways	Horse-feed [3]	Interest	Rents [4]	Tax [5]	Other Costs
Fenham	NE	1717	54.5	–	–	5.5	20.0	–	–	20.0	–	–
Sheffield	Yorks	1730–1	61.6	28.8	2.6	–	–	–	–	–	3.1	3.9
Longbenton	NE	1733	43.5	–	–	8.5	29.4	–	–	16.8	–	1.8
Gateshead Park	NE	1733	57.0	–	–	8.5	11.9	–	–	19.9	–	2.7
Salt Meadow Park	NE	1733	54.6	–	–	9.4	11.1	–	–	22.0	–	2.9
Tanfield	NE	1755	40.0	–	0.7	5.3	49.7	–	–	4.0	–	0.3
Lea Bransty	Cumb.	1773	52.9	10.0	–	10.6	21.2	–	–	–	–	5.3
Wylam Moor	NE	1773	39.1	4.5	3.4	6.7	34.5	–	–	10.1	–	1.7
Sheffield Park	Yorks.	1773	33.0	12.6	–	–	–	20.5	–	32.8	0.9	0.2
Bedington	NE	1778	51.2	1.1	3.1	2.7	14.0	–	5.3	5.3	–	17.3
Sheffield Park	Yorks.	1778	36.4	8.9	3.4	–	8.2	10.8	5.0	25.3	1.2	0.8
NE average	NE	1789	40.2	–	8.9	–	33.5	–	–	–	7.0	15.9
Alloa	Scot.	1798–9	58.5	6.3	2.1	–	11.8	19.6	–	1.7	–	–
Betlers Court	South Wales	1799	54.1	–	3.3	6.6	16.4	–	–	19.6	–	–
Plessey	Cumb.	1800	63.0	14.9	5.7	12.4	–	5.9	–	6.8	0.5	2.6
Elvet	NE	1801	47.5	8.5	6.8	18.6	1.7	8.9	–	2.6	1.0	4.2
Felling	NE	1811	39.2	29.3	1.7	0.5	4.5	–	–	6.8	–	12.3
Jarrow	NE	1811	54.6	9.5	7.7	2.1	3.6	5.9	–	3.6	–	15.7
Middleton	Yorks.	1813	64.9	16.2	–	–	4.8	7.1	–	–	2.7	1.9
Robert Town	Yorks.	1815	47.7	19.3	–	–	–	7.0	2.7	17.9	5.3	–
Jarrow	NE	1817	42.4	21.6	2.2	0.5	3.3	7.0	–	13.4	2.6	7.0
Burtonholm	Lancs	1818	54.3	6.6	3.6	–	14.3	–	–	19.1	–	2.1
Unnamed Bristol area	SW	1820–1	66.6	22.0	3.0	–	–	4.0	–	1.3	1.9	1.2
Cowpen	NE	1821	56.0	20.3	–	1.2	5.2	6.2	–	6.3	0.7	4.1
Jarrow	NE	1822	41.8	24.4	1.9	–	1.8	6.4	–	12.9	1.5	9.3

Black Park	North Wales	1825	55.0	3.8	1.2	3.7	2.5	—	3.8	30.0	—	—
North Hetton	NE	1830	49.3	16.8	—	—	7.5	11.5	—	12.6	—	2.3
Mean of collieries where items distinguished			50.8	14.3	3.6	6.4	14.3	9.5	4.2	13.5	2.3	5.3
Mean of all collieries			50.7	10.5	2.3	3.7	11.4	4.2	0.6	11.4	1.0	4.2

Notes:
1 All underground, winding, and banking wages.
2 All surface craftsmen and all materials consumed in operation and maintenance.
3 Where separately specified, otherwise this item must be subsumed under one of the other headings.
4 Rent of colliery, if leased, and rent of housing and farm land.
5 Land tax, poor, and highway rates, and voluntary contributions to poor funds, etc.

Sources:
Fenham 1717 — NEI Forster 40/4/1.
Sheffield 1730-1 — SCL Arundel Castle C193.
Longbenton, Gateshead Park, and Salt Meadow 1733: NEI Grand Allies 18/Parnership minute book 1727-38/48.
Tanfield Lea 1755 — NEI Forster 49/4/171-2.
Bransty 1773 — Wood thesis 1952, 46.
Wylam Moor 1773 — NEI Watson 8/10/194.
Sheffield Park 1773 — NEI Bell 46/13/no pagination.
Bedlington 1778 — NuRO Delaval ZDE 7/18/3.
Sheffield Park 1778 — SCL Arundel Castle S215/20-3.
North-east average 1789 — Beaumont 1789, 44.
Alloa 1798-9 — ScRO Mar and Kellie GD124/17/567/7.
Betlers Court 1799 — CLSG Miscellaneous 1.131/17-18.
Plessey 1800 — CuRO Senhouse D/Sen/19/6.
Elvet 1801 — NEI Buddle 5/51.
Felling 1811 — NEI Forster 49/8/85-6.
Jarrow 1811 — NEI Johnson 5/108.
Middleton 1813 — LCA Middleton MC34.
Robert Town 1815 — LCA 1546 19-20.
Jarrow 1817 — NEI Buddle 36/III/11.
Burtonholm 1818 — JRL Crawford and Balcarres 23/6/207.
Unnamed Bristol Area 1820-1 — BRO Ashton Court AC/AS 100.
Cowpen 1821 — NuRO Ridley (Blagdon) ZRI 35/5/1.
Jarrow 1822 — NEI Buddle 36/IV/no pagination.
Black Park 1825 — NLW Chirk Castle F/3853.
North Hetton 1830 — NEI Buddle Atkinson 45/1/no pagination.

that it was a very significant element in normal colliery operation. Very few collieries, except perhaps the smaller ones in the early part of the eighteenth century, failed to employ some horses for pumping, winding, underground haulage, or road or waggonway traction, so that the absence of costs of horse-feed must prompt the question of where this item has been concealed. Undoubtedly in a number of cases it was subsumed within the general waggonway or pumping costs, though in other instances the waggonway costs relate solely to maintenance, drivers' wages, or piece-rate payments to independent waggonmen employing their own horses.

With all these difficulties in interpreting the available colliery accounts, such conclusions as may be drawn from Table 9.2 must be treated with great caution. It is clear, however, that direct underground labour costs normally accounted for about half the cost of producing coal in this period, and there does not appear to be any trend over time, either upwards or downwards, in this proportion. Surface transport and rents accounted for a further quarter of costs, with craftsmen's labour and materials comprising up to one-eighth. The very high proportion of costs allocated to waggonway operation for Tanfield Lea in 1755 and Wylam Moor in 1773 may possibly be explained by the fact that both these collieries were at the extreme limit of workable transport distances from the staithes on the Tyne. Pumping rarely accounted for as much as ten per cent of total costs, though the transfer of horse-feed costs to other headings or the failure to account at all for small coal used in steam pump boilers may have led to some understatement of this element in costs.

Even allowing for the inconsistencies of colliery accounting procedures, it is also evident from Table 9.2 that collieries varied enormously in their cost structures and hence ultimately in their total costs. Even within a single colliery coal brought from different seams or different working areas of the same seam could vary substantially. A costing of 1797 for coal delivered to the staith from two seams at Cowpen colliery, Northumberland, for a vend of 1,600 chaldrons annually for a period of five years showed the Main Coal at 10s. 10¼d. per chaldron, and the Yard Coal at 12s. 2d. per chaldron.[11] At the Whingill colliery at Whitehaven in 1781 the cost of mining and delivering coal to the staith varied between the eight pits being worked from 1s. 2½d. per ton to 1s. 8¾d. per ton. Part of this difference was to be explained in terms of the varying distances of the pits from the staith. 'Leading' costs ranged from 4d. per three-ton waggon at the Lady Pit to 1s. 2d. at the How pit. But the How pit was one of the lower cost pits at 1s. 3½d. per ton, while the most

[11] NEI Johnson 12/28–9.

expensive pit to work, the Jackson pit, could lead its coal to the staith for the middling price of 10d. per waggon.[12] A similar range existed at the Lambton pits in Durham. An account of costs here in 1828 showed pithead cost ranging from 13s. 3d. per chaldron at the Charles pit to as much as 23s. at the Margaret pit. The mean of ten pits was 15s. 8d. To these varying working costs were added a further wide-ranging set of waggonway charges—from 2s 7$\frac{1}{2}d$. at Harraton pit to 4s. 8d. at Cocken pit to get the coal from pithead to staith on the Wear. All coal then bore a standard keel charge of 2s. 6d. per chaldron down-river to Sunderland.[13] On the Tyne in 1788 'A Calculation of laying the different Collieries upon the Staiths' for the principal seasale collieries showed costs ranging from 8s. 11$\frac{1}{2}d$. for Whitefield colliery to 13s. 0d. at Brandling Main colliery. These costs were dated specifically 28 January 1788. A mere ten days later on 8 February 1788 costs had changed appreciably, Whitefield rising to 9s. 5$\frac{1}{2}d$., and Brandling Main to 15s. 3$\frac{1}{2}d$.: there was little change, however, in the relative placings.[14]

For the share of the industry's output that was consumed in London there were several other substantial additions to mining costs. A very rough statement of 1829 prepared by the north-east coalowners for presentation by the Marquis of Londonderry to the House of Lords Select Committee that reported the following year illustrated very clearly the order of magnitude of these additions to FOB costs at Newcastle and Sunderland. Starting with a notional price of 14s. per chaldron as the price of coal at the riverside in the North-east including 3s. for fittage, there was then to be added 10s. for freight to London, 6s. for government taxes on the coastal trade, and 1s. 2d. for Orphans' Tax and metage in the Pool of London. All these additions raised the delivered cost in London to 31s. 2d. per Newcastle chaldron, appreciably more than double its cost on the staith in the North-east, and nearly five times the pithead cost. This price covered costs up to the point at which the coal was sold in London by the shipmaster, and the document went on to point out that there was probably a further 20s. to be added arising out of charges for unloading, wholesaling, and retailing in London before the coal reached the ultimate consumer.[15] The broad accuracy of this rounded estimate is borne out by a much more precise statement of the costs imposed on the London trade in an earlier memorandum of 1766. Taking a standard collier's cargo of 160 Newcastle chaldrons

[12] CuRO Lonsdale Colliery Reports not yet listed, 'Report on Lowther Collieries by John Bateman, 1781', no pagination.
[13] 'Cost of working the coal at the different Pits, Carriage, etc.', LEA not numbered.
[14] NEI Watson 8/8/245 and 8/11/110.
[15] NuRO Joint Coal Owners' Association 263, Minute book 1826–47, 58.

costing on board at Shields after payment of all Newcastle city and river dues as £152. 11s. 8d., this enumerates first freight to London and lighter costs in London amounting together to £174. 11s. 3d., then charges at London including coastwise duty, other City dues, factorage, metage, and the various presents required to ensure satisfactory unloading and sale. The latter amounted to a further £168. 11s. 4d. In this way coal that originally cost £120 at the staith on the Tyne, and £152. 11s. 8d. on board the collier at Shields, cost a total of £495. 14s. 3d. to the 'buyer' in London.[16]

The London trade, of course, was exceptional in so far as its scale had led to the erection of an elaborate, and therefore costly, market organization, while the extraordinarily narrow geographical concentration of the points of departure and arrival of the shipping route made it a temptingly easy target of government fiscal policy. It is easy to understand why, in these circumstances, the basic costs of production came to form such a minor element in the final price to the London consumer. Other coastwise trades bore similar, though normally lesser, burdens, and only landsale markets escaped the grasp of the national and civic tax collectors, the meters and the Lightermen. But this market, too, in its turn, was subject to the high costs of land transport. As we saw in chapter five, ton/mile overland freight rates could be as much as fifteen times those of coastal shipping, while even the much lower canal delivery costs imposed an effective limit to the radius of competitive sales. Thus, even using the new canals, in 1785 coal from Baddesley colliery in the Warwickshire coalfield that cost 5s. per ton at the pithead cost 8s. at Coventry, 17s. 8d. at Banbury, and £1. 2s. 8d., or four and a half times its pithead cost, at Oxford.[17] Similarly, in 1815, coal produced at collieries in Derbyshire and Nottinghamshire on the banks of the Erewash, Cromford, or Derby canals almost exactly doubled its pithead cost with the addition of canal carriage to Leicester.[18]

Finally, there is the problem of capital costs. The charging of interest is, of course, arbitrary in any business situation. Shareholders in a joint stock company do not technically receive interest on their investments, merely a share of profits if and when there are any. For this reason it would be inconsistent to charge interest as a cost. On the other hand, loan or debenture capital carries interest by definition, and it is clear that many mining ventures of the eighteenth and nineteenth centuries were financed in part or whole by loans. It is this dichotomy as much as any failure of accounting procedures that

[16] NEI Watson 8/10/145–8.
[17] WaRO Newdigate Additional CR764/264.
[18] NUL Drury-Lowe Dr E68/5.

probably explains the erratic treatment of interest in colliery accounts of this period. A survey of north-east mining costs of 1766, for example, for a hypothetical colliery producing 1,000 tens of coal with a capital of £4,000, accounted for five per cent interest.[19] Similarly, a calculation of the costs of the principal seasale collieries of the North-east of 1788 automatically included in the cost of each colliery an allowance of interest on its assumed capital at ten per cent.[20] A memorandum of 1821 concerning the colliery accounts on the Lambton estate argued that interest amounting to £1,065 (a notional five per cent) should be charged to the collieries because the sum of £21,300 had been borrowed by the estate for the sole use of the collieries and formed part of the capital employed in working them.[21] Broadly speaking, the evidence of colliery accounts, costings, and estimates suggests that interest was increasingly taken into account during the late eighteenth and early nineteenth centuries: there are very few references to interest charges during the first half of the eighteenth century, but such charges were common by the early nineteenth century. The reason for the omission of interest charges was often, as we saw in chapter six, that capital was borrowed in the course of estate management, even where it was primarily intended for mining investment. In cases where the estate, rather than a colliery on an estate, constituted the unit of accounting, interest was chargeable to the estate as a whole rather than to the colliery.

ii. *Prices*

If profits were to be made in mining, prices must exceed costs. But prices were determined as much by aggregate supply and demand as by costs. Throughout the period 1700 to 1830 the coal industry remained fairly intensively competitive, and demand was rarely volatile enough to cause prices to rise radically out of line with costs in any one market; and, if it did, the high profitability quickly attracted new entrants to the market. Efforts were constantly made, of course, to restrict competition and so prevent the margin between costs and prices falling. These took the form either of agreements between mineowners, most effective in the North-east, but rarely enduring many years at a stretch; or attempts by landowners to monopolize coal-bearing land or wayleave access to essential transport routes. All these restrictive practices were, before 1830, generally

[19] NEI Watson 8/10/145–8.
[20] NEI Watson 8/8/245.
[21] LEA MP12/2.

operative only within a single coalfield or trade route, and were subject, therefore, ultimately to the threat of inter-coalfield competition. In the long run, it remains true to say that marketing in the British coal industry before 1830 remained broadly competitive, so that prices were rarely allowed to range too far from costs. In this section, after an examination of the short-run determinants of coal prices in the eighteenth and early nineteenth centuries, some attempt will be made to trace their long-run movements in real as well as in money terms.

There were, in the first instance, price differentials arising from differences in the quality of the coal, and these differentials did not necessarily relate in any way to the kind of cost differences examined in the previous section. So long as domestic consumers preponderated in the markets for coal, then large brightly burning coal was at a premium. After its opening in the 1780s Wallsend colliery became synonymous with the best quality of household coal, though much coal from other Tyne and even Wear collieries was sold in London as 'Wallsend' since coal in this class fetched the best prices. A list of FOB prices for Tyne coals in February 1802 showed Wallsend alone fetching 27s. per chaldron and prices decreasing steadily to 18s. fetched by eight collieries. Wear coals started with 20s. for Lambton, falling to 16s. for 'Mr. Peareth's Harraton' and 'Mr. Wade's Leefield'.[22] In a list fixed by the Tyne Committee dated 30 July 1825, prices ranged from 18s. per Newcastle chaldron for Elswick colliery coal to 34s. for Percy Main; Wallsend stood second at 33s., with a mean of the thirty-five seasale collieries of 22s. 6d.[23] In a similar list of 1806 coals from Killingworth, Temple Main, and Walker collieries were most highly priced, with Percy Main, Bigges Main, East Kenton, and Wallsend close behind. In this year the range of prices in Newcastle was from 18s. to 30s.[24] Wear coals showed a much smaller range of prices: a list of 1813 ranged from 16s. per Newcastle chaldron to 22s.[25] With the decline in dominance of the market for household coal, other types of coals—coking coal and steam coals, in particular—became relatively more desirable, and relative prices adjusted accordingly.

Since labour formed such a significant element in coal costs, it is to be expected that prices would reflect changes in labour costs. In 1781, for example, John Curr, agent for the Sheffield collieries of the Duke of Norfolk, issued a printed notice to customers

[22] NEI Johnson 5/97.
[23] NuRO Joint Coal Owners' Association 263, Minute book 1825–6.
[24] NEI Watson 8/9/30.
[25] NuRO Joint Coal Owners' Association 263, Minute book, 1805–15, 242.

informing them of an increase in the price of the coal from the Sheffield Park colliery on account of the 'increased and daily increasing charges attending the working of the Park collieries.' Similarly in 1802, Staffordshire miners, offered high wages to migrate to Lancashire, were able to force their own employers to raise wages and allowances and to reduce the working week: this forced coalowners to raise their prices.[26]

Prices, of course, were also influenced in the short run by chance circumstances, particularly those arising out of weather and war. Complaints were frequent in London of the rise in the price of coal consequent upon a prolonged period of adverse winds that prevented the sailing of the east-coast colliers, or upon delay caused by the necessity to sail in convoy as a protection against privateers in time of war. Wartime loss of exports had a deleterious effect on the price of small coal sold overseas from the North-east. In 1804 it was reported from Newcastle that small coal was exported at from 13s. to 15s. 3d. per chaldron, while in 1807 much reduced exports fetched only 7s. per chaldron. 'It is evident . . .', wrote Buddle in comment on these figures, 'that neither we nor the Coal Trade at large will find effectual relief until our communication with the continent is restored, to which I trust the present *great* political events will ultimately lead us.'[27] Perhaps the greatest interference with the smooth flow of coal down the east coast was occasioned by the operations of the press-gang, which caused an immediate scarcity of keelmen and mariners (more to avoid the press than because of actual impressment) as much in times of threat of war as in actual war. In 1730, for example, when Britain was not involved in any war, Sir John Hussey Delaval's agent for his mines in Northumberland reported that a press had taken place which would put an immediate stop to shipping and raise the price of coal in London.[28]

But the most contentious influence on price levels was undoubtedly the combinations among coalowners. Though, as some evidence in chapter eight showed, owners in many coalfields combined for the purpose of raising prices, there is less evidence of their success in achieving this aim. In the North-east, however, partly because the combinations were much more persistent, partly because they have left some very comprehensive records as evidence of their activities, and partly because these activities directly affected the particularly articulate London consumers, we know much more about the impact

---

[26] SCL Arundel Castle S212; 'Memorandum re Meir Heath Colliery', Sept. 1802, StRO Sutherland D593/M/2/1/2.

[27] NEI Buddle 23/42.

[28] J. Crooks to Sir John Hussey Delaval, 10 May 1730, NuRO Delaval ZDE 4/6/24.

of combination in that coalfield upon the market price of coal. Generally speaking, of course, associations of producers take pains not to publicize their price-fixing activities, and it is certainly true that the minutes of the Joint Durham and Northumberland Coal Owners' Association of the early nineteenth century which are now accessible to the historians were not written at the time for public information. Nevertheless, the fact that they fixed prices in many years for the coals of every member colliery and entered these on printed forms suggests that knowledge of these fixed prices must have been fairly widespread. Within their own four walls they did not need to mince words. In June 1819 the first resolution of a joint meeting of the committees of the two rivers ran: 'That it is clear to this meeting that nothing but a limitation of the vend from both rivers can produce the effect of raising the price of coals in the London and coast markets to such a standard as to afford the ship owners a fair and adequate price for navigating their vessels, and enable them at the same time to pay the coal owner the standard price for his coals.'[29] That this conviction was born of long experience is confirmed by a statement of over one hundred years earlier in the House of Commons to the effect that the activities of the 'Regulation' in 1711 (see above p. 257) had driven up London prices from 11s. 6d. per London chaldron to 12s.[30]

The 'Regulations' and 'Limitations of the Vend' were, however, as we have seen, impermanent, and their ability effectively to sustain artificially high prices, even in the highly concentrated London market, must remain in question. In the generally deflationary conditions after 1815 the attempts by the north-east Coal Owners' Association to fix prices failed frequently. In February 1829, for example, they agreed 'that in the present state of the trade, each individual coalowner should accomplish his sales by adjusting his price to the value of his coal in the different markets as compared with coal from other collieries', which was simply a roundabout way of authorizing them to fix prices in competition with each other.[31] Less than a year later, however, in a petition to the House of Lords at the time of the hearings of that House's Select Committee, the Association defended its 'Limitation of the Vend' on the grounds that north-east output could so easily exceed what the markets could bear, 'restricted as the demand is by the present exorbitant oversea and coast duties, by heavy local charges and unnecessary and vexatious impediments to the free transfer of the coals from the ship

[29] NuRO Joint Coal Owners' Association, 263, Minute book 1819, 25–6.
[30] GPL Cotesworth CK/3/63.
[31] NuRO Joint Coal Owners' Association 263, Minute book 1826–47, 50.

to the consumer.' It claimed that the highest price ever received was
14s. per London chaldron, equivalent, after the addition of freight,
duty, and all other charges, to 44s. in London, and that this did not
enable its members to raise prices because 'the price must always be
regulated by competition with coals sent from other parts of England
and from Scotland and Wales'.[32] 'A restriction', wrote one north-
east mining agent in 1830, 'has a direct tendency to increase the
working of coal mines in all other places besides those connected
with the Tyne and Wear.'[33]

Knowing, as they must have done, what small quantities reached
London from other coalfields, and that it was through their own
efforts that inland coalfields had been specifically prohibited from
using canals to send coal by the cheapest route to London, these
arguments were decidedly specious, and the 1800 and 1830 Select
Committees had good reason to look closely into the possibilities
of bringing coal to London from coalfields other than the North-east.
Consumers in London were less easily convinced that it was competition rather than combination which set the level of prices. A petition
of London manufacturers of 1739 insisted that the recent high prices
for coal in London were due to the deliberate restriction of production in the North-east, while the master of a collier took the view at
the same time that the rise in prices between the early and the late
1730s was a direct consequence of agreement between coalowners.[34]
The breakdown of a regulation was more likely to show itself in
London prices than those in the North-east since the under-selling
that marked a return to open trading more often took the form of
giving over-weight than of actual price reduction.[35]

The behaviour of prices themselves makes it difficult to adjudicate
with any confidence between the competing claims of producers that
they really had very little control over prices, and those of consumers
that they were being exploited by the price-rigging activities of
producers' combinations. In the short-run prices certainly tended to
fluctuate in a way that can scarcely have been desired by the producers and which is hardly indicative of rigid control by them.
Table 9.3 sets out monthly prices in London for a number of collieries
in 1821 to illustrate the short-run movements. 1821 was not a year
of open trade, yet the fluctuations in price of particular coals from
month to month was not very consistent. On the other hand some
fairly sharp price changes in London have been directly linked to the

[32] NuRO Joint Coal Owners' Association 263, Minute book 1826–47, 67–8.
[33] N. Stewart to Lord Lambton, 3 May 1830, LEA MP11/7.
[34] NEI Buddle 14/251–2, 265–70.
[35] William Brown to Carlisle Spedding, 30 Apr. 1750, NEI Brown 16/1/4.

Table 9.3. *Monthly prices in London of coal from
selected north-east collieries, 1821*
(prices per Newcastle chaldron)

Month	Collieries							
	Hebburn		Adairs Main		Heaton		Killingworth	
	s.	d.	s.	d.	s.	d.	s.	d.
January	39	0	37	6	40	6	37	4
February	37	6	36	1	37	1	37	7
March	39	10	36	4	39	11	40	0
April	40	1	36	4	40	0	39	10
May	39	4	35	5	38	8	38	0
June	39	11	37	0	40	0	39	4
July	39	11	37	7	39	6	39	7
August	39	9	37	0	39	4	38	9
September	41	6	37	6	40	9	39	9
October	43	5	39	11	43	0	43	1
November	42	3	39	6	42	7	42	4
December	41	10	38	5	42	2	41	8

Source: NuRO Joint Coal Owners' Association 263 Minute book 1821–3, 94–5.

institution or withdrawal of a regulation in the North-east, and where
these can be clearly substantiated by reference to actual price movements, the argument looks good. The sharp rise in London between
1700 and 1703, for example, has been specifically attributed to
combination in the North-east, and all available South of England
price series certainly show a very marked rise over these few years.

In an effort to show both short- and medium-run price movements
of this kind, as well as to trace the long-run trend of coal prices, an
index of coal prices has been constructed in Table 9.4. This embodies
all the available long series of prices that meet the requirement of
running through one or more of the base-periods chosen for the
purpose. No price index is ideal, and this one necessarily has obvious
shortcomings. The series utilized are all composed of mean annual
prices, means of prices that might, as we have seen, fluctuate quite
substantially during the course of a year. But the most serious weakness relates to the balance between coalfields. As with many of the
documentary sources for the history of the British coal industry in
this period, the price data relate very heavily to the north-east coalfield. This is the case with all the London and South of England
contract series, and with many of the pithead and Newcastle series.
This imbalance is regrettable but unavoidable. It does mean,
however, that for practical purposes this is an index of north-east

Table 9.4. *Index of coal prices, 1700–1830*

Year	Index 1 (1720–9 = 100)	Linked Index (1770–9 = 100)	Year	Index 1 (1720–9 = 100)	Linked Index (1770–9 = 100)
1700	95.0	74.8	1743	113.8	89.6
1701	109.0	85.8	1744	113.4	89.2
1702	124.8	98.2	1745	114.4	90.1
1703	120.6	94.9	1746	112.1	88.2
1704	117.0	92.1	1747	109.3	86.0
1705	106.4	83.7	1748	107.5	84.6
1706	100.0	78.7	1749	105.3	82.9
1707	112.0	88.1			
1708	115.8	91.1	**Index 2**		
1709	116.5	91.7	(1770–9 = 100)		
1710	116.7	91.8	1750	80.9	80.9
1711	98.0	77.1	1751	83.2	83.2
1712	99.0	77.9	1752	84.9	84.9
1713	100.0	78.7	1753	85.0	85.0
1714	98.2	77.3	1754	92.3	92.3
1715	94.5	74.4	1755	102.5	102.5
1716	100.5	79.1	1756	104.3	104.3
1717	104.5	82.2	1757	101.0	101.0
1718	105.8	83.3	1758	100.6	100.6
1719	103.0	81.1	1759	97.8	97.8
1720	101.9	80.2	1760	99.4	99.4
1721	99.3	78.1	1761	100.7	100.7
1722	98.0	77.1	1762	96.9	96.9
1723	97.7	76.9	1763	99.6	99.6
1724	99.3	78.1	1764	99.1	99.1
1725	102.4	80.6	1765	92.3	92.3
1726	100.4	79.0	1766	91.0	91.0
1727	98.4	77.4	1767	90.3	90.3
1728	103.5	81.5	1768	89.5	89.5
1729	99.8	78.5	1769	91.3	91.3
1730	107.6	84.7	1770	98.5	98.5
1731	100.4	79.0	1771	98.8	98.8
1732	100.8	79.3	1772	93.0	93.0
1733	101.9	80.2	1773	91.5	91.5
1734	99.9	78.6	1774	93.8	93.8
1735	101.0	79.5	1775	100.9	100.9
1736	99.4	78.2	1776	103.5	103.5
1737	101.8	80.1	1777	107.1	107.1
1738	102.1	80.4	1778	106.4	106.4
1739	118.3	93.1	1779	109.4	109.4
1740	111.0	87.4	1780	108.5	108.5
1741	108.9	85.7	1781	111.5	111.5
1742	108.0	85.0	1782	101.7	107.7

Table 9.4. (*cont.*)

Year	Index 2 (1770–9 = 100)	Linked Index (1770–9 = 100)	Year	Index 3 (1820–9 = 100)	Linked Index (1770–9 = 100)
1783	94.3	94.3	1806	106.5	145.4
1784	100.7	100.7	1807	108.5	148.1
1785	100.9	100.9	1808	110.8	151.3
1786	99.0	99.0	1809	122.4	167.7
1787	99.7	99.7	1810	112.0	152.9
1788	98.2	98.2	1811	119.1	162.6
1789	104.7	104.7	1812	116.7	159.3
			1813	125.9	171.9
	Index 3		1814	126.4	172.6
	(1820–9 = 100)		1815	115.7	158.0
1790	77.3	105.5	1816	107.0	146.1
1791	78.0	106.5	1817	105.2	143.6
1792	81.0	110.6	1818	103.3	141.0
1793	84.4	115.2	1819	101.6	138.7
1794	90.6	123.7	1820	102.8	140.3
1795	79.7	108.8	1821	103.8	141.7
1796	78.6	107.3	1822	101.9	139.1
1797	79.8	108.9	1823	103.7	141.6
1798	93.8	128.1	1824	100.3	136.9
1799	100.0	136.5	1825	96.5	131.7
1800	89.8	122.6	1826	92.0	125.6
1801	88.7	121.1	1827	94.7	129.3
1802	94.2	128.6	1828	96.4	131.6
1803	101.5	138.6	1829	93.0	127.0
1804	104.3	142.4	1830	93.4	127.5
1805	107.1	146.2			

Note on method. In an effort to cope with the problem of distortion in indexes covering long periods, this index has been constructed initially in three separate sections—1700–49 (base period 1720–9), 1750–89 (base period 1770–9), and 1790–1830 (base period 1820–9). These sectional indexes should be used for the study of short- and medium-run price fluctuations. To facilitate the examination of long-run price movements, and to permit comparison with the available general prices indexes, however, the three indexes have been linked together into a single index with a base period 1770–9 in the following manner: the sectional indexes were extended to provide overlapping decades (1745–54 and 1785–94) and the ratios of the means of these ten-year periods applied to convert the first and third sections at the base period of the second.

The following price series have been drawn on. Because there could be no valid way of doing so, no attempt has been made to weight the series. A number of available series have had to be discarded because, though they provided fairly long runs of prices, they did not extend sufficiently into one or other base period. Because of the varying units of measure employed in the series used, each series was first reduced to an index before striking means of the series within each period.

Sources:

Series	Years covered	Location
1. Eton college	1700–1830	Beveridge 1939, 146–7.
2. Westminster college	1700–1830	Beveridge 1939, 194–6.

[*See opposite page for Sources cont.*]

coal prices, and we are left with no means of gauging how representative it is of price movements in other coalfields.

The isolation of each coalfield and its markets from all others in the eighteenth century might lead us to believe that there was no reason why their prices should move in broad sympathy. Yet, in the last resort, there was some potential competition between coalfields, as the north-east owners and their London customers realized: if prices in any one coalfield moved sharply out of line with those in others new possibilities of inter-coalfield competition would open up. This was particularly true of the Irish trade, the Bristol Channel trade, and of some markets in the export trade. It was even possible in the London market. 'In 1828', reported a commentator of the early 1840s, 'they [the north-east Joint Coal Owners' Association] fixed the prices too high, the consequence was an immediate influx of coals from Scotland, Wales and Yorkshire to London.'[36] Given that labour costs—of craftsmen's and managerial labour as well as

Series	Years covered	Location
3. Navy, London	1700–1826	Beveridge 1939, 578.
4. Oxford colleges	1700–89	Kindly provided by Dr D. P. O'Brien from the Beveridge MSS in
5. Cambridge colleges	1703–89	the library of the London School of Economics.
6. Somerset pithead	1709–73	Bulley 1953, 51.
7. Chelsea Hospital	1715–93	Beveridge 1939, 313.
8. Greenwich Hospital (ordinary)	1716–94	Beveridge 1939, 313.
9. Winchester college	1745–94	Beveridge 1939, 90.
10. Newcastle (Main Team)	1741–94	Beveridge 1939, 267.
11. Lord Steward's Department	1761–1829	Beveridge 1939, 436.
12. London	1769–79	*First SC Coal Trade* 1800, 588.
13. Navy, Portsmouth	1771–94	Beveridge 1939, 591.
14. Tanfield Moor	1792–1830	NEI Buddle 22/280, and 51/335.
15. Somerset (Midsomer Norton)	1795–1830	Bulley 1953, 51.
16. Newcastle (Wallsend)	1798–1828	Beveridge 1939, 267.
17. Greenwich Hospital (Wallsend)	1798–1828	Beveridge 1939, 295.
18. Birmingham	1800–28	von Tunzelmann 1978, 96.
19. Liverpool	1800–30	von Tunzelmann 1978, 96.
20. Newcastle	1801–30	NEI Watson 5/26/2.
21. London (Wallsend)	1805–24	DuRO NCB/I/JB/2435.
22. London (Holywell)	1805–24	DuRO NCB/I/JB/2435.
23. London (Tanfield)	1805–24	DuRO NBC/I/JB/2435.
24. London	1805–30	Mitchell 1962, 482.
25. Sunderland	1811–30	Gayer, Rostow & Schwartz 1953, I, 195, 232.
26. London	1813–30	Porter 1847, 280.
27. London	1813–30	DuRO NCB/I/X/154.
28. Newcastle (Wallsend)	1817–28	*SC Lords Coal Trade* 1830, 8.
29. Newcastle (Manor Wallsend)	1820–30	*SC Lords Coal Trade* 1830, 8.
30. Newcastle (Heworth)	1821–30	*SC Lords Coal Trade* 1830, 8.

[36] 'A brief compendium of the natural, political and commercial history of coal', undated MSS (probably early 1840s), NuRO NCB First Deposit NCB/I/X/154.

of underground and 'oncost' labour—formed such a major element in coal prices, the mobility of labour itself was some guarantee of at least some sympathy in the movement of coalfield wage rates. Evidence for this mobility of mining labour is reviewed in the next chapter. There are some grounds, therefore, however slender, for believing in the general sympathy of price *movements* between coalfields, though absolute price *levels* may have differed substantially from one to another. The mean of the Liverpool and Birmingham prices (nos. sixteen and seventeen in the list of source series to Table 9.4) has been compared with the movement of Index three: this comparison shows exactly the same percentage of price rise between 1800–4 and 1811–14. But while the general index falls quite substantially from the 1813–14 peak to the late 1820s, the Liverpool and Birmingham mean remains at roughly the same peak. While it might be possible to explain these differing trends, their existence underlines the need for caution in applying this price index to coalfields other than the North-east.

Further, many of the series in Table 9.4 are South of England wholesale or contract prices, particularly those covering the early part of the period. South of England prices clearly contain an element of freight charges and possibly taxes, and the former could fluctuate independently of mining costs; the latter were generally steady in spite of minor adjustments from time to time. Contract prices arranged by institutions were obviously less flexible in the short run than normal market prices; but neither contract nor wholesale prices could avoid reflecting general price trends in anything other than the short run. The series used, therefore, are reasonable reflections of the movements of north-east coal prices in every respect other than the very short run, though some take account of factors beyond the mere production of coal. At the same time, given the role of transport developments in the expansion of the industry, there is a positive virtue in an index which, whether by design or not, takes some account of waggonway and shipping costs.

So far as the short- and medium-run fluctuations are concerned, the index presents some slightly puzzling features. It does not, for example, reflect the impact of war consistently. War was likely to affect coal prices in a number of ways: by raising demand for coal in the armaments and shipbuilding industries, and by disrupting shipping through privateering activities, the need for convoying, and the activities of the press-gang. War, too, was generally inflationary: this was particularly true of the French wars between 1793 and 1815, though war was not the sole explanation of this inflation. The wars of Jenkins's Ear and Austrian Succession (1739–48) experienced some mild inflation of coal prices, as did the War of American Independence (1775-83); but the Seven Years War (1756-63) is barely detectable in the movement of coal prices. The War of Spanish Succession (1702-13) was a time of more violent price movements, but we should perhaps be hesitant in attributing these wholly to the war: the index is particularly thin at this period and too much reliance should not be placed on the sole movements of some South of England contract prices.

Part of the explanation of the price movements of the early eighteenth century may, therefore, lie in the market-rigging activities of north-east coalowners. The objective of all 'regulations' was to increase profits. 'In a Regulation profit is £1 11s. 2¼d. per ten', commented a viewer in the mid-eighteenth century. 'In a contesting trade there is a loss of 16s. 9d. per ten.'[37] The sharp rises and falls of coal prices in the first decade of the century do indeed coincide very closely with the formation and collapse of the early associations of north-east coalowners described in chapter eight, but movements after 1726 do not show the secular upward trend that was surely the objective of the Grand Allies. Their successful forcing of the closure of the Old Western Way—their competitors' main outlet to the Tyne —in 1738 was briefly reflected in the London price movements. A pamphlet of 1739 attributed the price rise of that year to the actions of 'the Grand Allies and other owners of mines from whence much more than half the normal vend might, and would be supplied, did not their Practices forbid'.[38] The broad stability of prices during the late 1720s and 1730s might, however, have reflected the success of the Grand Allies in maintaining price levels in the face of stagnant demand and the threat of rising output. Nor does the inauguration of the 'Limitation of the Vend' in 1771 appear to have had any immediate impact on the general price level. Unfortunately information about the periods of non-regulation between 1771 and 1805 is too vague to be of use in interpreting the short-run movements of north-east or London prices. The 'Limitation' was said to have been lifted in 1782, and there was certainly a ten per cent drop in prices to 1783, but prices seem almost to have recovered again in 1784 and 1785, when the trade was believed still to have been open.[39] The lifting of the regulation of prices at frequent intervals during the early decades of the nineteenth century and its reimposition as frequently can just be perceived by reductions and recoveries of

[37] NEI Watson 8/10/54, quoted by Cromar 1978, 206.

[38] Anon., *Enquiry into the Reasons of the Advance in the Price of Coals this Seven Years Past* (1739), quoted by Sykes thesis 1928, 35-6.

[39] For the question of suspensions of the 'Limitation' after 1771, see Sweezy 1938, 39-40.

prices, but these are mostly too small to attribute to this sole cause with confidence. Perhaps the most striking evidence of the effectiveness of combinations of owners in maintaining price levels is the way prices fell sharply when government began to enquire closely into price-rigging practices. This was apparent in both 1710 and 1800, though once again we should remind ourselves that the market may also at those times have been responding to other pressures.

Turning from short-run fluctuations to secular price trends, we find that the difficulties of tracing trends in coal prices are more than matched by those of tracing general price trends in the eighteenth and early nineteenth centuries. Yet it is of no little interest to discover whether, in the face of all its technical problems, the British coal industry was able to maintain, and even increase, its output at prices that were constant in real terms. This is a question of considerable importance. The supply of coal was fundamental to virtually all the key sectors of industrial development after the mid-eighteenth century—the iron industry, the cotton industry, the non-ferrous metal industries, and steam-power wherever it was applied. The rate of expansion of demand from these sources has already been examined in chapter seven, and it is evident that, price considerations apart, the industry was able to respond continuously to these increases in demand. Yet the coal industry was necessarily subject, all other things being equal, to constantly rising marginal costs: output could only be maintained, let alone increased, by even deeper and most costly mining, with longer hauls underground and on the surface. Unless this tendency towards rising costs was offset by falling labour costs—and in chapter eleven it is argued that this did not occur—the tendency in the mining industry must have been for real costs to rise. Only constantly improving technology could offset this tendency, and the purpose of comparing trends in coal prices with those of general prices is to discover to what extent the industry was able to combat the tendency towards rising marginal costs.

For the eighteenth and early nineteenth centuries there are a number of general price indices available to the historian. Some are better than others, but all have grave weaknesses; where they duplicate each other they do, however, display a reassuring conformity with each other. They are, at all events, the only ones that are available.[40] Their frailty, however, combined with that of the index of coal prices reproduced in Table 9.4, suggests that it would be unwise to attempt any statistically sophisticated exercise of comparison between them, and to restrict such comparison to the simplest possible approach. For this purpose the turning-points

[40] M. W. Flinn, 'Trends in real wages, 1750–1850', EHR, 2nd ser. 27 (1974), 399–404.

employed in an earlier article will be used here since these provide ready-made, rough guides to general price movements.[41]

For the first half of the eighteenth century only three general price indices are available.[42] The mean of these shows a 4.8 per cent price fall between 1700–4 and 1750–4: during this period the coal price index indicates a fall of 8.7 per cent, not a great difference, but not, however, a real increase. The first quinquennium of the eighteenth century, however, was a period when prices may, as we have seen, have been influenced by corporate price-rigging activity, and if the purpose of a comparison is to ascertain the long-run impact of rising marginal costs and technological change on the real cost of coal, it might be wiser to shift the basis of comparison to a quinquennium of lesser short-term fluctuation. A comparison of 1715–19 with 1745–9 shows the general price change, measured as above, as a fall of 3.3 per cent, and the coal price change a rise of 5.1 per cent—again, not a great difference, but a clear rise in real terms. Given, however, the frailty of both indices of coal and general prices and the small magnitude of change indicated, it would probably be wise to conclude that, in real terms, coal prices changed very little during the first half of the eighteenth century.

After mid century, while the increase in the number of coal price series serves to improve the quality of that price index, the measurement of general price movements becomes more complex. There was a distinct upward trend in prices which became rapid after the early 1790s. The acceleration of inflation from this point was associated, of course, with the wars against revolutionary and Napoleonic France, and, since the war inflation was followed by a post-war deflation, it is probably wisest to treat the latter phase of price change separately. Unfortunately, though the three original general price indices are joined from 1729 by a fourth, there is distressingly little agreement between the four about the extent of the price rise from the early 1750s to the early 1790s. Their assessments of the price rise from 1750–4 to 1788–92 range from 11.1 per cent to 46.5 per cent. The lowest of these is least likely to be an accurate reflection of the price change, and the mean of the remaining three shows a rise of 39.8 per cent. The mean of all four is 32.7 per cent. We are not likely to be very far from the truth if we assume a general price rise between these two quinquennia of between thirty-five and forty per cent. The rise in coal prices over the same period amounted

[41] Ibid., 397–9.
[42] E. W. Gilboy, 'The cost of living and real wages in eighteenth-century England', *Review of Economic Statistics*, 18 (1936); E. B. Schumpeter, 'English prices and public finance, 1660–1822', *Review of Economic Statistics*, 20 (1938).

to 23.4 per cent. By almost all acceptable estimates of the price changes over this period it seems that, in real terms, the price of coal probably fell slightly.

Though prices in general rose more steeply after the outbreak of war in 1793, we are somewhat better placed to measure the movement. Additional, and in at least one case, improved general price indices become available, and, so far as the inflationary period up to around 1813–14 is concerned, they agree more closely on the scale of the secular price rise. The six indices available for this period show prices rising generally from 1788–92 to 1809–15 by between sixty-five and eighty-five per cent, with a mean rise of 74.1 per cent. During the same period the coal price index rose by 54.6 per cent. Even allowing for the frailty of indices, it seems probable that coal prices did not rise as fast as other prices during this period, though the gap may not have been a very substantial one.

After the peak of 1813–14 prices in general fell until towards the middle of the century. Though there continued to be fairly sharp, short-run cyclical fluctuations of prices, the secular trend was at first fairly steeply downwards, but after the mid-1820s the price fall slowed down to level off by the mid-century. The two methodologically soundest indices that are available for the first half of the nineteenth century show prices falling from 1809–15 to 1826–30 by between 34.1 per cent and 40.1 per cent, with a mean fall of 37.1 per cent. Using the same method of measuring, coal prices fell by only 21.2 per cent. This indicates that, in real terms, the cost of coal is likely to have risen a little during the period of post-war deflation up to 1830, though it is obviously difficult to assess how far this real increase went towards offsetting the decline in real cost during the wartime inflation. This difficulty does, however, at least suggest that the change in the cost of coal between the 1790s and the 1820s was probably very slight: had it been larger one way or the other the change would probably have revealed itself in even these rough statistical measures.

The price movements discussed in the preceding paragraphs are set out in Table 9.5. No doubt somewhat different results could be obtained by ringing the changes on the indices used, and by substituting different turning-points. But the available price indices do not, for the most part, disagree very significantly in their measurements of general price changes, and the turning-points shown in Table 9.5 are real ones in the secular price history of the eighteenth and early nineteenth centuries. Any shift very far away from them would create a fresh set of methodological problems. The conclusions to which the data in Table 9.5 point are, first, that up to the secular

Table 9.5. *Comparison of coal and general price movements, 1700–1830*
(percentage change)

Period	Change in general prices (means of indices)	Change in coal prices
1700/4–1750/4	−4.8	−8.7
1746/50–1788/92	+32.7	+23.4
1788/92–1809/15	+74.1	+54.6
1809/15–1826/30	−37.1	−21.2

Sources: See text pp. 308–10. Coal prices are derived from Table 9.4
The general price indices used in this table are as follows:
1700/4–1750/4:   Gilboy; Schumpeter; Phelps Brown and Hopkins.
1750/4–1788/92:   Tucker; Gilboy; Schumpeter; Phelps Brown and Hopkins.
1788/92–1809/15:   Silberling; Tucker; Gilboy; Schumpeter; Gayer, Rostow, and Schwartz; Phelps Brown and Hopkins.
1809/15–1826/30:   Gayer, Rostow, and Schwartz; Rousseaux.
For the location of these standard indices, see M. W. Flinn, *EcHR* 2nd ser. 27 (1974), 412–13.

peak of prices in the second decade of the nineteenth century, coal prices rose less steeply than other prices; and, second, in the post-war deflation, coal prices showed greater resistance to decline than other prices. But it does seem unlikely that, over the whole of the eighteenth and early nineteenth centuries, the net outcome of price movements was any real increase in coal prices; if anything, the reverse is more likely to have been the case.

This stability, or possible marginal decline in real coal costs over the whole period is an achievement of considerable moment not merely for the coal industry itself, but for the whole economy in this key period of British economic history. A discussion of the wider implications of these trends must be deferred until the concluding chapter, but from the point of view of the history of the coal industry itself, the important point is that the general and remorseless tendency within an extractive industry towards diminishing returns and rising marginal costs was, somehow or other, but principally by means of technological advance, overcome. In spite of the need to go ever deeper, and to carry coal even further both underground and on the surface, the real costs of mining coal were unlikely to have risen significantly in the long run and may even have fallen.

iii. *Profits*

The art of mining in a capitalist system, it has been said, lies in extracting useful minerals from under the ground at a profit. Without profit there is no purpose in mining. Profit in the short or long run was what the coalowner of the eighteenth and early nineteenth centuries was interested in, and it was the business of his employees and advisers—his managers, agents, and viewers—to keep him informed by means of accounts and reports about all aspects of the mining enterprises that bore on profitability. Not surprisingly a high proportion of the mining records of this period on which much of this book is based were concerned, directly or indirectly, with profit. Yet profits were not always made in mining. Because of the uncertainties of mining—those arising out of the geological imponderables as well as those created by the needs of drainage and ventilation—much initial investment was speculative. Costs might be, as they often were, estimated in some detail, but contingencies were unknowable. A colliery was opened, for example, by John Turner in 1818 at Hazel Stoke on the Marquis of Anglesey's land in Staffordshire. It neither paid royalties to the landowner nor made any profit, and closed six years later.[43] There must have been many such ventures whose lack of success and short lives have left no record in the archives.

To add to the uncertainties, coal prices in the market were volatile in the short-run, so that even a fairly wide gap between estimated costs and anticipated prices could vanish in the vicissitudes of the market and the hazards of underground working. Investment in mining, according to William Cotesworth, 'cannot be undertaken without the Hazard of an Excessive loss'.[44] Buddle outlined the element of chance in mining when he pointed out that 'perhaps no stronger Proof of the great Risk can be adduced than that it [a coal mine] is a property which cannot be insured, either against Fire, Water or any other Accident. We have never been able to effect an Insurance on a Coal Work.'[45] This point had been made before,[46] but was apparently no longer valid by 1827 when the Norwich Union insured Tanfield Moor colliery for £3,640.[47] Even so experienced an engineer as Telford apparently found the risks of mining too much for him. 'Let me beg of you', he wrote to William Hughes in 1820, 'on your own account and that of your family, not rashly to engage in coal mining. I have paid severely for speculation of this sort, first by the uncertainty and risque of the works, and secondly by becoming entangled with partners—it is easy to get engaged, but vexation and ruin frequently are the result.'[48]

[43] StRO Anglesey D603/M/2.   [44] Quoted by Ellis thesis 1975, 67.
[45] Quoted by Wood 1971, 233.
[46] Beaumont 1789, 46.
[47] DuRO NCB First Deposit NCB/I/JB/774.
[48] Thomas Telford to William Hughes, 6 June 1820, NLW Chirk Castle F/7486.

The risk element in mining was incalculable and present even in mines that, in the event, made substantial profits year after year over several decades: a run of successful mining could be terminated any minute by inundation, explosion or faults. A letter from the Earl of Egremont's agent in 1824 illustrates very well the ways in which the uncertainties of mining could prevent profits being made: 'I now address you', he wrote,

concerning the Aspatria West Moor Coallery. We took it for 14 Years, and whereof 9 have expired and 5 remaining. We have now lost above £3,000 by it, the first Year we had paid £150 Rent without ever getting any Coal. We have now wrought the last three Years in a band of Coal about $7\frac{1}{2}$ Foot high, but it is so disturbed with hitches and geld Ground, and hemed in on one side by a Dyke, on the other by stone lying in the place of Coal and we have so much Water to lift, that with one thing and another we are verey likely to loose Money by it this Year exclusive of the Rent. We have got it vewed by a Coal Agent and he thinks that the Coal where we are now working may perhaps last this year or may not. When we took it Coals sold for 8/6d. per Ton. They are now selling at 6/6d. and very little demand for them, as there are so maney new Coallerys opened since we began. We think very hard to loose so much Money by it and no prospect of doeing better in this spread of Coal where we are now working. It may on some other part of the Moor that is unexplored be lying not so much disturbed, otherwise it is not worth the looking after. We believe there is no Coal near where we are now working worth looking after, as we have boored about 50 Fathoms and not found any workable Band. . . . I think they would have given it up long since but I always expected that it would have opened out better, so it would if the Stone Coal had not come in on one side, such a thing, I think, as never before hapened in any Coallery to such an extent.[49]

More usually, however, failure to make profits arose from over-optimistic assumptions about working and marketing conditions. The lessees of the Low Moor colliery near Barnsley in Yorkshire informed the owner that for several years they had invested between five and ten thousand pounds annually. By 1806 they had laid out a total of £46,000, but could still not get the coal on to the boats on the Barnsley Canal at a cost less than the current selling price. For this losing situation they blamed both the high level of royalties and high freights on the Barnsley Canal, though both must have been exactly predictable before any investment was made.[50]

To compensate for the risks and losses, profits had to be high at least in some collieries and in some years, otherwise capital would not have been ventured in mining. Moderate rates of profit equal to

[49] J. Brown to Earl of Egremont, 19 Jan. 1824, CuRO Leconfield D/Lec Box 41.
[50] Joseph Dawson to Walter Spencer Stanhope, 28 Mar. 1806, SCL Spencer Stanhope 60579.

what could be gained in other industries would not have been sufficient to attract capital so long as ventures like Aspatria and Low Moor suffered persistent and apparently unpredictable losses. Good profits could clearly, even in unfavourable circumstances, be made easily, as a letter of 1743 illustrates. 'The Duke of Hamiltons affairs at Bowness [West Lothian, Scotland] goe on in a very heavy maner, and the oncost above and below ground ar swelled to an exorbitan hight, and yet in spite of all Mr. Walkershaws sillness the profit on the whole workes in 18 months Mr. Walkershaws time amounts to no less than £1,459 10s. sterling.'[51] The necessity for relatively high rates of profit somewhere in the industry was emphasized by the inevitable tendency of profits in any one colliery to decline sooner or later as seams were exhausted or the working out of the higher or more easily worked seams forced deeper and more expensive working. All collieries were ultimately worked out, at which time investment in sinking, driving levels, and 'dead stock' was written off. Thanks to multiple shafts and a succession of workable seams some collieries enjoyed very long lives, but others expired soon after birth.

There are no really satisfactory ways of calculating profit in mining enterprises of this period from the data available in contemporary accounts. There were no generally accepted accounting methods at the time, and profits might be estimated or calculated in a wide variety of ways. At Ford colliery in Northumberland in 1750, for example, a computation showed a profit of 7s. 2d. accruing to the owner in a single day from the labour of six hewers, with total daily costs amounting to £1. 3s. 10d.[52] At other collieries profit was calculated weekly—at Griff in Warwickshire in 1701–2, for example; at Wollaton in Nottinghamshire between 1732 and 1749, and again from 1778 to 1784; and at Hewerhill in the North-east in 1808–9.[53] On the Sutherland estates in Staffordshire, however, for Pooldole colliery in the 1780s and 1790s, Meirheath colliery in the 1790s, and Priorfield colliery between 1817 and 1825, profits were accounted for fortnightly. This was not, however, a consistent estate practice, for at Knowles colliery on the same Staffordshire estate, profit was returned at six-monthly intervals.[54] Elsewhere, as at Trowell colliery in Nottinghamshire in the 1730s and 1740s, and at Mostyn colliery in Flintshire in the 1820s, monthly profit

    [51] (?) Elphinstone to unknown recipient, 2 Mar. 1743, NLS Dundas of Dundas 80.1.4/232.
    [52] NuRO Delaval (Hastings) 650/I 8.
    [53] WaRO Newdigate of Arbury CR136 V.131; NUL Middleton Mi Ac 133, 136; NEI Watson 5/10/22.
    [54] StRO Sutherland D593 M/11/1/1; M/8/1/1; M/10/1/2; M/12/1.

statements were the rule.[55] More unusually, and certainly less inform-
atively, a calculation by John Blenkinsop of profit at Flockton
colliery in Yorkshire in 1816 was shown per acre of coal worked.[56]

More commonly, and rather more usefully, profit was calculated,
for the information of coalowners, per unit of output. In the North-
east estimates and returns of profit were usually made either per
chaldron of coal produced, as at the Grand Allies' collieries in 1727
and 1733, at Sheriff Hill colliery in 1804, and at Bigges Main colliery
in 1805, or per ten, as at Northwood colliery in 1753 and Tanfield
Lea in 1755.[57] At a small landsale colliery in Durham, however,
a return of profit in 1734 was shown per score of corves produced.[58]
Similarly, in other coal fields, profit was calculated according to the
particular unit of measure used. Thus at Hollands Pit in Shropshire
in 1747 profit was returned per waggon, and at Lanmorlais colliery
in South Wales in the 1770s per weigh.[59]

Whatever period or unit of output profit was related to, however,
there are problems of attaching meaning to the figures produced.
The many statements of profits in the contemporary records of
mining enterprises are based on a simple subtraction of an aggregate
of costs from the revenue derived from the sale of coal. But, as we
have seen earlier in this chapter, the elements that entered into the
aggregated costs were somewhat arbitrary. The failure consistently
to distinguish capital from current costs, the normal omission of any
allowance for depreciation, or of interest on loan as opposed to share
capital, mean that it is not common to find profit statements that
have taken any precise account of capital costs. Furthermore,
variable capital and the 'running investment' identified in chapter
six were indeed often entered alongside, and not distinguished from,
running costs like wages, probably because they often consisted
mostly of wage-costs; initial fixed capital was occasionally treated in
the same way too.

The uncertainties of profit-and-loss accounting in this period are
nicely illustrated by papers produced in a lawsuit over the Stevenston
coal and salt enterprise at Saltcoats in Ayrshire in 1800–1. Here, five
different calculations of profit in a single year were made, the
principal cause of difference being the valuation of stocks of coal.
The enterprise's books showed a profit of £4,270; the defendant in
the case, evidently an aggrieved partner of the landowner in the

[55] NUL Middleton Mi Ac 35; UCNW (Bangor) Mostyn 6990.
[56] NuRO 962/52.
[57] NEI Grand Allies, Partnership Minute book 1727–38, 18/vol. not numbered/26–7,
74–6; NEI Watson 8/8/196 and 8/8/430–1; NEI Forster 49/4/172, 207.
[58] NEI Forster 49/5/66.
[59] ShRO Madeley Parish 2280 3/13; NLW Maybery 202.

enterprise, claimed that it should be £3,943; while separate statements by independent viewers according to different criteria assessed the profits variously at £2,619, £2,290, and £1,025. The last of these, therefore, determined the profit for one year's operation at slightly less than one-quarter of the figure actually shown in the books.[60]

In contrast to this confusion, an abstract of the accounts of the Vane-Tempest collieries for the five-year period 1814–18 shows a clear grasp of most of the issues raised in the foregoing. This statement is mainly devoted to an account of 'Extraordinaries, or Expenditure in extending the Workings in the Leashold Collieries, etc., no Part of which is included in the Yearly Valuations of live or dead Stock on the Colls., with other Sums paid not being usual Charges in Collieries.' These include 'interest and discounts', 'law expences', 'sinking pits', 'new buildings', 'expences in London p. agents', and 'receipt stamps'. Over the five-year period these amounted to £27,946. 16s. 5d. which, deducted from the gross profit figure of £109,776. 15s. 11¼d. left what was called 'Ordinaries' of £81,829. 19s. 6¼d. From this latter figure, however, a further deduction of £28,094. 4s. 8¼d. arising from the increase in the value of stock was made, leaving 'cash [i.e. net] profits' of £53,735. 14s. 10d., or an annual average of £10,747. Here, therefore, was an account which did take account of interest, though 'running investment' in the shape of new shafts and new buildings was treated as current expenditure, and deducted annually from gross profits. The inclusion of 'increase of stock' in the deductions from gross profits shows, however, that account was taken of depreciation, since this was clearly the net outcome of the changes in annual valuations.[61]

Though explicit statements are rare, other profit-and-loss accounts did occasionally also allow for interest charges. An estimate of the profit to be obtained from the working of Benwell colliery on Tyneside in 1777 showed gross profit at £5,125 which was derived from selling for £10,775 coal that had cost £5,650 to produce. But from this gross profit deductions for interest on the capital sunk in winning the colliery and an allowance of 25s. per ten for rent (royalty) left net profit at £3,375, still a substantial margin over costs.[62] Similarly, a computation by the Grand Allies for the operation of Heaton colliery for the year 1736 included as a cost interest on £30,000 at five per cent. In projecting the estimated profits from the operations of this colliery through the next five years,

---

[60] ScRO Court of Session CS96/640, Appendix, 31.
[61] DuRO Londonderry D/Lo/B41.
[62] NEI Watson 8/11/120.

the annual interest charge is shown as diminishing each year until in 1741 'the principall', amounting now only to £2,276, is deducted from the estimated annual profit. This reduction of the principal was achieved by using the net profit each year to reduce the principal. The calculation thus showed that it was possible to repay the entire capital, with interest, within five years, from the profits. Thereafter there would be no interest to pay.[63]

In reviewing the many statements of weekly, monthly, or annual profit made by colliery undertakings in this period, the problem is to know whether they reflect the muddled procedures of the Stevenston enterprise, or the advanced accounting of the Londonderry estate. From the bare statements that are all that are mostly available it is seldom possible to be sure. It seems probable that statements prepared for the larger estate operations by the early decades of the nineteenth century really do reflect net profit in the manner of the Londonderry accounts, though the eighteenth-century statements of smaller undertakings may often have been more haphazard and incomplete. In these latter statements the tendency would almost certainly be to overestimate profits.

With these reservations in mind we may now turn to Tables 9.6 and 9.7 where the longest-running available series of profits have been tabulated. For convenience they have been separated into two tables covering the separate earlier and later periods into which they fall. It should be noted first that not all series fall exactly into calendar years. Where they do not, they have been allocated to the calendar year in which the greater part of the accounting year falls. No attempt should be made to relate one series to another since, as we have seen, each series is probably calculated on a quite different basis from the others; but it would not be unreasonable to assume that each series is internally consistent in its method of calculation so that its short-run fluctuations and long-run trends are reasonable indicators of the real fortunes of the collieries or enterprises concerned.

The series in these Tables point to several conclusions. For the most part, though some collieries experienced steady profits for several years at a stretch, profits fluctuated fairly sharply in the short run. The experience of Middleton colliery in Yorkshire and Garesfield colliery in the North-east was particularly severe in this respect. These short-run fluctuations might be expected to relate to the vicissitudes of the trade cycle, but even after allowing for the lag of the fluctuations in some series owing to the vagaries of the accounting year employed there is remarkably little correspondence

[63] NEI Grand Allies, Partnership minute book, 1727-38, 100-1.

Table 9.6. *Annual profits and losses at selected collieries, 1709–42*
(To nearest £. Losses (−))

Year	Collieries			
	Benwell colliery (NE)	Coudon Cleuch colliery (Scot.)	Sheriffhall colliery (Scot.)	Ford colliery (NE)
1709	2,228			
1710	2,721			
1711	2,594			
1712	1,784			
1713	1,387	699		
1714	1,852	838	2,627	
1715	1,489	1,063	5,320	
1716	949	1,237	7,749	
1717	609	1,449	121	
1718	−317	1,508	5,244	
1719	686	135	207	20
1720	168	163	110	7
1721	916	172		−1
1722	−152	74	177	14
1723		−27	−24	
1724		−15	−712	
1725		−26	101	
1726			107	
1727				
1728				
1729		142		
1730		224		
1731		257		
1732		255		
1733		326		
1734		179		
1735		326		
1736		140		
1737		186		
1738		77		
1739		18		
1740		−40		
1741		−58		
1742		−31		

Sources:

Benwell colliery 1709–22	NuRO Benwell Manor MBE IV.5.
Coudon Cleuch colliery 1713–42	ScRO Buccleuch GD224/Boxes 54–5.
Sheriffhall colliery 1714–26	ScRO Buccleuch GD224/Boxes 51–3.
Ford colliery 1719–22	NuRO Delaval (Hastings) 650/I 6.

between the good and bad years of individual undertakings. In Table 9.6, for example, while Coudon Cleuch and Sheriffhall collieries in Scotland were enjoying a good year in 1718, Benwell in the North-east suffered its worst year in the fourteen years for which the series runs. Similarly, while Garesfield and Pontop collieries

in the North-east both had a bad year in 1818, available series
relating to other collieries do not suggest that this was generally
either a good or a bad year.

Several of the series illustrate what must have been a fairly common
experience in the history of colliery undertakings. After a run of
good years, profits enter a decline which seems to signify that the
colliery's profitable life is coming to an end. This appears to be the
situation at Benwell colliery in the early 1720s, and at Coudon
Cleuch and Sheriffhall collieries in the mid-1720s. Care should be
taken, however, in arriving at this interpretation, as the revival of
Coudon Cleuch's profits in the 1730s shows, though the profit
series there repeats in the late 1730s and early 1740s the decline of
the early 1720s. We knew, too, that Benwell colliery on Tyneside
came back into profitable operation more than once in the following
century. A likely explanation for this kind of cyclical behaviour in
profits would be the investment pattern. An initial injection of
capital would inaugurate such a cycle of profits, but as the workings
opened up by this investment are exhausted, a fresh spurt of output
and profits must await a new wave of investment, possibly even by
new operators.

In contrast to the short profit bonanzas of some undertakings,
others were able to sustain good, if fluctuating, levels of profit for
long periods. There is no particular pattern discernible here. The
profits of the Bridgewater collieries, for example, clearly separated
in the accounts from those of the canals, which fluctuated fairly
sharply throughout the thirty-nine years of the available series, were
none the less consistently substantial from the early 1790s. The
immense profits during the first decade of the nineteenth century
are difficult to explain. True, prices, according to Table 9.4, rose
sharply between 1801 and 1803, but scarcely sufficiently to explain
the quadrupling of profits. And prices continued to rise, though not
fast, between 1803 and 1809, when Bridgewater profits declined.
The situation, however, was one in which the frailties of the index in
Table 9.4 may be seriously misleading. The index, as was noticed, is
heavily based on north-eastern prices, while those in Manchester may
have been determined to a large degree by the Duke of Bridgewater's
prices, since at that time he was probably the largest supplier on the
Manchester market. It will be recalled that in 1759 he had committed
himself to maintaining a quayside price in Manchester of 4*d*. a cwt.
for forty years. This period expired in 1799, and the Duke would
have been less than human had he continued to sell coal at this
artificially low price when freed from the statutory constraint. But
this explanation of the enormous rise in his profits from 1799 leaves

Table 9.7. *Annual profits and losses at selected collieries, 1763–1830*
(To nearest £. Losses (−))

Year	Collieries						
	Bridgewater collieries (Lancs.)	Balbirnie colliery (Scot.)	Fordel colliery (Scot.)	Lount colliery (E. Mids.)	Sheffield colliery (Yorks.)	Burlow colliery (E. Mids.)	Wollaton colliery (E. Mids.)
1763		929		−68		−3	
1764		1,004		−88		71	
1765		1,122		−239		23	
1766		1,039		5		25	
1767		930		−71		15	
1768		1,035		28		−15	
1769		898		−491		24	
1770		824		−1		98	
1771				104		−16	
1772	198		598	88		−45	
1773	−212		512	48		−91	
1774	1,962		267	−161		−54	
1775	570		428	181		−138	
1776	2,422		777	116			
1777	1,040		851				
1778	998		1,091				
1779	584		278				
1780	3,339		1,226		674		
1781	939		652		567		
1782	1,425		957		580		
1783	933		1,306		570		1,739
1784	2,543		399		991		1,072
1785	312		923		1,185		2,392
1786	905		1,250		1,375		1,939
1787	2,171		648				1,445
1788	1,728		2,215				2,541
1789	1,826		2,313				2,000
1790	1,934		4,863				2,206
1791	2,617						

Year	Pontop colliery (NE)	Tanfield Moor (NE)	Middleton colliery (Yorks.)	Lothian collieries (Scot.)	Garesfield colliery (NE)	Haigh colliery (Lancs.)	Townley colliery (NE)	Alloa colliery (Scot.)	Sheriffhall colliery (Scot.)	Curwen collieries (Cumb.)
1792	5,660									
1793	3,114									
1794	1,760									
1795	2,867								311	
1796	3,544			462					371	
1797	4,181			843					58	
1798	2,407			502					354	
1799	5,644			528					975	
1800	6,024		−1,883	309					1,028	
1801	7,811		976	450					152	
1802	15,345		1,574	725					691	
1803	24,301		3,119	979					1,021	
1804	21,938		2,274	2,415					646	
1805	20,225		1,563	2,407					972	
1806	13,427		5,241						776	20,889
1807	11,245								490	13,028
1808	8,769								508	8,973
1809	7,254									3,983
1810	16,753									2,796
1811										11,633
1812						2,773				6,872
1813					7,599	3,175	8,000	6,867		4,313
1814					8,661	3,021	6,000	3,669		
1815	6,747				9,635	3,080	6,000	3,714		
1816	5,899				3,176	4,234	12,000	3,066		
1817	2,246				6,418	5,350	8,000	3,762		
1818	−2,035				5,426	3,395	12,000	4,122		
1819	2,446				4,789	3,095	8,000	3,288		
1820	2,209				3,321	2,963	6,000	3,027		
1821	655				1,576	4,579	4,000	3,640		
1822					4,745			3,463		
1823					8,125			3,999		
1824		6,374			10,788			3,694		
1825		4,490			6,956		5,066	437		
1826		3,747			7,964		3,626			
1827		5,591			6,487		5,848			
1828		2,934			7,340		5,924			
1829					7,166		1,829			
1830					4,606		5,675			

unexplained their subsequent decline only a few years later. There was, moreover, for whatever reason, a boom in total shipments of coal from the Worsley colliery down the canal to Manchester at this time. Shipments which had averaged 75,000 tons yearly during the 1790s ran at over 100,000 tons in 1800–2 and 1804.[64]

For the most part, the varying fortunes of individual undertakings in the short- and the medium-run must be explained less in terms of national or regional trade conditions than in terms of their immediate geological and investment circumstances. It was the lucky strike, the good fortune in avoiding hazards or disasters, and the well-planned investment, that determined profitability in the short- and medium-run even where the viability or otherwise of an undertaking in the first place was the net outcome of a wider range of determinants like distance from markets, the depth and thickness of seams, and the problems posed by drainage and ventilation. It remains true, of course, that expert advice of the kind supplied by the best viewers of the North-east could reduce the element of chance and luck in mining.

The annual series of colliery profits illustrated in Tables 9.6 and 9.8 are supplemented by a great many random statements for single years. Apart, however, from indicating orders of magnitude, these random statements are not very informative. In an attempt to make some of these random statements about profit more meaningful a number of estimated or actual profits have been set out in Table 9.8. Calculating profit as a percentage of total costs, they show an

---

Sources: (Table 9.7)

Balbirnie colliery, 1763–70	ScRO Balfour of Balbirnie 315.
Lount colliery 1763–76	C. P. Griffin thesis, 33.
Burlow colliery 1764–76	Daniels and Ashton 1929–30, 128.
Duke of Bridgewater's collieries	LaRO Bridgewater NCBw 6/1–2.
Fordell colliery 1772–90	ScRO Henderson of Fordell GD172/835/1.
Sheffield colliery 1781–7	SCL Arundel Castle S196.
Wollaton colliery 1783–90	NUL Middleton Mi Ac 120.
Sheriffhall colliery 1795–1808	ScRO Buccleuch GD224/986/1.
Marquis of Lothian's collieries 1796–1805	ScRO Lothian GD40/V/83.
Middleton colliery 1800–6	NEI Watson 9/1/no pagination.
Middleton colliery 1813–30	LCA MC34.
Curwen collieries 1806–13	Wood 1971, 232.
Haigh colliery 1812–21	JRL Crawford and Balcarres 23/14/10/608–9.
Towneley colliery 1813–22	DuRO NCB First Deposit NCB/I/SC/466(1). (These are distributed, not actual profits.)
Towneley colliery 1825–30	DuRO NCB First Deposit NCB/I/SC/466(4).
Alloa colliery 1814–26	ScRO Mar and Kellie GD124/17/587/16.
Garesfield colliery 1815–21	NuRO Armstrong 725/F/17/22.
Pontop colliery 1815–21	NuRO Armstrong 725/F/17/29.
Tanfield Moor colliery 1824–8	NEI Buddle 27/no pagination.

[64] LaRO Bridgewater NCBw/6/1, 2.

unweighted mean of 28.6 per cent, with the estimates, not surprisingly (since it is always tempting to assume that they will have tended to be over-optimistic), yielding a marginally higher mean than the actual accounts. In so far as the profits recorded in this table are representative of the industry as a whole in this period, they show a marked rise during the years of the French Wars after 1793. Profits recorded up to 1792 averaged 25.0 per cent, but rose during the war period to 30.5 per cent. In the post-war period from 1815 to 1830 the average fell again marginally to 29.9 per cent. With the exception of a small number of collieries that were clearly unusually unprofitable, the rates illustrated in this Table are, however, fairly consistent. None of the collieries made losses, though one or two came near to doing so, and few made profits of over fifty per cent. We should bear in mind, however, that, as Tables 9.6 and 9.7 revealed, it was not entirely uncommon for collieries to make losses from time to time. We should clearly not go far from the facts if we say that collieries in the eighteenth and early nineteenth centuries generally made a profit approaching thirty per cent of their costs.

A more meaningful measure of profits might, however, be their relation to capital invested. Though there is, as we have seen in this chapter and chapter six, a certain amount of information relating to both investment and profits, the two sets of data are very rarely available for the same enterprises at the same time, so that there is no possibility of formulating any valid generalizations in this area. A survey of Wylam colliery on Tyneside in 1826, for example, estimated annual profit at £1,850 and valued the colliery at £25,879, a return on capital of 7.1 per cent, but the assessment was a valuation based on the probable future earnings of the colliery rather than an exact statement of actual investment, and as Table 9.8 shows, Wylam was one of the less profitable enterprises of the period.[65] That the subject was of interest to contemporaries is witnessed by a report of Buddle's on Elswick colliery in Northumberland in 1809. Having taken careful account of the total capital sunk in the undertaking he went on to calculate that a vend of 14,000 chaldrons per year would be necessary to produce a profit that would both redeem the capital in $37\frac{1}{2}$ years and yield a return on it equal to fifteen per cent per annum. A vend of only 10,000 chaldrons would redeem the capital in a similar period but show a return of only ten per cent on the investment.[66] The implication of his calculations is that he considered fifteen per cent to be an appropriate return for the period, and this is borne out by Francis Thompson's report to the

[65] DuRO NCB First Deposit NCB/I/TH/6(3).
[66] NEI Miscellaneous 63 ZC/48/1.

Table 9.8. *Rates of profit, selected collieries, isolated years, 1717–1830*
(profits as percentages of total costs)

Year	Colliery	Mining region	Actual (A) or estimated (E) profit	Rate of profit	Source
1717	Fenham	NE	E	22.7	NEI Forster 49/4/1.
1720	Bucksnook	NE	A	3.6	GPL Cotesworth CG/4/157.
1740	Elswick	NE	E	13.6	NEI Forster 49/4/56.
1743–8	Cowclose	NE	A	16.8	DuRO Strathmore D/St/104.
1752–3	Geo. Weld's	W. Mids.	A	43.3	ShRO Forester 1224/173.
1773	Bransty	Cumb.	A	30.1	Wood thesis 1952, 47.
1773	Sheffield Park	Yorks.	A	13.1	SCL Arundel Castle S215/20–2.
1779–92	Ardeers	Scot.	A	21.9	ScRO Court of Session CS96/638/767–8.
1783–5	Coalpitheath	SW	A	49.2	NUL Middleton Mi Ac 129a.
1783–98	Misk	Scot.	A	4.2	ScRO Court of Session CS96/638/3/1935.
1786	Gateshead Park	NE	E	35.3	NEI Watson 8/11/74.
1787	Sheriff Hill	NE	E	17.3	NEI Watson 8/11/98–9.
1790	St. Anthony's	NE	E	54.0	NEI Watson 8/8/275.
1795	Pontop Pike	NE	A	30.9	WaRO Seymour of Ragley CR114a/252.
1799–1800	Vane-Tempest collieries	NE	A	39.6	DuRO Londonderry D/Lo/E390–6.
1801	Elvet	NE	E	24.9	NEI Buddle 5/51–2.
1801	Hardy	E. Mids.	A	10.0	DeRO Pashley 267Z.

1801	Cowpen	NE	E	39.1	NEI Watson 8/8/300.
1803	West Denton	NE	E	7.8	NEI Watson 8/8/318.
1803	Willington	NE	E	43.5	NEI Watson 8/8/303–4.
1804	Sheriff Hill	NE	E	33.2	NEI Watson 8/8/196.
1804–9	Heanor	E. Mids.	A	56.5	DeRO Heanor Colliery 1832Z.
1806	Felling and Carr's Hill	NE	E	33.3	NEI Watson 8/9/64.
1807	Heaton	NE	A	34.2	NEI Buddle 32/III/90–1.
1808	Hewerhill	NE	A	48.0	NEI Watson 5/10/22.
1811	Alfreton	E. Mids.	E	30.2	LCA 1546/1.
1811	Felling	NE	E	30.0	NEI Forster 49/8/85–6.
1815	Robert Town	Yorks.	E	0.4	LCA 1546/1.
1815	Newbottle	NE	E	26.9	NuRO Armstrong 725/F/17/118–20.
1816	Rothwell Haigh	Yorks.	E	14.4	NuRO 962/30–2.
1816	Flockton	Yorks.	E	54.5	NuRO 962/1/52.
1817–18	Jarrow	NE	A	19.5	NEI Buddle 36/III/11, 50.
1818	Burtonholm	Lancs.	E	52.8	JRL Crawford and Balcarres 23/6/209.
1818–20	Cowpen	NE	A	10.9	NuRO Ridley (Blagdon) ZRI 35/5/1.
1823	Hetton	NE	E	32.1	NuRO Wilson (Forest Hall) ZWI/4/341–4.
1824–8	Tanfield Moor	NE	A	32.5	NEI Buddle 37.
1825–30	Towneley and Whitefield	NE	A	24.3	DuRO NCB First Deposit NCB/I/SC/466(4).
1826	Wylam	NE	E	12.6	DuRO NCB First Deposit NCB/I/TH/6(2).
1827	Hetton	NE	E	36.4	NuRO Wilson (Forest Hall) ZWI/4/385–6.
1829	Hetton	NE	A	50.2	NEI Forster 49/8/189.
1830	North Hetton	NE	A	19.2	NEI Buddle Atkinson 45/1/no pagination.

1800 Select Committee that, after the institution of the 'Limitation of the Vend' in 1771, Washington colliery in County Durham, of which he was at the time manager, was able to return 'better than 15 per cent upon the capital of £15,000 expended on that Colliery'.[67] This magnitude of margin was further confirmed by a letter from Buddle in which he estimated that the total profits from all the Tyne collieries in the year 1807 amounted to £150,000, and that represented very nearly seventeen per cent of the total investment of £883,000. The roundness of the figure for profit suggests that this was a very rough guess, and indeed he was reported in 1828 as estimating a return of only eight per cent on capital invested in Tyneside mines.[68]

Unsatisfactory though these various measures of profit are, they are just sufficient to suggest that coal-mining was generally a very profitable business for those fortunate enough to occupy coal-bearing land or willing to risk the relatively large sums of capital essential for successful enterprise. It scarcely needs proving that a small number of landowning, mainly artistocratic, families made substantial fortunes in the eighteenth and early nineteenth centuries out of their coal-mining ventures. The £3,000 a year gained from mining by the Earl of Crawford and Balcarres in the early 1820s and the £2,600 a year averaged by the Earl of Mar and Kellie for twenty-three years up to 1818 from his were good incomes by early nineteenth-century standards, but they were small beside the £13,635 averaged by the Duke of Bridgewater in the first decade of the nineteenth century and the almost identical income averaged by Sir Henry Vane-Tempest in the same period. In consequence of investment in 'extraordinaries' and stocks, the income of the Vane-Tempest family from mining ran somewhat lower—averaging £10,747—in the immediate post-war years, but by the time the Marquis of Londonderry had taken over the estate and added to its resources, his annual income from his collieries was estimated at £30,000. Though his neighbour, Lord Durham (Lambton), achieved this income in isolated years during the 1820s, his average income from mining between 1824 and 1828 was only £17,500. The Lowthers, now the Lords Lonsdale, were drawing annual profits in the early years of the nineteenth century sufficiently close to £30,000 to be able to offer their viewers bonuses when this level was reached.[69]

[67] *First SC Coal Trade* 1800, 542.
[68] J. Buddle to G. Silvertop, 27 Aug. 1808, NEI Buddle 23/44; NEI Watson 5/26/42.
[69] JRL Crawford and Balcarres 23/14/10/85; ScRO Mar and Kellie GD124/17/581/8; LaRO Bridgewater NCBw/6/1–2; DuRO Londonderry D/Lo/390–6, B38, B41, B310(7); H. Stephenson to Lord Durham, 26 Jan. 1829, LEA MP12/not numbered; Wood thesis 1952, 150.

Perhaps the most dramatic fortune was that won by William Russell, the Sunderland merchant, who took the lease of Wallsend colliery from the Dean and Chapter of Durham Cathedral in 1787. At first the rents on this relatively new colliery were low, while profits on the very high quality of coal won were high. Even after a serious disaster in 1802 the colliery was still yielding an annual net profit of between £30,000 and £60,000. Profits in the early nineteenth century ran at over 100 per cent of costs: in 1809, when operating costs came to just over £50,000, gross revenue amounted to £110,000. Between 1787 and 1810 Russell bought estate in County Durham to the value of almost £750,000 entirely from the profits of a single colliery, albeit probably the best-known name in coal at that period.[70]

It is therefore hardly surprising to find that the early nineteenth century was a great period for the building and rebuilding of stately homes by the coal magnates of the North-east. William Russell bought Brancepeth Castle in 1796 for £75,000 and his son, starting in 1817, spent a further £120,000 rebuilding it. William Henry Lambton, the father of John George, the first Lord Durham, built Lambton House in 1797 and his son greatly enlarged and castellated it, renaming it Lambton Castle, in 1833. The Liddells engaged Nash to build Ravensworth Castle for them in 1808 and enlarged it in 1822. Across the Pennines Lord Lonsdale employed Robert Smirke to design Lowther Castle for him in 1806. The mania for castles in this period owes much to the revival of interest in medieval chivalry, and the desire to proclaim roots in ancient lineages manifested in this return to mock-feudalism seems to have been a characteristic of the group of aristocratic radicals of which Lord Durham was a leading member. This explanation of castle-building by coal magnates is perhaps less fanciful than one that sees the castles as the embattled defences of the employing class against the rising aggression of its infinitely poorer and less well-housed workers.[71]

The great coalowning magnates of this period did not formally indulge the practice of twentieth-century businesses of transferring a portion of their profits each year to reserve in order to build up a fund from which to finance future investment, but in the case of the family enterprises of the kind represented by these magnates this is effectively what happened. Investment in their undertakings was largely if not wholly provided out of past profits, and, if the

[70] Hughes thesis 1963, I, 2–3. Hughes had access to the Hamilton-Russell papers at Brancepeth Castle not accessible to the present researchers.

[71] Details from N. Pevsner, The Buildings of England: County Durham (London, 1953). For the revival of chivalry, see M. Girouard, The Return to Camelot (New Haven, Conn., and London, 1981).

industry was to continue to expand and take advantage of the newest technology, profits had to be large enough not merely, as we have seen, to compensate for the high risks involved, but also to provide future capital. By the early nineteenth century, the capital requirements of viable mining enterprises were large by the general industrial standards of the day, and only generous rates of profits would suffice to allow for ploughing-back. Though in the non-landowning sector of the industry, which, as we saw in chapter six was important and possibly growing by the early nineteenth century, some savings from much wider sources were canalized into mining, the same principle still broadly operated. The mining industry, in the main, was financed from ploughed-back profits, and profits had to be on a scale that made this possible.

Chapter 10

The Organization of Mining Labour

i. *The nature of the labour force*

Commentators from outside the mining industry are apt to describe all those who work in it collectively as 'miners', yet the diversity of skills and occupations in the industry of the eighteenth and early nineteenth centuries as well as of today was so great as to make any single designation unhelpful. A principal division, of course, was that between surface and underground workers, but even in these divisions sharp distinctions of skills, pay, and status existed.

Underground, the work-force may be divided between those who cut and moved the coal—the production workers; and those who prepared and kept the workings in a state that permitted continuous production—the maintenance staff. On the production side there were broadly four tasks to be done—cutting, loading, hauling, and hooking whatever coal container was used on the winding rope. The number of hewers effectively determined the size of the remainder of a colliery's work-force. They were the élite of the underground work-force, worked the shortest hours, and were generally the most highly paid apart from the supervisory and managerial staff. They got coal down from the coalface and were not normally concerned with moving it beyond their own need for working space. In some coal-fields, however, as in Cumberland in the mid-eighteenth century, hewers (there called haggers) did in some situations haul the coal they had cut some or all the way to the shaft bottom.[1] In pillar and stall working, each hewer normally worked on his own and in his own stall; but with longwall working, several hewers worked together side by side on a long face and some co-ordination of processes was clearly essential. In longwall working in the mines of the Carron iron company in Scotland Gabriel Jars observed during the 1760s that face-workers operated in two specialized groups. A morning shift cut the lower veins of a seam with picks, while an afternoon shift brought down the upper veins with crowbars and hammers. Since the veins or strata of the seams would contain different types of coal, this shift system permitted the separation of the different coals

[1] 'Memorandum on the running of collieries, Nov 1756', CuRO Lonsdale D/Lons/L/Acc.629.

during hauling and winding.[2] In Derbyshire even greater division of labour prevailed for longwall working. There the face was first undermined by 'holers' using picks, who then gave way to 'hammermen' or 'drivers' who brought the coal down with the aid of wedges. 'Remblers', who broke up the large blocks of coal produced by this method finally took over before the coal was ready for the 'harrers' who dragged the corves, leaving the space cleared to the 'timberers' who shored up the roof with props.[3] In Shropshire longwall working the face was undercut by 'holers' and the coal brought down by wedges driven in along the roof by 'getters'. A team of such specialists each worked a section of the longwall coal face, called in Scotland a 'space' or a 'room', of about ten yards.[4]

Once cut, coal had to be loaded into corves, tubs, or waggons for hauling, and the name given to the class of workers who did this work varied with the method of hauling employed. Those who hauled by their own power, whether by pulling sledges or by pushing wheeled vehicles were generally called putters, but where hauling was horse-powered the work was done by rolley-drivers or inbye-drivers. In the loading operation they might be assisted by fillers or shifters, while the transfer of the corves or tubs from the haulage rolleys or sledges to the winding rope at the bottom of the upcast shaft would be done by 'onsetters'.

The labour force concerned with the preparation and maintenance of the underground workings may similarly be divided into those who opened up new workings—something that required to be sustained constantly if a mine was to be kept in operation, and those who maintained existing workings in a state that permitted continuing work. In some colliery districts and in the smaller mines the work of opening new faces might be undertaken by the hewers themselves and in these circumstances there might be agreed rates of pay for this work. In other districts and in the larger collieries specialized teams, as in sinking, were engaged for driving levels or headings. The main servicing tasks were concerned with ventilation and keeping the roadways clear for hauling. The key job in ventilation was that of the furnaceman who fed the furnace either underground or at the pithead to ensure regular and vigorous 'coursing' of the air underground. With the development of Spedding's air courses from the mid-eighteenth century, and of Buddle's more elaborate split courses in the early nineteenth century there was an increasing need for trap-doors operators ('trappers'). Though normally young boys,

[2] Jars 1774–81, I, 267.
[3] VCH Derbyshire, II, 354.
[4] Brown 1962, 16; Payne 1961, 80.

their task was of vital importance if the dangerous gases were to be removed from deep and extensive workings. When thought desirable, 'firemen' were sent down before shifts started work after weekends or holidays, to ignite gases that had accumulated in roofs or goafs. Roadways were cleared of roof-falls, waste, or other obstructions by 'wastemen' who were also responsible for checking the state of gas and roofs in the goafs. In the larger pits tramway or rolley-way maintenance men might also be necessary.

At the surface the tasks were more varied though there was seldom the call for large numbers of any class of worker as there often was underground. Workers in charge of the horse-gins for drawing water or coal were simply 'horse-keepers' or 'gin-drivers', while pumping- and winding-engines were looked after by 'enginemen' or 'brakemen'. 'Bankmen' or 'banksmen' unloaded the corves at the pithead, either unloading the coal into waiting wains or waggons, or tipping the coal on the bank. In the mines of the North-east from the 1770s onwards as well as in some other coalfields, as was described in chapter 3 above, screening was increasingly undertaken, normally at the surface, and this, of course, also called for specialist workers. The wain and waggon drivers who finally took the coal away from the mines were mostly self-employed, and so not on the books of the collieries. But the general maintenance of the colliery, its roadways, shafts, and equipment, called, particularly in the large collieries, for a varied and sometimes numerous staff of craftsmen. Many collieries employed resident masons, smiths, engine-wrights, and joiners, and some even brick-makers and sawyers. And many collieries were obliged to employ a number of general labourers, odd-job men, and carters.

The distribution of the work-force between the whole range of specializations is well illustrated for the principal north-east collieries by a return of 12 March 1812. While this return sets out what purports to be the labour force in all categories of workers at each of the collieries, it is clearly far from complete. For two collieries no workers are enumerated apart from hewers, though many other workers must also have been employed. Other entries show a similar implausible incompleteness. None of the collieries are shown as employing any corvers, yet a statement of 1808 referred to nine master corvers with fifty-four journeymen and twenty-eight apprentices employed in Tyne collieries alone.[5] The entries for Temple Main and Elswick collieries, however, appear to be complete, and the staffing of these is set out in Table 10.1. In these two collieries together, 72.5 per cent of the work-force was underground, though, as might be expected, the proportion of underground workers was

[5] NuRO Joint Coal Owners' Association 263, Minute book 1805-15, 98-9.

Table 10.1. *Workforce at Temple Main and Elswick collieries,*
12 March 1812

Category of worker	Temple Main	Elswick
Hewers	106	40
Putters	42	20
Inbye-drivers[1]	16	–
Rolley-drivers	75	11
Trappers	22	1
Overmen	4	1
Deputies	5	2
Wastemen	9	–
Shifters	10	3
Onsetters at shaft	4	1
Cranesmen	6	2
Onsetters at crane	4	1
Bankmen	8	2
Furnace keepers	2	–
Underground waggonway wrights	2	–
Tramway layers	2	–
Rolleyway keepers	6	1
Horse-keepers	6	2
Keekers[2]	2	–
Waggonmen and trimmers	18	–
Brakemen	6	2
Firemen	3	1
Masons	1	–
Wrights and joiners	6	–
Engine wrights	2	3
Smiths and horseshoers	10	2
Sawyers	2	–
Labourers	12	3
Cartmen	7	2
Brick-makers	4	–
Wailers[3] and screeners	37	5
Offhandmen[4]	1	–
Total underground	312	83
Total surface	128	22
Total	440	105

Notes: [1] Inbye simply meant in the workings away from the shaft.
[2] An inspector, a class of overman.
[3] A worker who picked out stones, slates, or rubbish from waggons that had escaped the notice of screeners, and who was generally a boy.
[4] A general expression denoting any workman who was not a hewer or putter.

Source: NuRO Joint Coal Owners' Association 263, Minute book 1805–15, 167.

lower in the larger colliery where a larger permanent staff of maintenance workers was employed. Small collieries probably engaged
self-employed craftsmen for maintenance work as and when work
was needed. Similarly, hewers formed a smaller proportion both of
the underground and total workforce at Temple Main (34.0 per cent
and 24.1 per cent respectively) than at the smaller Elswick colliery
(48.2 and 38.1 per cent). The ratio of hewers to the total work-force
was important since the regulation of employment in north-east
collieries by the Coal Owners' Association in the early nineteenth
century was usually achieved merely by determining the number of
hewers each colliery might engage. These proportions of underground to surface workers were confirmed by what appears to be
a very exact return of the workforce at Willington, Heaton, and
Burdon Main collieries on Tyneside in 1828. With little difference
between the proportions of underground and surface workers at each
colliery, the average for all three was 71.8 per cent underground. For
all Tyneside collieries another 1828 statement gave 71.0 per cent
of all workers employed underground.[6]

As a general rule, the smaller the colliery, the narrower the range
of specialist workers employed. At the bottom of the range of size
—pits where only one or two men worked—it is probable that
there was no division of labour at all: all tasks were done by a single
worker, which must have severely reduced productivity. In the larger
mines the variety of specializations called for a wide range of degrees
of skill and strength. Both above and below ground there were possibilities of making use of the lesser strength of women, girls, and
young boys, and their employment underground was not, of course,
prohibited until 1842. The Children's Employment Commission of
1842 found women and girls employed underground only in the
Yorkshire, North Lancashire, South Wales, and eastern Scottish coalfields.[7] There is some evidence from the early eighteenth century
that girls occasionally worked underground in the North-east, and
that the practice may have been more common there on Wearside
than on Tyneside, but it seems that it had already ceased by about
1720. A woman was among those killed underground by an explosion
at Fatfield colliery on Wearside in 1708.[8] By the early nineteenth
century Matthias Dunn, the north-east viewer, was so unused to
women working underground that when he visited the Lancashire
coalfield in 1825 he found their presence there so unexpected and

---

[6] NuRO Wilson (Forest Hall) ZWI 5/176-7.
[7] *Children's Employment Commission* 1842, 24-35.
[8] 'The Pitman's Pay', MS poem in NuRO Society of Antiquaries ZAN M18/18/19-21;
Matthias Dunn, 'History of the Viewers', MS in NEI Bell 15/1/13; H. and B. Duckham
1973, 36.

apparently amusing, that he wrote about them at some length to Buddle. 'The first pit that I went down', he commented, 'was 85 fathoms and I was not a little amused to find the Onsetter sported a pair of golden Ear rings, being a very fine figuring wench of 24 in the following costume—*shift* of flannel, a pair of huge white flannel Trousers, a short bedgown and overall, a *Smock-sark* of flannel— her head was bound by a cotton round Cap, underneath which peeped as handsome a set of Curls as need be sported. The seam is 4 feet high, and the putters principally girls, being all furnished with Trousers and mostly jackets. I regretted much that I had not a No. Country companion to share the joke. The women of Whitehaven (from I suppose their petticoat dress) do not interest one half as much.'[9]

Women clearly worked underground in the Cumberland coalfield. Of the 453 workers on the payroll of the Lowthers' Howgill colliery in 1802, 124 were women. Some, employed as slate-pickers, gin-drivers and grooms, clearly worked on the surface, but those described as fillers, hookers, tram-drivers, and gate-watchers among other tasks —62 per cent of the women's work-force—equally clearly worked underground. It is assumed that this coalfield had abandoned the underground employment of women and girls by 1842. There is evidence too, in spite of their reported absence in 1842, of their employment underground some thirty years earlier in Shropshire. The Madeley parish register recorded the deaths of two girls underground in 1808 and 1809.[10] In South Wales no evidence has come to hand of women working underground in Glamorgan. The only evidence of the death of a woman underground in the records of the Glamorgan coroner's inquests related to one who fell down a pit-shaft. In neighbouring Pembrokeshire, however, at the western extremity of the coalfield, women were employed in sufficiently large numbers at Moreton, Begeley, and Ridgeway collieries during the 1770s to indicate that some, at least, must have worked underground. It seems likely, however, that the great majority of the women underground workers reported in South Wales to the Children's Employment Commission were all confined to the eastern sector of this coalfield.[11]

Almost half of the women employed underground in 1842 were in the east of Scotland—about 2,000 out of less than 5,000 in the whole country.[12] There they were mainly engaged as bearers (putters),

[9] M. Dunn to J. Buddle, 26 Apr. 1825, DuRO NCB First Deposit NCB/I/JB/431.
[10] Brown 1962, 14.
[11] Roberts thesis 1953, 165–6; NLW Picton Castle 4076.
[12] Hair thesis 1955, 226.

often drawing coal cut by husbands or fathers, and mostly out-numbering the hewers. At Loanhead colliery in Midlothian in the mid-eighteenth century, female bearers were almost twice as numerous as 'coalliers' (hewers), and at Pitfirrane colliery in Fife in 1771, twenty-two female bearers worked for sixteen colliers. At Prestongrange colliery in East Lothian, of the twenty-four bearers who worked for fourteen colliers, twelve were colliers' wives.[13] The labour of bearing was unbelievably hard and damaging to the health. It is hard to understand why the employment of women for this work should have been so concentrated in the Firth of Forth area; their employment in this capacity seems to have been rare and rather random in all other coalfields. Even in the Forth area there were those who opposed their employment underground as early as the 1790s. In 1793 Lord Dundonald, himself the owner of mines at Culross on the upper reaches of the Firth, called for 'a Stop . . . to the *barbarous* and *ultimately expensive method* of converting the colliers' wives and daughters into *beasts of burthen*, and causing them to carry coals to the pit bottom or to bank on their backs.'[14]

The most harrowing account of female underground employment, however, comes from Lancashire towards the end of the eighteenth century. In 1771 John Hodson was killed by a stone fall in an accident in Orrell colliery near Wigan, a loss that severely mentally disturbed his wife, leaving his nine-year old daughter, Betty, to provide for and look after her sick mother and two younger brothers. When old enough she took work underground and for eleven years worked, sometimes undertaking double shifts, to support her family. The two younger brothers died in 1782, and her mother in 1788, in which year Betty herself was forced to give up her underground work, worn out 'by grief, poor food and excessive fatigue'. A neigh-bouring gentleman, William Banks, took her into his household, where she remained for the next twelve years and possibly longer as a domestic servant.[15]

Women who worked underground are likely to have comprised less than four per cent of the mining labour force in 1830 though a greater proportion in those coalfields where they were to be found at all. In Scotland they may have amounted to about twelve per cent, though their concentration in the east of Scotland might have

[13] ScRO Clerk of Penicuik GD18/990/8; NLS Cadell of Grange 37/1; NLS Prestongrange Colliery 3720/2.

[14] Dundonald 1793, 55.

[15] P. E. H. Hair 1969. Hair's account, backed by some able detective-work in local records, is drawn from a pamphlet of 1795 by Hannah More, *The Lancashire Collier Girl*, which in turn borrowed heavily from an article by Joseph Budworth in *Gentleman's Magazine* for March 1795.

raised their employment in that area towards twenty per cent. In Lancashire, the other mining region of heavy concentration of women's labour, women may possibly have accounted for six per cent of the labour force. In Yorkshire and South Wales, therefore, the proportion of women working underground in the total work-force may have been rather lower than the national average of about four per cent. As proportions of the underground work-force, of course, all these percentages should be raised by between one-quarter and one-third, making, for example, women just over five per cent of the underground work-force for the whole country in 1830. These figures are necessarily the very roughest of orders of magnitude, given the almost total absence of the relevant data.

Nothing at all of any statistical value may be said about the pro-portions and distribution of the women's labour force in the early eighteenth century, and statements, which have appeared from time to time about trends during the eighteenth and early nineteenth centuries in the underground employment of women can have no basis in fact. All we know is that in some mining regions like the North-east, the western sector of South Wales, the West Midlands, and Cumberland, where there is some evidence of the employment, often rather exceptional, of women underground, the practice was abandoned during the period—apparently very early in the North-east, and rather late in Cumberland. As to whether there was an increase relative to the total size of the regional labour force in Lancashire, Yorkshire, and the East of Scotland, it is quite impossible on the present evidence to say. Some women, of course, were employed as surface workers, particularly as screeners after the process was introduced in the late eighteenth century. They were also employed as 'wailers', picking out stones and slates from the hewn coal; as 'hailers', pulling keels on the Wear from the towpath; at sweeping out the Tyne keels between voyages; and, most sur-prisingly in one instance, as an 'above-ground agent', at the Lowthers' Whingill colliery in Cumberland in the 1780s.[16] Since most surface workers were craftsmen or other skilled workers, however, it is un-likely that women ever formed a substantial proportion of the surface labour force. In most coalfields and for most of the eighteenth century they were probably entirely absent on the surface.

In contrast to the highly localized employment of women and girls underground, the use of boys' labour underground was general. They undertook a variety of jobs, though most were connected in

---

[16] NEI 48/MS dated 1804 at rear of unnumbered volume of pamphlets; NEI Miscellaneous 60/ZA/3a/49a, 55; 'Report on [Lowther] collieries by John Bateman, 1781', CuRO Lons-dale Colliery Reports not yet listed.

one way or another with hauling; but they were also used to operate trapdoors in ventilating courses, to bale water, and to drive horses for all purposes. In bord and pillar working it was sometimes possible for a boy to 'put' for his father. This situation, often cited by way of mitigation of the basic inhumanity of condemning sub-teenage boys to long hours of heavy underground work, on the assumption, by no means proven, that a father might be in some way a more humane master than an unrelated hewer, could by no means prevail generally. In the working lives of both father and son there should be no more than a few years at most when such a relationship at work could operate; some young boys would be orphans; and some hewers would be unmarried or have no sons, or more sons than could work with them. It probably has to be accepted that most young boys worked underground as independent employees. Boys normally entered underground employment between the ages of seven and ten, though probably in general nearer the upper end of the scale than the lower. In North Staffordshire it was rare for boys to be employed under the age of thirteen, but in South Staffordshire boys commonly began working underground between the ages of seven and nine.[17]

When the widespread employment of young boys, the arduous nature of hewing at which most adult males underground were engaged, and the high accident-rate are all taken into account, the conclusion seems inescapable that the labour force in mines must have been young in relation to the population. There would seem to be much truth in the words of the old miners' song:

> I am an old miner aged fifty and six . . .
> Aa can't get employment 'cos me hair it's turned grey.[18]

It is, unfortunately, extremely difficult to put this assumption to any kind of test. In the eighteenth century not everyone could state their age accurately, and in the nineteenth century none of the censuses before 1841 enumerated the population reliably in age-groups. The experience of Thomas Wainwright, pensioned off at the age of ninety-one when Lawwood colliery in south Yorkshire closed down in 1828 was, of course, exceptional.[19] Two studies of the age-structure of the mining labour force have, however, come to light, and in default of fuller information, they offer the best available guide. They relate to the entire labour force, male and female, underground

[17] VCH Staffordshire, II, 102.
[18] M. Dawney (ed.), Doon the Wagon Way: Mining Songs from the North of England (London, 1973), no pagination.
[19] Mee 1976, 50.

and surface, of the Lowthers' Howgill colliery at Whitehaven in 1802; and to eighty-nine of the ninety-two underground workers killed in the terrible explosion at Felling colliery on Tyneside in 1812 whose ages were recorded. The ninety-two miners killed in that disaster accounted for 76 per cent of the entire morning shift, and there is no reason to suppose that the age-structure of the casualties differed materially from that of the whole underground work-force. These age-structures are set out in Table 10.2 beside that of the male population of England and Wales in 1841 over the age of ten. It has been necessary to omit workers under the age of

Table 10.2. *Age-structure of the mining labour force, early nineteenth century*
(Workforce and population in ten-year age-groups, as percentages of totals over age ten.)

Age-group	Howgill colliery 1802	Felling colliery 1812	England and Wales 1841
11–20	22.2	48.7	28.7
21–30	12.7	21.8	23.1
31–40	16.7	15.4	17.3
41–50	18.4	7.7	13.0
51–60	14.7	3.8	8.5
61–	15.3	2.6	9.4

Note: The percentages of the England and Wales male population in 1841 are for ten-year age-groups one year younger than those of the collieries, viz. 10–19, 20–9, etc.

Sources: Howgill colliery 1802: Wood 1972, 308.
Felling colliery 1812: Hodgson 1813, 13–15.

eleven from this table since there are no data for individual years of age in the 1841 census. In fact, ten of those killed in the Felling explosion were aged between eight and ten, though at Howgill only three of a workforce nearly five times as large were in this age-group. The analysis of the Felling casualties certainly bears out the belief that underground work was preponderantly for young adults: only 14.1 per cent of those killed underground in Felling colliery were forty years or older, compared with 30.9 per cent in the whole population over age ten. It does not seem unreasonable to suppose that a high proportion of those over age forty employed at Howgill colliery in 1802 were surface workers. Only five of those killed at Felling were over fifty, though John Pearson and Isaac Greener, both hewers, were sixty-four and sixty-five respectively. Howgill colliery contrived to employ twenty-four workers over the age of seventy, six of whom were over eighty; they must surely have been surface workers.

ii. *Recruitment and training*

Since the mining industry was already long established at the opening of the eighteenth century in all the mining regions to be exploited before 1830 there was a labour force already in existence where it was needed. And since the nature of mining investment was such that sudden bursts of growth were scarcely possible, the gradual growth of demand for mining labour, could, in many situations, be met by the natural increase of the existing work-force. Indeed, this was an ideal ardently pursued by employers. 'Our peculiar race of pitmen . . . can only be kept up by *breeding*', wrote Buddle in 1842. 'It never could be recruited from an *adult population*.' He took the view that if boys were not initiated into pit-work before the age of thirteen or fourteen 'they never will become colliers'. 'I myself was initiated into the mysteries of pit-work when not quite six years old' he wrote on another occasion.[20] The Children's Employment Commission of 1842 established from the biographical questioning of witnesses that coal-mining in Britain was very much a family occupation, and that colliers were born, not made. 'I am a regular bred collier', replied on Staffordshire witness, 'and my father before me.' Accordingly colliers tended automatically to put all their sons into the industry at an age too early for them to have made up their minds to look for another occupation. Once in the industry, few left for other ways of life. There was thus normally little call or desire for adult recruitment. Buddle, indeed, saw a sharp and essential distinction between a 'collier', who was any man who worked underground, and a 'pitman', a collier skilled by long experience of underground working. 'Is he a regular-bred pitman?' was Buddle's first question about a miner. 'We speak of a good pitman as we would of a good seaman. . . . Therefore we had a middling good pitman, a thorough good pitman, and a pitman.'[21]

The particular brand of experience Buddle had in mind was not merely the manual skills of the hewer and the fireman, the vast and important business of the care of horses, or the particular muscular development that all forms of underground labour demanded, essential as these were. It was the experience colliers gained in

---

[20] J. Buddle to H. Lambton, 16 and 28 May 1842; and *Morning Post*, 25 June 1842, quoted in Hiskey thesis 1978, 16.
[21] Hair thesis 1955, 48–9; *SC Accidents* 1835, Q.1996.

distinguishing between different qualities of coal in the near complete darkness of underground working—an ability to sense or feel, by the way the mineral responded to a blow from the pick, the nature of the 'metal'. This ability, put to the service of sending up to the surface only coal of the quality and size called for, could not be taught and could be acquired only by long experience at the coalface. Even more important, however, was the sense of danger. Pits were extremely dangerous places. Danger came from gases, roof falls, and flooding. There were, however, some warning signs to be read by the experienced—the creak of a creep, the telling smell of a build-up of gas, or the changing colour of the candle or lamp's flame. There was even premonition, a sensitivity not to be despised in the threatening atmosphere of a pit. It was an intuitive response to these features of the mining environment that turned Buddle's colliers into pitmen. Without these aspects of experience in its work-force a mine would be less productive and more than usually dangerous.

If pitmen were born and not made, and adult recruitment was undesirable, then the growing demand for coal must be met in all coalfields either by corresponding increases in the productivity of labour, or by the natural increase of the existing work-force. Given the more than ten-fold increase in coal production between 1700 and 1830 it is unlikely that increases in productivity could go far in bridging such a gap, and while the possibility that the fertility of mining communities exceeded that of the population at large cannot be ruled out, it is beyond possibility that the mining community multiplied itself on a scale anywhere near commensurate with the growth in output. In spite, therefore, of the virtue of 'breeding' its own work-force, the mining industry was obliged in times and places of more rapid growth, to look beyond its own immediate resources for a supply of labour. 'There is not a collier to be found out of employment', wrote John Powell's agent to him about the South Wales coalfield in 1824, 'and many now wanted in the neighbourhood.'[22]

The premium on experience being so high, an employer looking for additional miners was under strong temptation to look covetously at his neighbour's work-force. There is little doubt that much poaching went on and that the 'bond' system in general use in the North-east and described in the next section of this chapter was designed, at least in part, to minimize this evil. Indeed, in an endeavour to reduce a high turnover rate of workers, the Lowthers attempted to introduce a similar system in their collieries at White-

[22] Thomas Ellwood to John Powell, 12 Nov. 1824, NLW Maybery 1125.

haven in the early nineteenth century, though apparently without success.[23] Sir John Hussey Delaval's agent, John Crooks, reported to him in 1778 that the Lambtons' agent from Wearside had come to Hartley colliery in Northumberland to find miners. Crooks remonstrated with the Lambtons' chief agent and it was agreed that they should not take more than two workmen from each other's collieries each year. But Crooks complained that this agreement was not kept when Lambton colliery bound nineteen men and one boy from Hartley. Hartley lost experienced pitmen to other collieries, too—fifty-five men and two boys in all in that year—which obliged Crooks to retaliate by poaching thirty-six men and eight boys from elsewhere.[24]

Poaching was achieved by bribes of various kinds. In the Northeast the level of fees, or 'binding money', offered at the time of the annual bindings, were an obvious method. John Bryers, the Delavals' agent in the early nineteenth century, advised in 1803 that binding money would have to be increased because a great many miners had left. Alternatively, higher rates of pay could be offered. Lord Stafford lost eight miners from his Meirheath colliery in Staffordshire in 1802: they were tempted by offers of high wages in Lancashire. Sir James Clerk of Penicuik offered bounties and higher wages to free workers at neighbouring collieries to come and work at his Loanhead colliery in Midlothian in the 1760s and 1770s. Poaching was also rife in the Wrexham district of the North Wales coalfield during the mid-eighteenth century. 'One of the persons that sunk the new pit down for me', complained one owner to another in 1750, 'who goes by the name of Edward Davies . . . thought fit last Monday to leave his work without giving any warning at all, and am informed by his father . . . that he is now actually at the black park [Black Park colliery, near Wrexham], by which tis plain that what I told you lately of the black park workmen endeavouring to inveigle my workmen away was matter of fact. . . . If the said Davies is to be countenanced at the black park, where there is much more . . . wages given . . . most of my workmen will leave me in the same manner.'[25]

Under pressure, in an age of expansion, from a persistent shortage of labour, miners could be, and were, tempted to move from colliery to colliery in search of better terms, to move from dangerous to safer pits, or to get away from an unpopular employer. The agent at Hartley colliery in Northumberland expressed the belief in 1805,

[23] Wood 1972, 57.

[24] J. Crooks to Sir John Hussey Delaval, 12 Nov. 1778, NuRO Delaval ZDE 4/4/6.

[25] J. Bryers to Sir John Hussey Delaval, 20 Sept. 1803, NuRO Delaval ZDE 4/25/27; StRO Sutherland D593 M/2/1/2; ScRO Clerk of Penicuik GD18/1105, 1116; Thomas Meredith to Mr Lovat, Steward at Chirk Castle, quoted by Lerry 1968, 16.

wrongly in the event, that he would have no serious difficulty in retaining his workers, since 'our colliery is good work, very safe from fire or accidents of any kind, and I believe has a good character for quietness and comfort for the workmen'.[26] But in spite of determined efforts to prevent movement there is a great deal of evidence of migration not only within coalfields, but between coalfields. In some cases, of course, the drift was in response to a particular effort to bring skilled workers into a coalfield short of special skills. It was for this reason that Sir Richard Newdigate's accounts in January 1703 showed that he 'paid to John Bedder going into Shropshire to get 20 men' to teach the Warwickshire miners at his Griff colliery the arts of the longwall technique, as also did Sir Humphrey Mackworth at the same time to his miners near Neath in South Wales, 'many of them above two hundred miles from Home'.[27]

The partnership operating the Measham and Swannington collieries in Leicestershire in the 1720s recruited skilled workers from Warwickshire and Derbyshire as well as from Shropshire. Their travel expenses were refunded, 2s. 6d. 'hire money' paid to each of them, beer offered them on their arrival, and accommodation found for them. Thirty-seven miners were brought in this way to Swannington colliery alone in 1727. Ironically they included 'Griffmen' who may have been among those attracted with some effort and expense to Griff colliery earlier. Wallsend colliery on north Tyneside paid out £20 in 1811 for colliers' removal expenses. The Gadlys company, a lead-smelting company, was said to have imported 'large numbers' of miners from Staffordshire and the North-east to work in its coal-mines at Bagillt in Flintshire in the 1740s.[28]

It may be more than a coincidence that many of these examples of inter-coalfield migration are drawn from the first half of the eighteenth century. This was a time when several coalfields were striving to expand production and when skilled labour may have been in particularly short supply. It is possible that by the early nineteenth century some degree of self-sufficiency had been achieved in these coalfields by which they were able to generate their own increase of skilled labour. It may therefore have been a sign of the times that by this period miners around Wrexham were willing to strike against the importation for 'foreign' labour.[29] Certainly, during the French wars of the early nineteenth century, when labour was particularly scarce, the Cumberland coalfield suffered acutely from

[26] J. Bryers to Sir John Hussey Delaval, 20 Oct. 1805, NuRO Delaval ZDE 4/27/88.

[27] White 1969–70, 536; White thesis 1969, 125; Roberts thesis 1953, 162; Trott 1969, 63, quoting pamphlet of 1705.

[28] C. P. Griffin thesis 1969, 75–6; Scott thesis 1946, 21; Rogers 1963, 125.

[29] Rogers 1963, 133.

labour shortage and advertised for labour as far afield as Newcastle, Manchester, and Scotland. Yorkshire employers advertised similarly in Black Country newspapers, as did some of the new Forest of Dean companies.[30] These wartime scarcities may explain why the proportion of women workers was so high in the Lowther mines at this period. In the North-east outlying collieries like Walbottle and Whitley frequently advertised for labour in the early nineteenth century.[31] To staff his projected mine at Brora in Sutherland the Earl of Stafford arranged in 1814 to transfer miners from pits on his Staffordshire estate. Their removal, which was to be mainly by sea from London to Inverness, was to be at Lord Stafford's expense; they were to have houses and gardens in Sutherland rent-free; and if the Brora mine closed down within seven years they were to be returned to Staffordshire at his expense. The Earl's Sutherland agent also recruited colliers from the south of Scotland and Wales. Wives, however, did not accompany the Staffordshire miners and pay and living conditions in Sutherland left much to be desired. Evidently the Staffordshire miners drifted back home, for by 1820 the Earl's agent reported that the Brora mine was being successfully operated by native Sutherland labour.[32]

Migration of skilled workers within coalfields is less easy to trace, though there can be little doubt that it was lively. The fortunate survival of a document of 1805 provides an instructive insight into this movement. The bond system in the North-east, while it prohibited change of employment during the twelve-month operation of each bond, allowed movement at each annual binding. Indeed, in 1805 the Joint Coal Owners' Association specifically laid down that colliery recruitment should be restricted at each binding to no more than ten men and twelve boys from any other colliery. The 1805 document is an exact statement of the movement of hewers between Tyneside and Northumberland collieries at the autumn binding of that year. It shows the numbers leaving and joining each of thirty-seven named collieries, as well as general statements about Wearside and 'landsale' collieries. We know, from other sources, that in 1805 a total of about 2,300 hewers were bound on Tyneside and in Northumberland. Of these, 650 left the collieries to which they had been bound in the previous year, and 723 were taken on from different collieries, a 'general post' of between 28 and 31 per cent in a single year. The difference between those leaving and those

---

[30] Wood 1971, 220–1; Hair thesis 1955, 28–30.
[31] Scott thesis 1946, 21.
[32] J. German to J. Burgess, 21 and 28 Nov. 1814, StRO Sutherland D593 M/2/2/2; E. Richards, *The Leviathan of Wealth* (London, 1973), 176–7, 226–7.

joining is largely explained by a net drift from Wearside. Seventy-four hewers left Tyneside and Northumberland collieries for Wearside at this binding, but 156 joined from there. The turnover varied substantially from colliery to colliery. Walbottle colliery, for example, lost only nine out of its force of sixty hewers, gaining nine outsiders in exchange, while the Brandling colliery lost forty of its seventy-seven hewers, taking on only twenty-five in their place. Many of the individual moves were over short distances between neighbouring collieries, like the two hewers who moved from Wallsend to Bigges Main, but with much housing tied to individual collieries, many of these moves must have involved changing homes. Other moves were over long distances, and, given the impossibility of long daily journeys to work, must certainly have involved moving house. Three hewers, for example, moved from West Kenton colliery, north-west of Newcastle, to Cowpen colliery in Northumberland, a distance of about ten miles, and six moved to Wylam colliery from East Kenton colliery. Those who moved between Tyneside and Wearside, of course, probably moved the greatest distances. Nevertheless, it is not surprising that the more outlying collieries like Pontop and Walbottle showed relatively low rates of turnover.[33]

Hewers, of course, were less than one-third of the total labour force, but there is no reason to suppose that other mineworkers were less mobile than them. The number of miners changing employment in 1805 was, in short, astonishing; but 1805 was almost certainly not a typical year in this respect. It was the year after binding money had reached a peak sufficiently high to bring the north-east owners together once again in a combination that gave priority to collective action to bring it down. The rise in the levels of binding money owed much to the renewal of war in 1803 and its resultant scarcity of labour. While the sums offered as binding money from colliery to colliery rose broadly in sympathy, the general rise could only be brought about by competitive bidding between employers that heightened both the temptation and the opportunities for miners to move from one colliery to another. Indeed, the very existence of the document that has made this study of inter-colliery movement possible suggests that the situation in that year was exceptional. Though the survival of documents can be rather random it remains the fact that no similar document has survived for any other year, though there is extant a very comprehensive set of records from the north-east Coal Owners' Association from 1805. It would not be

[33] NuRO Joint Coal Owners' Association 263, Minute book 1805–15, 3; NEI Watson 5/9/16. A similar statement for the same year in rather more summary form, but covering the 1,589 hewers in the Wearside collieries as well, exists in NEI Buddle 14/197–9.

unreasonable to suppose that it was the unusual extent of inter-colliery movement in 1805 that led to the commissioning of this statistical study.

But even inter-colliery movement at a substantially lower level than that occurring in 1805 would still be brisk, and must be assumed to be a normal condition. Some movement would naturally result, as it inevitably does today, from the exhaustion of mines. Further movement resulted from enforced transfers by owners. In 1806 Percy Main colliery on north Tyneside was obliged to close temporarily on account of creep. Some of the colliers, boys, and horses were transferred to neighbouring Flatworth colliery, and the remainder left free to find employment where they could, though it was agreed within the association that any colliery taking them on must also take horses in proportion. Men, boys, and horses transferred in this way were recallable at one day's notice.[34] Workington colliery in Cumberland in successive years from 1809 to 1812 lost 147, 108, 81, and 50 employees, replacing them respectively with 154, 102, 119, and 111 newcomers. Of fifty-six colliers employed at Walker colliery on north Tyneside in 1781, only ten were still in employment there ten years later, and only one by 1796. Wastage by retirement, ill-health, and casualties would have accounted for a proportion, but by no means all, of these departures. When Halbeath colliery in Fife was trying to attract a labour force in the late 1780s neighbouring coalowners were obliged to bribe their own miners with gifts like bedsteads 'in order to *encourage* them to stay'.[35]

There is no shortage of evidence, too, of wastage by the drift of workers out of the industry, or at least out of the coalfield of their initial employment. This was always a danger when pits were closed down, even temporarily. Buddle expressed reluctance to lay off men when production was held up in 1803 by a keelmen's strike. 'They will immediately disperse thro the country', he wrote 'and be very difficult to collect in case of need.' Some left the district: a correspondent of Buddle's in 1812 spoke of desertion from collieries resulting from a 'proneness to emigration'.[36] Others simply deserted their collieries without giving notice or reason. 'We had a most disagreeable account yesterday at Hartley', Sir John Hussey Delaval was informed in 1778. 'About 8 of our colliers had run away. . . . John Crooks is in pursuit of the colliers, and I hope will be able to

[34] J. Buddle to George Waldie, 17 Aug. 1806, NEI Buddle 15/152–2.
[35] Hair thesis 1955, 38; Payne forthcoming, 14.
[36] J. Buddle to M. Russell, 18 May 1803, NEI Buddle 15/14–15; W. Potter to J. Buddle, 8 June 1812, NuRO Joint Coal Owners' Association 263, Minute book 1805–15, 216.

bring them back to their work.' In October 1805 the agent at Hartley colliery drew up an analysis of the twenty-eight hewers he had lost during the previous twelve months. Eight had gone off to sea, three absconded to Scotland, two had died, four had become old and infirm, one had been discharged for bad conduct, seven had been transferred to other jobs at the colliery, and three had been transferred to other collieries.[37]

Almost all the inter-coalfield and inter-colliery movement examined in the preceding paragraphs amounted to little more than a reshuffling of the existing skilled labour force: none of it could increase the total labour supply at a rate faster than that of the natural increase of the mining community generally. Yet the rate of increase of the industry's output was such that there must have been some augmentation of the work-force from sources outside the industry. Irish immigrants to the industry were found in Kilmarnock in south-west Scotland in 1798, while the Lowthers' agent wrote to Buddle from Whitehaven in 1823 that 'the majority [of his workforce was] composed of Irish and other trampers that turn only to us when no other employment could be had.'[38] Howgill colliery at Whitehaven employed in 1802 forty-four workers whose place of origin was in Ireland, forty-one in Scotland, twenty-one in Northumberland and Durham, and forty-three in other counties outside Cumberland.[39] In the early eighteenth century the Tyne keelmen were heavily recruited from Scotland, particularly from the Forth area. A census of the Tyne keelmen of 1740 revealed that 55 per cent were Scottish-born, and only 39 per cent were born in Newcastle. Thirty years later half were still estimated to be of Scottish origin.[40]

Hair examined the marriage registers of a number of north-east parishes where mining was concentrated for the years between 1798 and 1812. He found that ten per cent of male colliers marrying gave as their birthplaces parishes outside the coalfield, and assumed that they were likely to have been the sons of agricultural labourers. One-quarter of miners' wives came from non-colliery parishes.[41] In south-west Lancashire, where Langton had estimated that about 1,000 miners must have been recruited from outside the industry in the last twenty years of the eighteenth century, a high proportion of the new entrants were recruited very locally. During the last sixty years of the eighteenth century, of forty-two miners in the

[37] Memorandum dated 27 Oct. 1805, NuRO Delaval ZDE 4/27/90.
[38] J. Peile to J. Buddle, 18 Oct. 1823, DuRO NCB First Deposit NCB/I/JB/1063.
[39] Wood 1971, 221; and 1972, 307.
[40] TWRO Tyne Keelmen Acc. 394/29; Fewster 1957, 28.
[41] Hair thesis 1955, 60–73.

parish of St. Helens whose fathers' occupations can be traced through the parish registers, thirty-four were also miners, and the remaining eight were labourers, nailers, carpenters, blacksmiths, tailors, and pipe-makers.[42] At the opening of the eighteenth century Sir Humphrey Mackworth even took on prisoners to man his mines in South Wales. In 1700 seventeen prisoners pardoned by the King on condition that they apprenticed themselves to Sir Humphrey were sent by ship from London to Neath. A group of Glasgow merchants who formed themselves into a joint stock company for mining in 1825 announced that they intended to train their labour force entirely from men who had not previously been colliers: it is not known whether they went ahead with this unpromising project and with what success.[43]

In spite of some adult recruitment from other occupations, however, entry to the mining labour force was predominantly in early youth. Indeed, though evidence on this point is lacking, it is quite probable that adult recruitment was rarely into the skilled underground grades at all, and principally into the miscellaneous service jobs. The typical underground worker was male, and was recruited into the industry throughout the eighteenth and early nineteenth centuries between the ages of eight and ten though occasionally younger. His training for the skilled and more highly paid jobs was simply through familiarity with the work acquired by working closely with such workers. In both bord and pillar and longwall working the 'career' grade was the face-worker who cut the coal. The hewer in the North-east, the hagger in Cumberland, was the basic production worker: all other workers were secondary and supportive.

The eight-year-old entrant to the industry would work his way through these supportive grades in about ten to twelve years. This progression was described in a north-eastern account of the early years of the nineteenth century:

Boys enter the subterranean workings at the age of 7 or 8, sometimes as early as 6. They are first Trap door keepers, being employed to open and shut doors fixed for conducting air round the works, while the Coals are passing through them from the workman to the Shaft; their wages are 6d. a day: they continue in this situation 4 or 5 years when they become what are termed lads or foals supplying the inferior place at a machine called a Tram, where two are employed, and made use of to convey the Coals from the workmen to the Pit mouth: their wages from 9d. to 12d. per day according to the earnings of the Tram

[42] Langton 1979, 194–9.
[43] Trott 1969, 65; W. Grafton to J. Buddle, 28 Nov. 1825, DuRO NCB First Deposit NCB/I/JB/544.

which is paid a certain price per score or 20 Baskets of Coals in proportion to the distance of the workings from the Shaft. In this state they continue 2 or 3 years when they become half-marrows receiving a moiety of the earnings of the Tram which brings them from 14 to 16*d.* per day. In this capacity they continue about [blank] years, when they reach the class of Headsmen, putting the Tram with a lad or foal and receiving about two thirds of the wages of the Tram. As Headsmen they continue about two years when they become Put and Hewers, half of their time employed at the Tram and the other half in working the Coal, their wages from 2*s.* to 2*s.* 6*d.* per day. They seldom continue more than one year in this situation when they commence Hewers, constantly employed in working the Mine: their wages from 2*s.* 6*d.* to 3*s.* per day.[44]

There was, of course, a further progression accessible to a small number of the experienced, literate and numerate hewers, to the supervisory grades of overman, deputy, and, ultimately, viewer. The age-structure implied in the above account is broadly borne out, allowing for variations in terminology, by the sole source of information that lists both occupations and ages—John Hodgson's list of the ninety-two miners killed in the explosion at Felling colliery on Tyneside in 1812. The occupations of the eighty-nine workers for whom both sets of data were given are set out in Table 10.3. Apart from one trapper whose age was thirty, and who must have been allocated to this light work on account of disability or ill-health, all trappers were in the age-range eight to fifteen: the oldest putters were twenty-three; and the youngest hewers were twenty.

So far as underground labour was concerned, then, the supply of the various kinds of labour was managed by balancing the periods of time spent by boys and youths working through the progression to become hewers. We lack information, unfortunately, about the training for the other miscellaneous jobs underground. These either involved less skill or less strength than hewing, and they may have been filled by men unable to continue as hewers through age or injury, or they may have been places more easily filled by adult recruits. On the surface some of the workers were craftsmen whose entry to the industry was through traditional apprenticeship. Most carters and waggonmen were self-employed smallholders or tenant farmers.

For a very high proportion of those employed, the mining labour force until well into the nineteenth century was a self-sustaining

---

[44] 'Queries concerning the State of the Pitmen on the River Tyne by Sir Jno. Swinburne Bt., with Replies thereto by Jno. Thomin of Denton Hall', n.d. but MS noted as copied in September 1807, NEI shelf 48, MS addition to collection of pamphlets. The essential accuracy of this account is confirmed by 'The Pitman's Pay', a bound MS poem by Thomas Wilson, apparently written about 1826–30, but referring to times about forty-five years earlier in the Gateshead area. (NuRO Society of Antiquaries ZAN M18/18.)

Table 10.3. *Occupations of underground workers by age-groups, Felling colliery, 1812*

Age-group	Occupation	Numbers
10 and under	Trapper	9
	Waggon driver	1
	Putter	1
11–15	Trapper	6
	Waggon driver	4
	Putter	10
	Lamp-keeper	1
16–20	Putter	13
	Craneman	1
	Crane onsetter	1
	Hewer	2
21 and over	Putter	3
	Hewer	32
	Shifter	1
	Horse-keeper	1
	Braking inclined plane	1
	Deputy	1
	Trapper	1

Source: Hodgson 1813, 13–15.

closed community. Entry was at an extremely early age not so much because employers were callous—though many were—but because there was a positive belief that skilled 'pitmen' could only be created by an early acculturation in the environment of the mine. Training was not, as it might be today, in a set of specific skills and the acquisition of a specific body of information, but by familiarity with and total immersion in the routines, skills and dangers of the mine.

iii. *The terms of employment*

If a dozen years were necessary for the training of a skilled, experienced hewer, the employer's interest was strongly directed to retaining his services once trained. The output of a colliery was directly related to the number of hewers, and while individual employers might increase their force of hewers by poaching or otherwise attracting skilled hewers from other collieries, for the industry as a whole the work-force of hewers could be increased only after a lag of twelve years subsequent to increasing the intake of boys, or by recruiting hopelessly inefficient adults. New collieries, it was said, tended to attract all the 'disorderly characters' and the 'scum of the others'.[45] A supply of skilled labour, particularly hewers, was a prerequisite of staying in business as a mineowner, and, in the context of labour relations in the eighteenth and early nineteenth centuries, it is not surprising to find employers exploiting a sympathetic legal environment to prevent their skilled workers deserting them.

Various forms of contract were tried. Their purposes were generally to make it an offence for a worker to leave his employment before the end of a contracted period—normally a year, or longer. In the event of breach of contract an employer was able, in the eighteenth and early nineteenth centuries, if able to trace a deserter, to enlist the aid of the law in forcing the deserter to return and work out the remainder of his contracted period. In 1805 several of the Hartley miners 'having absconded lately', were said by some of their friends to have gone to work near Haddington in East Lothian. The Delavals' agent was advised that the best way of discovering the whereabouts of bound pitmen suspected of deserting to Scotland was to insert advertisements in Edinburgh newspapers giving descriptions of them.[46] More drastic action was taken in Nottingham early in the eighteenth century. The Nottingham justices ordered on 13 January 1717 that 'John Dennis of Alsworth in the parish of Nuttall, coalminer, appearing to the Court to be a servant of the Rt. Honble. Thomas Ld. Middleton at his coalmines and to have departed his service without consent and contrary to his agreement at being hired, This Court doth order the Mr. of the House of Correction to take the body of the said John Dennis into his Custody and to keep him to hard labour and give him correction for one month from this day.'[47] Absconding workers were not always pursued so relentlessly: much depended on the relationship between supply and demand within a particular occupation. When questioned about keelmen breaking their bonds and running away, a fitter in 1768 answered that he knew of hundreds, but that none of these were taken up by warrants from Justices of the Peace. Probably there was a ready supply of replacement Scottish immigrants.

Period labour contracts were not unique to the mining industry in this period. Long-term bonds were common in salt-making and file-making, and were widespread for agricultural workers. Sir Humphrey Mackworth bound his workers at his Neath collieries

[45] Hair thesis 1955, 39, quoting 'The Pitman's Pay'.

[46] J. Bryers to Sir John Hussey Delaval, 21 June 1805, quoted in Foster thesis 1948, 34; D. Stenhouse to J. Carr, 13 July 1805, NuRO Delaval ZDE 7/6/25.

[47] Quoted in A. R. Griffin thesis 1969, I, 19.

in the early eighteenth century as 'covenant servants' to serve him for a term of one or more years, and we have already seen that he was willing to take convicts as apprentices in a form of indentured labour similar to that used widely in the transatlantic colonies at that period.[48] Colliers in Yorkshire were contracted by similar annual 'agreements'. All the Fentons' miners over the age of eighteen signed the following agreement in 1794:

> We whose names are underwritten do agree to serve Wm. and Thos. Fenton Esqrs. from the day of the date hereof for and during one year as Colliers and Hurriers at Stanley Colliery, and to work at the said colliery regularly, and every working-day if our health permits, and the Colliery be in working condition— And should we want to leave working at the said Colliery at the Expiration of the above Time, we agree to give three Months' Notice to the Agent at the said Colliery, or to serve Three Months after the Expiration of the said year. Also we who are Colliers [i.e. hewers] do agree that when any other Collier shall have occasion to hurry by reason of a Hurrier or Hurriers being wanting to give him every one of us one Corf of Coals to mend his wages.[49]

Similar bonds were widely used in south-west Lancashire in the second half of the eighteenth century.[50]

Where formal contracts of this kind were not customary, employers occasionally agreed together within coalfields to require a certificate of release signed by a previous employer before taking on a new worker. Such an agreement was made between charter-masters, the effective employers of labour, in Staffordshire in the 1790s. No miner, they agreed, was to be employed without the production of a note of discharge from his last master. A miner who had been formally discharged in this way and who obtained work with another charter-master was, on application from the old master, to be immediately dismissed and the new master to pay £10 to the old master.[51] Agreements of this kind rarely survived the first occasion when labour was short. In the North-east the owners attempted in 1765 to introduce a clause into their annual contracts requiring the production of a certificate of release from a former employer before a miner could engage with a new one. The miners went on strike rather than accept this, believing that 'no coalowner would give such a certificate' and that the terms amounted to 'a binding during the will of a master'. The 1765 strike involved other issues as well, and the owners dropped this clause at its termination, going so

---

[48] Trott 1969, 64–5.
[49] J. Goodchild, 'The coal mining industry of the lower Calder valley, 1700–1860', WMDL undated typescript, 9.
[50] Langton 1979, 194.
[51] StRO Sutherland D593 M/2/1/2.

far as to claim that such an agreement had never been made between them.[52]

It was in the North-east, not surprisingly, that the annual contract assumed its most sophisticated form, though it was not apparently used there until the very late seventeenth century. The first known bond was made between the Hon. Charles Montague and his miners at Benwell colliery on Tyneside in 1703. This set out the wages and allowances payable, and bound the miners to continue in work at the colliery for the ensuing twelve months. Miners were liable for a penalty of 40s. for breach of any clause of the bond. The primitive and limited nature of this bond suggests that the system had not long been in existence. There is very little direct evidence of the practice of binding during the first half of the eighteenth century, but it is clear that by the 1760s bonds were in general use throughout the north-east coalfield. Each colliery had its own exact form of bond, but piecemeal negotiation of their terms had given the miners some voice in their own terms of employment that had resulted in the bond not being quite so one-sided in the safeguards it provided for the signatories. The employers, too, for their part found the need to build in more safeguards, so that the bond rapidly developed into a complex document. One of Wallsend colliery in 1791, for example, runs to three quarto pages of small handwriting, embodying sixteen clauses.[53]

By the early nineteenth century bonds had become fairly uniform and standardized. In 1811, following a major dispute, the coalowners agreed to employ 'an able barrister at law who is connected with the Coal Trade and has no interest therein' to draw up a standard form of bond. Copies of this were to be kept at each colliery in the North-east and by 'such individual of the men as they themselves shall appoint'.[54] It seems, however, that it was not until 1826 that a single printed form was produced for the use of all collieries. Besides stipulating the fundamental commitment to one year's work at the colliery in question, and setting out full details of wages and allowances, the bonds now also included clauses denying the right to strike or leave work for any reason other than ill-health, requiring the miners to keep the colliery-owned houses they lived in in good repair, and to vacate their houses on the termination of employment at the colliery, providing for arbitration in disputes about the quantities of coal on which piece-rates were paid, and penalising

[52] Webb 1921, 5–7; Welbourne 1923, 22; Scott thesis 1946, 36; Cromar 1979, 53.

[53] NEI Buddle 18/21–3.

[54] 'Proposals for regulating the contracts between the Coal-Owners and their Pitmen on the Rivers Tyne and Wear, and of Hartley, Blyth and Cowpen', dated 3 Jan. 1811, NuRO Joint Coal Owners' Association 263, Minute book 1805–15, 147–50.

miners for sending up inadequately filled corves or coal containing an excessive proportion of rubbish. In return for all these obligations the miner obtained security of employment for one year, though the owner retained the right to close his colliery for any reason during the year. In this event, however, miners were to receive lay-off pay at rates not far short of what could be earned in full work, and were free to take work elsewhere. Disputes were to be referred to the arbitration of a small number of viewers to be nominated by the parties to the dispute, and both parties had the right of appeal to a Justice of the Peace in the event of breach of the agreement.[55] In reflection of the owners' pressing need to secure their labour supplies in situations when demand often exceeded supply, a sum of money, known as 'binding money', was paid to the miner when he signed. Binding money was not mentioned in the 1703 Benwell bond, but by the second half of the eighteenth century, 6d. or 1s. was the usual sum.

Since the purpose of binding was to secure for at least a year the labour of skilled miners, in general it was the more skilled grades of workers that were bound. It goes without saying that hewers were the first in this category, but by the opening years of the nineteenth century horse-keepers, bankmen, deputies, cranemen, onsetters, waggon, and inbye-drivers were regularly bound. The list did not include any occupations normally undertaken by boys or youths, though putters were bound collectively in the teams that operated trams. Thus the numbers bound at any one colliery would fall some way short of the whole labour force. Keelmen, too, were bound by very similar bonds to their employers, the fitters.[56]

Binding was formally undertaken on a specific day of the year, normally the Saturday nearest to fourteen days before the expiry of the old bond. As the day approached both sides began feeling their way, the miners stating their terms for the new bond with careful regard to the conditions of supply and demand in the labour market, and the owners sounding out each other to discover the terms their competitors were willing to offer or considering the possibilities of a united front. The 'binding book' was opened several days before the formal binding day. Miners signed the bonds individually and the owners always tried hard to get some to sign early to encourage others. As an inducement to sign, agents sometimes offered an extra guinea to the first to sign and half a guinea to the second. In general,

[55] See, e.g., the draft bond for Kenton and Coxlodge collieries, 1808, NEI Watson 9/13/no pagination.

[56] See keelmen's bond dated 24 Dec. 1795 signed by thirty-two keelmen in the service of David Crawford, fitter, NuRO Society of Antiquaries ZAN M19/26.

however, the miners tried to delay signing in the hope of some improvement in the terms offered. As the deadline for signing approached the miners often drifted into the towns, particularly into Newcastle, where they could keep in close touch with each other, and where the colliery agents were circulating offering drinks to attract signatures. The process is well illustrated by events at Hartley colliery in Northumberland in October 1804. The agents had worked hard at getting the men to sign: one had stayed up all one night persuading the miners. Eventually a compromise was reached: the agents offered 'a great advance upon last year' and the men dropped the remainder of the demands that had originally been set out in a petition to the owner. The following night twenty-five had signed by midnight and the rest quickly followed suit in the morning. When the news of the Hartley binding circulated, agents at neighbouring collieries came over to discover the terms so that they could offer similar terms to prevent the loss of their best men.[57]

By the late eighteenth century the act of binding had been turned into something of a ceremony. Many miners could not actually sign their names and their assent was given by stretching their arms over the agent's shoulders to touch the pen as he put a cross to their names. Those that could not sign, of course, mostly could not read the bond either, and there was inevitably much ignorance of the 'small print' of what was formally being agreed to.

During the second half of the eighteenth century and the early nineteenth century there were two issues that raised major problems over binding. First was the time of the year fixed for binding day. This was of some importance since binding during a slack season would tend to favour the owners, and a busy season the miners. When binding was developing into a serious form of negotiation during the first half of the eighteenth century a date in October had come to be accepted as the rule. Generally this favoured the miners, since the London and east-coast buyers were stocking up at that time for the winter and east-coast sailings, though still at their peak, would soon begin to fall off. This was no time of the year for owners to lose their skilled workers. Conscious of their disadvantage as bargaining at binding time became tougher, in 1765 the owners decided unilaterally to switch binding time from October to January. This move contributed to sparking off the strike of that year and appears not to have been successful. The Wallsend bond of 1791 was dated 12 October, and in 1808 the date was still 15 October.[58] In the following year, however, the Joint Coal Owners' Association

[57] J. Bryers to Sir John Hussey Delaval, 18 Oct. 1804, NuRO Delaval ZDE 4/26/67.
[58] NEI Buddle 18/21-3.

decided once again to attempt to switch the binding date to January. Accordingly they agreed in September to bind the miners in October for three months only, and to resume yearly binding in January 1810, the quietest time of the year for shipping.[59] The miners resisted this with a strike beginning on 18 October 1809. The strike was prolonged and violent. The Dragoons were brought in and nearly 300 arrests were made. Eventually a compromise was reached whereby the binding day was moved to April. This new binding date, which remained in force until after 1830, clearly did not satisfy the owners since in 1831 they made an attempt to substitute monthly for yearly bonds.

The second troublesome issue concerned the amounts payable at signing, known as the 'binding money'. In general only adult workers signed bonds, and the rates of binding money varied according to the class of workers. Hewers commanded the highest rates, and sledge and waggon drivers the lowest; but, among the hewers, the very highest rates were offered to young unmarried men, presumably because they were more mobile and with a longer working-life ahead of them, and so worth a greater bait to retain their services. Rates were also fixed for 'trams', which referred to the whole team operating a tram. In the 1760s and 1770s binding money appears to have been rather nominal, at 6d. or 1s., but by 1789 sums of half a guinea or one guinea were being paid in the Blyth area.[60] The French wars from the 1790s, however, changed this situation as recruitment for the armed forces created a real scarcity of labour. By 1800 sums of twelve to fifteen guineas were being quoted for hewers on Wearside, but peace in 1802–3 brought the price down somewhat: four guineas for a married hewer were paid at Hartley colliery in 1803. But the resumption of war in late 1803 drove binding money up to astronomical heights, and in October 1804 fifteen to twenty guineas were being paid on Wearside, and anything from twelve to twenty guineas in the Blyth district on the Northumberland coast.[61]

At these levels binding money represented a bonus amounting to up to half a miner's normal annual wages, and while this extraordinary situation may have been a true reflection of the state of supply and demand for mining labour in the North-east after the

[59] NuRO Joint Coal Owners' Association 263, Minute book 1805–15, 121.

[60] Bond dated 22 Oct. 1763 for Pontop Pike, Harperley, and Collierly collieries, quoted in Scott thesis 1946, 11–12; bond dated 7 Oct. 1774 for Byker Hill colliery, NuRO Society of Antiquaries ZAN M17/21; J. Crooks to Sir John Hussey Delaval, 15 Oct. 1789, NuRO Delaval ZDE 4/6/19.

[61] Beastall 1975, 42–4; J. Bryers to Sir John Hussey Delaval, 9 Oct. 1803, NuRO Delaval ZDE 4/25/29; and 25 Oct. 1804, 4/26/69.

resumption of war, it was not one that the owners were willing to tolerate. The undignified scramble for skilled workers and the torrents of drink poured out in bribes—'such a scene of confusion and mischief as perhaps was never before experienced among all the collieries'—had to stop.[62] Well in time for the 1805 negotiations the owners had organized themselves to act as a united body. The available documentary evidence does not make it wholly clear to what extent the 'Committee of Coal Owners of the Rivers Tyne and Wear' that met on 10 September of that year was an entirely new combination, or whether it was merely a continuation of the organization founded in 1771 and known as 'the Limitation of the Vend'; but a new minute book was opened by the 10 September meeting, and this began a series that continued without break through to the 1840s.

In the early meetings from September 1805, apart from constitutional matters, the new committee, if it was such, was heavily preoccupied with the question of binding. First, it tried to instil some order into the conduct of the binding negotiations. A whole series of regulations was agreed to. Binding was to take place only at colliery offices, and the offer of drinks to miners as an inducement to sign, 'except the usual allowance of liquor which is only to be given at the colliery office on the days of binding', was to cease. Several categories of workers were no longer to receive binding money. Poaching was to be outlawed, and inter-colliery movement limited to not more than ten men and twelve boys from any one colliery. Owners were not to allow their agents, viewers, or overmen to go to Newcastle on the Saturday in the middle of the hiring period. More urgently, however, they agreed to stand firm for a reduction of the extravagantly high binding money of 1804. They appear to have been successful in fixing a level of three guineas for Tyneside and five guineas for Wearside hewers, high figures still in relation to pre-war levels, but between one-quarter and one-fifth of the 1804 level. In the following year they carried the process further, reducing the money to one guinea for Tyneside and two for Wearside. They maintained this level in the ensuing years until 1812 when they reduced it further by fifty per cent. Finally in 1826 they decided to abolish binding money altogether, a decision that inevitably sparked off a reaction from the miners. Keelmen's binding money had been sharply reduced in 1819 and stopped altogether in 1822.[63]

[62] J. Bryers to Sir John Hussey Delaval, 25 Oct. 1804, NuRO Delaval ZDE 4/26/69.
[63] *Address of the Keelmen of the River Tyne*, handbill dated 9 Oct. 1822, NEI Bell 15/13/590.

Binding money was always an element in labour costs. Accounts of Brockwell colliery of 1785 and of Sheriff Hill colliery of 1787, when binding costs were still fairly nominal, showed pitmen's binding money amounting to 1.0 and 1.7 per cent of the estimated working and leading costs respectively.[64] But when binding money was bid up to the extreme heights of the early years of the nineteenth century it became a major item of costs. At the Penshaw and Eden Main collieries in County Durham in 1803 a drinks bill of £249. 17s. 6d. and incidentals of £46. 4s. 6d. were added to binding money of £636. 6s. 0d. to make a total bill for binding of £932. 8s. 0d. 'It had been such a week for expence in liquor', wrote the Hartley agent at this time. At the Lambton collieries the bill for drinks alone at binding time rose steadily during the war period—£198 in 1797, £221 in 1798, £287 in 1799, and £430 in 1803. The total bill for binding 612 men at the Lambton collieries in the peak year of 1804 amounted to £8,335. 8s. 10d., and included £685. 6s. 2d. for drink—more than £1 worth per head at a time when beer probably cost no more than 3d. per pint. By 1811, however, binding costs were back to their pre-war normal. At Felling colliery in 1811 John Straker, the viewer, estimated that binding costs, at £135, would amount to less than one per cent of workings costs.[65]

In general, the miners favoured the bond system and, as we have seen, resisted changes of substance to it. In an age when combinations were generally persecuted by both employers and government, the annual bindings provided an opportunity for collective bargaining about wages and conditions of employment. It will have been noticed that the most vigorous and successful bargaining occurred in the early years of the nineteenth century at a time when trade unionism was most specifically outlawed. Though collective action by the owners that was almost certainly technically illegal succeeded in reducing substantially the financial advantages that the miners had been able to extract from their temporary scarcity, the formal proposals put forward by the owners in 1811 embodied valuable provisions for arbitration by viewers and appeal to Justices of the Peace. If the latter would traditionally have been unsympathetic to workers' grievances, the arbitration of consultant viewers was a more effective protection to the miners. In short, the experience gained in the negotiations for the annual bindings was a valuable education for both

[64] NEI Watson 8/11/60, 99.

[65] NEI Buddle 8/88; J. Bryers to Sir John Hussey Delaval, 16 Oct. 1803, NuRO Delaval ZDE 4/25/32; NEI Buddle 13/60, 88; NEI Forster 49/8/85-6.

employers and workers in the decades running up to the creation of formal trade unions.[66]

North of the border in the Scottish coalfields miners were less well placed for collective bargaining for most of the eighteenth century. There an anachronistic system approximating to serfdom operated. As Duckham has shown, the link with serfdom was not an ancient one, being the product of acts of the Scottish parliament of 1579, 1597, 1606, 1641, 1660, 1672, and 1701. It seems that the prime purpose of the earlier acts was the control of vagrants, for effectively they gave power to vagrants to bind themselves for life to coalmasters, and to coalmasters to bind vagrants for life. Legally the miner was not bound to an owner for life; the law merely prevented him from leaving his employment without the employer's permission. The result of this technicality, however, was a form of life servitude. This right over the life of an adult was extended, again effectively, to allow employers to claim the same right over the children of a worker so bound. The act of binding was legalized simply by entering the 'recruit's' name in a book and by the payment of 'arles', a small bounty. The binding of the child of a bound miner was confirmed by giving similar arles at the child's birth. The binding of a second generation was always of doubtful legality, since technically a 'life' bond was not good until a miner had worked for the owner to whom he was bound for a year and a day. The 1606 act had prohibited the movement of miners to new employment without a certificate of release from their previous employment, though an employer had the right to move a miner from colliery to colliery within his estate.[67] The Scottish miner's 'serfdom' was restricted to the field of employment: miners were free to acquire or lease property, including mines, and might be admitted as burgesses of boroughs. They were paid wages, as were free workers, and though Duckham believes that, in general, these were above the level of those paid to free workers in other industries, their lack of freedom to withdraw their labour must have weakened their bargaining power in wage negotiations. The system did not, however, despite the chronic shortage of labour it engendered, offer any security of employment to the bound miner. Sir John Clerk summarily dismissed a collier he described as 'worthless' in 1752, sending half his family away with him, but keeping the other half he considered useful to him.[68]

[66] Apart from the sources cited, this account of the practice of binding in north-east collieries is based mainly on Louis 1929–30; Scott thesis 1946; and P. E. H. Hair 1965.

[67] See, for example, the lawsuit of miners in the service of the Marquis of Lothian in 1762. (Printed memorial dated 8 Feb. 1762 in ScRO Clerk of Penicuik GD18/1096.)

[68] George Lockhart to Sir John Clerk, 26 Mar. 1752, ScRO Clerk of Penicuik GD18/1087.

This system was brought to an end in two stages by acts of 1776 and 1799.[69] By the former, life binding of new entrants was to be prohibited. Bound men already in the industry under the age of twenty-one, and between the ages of thirty-five and forty-four were not to be free of their life bonds for a further seven years, and those forty-five and over for three years. Those of the most productive age—from twenty-one to thirty-four—were to wait ten years more for freedom; at all ages, however, freedom could not be obtained until all debts to the owner had been paid off—a very limiting restriction. Not until 1799 was this restriction removed by the effective cancellation of all debts. It is unlikely that the abolition of mining serfdom was the result of either pressure from the miners themselves or of humanitarian zeal. True, there were some murmurings from the miners in 1762, but 'emancipation', wrote Duckham, 'was the result of a steadily growing labour shortage'. Indeed, Sir James Clerk of Penicuik admitted in 1772 that the servitude of miners was 'the real cause of the present great scarcity of hands we all justly complain of'.[70] The *de facto* ending of the perpetual bond in Scottish mining was, in the event, a by-product of an act whose principal aim, though much modified in its passage through Parliament, was to call a halt to the rising cost of mining labour by the control of combinations and the regulation of wages by Justices of the Peace. Though the Anti-Combination law of 1799 applied equally in Scotland as south of the border, its incompatibility with some of the principles of Scots common law rendered it practically useless in Scotland, and the 1799 mining labour act, introduced originally as a bill 'to prevent combinations among colliers . . .', may have gone some way to fill the gap and meet the needs of employers, as they saw them.

In fact, the system of servitude did not guarantee a supply of labour capable of matching the almost three-fold expansion of production in the Scottish mining region during the second half of the eighteenth century. Miners bound so inflexibly could hardly be expected to be enthusiastic workers. Sir John Clerk had tried to remedy this lack of enthusiasm for work early in the century by an 'Agreement with the Coaliers as to their working whole days', though it must be doubted whether this 'agreement' was anything other than a unilateral decree since it consisted of a series of disciplinary and punitive measures.[71] Some miners absconded, taking the risks of recapture and punishment. John Kirkwood, a miner 'born and

---

[69] 15 Geo.III, c.28; and 39 Geo.III, c.56.
[70] Duckham 1969, 193–4.
[71] ScRO Clerk of Penicuik GD18/995.

bred under the said sr John [Clerk]', suffered such a fate in 1702. When recaptured he was obliged to sign a new bond which pledged him:

1º. To study and know the principles of Christianity more than ever I did formerly, to learn my catechism, to learn to read and write, and to be more frequent in prayer than ever formerly. . . .

2º. To be at my work daily by four a clock in the morning.

3º. To refuse to do nothing which either the said Sr John or his Lady shall command.

4º. To go to bed every night by eight a clock at farthest.

5º. Never to leave the said Sr John Clerk his work without his consent and till he provide no work in some other place.[72]

Two colliers similarly deserted the Dundas's colliery in West Lothian in 1727. One had been particularly difficult to his employer, and the grieve asked the owner to 'order some exemplary punishment for that villain. If he is not punished effectively, others will not abide by the works. Whipping or the Correction house, if either can be procured, would be very proper for him.'[73]

By the third quarter of the eighteenth century it is clear that servile labour in the Scottish mines had to be supplemented by free labour. Sir James Clerk of Penicuik was accused in 1765 of poaching miners from neighbouring Hawthornden colliery, something that was possible only with free labour. In 1771, too, Sir James was offering bounties to miners entering his service from other collieries.[74] Miners were certainly brought in from north-east England. One Midlothian coalowner had observed as early as 1703 that 'most of the sinkers or mynders in my works are Newcastle men, ych I bring from thence, feanding them incompariblie befor ours both for work, honnestie and civilitie', though it is perhaps surprising that this did not lead him on to further conclusions about the merits of free labour. Ninety years later Lord Dundonald confirmed this experience very closely. 'A Newcastle Collier', he wrote in 1793 with reference to migrant miners in Fife and comparing them with local Scots miners, 'while he works, works hard; is stripped to the skin; does not *take snuff, consider,* and *cool upon his work,* but *pushes out quantity* on which a master's profit *depends.*'[75]

The system of serfdom, then, was abandoned primarily because it did not meet the industry's requirements in the circumstance of the

[72] ScRO Clerk of Penicuik GD18/1007/1.

[73] P. Maxton to G. Dundas, 21 Nov. 1727, NLS Dundas of Dundas 80.1.3/55.

[74] W. A. Drummond to Sir James Clerk, 7 Mar. 1765; and Petition of Peter Brown to Sir James Clerk, 26 Mar. 1771, ScRO Clerk of Penicuik GD18/1105, 1116.

[75] W. Biggar to Sir John Clerk, 15 May 1703, ScRO Clerk of Penicuik GD18/1016/3; Dundonald 1793, 52.

late eighteenth century.[76] It was replaced mainly by one-year bonds on the lines of those of north-east England, though other schemes were also tried. At Govan colliery outside Glasgow William Dixon bound his miners to raise a fixed quantity of coal per year, while at the Earl of Mar and Kellie's Alloa colliery in Clackmannan, bonds of various durations were signed. Only two months after the 1799 act had become law twenty-three miners deserted to seek employment in Glasgow. Thirteen of these were under bond until 1807, and the remainder had bonds still to run for periods ranging from three of fourteen years. Of thirty-five bound miners at Loanhead colliery in 1813, twenty-six were engaged on one-year bonds, but five were on two-year bonds, three on three-year bonds, and one on a five-year bond.[77] Though the longer bonds look not unlike the life bonds they replaced, it must be assumed that they had been entered into voluntarily by the miners concerned.

iv. *The size and productivity of the labour force*

In the absence of any formal estimates of the workforce of the mining industry in the eighteenth and early nineteenth centuries, and with the guidance of only a very few random accounts, the enumeration of the total labour force in collieries, coalfields, mining regions, and the whole country is almost impossible. Collieries varied enormously in the numbers employed, and it is never possible to know whether the figures available for random collieries at random dates are typical for their period and coalfield. There probably were mines worked by single workers in most coalfields, but the nature of such minute enterprises has deprived us of written confirmation of the fact. Indeed, in the nature of things, the records that survive today as guides to the numbers employed are probably more likely to relate to the larger than to the smaller enterprises. In the early eighteenth century, when collieries often consisted of numerous shallow pits, relatively few miners were able to work in each pit. At Sir Humphrey Mackworth's Neath collieries in South Wales in the opening years of the eighteenth century only seven miners worked to a pit—three 'cutters' and four waggoners—and at Griff colliery in Warwickshire at the same time eight pits were worked, each employing between eight and sixteen men. Seaton colliery in Cumberland

---

[76] Except where otherwise indicated, this account of eighteenth-century 'serfdom' in Scottish mines is based mainly on Duckham 1969c and 1970, chaps. 9 and 10; Campbell 1979, 9–17; T. C. Smout, *A History of the Scottish People* (London, 1969), 430–40; and J. L. Gray 'The law of combination in Scotland', *Economica*, 8 (1928).

[77] 'Memorial re contracts with colliers, 13 Aug. 1799', ScRO Mar and Kellie GD124/17/570; ScRO Clerk of Penicuik GD18/1148/107.

was worked in 1745 by fifty-seven 'haggers' and thirty four 'trailers' in five pits, the largest of which employed twenty-seven workers in all.[78]

In the North-east in the early nineteenth century the apparently more plentiful data are particularly difficult to use. Occasional statements give some indication of the scale of the unit of employment. In 1812, for example, a return of five collieries reads as though it relates to the whole labour forces and not merely the bound portions. In three of these, Fawdon, Kenton, and Willington, the work-force exceeded 500, while at the last named it numbered 709.[79] Many of the available returns are for the numbers of men bound each year but, as we have seen, several categories of workers were not engaged by binding, so that these returns are incomplete. Most extant data, however, relate only to the number of hewers bound, and it would be useful to have some indication of the proportion that the hewers held to the total work-force of a colliery. Two statements only appear to provide exactly this information. A list of the work-force of Jarrow colliery on 5 March 1812 enumerates the workers in twenty-five different categories which gives every appearance of including all likely occupations up to the point at which the coal was carried away from the bank. Ninety out of a total of 406, or 22.2 per cent, were hewers.[80] There is also a return of all Tyne seasale collieries for 1820 which divides the total work-force into six categories, one of which is 'hewers'. The average for each colliery was 342 in total, with 94 hewers per colliery. The largest of these collieries was Percy Main, with a total work-force of 631; the smallest was Whitley with 141. The thirty-five collieries employed a total of 11,954 men and boys, of whom 3,301, or 27.6 per cent, were hewers.[81] This proportion is broadly borne out by a return of the work-force at Willington, Heaton, and Burdon Main collieries in 1828. The work-force at these three north Tyneside collieries ranged from 389 at Heaton to 618 at Willington and totalled 1,440, of whom 321, or 22.3 per cent were hewers. By way of comparison it may be noted that at the Lowthers' Howgill and Greenbank collieries in Cumberland in 1705, haggers (hewers) constituted 23.6 per cent and 25.0 per cent respectively of the total work-forces.[82] If hewers are assumed to have constituted one quarter of the total

[78] Trott 1969, 63; White thesis 1969, 148; CuRO Lonsdale D/Lons/W/Collieries and the Coal Trade, 25.
[79] NEI Forster 49/18/143.
[80] NEI Easton 17/7/65.
[81] NEI Buddle Atkinson 45/5/no pagination; also in NuRO Wilson (Forest Hall) ZWI 5/177.
[82] NuRO Wilson (Forest Hall) ZWI 5/176; Beckett 1981, 65.

colliery work-force in the North-east of the early nineteenth century we shall not be very far wrong.

The collection of statistics relating to the number of hewers employed in the North-east was stimulated by the very high binding fees of 1804, and on the return of these fees to normal levels within a few years interest in the compilation of these returns seem to have waned. However, for the years 1804–9 there are exact and fairly complete returns of the numbers employed in each of the three districts, and these are set out in Table 10.4. Apart from illustrating

Table 10.4. *Numbers of hewers bound at north-east collieries, 1804–9*

| Year | Colliery districts | | | |
	Tyne	Wear	Hartley and Blyth	Total
1804	2,231	1,557	304	4,092
1805	2,041	1,389	264	3,694
1806	2,006	1,303	267	3,576
1807	1,931	1,211	252	3,394
1808	1,968	n.a.	253	n.a.
1809	1,980	n.a.	244	n.a.

Sources: Returns for Tyne and Hartley 1804, NEI Johnson 5/25; for Wear 1804, NEI Watson 5/9/16/7; for Tyne and Hartley 1805, NEI Watson 5/9/16/5; for Wear 1805–7, NEI Johnson 5/95; and for Tyne and Hartley 1806–9, NuRO Joint Coal Owners' Association 263, Minute book 1805–15.

the sharp (9.7 per cent) fall in employment following the enormous binding fees of 1804, and the continuing fall over the four-year period (17.1 per cent by 1807), these returns suggest (assuming a trend on Wearside comparable to those in the other districts) a fairly stable employment of hewers for the whole mining region of about 3,400 in the years 1807–9. This would imply a total employment of all grades of mineworkers in the North-east at this time of about 13,600. Relating the numbers employed in the years 1804–7 to the estimated output of the region (derived from the annual figures underlying the means and estimates in Table 7.3 and Table 1.4) produces output per man-year figures for the whole force of mineworkers ranging from 269 tons in 1804 to 315 tons in 1806. It does not seem unreasonable to suppose that the reduction of the workforce in this period was associated with a rise in productivity. By the late 1820s when the north-east coastal shipments had increased from the late 1810s by 40.4 per cent, a further isolated statement estimated numbers employed in the whole mining region as 21,250 implying an output per man-year over the whole labour force of 292 tons, a level broadly consistent with the figures for twenty years earlier.[83] These calculations therefore give some confidence for supposing that the labour returns of this period are reasonably accurate.

Information about the size of the work-force in other mining regions is unfortunately even sparser than for the North-east. Contemporary estimates are almost non-existent. In Cumberland in 1815 it was estimated that the Whitehaven collieries employed 900 workers and the Workington collieries 400; but there were other coal-producing areas in this coalfield at that time so that these figures do not represent the whole work-force.[84] The Forest of Dean mines appear to have provided work for about 450 men, boys and women in 1788, but again there are no reliable estimates of output at that time to which to relate this total.[85] At any likely level of output for that coalfield, however, it is scarcely possible for labour productivity there to have exceeded half that of the North-east. An estimate for the Bristol and Somerset coalfields in 1800 suggests that between 4,000 and 4,500 men were required to produce an annual output of 300,000 tons—an output per man-year of a mere 67 to 75 tons, though Bulley had estimated approximately 100 tons average over the whole work-force for the beginning of the eighteenth century.[86] Hewers at the small Cluny colliery in Fife in a 52-week period in 1751–2 produced a daily average of 0.94 tons, equivalent to a yearly output of about 253 tons. Since hewers are likely to have comprised nearly 40 per cent of the total labour force in this type of mine in Scotland at this period, the annual output per worker must have been in the region of 100 tons.[87]

Variations over time in the size of the labour forces of the different mining regions, however, depended in the long run upon the rate of growth of the output of individual regions, and in the short run upon the year-by-year fluctuations of the trade cycle. In those coalfields that engaged labour by yearly bonds or contracts employment is unlikely to have fluctuated much within each twelve-month period. Employment returns in the North-east for the early years of the nineteenth century, however, show that the fluctuations from year to year could be quite pronounced. In that coalfield, of course, they were, at that time, subject to detailed manipulation by a powerful employers' organization. Each of the seasale collieries was allocated a quota of hewers to be employed each year in the

[83] NuRO Wilson (Forest Hall) ZWI 5/177.

[84] 'Notebook containing replies to Mr Lyson's queries on the Whitehaven collieries, 1815', CuRO Lonsdale/Colliery reports not yet listed.

[85] Fisher 1978, 22.   [86] Davis thesis 1959, 55; Bulley 1955, 32.

[87] Thomson thesis 1981, Table 6.

knowledge that this allocation would determine the size of the total work-force. Landsale collieries, not subject to the output restrictions of the 'vend', were uncontrolled, and their work-forces were assumed to be available, as a minute of 13 October 1807 of the Joint Tyne and Wear Committee of the Coal Owners' Association made clear, for topping up the workforces of the seasale collieries in years of labour shortage.[88]

If labour productivity in the North-east could be assumed to be typical of other coalfields it would be a simple matter to estimate the sizes of the labour force in each mining region by reference to regional output estimates. But it is certain that there must have been substantial regional variations in productivity, and likely that north-east productivity was high by the standards of other regions. At about 290 tons per man-year for the whole workforce in the early decades of the nineteenth century, annual output per hewer would have been about 1,160 tons, or about 4.3 tons per shift. According to Gabriel Jars, however, a north-east hewer in 1765 normally produced between six and seven tons per shift.[89] This seems to be very high. For Scotland about this time Duckham estimated that a pair of face workers (coallier and bearer) might produce between 1.5 and 2.5 tons per day, or less than one-half that of the north-east hewers.[90] In the Black Country of south Staffordshire estimated output per hewer in 1815 was 38 cwt. per shift or about 513 tons over a working year of 270 days.[91] An estimate of 250 tons per year over the whole mining force, which might therefore still be on the high side, would indicate a total employment in the British mining industry in 1800 of about 58,000 and in 1830 of 121,500. If output per man-year was only 200 tons, a total labour force of 152,000 in 1830 would have been necessary. These totals may be compared with an estimated 375–400,000 workers in the cotton industry in 1831.

It would, however, be misleading to consider employment in the coal industry exclusively, as we have so far, in terms of colliery employment. Coal at the pithead was economically almost valueless, and, as we have seen, transport to the consumer was an integral part of the business of coal production. While there are sufficient estimates of the numbers of keelmen on the rivers Tyne and Wear and of seamen manning the east-coast collieries, we know virtually nothing about the numbers employed on the waggonways even of the statistically minded coalowners of the North-east, let alone

[88] NuRO Joint Coal Owners' Association 263, Minute book 1805–15.
[89] Jars 1774–81, I, 193.
[90] Duckham 1970, 275–6.
[91] 'On Dudley coal mines, 1815', MS volume in NuRO Society of Antiquaries ZAN M14 A9/8.

those of other regions, while the scale of labour employed moving coal along the rivers and canals of the rest of the country is similarly quite beyond the possibilities of estimation. An estimate of the labour involved in the Tyne coal trade of 1792 listed 103 fitters and runners, 1,000 trimmers and ballast heavers, 500 pilots and foymen, 946 shipwrights and keel-builders, 1,100 purveyors for ships and keels, and 2,000 coal factors and clerks, all in addition to 1,547 keelmen, 8,000 seamen, and 6,704 pitmen and boys estimated to work in the mines of Tyneside.[92] It is not beyond the bounds of possibility that the work-force employed in the late eighteenth and early nineteenth centuries to cut coal and raise it to the surface was equalled, if not exceeded by, that necessary to convey it from the pithead to the consumer.

[92] Holmes 1816, 234–5, quoting estimates by 'Dr Macnab'.

Chapter 11

Wages and Industrial Relations

i. *Hours of work*

The assessment of the amount and rewards of the work of miners at any time during the eighteenth and early nineteenth centuries, let alone their trends over time, is extremely difficult. Information is seldom more than random and fragmentary, and even when series of colliery wage-sheets are available they are mostly for rather short runs and it is always difficult to interpret them in a way that makes possible comparison with other collieries and other periods. The working day varied from one group of workers to another and there is some evidence that the number of days worked varied substantially from pit to pit, though it is likely that irregularity in this respect was greater in small than in large collieries. In some, perhaps most, coalfields, mining was often not a full-time occupation. There is unfortunately very little information about the extent of part-time work. In Staffordshire, for example, mining for some was associated with smallholding, while others left off mining periodically to switch to agricultural work or carting.[1]

Though single-shift working seems to have been the most usual work-pattern in the eighteenth century, random evidence indicates that two shifts were not uncommon. The more extensive division of labour in longwall working, in particular, encouraged shift-working. There is evidence for its adoption for longwall working, for example, in Scottish mines in the 1760s and in the Leicestershire coalfield by 1830. In the latter area hewing and hauling were concentrated in the first shift, while the second shift was utilized for stacking 'sleck' in the goaf, a process known as 'gobbing', and for resetting the roof props. In Scotland, according to Gabriel Jars, the workers were divided into two groups: a morning shift that undercut the seams, and an afternoon shift that brought the coal down with crowbars, wedges, and hammers. In view of this arrangement it is possible that shift-working may have been found in other longwall districts, but we lack positive evidence.[2] Sir Roger Newdigate planned for two twelve-hour shifts when he reopened Griff colliery in Warwickshire

[1] *VCH Staffordshire*, II, 101.
[2] Jars 1774–81, I, 267; C. P. Griffin 1978a, 67; Hair thesis 1955, 144.

in the early 1770s and Middleton colliery in Yorkshire worked two shifts in the late eighteenth and early nineteenth centuries. Possibly, too, the introduction of panel working in the North-east at the beginning of the nineteenth century was the means of introducing shift working there. Buddle planned for two shifts at the new Elswick colliery which was being won between 1804 and 1808, as well as at Tanfield Moor colliery in 1825 to keep up output. Benwell colliery, normally worked single shifts in the early nineteenth century, but if one pit was closed following an accident, or for any other reason, another pit was put on double shifts. Howgill colliery at Whitehaven employed haggers (hewers) on a three-shift system in one pit in 1802.[3] This implies a shift of no more than eight hours, and although, as we shall see, it was not uncommon for hewers to work shorter hours than this, it was rare for other classes of workers.

A principal difficulty in establishing the length of a miner's working day in this period is that it was often determined not by the clock but by the length of time it took to cut and haul a predetermined quantity of coal. Sir John Clerk, for example, ordered in 1704 that the 'coaliers' (hewers) at his Loanhead colliery in Midlothian 'shall work whole days, to witt twelve hours space each day of the week at least as many hours dayly as may furnish to their bearers twelve hours work dayly to bear our yr. masters wrought coals.'[4] In the North-east at the time of Gabriel Jars' visit in 1765 hewers, paid at piece-rates, worked as long as they pleased, the length of their working day being determined by the quantity of coal they were content to produce. 'He gets perhaps 15–25, even 30 baskets of coal', commented Jars, 'mostly 20–25—each basket weighing 6 quintals of 112 lbs each.' To produce these quantities the hewer 'mostly works only six or seven hours in each twenty-four'.[5] In 1816 Buddle spoke of the newly invented Davy lamp as burning for the full six hours of a collier's shift.[6] A rather unreliable source from the 1820s, however, spoke of hewers working a specific shift or 'turn' of eight hours and then sometimes being required to stay down longer to assist their putters.[7] In the eighteenth century Somerset shifts ranged from six hours at Radstock in 1792 to about nine hours at James Twyford's mines in the early years of the century, though here, as in the North-east, the length of the working day was usually

[3] Memorandum, n.d. (probably 1773), WaRO Newdigate of Arbury unnumbered; Rimmer 1955, 41; DuRO NCB First Deposit NCB/I/JB/2034/55; NEI Buddle 22/201, and 21/221.
[4] ScRO Clerk of Penicuik GD18/995/25.
[5] Translated from Jars 1774–81, I, 193.
[6] Newspaper cutting of letter from J. Buddle, 1 June 1816, NEI Bell 14/5/378.
[7] Anon., *A Voice from the Coal Mines* (South Shields, 1825), 13.

regulated by the obligation to produce a quota of coal.[8] In early eighteenth-century South Wales an eight-hour day for underground workers appears to have been most usual, as it also was at Brandlings' Middleton colliery in Yorkshire in the early nineteenth century. In the Lowther collieries in Cumberland a nine-hour shift was worked at the beginning of the nineteenth century.[9] Hair found a disparity between the length of the hewers' working day in the North-east and in all other coalfields. In the former, eight hours was quite the most usual, though as little as six to seven hours was worked at Walker colliery in 1765, as Gabriel Jars had pointed out, and up to ten hours was known at other collieries. In Scotland, however, in the late eighteenth and early nineteenth centuries, he found anything between eight and fourteen hours in Ayrshire and from ten to twelve hours at the Earl of Mar and Kellie's Alloa colliery. Twelve hours was customary in the Staffordshire, Shropshire, Bristol, and Forest of Dean coalfields.[10] The comparatively short working day of the north-east hewers might be explained in terms of their exceptionally high productivity.

The evidence for the length of the working day, is therefore, patchy and somewhat disparate. Only in the North-east is a clear distinction made between the working-day of the hewers and that of other underground workers. In other coalfields we are left to assume that no significant occupational differences existed. In all coalfields it must be assumed that all workers concerned with winding— onsetters, banksmen, and enginemen—worked at least as long as the putters, and indeed, as long as there was anyone down the pit to be brought to the surface at the end of their shifts. Buddle reported in 1825 that surface workers in the North-east normally worked in summer from 6.0 a.m. to 6.0 p.m. with one and a half hours off for meals—a ten and a half hour working day. In winter work was restricted to the hours of daylight.[11] There is insufficient evidence to indicate whether there was a lengthening or shortening of the working day over time. In the absence of specific comment on this subject during the early nineteenth century it is unlikely that there was any very marked trend one way or the other.

Where single shifts were worked the day's work was started very early: 2.0 a.m. was not unknown, and 3.0 or 4.0 a.m. was usual. John Kirkwood, it may be recalled, Sir John Clerk's recalcitrant miner at his Loanhead colliery, was obliged to commit himself in

[8] Bulley 1955, 35.
[9] John 1943, 102; LCA 1546/10–12; Wood 1972, 61.
[10] Hair thesis 1955, 145–7; StRO Sutherland D593 M/2/1/7.
[11] SC Combination Laws 1825, 565.

1702 'to be at my work daily by four a clock in the morning.' Somerset miners commonly started work in the early eighteenth century at 3.0 or 4.0 a.m. while Jars found underground workers at work from 2.0 a.m. in 1765. The times of deaths from pit accidents in south-west Lancashire as stated in the records of coroners' inquests were always between midnight and midday.[12] To make such early starts before daybreak even in summer, and at a time when relatively few workers would possess clocks or watches, some system of calling or 'knocking-up' was necessary. In the North-east in the late eighteenth century a 'caller' was employed to go round the pitmen's houses every morning waking up their occupants. The time appointed for this was called the 'calling course', and if there was no caller available, the calling course had to be kept by one member of each family. The purpose of working such 'unsocial' hours was clearly to allow the underground workers to enjoy some daylight after their shift was finished. An eight-hour shift would bring miners to the surface by midday, and even a twelve-hour shift would still leave some afternoon or evening daylight most of the year. In early eighteenth-century South Wales underground workers who came back to the surface by 11.a.m. 'moonlighted' in the afternoons by loading coastal vessels.[13]

By the standards of working hours in other industries in the eighteenth and early nineteenth centuries, miners, even when they worked up to twelve hours, enjoyed a comparatively short working day, and those who worked for as little as eight hours, an unusually short working day. To what extent was this difference increased or reduced by the length of the working week? It was, of course, usual until well into the nineteenth century for industrial workers to work a full six-day week. How long was the miners' working week? As usual, there are difficulties about making precise statements about this. Not all miners were full-time workers, particularly in the earlier part of the period and in the smaller mines. At the New Pit of Erddig colliery near Wrexham in North Wales there were five 'cutters' who worked with their 'partners' (haulers) in 1718. Almost all worked irregularly, as did twelve labourers at the same pit. The winder, Simon Hughes, regularly worked six 'turns' (shifts) each week, sometimes seven, and in one week when he worked six shifts he also worked through one night 'winding sleck'. During the week beginning 23 June 1718 one cutter worked seven shifts, one six, and another only one. Generally it is not possible to detect any regular working

[12] ScRO Clerk of Penicuik GD18/1007/1; Bulley 1955, 35; Jars 1774-81, I, 193; Langton 1979, 295 n.197.
[13] John 1943, 102.

pattern: the pit was a small one and the date early. Miners at Newbold in Derbyshire in the mid-eighteenth century rarely worked for
six days each week, and often not even for five days.[14] Five days,
however, were worked regularly in south Yorkshire mines in the late
eighteenth century,[15] and Sir John Clerk tried to force a six-day
week at Loanhead colliery at the beginning of the century by
threatening to fine absentees. He was clearly committing himself to
an uphill struggle, since Lord Lothian wrote in 1762 that Midlothian
miners 'refuse to work any more than three days in the week, and so
become idle all the rest'.[16] Sir John Hussey Delaval's agent reported
to him that the pits at Hartley colliery in Northumberland in March
1778 had worked only ten days in a fortnight. At the neighbouring
Cowpen colliery in 1830 five or six days was usual, but in two weeks
only four days were worked, in three only three, and in one none.
When planning work at the new Elswick colliery before its opening
in 1808 Buddle assumed that a five-day week would be worked.[17]

The evidence of wage-books confirms this general pattern. At
Moreton colliery in Pembrokeshire in 1777 six days was the normal
week's work. In one eight-week period nineteen out of forty workers
worked an average of between five and a half and six and a half shifts
each week; another nineteen, including all the eight women, worked
between five and five and a half shifts on average, while two men
actually worked seven and a half shifts in one week. Less than five
shifts in a week was not common here, and, when it was, is probably
to be explained by illness.[18] Similarly at Knowles colliery on the
Earl of Stafford's estate in Staffordshire, hewers normally worked
six or seven shifts a week during 1795, though in January of that
year few worked more than three and a half shifts in any one week,
and again short weeks were worked in late May and early June.
When short weeks were worked, it was usually Mondays, Tuesdays,
and Wednesdays that were taken off. Hewers in continuous work
averaged exactly five days a week during the first half of the year.[19]
At Darnall Common colliery in Yorkshire, on the other hand, many
miners worked twelve days each fortnight with great regularity
throughout 1769. A similarly regular twelve-day fortnight was
worked throughout 1817 at the Drynole pit, Upholland, in Lancashire.

[14] ClRO Erddig D/E/736; Hardy 1955–6, 159.
[15] Cox thesis 1960, 125.
[16] ScRO Clerk of Penicuick GD18/995; Marquis of Lothian to the Sheriff Depute of
Edinburgh, 13 June 1762, ScRO Clerk of Penicuik GD18/1095/4.
[17] J. Crooks to Sir John Hussey Delaval, 17 Mar. 1778, NuRO Delaval ZDE 4/4/5; NEI
Watson 5/9/70; DuRO NCB First Deposit NCB/I/JB/2034/55.
[18] NLW Picton Castle 4076.
[19] StRO Sutherland D593 M/12/3/2.

At Owlcotes colliery in Derbyshire the banksman worked for six days in twenty out of the first twenty-six weeks, and only missed ten working days in the remaining six. The gin-driver had a very similar record.

These, however, were indispensable workers if a small mine was to operate at all, and the hewers may not have worked quite so consistently. Fourteen hewers at Skelmersdale colliery in Lancashire worked on average of 5.6 days each week in 1799. At Rothwell Haigh colliery in Yorkshire hewers were offered an extra sixpence a day in 1817 if they worked six days a week.[20] The daily wage-sheets of the Curwens' Workington colliery in Cumberland for 1800–1 reveal that while many workers regularly worked for six days each week, a not inconsiderable proportion of the workforce worked much less regularly. On one seam in the John Pit, two out of five hewers worked eleven out of fourteen days in the fortnight ending 2 August, two worked eight days, and one three. At the same pit in the fortnight ending 17 January 1801 four out of eleven miners worked the full twelve days, three worked eleven days, two worked eight days, and two four and two days respectively. The pattern of the majority working five or six days each week was the norm.[21] In a 35-week period from April to December at Cluny colliery in Fife during the year 1751 the number of hewers working varied from nine to fifteen, with an average of 12.1. Out of a total of 422 man-weeks worked, 222, or 52.6 per cent, were worked in six-shift weeks, and a further 118, or 28.0 per cent, in five-shift weeks. The remaining 82, or 19.4 per cent, were worked in one- to four-shift weeks. The mean working week consisted of 5.2 shifts. In the North-east, where wages were normally paid fortnightly on alternative Saturdays, pay-day was rarely worked, and the eleven-day fortnight was the norm. It is, of course, never possible from the evidence of wage books to determine whether short weeks were due to absenteeism or sickness. At Wallsend colliery in 1813 Buddle estimated that 13.3 per cent of his labour force would be absent at any time through sickness.[22] 'Fundamentally', commented Hair, 'the tradition of the short week in mining was based not on economic circumstances, but on an attitude of mind—the colliers disliked the underground labour and wished to minimise it.'[23]

Much evidence, therefore, points to an average of five and a half days per week where regular working was the rule in the larger

[20] SCL Oborne OR7–8; LaRO Bankes of Winstanley DDBa/19; NUL Manvers M4648–9; Langton 1979, 206–7; LCA 1546/30.
[21] CuRO Curwen D/Cu/6/19.
[22] KM Rothes 40/81/7; NEI Buddle 33/IV/52.
[23] Hair thesis 1955, 150, 156.

collieries of the eighteenth century, and there does not appear to have been any noticeable departure from this norm in the early nineteenth century. When less than that was worked it was mostly when an entire colliery work-force was off work on account of holidays or a pit closure because of slack sales or some contingency like flooding or a dangerous concentration of gas. Opportunities for holidays were sought as a means of breaking up the drudgery and unpleasantness of long spells of underground work. In the North-east the younger pitmen in particular insisted on 'gaudy days' on such occasions as on hearing the first cuckoo, when the peas and turnips were ready for lifting, or when a pit-mate was getting married, though these days were generally spent at public houses.[24] The most universally observed holiday, however, was over Christmas and the New Year. Buddle closed Heaton colliery, for example, in 1808 from Christmas Eve until New Year's Day inclusive to 'allow time for making the necessary repairs about the machines, etc.' and in 1822 he wrote that the pitmen's holidays would begin on 31 December and would last for two or possibly three weeks.[25] The bond signed by the miners at Kenton and Coxlodge collieries on Tyneside in 1808 specifically allowed the owners to close the workings around Christmas time for up to fourteen days without paying any wages except to men engaged on maintenance work.[26] There is little doubt that a long break at this time of the year served the interests of the employers better than those of the workers. Apart from providing a valuable interlude for necessary maintenance it prevented the accumulation of stocks at a time of slack shipping. There is evidence that the miners did, indeed, object to being laid off, unpaid, for a period so long that they were forced into debt.[27]

In the North-east where the information is fullest, it seems likely that miners could work up to an average of five and a half days a week for possibly the equivalent of forty-eight or forty-nine weeks of the year—a total of perhaps 265–70 days each year. The actual number of days worked in a year depended very much on the number of days on which a colliery was closed for one reason or another. A printed statement published by the north-east employers in the furtherance of their cause in the labour dispute of 1831 stated the number of days worked at each of the Tyne collieries in the twelve months ending 28 February 1831. Apart from Felling colliery which worked for only 164 days, the range of days worked at the

[24] Thomas Wilson, 'The Pitman's Pay', MS poem in NuRO Society of Antiquaries ZAN M18/Part 3/13, 37.
[25] NEI Buddle 32/119; J. Buddle to W. M. Pitt, 30 Dec. 1822, NEI Buddle 22/85.
[26] NEI Watson 9/13/no pagination.
[27] Anon., A Voice from the Coal Mines (1825), 34.

remaining thirty-seven named collieries was from 221 days at Backworth colliery to 286 at Mount moor, Pontop, and Garesfield collieries. The mean was 252 days.[28] This is slightly less than estimates of the number of days worked by colliery horses: horses could not work without men to drive them and coal to draw. A costing of 1810 and 1811 for Coxlodge and Hebburn collieries on Tyneside assumed that waggon horses would average a ten and a half day fortnight, or 273 days in the year.[29] For hewers who worked eight hours a day, a 270-day year amounted to a working year of 2,160 hours, and for others miners working a twelve-hour day up to 3,240 hours. Miners in coalfields outside the North-east achieved a working year close to that of the non-hewers in the North-east. For purposes of comparison it is likely that a late twentieth-century industrial worker on a five-day week with three weeks holiday, the equivalent of a further week at Christmas and the New Year, and other occasional public holidays, would work for about 235 eight-hour days each year, or 1,880 hours in the year. A hewer's working year in the North-east was unlikely, therefore, to have been substantially longer than that of his late twentieth-century successor, though his work was, of course, enormously more arduous, unpleasant, demanding, and unhealthy. All other types of mineworkers worked very much longer hours than are worked today, though no longer, and possibly even slightly shorter hours, than those of workers in other industries in the same period.

ii. Methods of wage payment

The remuneration of miners in the eighteenth and early nineteenth centuries was extremely complicated, a fact which makes the determination of levels and trends difficult, if not impossible. The first difficulty lies in the fact that some classes of workers were paid at daily or weekly rates, others at piece-rates, and it is notoriously difficult to trace trends in earnings from piece-rates.

The variety of methods of payment may be illustrated by a statement of 'working prices' at the Lambtons' Penshaw and North Rainton collieries in County Durham for 1801 and 1805. Hewers were paid, as was traditional in the North-east, a piece-rate 'per score', meaning per score of corves. The size of corves varied, however, from colliery to colliery between sixteen and twenty pecks, though the twenty-peck corf had become fairly standard by the early decades of the nineteenth century. At Penshaw and North

---

[28] NEI Watson 5/26; NEI Buddle 40/30.
[29] NEI Johnson 5/113.

Rainton collieries a marginally higher rate was payable to hewers for coal cut 'under the top' than for that cut 'at the stone'. The opening up of headways was paid per yard. There was a supplement for 'double working', when two hewers worked side by side in a single bord. Piece-rates were also payable for drawing (removing) props, building stoppings, corving, and sledding. Daily rates were paid to rolley-drivers, onsetters, horse-keepers and waggon-drivers, and weekly rates to overmen.[30] Hewers' piece-rates at Hebburn colliery on Tyneside in 1827 were even more sub-divided. Hewing 'in the Whole [in a virgin seam] with a 20-peck corf, including Ramble [a thin stratum of shale above the coal which fell when the coal was cut and got mixed with the coal] and double working' earned 69d. per score; similar hewing 'in the Broken' [pillar working] 63d.; while the production of small coal 'in the Whole' and 'in the Broken' earned less than half of these rates. All rates were conditional upon 'separation' of round from small coal. It was at this colliery that Buddle reduced hewers' rates substantially in 1812 when it was found safe to revert to the use of candles after a period of working with steel-mills. Evidently working in the poor light of the steel-mills reduced hewers' output and called for higher piece-rates.[31]

At Hetton colliery in north-east Durham in 1827 hewers were paid a flat rate for both round and small coal, but with a higher rate for cutting 'headways' (with the 'cleat' or grain of the coal) than for cutting 'boardways' (across the cleat). At the Lowthers' Whitehaven collieries in 1756, haggers (hewers) were paid '1d. per Corf (or Basket) in the Main or Prior Band (wch is 2½ yards or 10 Quarters high), 1½d. or 2d. per Corf in the Bannack Band which is about 2 yds High, with a Mettle in the middle of it called Bannack of about 9 Inches in some places 12 Inches thick, according to the hardness of Coal and thickness of the Bannack.' At Birley colliery in Derbyshire in 1809 hewers received 20–1d. per dozen (corves?) for small coal and 23–4d. for hard coal. At nearby Harberlands colliery in 1795 hewers had received 12d. per dozen for small coal and 18d. for great coal.[32]

Rates for putting could be equally complex. In 1830 a meeting of viewers at the Newcastle offices of the Joint Coal Owners' Association decreed that 'in future the price per Score for putting a 20 peck corve shall be 1s. 2d. until the average distance exceed 100 yards from each shaft or Crane, and one penny advance for every 20 yards

[30] NEI Buddle 8/95–6.
[31] NEI Buddle 41/160; and 40/202.
[32] NEI Weeks 66/12; NEI Buddle 51/21; CuRO Lonsdale D/Lons/L/Acc.629; NUL Manvers M4737; DeRO Sitwell 1000/Coal Box 4/9M.

put beyond that distance, and that the putters find their own greese, candles and soams [traces for drawing tubs].'[33] While the owners' association in the North-east was able to ensure standard rates, however complex, across the whole coalfield, this standardization almost certainly did not prevail in other coalfields, even where associations of owners existed. In Derbyshire, for example, a statement of rates paid at fifteen collieries in 1826 showed enginemen paid sometimes by the day and sometimes by the week: daily rates ranged from 31d. to 40d., and weekly rates from 10s. to 21s. Banksmen at most collieries were paid at daily rates that ranged from 36d. to 54d., but at some collieries they were paid by the ton of coal banked at rates that ranged from 2½d. per ton to 3¼d.[34]

Payment by piece-rate involved exact measurement of quantities produced, and the identification of corves sent to the surface by individual hewers. In nineteenth-century Somerset corves were identified by means of wooden tallies about fourteen inches long which must have been notched distinctively for each hewer.[35] Such a system is likely to have been in general use. At Clydach colliery in South Wales corves were weighed at the pithead in the early nineteenth century as a preliminary to accounting for payment to hewers. But the miners objected to the weighing being done some distance from the pithead since this gave scope for pilfering by people living nearby before their corves were weighed. The management turned down this demand arguing that if they conceded this the next demand would be for miners to appoint their own weighers.[36] A system of checkweighmen seems not to have been evolved in any coalfield before 1830.

The payment of wages was, however, complicated by further differential rates for special circumstances. Leicestershire collieries in the early eighteenth century rated night work one-sixth more highly than day work, though in the context of colliery work at this period, when 'day' work might start in the very early hours of the morning, 'night' work is likely to have covered more hours before midnight than after.[37] In some collieries in eighteenth-century Scotland production bonuses were paid, possibly to increase the incentive for hewers on life bonds. At Grange colliery in Midlothian hewers producing thirty carts of great coal or more in a fortnight received bonuses of 1s., and similar premiums for high individual outputs were paid in the 1780s at Halbeath colliery in Fife. At

---

[33] NuRO Joint Coal Owners' Association 263, Minute book 1826-47, 73-4.
[34] DeRO Miller Mundy 517.
[35] Bulley 1955, 36.
[36] J. Scale to J. Jones, 29 May 1823, NLW Maybery 3332.
[37] C. P. Griffin thesis 1969, 79.

Cluny colliery in Fife scaled bonuses were given to the six hewers who produced the greatest quantities in each calendar year. To ensure steady working, however, these awards were conditional upon daily output never falling below a certain minimum.[38]

A custom that renders the historical analysis of the wages of certain classes of miners virtually impossible, however, was group payment. This took two forms. In areas—mainly those worked by the longwall method—where underground work was contracted through charter-masters, the payment of miners' wages became the business of the charter-master instead of that of the owner or lessee. Though there is little doubt that miners contrived to secure some regularity in rates of pay under charter-masters, it is equally probable that wage determination was less formal than in, say, the large collieries of the North-east. The smaller scale of operation of charter-masters, too, has ensured that, so far as can be traced, no documentation of the relationship of charter-masters with their miners has survived from the period 1700 to 1830. In consequence, while, as we saw in chapter 2, some evidence of the rates paid by owners to charter-masters has survived, the wage rates paid by charter-masters in this considerable sector of the industry remain largely beyond the historian's reach. The second area of group payment lay in the pay of the young or subsidiary workers. Bearers in the Scottish mines of the eighteenth century were commonly regarded by employers as the assistants of the hewers, and were, of course, often their wives or daughters. In these cases the hewer's pay often, though not invariably, included that of his bearer. Piece-rates for hewers at Cluny colliery in Fife, for example, were reduced by $1\frac{1}{2}d.$ a load in 1752 when the owner, the Earl of Rothes, undertook to pay bearers directly. In the North-east 'foals' and 'heedsmen' (the younger putters) were commonly paid through the hewer for whom they worked. At the Mostyn colliery in North Wales in 1828, cutters were paid in pairs, presumably because they worked together.[39]

The vicissitudes of the trade cycle or seasonal trade fluctuations occcasionally obliged employers to reduce or cease production temporarily, and it was one of the advantages of the yearly bond in the North-east that it guaranteed some income, albeit a reduced one, to bound miners in such periods. A Washington colliery (Durham) bond of 1812, for example, guaranteed 2s. 6d. per day lay-off pay for men, and 1s. for boys, at a time when a hewer in normal work might earn in the region of 4s. per day. These rates were payable

---

[38] NLS Cadell of Grange Box 12/1; Payne forthcoming, 14; KM Rothes 40/88.

[39] Thomson thesis 1981, 53–4; 'The Pitman's Pay', NuRO Society of Antiquaries ZAN M18 18/part 2/28; UCNW (Bangor) Mostyn 6990.

only in lay-offs of more than three days, and those receiving the payments were entitled to seek work elsewhere: if they secured full-time work, they forfeited their lay-off pay, but in the event of their obtaining only half-time work elsewhere, they retained an entitlement to a lay-off rate of 1s. 6d. per day for men and 9d. for boys. Such a provision was, indeed, exactly in accordance with the proposals for regulating all north-east bonds set out by the owners in 1811. This clause in the bonds was often abused by owners who brought miners back to work for a day or two after each three-day lay-off and then laid them off for a further three-day period.[40]

This guarantee of pay in a lay-off was matched, however, by an obligation to regular work. Absenteeism under such an arrangement led not merely to loss of pay, but to a fine as well. The newly consti-tuted Joint Durham and Northumberland Coal Owners' Association standardized a practice of fines very speedily. In 1806 the owners agreed that the penalty 'for lying idle' for other than health reasons should be 2s. 6d. per day, confirming this forfeiture in 1808 and embodying it in the formal proposals of 1811. A similar forfeiture was exacted at Grange colliery in Midlothian in the 1770s when the fine for a day's absence was 6d.[41]

Absenteeism was not the only source of deduction from wages. Hewers, because they were paid at piece-rates, were most subject to this danger. Corves could be underweight or contain more than an acceptable maximum of stone. Since there was no weighing of corves underground, the weight being judged at loading from the height to which coal was piled in the corf, there must inevitably have been scope for differences and exploitation here. At Loanhead colliery (Midlothian) in the 1770s five tubs in every hundred were routinely deducted from the accounts of each hewer to allow for deficient measure. A statement of 'general customs' at Wallsend colliery on Tyneside in 1792 listed routine penalties as follows:[42]

	s.	d.
For every Corf of Foul Coals		6
For Sticking the Candle above the band	1	0
For having the Bords too wide	1	0
For having the Nicking up more than 16 Inches Wide	1	0

[40] Scott thesis 1946, 14–15; NuRO Joint Coal Owners' Association 263, Minute book 1805–15, 147–9; NEI Forster 49/18/10. And see chapter 10, p. 353.

[41] NuRO Joint Coal Owners' Association 263, Minute book 1805–15, 37, 93, 147–9; NLS Cadell of Grange Box 12/1.

[42] Evidence of A. Hardner, Superintendent of Loanhead colliery in case of Warner v. Cunninghame, 1800–1, ScRO Court of Session C596/638/1833–4; NEI Buddle 18/15.

s. d.

For having the Kerving about [above?]
14 Inches high   1 0

At Jarrow colliery in 1825, no less than eleven kekers were employed to check the weights of the corves brought to the surface. To justify their wage, the miners claimed, they were obliged to be over-zealous in fining hewers. Underweight corves could arise, in any case, from spillage in hauling and winding, and the miners asked for measurement at the pit bottom. The same source suggested the hewers' fines in the North-east averaged 1s. per week, or up to 4–5 per cent of weekly earnings. In a statement put out to refute some of the miners' claims, the owners nevertheless agreed with this assessment of the level of deductions.[43] Fines at one of the Lowthers' Cumberland collieries amounted in total to £56. 2s. 1¾d. over the period 1713–33, but it was the practice there to offer the fines to the miners' welfare fund, as it was also at Meirheath colliery in Staffordshire in the 1790s.[44] Similarly, fines at the Duke of Bridgewater's Lancashire collieries were used to provide housing. One row of miners' cottages was known, from the 2s. 6d. fine for late arrival at work, as 'Half Crown Row'.[45] It should not, of course, be thought that disciplinary fines were unique to the coal industry. They were a very common feature of labour management in this period when they were justified on the grounds of the need to train hitherto undisciplined work-forces in the routines and disciplines of industrial work.[46]

Finally, it was customary in many coalfields for underground workers to provide their own candles or lamp-oil which must have called for an outlay from their wages of a few pence each week. At the new Hetton colliery in east Durham in the 1820s a report by two viewers noted that 'the overmen are paid very moderate wages by the company but they seem to be very amply paid by the profit they derive from finding the workmen with candles.' Hewers at Wallsend and Hebburn collieries on Tyneside in the early nineteenth century provided their own candles and gunpowder. At Hebburn, however, in the 1820s after the introduction of the Davy lamp, and presumably to encourage the use of the safety-lamp rather than

[43] Anon., *A Voice from the Coal Mines* (1825), 8, 14–15; *Brief Observations in Reply to 'A Voice from the Coal Mines'* (Newcastle, 1825), 5.

[44] CuRO Lonsdale D/Lons/W/Collieries and the Coal Trade, 26; StRO Sutherland D593 M/2/1/7.

[45] Challinor 1972, 18.

[46] See, e.g., R. S. Fitton and A. P. Wadsworth, *The Strutts and the Arkwrights* (Manchester, 1958), 232–40; S. Pollard, *The Genesis of Modern Management* (London, 1965), 181–92.

candles, the employer provided lamp-oil free. Working tools were normally, but not invariably, provided by employers. At Paulton colliery in Somerset, however, in the early eighteenth century, hewers were expected to provide their own tools.[47]

Offsetting these deductions and further distancing rates of pay from the real emoluments of miners were a number of benefits and payments in kind. Broadly, these fall into three categories: housing, coal for domestic use, and corn. Customs relating to the provision of housing varied from coalfield to coalfield and colliery to colliery. Since collieries could not be located handily for existing housing, and long walks to work were impracticable, owners were frequently obliged to provide housing for colliers. Though in periods of expansion of the labour force or of the establishment of new collieries it was occasionally possible to find temporary lodgings for workers brought in from other areas, mostly the need could be met only by new building. The study of investment in chapter 6 showed how frequently this was undertaken. There seems to have been no fixed customs as to whether owners provided free housing, or charged rents, possibly less than economic rents, for housing they erected and owned.

A free allowance of coal was probably more common. Miners received a weekly allowance at Middleton colliery in Yorkshire in 1819, at Sefton colliery in Lancashire in the 1750s and at nearby Orrell colliery in the 1770s, at Meirheath colliery in Staffordshire in the 1790s and the early nineteenth century, at several Somerset collieries in the early nineteenth century, and in Scotland at Lochgelly colliery in Fife in the 1790s, at the Marquis of Lothian's collieries in Midlothian in the 1740s, and at the Earl of Rothes' collieries in Fife in the 1750s. At Grange colliery in Midlothian miners received a free supply of firewood each fortnight. In some of these collieries, and doubtless in many others, too, the coal allowance was hedged around with restrictions. Though coal at the pithead was plentiful and cheap, miners were not allowed to help themselves, since it was found that they exceeded their allowance and sold what they did not need for themselves. In some collieries the allowance was made only to married colliers. At others a cash allowance of 6d. or 1s. a week was available in lieu of coal if this was preferred by the miners. At Orrell colliery in Lancashire there were two grades of allowances: hewers and some skilled surface workers received larger allowances than other grades of workers.[48] In some collieries,

[47] NuRO Wilson (Forest Hall) ZWI 4/378; NEI Buddle 33/IV/327; 40/202; 41/160; Bulley 1955, 38.
[48] NuRO 962/10–12; WiRO Leigh D/D Lei B1/A4/9; StRO Sutherland D593 M/2/1/1,

however, the miners' coal allowance was not free. At Winstanley in Lancashire, miners were charged the full market price for coal in the mid-eighteenth century, while in the Grand Allies' mines in the North-east early in the eighteenth century, as at Ouston colliery there a century later, miners were charged for their coal but at a price substantially less than the market price.[49]

These basic and widespread additions in kind to wages were supplemented by occasional gifts. Ale was sometimes presented, either as a regular allowance, as in the Black Country in the early nineteenth century, or as seasonal bounty, as at the Earl of Rothes' Strathore colliery in Fife where it was given in the 1730s at Martinmas and, with a whole ox, at Christmas. Christmas feasts given by employers for their miners were quite common, but the £1. 15s. expended by the Duke of Norfolk on the Christmas 1790 feast for the miners of Thorpe Hesley colliery in south Yorkshire suggests only moderate conviviality.[50] Elsewhere ale was given, as at Griff colliery in Warwickshire, in the early eighteenth century, after some particularly difficult or unpleasant work such as blasting through rock with gunpowder or working in very wet conditions. The Lowthers' Whitehaven mines in the mid-eighteenth century periodically laid out cash 'given to workmen to drink when any Bargains are made with them, or at finishing their work which is claimed as a due, besides casual gratuities given by the Underground Stewards by way of Encouragement to the Workmen to venture more boldly into dangerous places.' In the very dear year of 1801 Earl Fitzwilliam distributed gratis to his Wentworth colliers 8,970 herrings, 2 tons of rice, 90 stone of flour, 10 loads of wheat, and 51½ loads of potatoes.[51]

Subsidized bread grain was provided at various times in some coalfields. The evidence for this practice, however, is patchy, and it is possible that the provision was made only at times of exceptionally high grain prices as a way of avoiding an increase in wages which would have been hard to recoup when grain prices fell again. In 1795, a year when grain prices rose sharply, Sir John Hussey Delaval acceded to a request from his Hartley miners in Northumberland to supply rye at 8s. per boll 'as other collieries do' at a time when

7; NLS Minto 13,300; NLS Miscellaneous 2980/28; KM Rothes 40/88; NLS Cadell of Grange Box 12/1; Bulley 1955, 38, 41; Langton 1979.

[49] LaRO Molyneux of Sefton DDM 4/6; NEI Grand Allies 18/Partnership minute book 1727-38, 59; NEI Miscellaneous 60/ZB/8.

[50] NuRO Society of Antiquaries ZAN M14 A9/8; KM Rothes 40/83/2; Smith thesis 1974, 88.

[51] White thesis 1969, 171; 'Explanations of the Coal Accounts, Nov. 1756', CuRO Lonsdale D/Lons/L/Acc.629/3; Mee 1975, 153.

the market price was 10s. 6d. In Cumberland Sir James Lowther established a granary in Whitehaven from which oats were released for sale at less than cost to miners only when the open market price rose above 5s. per Cumberland bushel. Similarly, Charles Brandling subsidized the sale of wheat and oats to his miners at Middleton colliery near Leeds. In 1796 wheat he bought at 38s. a load was re-sold to miners at 24s. In 1800 one of the two or three peak years of corn prices during the whole period of the French Wars, the Lambtons expended £2,377. 6s. 9d. in subsidizing the sale to their colliers of rye purchased for £6,495. 9s. 9d. This was a very large expenditure for that period.[52]

The Joint Coal Owners' Association of the North-east, coming into existence during this wartime period of wildly fluctuating grain prices, tried to stamp out the practice of subsidizing prices by prohibiting in 1805 the supply by any member colliery to its miners of rye or any other hard bread grain. Medium high prices prevailed in 1805, but when the highest peak of corn prices was reached in 1812, the Association, faced with the problem of deciding between subsidizing food prices or raising wages, opted for a form of 'Speenhamland' allowance. It resolved that when the average price of wheat in Newcastle market was 35s. to 45s. per boll, each miner's family was to receive over and above their normal pay 9d. per week for every child or individual not in employment unless the earnings of the whole family amounted to 5s. per head per week. When the average price of wheat was 28s. to 35s. the allowance, under the same conditions, would be 6d. Single men, or married men with only one child, would be ineligible for this allowance if their earnings exceeded 15s. per week.[53] Almost certainly this scheme was designed to take account of exceptionally high food prices without actually increasing wage rates, and would have been discontinued when prices fell again in 1814.

The provision of food at subsidized prices, though certainly undertaken by employers as an alternative to raising wages, was none the less a form of increased payment to workers; yet it came perilously close to 'truck', which has been much condemned. Mining communities inevitably were remote from existing settlements, and their divorce from an agricultural background rendered them quite dependent upon shopkeepers. But shopkeepers did not immediately move in following the risk of individual mining communities, and if employers did not fill the gap by retailing at least the basic foodstuffs,

---

[52] J. Crooks to Sir John Hussey Delaval, 20 Apr. 1795, NuRO Delaval ZDE 4/6/58; Rimmer 1955, 44; Wood thesis 1952, 44; NEI Buddle 13/11.

[53] NuRO Joint Coal Owners' Association 263, Minute book 1805–15, 3, 235–6.

miners might well have experienced very great difficulty in provisioning themselves. There is every reason to believe that in many instances they welcomed this service by employers; yet it is clear that it gave rise to endless possibilities of exploitation of workers by the less scrupulous employers or their servants. Exploitation in this area took two forms; either an employer's shop took advantage of the monopoly position conferred on it by its remoteness from competitors to charge excessive prices; or employers took advantage of their workers' need for basic foods to pay part of their wages in goods, possibly over-valued or of inferior quality. In an eighteenth- and early nineteenth-century context colliery shops provided a further possibility of exploitation. When, as was so often the case in this period, coins of small denomination were in short supply, it seemed sensible to transact business in the shop on paper and make appropriate deductions from the miner's pay. This process all too easily allowed the miner to slide into debt, and in eighteenth-century Scotland, in particular, but also to some extent in other areas, an employee could not leave his employer's service so long as his debts remained outstanding.

Actual evidence of these forms of exploitation is, none the less, extremely difficult to find. John Brocksopp, a Derbyshire coal-owner, paid his miners partly in beef from his own farm in 1793–4, but we do not know whether the price was fair or the beef wanted. In 1822 J. C. Curwen's miners in Cumberland petitioned against part-payment in goods, though there is no evidence of the practice in the neighbouring Lowther collieries. In contrast to the subsidized grain sales during the French Wars of 1793–1815 a workman at Bilston in Staffordshire deposed on oath before a magistrate in 1830 that flour sold in employers' shops for 3s. 4d. per stone could be bought elsewhere for 2s. 8d., but it is not certain that the deponent in question was actually a miner. Lord Dundonald accused fellow-coalowners in Scotland in 1793 of the 'dirty and *mean practice* of . . . supplying their workmen frequently at an advanced price with Oatmeal, Salt Herrings, Salt Beef, Cheese, Butter, Candles, Soap and such articles.' In 1823 the viewer of Tantobie colliery in the North-east persuaded the owner to allow his daughter to open a shop at the colliery. 'Since then', according to one observer, 'there has been nothing but oppression and mischief between him, her and work-men.'[54] This is the only instance that has been traced of a truck shop for miners in the North-east. A Monmouthshire magistrate in 1816 estimated that the malpractices of mineowners' truck shops currently reduced the real earnings of miners by between 20 and 25 per cent.

[54] J. Armstrong to W. M. Pitt, 18 Jan. 1823, NEI Buddle 22/103.

There is some evidence that the worst exploitation through truck shops was to be found after 1815 in the Staffordshire and South Wales coalfields, and within those coalfields particularly in the collieries operated by iron companies.[55] But even in the Black Country of south Staffordshire, the source of some of the most persistent reports of exploitation by truck shops, it was noticed in 1822 that 'the practice of paying miners otherwise than in money is by no means general practice.'[56]

Perhaps not surprisingly, actual colliery records of the eighteenth and early nineteenth centuries contain virtually no references to truck shops or their activities, beyond the record of miners' indebtedness, though this could arise for reasons other than truck retailing. The accounts of one such shop, however, have survived. It was operated by Newton, Chambers and Company, a Sheffield iron-making company that also worked coal-mines. The extant accounts include a stock valuation taken on 27 March 1817, and the 'slates' of a number of customers during the years 1807–10. The shop stocked a very large range of textiles, foodstuffs, and household goods to the value in 1817 of £2,098. 15s. 4d. Some items, such as silk handkerchiefs and lace, might suggest that the shop numbered middle-class customers among what must otherwise have been a mainly working-class clientele, but a very large stock of candles is perhaps an indication that it was, nevertheless, mainly patronized by miners. The accounts, indeed, include a list of debts owed specifically by colliers at 15 June 1811. The debts range from 4s. 9d. to £6. 10s. 8½d., with an average debt of £2. 4s. 5d.

Only one of the 'slate' accounts can be positively identified with the miners in the list of debts. Between July and September 1807 Samuel Taylor, collier, made almost daily purchases. Many of the payments unfortunately are for unspecified goods. The only separately itemized goods include candles, sugar, salt, cheese, oatmeal, bacon, flour, yarn, and a brush. During the ten-week period for which the account runs, Taylor bought no less than 60 lb. of candles, mostly at 9d. per lb., an expenditure of 4s. 6d. per week on this item of working equipment alone. In ten weeks between 4 July and 12 September he spent a total of £25. 8s. 4d. Every fortnight, presumably on pay day, he paid something on account, but the amount 'left over' after these fortnightly settlements grew from £5. 15s. 3½d. in mid-July to £9. 0s. 0d. in mid-September. But

[55] Stephens 1977, 232; Hilton 1960, 19–39, 95–6, 99–100; Dundonald 1793, 55; Wood thesis 1952, 136.

[56] Meeting of principal iron and coal masters, Bilston, 23 Apr. 1822, quoted in Aspinall 1949, 354–5.

expenditure at a rate of more than £2. 10s. per week is misleading, since many of the items against his account, totalling £9. 3s. 10d., are simply put down as 'Rodger', or in one instance as 'J. Rogers'. There were three colliers in the debt list called 'Rodger', and one called Joseph Rodger, so that it is likely that for some reason, perhaps because Rodger was a close relative or a lodger, his account was included in that of Samuel Taylor. If this is correct, then Taylor's average weekly expenditure on its own was just over £1. 12s. per week, a sum that must indicate a household in which he was not the sole wage-earner.[57]

The cash element in wages net of deductions and bonuses was usually paid fortnightly, though not all coalfields followed this plan. Collieries around Swansea paid their miners monthly, but in Scotland weekly pay seems to have been more usual. Buddle arranged for the hewers at Tanfield Moor in the North-east to be paid fortnightly in 1822, but for other grades of workers to be paid monthly. At Tarbock colliery in Lancashire in 1750 wages were paid only every six weeks.[58] A practice prevailed in some coalfields, however, of paying miners on the regular weekly, fortnightly or monthly pay days only 'subsistence money', a portion of the pay due to them sufficient to meet their day-to-day subsistence requirements, and paying the balances due to them at longer intervals. 'This mode of paying them', wrote the Earl of Dundonald in 1793, 'made them economical, and the arrears enabled them to provide themselves with good *clothes, household furniture*, etc., and to lay in a supply of beef for their families in November.'[59] Subsistence payments to miners at Griff colliery in Warwickshire in the first years of the eighteenth century might be as little as 2s. per week, though even that sum might represent as much as 40 per cent of a week's pay at that time. In early eighteenth-century South Wales the balances after the weekly payment of subsistence money were paid at four- to six-week intervals. At Meirheath colliery in Staffordshire in the 1790s it was the practice for the employer to keep back the equivalent of each Saturday's wages until the completion of an 'agreement' which is likely to have been for a whole year, presumably as a precaution against desertion.

In these ways owners were normally in debt to their miners. When Lord Mansell inherited his collieries in 1707 he found that

[57] SCL Newton Chambers TR 332, 345. This set of accounts must be one of very few sets, if not the only set, relating to a company shop in any industry for this period.

[58] CuRO Lonsdale D/Lons/W/Collieries and the Coal Trade/38/7; ScRO Court of Session C596/638/1518; J. Buddle to W. M. Pitt, 30 Dec. 1822, NEI Buddle 22/87; Langton 1979, 210, n. 196.

[59] Dundonald 1793, 66–7.

he owed £750 to his Swansea colliers.[60] At the relatively well regulated collieries of the North-east payment was usually made on Fridays or Saturdays in the colliery office, though payment at public houses by viewers or overmen was not unknown. At Stevenston colliery in Ayrshire at the end of the eighteenth century the men were paid on Saturday night at the grieve's house.[61] Arrangements for pay through the charter-masters of the longwall districts of the English midlands were almost certainly less formal and less satisfactory. Here pay was often distributed by the butty in a public house, possibly one owned by the butty himself, and some expenditure on drink was virtually a condition of payment.

There were situations in which miners found themselves indebted to their employers, though it is rarely clear how this indebtedness arose. It is unlikely that credit at company or truck shops was the sole cause. In some instances employers advanced money to newly recruited workers to enable them to establish themselves and their families, but this, in turn, could hardly account for very large sums. A list of thirty-five colliers at Loanhead colliery, Midlothian, in 1813, reveals only two not in debt to their employer, twenty owing over ten pounds each, and nine owing over twenty pounds. The largest debt, £33. 6s., owed by Alexander Young, represented a substantial proportion of a year's earnings. Most were repaying at the rate of 1s. per week, but against Alexander Young's name is the comment 'refuses to pay anything'. Had he been aware of the fate, fifty years before, of his fellow-miner, James Spence, of Hartley colliery in Northumberland, he might perhaps have been more co-operative. In 1764, being unable to repay his debt to his employer, Sir John Hussey Delaval, Spence was obliged to assign to him all his furniture and household goods.[62]

iii. *Levels and trends of wages*

It is easier to examine the complexities of the methods of payments of miners' wages in the eighteenth and early nineteenth centuries than it is to trace trends in their levels. Wage books and other documentary statements may quote either piece-rates or quantities produced, leaving it difficult to determine actual earnings, or may record earnings for very variable working weeks. In other instances, group payments from those to a hewer that include his putters' or bearers' wages without making it clear how many individuals were involved,

[60] White thesis 1969, 174; StRO Sutherland D593 M/2/1/7; John 1943, 102.
[61] ScRO Court of Session C596/638/1518.
[62] ScRO Clerk of Penicuik GD18/1148/107; NuRO Delaval ZDE 7/6/9.

to those to a butty for his whole working gang are almost useless for the purposes of tracing trends in wages. There are, in any case, few long series of wage books extant for this period. There were, in addition, so many different grades of labour involved in all but the smallest mines that the problem of comparing like with like is acute. And it is virtually impossible, as we have seen, to assess what could be the very variable extent of non-monetary emoluments.

None the less, the question of the extent to which miners benefited or suffered from the great expansion of their industry in the eighteenth and early nineteenth centuries is of prime interest, and some attempt should be made to answer it. The only practical way to achieve this seems to be by concentrating on the movement of the wage rates of a single class of workers easily identifiable in all mining regions, and whose rates of pay are quoted with some frequency. For this purpose the hewer is the obvious choice, and the method chosen for illustration in Table 11.1 has been to note down all available random quotations of hewers' wage rates in (old) pence per day, distinguishing between mining regions, between which, as may be seen and is to be expected, there were often substantial differences. It should be noted that most of the entries in this table are drawn from the records of separate collieries. There are few chronological series, and variations between mining regions or from year to year within a single mining region reflect differential levels from colliery to colliery rather than short-run fluctuations. A Table put together from random data in this way can only reflect secular movements in the broadest possible way.

Table 11.1 is therefore, not easy to interpret, but one or two features may be observed. In the first quarter of the eighteenth century it seems that hewers stood to earn between 10 and 15 pence per day, though most rates fall in a narrower band between 12 and 14 pence. By the last quarter of the century rates seem to have risen to roughly double that rate, with the majority of rates centering around 24 pence per day. By the end of the French Wars in 1815 rates seem to have roughly doubled again. This is closely in line with Bald's view of 1808 that hewers' wages in Scotland had doubled between 1715 and 1785, and doubled again between 1785 and 1808. Though the evidence becomes less unequivocal, wages seem mostly to have retained their wartime level through to the late 1820s. While it is possible that the rates of pay of the less skilled workers did not match these trends, there is every reason to suppose that the wage rates of skilled underground and surface workers followed these trends in reasonable sympathy.

Taking into account, therefore, solely cash payments, there are

Table 11.1. *Hewers' wage rates, 1700–1830*
((old) pence per day)

Year	Mining regions									North-east	
	Scotland	Cumberland	Lancashire	North Wales	South Wales	South-west	West Midlands	East Midlands	Yorkshire	per score	per day
1700	12					12–14					
1701	12½										
1703					15						
1709		10									
1715	14–20										
1716		10									
1718				12							
1721								12–14			
1726								18			
1730	8		10							12	
1740											18–22
1742											18–22
1746	7										
1747	8½										
1749										12	
1751–2	13										
1763			18–20								
1765			13½								
1766								20			
1770	20										
1774			12½		18						
1777					16						
1780	25										
1790	27½, 36										

Year								
1792						20	30	28
1795							24	24
1796	38	30						
1797	38						38	38
1798			36½					
1799								
1800	35	36, 51			30			52½
1801								
1804	36							68
1805							38	68
1806					36			
1807	30-6				40			
1809							48	
1810	37½							68
1811	59							49
1812	48-59	21-6						40
1813	48				36			58½
1814	49½, 51						48	
1815	54							47½
1816	55		56½					46½
1817	48					24		61½
1818	44							
1819	47					60		
1820	41½, 45							49½
1821	39							
1822	42, 44						30-6	
1823	43, 44½							
1824	50			47½			24	
1825	63, 67½							
1826	60							66
1827	51							
1828	51							
1829	51							
1830	51	40-66				24		38

[See p. 390 for Sources]

reasonably solid grounds for believing that the period 1700 to 1830 witnessed a substantial improvement in the hewer's standard of living. While prices in general may have risen over the whole of the first ninety years of the eighteenth century by about one-third, the hewer's wages may roughly have doubled. Similarly, while general prices rose further during the war period from the early 1790s to the early 1810s by perhaps 70 or 80 per cent, the hewer's money wage doubled again, leaving him a further gain in real terms. And when, after 1813, prices generally fell by perhaps one-third by 1830, the hewer's money wage fell no more than marginally, and may not have fallen at all. 'A small decrease of wages has taken place since the peace in 1815' reported Buddle in 1830, 'not considerable, but there has been a decrease.'[63] Within these very broad secular trends there were, of course, sharper short-run fluctuations. The great scarcity of skilled workers on the resumption of war in 1803 led, as we have seen, to an immediate sharp rise in wages in the North-east, though the owners took the opportunity of slacker demand later in the same decade and in the post-war depression to push wage rates down again. And in the exceptional years 1803–4 wages were sharply supplemented by 'binding' fees that may have added 25 per cent or more to annual earnings.

A number of random statements of earnings for the late eighteenth and early nineteenth centuries broadly confirm the daily rates quoted in Table 11.1. Hewers at Lochgelly colliery in Fife, for example, earned about £40 each in the whole year 1790. Average earnings of all 292 underground men (not including boys) after deducting 'offtakes for candles, etc.', at Jarrow colliery on Tyne-

---

Sources: *Scotland:* Duckham 1968a, 116; Hair thesis 1955, 351–3; Payne 1961, 81–2; Campbell 1979, 19.

Cumberland: CuRO Curwen D/Cu/6/19; Wood thesis 1952, 41–2, 135.

Lancashire: LaRO Bankes of Winstanley DDBa; Langton 1980, 200–10.

North Wales: UCNW (Bangor) Mostyn 6990.

South Wales: Roberts thesis 1953, 193–6; John 1950, 81–2.

South-west: Bulley 1955, 39–40.

West Midlands: StRO Sutherland D593 M/2/1/7; *VCH Staffordshire*, II, 102; Aspinall 1949, 354–5.

East Midlands: C. P. Griffin thesis 1969, I, 100, 116, 75–9.

Yorkshire: LCA 1546/10–12; NuRO 962; LCA 1546/30.

North-east: The daily rate is the more reliable guide to daily earnings. It was often assumed that hewers produced about a score a day, but in 1813 Buddle asserted that a hewer would produce 28 corves (1.4 score) per day on average. (NEI Buddle 33/IV/51.) NEI Miscellaneous 60/ZB/8; Watson 5/26; Bell 15/1/8; NEI Buddle 8/95–6; 13/76, 98–102; 17/204; 18/57; 25/3, 43; 33/IV/90, 324, 327; 36/I/146–7; 36/II/136; 41/160; 46a/145; NuRO Joint Coal Owners' Association 263 Minute book 1805–15; NuRO NCB First Deposit NCB/I/JB/681; W. Green 1865–6, 205; NuRO Society of Antiquaries ZAN M14 A9/8.

[63] *SC Lords Coal Trade* 1830, 36.

side in 1814 were 20s. 6d. per week, and at neighbouring Hebburn colliery 20s. The weekly earnings of banksmen at two other Tyneside collieries showed that their earnings were well above average. Wallsend colliery banksmen averaged £1. 9s. 1d. per week in February 1812 and those at Heaton colliery in August 1807 averaged £1. 10s. 5¾d. Wastemen—workers who kept underground roads clear—at the latter colliery averaged £1. 4s. 9d. Banksmen at Burtonholm colliery in Lancashire in 1818 earned 24d. per day, but horse drivers there earned 36d., blacksmiths 40d., and enginemen 30d.[64]

A printed statement of 17 March 1831 purported to give the 'net average weekly earnings of the Pitmen on the Tyne for the Year ending 28th February 1831'. Its precision suggests accuracy, but the fact that it was produced in support of the employers' case in an industrial dispute inevitably casts some doubt on it. For what it is worth, however, it lists average earnings of '1st class', '2nd class', and '3rd class' miners at each of thirty-eight Tyneside and Northumberland collieries. The earnings of '1st class' miners, presumably fully able hewers, ranged from 14s. 9d. at Low Moor and South Moor collieries to 24s. 9d. at Mount Moor colliery, with an average of 18s. 4½d. These earnings were for an average working year of 252 days. Assuming an average working week of 5½ days, or a total of 46 working weeks in the year, this shows average daily earnings at 40¼d., low by the indications of Table 11.1, but it should be remembered that these earnings are net of various deductions. '2nd class' miners averaged 15s. 4d. per week, and '3rd class' miners 14s. 10½d. A note at the foot of the Table pointed out that 'those men who earn the lowest wages are generally old Men who have large Families that are earning great Wages in the Colliery besides. That is, Boys from 7 to 12 Years of Age are employed to shut and open the Doors in the Mine, under the Denomination of Trappers, at 10d. per Day; from 12–16 they become Waggon-drivers at 14d. per day; or Putters, two Boys to a Tram: after the Age of 16, if Putters are able to put a Tram alone, they earn fully as great Wages as the Hewers themselves. They have Medical Attendance, a House, Garden, Coals, gratis, except the Payment of 1s. per Month towards the Expense of leading the latter.'[65] A South Wales agent, writing to John Buddle in 1825 to ask him if he could procure twenty northeast miners for his Coed Talon colliery, pointed out that, though 'our Welsh miners are a very idle set', they earned 20s. to 24s. per

[64] NLS Minto 13,300; NEI Forster 49/16/7; NEI Buddle 33/III/276; and 32/I/247; JRL Crawford and Balcarres 23/6/207.
[65] NEI Watson 5/26.

week: hard-working Tyneside miners, he was sure, could earn 30s. in South Wales, and would be provided with cottages and gardens as well.[66] Underground supervisors earned more than hewers. Five oversmen at Lochgelly colliery in Fife averaged earnings of £40. 7s. 6d. during the twelve months ending 1 December 1792. Overmen in the Lowthers' Whitehaven collieries were said to earn £100 per annum in 1823, while deputies earned 25s. per week, plus an allowance for candles and oil.[67]

Finally, two statements in the records of the Coal Owners' Association set out the total earnings of miners in Tyne and Wear collieries in the year 1815, distinguishing between underground and surface workers. At thirty-two Tyne and Northumberland collieries, 5,040 underground workers, including presumably the lower-paid putters and trappers as well as the hewers, averaged £43. 18s., while 1,968 surface workers averaged £36. 12s. The corresponding earnings at ten Wearside colliery groups were £40. 5s. for 2,276 underground workers and £43. 18s. for 1,220 surface workers.[68] Both these documents make a feature of the number of 'average' wage-earners in each family, since the Association was anxious to draw attention to household earnings. The Wear owners' case was somewhat diminished by their assumption that all miners' households averaged five members exactly, of whom two were employed in the mines. The Tyne owners achieved a greater degree of verisimilitude by varying the household size at each colliery from as low as three members to a maximum of 5.5. The mean was 4.75, with a mean of 1.95 members in each household employed in the mines. This interest in family earnings was further illustrated by a 'statement of earnings of six of the best families at Cowpen colliery, 5 April 1830–5 April 1831.' These six families averaged 4.3 working members, and their household earnings averaged £165. 14s. 6d. The hewers among them averaged £47. 14s.[69]

Apart from this evidence drawn from strictly comparable sources, other more random evidence confirms the broad trends it reveals. The wage books of three Leicestershire collieries, for example, enabled C. P. Griffin to observe trends in the wage rates of thirteen different classes of mineworkers for six-day weeks between 1721–7 and 1763–76. During this half-century in which prices in general rose very little, he found that all money wage rates rose. The smallest increase was 20 per cent, while many rates doubled. The mean increase (unweighted) was 67.8 per cent.[70]

[66] J. Gray to J. Buddle, 27 June 1825, DuRO NCB First Deposit NCB/I/JB/575.
[67] NLS Minto 13,300; J. Peile to J. Buddle, 3 Nov. 1823, DuRO NCB First Deposit NCB/I/JB/1064.
[68] NuRO Joint Coal Owners' Association 263, Minute book 1805–15, 261–4.
[69] NEI Watson 5/9/74.   [70] C. P. Griffin thesis 1969, I, 116.

There is a widespread belief that by the late eighteenth and early nineteenth centuries miners were more highly paid than workers in other industries. Langton has pointed out how in Lancashire wage rates for underground workers were well above those of craftsmen in other industries,[71] while in Scotland Bald took the view in 1808 that miners' wages were double those of 'common labourers'. There is a need to compare like with like, however. Comparison of actual wage rates is difficult on account of the wide range of rates in other industries and the need to compare, say, a hewer's wage with that of a skilled, adult male worker in other industries, not that of less skilled, or female, or juvenile labour in other industries. In the 1810s, for example, when hewers were earning between 4s. and 5s. per day, male fine spinners in the Lancashire cotton industry were making 32s. per week, and coarse spinners 24s., almost certainly for six-day weeks, very comparable rates of pay. Handloom weavers, however, though not all adult males, whose earnings at their peak in the early 1810s may have come close of those of skilled miners, suffered, as is well known, a persistent decline during the next twenty or thirty years, while miners' wages held up fairly well. Male adults in various branches of the factory cotton industry of Lancashire and Cheshire, however, were still, according to one source, taking home weekly earnings of between 23s. and 29s. in 1833, but according to another only about 20s.[72] In the iron industry wage rates for adult male workers did not appear to be greatly lower than those of miners. In the 1770s and early 1780s, for example, furnace 'keepers' at the Coalbrookdale Company's Horsehay furnaces in Shropshire earned an average of about 25d. per day and fillers about 23d., very much what hewers were paid at that time. By the mid-1790s smiths at Boulton and Watt's Soho works were earning between 15s. and 18s. per week, again about the same as hewers. The highest grades of metal-workers in the Sheffield area earned about 25s. per week in 1830.[73] These comparisons suggest that the more highly paid grades of mining labour were, by the late eighteenth and early nineteenth centuries, at least as well paid as comparable grades of skilled adult workers in other industries, and possibly marginally better paid.

Contemporaries were in no doubt about the position. Sir John Hussey Delaval's agent informed him in 1805 that miners earned

[71] Langton 1979, 209–10; Bald 1808.

[72] F. Collier, *The Family Economy of the Working Classes in the Cotton Industry, 1784–1833* (Manchester, 1964), 60–1, 66, 69; *Report of Select Committee on Manufacturers' Employment*, PP 1830 (590) X.221, 4.

[73] T. S. Ashton, *Iron and Steel in the Industrial Revolution* (Manchester, 1924), 190–2; A. Raistrick, *Dynasty of Ironfounders* (London, 1953), 119; *Report of Select Committee on Manufacturers' Employment*, 1830, 5.

'double that of most other descriptions of working men'. 'It is certain that the ratio of wages among the pitmen', wrote a correspondent to a Newcastle newspaper in 1812, 'is much higher than that among most classes of the labouring poor.' He quoted from a report of the Society for Bettering the Condition of the Poor, which asserted that 'high wages of the collier . . . furnished [him] with the power of obtaining more than the necessaries of life'.[74] The miners themselves, too, believed that they were among the better-paid industrial workers, as a Durham folk-song of the period illustrated:

> Collier lads get gold and silver,
> Factory lads get nowt but brass.
> Who'd be bother'd with a spindle bobber
> When there are plenty of collier lads?[75]

This pride was echoed in another north-east song from a collection of 1812 that may have referred to the high binding fees of a few years earlier:

> When I cam te Walker wark
> I had no coat nor ne pit sark.
> But now aw've getten twe or three,
> Walker pit' denn well for me.[76]

To some extent the relatively high level was a recognition of the dangerous nature of the work. 'The Miners could not be entitled to as high wages', wrote a correspondent to Buddle in 1827, 'if instead of a dangerous and unwholesome, they worked in a safe and wholesome air.'[77]

It remains to look briefly at the wages of the keelmen and the seamen who were associated so closely with the miners of the North-east. The keels were owned by the fitters who were therefore the employers of the keelmen. Like the miners, the keelmen were bound by the year, and were paid as a crew by the voyage. Their wages included payment for unloading the coal into the colliers, but, since the colliers were loaded through port-holes which lay at varying heights above water level as the vessels took on their cargoes, there were additional payments for throwing the coal when the port-holes were above certain heights, and for loading foreign vessels. In the

---

[74] J. Bryers to Sir John Hussey Delaval, 13 Oct. 1805, NuRO Delaval ZDE 4/27/86; newspaper-cutting of a letter from Philoiktos, 2 June 1812, in NEI Bell 15/11/74.

[75] D. Douglass, *Pit Talk in County Durham* (History Workshop Pamphlet), 10 (1973), 11.

[76] Hair thesis 1955, 370, quoting from *Bell's Northern Bards* (1812).

[77] Sir Thomas Clarges to J. Buddle, 10 July 1827, DuRO NCB First Deposit NCB/I/JB/304.

1760s the basic payment per keel was 14s. 6d. plus beer (or 2d. extra in lieu of beer), while in 1822 a calculation of payments made to the keelmen operating from the Tanfield Moor colliery's staith allowed £1. 3s. 6d. per voyage. In that year the crews averaged only 2⅖ tides or voyages per week, and the estimated weekly earnings per man averaged 17s. 2d. Buddle was prepared to assert as late as 1830 that keelmen, when in full employment, earned higher wages than miners; but by that date the qualification might have been crucial.[78]

Seamen were paid by the voyage and it must be supposed that their wage rates took into account the subsistence they received aboard as well as of the undoubted risks of drowning, privateers, and the press-gang. Davis estimated that a collier seaman on the east coast run could expect to earn a very regular 30–5s. a voyage between the late seventeenth century and the 1770s.[79] By 1792, however, the standard wage on the east coast run was 50s. per voyage, yielding a yearly earning of £20, or 8s. per week round the year. This could not be considered high by any standards and with the rise in prices towards the end of the eighteenth century there was an active movement for higher wages. The demand in 1792 was for four guineas a voyage, though after the intervention of the military it seems that a settlement was reached at £3.[80] But the ensuing wars against France placed a premium on the labour of skilled seamen and, for those who managed to avoid impressment, good wages could apparently be earned. On the return of peace in 1815, and with the sharp drop in the general price level, the owners looked to reduce these wages. In the strikes that followed this move in 1815 the seamen, in addition to demanding five guineas per voyage, also insisted on the dismissal of the foreign seamen who had been recruited to keep up the manning of colliers during wartime, as well as a minimum manning level of five men and a boy for every one hundred tons. Such a scale would push up to at least thirteen the crew of the average collier. It seems clear that to counter the high wage rates and scarcity of labour during the war the owners had reduced manning levels. Eventually the seamen accepted an offer of £5 per voyage, but failed to secure a guaranteed minimum manning level.[81]

iv. *Industrial relations*

The success of the miners in securing persistent gains in real wages during the period 1700 to 1830 and in raising them to a level as high

[78] Jars 1774–81, I, 205; TWRO Tyne Keelmen 394/42; *SC Commons Coal Trade* 1830, 307.   [79] Davis 1962, 134.
[80] Aspinall 1949, 9–16.   [81] Milne 1977, 228–31.

as, if not higher than, those of the better-paid workers in other industries might seem to suggest that they had learned to make effective use of their power in collective bargaining. There was, needless to say, some truth in this, as we shall see; but in concentrating for a while on the ways in which the miners developed the arts of collective action, it should not be forgotten that the period during which these arts were learned was also one of the most rapid expansion of coal production. The supply of skilled mining labour lagged behind this growth and its scarcity certainly contributed to the steady rise in its rewards. Nor should collective action be equated during most of this period with trade unionism: not until the last few years before 1830 can formally established trade unions be clearly identified. Many aspects of the existence and activities of trade unions were formally made illegal during the eighteenth century. But though it was only during the years 1799 to 1824 that they were absolutely proscribed by law, many organizations that can only be described by that name certainly existed, if only ephemerally. The widespread use of the annual bond in mining, which created formal annual occasions for wage bargaining, and the compactness, exclusiveness, and cohesion of mining communities under the leadership of experienced hewers ensured that miners would negotiate collectively rather than individually. Thus, while there is little evidence of the existence of formal trade unions among mineworkers before 1825, there is plenty, both direct and implicit, of collective activity by miners in the traditional fields of union activity— negotiations over wages and the conditions of work and employment.

In the documentary evidence of miners' collective activity in the eighteenth and early nineteenth centuries a distinction may just be made between references to 'combinations' and those to 'unions', though both expressions relate to similar types of activity. Combinations were informal and ephemeral; unions were formal and gave themselves titles, and, though they were often almost as ephemeral as the combinations that preceded them, aspired at least initially to permanence. Combinations were evidently more rudimentary forms of the type of organizations that later evolved into unions, though throughout the period up to 1830 neither form of organization ever transcended local, or coalfield, status.

The evidence of scattered and probably ill-organized activity from early in the eighteenth century suggest that combinations may have been pushed into temporary existence by various provocations, but the earliest documentary reference to specific combinations among miners comes from Scotland later in the century. The survival of a brief cashbook entitled 'Collections of the Coalliers in Scotland at the several meetings aforementioned' refers to a series of meetings in Dalkeith, Midlothian, between 1769 and 1771.[82] Unfortunately entries in this book are insufficient to determine whether the 'coalliers' in question were running a friendly society of the type examined in chapter 12, or whether this was indeed an organization to confront the employers. A circular issued by the Scottish coal-owners in 1797, however, referred quite explicitly to what they believed to be a combination of miners formed to raise wages by refusing to work, and the records of the Earl of Mar and Kellie's Alloa colliery refer in 1799 to the existence of a similar combination which held meetings underground (literally) to co-ordinate strike plans in a campaign for higher wages. There is evidence, too, of combinations among the miners of Ayrshire organizing strikes in 1793 and 1798.[83] Other combinations were reported at the time of the negotiations for the 1809 binding in the North-east, and among the miners at Whitehaven in Cumberland in 1811. The latter 'meet publickly now twice a week to collect subscribers and to swear them to be true to each other. . . . Their number is near 200'.[84]

Activities of this kind, particularly those that flourished during the period of the Anti-Combination Laws of 1799–1824, operated in the face of considerable hostility from the law as well as from employers. Their protection lay in the ephemeral and amorphous nature of their organizations; it was hard, if not impossible, for magistrates and employers to substantiate their existence and pin down their leaders. But the need for circumspection at least discouraged the formation of more formal workers' organizations during this period—discouraged, but not entirely prevented. The existence of a set of 'Articles, Rules, Orders and Regulations' of 1811 'to be observed by, between, and amongst the Friendly Associated Coal Miners within the Township and Parish of Wakefield [Yorkshire] . . . and in the Townships and Places in the neighbourhood thereof' may have indicated an organization having more the character of a friendly society than of a trade union, though the former was frequently used as a cover for the latter, but a Yorkshire labour historian believes that a formally organized union was behind a strike of miners in the Leeds and Bradford area in 1819.[85] A similar train of events may be traced in Lancashire. A number of friendly societies, of which the Brotherly Union Society formed at Pemberton

[82] ScRO Court of Session C596/2193.

[83] ScRO Leven and Melville GD26/V/369; ScRO Mar and Kellie GD124/17/570; Campbell 1979, 13.

[84] Wood 1972, 57.

[85] Machin 1958, I, 30–1.

in October 1794 was typical, had come into existence by the end of the eighteenth century and were almost certainly being used to disguise 'industrial' activities. On 18 August 1818, however, seven hundred Lancashire colliers met together at Kersall Moor to form the Union of all Trades which enjoyed only the briefest existence and very modest success.[86] In 1818 two Scottish miners' leaders were charged in the High Court in Edinburgh with organizing an 'illegal combination amongst great numbers of operative colliers in various places in the counties of Ayr and Lanark.' The combination in question had been widespread, embracing thirty-eight collieries and up to 2,000 miners. A three-week strike at several Glasgow collieries had been successful in procuring wage increases. In Ayrshire, however, the arrest of the combination's leaders forestalled strike action.[87]

Though the repeal of the Anti-Combination Acts in 1824 and the modification of the repeal in the following year removed the stigma and handicap of illegality from trade union activity, inexperience, poor communications, and slack trade as well as continuing hostility from employers prevented the burgeoning collective activity after 1825 from achieving much success or permanence. In the burst of trade union activity that followed the legislation of 1824–5 trade unions were noted, with some apprehension, by employers and viewers in many coalfields. 'Every class of our workmen is combining', reported John Buddle in 1825, drawing his information from the friendly landlord of the public house where trade unionists met, 'and are one after another compelling us to advance their wages.' They did, indeed, form a United Association of Colliers on the Rivers Tyne and Wear which engaged a solicitor to advise it on the terms of the bond. The formation of the Colliers of the United Association of Durham and Northumberland was also reported in 1825, to be followed by that of the Pitmen's Union of the Tyne and Wear in 1829.[88] Similar unions emerged in Yorkshire in the Sheffield area in 1825, and in South Wales, where the agent at Clydach colliery reported in 1827 a stoppage resulting, he claimed, from 'the abominable system of combinations which has crept into our Works', and which was infiltrated in 1830 by the Friendly Associated Miners' Union of Lancashire, a solitary example before 1830 of inter-coalfield co-operation. This union may or may not be identified with the

---

[86] Challinor 1972, 22–3.
[87] Campbell 1979, 52–7.
[88] J. Buddle to C. Tennyson, 2 Apr. 1825, DuRO NCB First Deposit NCB/I/JB/1444; NEI Buddle 36/IV/127–8; Scott thesis 1946, 48–54; Webb 1921, 26–8; Buddle's evidence to *SC Combination Laws* 1825, 1–2.

Friendly Society of Coal Mining also created by the miners of south Lancashire in 1830.[89]

Whatever the degree and sophistication of organization, however, when it came to differences between employers and employees, the miners and their associated workers, the keelment and the seamen, were demonstrably capable of acting collectively from an early date. Strikes—'sticks', or 'steeks'—were of frequent occurrence throughout the eighteenth and early nineteenth centuries. Keelmen—'the Bane of the Trade', according to Buddle[90]—were reported as striking in 1708, 1710, 1719, 1738, 1740, 1746, 1750, and 1771, though little is known about the causes and outcome of these actions. Indeed, the mayor of Newcastle described the keelmen in 1746 as being 'too ready to rise and become tumultuous upon the least pretence'.[91] The earliest reports of miners making use of the strike weapon come from the Bristol coalfield in 1738 and from Scotland, where Lord Elphinstone's miners struck in 1743.[92] The most serious of the early strikes was mounted, however, by the Tyne miners in 1765 when the owners attempted to impose a Scottish type of interminable bond by agreeing between themselves not to bind any miner from another colliery who could not present a certificate of release from his previous employer. While taking strenuous action to drive the miners back to work, the employers decided to drop a demand which the miners were clearly determined to resist fiercely.

There were further reports of strikes at the Earl of Scarbrough's Lumley colliery in Durham in 1780 and 1781, and at the Coalpitheath colliery in Bristol coalfield in 1783,[93] but it was the year 1792 that witnessed the most widespread troubles. Concerned, no doubt, about rising food prices, 4,000 Somerset miners struck, successfully, for higher pay, as did the Duke of Norfolk's miners at Sheffield and those in the Bristol, Lancashire, and north-east coalfields, as well as the seamen manning the colliers at Shields. They were followed by Sir John Hussey Delaval's miners at Hartley in Northumberland who looked for improved hewing rates and a weekly allowance for miners who 'receive any capital hurt'.[94] The Hartley miners threatened to strike again in 1798 in an endeavour to win higher rates on account

[89] Machin 1958, I, 35; E. Frere to John Powell, 9 Jan. 1827, NLW Maybery 3542; Roberts thesis 1953, 211; J. R. Harris, 'The Hughes papers: Lancashire social life, 1780–1825', THSLC 103 (1951), 25–6.

[90] J. Buddle to W. M. Pitt, 26 Feb. 1823, NEI Buddle 22/154.

[91] Fewster 1957, 33; W. Brown to C. Spedding, 30 Apr. 1750, NEI Brown 16/1/4; Turner 1915–16, 544.

[92] Turner 1921–3, 13; Lord Elphinstone to (?), 2 Mar. 1743, NLS Dundas of Dundas 80.1.4/232.

[93] Beastall 1975, 32–3; BRO Ashton Court AC/AS 97/10.

[94] J. Crooks to Sir John Hussey Delaval, 13 Feb. 1793, NuRO Delaval ZDE 4/6/40.

of the greater hardness of the coal they were working on. They pressed for the engagement of two men from neighbouring collieries to arbitrate on rates. Delaval's agent offered the employment of viewers as arbitrators, and the miners finally, though reluctantly, accepted this in response to an offer of increased rates.[95] In spite of the enactment of the Anti-Combination Laws in 1799, a further strike at Hartley was not averted in 1800, but unfortunately there is no information about its causes and outcome.[96]

This was indeed but the first of many strikes during the period when workmen's combinations were explicitly illegal. In a period of acute scarcity of skilled labour, the employers' needs could not be met by imprisoning large numbers of miners. And so strikes continued, and were met by the same combination of concession and resistance as before 1799. While the Anti-Combination Laws were in force there were strikes at Cowpen colliery in Northumberland in 1805 when the owners arbitrarily stopped the free coal allowance to miners and put a guard on their coal stocks to prevent pilfering; on Tyneside at binding time in October 1809; on the Wear in the following year—'a most obstinate stick', according to Buddle; at the Earl of Stafford's Meirheath colliery in Staffordshire in pursuit of higher wages in 1815; at collieries in the Leeds and Bradford district of Yorkshire in 1819, which achieved some success when the magistrates decided not to act against the miners on the grounds that the masters' combination was as illegal as the miners; and at Clydach colliery in South Wales against irregularities in weighing.[97]

The most serious strikes of the period of the Anti-Combination Laws, however, were those of the keelmen of 1819 and 1822. As we saw in chapter 5, by the second decade of the nineteenth century the position of the Tyne keelmen was being seriously undermined by the direct loading of colliers below Newcastle from spouts and drops. They were therefore extremely sensitive to any additional threats to their livelihoods, so that when in October 1819 the coalowners began, in spite of legislation to the contrary, to press the sale of their coal to shipmasters by giving over-weight in the keels, the keelmen struck in protest against the absence of extra payment for shifting extra amounts from the keels to the colliers. They also wished to restrict the use of spouts. The strike brought some increase in the keelmen's rates, but no action against spouts. The failure of the

[95] J. Bryers to Sir John Hussey Delaval, 5 Aug. 1798, NuRO Delaval ZDE 4/23/60.

[96] T. Fenwick to Sir John Hussey Delaval, 5 May 1800, NuRO Delaval ZDE 4/24/22.

[97] J. Bryers to Sir John Hussey Delaval, 24 Mar. 1815, NuRO Delaval ZDE 4/27/33; Scott thesis 1946, 42–3; *SC Combination Laws* 1825, 2; J. Loch to (?), 1 Feb. 1815, StRO Sutherland M/2/2/2; Machin 1958, I, 31–4; J. Scale to J. Jones, 29 May 1823, NLW Maybery 3332.

Common Council of Newcastle to honour an undertaking given at the time of the settlement in 1819 to look into the problem of the spouts, led to a further, and in the event, much more serious, strike in 1822.[98] This strike, beginning in early October, and known in the lore of north-east labour relations as 'the long stop', lasted for ten weeks and ended only with the total defeat of the keelmen. The keelmen's position was weakened by the fact that the withdrawal of their labour primarily affected only the owners above the bridge at Newcastle, since most of the below-bridge owners were already loading directly and were willing to assist the above-bridge owners with compensation to strengthen their resolve not to make concessions to the keelmen. The keelmen, for their part, offered to compromise by agreeing to allow colliers to take on a proportion of their cargoes at spouts: this was quite a usual practice already, since the complete loading of colliers at the spouts set them too low in the water to navigate the narrow, shallow river channel. The strike was accompanied by some violence between the above-bridge keelmen who were not threatened by the spouts and the below-bridge men whose livelihoods were most in jeopardy. The manning of keels by naval personnel with military protection finally broke the keelmen's resistance, and in December they returned to work with no tangible gains.[99] 'This is the first battle the coalowners ever gained over the turbulent body [of keelmen]', wrote Buddle on 13 December.[1]

The formation of legal unions from 1824 briefly intensified strike action, as, for example, in Yorkshire and Scotland. In the latter area an Association of the Operative Colliers of Lanark, Dunbarton, and Renfrew had been formed in 1824 and quickly achieved substantial wage increases and reduced hours of work in Renfrew and Ayr. At the Redding and Brighton collieries on the border of Stirlingshire and West Lothian the owner, the Duke of Hamilton, refused to concede wage increases. After a four-month-long strike accompanied by some violence against blacklegs, the miners were obliged to return to work without any gains.[2] Already by 1825, with some modification of the freedom to form unions conceded in 1824, the environment was becoming more hostile again, and the low level of demand following the financial crisis of 1825–6 discouraged major strike action in the late 1820s. Serious labour problems began to build up, however, in 1830, a year of widespread social disturbance. A major

---

[98] Printed notice, 20 Oct. 1819, TWRO Tyne Keelmen 394/42.
[99] Rowe 1969.
[1] J. Buddle to W. M. Pitt, 13 Dec. 1822, NEI Buddle 22/81.
[2] Campbell 1979, 62–73.

confrontation was delayed until the following year, but the coal strike of 1831 falls outside the scope of this volume.

In negotiating with owners and organizing strike action in the eighteenth and early nineteenth centuries miners were handicapped by a lack of enduring organizations. In the North-east, and to a lesser extent in other coalfields, negotiations for the annual binding, however, created, at least from the later eighteenth century, situations in which employers were forced to negotiate; and this formalizing of contacts was a valuable experience for both sides in the practicalities of modern industrial relations. But the binding negotiations, though they contributed on both miners' and employers' sides to the formation of combinations, also served not infrequently to polarize attitudes and exacerbate relations. There is much evidence, however, that the miners approached negotiations with employers with much realism and responsibility. Sir John Hussey Delaval's agent, for example, in an excess of zeal during a strike at Hartley colliery in 1800, was anxious to persuade the magistrates to break the strike by committing the leaders to gaol under the Riot Act: but he was obliged to admit the impossibility of doing this since the miners' behaviour was entirely restrained, and, conscious of the riot law, they never assembled in gatherings of more than twelve.[3] When Bristol miners crossed the Avon in 1792 to stop pits working in Somerset 'they behaved very orderly, but said they were determined to carry their point.'[4] And when negotiations over special rates for working in difficult conditions at the Lambton collieries broke down in 1810, the hewers agreed to the arbitration of two independent viewers. The arbitrators found for the owners, and the hewers accepted the decision.[5]

Approaches were often initiated by means of a petition, an appropriate enough procedure for subjects supplicating a sovereign body like a parliament, but deferential in the context of employee-employer relations, though entirely in keeping with the formal traditions of class relations in the eighteenth century. In 1700, for example, the 'Cutters and Drivers of Coal belonging to the several Works of Briton Ferry' petitioned their employer, Sir Thomas Mansel, against a contemplated reduction of output and wages.[6] In the North-east petitions were apparently a common method of approach to the annual binding negotiations. Hair has traced such a petition from the miners of Bigges Main colliery on Tyneside in

[3] T. Fenwick to Sir John Hussey Delaval, 5 May 1800, NuRO Delaval ZDE 4/24/22.
[4] Capt. George Monro to Henry Dundas, 9 Aug. 1792, quoted in Aspinall 1949, 6.
[5] NEI Buddle 34/II/61–2.
[6] Phillips 1931–2, 76.

1805 requesting higher prices for hewing, higher wages for other workers, increased binding money, increased pay for miners off work through sickness, and the appointment of one John Storey as a 'Boansetter'.[7] At other times, believing that the justice of their cause must lead to the triumph of right, the miners employed lawyers in the role of public relations officers to draft broadsheets, pamphlets, and newspaper announcements. This tactic was employed by the keelmen in the early stages of their last struggle in 1822, and was also adopted by the miners of Cowpen colliery in Northumberland in 1805.[8]

It was a fact, however, that peaceful persuasion was capable of achieving only limited results so that in many instances the miners felt constrained to adopt a more threatening attitude. Persuasion by the reduction of output—the eighteenth-century equivalent of 'working to rule'—was sometimes attempted. For piece-workers this had the advantage of not breaching contracts. This method was evidently employed on a wide scale in Scotland in 1797 and on Tyneside in 1825.[9] In Scotland, the limiting of output was achieved by the enforcement of a rigorous 'closed shop' among the hewers which was moderately effective between the 1790s and the mid-1820s. Hewers monopolized the actual production of coal and none were admitted to the status of hewer except those that the hewers' associations chose to accept. This control over the key labour supply by the workers rather than by the employers was not seriously challenged by the Scottish coalowners until the 1820s when, in response to the massive growth of demand from the iron industry, they began to dilute the hewing 'aristocracy' by floods of inexperienced miners recruited from the ranks of labourers, handloom weavers, and Irish immigrants. Thus were sowed the seeds of stormy labour relations after 1830.[10]

The strike weapon, the obvious resort, was, however, in the context of the eighteenth and early nineteenth centuries, surrounded by difficulties and constraints. In the absence of durable organizations or even of a tradition of union loyalty, there was an ever-present problem of securing a sufficient backing to confront an employer with an effective withdrawal of labour. Solidarity was sought by the administration of oaths at the semi-masonic rituals of brotherings,[11] but much effort had to be devoted to persuade fellow-miners to

[7] Hair 1965, 5.
[8] Rowe 1969, 113; J. Bryers to Sir John Hussey Delaval, 24 Mar. 1805, NuRO Delaval ZDE 4/27/33.
[9] ScRO Leven and Melville GD26/V/369; NEI Buddle 36/IV/127.
[10] Campbell 1979, 13–17, 72–6.
[11] SC Combination Laws 1825, 2; Campbell 1979, 41–2.

join strikes to make them effective. 'The miners of Ayrshire,' wrote a coalowner in 1793, 'have among them what they call "brother-ings", which seems to be something like the mason-word. It is some solemn oath or engagement, to stand by each other. . . . The effect is, that they are generally united, and if the majority in the pit agree to make an idle day the rest must do the same.'[12] Some attempts were made to raise strike pay. Buddle reported that the Jarrow miners on strike in 1825 expected to receive 15s. per week from their union.[13] Friendly society funds were occasionally used improperly for this purpose, as at Tipton in the Black County in 1822 and during the Tyne keelmen's strike of the same year, while begging in neighbouring towns was even resorted to. After the formation of formal, legal unions in 1824, strike funds became available, and, exiguous though resources must have been, mutual financial support was occasionally made available.[14] Miners at Plessey and Hartley collieries gathered a subscription in support of the Cowpen miners in 1805, and the Tyne miners offered financial assistance to the keelmen in 1822. The miners at Redding in Stirling-shire were supported by subscriptions from several other Scottish coalfields.[15]

In the last resort, however, the enforcement of a strike not infrequently led to tougher methods of persuasion. Owners had to be prevented, by the extension of a dispute with one owner to all collieries in a district, from helping each other, while deliveries from stocks had to be stopped to bring financial pressure to bear on owners. The latter technique was tried, for example, by Wednes-bury and Tipton miners in the Black Country in 1821. Threats of violence were not uncommon in the effort to close neighbouring, competing collieries during a strike. The Cowpen miners in Northumberland, for example, were said in April 1800 to be setting out to the neighbouring Hartley colliery armed with bludgeons to bring out the miners there. The Clydach miners in South Wales were reported in 1823 to have broken the windows of fellow-workers who failed to join their strike. When the miners at Hebburn colliery on Tyneside refused the owners' offer for binding terms in 1826, in an effort to prevent the owner taking on others in their place 'they send out parties daily to watch all the roads leading to the Colly. and stop and intimidate all strangers and men from other Colls. from

---

[12] Anon., *Considerations on the present scarcity and dearness of coals in Scotland* (Edinburgh, 1793), quoted by Campbell 1979, 14.

[13] NEI Buddle 36/IV/130.

[14] Aspinall 1949, 356; Rowe 1969, 118; NEI Buddle 36/I/128.

[15] J. Bryers to Sir John Hussey Delaval, 24 Mar. 1805, NuRO Delaval ZDE 4/27/33; J. Buddle to W. M. Pitt, 10 Nov. 1822, NEI Buddle 22/66; Campbell 1979, 68.

coming near the place.' Blacklegs were reported to have had their ears cut off during a strike near Edinburgh in 1823.[16]

Finally, if a show of force was ineffective, working was prevented by the outright blocking of pits. Two miners, for example, were convicted in 1789, after pleading guilty, of attempting to set fire to Shiremoor colliery on Tyneside and damaging a building there in the course of a strike.[17] At about that time it was reported that, in order to 'lay in' other collieries, Wearside miners on strike would 'hang on a corf, filled with stones, at the same time hanging on a clag. The weight of the corf moved the gin, and as the former descended, the latter gained velocity, until the clag, flying out in the air, knocked away the supports of the gin, and laid it on its side, thus rendering it totally unfit for use, and thereby putting a stop to all work for some time to come.' This practice had evidently ceased by the 1820s.[18] Keelmen were known to sink keels during the strikes. During a strike in Shropshire in 1821 pumping engines were put out of action and blacklegs threatened, while Wigan miners on strike in 1792 supported their pay demands with threats of 'pulling up the engines, throwing down the wheels and filling in the pits'.[19]

Violence of these kinds, however, was probably rare, anger and determination being expressed by the miners more often in the form of what was described by magistrates in this period as 'riotous assembly'. Indeed, action by miners in pursuance of their desire for better wages and conditions of employment was severely circumscribed by the resources of the law and the use of the military available to their employers. Collective action by owners, to be sure, was much easier to organize than among miners. There were fewer of them and they had fewer problems of communication and meeting. Many coalowners, in any case, were magistrates. Even during the period of the prohibition of combinations, while rarely failing to invoke the full resources of the law against illegal combinations of the miners, the equal illegality of their own combinations seemed not to matter to the authorities. The Joint Durham and Northumberland Coal Owners' Association was particularly active during the last twenty years of the Anti-Combination Laws not so much in opposing miners' combinations under the laws of 1799 and 1800, as in using their own collective strength in countering the

[16] J. Bryers to Sir John Hussey Delaval, 29 Apr. 1800, NuRO Delaval ZDE 4/24/61; J. Scale to J. Jones, 31 May 1823, NLW Maybery 3333; NEI Buddle 41/109; Campbell 1979, 62.
[17] NuRO Quarter Sessions QSO 13/211–3.
[18] 'The Pitman's Pay', NuRO Society of Antiquaries ZAN M18 18/Preface 6–8.
[19] Metcalfe 1937, 13; A. C. B. Mercer, 'The Cinderloo affair', Shropshire Magazine, 17 (1966), 22–3.

activities of the miners. Thus in 1809 the Association's management committee agreed that 'the expence attending the late stop of the keelmen to be paid out of the general fund of the Trade', and in 1825 the Tyne committee, considering a strike of miners at Jarrow colliery, agreed that 'the owners of Jarrow colliery should receive the support of the Coal Trade at large to protect them against such illegal conduct of their workmen.' In the following year both Tyne and Wear committees joined to raise £1,000 to compensate the owners of Jarrow colliery for their losses in resisting the strike. In the great struggle of the keelmen against the spouts in 1822 the Tyne committee decided to leave owners to fight the keelmen individually, but 'with the understanding that they [the Association] will bear the expence of any law proceedings that may arise on this occasion out of the general fund of the Trade'.[20]

Employers saw nothing wrong in victimization—the dismissal of 'ringleaders', the leaders of combinations or unions. It was to be a long time before unions were strong enough to combat this weapon of the employers. Employers in most coalfields and at all periods believed that their best hope of securing submission of their workers lay in refusing to employ strike leaders. Lord Elphinstone ordered that leaders of the strike at his Scottish colliery in 1743 be discharged. The agent at Coalpitheath colliery in the Bristol coalfield was advised in 1783 not only not to re-employ the ringleaders of a strike but also the husbands of 'the most outrageous women'. Strike leaders were not taken on after the Yorkshire miners' strike of 1819 or after the Jarrow colliery strike of 1826. The keelmen's strike of 1822 was partly a consequence of the failure of a number of fitters to honour their undertaking after the 1819 strike that there should be no victimization.[21] The occupation by miners of tied houses provided employers with a further weapon. It was, of course, a corollary of dismissal that a miner lost his right to continue occupying a colliery house. There is very little actual evidence of the use of eviction as a weapon in the hands of employers, but it is unlikely that they always resisted such a temptation. Buddle recorded in his working diary of Hebburn colliery that in the strike of 1826 he sent eviction notices to union leaders, giving them only two days to leave their colliery houses. Four days after serving the notices he had three men evicted by the parish constable aided by six constables from

[20] NuRO Joint Coal Owners' Association 263, Minute book 1805–15, 127; 1822–3, 21, 55, 57, 63–5; 1825–6, no pagination, minutes for 12 and 19 Nov. and 3 Dec. 1825, 14 Jan. 1826.

[21] Lord Elphinstone to (?), 2 Mar. 1745, ScRO Dundas of Dundas: (?) to J. Smith, 25 July 1783, BRO Ashton Court AC/AS 97/10; Machin 1958, I, 32–4; NEI Buddle 36/IV/130; Rowe 1969, 111.

Newcastle. Three days later the strike collapsed and the miners accepted binding on the employer's terms.[22]

Trouble-makers among the keelmen and seamen could be relatively easily disposed of by encouraging or allowing their impressment by the press-gang. When nearly 5,000 men were recruited for the navy from the Tyne and Wear between 1792 and 1800 alone, the fitters and shipmasters would have been less than human had they not encouraged some selectivity by the recruiting and impressing officers.[23] The 1719 strike of keelmen was allegedly broken by the impressment of leaders.[24] It is not easy to judge whether the dismissal and eviction of strike leaders was so common that it was scarcely worthy of notice in the records that have come down to us, or that it was not noticed because it was very rare.

At all events, the employers were so comprehensively supported by the law that they really had little need to resort to such tactics. As we have seen, the Anti-Combination Laws of 1799 and 1800 were rarely invoked, if only because the law in fact already provided a wide-ranging armoury of weapons for use by employers when they felt strong enough to risk the provocation that their deployment necessarily involved. The arrest of two miners from Flockton colliery in Yorkshire at the time of the 1819 strike, for example, was probably not ordered under the Anti-Combination Laws. They were sentenced to three months imprisonment 'for enticing colliers to enter into an illegal combination.'[25] But mining employment in most coalfields was organized within some system of bonds or agreements, and a strike in these circumstances necessarily involved breach of contract, giving employers an automatic opportunity for arrest and prosecution if they chose to take it. Sir John Hussey Delaval's agent at Hartley colliery was advised by a magistrate in 1800 that he could, if he wished, order strike leaders to appear before the magistrates at Tynemouth on the grounds that they had broken their contracts, and, if they refused to appear, the constables had power to arrest them, calling, if need be, for assistance from the military.[26] Where bonds were ineffective the Masters and Servants Acts provided comparable legal support, and the 1747 Act made specific and severe reference to miners, colliers, pitmen, and keelmen.[27] To make doubly sure, from the 1770s many north-east owners inserted a clause in their annual bonds obliging the men to agree to work without 'sticking or combining.' And the law against breach of contract was

[22] NEI Buddle 41/110–3. [23] Hair 1965, n.6.
[24] Metcalfe 1937, 10. [25] Machin 1958, I, 32–4.
[26] T. Fenwick to Sir John Hussey Delaval, 5 May 1800, NuRO Delaval ZDE 4/24/22.
[27] 20 Geo.II, c. 19.

indeed invoked on occasion against miners. When some putters at Hartley colliery set a limit in 1760 to the quantity they would drive in a day, the viewer prosecuted them and they were committed to the House of Correction for a month. This action invoked a strike aimed at securing their release. Warrants were also taken out against keelmen during the 1822 strike for the offence of bond-breaking.[28]

In the event of violence during strikes the employers were equally well protected. Probably in response to, rather than in anticipation of, physical damage to mine equipment during strikes, a series of acts was passed in the middle decades of the eighteenth century specifying offences and ordering severe penalties (up to seven years transportation) for drowning or setting fire to mines during industrial disputes.[29] In the last resort, however, almost any kind of demonstration or threatening activity by miners during strikes was sufficient to allow their arrest and imprisonment. Two miners were arrested during a strike at Walbottle colliery on Tyneside in 1789 and, after pleading guilty to 'riotous assembly', were fined 1s. and imprisoned for three weeks. During a strike of Wear miners in 1810 no fewer than 159 were imprisoned in the Bishop's stable in Durham city. During the Jarrow colliery strike of 1825 the viewer, Buddle, committed thirty-five trade unionists to the House of Correction. Later, when miners' wives tried to prevent blacklegs from returning to work, two of them followed their menfolk to prison for assaulting and hindering men from going to work. The strike was only ended on Christmas Eve on condition that the imprisoned miners were freed: it seems that the owners were able to intervene in the course of justice to the extent of having this demand complied with.[30]

The actual arrest of strike leaders, of course, was not necessarily an easy task for the parish constables of the eighteenth and early nineteenth centuries. But they could, and frequently did, enlist the support of the army and navy. The owners, for example, called in troops from Newcastle during a strike of Wearside miners in 1781. Four miners were arrested and subsequently imprisoned. When the Dragoons were called in during the Tyneside strike of 1809, nearly three hundred miners were arrested, though this was insufficient to end the strike. The intervention of the military on Tyneside in 1765 and at Wigan in Lancashire in 1792, however, was effective.[31] When the military were resisted, on the other hand, events could take a serious turn. On 2 February 1821, in the course of a strike over

[28] Hair 1965, 6; R. Brown to Sir John Hussey Delaval, 16 May 1760, NuRO Delaval ZDE 6/3/3; Rowe 1969, 113.

[29] 10 Geo.II, c.32; 17 Geo.II, c.40; 24 Geo.II, c.57; 31 Geo.II, c.42; 8 Geo.III, c.29.

[30] NEI Buddle 36/IV/130–8.

[31] Beastall 1975, 32–3; Scott thesis 1946, 42–3; Webb 1921, 7; Aspinall 1949, 9.

wage reductions in Shropshire, the yeomanry were sent in after engines had been put out of action and blacklegs threatened. Some two to three thousand miners assembled to resist them and answered the reading of the Riot Act with a shower of cinders. In the ensuing battle, subsequently known as 'Cinderloo', the yeomanry finally retaliated by opening fire, killing one miner, and mortally wounding another. Many prisoners were taken, of whom one was subsequently convicted and hanged and several sentenced to nine months hard labour.[32] There were no deaths in the conflict between keelmen, army and navy in the 'long stop' of 1822, but much serious fighting took place as keelmen endeavoured to stop the movement of keels down-river. A strike of colliers' seamen at Shields in 1815 was only broken by a combined operation of special constables, naval seamen, marines, and troops ordered by the Home Secretary.[33]

An interesting light on the use of the military by employers in the conduct of their industrial relations is thrown by a letter written by John Buddle in 1830 to one of Lord Durham's agents. The agent, H. Morton, had evidently suggested to Buddle the formation of a new 'Corps of Special Constables' in readiness for the labour troubles that were then foreseen.

Although I should deem the formation of such a Corps expedient in the event of any commotion among the Colliery population [replied Buddle], I doubt very much the prudence in the present satisfied and languid state of the whole body of colliery Labourers, of manifesting any appearance of apprehension or distrust of them by *openly* taking any measures of precaution.

At the same time, however, I think it might be prudent for us *privately* to organise and arrange a plan for raising a powerful body of Special Constables ready to be embodied on the shortest notice. Each Colliery might appoint leaders or officers from the Agents, Viewers, Overmen, Deputies,etc., and the whole plan might be communicated to the confidential persons amongst them in each concern with written instructions how to proceed on the shortest notice.

Stations might be fixed at the different Collieries as rallying points on any alarm being given and proper measures should be concerted for concentrating any part of the whole of the parties from the different stations, in case of need, at any particular point with the least possible delay. Of course, as many individuals would be mounted on horses and appointments could be provided for.

We ought each to form a list of the names of the persons proper to compose the Staff of our respective Corps, and to name our Stations. We ought also to ascertain how many men we can mount at each concern.

We, that is to say, yourself, Redhead, Stobart Morris and John Wade might meet privately in all this and digest a plan of general co-operation in case of need.

[32] A. C. B. Mercer, 'The Cindaloo affair', *Shropshire Magazine*, 17 (1966); 22–3; I. J. Brown, 'The miners' revolution', ibid., 19 (1968), 32.
[33] Rowe 1969, 115–19; Milne 1977, 230–1.

The whole Staff of Special Constables might at any time be sworn in in a few hours, and I have never seen the least difficulty in getting as many 'Rank and File' for this sort of service as were necessary. They are always paid their ordinary wages and I have always found the best men prefer entering the ranks to protect their masters' property, to joining the mob.

The mounted men ought to have pistols, and no weapon, the sabre excepted, is equal to the common 'Pick Shaft' with a peg and string at the small end to form a handle or hilt—for either Horse or Foot—they ought to be painted like Constable Stores. The propriety of having a few Muskets at the head-quarters of each Colly. for the Foot is for consideration. I shall be pleased to confer with you further on this subject tomorrow at Newcastle.[34]

This seems to be preparation for class war with a vengeance, yet in the context of the usual nature of industrial relations for a long period before 1830 it was not especially dramatic. In the absence of formalized negotiations, labour relations were necessarily conducted against a background of near-violence. In the event, most of the activity took the form of noise, threats, and ritual confrontation, and casualties seem to have been surprisingly few. For all the mobilization and display of force, both sides showed a keen grasp of realities and a readiness to compromise. When stands were made, as by the miners against the introduction of leaving certificates in the North-east in 1765 and against January bindings in 1765 and 1809, or by the employers in defence of spouts in 1822, the choice of issues seems to have been rational. For all the array of weapons at the service of the employers, they conceded part or even the whole of the miners' demands on many occasions. Owners gave way to some or all of the miners' demands backed by strike action at Hartley colliery in 1793 and 1798, to the claims for binding money in the North-east in 1809, to the demands of the miners at Nant-y-glo colliery in South Wales in 1822, and doubtless on many other occasions that have not found their way into the records.[35] Miners were, as we have seen, generally successful in driving up their wages, though it may never be possible to judge how far this success was due to militancy and how far to the failure of the supply of skilled labour to match the persistent growth of demand for it. Certainly trade unionism, in so far as that phrase implies some degree of both permanence and at least regional organization, played virtually no part at all in labour relations in the mining industry before 1824. None the less the miners demonstrated throughout the eighteenth and early nineteenth centuries a real flair for extemporary organiza-

[34] J. Buddle to H. Morton, 10 Dec. 1830, LEA MP11/10.

[35] J. Crooks to Sir John Hussey Delaval, 13 Feb. 1793, NuRO Delaval ZDE 4/6/40; J. Bryers to Sir John Hussey Delaval, 5 Aug. 1798, ibid., 4/23/60; Scott thesis 1946, 40; Aspinall 1949, 352–3.

tion as occasion demanded. The peculiar isolation of both working and living environments as well as the discipline demanded by the dangers of the occupation no doubt contributed considerably to this ability. It is to these aspects of the miners' lives that we must now turn.

Chapter 12

The Mining Community

i. *Health and accidents*

Mining was, as it remains today, a dangerous occupation. To the normal, industrial dangers of working with heavy machinery were added those inherent in underground work—roof falls, flooding, the problems of explosive and toxic gases, and the remorseless destruction of miners' respiratory systems by work in dust-laden atmosphere. And in the period up to 1830 there were no legislative safety controls or government inspectors. Safety levels were set by viewers who, in many instances, set high standards and enforced them with vigour; but viewers were servants of the owners who rarely came face to face with their workers or with the dangers faced daily by them, and who were in the business of mining for profit. For economic reasons, then, mining was often carried on in conditions that were less than perfectly safe. Occasional accidents involving loss of life were accepted as unavoidable by all concerned—owners, viewers, and the miners themselves. This resignation to a running toll on the lives of miners was abetted by an inadequate scientific understanding of the conditions that gave rise to accidents and by equipment insufficiently robust to withstand the forces unleashed by explosions and inundations.

The limited scale of mining in the early eighteenth century seems normally to have kept accidents and fatalities to fairly low levels, but an accident at Bensham colliery on Tyneside in 1710 which, rather exceptionally for the period, killed no less than seventy-five miners was a stern warning of the dangers that lay ahead. By the end of the eighteenth century and the early years of the nineteenth, with the increase in scale and depth of pits, especially in the North-east, disasters mounted to reach a scale that began, even at that relatively callous period, to cause anxiety, if not to the acquiescent miners themselves or to their employers, at least to humanitarians in the mining areas. Disasters involving severe loss of life became monthly rather than annual occurrences.

Although official statistics relating to deaths from accidents in mines were not collected and published until the mid-nineteenth century,[1] there is, at least for the North-east, a great deal of random

[1] Hair 1968, 545–6.

information on the subject, particularly for the late eighteenth and early nineteenth centuries. While this information reveals a scale of mortality that was horrifying and would be wholly unacceptable in the twentieth century, it is none the less seriously incomplete as a record of colliery fatalities. Probably most major accidents were noted, as were a great many involving only one or two deaths, but some of the smaller accidents, as well as all accidents in some coalfields, seem to have left no record.

The best-known and most widely quoted estimates of mining fatalities were those prepared for the Select Committee on Accidents in Mines of 1835. This committee estimated that there had been 1,125 deaths in the North-east during the preceding twenty-five years and 954 in all the remaining coalfields put together.[2] The committee's estimate, in its turn, was drawn from returns from coroners in England and Wales that had been published in the previous year.[3] The returns enumerated 949 deaths, but admitted to being seriously incomplete. No returns were received from coroners in Durham, Northumberland, Leicestershire, Worcestershire, Glamorgan, and several colliery districts of Lancashire. The absence of returns from the North-east is explained by the custom of not holding inquests on miners killed at work until these were expressly ordered in August 1814. There can be no doubt that this order was provoked by the campaign for mine safety initiated in the previous year.[4] More seriously, it was a return, as its title indicated, of deaths from cokedamp and firedamp only. A particularly conscientious return from the West Riding of Yorkshire gave some indication of the extent to which this limitation left the enumeration far short of the actual total of mining fatalities: this recorded 23 deaths from chokedamp, 93 from firedamp, and 230 from other causes. If the coroners in other counties made their returns (none of which were differentiated in this way), as they were requested, strictly in terms of deaths from chokedamp and firedamp only, they must seriously have undercounted all mining fatalities. The absence of Scotland from the return was a further major omission: no attempt seems to have been made at any time before 1835 to estimate the scale of mining fatalities in Scotland.

For the North-east the 1835 committee relied, in the absence of returns from the coroners, on the work of John Sykes. A list

---

[2] *SC Accidents 1935*, iv.

[3] *Return of the Number of all Persons who have been lost or destroyed by Choke Damp and Fire Damp in Mines and Collieries in the different Counties of England and Wales . . . from Returns made by Coroners since the Year 1810*, PP 1834 (595) XLIX.371.

[4] Handbill by 'A Looker On', *Colliery Juries and Inquests* (n.d. but almost certainly 1815), in NEI Bell 14/8/59-60.

of fatal accidents in the North-east compiled by Sykes and covering the whole period from the late seventeenth century to 1830 gives the appearance of completeness and care in compilation.[5] Sykes published his list in 1830, but in 1835, presumably with the needs of the Select Committee of that year in mind, he revised it and brought it up to the end of 1834. His revision appears on a copy of the 1830 pamphlet annotated in his own handwriting.[6] While the 1835 committee estimated 1,125 fatalities in the North-east for the period 1810 to 1834, Sykes's original list enumerated only 790. Though his 1835 annotations added a further 126 up to the end of 1834, they contain no entries between November 1808 and August 1830. Further, it cannot be known whether the 1835 committee took into account the 101 lives lost in the Wallsend disaster of 18 June 1835. A further list of North-east fatalities, claiming to be the most complete list 'that has ever yet appeared in print', and covering the period 1799 to 1840, was prepared by J. R. Leifchild for the Children's Employment Commission of 1842. This was avowedly based on Sykes's work but supplemented by information from James Mather of South Shields and a number of viewers. For the period 1810 to 1834 Leifchild enumerated 958 fatalities.[7]

The 1835 committee was certainly wise not to accept Sykes's list as complete, though it had no basis other than guesswork for correcting it. Where independent information is available, Sykes's list can be shown to be fallible. He makes no reference, for example, to an explosion in a Gateshead colliery in the year 1700 in which over one hundred men were reputed to have lost their lives.[8] His list for the year 1815 enumerated five accidents in which 166 miners lost their lives. But a record kept by Buddle for that year listed thirty-three accidents involving the loss of 198 lives.[9] The difference is to be explained by the inclusion in Buddle's list of a larger number of accidents involving only one or two deaths.

Sykes's list may be shown to be incomplete also by reference to returns collected from both Tyneside and Wearside collieries by the

[5] Sykes 1830, 1–4. Sykes incorporated his data on mining accidents in his *Local Records* of 1833. An identical list to Sykes's, but omitting his accidents not caused by explosions, and covering the period October 1805 to November 1828, was published in a broadsheet *The State of the Coal Mines* (Newcastle, n.d. but probably 1829) (copy in NuRO 602/25/12), and copied in the *Tyne Mercury* for 12 May 1829 (copy in NuRO 602/25/13). It is probable that this broadsheet was produced for the benefit of the Lords Select Committee that reported in 1830.

[6] Annotated copy of Sykes 1830 in NEI Forster 49/19/no pagination.

[7] *Report of Children's Employment Commission* 1842, 547. Leifchild's list was reproduced by Dunn 1848, 237; and by H. and B. Duckham 1973, 15.

[8] J. Clephan, 'Coal-mining in old Gateshead. Explosion in "The Stony Flatt" ', *AA*, n.s. 11 (1886), 224.

[9] NEI Buddle 30/3–38.

Joint Coal Owners' Association covering the period 5 April 1811 to 31 July 1815. These returns were probably collected in the late summer of 1815 as a result of the agitation that led to the engagement of Sir Humphry Davy to investigate the possibility of designing a safety-lamp. During this period of four and one-third years, according to Sykes, there were twelve fatal accidents which cost a total of 358 lives; but the Association's table show that there were accidents involving fatalities in no less than thirty-one out of thirty-three collieries listed as having made returns, involving the loss of 440 lives. It seems likely that Sykes's list included only major accidents and principally (though not exclusively) those caused by explosions. But even the Association's Table, in respect of which Hair was inclined to believe that 'it is unlikely that there were any deliberate errors' may not have been complete. They did not, of course, include landsale collieries. Then, as Hair pointed out, some seasale collieries did not submit returns. Six major Tyneside collieries and three Wearside collieries or colliery groups, including all the Vane-Tempest mines, failed to make returns, and though none of these collieries figure in Sykes's list, or in Buddle's 1815 list, the gap in Sykes's annotations covering this period may conceal fatalities there. When thirty-one out of the thirty-three collieries actually making returns reported fatal accidents within this period, it seems improbable that all the nine that failed to make returns escaped without any fatalities. And those not making returns cannot wholly avoid the suspicion that they had something discreditable to conceal.[10]

Another source of error in the Association's 1811–15 tables is revealed by comparison with a copy of the only one of the extant individual returns from which the tables were compiled. Hebburn colliery, which sent in a joint return with Jarrow, reported a total of eighteen deaths; but only sixteen were reported in the Tyneside table. Since in all other respects the table reproduced all the details from this individual return correctly, it may amount to no more than a minor clerical error. It happens, however, like all the other reports, to under-count the actual fatalities.[11]

Occasional references in coroners' records reveal mining deaths that have not found their way into any of the known accounts. The Wigan coroner's records, for example, refer to three mining deaths in that eight-year period for 1804 to 1811. Those for the Liberties of Cockermouth and Egremont, which include all the Cumberland mining district, cover the whole period from 1700 to 1830 with

[10] The Tyneside table is in NuRO Joint Coal Owners' Association 263, Minute book 1805–15, 263–4; and the Wearside table in ibid., 261–2.
[11] NEI Forster 49/16/6.

only a five-year gap in the late 1740s. They record the deaths in mining accidents of eighty-three miners, half occurring after 1800. There are similar coroners' records of mining deaths in the Coventry area from 1727 to 1752 embracing probably all the then-active area of the Warwickshire coalfield; and for Gloucestershire for the years 1795 and 1818 which cover the Forest of Dean and Bristol coalfields. Shropshire coroners' records reveal that in the first twenty years of the nineteenth century no fewer than 267 men and boys were killed in mining accidents in that county.[12] Apart from isolated press reports, these coroners' lists are, so far as is known, the sole records of deaths from mining accidents outside the North-east.

Press reports are an unreliable source, however, if only because, as the *Newcastle Journal* reported in the wake of a major disaster at Fatfield colliery on Wearside in March 1767,

as so many deplorable accidents have lately happened in Collieries, it certainly claims the attention of Coalowners to make a provision for the distressed widows and fatherless children occasioned by the Mines, as the catastrophe from foul air becomes more common than ever; yet, as we have been requested to take no particular notice of these things, which in fact could have very little good tendency, we drop the further mention of it.

'It is from such injunctions laid upon newspaper editors', wrote John Sykes in the preface to his 1830 list, when quoting this comment, 'that these occurrences for a great number of years were kept as much as possible from the publick.' Yet, when Sykes added annotations to his list in 1835, he wrote in his own hand on the first page: 'Only 50 copies printed. Not for sale.' Reticence remained the rule, it seems, right through to the 1830s.[13]

Table 12.1 sets out the fatalities over the whole period from 1710 to 1834 in the North-east as recorded by Sykes in 1830 but including his hand-written additions of 1835. The Table is useful for indicating the trend of fatalities over time, but does, of course, seriously underestimate their scale. Table 12.2 lists mining fatalities recorded by coroners over the whole period in the counties of Glamorgan and Cumberland, and is much more likely to be more accurate. While the Glamorgan record covers the greater number of accidents in the South Wales coalfield, it cannot, however, be fully comprehensive on account of mines lying just outside the Glamorgan county boundary in Pembrokeshire, Breconshire, and Monmouthshire.

[12] WiRO Coroner's Court Records AB; CuRO Leconfield D/Lec/CR Coroners C; CoRO Private Accession 136/1; GRO D260; *Shropshire County Records, X, Quarter Session Roll* (n.d.), cited by Hair 1968, 556.
[13] NEI Forster 49/19/no pagination.

Table 12.1. *Accidents involving fatalities in north-east mines, 1710–1830, according to John Sykes*

Period	Number of accidents	Number of fatalities	Annual average number of fatalities
1710	1	75	—
1711–42		none recorded	
1743	1	17	—
1744–54		none recorded	
1755–9	2	20	4.0
1760–4	2	6	1.2
1765–9	5	68	13.6
1770–4	1	5	1.0
1775–9	2	26	5.2
1780–4	7	16	3.2
1785–9	5	13	2.6
1790–4	6	90	18.0
1795–9	8	67	13.4
1800–4	1	15	3.0
1805–9	10	111	22.2
1810–14	8	197	39.4
1815–19	13	292	58.4
1820–4	11	162	32.4
1825–9	15	133	26.6
1830	1	42	—

Source: Sykes 1830, 1–4, including additions from annotated copy dated 24 June 1835 in NEI Forster 49/19. The 1835 annotations added 188 deaths to the total of 1,246 for the period 1710 to 1834 shown in the original list of 1830.

Working from the Coal Owners' Association's tables for 1811–15 Hair showed that deaths in the North-east averaged annually 8.1 per 1,000 employed in those years. His estimates for other coalfields produced annual fatality rates for Shropshire between 1800 and 1819 of 4.4 per 1,000, and for the Black Country in 1838 of 7.0 per 1,000. In Hebburn and Jarrow collieries, however, the rates for 1811–15 were 14.3 and 4.9 per 1,000 employees per annum respectively.[14] For purposes of comparison, the figure for the whole of Britain for 1980/1 was 0.17 per 1,000 employed. Hair attributed the high fatality rate in the Black Country to the hazards of roof falls when working the quite exceptionally thick seams of the Ten Yard Coal, and the even higher rate in the North-east to the extreme

[14] NEI Forster 49/16/6. The number of workers employed at Hebburn in 1812 is given in NuRO Joint Coal Owners' Association 263, Minute book 105–15, 167; and for Jarrow in NEI Easton 17/7/65.

Table 12.2. *Coal-mining fatalities in Glamorgan county and the Liberties of Cockermouth and Egremont, Cumberland, 1700–1829*

Period	Glamorgan	Cumberland
1700–9	1	0
1710–19	0	3
1720–9	0	1
1730–9	3	4
1740–9	5	1[1]
1750–9	17	5
1760–9	5	5
1770–9	19	8
1780–9	54	8
1790–9	62	6
1800–9	45	9
1810–19	39	11
1820–9	25	21

Note: [1] The years 1745–9 are missing from the record.
Sources:
Glamorgan: Roberts thesis 1953, 179, from records of Coroner's Inquests and local press reports.
Cumblerland: CuRO   Leconfield   D/Lec/CR, Coroners C.

gassiness of the pits there which led to such a high number of explosions.[15] His view of the differences between the hazards of mining in the two areas is confirmed by a north-easterner's report on the Black Country mines of 1815:

From all the accounts we were able to procure it appeared that accidents by fire were neither so numerous nor any way comparatively so destructive of human life as the mines of this neighbourhood. An eminent surgeon in Dudley after considering the case maturely thought that the number of persons annually burned by explosions of gas did not exceed 50, and that not more than one-tenth of that number died either by the effects of burning or by suffocation in the after damp. We obtained a list of the men and boys who had been burnt to death in Lord Dudley and Ward's collieries at Netherton in the space of about sixteen years which amounted to twelve men and five boys in 30 collieries, and these collieries are considered the most dangerous of all the Dudley mines. The greatest number of fatal accidents which befall the miners in these collieries is occasioned by masses of coal and stone falling from the upper parts of the mine upon the men: and certainly nothing can appear more horrible than one of these

[15] Hair 1968, 550; National Coal Board, *Report and Accounts* 1980/1.

gloomy chambers fifty-six feet in length, 36 in breadth and 30 feet high. The roof being of schistus is of a lighter colour than the coal. . . . Huge masses of the schistus in the parts that are wrought out everywhere lie on the floor.[16]

Thus, in a lifetime of, say, forty years of underground work in the late eighteenth and early nineteenth centuries, a miner might experience a chance of anything between one in twenty and (according to the Hebburn figures) one in two, of being killed at work. All these figures underestimate the risks of underground work since they are based on employment figures that include surface as well as underground workers. As we saw in chapter 10, underground workers might amount in the larger collieries to almost 75 per cent of the total labour force. A very high proportion of all fatalities occurred underground, so that the risks to the underground work-force might be raised by almost one-third.

Tables 12.1 and 12.2 concur in demonstrating a sharp acceleration in the number of fatal accidents in mines from the last two decades of the eighteenth century. When the increase of output is taken into account, however, it is no longer so clear that the accident rate increased, at least if measured by the tonnage of output. In the 1750s and 1760s, fatal accidents in the North-east ran at approximately 3.0 per million tons of coal produced, in South Wales at 15.7, and in Cumberland at 2.9. By the first decade of the nineteenth century the corresponding rates for these three mining regions were 3.2, 2.6, and 1.6, and by the 1820s 4.3, 0.6, and 3.8. Apart from the fact that the South Wales figure for the 1750s and 1760s was pushed out of line by an unusually high number of fatalities in the 1750s (the figure for the 1760s alone is roughly 3.1), these figures do not suggest that the production of coal was becoming more costly in terms of human life; but neither was safety being noticeably improved. Unfortunately the almost total absence of reliable employment estimates makes it impracticable to attempt to estimate changes in rates of fatal accidents per unit of employment over long periods. Using the most reliable estimates of the workforce in the North-east, and assuming that the shortfall in the enumeration of fatalities in the *Report* of the 1835 Select Committee remained roughly constant, Hair has shown that the annual fatality rate per 1,000 employed in the North-east fell from a peak of 4.4 in the years 1815–19 to 1.3 in the late 1820s. The former may, as we have seen, be barely half the true rate, but the trend that these figures show may have been real and a consequence of the progressive adoption of the safety-lamp.[17]

---

[16] NuRO Society of Antiquaries ZAN M14 A9.   [17] Hair 1968, 551.

Whatever the trend in the North-east's accident rate after 1815, immediately before that year there was a sharp increase in fatalities. It is true that the figures were boosted by the terrible disaster at Felling colliery in 1812 when ninety-two miners lost their lives, but the toll of deaths was also raised by three other serious accidents in 1812–13 that each involved more than twenty deaths. Then, in May and June of 1815, there occurred two further major catastrophes. On 3 May Heaton colliery was suddenly flooded by an inundation from a breakthrough into an old working and seventy-five miners were drowned; and on 2 June fifty-seven miners were killed by an explosion in Newbottle colliery on Wearside. If the visit of Sir Humphry Davy to Newcastle in August of that year was not directly connected with these tragic events there can be no doubt that both he and George Stephenson, working simultaneously on their safety-lamps during the second half of 1815, must have drawn an added sense of urgency from them. The whole chain of events leading from Clanny's experiments in 1813 to the invention of the safety-lamps in the autumn of 1815 cannot but have been closely linked to the alarming scale of fatalities between 1812 and 1815. The same concern surely lay behind the collection of accident statistics by the Coal Owners' Association in 1815, the first known attempt in the history of coal-mining to compile such records.

In his evidence to the 1835 Select Committee Buddle asserted that 92 per cent of all north-east fatalities since 1710 had resulted from explosions.[18] This is a correct calculation from Sykes's 1830 list. The overwhelming role of explosions in north-east mining fatalities implicit in these figures was also supported by Leifchild's 1842 statistics which attributed 84.7 per cent of fatalities between 1799 and 1840 to explosions. But these lists tended to ignore accidents arising from other causes, and in a pamphlet of 1814 Buddle committed himself to the view that 'on an average, through this district, I believe that the ordinary and unavoidable casualties in collieries occasion more calamaties than explosions of inflammable air.'[19] The details of accidents in the North-east during the year 1815 among his own papers also bear out the latter statement, while in other coalfields, for which coroners' records permit some analysis, explosions and chokedamp, as Table 12.3 shows, were responsible for an even smaller proportion of total fatal accidents. Fatal accidents in mines occurred from a wide variety of causes, of which explosions were only one. Accidents in shafts arising from rope and chain breakages, roof falls, flooding, fire, and rail accidents were frequent causes of the deaths of miners working underground.

[18] *SC Accidents* 1835, iv.   [19] Buddle 1814, 23.

Table 12.3. *Cause of fatalities in coal-mines, various districts, 1700–1830*

District	Period	Falls in shaft		Roof falls		Explosions and chokedamp		Others[1]	
		number	%	number	%	number	%	number	%
Cumberland	1700–1830	21	25.3	32	38.5	11	13.3	19	22.9
Gower	1700–1832	–	16.2	–	33.8	–	34.8	–	15.2
Warwickshire	1727–52	10	41.7	10	41.7	0	0.0	4	16.6
Gloucestershire	1795 and 1818	8	34.8	3	13.0	5	21.7	7	30.5
North-east	1815	20	9.8	14	6.8	93	45.4	78	38.0

Note: [1] Includes mainly inundations, underground waggonway accidents, bursting boilers, and other surface accidents.

Sources: Cumberland: CuRO Leconfield D/Lec/CR/Coroners C.
Gower: Roberts thesis 1953, 180.
Warwickshire: CoRO Private Accession 136/1.
Gloucestershire: GRO D260.
North-east: NEI Buddle 30/3–29.

Fatalities were not, of course, the sole tragedies of mining accidents. Many accidents injured miners, leaving some maimed or handicapped for life. 'When there is a catastrophe of this kind', said Buddle in 1830, 'there are not only a great many killed, but a great number wounded and disabled for life; it always produces an immense number of cripples.'[20] The feeble resources of the medical profession at the time restricted rehabilitation after accidents. But in an age that took relatively little interest in recording deaths from mining accidents, it is hardly to be expected that much notice would be taken of mere injuries. We have, indeed, only the rarest of glimpses of the extent of injuries from mining accidents. The most comprehensive is afforded by the returns collected for the years 1811–15 by the north-east Coal Owners' Association. Collieries were asked to report the 'number who have suffered accidents and received smart money or parochial relief for one year ending 31 December 1814'. On the Tyne all but two of the collieries making returns recorded injuries, and at some collieries the numbers were large. Percy Main colliery, for example, recorded one hundred injured, and Walbottle colliery no less than 165. In all, twenty-one collieries reported 599 miners as receiving injuries sufficiently serious to keep them off work, and only three reported no injuries. On Wearside six collieries or owners reported a total of 232 miners injured, while the Lambton collieries differentiated between 120 miners injured in accidents (and included in the total of 232) and 281 miners 'sick'. A further category of the 'number who have become superannuated or disabled and received parochial relief or supported by the Fund', showed forty-seven on Tyneside and fifteen on Wearside. It seems that the former category related to those temporarily put off work by injuries during the year 1814, and the latter to both retirals and those permanently prevented from working as a result of injuries.[21]

One form of injury, however, went virtually unnoticed in the eighteenth and early nineteenth centuries. Much attention has rightly been devoted during the later nineteenth and twentieth centuries to the permanent damage caused to the respiratory system by working in the coaldust-laden atmosphere of ill-ventilated mines. Pneumoconiosis was belatedly recognized, and preventive measures ultimately taken; but before 1830 this seriously debilitating condition was hardly observed, let alone identified. 'In old age asthmatical complaints are, I think, more frequent among Pitmen than their poor neighbours employed in other avocations'—a comment made

[20] SC Lords Coal Trade 1830, 33.
[21] NuRO Joint Coal Owners' Association 263, Minute book 1805–15, 261–4.

in 1807—is the sole reference to respiratory conditions traced in the whole vast corpus of mining records of the eighteenth and early nineteenth centuries.[22]

Not until 1813 was the attention of the medical profession drawn to the unique condition of miners' lungs. In that year Dr G. Pearson identified the black colouring in the bronchial glands and lungs of miners as charcoal. A condition known popularly as 'black spit' and in the medical literature as 'melanosis' had been observed for some time, and was believed to be created by secretion from the blood. Pearson was the first to demonstrate that it was, in fact, caused by coal-dust that had entered the lungs by breathing. The condition was systematically studied during the 1820s by William Thomson, an Edinburgh doctor, who had the opportunity to carry out autopsies on miners, but the results of his investigations and those of his Edinburgh colleague, Dr J. C. Gregory, were not published until the 1830s. The first vital step in the identification of the condition and its cause had been made; but before 1830, as indeed for long after, there was no relief whatever for the miners whose lives were shortened by it nor any consideration given to the problem of air pollution underground.[23]

ii. *Miners' welfare*

The dangers and health hazards to miners raised welfare problems beyond the scale of other occupations, and in the eighteenth and early nineteenth centuries there was, of course, no state provision for industrial injuries nor for widows and dependent relatives beyond the meagre aid of parish poor-relief. In almost all mining communities, as some surveys examined in the next section reveal, there were widows and orphans, and though some of these may have been the simple consequence of the normal low expectation of life of this period, many explicitly acquired this dependent status as a result of mining accidents. The 1811–15 survey of the north-east mining population, for example, specifically categorized 'widows and dependent relatives' in a column adjacent to the enumeration of 'lives lost by accident'. Tyneside in this period counted no fewer than 464 such widows and other dependants, and Wearside 110, though the latter return was seriously incomplete.[24]

In many instances coalowners accepted some responsibility for the dependants of those killed in accidents in their mines. Very early

---

[22] NEI 48/MS report at end of bound volume of pamphlets.
[23] This paragraph is based entirely on Rosen 1943, 195, 248–52.
[24] NuRO Joint Coal Owners' Association 263, Minute book 1805–15, 261–4.

in the eighteenth century sick or injured miners at Griff colliery in Warwickshire were offered allowances of up to half their normal pay, while the Wilkins partnership in Leicestershire awarded cash allowances to the dependants of miners killed in pit accidents, to those prevented from working as a result of accidents, and even during periods of enforced unemployment. At the Lowther collieries in Cumberland in the same period payments were made from the fund accumulated from fines. A single payment of 10s. was made to a dependant on the death of a miner, and sums of between 2s. 6d. and 5s. were paid for injuries. Smaller amounts were payable in the event of sickness and for burials.[25] Similar schemes operated elsewhere in the late eighteenth and early nineteenth centuries. At the collieries on the Earl Fitzwilliam's estate in south Yorkshire payments to injured miners ranged from 1s. 6d. to 7s. per week, while widows received weekly pensions of 2s. 6d. with additional allowances for children not yet earning. In what was clearly an exceptional act of generosity, when Lawwood colliery ceased to operate in 1828, Thomas Wainwright, forced into unemployment at the age of ninety-one, was granted an allowance of 12s. per week.[26] In the North-east payments of this kind were normally left to the discretion of viewers and managers. A demand by Hartley colliery miners in 1793 for an allowance of 5s. per week for pitmen injured in the mine was supported by an assertion that this was the rate paid by Tyne and Wear collieries.[27] In his evidence to the Lords Select Committee that reported in 1830 Buddle suggested that the private charity of coalowners in making provision for widows and injured miners probably ran 'to a much greater extent than they are even themselves aware of'. After a major disaster at his Plane pit in 1823 when fifty-six miners lost their lives, Lord Londonderry paid out over £2,000 to victims and dependants during the ensuing four years.[28]

It is not, of course, possible to demonstrate that *ex gratia* payments of this kind were general throughout the industry, though they appear to have been fairly common. They can rarely be described as generous, but account should be taken of non-monetary supplements in the form of low-rent or rent-free housing and coal supplies. Speaking in 1830 about the dependants of miners killed in pit accidents, Buddle said that 'it is not within my knowledge that any coalowner ever disturbed a widow, after an accident of

[25] White thesis 1969, 173; C. P. Griffin thesis 1969, 88; CuRO Lonsdale D/Lons/W/Collieries and the Coal Trade, 26.
[26] Mee 1976, 50–1.
[27] J. Crooks to Sir John Hussey Delaval, 11 Feb. 1793, NuRO Delaval ZDE 4/6/39.
[28] SC Lords Coal Trade 1830, 33; Heesom 1974, 245.

that sort, or put her out of her house; they have their houses and fuel continued to them as long as they live.'[29]

In a number of instances coalowners supplemented the cash allowances they made by the provision of medical attention. 'It is the practice of some collieries', ran a report from the North-east of 1807, 'tho by no means general, to give a Surgeon a certain yearly sum for drugs and attendance on such of the pitmen or their families who may have suffered from any accident happening in the Colliery, but in all other disorders they provide themselves with Medical Advice.'[30] Such a 'Surgeon to ye colliers' was paid a retainer at Griff colliery at the beginning of the eighteenth century, while another was paid a total of £7. 7s. for his services to the colliers of Pencaitland colliery, Midlothian, between May 1787 and June 1794. This was a trifling sum beside the annual payments made at almost the same period by J. C. Curwen for medical treatment of the colliers at Harrington colliery in Cumberland. Over a six-year period from 1792 to 1797 annual payments averaged £81 per year.[31]

Many owners looked further than the immediate needs of their work-force in support of the wider community. Some, like the owner of a Gloucestershire colliery, who allocated £100 for this purpose in 1820, made periodic donations to 'the Poor' in addition to the routine payment of the poor rate. In 1806 the Lambton collieries spent £10 on New Year's gifts for children.[32] The most usual form of charitable gifts from coalowners, however, was coal itself. The Tyne coalowners, for example, in 1824 acceded to a request from the Vicar of Newcastle for an annual donation of a keel of coals for the town's Lying-in-Hospital, while in Derbyshire thirty-seven poor people in Sherborne were given coal in March 1795 by the owner of a local colliery. The coal was accompanied by gifts of flour and money. At Aberpergwm in South Wales winter gifts of coal to the poor seem to have been a regular practice. 'I think it is too soon to send coal to the poor people', wrote the manager on 20 November 1811, 'as the weather is extremely mild. About Christmas would be more suitable to them, I think.' In Warwickshire, probably to celebrate the reopening of Griff colliery in 1775, the presentation of coal to 300 poor inhabitants of Coventry was turned into a splendid ceremony. Six boatloads of coal were sent

[29] SC Lords Coal Trade 1830, 33.
[30] NEI 48, MS report at end of bound volume of pamphlets.
[31] White thesis 1969, 173; ScRO Hamilton of Pencaitland RH15/119/18/4; 'Account book for medical treatment of colliers at Harrington Colliery at the expense of J. C. Curwen', CuRO Curwen D/Cu/Additional/not numbered.
[32] BRO Ashton Court AC/AS: NEI Buddle 13/125.

by canal to the city, each boat bedecked with flags and accompanied by music from 'a French Horn, Hautboy, Violin and Basoon'.[33]

Clearly the provisions made for needy colliers and their dependants varied enormously from colliery to colliery, and there may have been many owners whose humanity did not extend to this kind of care. From the latter years of the eighteenth century it became more common for miners to make their own provision for these contingencies by means of friendly societies. 'The first and principal object' of the Workington Coal Miners' Society of 1793 'was to make provision for unfortunate sufferers from accidents which occasionally happen in the works, and which no skill or attention can at all times prevent. It proposes also relief against the common infirmities incident to human nature.'[34] In some instances, as for example with the Tyne keelmen, the friendly society was founded on the initiative of the employers, while in other cases the employers made some financial contribution. All miners' friendly societies were local in character, but there is evidence that they were widespread. Such societies existed in Cumberland, for example, at Harrington at least from 1808, while one at Workington was founded in 1793. In Scotland societies had been founded at Rosewell in Midlothian in 1802, at Niddrie in 1806, and at Inveresk and Millerhill in 1823. The proliferation of societies within such a small area suggests that they were restricted to workers at individual collieries. Similarly in Somerset, where a 'brotherly society' had been founded at Pensford in 1769, other societies followed in several places in the early nineteenth century.[35] Earlier societies, such as one founded for the Clerk of Penicuik miners at Loanhead in about 1755 and the Tyne keelmen's fund started as early as 1699, evidently owed much to the initiative or administrative assistance of the coalowners.[36] Northeast viewers, too, organized their own friendly society in 1810. Subscriptions were £5. 7s. per year, with an entrance fee that varied according to age.[37]

Friendly societies were financed by small weekly subscriptions collected from each miner supplemented in some cases by subscriptions from the employer. The mid-eighteenth-century scheme at Loanhead in Midlothian, for example, required each 'coallier' to pay

[33] NCRO Edge DDE22/21; R. Williams to Ann Williams, 20 Nov. 1811, NLW Aberpergwm 60; Thomas Hutchins to Sir Cavalier Newdigate, 22 June 1795, WaRO Newdigate of Arbury CR136/B1771.

[34] CuRO Curwen D/Cu/6/25, 58.

[35] CuRO Curwen D/Cu/6/58; D/Cu/additional/Compartment 6 and 'Colliers Society subscription account books' (not numbered); ScRO Assistant Registrar of Friendly Societies for Scotland FSI/3/23, 35, 17/147, 165; Bulley 1955, 43.

[36] ScRO Clerk of Penicuik GD18/1132; Dendy 1901, 154–5.

[37] NEI Watson 5/26.

in one shilling each year in addition to a weekly subscription of two-pence. These payments were to be deducted from wages by the grieve, and the employer committed himself to add 2s. 6d. weekly. J. C. Curwen agreed to supplement the income of the Workington Miners' Society to the extent of three-tenths of the whole sum sub-scribed by members. Similarly, a general north-east fund set up under the auspices of the Coal Owners' Association in 1812 to replace numerous small, local societies, was to be financed by payments from miners of $\frac{1}{4}d$. in the shilling of their wages and $\frac{1}{4}d$. or $\frac{1}{2}d$. per chaldron shipped from the employers.[38] Other societies depended entirely upon funds collected from the colliers themselves. The 1818 rules of Kilmarnock Coal Cutters Society, for example, called for entrance fees ranging from 3s. for those aged 16–29 to 8s. for those aged 35–9. Entrance at age 40 or over was not permitted, and all members were required to be 'of good character [and] healthy'. Regular subscriptions were 2s. per quarter. The Benevolent Society of Craighall laid down similar conditions, though entry fees were rather higher (but with some remission if the applicant was a son of an existing member) and entry was permitted up to the age of 45.[39]

Employers' motives for adding to their costs in this way were rarely made explicit. It would have been uncharacteristic if they had stemmed wholly from humanitarianism. No doubt they were, in any case, under some pressure to reduce the claims made on local parish funds. One of Buddle's correspondents in 1812 suggested a possible motive when, in supporting the proposals currently before the Joint Coal Owners' Association, he argued that a fund liberally assisted by the owners would be 'an incitement to increase the number of that useful description of workmen, and, by making their desertion from the quarter the cause of exclusion from the privileges of the institution, prevent that proneness to emigration . . .' The fund, he continued, 'would surely have a tendency to civilize such eccentric mortals as pitmen and keelmen generally are'. 'Civilizing' was clearly an important motive behind the Loanhead scheme of 1755, since many of the rules provided for the payment into the fund of fines for absenteeism, swearing, drunkenness, or threatening behaviour.[40]

Funds so collected were used for two main purposes: to pay for the services of a surgeon, and to pay a range of benefits in the form of either lump sums or weekly allowances to widows or to miners

[38] ScRO Clerk of Penicuik GD18/1132; CuRO Curwen D/Cu/6/58; NuRO Joint Coal Owners' Association 263, Minute book 1805–15, 215.

[39] ScRO Assistant Registrar of Friendly Societies for Scotland FS1/2/41, 17/8.

[40] W. Potter to J. Buddle, 8 June 1812, NuRO Joint Coal Owners' Association 263, Minute book 1805–15, 216–17; ScRO Clerk of Penicuik GD18/1132.

themselves in the event of injury, sickness, or unemployment. Some societies, like the Camerton Society in Somerset, employed part of their funds to retain the services of a doctor who attended sick and injured miners in their homes. In the North-east, 'in Collieries where no Surgeon is found by the owner, the pitmen frequently contribute a weekly sum to establish a fund as a yearly salary to a professional man for his attendance on all occasions'. The 'keelmen's groat', the 4*d.* per tide collected from each keel, was used in part to support the Keelmen's Hospital founded in 1701.[41]

Otherwise, society funds were used to pay out a range of cash benefits according to prescribed scales. The early fund at Loanhead colliery in Midlothian paid in 1737 £18 Scots (30s.) on a man's death, and two-thirds of that sum on a woman's death. By the 1750s, while the rules of the fund remained vague, apparently to the point of leaving it to the managers to determine rates of benefit, a widow's allowance of 30s. per year was payable, though this was not to be paid in the first year of widowhood, perhaps because the lump sum payment was held to cover that period.[42] By the early nineteenth century benefit scales had become more formalized. In 1818 the Kilmarnock Coal Cutters Society paid 5s. 6d. weekly to members of at least three months' standing who were confined by sickness to their bed or room, and 4s. to those unable to work but able to get about. These degrees of incapacity had to be certified by a doctor fortnightly. Both these rates were reduced to 2s. weekly after six months. At death (not necessarily as a result of a pit accident) a sum equivalent to 10d. for every member of the society was payable to the next-of-kin. Another Scottish fund, the Benevolent Society of Craighall, paid 4s. per week in 1830 for the first thirteen weeks of certified sickness, 3s. for the next thirteen weeks, 2s. for a third period of thirteen weeks, and 1s. 6d. thereafer so long as the ailment lasted. Funeral benefits of £3 were payable for either a member or his wife, and 15s. for the burial of a child providing that it was not stillborn or illegitimate.[43] The Workington Miners' Society, with the aid of a substantial employer's contribution, offered very liberal benefits in the early years of the nineteenth century. A miner off work through injury received 15s. per week for the first twelve weeks, 8s. for the next twelve weeks, and 5s. thereafter. There was a funeral allowance for members and their families and an allowance of one guinea to married women, presumably

[41] Bulley 1955, 43; NEI 48/MS report at end of bound volume of pamphlets; NEI Miscellaneous 60 ZA/3a/45.

[42] ScRO Clerk of Penicuik GD18/1048, 1132.

[43] ScRO Assistant Registrar of Friendly Societies for Scotland FSI/2/41, 17/8.

employees rather than wives, on the birth of a child. Other rather unusual allowances, such as five guineas to a collier on his marriage have a handwritten note attached to them in the rule book indicating that, in fact, they were not paid.[44]

In the North-east, the Miners' Society founded on the initiative of the Coal Owners' Association and covering miners in all collieries on Tyneside, Wearside, and in Northumberland, paid more generous rates than the Scottish societies, perhaps because the miners' contributions were supplemented by a levy on the employers. In the event of sickness as well as in old age when unable to work, members drew 7s. per week for up to thirty weeks, and thereafter 3s. 6d. On the death of a member a funeral benefit was paid on a sliding scale rising from £1 for a member of one year's standing to £5 for one of five years' membership. Up to £3 was payable for the funeral of a member's wife.[45]

Scales were fixed at rates that were a compromise between what was considered necessary to live on in the absence of wages, and what the funds could afford. These rates, as we have seen, were rarely more than one-third of the wages of a hewer in regular work. None the less the financial position of the societies was often precarious. In the four years 1815–18 the expenditure of the Keelmen's Society regularly exceeded its income. During this period the fund was supporting 138 superannuated members, 182 widows, twenty-two sick keelmen, and six orphans, large numbers of dependants for an occupational group that probably numbered less than one thousand at that time. Yearly income averaged £2,108, and expenditure £2,210, an excess of 4.6 per cent. In contrast, the Harrington Colliers Society in Cumberland enjoyed an income in 1808 of £87. 15s. 10d. while expenditure amounted only to £41. 3s. 2½d. Though the gap had closed somewhat a decade later, the society's accounts for 1817–24 still showed an ample surplus of income over expenditure in every year.[46]

iii. *Housing*

The situation of most coal-mines in the eighteenth and early nineteenth centuries commonly made it unavoidable for owners to provide housing for their miners. The location of mines was necessarily

[44] CuRO Curwen D/Cu/6/58.

[45] *Articles, Rules and Regulations to be observed by the Miners' Society* (Newcastle, 1817).

[46] NuRO Joint Coal Owners' Association 263, Minute book 1819, 37; CuRO Curwen D/Cu/Additional/Compartment 6, and 'Colliers Society Subscription accounts books' (not numbered).

dictated by geological facts rather than social convenience, and the impracticability of long journeys to work required housing adjacent to collieries rather than in the nearest villages. The housing problem created by the development of collieries is well illustrated by the growth of population in the parish of Hetton, County Durham, following the winning of Hetton colliery in the early 1820s. The parish's population in 1801 had been a mere 253, but with the opening of the colliery it had risen in 1821 to 994. Development during the 1820s, however, produced a population in 1831 of 5,951. Housing for miners, of course, required land, and the Hetton Company leased the colliery and did not initially own any land. However, it set about buying land, and in 1823 it bought 28½ acres. By 1827 it had acquired 158 acres and had built 110 houses.[47]

Virtually all collieries in the North-east were forced to take similar action. 'In almost every colliery on the Tyne', ran a report of 1807, 'pitmen are provided with houses by their employers . . . The Occupiers of Collieries made a point of situating the houses as near to the concern as possible; but as the Mine becomes exhausted the distance from the houses to the pits gradually increases, and in some cases extends to 2 or 3 miles.'[48] It seems that on Wearside in the early nineteenth century it was customary to pay miners a travelling allowance when it was not possible for an owner to provide housing close to a colliery. In 1819, as the adoption of steam-power permitted the reduction in the number of horses employed at Rainton colliery on the Vane-Tempest estate, Buddle proposed to convert some stables into pitmen's cottages primarily in order to reduce expenditure on travelling allowances.[49] Twenty-three houses for colliers were among the assets of Loanhead colliery in Midlothian in 1737, seventeen at Cluny Colliery in Fife in 1752, 200 at the Lowthers' Whitehaven collieries in 1788, and 297 at the Marquis of Stafford's colliery at Shelton in Staffordshire in 1796. William Fenton, the Yorkshire coalowner, owned ninety-one miners' cottages in the township of Rothwell in 1816.[50]

Housing was, therefore, both a common and substantial element in mining investment. A valuation of the fixed assets of the collieries owned by the Grand Allies on Tyneside in 1791 listed workmen's houses at £2,280. 16s., or 6.3 per cent of the total assets.[51] Forty pitmen's houses erected at Hartley Main colliery in 1804 were

---

[47] Sill 1979, 3–8.
[48] NEI 48/MS report at end of bound volume of pamphlets.
[49] Heesom 1974, 247.
[50] ScRO Clerk of Penicuik GD18/1066; KM Rothes 40/81/8; Wood, thesis 1952, 42–3; StRO Sutherland D593 M/2/1/1; Goodchild typescript (n.d.), 10., WMDL.
[51] DuRO Strathmore D/St/117.

expected to cost, at £35 each, a total of £1,400. Houses built for Jarrow and Hebburn collieries in 1817 cost £50 each when built of brick but £116 when built of stone, while two houses put up for miners at Lambton colliery in 1805 cost £68 each.[52]

Rents were rarely calculated on an economic basis. Houses, indeed, were frequently provided free, as they were at the Lowther collieries in Whitehaven in the late eighteenth century, at Coed Talon colliery in South Wales, at some Somerset collieries in the 1820s, and at Lochgelly and Grange collieries in Scotland in the 1790s.[53] At the last colliery only married miners were entitled to rent-free housing in the late eighteenth century; single men paid 3d. per week. Colliers at Loanhead in Midlothian paid 2d. per week in the 1750s for their houses, but at Trefarclawdd colliery in South Wales the usual rent in 1808 was two guineas per year, or nearly 10d. per week.[54] Rents were general in the North-east and were deducted at source. The amounts charged, however, were generally low: according to Buddle both house and coal were provided by employers around 1830 for 3d. per week.[55]

It is easier to document the building and letting of miners' housing than it is to determine the nature of the houses built and occupied. The relatively short lives of collieries, and therefore of the housing associated with them, has always been assumed to have led to cheapness and jerry-building. The historian's problem, however, is less the absolute quality of miners' housing than the quality relative to housing available for comparable workers in other industries during the same period. Because both of the geographical shifts of mining and of the rising standards of expectations in housing, it is extremely unlikely that any of the houses built specifically for miners before 1830 still stand anywhere today. One would hardly expect to find running water in working-class housing in this period, and the water-closet was still a luxury available only to the urban wealthy. Thus housing consisted of little more than four walls, a roof, a fireplace, a door, and one or two windows.

Most miners' houses in this period were built in rows—short ones of six or seven houses, often built parallel with cross or head-rows, or long ones, like the 180 houses in two rows running for over

[52] NEI Watson 8/8/419; NEI Forster 49/16/8; NEI Buddle 16/12.

[53] Wood thesis 1952, 42–3; J. Gray to J. Buddle, 27 June 1825, DuRO NCB First Deposit NCB/I/JB/575; Bulley 1955, 41; NLS Minto 13,300; NLS Cadell of Grange Box 12/1.

[54] Wood thesis 1952, 42–3; NLS Cadell of Grange Box 12/1; ScRO Clerk of Penicuik GD18/1080; NLW Wynnstay 106.

[55] SC Lords Coal Trade 1830, 36; and see NEI Buddle 40/202; NuRO 962/10–12; NEI Miscellaneous 60 ZB/8.

half a mile built by the Hetton Company in the mid-1820s to form the community of Easington Lane.[56] A plan of housing on south Tyneside in 1817 showed back-to-back houses, the 'fore house' measuring 15 feet by 18 feet in ground plan and 12 feet high, presumably to allow for two floors, and the 'back house' merely 10 feet deep on its frontage of 18 feet, and with a sloping roof that severely limited head-room in the upper floor. It would just have been possible to divide these houses into two rooms on each floor, if desired.[57] Pitmen's houses built at the Earl of Scarbrough's Lumley colliery on Wearside in the 1770s were single-storey, ten feet high, and seventy-two square feet in area. These were exceptionally small: they could have consisted of no more than a single room eight feet by nine—a mere cubicle. Though built of local stone with brick floors and pantile roofs, they cost only £15 each.[58] In sharp contrast to this poverty, two rows of cottages erected by the Earl of Moira at his Moira colliery in Leicestershire were positively luxurious. The nineteen houses in two stone-built terraces erected in 1811 had long gardens with earth closets and ashpits at the bottom. Each house contained a large front room on the ground floor with a parlour and kitchen at the back, and two large bedrooms upstairs. The Butterley Company in Derbyshire, too, which provided houses for its colliers and iron-workers, built houses in long terraces of twenty to fifty houses. Each house had two rooms downstairs and two upstairs, with both front and back doors. They enjoyed large gardens and each house had its own privy and coalshed in its back yard. A total of 530 square feet in four rooms contrasted sharply with the 72 square feet at Lumley.[59] A detailed study of many rows built by the iron companies for their ironworkers and colliers in the valleys of the eastern sector of the South Wales coalfield between the 1790s and 1830 reveals that two-storey, four-roomed houses were the most usual form of industrial housing. Some rows were reduced in size either by being built back-to-back or by having a 'catslide' roof which reduced ceiling space at the back.[60]

In what degree of comfort did miners live in these houses? Only a single document has come to hand that throws some light on the furnishings and equipment of a miner's house in the eighteenth century. When surrendering all his goods and chattels to his

[56] Sill 1979, 9.

[57] NEI Forster 48/16/8.

[58] Beastall 1975, 28.

[59] C. P. Griffin thesis 1969, II, 507; P. Riden, *The Butterley Company, 1790–1830* (Chesterfield, 1973), 31.

[60] Iron Industry Housing Papers, Nos. 1–8, University of Wales Institute of Science and Technology, Department of Architecture, n.d.

employer, Sir John Hussey Delaval, in 1764 in discharge of his debt, James Spence of Hartley colliery enumerated

two Close Beds and Bedding, one open Bed and Bedding, one Dresser and Cupboard, seven pewter Dishes, six Delf Dishes, twelve Delf plates, one Oak Cupboard, one Chest, two Chairs, one Table, one small Ditto, Two large Boiling pots, one small Ditto, one Water Sheel, one Milk Can, one Spinning Wheel, one Frying pan, one Girdle, one pair of Teamses, one Box Iron and Heaters, six Wood Trenchers, three White Delf Basons, one Looking Glass, one pair of Barrs, one Wood Bowl, one Chimney Crook, and three wood Stoves.

His house was not badly equipped.[61]

Detailed surveys allow us to discover just how many members of miners' families occupied these houses. Fordell colliery in Fife owned 104 houses when its private census was taken on 3 September 1814. Families ranged in size from one to thirteen, though the largest number inhabiting a single house was ten. Families of over ten were allocated two adjacent houses. Thus, Thomas Drysdale and his family, consisting of himself, his wife, five sons, and four daughters, occupied Nos. 1 and 2, Eastmuir houses, North row west end, with one fireplace in each house; and Thomas Muir Nos. 1 and 2, The Saltery, with his wife, three sons, and eight daughters. Most of the single occupants were widows, and the small number of houses occupied by single men suggests that priority was given to married men with families. Out of the 104 houses, six were occupied by widows living on their own, three by single men, nine by widows with children, and one by a widow with a lodger. The mean household size was 4.2 persons. It seems probable, however, that terraces were built of houses of varying sizes. The mean household size of Eastmuir, South row, for example, was 3.3 persons, but of Cuttle-hill, north end, 5.6 persons.[62]

Similar surveys, though not related specifically to housing, generally bear out these statistics of miners' households. A census of the miners and their families of Hartley colliery in Northumberland taken on 1 June 1757 showed 67 family households with a further 14 single men and two widows. Of the 67 family households, 58 were headed by married couples with a total of 142 children. In addition there were two widows with 8 children, and 4 widowers with 5 children. There were 3 households of single men with 7 dependent relatives (parents and sisters). The mean family size of the family households was 4.3, but we do not know whether the single men and widows without dependants lived separately or with

[61] NuRO Delaval ZDE 7/6/9.
[62] ScRO Henderson of Fordell GD172/848.

other families.[63] Another survey of the collier families at Preston-grange colliery (East Lothian) in April 1748 showed 21 family households with 45 children. Only two single men were listed, and there is no mention of widows. Ignoring the two single men, the mean family size was 4.1. Finally, a survey of the families at Jarrow and Hebburn collieries on Tyneside dated 21 July 1815 showed that the 'average number of individuals in each family' was 5.1 at Jarrow and 4.5 at Hebburn.[64]

iv. *Leisure*

What kind of people were miners and their families? What was the quality of their lives ouside the pit? These questions imply that in some ways miners were different from other social and occupational groups in eighteenth and early nineteenth-century society, and the differentiation is a legitimate one. To a very considerable degree they lived in isolation from other people in housing specially built for them close to their pits and away from existing settlements. Their hours of work differed from those in other industries; very often they worked while others slept. Down the pit they were in a unique environment of danger in which injury and death were so commonplace that they tended to attract little notice. The working groups in most coalfields were exclusively male, and there were few opportunities for the women either to share in the work or to find work independently. Miners looked different, at least as they came away from work, since there were no pithead baths or running water in their homes, and getting the coal-dust out of the skin must have been very difficult. For all these reasons, miners were very clannish, a form of group cohesion that manifested itself both in intense loyalty to their local combinations, friendly societies, and trade unions, but also in a distinctive world of folk-lore. These strong mutual bonds were reinforced by the almost unbreakable heredity of the trade.

The reaction of the outside world to the introversion of the mining communities was inevitably, for the most part, hostile. Knowing little of the nature of the miners' working life and appreciating few of its dangers, outsiders tended to view miners as uncouth, dirty, irreligious, and drunken to such an extent that it became an axiom of general folk-lore that miners were not like ordinary folk: they were not civilized. It is no easy matter to separate truth from fiction in contemporary accounts, not least

[63] NuRO Delaval ZDE 7/6/2.
[64] NLS Prestongrange colliery 3720/17; NEI Forster 49/16/6-7.

because, as we have seen, the nature of miners' work and lives did indeed set them apart from their neighbours. Critics were almost invariably from the middle or upper classes, the circumstances of whose lives and upbringing made it easier for them to set rigid standards of public behaviour and whose own misdemeanours could more easily be concealed from public observation. Sir John Clerk of Penicuik, for example, expressed himself anxious, in his unilateral 'agreement' with the 'coalliers' of his Loanhead, Midlothian, colliery of 1703 to 'guard against' the 'profaneness and immorality, particularly excessive drinking and tipling, fighting and flyting, cursing and swearing, or taking the Lord's name in vain' of the miners.[65]

Above all, the miners' way of life appealed least to the early nonconformist leaders of the eighteenth century. Visiting the mining village of Plessey, near Hartley on the Northumberland coast, Wesley spoke of the colliers as being 'in the first rank of savage ignorance, and wickedness of every kind', while Whitefield, who had ideas of missionary work among the North American Indians, was advised by friends in Bristol, 'What need of going abroad? Have we not Indians enough at home? If you have a mind to convert *Indians*, there are colliers enough in Kingswood.' The Methodist Magazine of 1815, referring to the miners of both Newcastle and Kingswood (the latter nearly always singled out for obloquy by the Methodists, presumably because they were conveniently near to a major centre of Methodism), believed that

> Wild as the unataught Arab's brood,
> The Christian savages remain . . .[66]

To be fair to both miners and evangelicals, the extreme language of this latter needs interpreting. 'Savage ignorance' meant some lack of knowledge of the Bible, while 'wickedness' generally meant taking part in some kind of games on Sundays. More moderately, an account of north-east miners of 1804 asserted that 'intemperance is a leading feature in the Character of a pitman', and went on to assume that this vice was at the root of all trade union action.

At a very early period in life the Children attend the haunts of their Father at public houses where encouraged rather than checked in their growing fondness for liquor they become almost from infancy habituated to frequent intoxication, spectators and often actors in those rude scenes which accompany drunkenness. To gratify themselves in the indulgence of this favourite passion they fail not

[65] ScRO Clerk of Penicuik GD18/995/25.
[66] Welbourne 1923, 18, quoting from Wesley's *Journal*, III, 71; and Hair thesis 1955, 286–8, quoting from J. Gillies, *Life of Whitefield* 1772, 36, and the *Methodist Magazine* 1815, 581.

to avail themselves of every act in their power to enhance the price of their labour, and in all transactions with their employers readily sacrifice the principles of truth and honesty to promote their own selfish designs.

Miners' wives were described as being 'strangers to cleanliness, frugality or economy'.[67] Translated from the extremes of contemporary moral preaching, these comments really meant that miners' public houses were noisy places, their homes not always spotless, and that miners' pay allowed a few luxuries in their diet.

Other contemporary evidence, however, suggests that it is very difficult to generalize about miners' ways of life. There were enormous differences between communities. Lord Dundonald, for example, claimed that, unlike mining communities in other parts of Scotland, his Culross, Fife, miners were 'steady, sober men of principle, well clothed, neat in their persons, and well supplied with household furniture'.[68] When Commissioners from the Factories Inquiry Commission of 1833 visited colliers' houses in Glasgow, however, they found 'the collier women were very clean in their apearance, and looked healthy. The children above ten, though many of them were black with coaldust, looked also healthy. The little ones were fat and rosy.' They found the houses 'usefully and cleanly furnished', and there was a handsome clock in one. Bald, the Earl of Mar and Kellie's viewer at Alloa, wrote in 1808 that the great ambition of his colliers was to own a mahogany chest of drawers and an eight-day clock. Similarly, Mackenzie in his 1825 *History of Northumberland* described miners' homes as 'remarkably clean and orderly'. Cobbett, too, had found miners' homes 'very clean, hardly ever without a chest of drawers'.[69]

Apart from furniture, miners liked to indulge in dress. A miner's budget of 1817 for a family of a man, a wife, and three children, showed over ten per cent of the weekly budget set aside for clothing.[70] In an age when a very high proportion of working-class budgets had necessarily to be allocated to food, this was a considerable expenditure. In the North-east, the traditional miner's working dress consisted of a pair of white or blue checked flannel trousers (it will be remembered that the women underground workers of Lancashire wore white flannel trousers), a blue checked shirt, a red tie, a jacket to match the trousers, square-toed shoes, and long grey knitted stockings. His hair was long and tied in a pigtail for working. The hair was wrapped round 'curlers' made of thin pieces of lead

---

[67] NEI 48/MS volume bound at end of volume of pamphlets.
[68] Dundonald 1793, 65.
[69] Campbell 1979, 22; Bald 1808, 139; Hair thesis 1955, 265–8, quoting Mackenzie and Cobbett.
[70] Campbell 1979, 22.

wrapped in paper which were only removed at the weekend when the hair was washed. It was let loose down to the shoulders on a Sunday when an entirely different set of clothes was worn. This consisted of blue velvet breeches, a white linen shirt, a shiny blue coat with a bright lining, a short waistcoat, long pink, purple or blue stockings and buckled shoes, and a hat with bands of yellow ribbons.

> When aw put on my blue coat that shines se,
> My jacket wi posies sae fine se,
> My sark sic sma' threed, man,
> My pigtain se greet, man,
> Odd Smash, what a buck was Boby Cranky.

> Blue stockings, white clocks, and reed garters,
> Yellow breeks, and my sheen wi' lang quarters,
> Aw myed wor bairns cry,
> Eh! Sartees! Ni! Ni!
> Sic very fine things had Bob Cranky.[71]

All this suggests both quite heavy expenditure, and a very considerable pride in appearance that runs counter to the evangelical picture of dissoluteness.

'The Pitman's Pay', the manuscript poem of the late 1830s that is such a valuable source of information about the working life and leisure of north-east miners, attributed the improvement over the previous forty years, as Thomas Wilson, its author, saw it, in the quality of the miners' home life to the spread of Methodist Sunday schools, the introduction of savings banks, and the availability of cheap publications spreading 'useful knowledge'.[72] Information about the role of the churches, particularly the nonconformist churches, however, is surprisingly scarce, having regard to their importance in mining communities by the middle decades of the nineteenth century, a scarcity particularly striking in the histories of nonconformity in both the North-east and South Wales. This seems to suggest that the principal growth of nonconformity in the mining communities might indeed be a feature of the decades immediately following 1830. Mining communities were obvious targets for the nonconformity of the eighteenth and nineteenth centuries since they did not fit into the parochial pattern of the Church of England and might easily be located a considerable distance away from a parish church; and there was always at least a nucleus in every pit community desirous of having the services of a church and the clergy. The immigrant 'poor coaliers and sailors

[71] Welbourne 1923, 18–19.
[72] NuRO Society of Antiquaries ZAN M18 18/Preface, 8.

of Scotch birth and education' in Whitehaven petitioned Sir James Lowther in the early eighteenth century for relief from rent on three acres they had been leased on which to build a church. They had raised £200 from their own resources to build their church and had brought a minister from Scotland. 'The opportunity of enjoying the Presbyterian religion is and has been', they said, 'a mighty inducement for Scotch people to come to the place and work in your Honour's works'.[73] Roberts found evidence of a great many nonconformist chapels in the western sector of the South Wales coalfield, though he, too, was unable to confirm what proportion of these came into existence before 1830.[74] In the North-east, however, a report of 1807 regretted that 'so little attention is paid to the duties of religion. The time which ought to be employed in attendance on divine worship is frequently spent in some frivolous pursuit or in the more pernicious practice of drinking at public houses'. But even here there was a church-going minority. 'Some of them are dissenters and these attend meetings much more regularly than others do the Church. Pitmen are not much given to Superstition.'[75]

It is similarly not easy to determine very precisely the extent to which mining communities were served by schools. Boys who entered the pits at the ages of eight, nine, or ten could expect to do little more than derive their education from the school of life and would have little opportunity even to master the elements of literacy. The willingness of employers to take on boys of this age must, of course, have had something to do with it as well, as had the belief that only by entering the pit at this young age could real 'pitmen' be bred. Certainly there were schools of sorts in many mining villages, and in some instances these were provided by the owners. At Coleorton in Leicestershire in the opening years of the eighteenth century, Lord Beaumont founded a school, and a century later, on the Vane-Tempest estate, Lord Stewart contributed towards the salary of schoolmasters at schools attended largely by miners' children at West Rainton and Shiney Row. He also provided the building for the latter school.[76] In the North-east, it was said in 1807, 'in general little attention is paid by the Colliers to the Education of their Children: the product of their labour is by them considered of more importance, and the interest of the Child is sacrificed to the

---

[73] Petition, n.d. but probably pre-1750, CuRO Lonsdale D/Lons/W/Whitehaven 21.

[74] Roberts thesis 1953, 160; and see E. T. Davies, *Religion in the Industrial Revolution in South Wales* (Cardiff, 1965).

[75] NEI 48/MS report at end of bound volume of pamphlets.

[76] C. P. Griffin thesis 1969, 537; R. Pallister, 'Educational investment by industrialists in the early part of the nineteenth century in County Durham', *DUJ*, n.s. 30 (1968).

selfishness of the parent'.[77] This reluctance to send their children
to school is not borne out by the miners of one unnamed colliery
in the North-east .at about this time: their terms for the binding
settlement of 1805 included a request for a school near the
colliery.[78]

The Sunday school movement of the late eighteenth and early
nineteenth centuries, of course, touched the mining villages. The
owner of a colliery in the Bristol area donated money in 1820 to
'the Sunday School', though not in the following year. Perhaps the
school experienced a similar lapsing of interest to those in the
North-east. 'While the institution was novel', wrote the 1807 reporter
on the subject of Sunday schools, 'they were numerously attended,
but as soon as that impression lost its influence they became less
frequented and no representations of the good effects of such institutions have been sufficient to call forth the authority of the Parent
to enforce regular attendance.'[79] Several schools had been founded
in the first flush of enthusiasm for the charity school movement in
the Somerset coalfield early in the eighteenth century, but it is not
known how long these survived. In the village of Camerton in that
coalfield, out of a total population of about 1,200 in 1828, 166
children attended six dame schools and a further fifty a Sunday
school.[80]

With this scanty evidence of schooling it is hardly to be expected
that there would be very high standards of literacy among miners.
Yet of 460 miners at Pittington colliery in County Durham in 1840,
no less than 228 were able to read and write, and a further 132 were
able to read only. There had obviously been substantial advances in
their education during the early decades of the century. Twenty-two
out of twenty-five miners at Byker Hill colliery signed the 1774
bond with their marks, and twenty-seven out of thirty-two of the
fitter, David Crawford's, keelmen similarly in 1795. By 1822 forty-
four out of 119 miners at Pontop Pike colliery were able to sign
their names fully at the yearly binding.[81] Some, no doubt a very
small minority of, miners, put their literacy to very good use and
were among the purchasers of books published by subscription in
mid-eighteenth-century Scotland.[82]

[77] NEI 48/MS report at end of bound volume of pamphlets.
[78] NEI Watson 5/9/21.
[79] BRO Ashton Court AC/AS 100; NEI 48/MS report at end of bound volume of
pamphlets.   [80] Bulley 1955, 48–9.
[81] DuRO Londonderry D/Lo/B256/49; NuRO Society of Antiquaries ZAN M17/21;
and ibid., M19/26; DuRO Strathmore D/St/320.
[82] P. Laslett, 'Scottish weavers, cobblers and miners who bought books in the 1750s',
Local Population Studies, 3 (1969), 7–14.

With fairly low levels of literacy, relatively few miners spending their limited spare time in church attendance, and their communities being often isolated from other settlements, miners were very much thrown on their own resources for filling their leisure. In the North-east they made the most of every opportunity in the eighteenth century for a celebration, and miners' weddings and christenings were great social occasions. Village weddings were attended by all, and volleys of gunfire accompanied the bride and bridegroom into and out of the church. Christenings similarly grew large crowds, who, after 'getting up steam' at a public house, were regaled first with a substantial hot dinner and later with tea and supper. By the 1820s both these occasions were much quieter.[83] Between celebrations miners were great games players. In Somerset fives, played against the gable-end of the Bell Inn at Radstock or against the church at Midsomer Norton, was a favourite game. Cricket and rounders were popular in the early nineteenth century. In Cumberland cock-fighting, hound-trailing, and wrestling were popular. It was quite common for miners' cottages to be provided with gardens, and the cultivation of vegetables and even the keeping of a pig or a cow were quite common. 'A pitman is seldom without his pig or a hen or two', commented an 1807 north-east reporter. 'Gardens are becoming much more frequent than they were, and in some cases small considerations are paid for them. They are cultivated by the pitmen themselves.' Large gardens were attached to the miners' cottages built in the early nineteenth century by the Butterley Company in Derbyshire and by the Earl of Moira in Leicestershire.[84]

Though the evidence is scrappy and nebulous, there are signs that the social environment of mining communities was changing quite profoundly during the late eighteenth and early nineteenth centuries, and that the principal stimulus to this change was the substantial rise in real incomes. Homes were becoming more comfortable and better furnished, and although drinking remained the main social activity for the men, noisy, drunken occasions were becoming fewer. The more violent and cruel sports were slowly being replaced by gentler games. Literacy was rising, as was church attendance, though reading and church attendance were still minority occupations. Schools, friendly societies, savings banks, and trade unions provided a growing number of occasions and situations that gave miners themselves opportunities for responsible collective activity. But as the miners lost something of the 'wildness' that had kept them

---

[83] 'The Pitman's Pay', NuRO Society of Antiquaries ZAN M18/18/Preface, 22–4.
[84] NEI 48/MS report at end of bound volume of pamphlets; P. Riden, *The Butterley Company, 1790–1830* (Chesterfield, 1973), 31; C. P. Griffin thesis 1969, 507.

apart from other social groups, they lost nothing of their cohesion and loyalty to each other. The knowledge and skills of the true 'pitman' had been laboriously and only slowly acquired. He was deeply conscious of the value of his craft; and the ability, of the hewer at least, to determine, within the limits of economic necessity, his own hours of work, gave him a considerable pride of independence. That he was able by the early nineteenth century to match this independence with a well-furnished home and a set of sophisticated social institutions was the source of some gratification. It also gave him something to lose and therefore underlay a determination to fight, if necessary, to keep it. This rise in status goes a long way towards explaining the stormy labour relations that accompanied the great expansion of the industry after 1830.

Chapter 13

The Coal Industry and the Economy, 1700–1830

Throughout the period 1700 to 1830 the coal industry was one of Britain's major industries. In this respect it was unlike the cotton and iron industries which have hitherto dominated most analyses of the Industrial Revolution. The iron industry of the first half of the eighteenth century was minute compared with its nineteenth-century scale, and, starting from such small beginnings, had no difficulty in achieving a fast growth rate during the later eighteenth and early nineteenth centuries. The cotton industry displayed an even more extreme growth pattern during this period. The industry of the 1760s and 1770s was virtually a new creation since before that time cotton could, for lack of technical knowledge, be used in British cloth-making only in conjunction with other fibres. With the advantage of cheapness and novelty, this industry, too, was able to take off at a very high rate of growth. But the steady growth of the British coal-mining industry during the first half of the eighteenth century and the absence of major turning-points of the kind experienced by both the iron and cotton industries has distracted the attention of historians away from what was, none the less, an astounding record of persistent growth.

The output of coal, as we saw in chapter 1, increased by 75 per cent in the first half of the eighteenth century, trebled during the second half, and doubled again in the first thirty years of the nineteenth century. Over the whole period the expansion was ten-fold. How was this immense growth of an already well-established industry achieved?

We have already seen from chapter 9 that the growth was achieved with virtually no increase in real terms in the cost of production. While the iron and cotton industries were also successful in this way, they were not quite so susceptible as was the coal industry to the pressure of diminishing returns arising, in its case, out of the persistent exhaustion of the more easily mined seams. The increase in the supply of coal at prices that in real terms were constant or even diminishing was, of course, made possible by an unceasing flow of technical advances. The number and economic significance of these developments have been much underrated by historians in the past. Few of them were as dramatic or as immediate in their impact as, say, Arkwright's water frame, or the Darbys' coke-smelting, but their cumulative effect was decisive.

The calls on technology made by the mining industry in this period were broadly in two areas—the creation of an underground environment that permitted constant work, and the movement of hewn coal. These, it will be noticed, do not include the problem of actually extracting coal from the solid mass of mineral that confronts the miner at the face underground, and it is an interesting reflection on the history of the coal industry in this period that there were no advances in the technology of coal-cutting at all. In 1830, as in 1700, coal was brought down from the face by pick, wedge, and hammer. Because human muscle was as necessary in 1830 as in 1700 to cut coal there could be few major advances in the productivity of face workers. Some reorganization of the approach to coal-cutting such as that involved in the switch from bord and pillar to longwall working certainly contributed to the raising of productivity, and the use of gunpowder, had it been more than exceptional, might also have contributed; but for the most part coal was cut entirely by human power assisted by a few, unchanging hand tools.

Merely to maintain labour productivity underground in the face of the steady exhaustion of the more accessible seams called for deeper mining; and deeper mining, in its turn, required the exploitation of wider areas from a single shaft in order to economize on sinking costs. Both these needs multiplied the underground environmental problems of drainage and ventilation. It was in these fields that some of the most valuable innovations took place. Probably the single most important development in the mining technology of the period 1700 to 1830 was the invention and widespread adoption of the steam-pump. It was the introduction of this technique that made possible the expansion of the industry from a point early in the eighteenth century when other industries were still hamstrung by technological bottlenecks. The Newcomen steam-pump was not technically very efficient, but its main weakness—high fuel consumption in relation to the weight of water raised—was of minor importance at the pithead. And steam-pump technology did not stand still after the initial invention. Cylinder sizes grew and valve gear and boiler design were improved. By the third quarter of the eighteenth century engineers like Smeaton were increasing the engine's efficiency even before Watt made his valuable step forward in steam-engine design. By the early years of the nineteenth century a wide variety of steam-engines were available on the market for mining use, and collieries from the smallest and shallowest to the largest and deepest could select the most appropriate engine to keep their workings dry for regular work.

The other environmental hazard underground was gas, principally in the form of firedamp and chokedamp. Some serious accidents, like the explosions at Gateshead in 1700 and at Bensham in 1710, gave clear and early warning of the reality of the problems of deep mining. Great advances were made during the eighteenth and early nineteenth centuries in ventilation techniques, but none of them involved the novel application of scientific principles; they were never more than progressive improvements to long-established techniques, and were the achievements of working viewers. In spite of a number of unsuccessful efforts to harness steam-power to mechanical ventilation, the convection currents impelled by furnaces remained until 1830 the sole method of moving air through underground workings to drive out the dangerous gases. But great ingenuity was displayed by Carlisle Spedding and John Buddle in making the most effective use of the feeble currents set in motion by the convection furnaces. 'Coursing the air' and 'splitting the courses' were undoubtedly effective, and while serious explosions continued to be regular, melancholy features of mining throughout the nineteenth century, such evidence as is available suggests that they did not become more serious (in terms of lives lost per ton produced) as mining became deeper in the early nineteenth century, and may even have been reduced. The battle for ventilation, while far from being won in this period, was not actually lost in spite of a continuing intensification of the problems.

Part of the problem of ventilation, of course, was the question of lighting. Very little was needed to spark off an explosion in a concentration of firedamp, and most explosions were set off by the forms of lighting necessarily employed in underground work. A naked flame, the most widely used form of underground illumination, was the simplest way to ignite the gas. Until Carlisle Spedding devised the steel-mill in the 1730s, it was, indeed, the only form of underground lighting. Without the safety-lamp, the sole improvement in underground lighting in the century following the invention of the steel-mill, the deeper mining of the nineteenth century would have become unacceptably dangerous, and the supply of coal begun to dwindle. While Davy's safety-lamp was a true product of the application of scientific principles and methods to industrial technology, the same can hardly be said of Stephenson's almost identical and simultaneous lamp. Stephenson was a classic example of the ingenious craftsmen.

Between them, this important group of drainage, ventilation, and lighting developments allowed workable coal seams to continue to be accessible to miners throughout the eighteenth and early nineteenth centuries. Without them, continuous expansion of coal production would not have been possible. As essential as access to coal in allowing supply to respond to rising demand, however, were the means of getting coal cut at the face to the surface. As depths and hauling distances underground increased, so the cost of bringing coal to the pithead rose for any given method of hauling and winding. Human labour, as used in the early eighteenth century for much underground hauling and even still for some winding, could only have continued to suffice with a disproportionate increase in unit costs. The substitution of horse- for human-power lowered unit costs in spite of the fact that a horse cost two or three times as much as a human to employ: its productivity was more than as many times greater. And when improved rails with metal surfaces were substituted for the original wooden rails on the rolley-ways and waggon-ways underground, their productivity rose still higher. In winding, however, the switch to horse-power was a once-for-all gain, since, apart from small variations in design, horse-gins were scarcely susceptible to technical improvement. But the substitution of steam- for horse-power in winding towards the end of the eighteenth century led to another dramatic reduction in unit winding costs, and the steam winding-engine, once adopted, was capable of steady technical improvement. Guide rails, automatic surface tipping devices, and the use of flat ropes and later chains for winding further raised the productivity of labour and capital in the same period.

While the adoption of steam for pumping and winding in the early and late eighteenth century respectively were the most obvious and dramatic technological advances in mining techniques, numerous other developments, each yielding only marginal gains, but cumulatively producing significant reductions of average costs, were more than sufficient to combat the remorseless pressure of rising average costs.

All these advances in draining, ventilation, lighting, hauling, and winding made it possible to bring ever-growing quantities of coal to the surface at prices which, in real terms, did not increase in spite of the inherent tendency of mining costs to rise. But the most restrictive bottleneck in the business of mining in early eighteenth-century Britain was not merely getting coal to the pithead, but transporting it from the pithead to the ultimate consumer. The location of most potential consumers had been determined long before the opening of the eighteenth century with no regard to the supply of coal, and it is one of the best-known facts of the economic history of pre-industrial Britain that the cost of the overland carriage of coal for more than a few miles was prohibitive. True, the water carriage of coal was relatively cheap, but by no means all potential consumers of coal were conveniently located for water transport, and very few mines themselves were at the water's edge. Indeed, the long history of mining before the opening of the eighteenth century had ensured the exhaustion of most such favourably placed mines.

To liberate the supply of coal and to permit advantage to be taken of the steady and detailed improvements in the techniques of coal production during the eighteenth and early nineteenth centuries, the links between the mines and the consumers had to be improved and ton/mile costs reduced. As we saw in chapter 5, a series of both major and minor developments accomplished these connections. The water links were made more flexible and numerous by the improvement of river navigation and the construction of canals, and the gaps still left between mines and water bridged by the construction of innumerable short waggonways. The waggonways remained short because their ton/mile costs were still many times those of the water-borne transport of coal: indeed, an eighteenth-century waggonway might almost have been defined as the shortest distance between a mine and a navigable waterway. Short as they were, however, the productivity of the labour and capital employed on them was sufficiently greater than those of road transport to keep the delivered price of coal within the reach of at least some consumers. And as the output and consumption of coal rose throughout the eighteenth and early nineteenth centuries, a steady stream of improvements to the design of waggonways—the reduction of gradients by the use of cuttings, embankments, and bridges, inclined planes either self-acting or using horse-gins or stationary steam-engines—and to the rails themselves, substantially increased the productivity of horses and their keepers by reducing friction and wear and tear.

The evolution of stages of the wrought-iron waggonway rail of the early nineteenth century from the wholly wooden rail of the early eighteenth century considerably reduced ton/mile costs, and with this achievement it is hard to imagine what scope there would have been for further improvement of the horse-drawn waggonway. At just this point in time, however, steam-power, already familiar to mining engineers from its application to draining and winding, was successfully adapted to rail propulsion and, exclusively in the context of coal-mining, the modern railway was born. The advantages of the substitution of steam- for horse-traction on colliery waggonways in terms of ton/mile costs were easily demonstrable, and the adoption of steam-locomotives on the waggonways of the larger collieries together with the parallel improvement of the rails on which they ran was rapid after 1813.

Steam-traction led to some lengthening of the distances economically viable for the rail transport of coal, but the costs of the construction, maintenance, and operation of even steam-railways before 1830 left water-transport still appreciably cheaper in ton/mile terms. In the last resort it was the extension of inland navigation that was the most decisive single development that created the expansion of coal consumption. At $1\frac{1}{2}d$. per ton/mile, and in some instances as little as $1d$., the canal and river transport of coal compared very favourably with rates two, three, or even more times as high on the waggonways. This cost advantage ensured that until the major developments of long distance steam-railways after 1830 water transport would continue to be preferred, wherever possible, to rail transport for coal traffic. And in the field of water transport, coastal navigation, employing larger vessels than the rivers or canals, would continue to be preferred, wherever practicable, to river or canal transport. Railways and waggonways remained short before 1830, therefore, because it was mostly possible to bring canals sufficiently close to mines to leave the gap to be bridged by waggonways short.

In the more concentrated coalfields already relatively well served by waterways or conveniently placed for coastal navigation like many of the Scottish coalfields, or the Cumberland and North-east mining regions, canals and improved river navigation played almost no part in the growth of the eighteenth and early nineteenth centuries. In other coalfields, including those in which production grew rapidly, like South Wales, the East and West Midlands, Lancashire, and Yorkshire, the creation of water-transport facilities was crucial. In the eastern sector of the South Wales coalfield, for example, the distance of the accessible coalfield from the sea in the Bristol channel had almost totally barred developments before the construction of canals towards the end of the century. In this instance the coalfield was developed by the iron companies; but the huge expansion of iron-making there was itself only practicable after the construction of the canals. In other coalfields the coming of the canals permitted an extension of the developed area within the coalfields, often towards more easily mined, or better quality seams.

Technical developments in mining, then, made possible a steady increase in coal production at constant or even slightly falling prices. Meanwhile, the creation of cheap transport links between mines and potential customers so far reduced average ton/mile transport costs that coal could be delivered at acceptable prices to millions of new urban and industrial consumers. On the supply side, a long list of technological innovations, both major and minor, not only made it possible for the industry to respond to rising demand for coal, but actually created some of that demand by a capacity to deliver coal cheaply to an ever-widening circle of consumers.

Technological advances are easily identifiable, but it is possible that developments in organization, less obviously translated into economic gains, may also have contributed. Certainly the evolution of mine design and of methods of extraction helped to raise productivity, or at least to offset the losses incurred by deeper working. Longwall working involved a greater degree of division of labour and it must be presumed that its spread, combined with that of its modified forms of the panel working of the North-east and the narrow and wide banks of Yorkshire, made significant contributions to productivity. How far the economies of scale operated in mining is more difficult to assess. That they are likely to have done so is suggested both by the steady growth in the size of the unit of employment in most coalfields and by the concentration generally of the largest units in the North-east, the region of highest productivity. We saw in chapter 10 how the larger collieries developed a much greater degree of specialization of labour. More importantly, however, it was the larger collieries, and even the grouping of collieries in larger units of ownership, that produced the major viewers, the key figures in the development of mining technology. In this way there was a very positive link between the size of the unit of production and the pace of technical advance.

These shifts, in the economist's terminology, of the supply curve to the right account, however, for part only of the expansion of the industry. Much of the growth must be seen in terms of new sectors of demand, to an increase, in other words, in the per capita consumption of coal. The sheer rise of population of the order of about $2\frac{1}{2}$-fold between 1700 and 1830, of course, accounts for the part of this growth, and its increasing tendency to concentrate in towns where firewood was expensive and coal markets well organized probably led to expanding per capita coal consumption for urban domestic heating. But the principal new markets for coal were industrial, and the product of technological innovations in certain industries. Though experience varied from industry to industry, there was certainly a substantial net increase in demand from the 'old' coal-consuming industries—those that were already coal-users at the beginning of the eighteenth century. These fell into several groups—the non-ferrous metal industries, industries associated with building, with food and drink processing, and miscellaneous industries. The non-ferrous metal industries tended to grow only slowly during the eighteenth and early nineteenth centuries and their consumption of coal, never more than a small proportion of total consumption, declined in relative importance, though rising in absolute levels. The building industry consumed coal principally in the manufacture of bricks, tiles, and glass. House-building, a major sector of the whole building industry, necessarily grew very much at the pace of population, though the steady progress of urbanization no doubt contributed to some acceleration in the growth of demand for bricks for urban building. The building industry was diversified after the middle of the eighteenth century into more extensive industrial building and the building associated with road and waterway improvement. The demand for coal from the building industry certainly grew faster than population during the later eighteenth and early nineteenth centuries, but this sector of coal demand never grew to major significance. The food and drink trades, too—baking, sugar-boiling, distilling, and brewing—while increasing their consumption of coal at least in line with population growth, remained of relatively small signficance to the mining industry. Salt-making, in earlier periods a major customer for the mines, also declined in relative importance, not least on account of the growing dominance of rock-salt, and its much lower consumption of coal, over sea-salt. Beyond observing that demand was growing, probably faster than the growth of population, there is no possibility of assessing the consumption of coal in the wide range of miscellaneous coal-using industries—soap and other chemicals, dyeing, glass-making, lime-burning, and the manufacture of china and pottery.

The sources of demand that really lay behind the expansion of the mining industry were, of course, the new industrial uses—iron-making, gas supply, and the many and varied industrial uses of steam-power. Of these, quite the most important, and probably the largest single element in the growing demand for coal in the late eighteenth and early nineteenth centuries, was the iron industry. Of the whole increase in coal consumption in the last quarter of the eighteenth century, the rise in demand from iron-making accounted for 25.8 per cent, and in the first thirty years of the nineteenth century for a further 25.0 per cent. The new demand for coal for iron-making, of course, was not evenly distributed over all the mining regions. It was heavily concentrated in South Wales and the West Midlands, with some increase in Scotland, Cumberland, North Wales, and York-shire; but the South-west, East Midlands, Lancashire, and the North-east drew little benefit from this great surge of demand. The coal industry benefited initially from the early inefficiency of iron-making; but once the techniques of coke-smelting and puddling were widely diffused, interest began to be shown in the design of furnaces with a view to fuel economy. When blast furnaces consumed between four and nine tons of coal for every ton of pig iron they produced, there was scope for this. The invention by Neilson of the hot-blast process in 1828 quickly made an impact on the coal consumption of the iron industry, a process speeded up by the substitution after 1856 of Bessemer steel for puddled iron; but these innovations made their impact on the mining industry only after 1830.

Though the possibilities of using coal gas for street, factory, and domestic lighting had been demonstrated in the late eighteenth century, the practical problems of large-scale manufacture of gas and its safe distribution over wide areas were not solved immediately, and the growth of commercial gas consumption was a feature of the second and third decades of the nineteenth century. Once initiated, the growth of demand was very rapid as gas supply companies sprang into existence in most of the larger towns; but because of this chronology of growth the impact of these developments on the mining industry was slight before 1830.

The mining industry was responsible first for attracting and later for developing and diversifying the industrial use of steam-power. In chapters 3 and 4 we saw how steam-power was first employed for mine drainage, then for winding, and finally for waggonway traction. All these applications had relevance in areas of the economy beyond coal-mining. Steam-pumping was used in metal-mines as well as coal-mines, and was also transferable to the water-supply industry and to land-drainage; the rotary engines used in winding had many uses in manufacturing industry, above all in textile manufacture to drive the new spinning and weaving machines; and, though initially confined to colliery use, the possibilities of the steam-locomotive for public passenger and general industrial transport soon led to the dramatic railway construction manias of the middle decades of the nineteenth century. Nor should the first tentative applications of steam-power to water transport of the early nineteenth century be overlooked in this context. Ramifying from the mining industry, steam-power became a major consumer of coal, and there is much to be said for the view that in this way the industry, as a result of its own technological genius, created its own markets for much of its production. Unfortunately the very diversity both of applications of steam-power and of engine types and sizes prevents any precise quantification of its relative importance to the over-all demand for coal. What is certain is that because there were so few applications of steam-power outside coal-mining before about 1775, the impact of these developments on the demand for coal was almost wholly confined to the last quarter of the eighteenth century and after.

There was, therefore, in the interplay of supply and demand, a circularity that was characteristic of all economic growth. In the process of responding to early undramatic increases in demand spread generally over all consumers of coal, the mining industry turned to new technologies that, with their own evolutionary momentum, soon spread beyond their initial applications and created independent markets for coal. In contrast to this mechanism and supplementing it, entirely independent technological advances in the iron and gas industries, linked to those in coal-mining only through an intellectual climate favourable to research and innovation, won new markets in areas that could hardly have been conceived at the opening of the eighteenth century.

The ten-fold growth of an already well-established industry over a period of 130 years, or a near quadrupling of output in less than half that time from 1775 to 1830, suggests that the rise of the coal industry must have constituted a major element in the British Industrial Revolution. Yet the coal industry has rarely been regarded as playing a very significant role in that transformation, a view which is broadly confirmed by the undramatic nature of the growth of the industry and, not least because of the low value of the product, by the small share of the industry in the national product. If, to strike an extremely rough approximation to the average value of coal at the pithead around 1830, we assume a price of 6s. 8d. per ton, then the 30 million tons produced in that year would be valued at £10 million, or slightly less than 3 per cent of the estimated gross national product at that time. Thirty years earlier, the proportion was about 2.2 per cent. Looking at the industry in the context solely of the industrial sector, however, the picture appears a little different. In 1801, the output of coal accounted for approximately 9.2 per cent of the total output of the mining, manufacturing, and building sectors taken together, and marginally less in 1831. The decline of the coal industry's share by 1831 is merely a reflection of the great expansion of the whole industrial sector of this period. For a single industry these are very substantial proportions and must place the coal industry in the ranks of the three or four principal industries of the country in the early nineteenth century. It is worth bearing in mind, too, that although estimation of actual magnitudes is quite impossible, the coal industry certainly consumed a disproportionately large share of the nation's transport services in this period.

The importance of the coal industry to the economic development of the eighteenth and early nineteenth centuries, however, extended beyond its mere quantitative share in the nation's economic growth. Coal was a raw material of other major industries and without a supply of coal capable of virtually limitless expansion at constant prices, the growth of which these industries were otherwise capable must have been hamstrung. There has been much discussion, for example, about the problems of the iron industry in the last decades of its charcoal era. There is no longer such certainty as there was formerly that, with a progressive consumption of the nation's stock of timber, the remorseless rise in the price of charcoal was slowly strangling the charcoal iron industry. The industry's charcoal supply was provided by coppicing, a system that was capable of maintaining a constant supply of suitable wood for charcoal-making, and there is little evidence of a really damaging rise in its price until, in fact, well after the discovery of the coke-smelting process. It remains the case, nevertheless, that the charcoal supply could never, in seventeenth- and eighteenth-century Britain, have been capable of rapid and sustained expansion. Had the breakthrough of coke-smelting not been achieved, the dramatic growth of iron production that occurred in the later eighteenth and early nineteenth centuries could not possibly have taken place and the whole chain of developments dependent upon a supply of iron must have been held up in its turn. The response of the coal industry, above all in specific coalfields and at constant prices, was central to this development.

The same crucial role may be seen, too, in the range of developments based on steam-power. So important was the availability of coal for the power-supply in the textile industries that, as they gradually switched from human- and water-power to steam-power, they migrated to coalfield areas. The process may be seen almost in miniature in Lancashire, where the distances between the original water-power sites of machine cotton manufacture and the later steam-power sites more directly on the coalfield were not great; but the drift none the less is discernible. The process was repeated in Yorkshire, though here the switch to steam-power was, in general, almost a generation later. On the wider, national map, the crucial role of coal was demonstrated in the inability of the old areas of woollen cloth-manufacture of East Anglia and the West of England to match the new economics of steam-powered manufacture on the coalfield of west Yorkshire.

In these and other examples of the new coal-based industries, the role of the coal industry was largely passive. All that was required of it was to produce more coal without seriously pushing up its average price in the process. Thanks to the availability of seemingly inexhaustible reserves and the steady evolution of the techniques necessary to go deeper and further underground to bring the coal to the surface, it met these calls. The industry did, however, make a much more positive contribution to the acceleration of the rate of economic growth through its contribution to technology. In the process of responding to the increase of demand, the mining industry attracted the development of three of the key technological foundations of Britain's subsequent economic expansion.

The first of these in chronological sequence was steam-power. It is true that Newcomen's interest in devising his steam-pump in the early years of the eighteenth century was first inspired by the problems of draining the non-ferrous metal-mines of Cornwall. That he was aware of the applicability of his invention to coal-mines is apparent from the fact that almost all the pumps erected during the few remaining years of his life were installed in coal-mines. And it was in coal-mines that most of the subsequent improvements to Newcomen's original design were evolved. The early steam-pump found uses, of course, outside coal-mining, and it is not to be doubted that it would have been developed to its more advanced designs and uses of the nineteenth century whether or not it was employed in coal-mining. The mining industry must take the credit, however, for much of the speed and sophistication of the evolution of steam-engine design. The fact that a very high proportion of all steam-engines in use before Boulton and Watt, and a still large, if diminishing, proportion thereafter, were employed in coal-mines, indicates the source of the principal efforts to refine and improve design. It is even possible, as we saw in chapter 3, that the first efforts to make the decisive switch from reciprocating to rotary motion were made on the coalfields.

The second of the major technological contributions was the canal. Here again, it is possible that canals could, and would, have enjoyed an existence in Britain independently of the mining industry, but it was in the context of coal carriage that the viability of canal transport was first unequivocally demonstrated. The little known 'boatways' of Griff colliery in Warwickshire, the Sankey Brook and Bridgewater canals established by the 1760s the utility and economic advantage of canal transport for coal. Most of the early canals thereafter were constructed primarily, if not exclusively, for coal carriage; and if they also found customers outside the coal industry, their continued profitability hinged largely on their coal traffic.

But it was in the evolution of steam-railways that the coal industry made its greatest contribution to general economic development. The wooden waggonways from which the steam-railways of the nineteenth century evolved were, so far as is known, confined almost exclusively to colliery use, though towards the end of the eighteenth century and in the first decades of the nineteenth century tramways for more general traffic began to appear outside the coalfields. The contribution of the mining industry to railway technology, however, took two vital directions—the design of the rails themselves, and the application of steam-power to locomotion. In chapter 5 we saw how the economics of horse-traction led to the progressive improvement of wooden rail surfaces and then to the substitution of, first, cast-iron, and, later, wrought-iron, rails for wooden rails. When it came to the design of locomotives the development of wrought-iron rails was crucial, since the failures of the first locomotives from Trevithick onwards were due primarily to the inability of existing rails to support them. The evolution of efficient rails and all that went with them in track design—points, turntables, bridges, tunnels, and embankments—were the exclusive achievement of the coal-mining industry.

The links between Newcomen's steam-pump and the steam-locomotives of the early nineteenth century are obvious, and with the aid of historical hindsight we can be confident that once Newcomen had made the initial breakthrough, the steam-locomotive was bound to follow sooner or later. But it remains the fact that the steam-locomotive was wholly the product of the mining industry: it was developed at collieries very largely by colliery engineers to serve colliery needs. The first commercially successful locomotives were built and operated by Blenkinsop and Stephenson, both colliery engineers. Even Richard Trevithick, one of the very few early locomotive pioneers not directly employed in the coal-mining industry, demonstrated his first model on a colliery waggonway. For the first dozen years, important in taking the engineers through the early teething troubles of locomotive design and operation, steam-locomotion was employed almost exclusively in the context of collieries. When the time came for the extension of steam-powered railways to passenger and general freight traffic in the later 1820s and 1830s, the early, unavoidable stages of design evolution had already been passed through.

The new uses for coal and the innovations instigated by the expansion of coal-mining in the eighteenth and early nineteenth centuries all liberated the economy from the employment of energy sources in inelastic supply. The adoption of coke-smelting, which opened the door to a major new use for coal, released the iron industry from the tight constraints of a highly inelastic charcoal supply. Steam-pumping and -winding substituted coal energy for mainly horse-power. True, the supply of horses themselves was reasonably elastic, but an island country with a rapidly growing population was bound to find a point at which the demands on land utilization of horse-feed competed unacceptably with the production of food for humans. It is not easy to imagine how, even by 1830, the horses required to produce 30 million tons of coal could have been fed if all pumping, winding, and surface traction were to be powered by horses. The substitution of canals for road haulage and of steam-locomotion for horse-drawn waggons contributed equally to the avoidance of the bottleneck theatened by a greatly enhanced reliance on horse-power. Though these forms of avoidance of rising marginal costs were initiated within the coal-mining industry itself, their impact made itself felt in ever-widening circles of the economy. To describe the situation as 'a severe energy crisis', and to locate such a crisis rather precisely in the early 1780s, as the economist, Brinley Thomas, has recently done, is perhaps a little exaggerated; but there can be no doubt that growth in the British economy would have been slowed down had not a highly elastic coal supply been available to substitute for the inelastic supplies of other forms of energy.

In the space of the 130 years after 1700 the British economy had passed from dependence on human-, horse-, wind- and water-power for its energy needs to a high degree of dependence on coal. The change may have been a response to sheer necessity, but it was economically advantageous. Already in the early eighteenth century the existing energy resources were precarious. Human-powered machines—spinning-wheels, handlooms, and the ubiquitous wheelbarrow—were labour-intensive and of low productivity. Wind was always intermittent and so unreliable that its effective industrial use was minimal. Water-power, the prime source of energy for most heavy industrial purposes, was of rather severely restricted utility. Industrial locations in Britain with an adequate fall of water were restricted and confined to certain geographical areas that did not always coincide with other locational determinants. More serious, water-power was subject to seasonal fluctuations: the reduction of the flow in summer and occasional freezing in winter could bring production to a standstill, a major diseconomy in, say, blast-furnace operation. Even though water-power was 'free', there were many attractions in steam-power for the industrialist.

The end of horse-power in British industry may have been the least obvious prognostication at the beginning of the eighteenth century. Indeed, in mining itself, it had not long established itself as the prime source of energy in draining, winding, and surface transport. Its limitations, however, were its high capital and operating costs. So long as there was no substitute, it served its many purposes, and for some of these purposes it had a role to play until well into the twentieth century. But for others, as soon as steam-power demonstrated its adaptability and relative cheapness, the horse's days were numbered. This substitution would have happened whether the supply of horses and horse-feed were elastic or inelastic. In the event this elasticity was never seriously put to the test, though the high price of grain during the French wars of the turn of the eighteenth and nineteenth centuries certainly contributed to an acceleration of the pace of substitution.

The transformation to coal-based sources of energy was not complete by 1830, of course, but it had gone a long way. Coal energized iron-making almost entirely, as the fuel in smelting and puddling and to power the blast for furnaces and the rolling mills. By 1830 the cotton industry had very largely gone over to steam-power to drive the spinning mills and the rapidly growing power-weaving section: and a similar substitution was following, with a lag, in the woollen industry. Other key industries—non-ferrous metal-smelting, pottery, flour-milling, and brewing—were already largely steam-powered. In transport, of course, the process was only just beginning. The investment required to make the switch completely to steam-driven railways and from sail to steam on the seas, rivers, and canals was immense, and must necessarily be spread over a long period; but there was no doubt by 1830 that it was only a matter of time. The technology had proved itself and the supply of energy was guaranteed by a flourishing coal-mining industry.

At the beginning of the eighteenth century annual per capita coal consumption in Britain was probably slightly less than half a ton. Coal production rose throughout the eighteenth and early nineteenth centuries faster than population thanks to the discovery of ever-new uses for coal, and by 1800 per capita consumption had probably climbed to about 1.4 tons. By 1830 this had risen to just under 2 tons, not very far short of the level of the 1980s. The British economy that entered the Victorian era was indeed a coal-based one.

The coal industry does not fit easily into the pattern of British industrialization as it is conventionally understood. We can put precise figures to the numbers employed in only one or two of the mines of the early eighteenth century, but the levels of output of some collieries, above all in the North-east, indicate that the size of the unit of employment in the industry was already in some instances well beyond what is comprehended by 'pre-industrial' production. Winding and draining, though still horse- and water-powered, had already reached a degree of sophistication that placed the industry outside the scope of small-scale cottage industry, while the level of fixed capital investment demanded by the larger mines pushed the industry well into the modern industrial era. The adoption of steam-power in the second decade of the eighteenth century, half a century before James Watt, the traditional 'hero' of steam-technology, put his mind to the question, clinched the issue: the coal industry led the way in industrial revolution well in advance of its rivals.

When other industries followed coal along the road of mechaniza-tion, of high capitalization, and of growth in the scale of units of employment and organization, the coal industry responded both to the new demands for its product and to the challenge of continuing modernization. The pace of technological innovation did not abate, and some of the most valuable advances—steam-winding, the safety-lamp, and steam-locomotion—were evolved in step with the rapid technological development of other industries. The chronology of the coal industry's growth, however, was not of a pattern with that of much of the rest of the industrial sector. This nonconformity does not, of course, make nonsense of the idea of an 'industrial revolution' of the late eighteenth century; it does, however, blunt somewhat the concept of a preceding, 'pre-industrial' economy, and cautions against a too-rash acceptance of a concentrated 'take-off' towards the end of the eighteenth century.

Appendix A

Glossary

Adit. A drain from a mine using gravity and opening to a hillside or stream at a level lower than that of the mine sump. Called 'sough' in Lancashire, and 'day-level' in Scotland.

Balance (South Wales). A winding engine in which the weight of a tub filled with water was used to wind coal to the surface.

Bassett. An outcrop of coal. To outcrop.

Bearer (Scotland). A putter (q.v.) or underground hauler of coal.

Bear-mouth (Cumberland). Opening of a drift, or sloping entry to a mine.

Bell-pit. Shallow pit increasing in diameter with depth.

Bord. A stall or passage between pillars or stoops from which coal has been or is being taken. The coal pillars are left to support the roof.

Brattice. A vertical division of a shaft, made of wood, to allow for two simultaneous uses of a single shaft—winding and ventilation, or pumping and ventilation.

Butty. A charter-master (q.v.).

Cannel. A hard, bright-burning variety of coal mined in this period principally near Wigan in Lancashire.

Cavilling. Drawing lots to determine the allocation of bords or stalls between hewers.

Charter-master. A gang-leader or sub-contractor who accepted responsibility for supplying all the labour necessary to extract coal and raise it to the surface.

Chokedamp. A suffocating gas created by an explosion of firedamp (q.v.). Heavier than air, it quickly killed miners knocked to the ground by the force of an explosion.

Collier. 1. Generally, a miner. In some coalfields, a hewer. (In Scotland, 'coalier'.) 2. A sea-going vessel carrying a cargo of coal.

Corf. A basket for the underground movement of coal.

Course. The passage of ventilating air through underground workings guided by stoppings (q.v.) and trap-doors.

Craneman. An underground worker who lifted corves or other coal containers on to sledges or waggons for underground haulage.

Creep. The sinking of the base of a pillar into the floor of a working under the weight of the overlying strata.

Cribbing. A temporary wooden lining to a shaft during sinking intended to be replaced by tubbing (q.v.) later.

Crimp or *coal-broker*. Small middle-man in the London coal market often no more than a contractor (or 'undertaker') of the labour of coal-heavers or coal-whippers for unloading colliers.

Crush. The pressing of the top of a pillar into the roof of a working under the weight of the overlying strata.

Culm. Generally, small coal. In South Wales, the small coal of anthracite.

Curving or *kirving.* Making vertical cuts in a coal face preparatory to under-cutting and bringing down the coal by wedge.

Day-hole (Scotland). Mouth of a drift or sloping entry to a mine.

Day-level (Cumberland and Scotland). A drift, or sloping entry to a mine or an adit (q.v.).

Dead stock. The fixed, irremovable equipment of a colliery.

Deputy. Underground worker responsible for safety, principally in connection with the propping of the roof.

Dib-hole. Sump at foot of a drainage shaft.

Drop. A mechanical contrivance for lowering a full waggonway waggon at a staith into the hold of a collier to minimize breakage of great coal.

Factor. A London agent of a north-east coalowner, who acted on commission as middleman between shipmasters and the principal coal buyers.

Firedamp. Explosive gas released from coal seams. Lighter than air, it collected under roofs of mines.

Fireman. A worker whose task was to descend pits ahead of working shifts and ignite firedamp that had collected in the roof.

Fitter (North-east). A Newcastle shipping agent who arranged the sale of coal to shipmasters on behalf of a coalowner, owned keels, and employed the keelmen.

Freighting (North-east). The speculative shipment of coal by coalowners at their own risk for sale in London or at other ports at whatever price could be obtained, in contrast to the usual practice of a sale negotiated by a fitter to a shipmaster.

Furnace. A brazier holding a coal fire suspended in, or at the foot of, a pit shaft to create an up-draught of air for ventilation.

Gale (Forest of Dean). A grant of right to mine coal in a designated area.

Garland. A spiral drain running round the perimeter of a circular shaft.

Getter (Yorkshire). A hewer (q.v.).

Gin. An engine, usually a wooden-framed, horse-drawn machine, for pumping or winding.

Goaf, or *gob.* Underground space cleared of coal in the course of longwall (q.v.) working, and used for stacking slack or waste small coal.

Hagger (Cumberland). A hewer (q.v.).

Hewer. A miner who cut coal from the face.

Hurrying (Yorkshire). Hauling underground.

Hutching (Forest of Dean). Hauling underground.

In-bye. In the workings away from the shaft bottom.

Jud. The coal face between two vertical cuts or 'curves' (q.v.).

Kibble. A large bucket (generally square in section) used to lift water out of mines.

Kirving. See 'curving'.

Landsale. That part of a colliery's output sent to market by overland transport. A 'landsale' colliery was one that concentrated its production on markets reached by overland transport.

Leading. Carriage by horse-drawn cart or wain.

Level-free. A mine so situated that it could be drained by adit (q.v.).

Live stock. The removable (and saleable, if necessary) equipment of a colliery.

Longwall. A method of working in which a seam was worked along a long face. The roof in the space cleared was propped with timber and ultimately left to collapse as the props were moved forward to newly cleared areas.

Meter. An official appointed by the City of London to measure for taxation purposes the coal as it was unloaded from colliers to lighters in the Thames.

On-setter. An underground worker who hooked corves or other coal containers to the rope or chain at the shaft bottom for winding to the surface.

Overman (or *oversman*). A mine manager under a viewer (q.v.).

Putter (North-east). An underground hauler of coal by any form of transport.

Rolley-way. Underground tramway for hauling coal using wheeled sledges.

Roof-bending. A technique devised by John Buddle junior for allowing the roof of a cleared space to fall gradually without fracturing the overlying seams.

Seasale. That part of a colliery's output sent to market by sea transport. A seasale colliery was one that concentrated its production on markets served by sea transport.

Spout. A chute that allowed coal from waggonway waggons to be loaded at a staith directly into sea-going colliers.

Staith. A quay for transferring coal from a waggonway to a keel, generally with facilities for storing coal.

Steel-mill. An invention of the 1730s for providing light underground that was believed to be less dangerous than the naked flame of a candle or a lamp. The light was produced by flint pressed against a rapidly rotated grindstone.

Stopping. A solid wooden frame to seal off the movement of air through an underground roadway.

Trailing (Cumberland and South Wales). Hauling underground.

Tramway or *plateway.* A railway for horse-drawn waggons using L-section iron rails and waggons with flangeless wheels.

Tubbing. The lining of a shaft made with wood, bricks, stone, or cast-iron segments.

Turn. A shift, or day's work.

Vend. (North-east). The quantity of coal marketed either by individual collieries or by all seasale (q.v.) collieries by coastal shipment. From 1771 this quantity was regulated by agreement between coalowners.

Viewer. A mine manager, or consultant engineer. See chapter 2, section 4 for the range of activities embraced in this occupation.

Waggonway. A railway for horse-drawn waggons using rectangular wooden (later iron) rails and waggons with flanged wheels.

Wasteman. An underground worker responsible for inspecting goafs (q.v.) and keeping bords (q.v.), levels, and roadways clear of roof falls.

Wayleave. A right to cross land in somebody else's ownership for the purposes of transporting coal.

Whimsey. A small Newcomen-type engine adapted to rotary motion for winding.

Win. To create a colliery in a state of readiness to extract coal.

Appendix B

Weights and Measures

Wherever possible in the tables weights have been converted into *tons* of 2,240 lb., and in some tables, for purposes of comparison with modern measures, weights have also been quoted in *tonnes* of 1,000 kilogrammes. In the period 1700 to 1830 most mining regions employed their own measures. Most of these were measures of volume rather than of weight, if only because they related initially to forms of transport which could not be standardized, and they often varied substantially from one part of a coalfield to another, from one type of coal to another, from one period to another, from one colliery to another, and even from day to day depending upon whether the coal was wet or dry. All measures in the following table are related to their own regions. While the twentieth-century mind might see nothing but disadvantages arising from variable measures, in the eighteenth century flexibility offered some virtues: quantities could be altered to reflect the bargaining strength of buyers or sellers; the rigidity of the 'Vend' or of 'regulations' could be relaxed to give advantage to individual sellers; the revenue could be more easily defrauded; and miners on piece-rates could be under-paid.

Basket (Lancashire): normally 120 lb., but see Langton 1979, 243–4 for possible variations.
Basket (Scotland): normally 5 cwt.
Boll (North-east): $\frac{1}{24}$th of a Newcastle chaldron = 247.3 lb. = 2.208 cwt.
Cart (Scotland): varied between 7 and 15 cwt., but was usually 10 or 12 cwt.
Chaldron. 1. *Newcastle chaldron* (North-east): though a variable weight until the late seventeenth century, this had settled down by 1700 to 53 cwt. which it remained thereafter.

    2. *London* (or *Winchester*, or *Winton*, or *Imperial*) *chaldron*: used for the measurement of coal from the North-east in the London and south-coast trades. Like the Newcastle chaldron it had settled by 1700 normally at one-half (26.5 cwt.) of a Newcastle chaldron, though it could rise a little above this level. In 1785 it was said, for example, that the Newcastle and London chaldrons were in the proportion 15 to 8.

    3. *Scottish chaldron*: extremely variable, and could be anything between 1.5 tons and over 5 tons. At Pitfirrane colliery in Fife, for example, it was 44.5 cwt.

Corf (North-east): a measure of capacity varying between 16 and 20 pecks. In a memorandum of 1785 a 20-peck corf at Newbottle colliery was defined as measuring 34.5 inches diameter at the top, 33.5 inches at the bottom, and 26.645 inches high. (NEI Johnson 5/7.)
Dozen (Yorkshire): 30.6 cwt.

Load (Scotland): normally 2–2.5 cwt., but could be between 2.5 and 4 cwt. in Fife.

Load or *Cartload* (Staffordshire): 25 cwt. of 120 lb. = 26.8 cwt. of 112 lb.

Load (Yorkshire): 27 cwt.

Sack or *Seam* (Gloucestershire): one-eighth of a ton.

Ten (North-east): a most confusing measure which, though widely used in certain contexts in the North-east, remains of uncertain and varying size. It has often been assumed (for example, by Nef 1932, II, 377) to be ten Newcastle chaldrons, or 26.5 tons, but this is unlikely to be correct even for the early eighteenth century. At that period Ellis assumes that there were two different tens: a 'leading' ten, used for measuring coal carried by waggon, and a 'vending' ten, used mostly in leases, the latter being between five- and six-eighths of the former. (Ellis thesis 1975, 58.) One of these tens (presumably the vending ten) was accounted in 1712 to consist of 440 bolls (q.v.). (C. Bewick to W. Ramsey, 2 Dec. 1712, GPL Cotesworth CK/3/68.) By the early nineteenth century, however, north-east records speak only of one kind of ten, though it was not constant. One account sets it quite specifically at $18\frac{1}{3}$ chaldrons, or 48.58 tons. (NEI Easton 17/4/no pagination.) Another sets it at $17\frac{5}{12}$ chaldrons, or 46.2 tons. (NEI Buddle 25/III/17.) But in 1802 the ten was said to range in Tyne collieries from 418 bolls (46.15 tons) to 550 bolls (60.72 tons), and in Wear collieries from 418 bolls to 440 bolls (48.58 tons). (NEI Buddle 14/425.)

Ton: in the text and tables of this book 2,240 lb., and generally the same by the early nineteenth century in coalfield usage, but care is necessary. At Deebank colliery in Flintshire in 1817 a 'collier's ton' was defined as 30 cwt. each of 120 lb. (NEI Buddle 6/204.)

Tonne: in the tables of this book 1,000 kilogrammes.

Waggon (Cumberland): normally (possibly a *Whitehaven waggon*) 45 cwt. (CuRO Lonsdale D/Lons/W/29.) A *Workington waggon* was said in the early nineteenth century to be 44 cwt. (NEI Buddle 1/13.) On the other hand, in 1823 J. Peile, the Lowthers' agent, defined the Cumberland waggon as two-thirds of a Newcastle chaldron, or 35.33 cwt. (J. Peile to J. Buddle, 28 Mar. 1823, DuRO NCB First Deposit NCB/I/JB/1060.) A memorandum of *c.*1805 among the Buddle papers, however, assessed a Whitehaven waggon 'at the Custom House' at $1\frac{1}{4}$ London chaldrons, or 33.125 cwt. (NEI Buddle 14/196.) Wood assumed the waggon to be two tons. (Wood thesis 1952, 52–3.)

Waggon (Yorkshire): 46 cwt. (3 waggons = 2 (Yorkshire) loads.)

Weigh or *Wey* (South Wales): increased steadily during the eighteenth century. Starting in the early eighteenth century at about 5 tons, it had reached 8 tons by 1775, but was stabilized by the early nineteenth century at 10 tons. (John 1960, 189.)

Bibliography

A. *Manuscript sources*

The manuscript collections used in this study are listed below under the archives in which they are housed. Reference numbers for collections, where these have been allotted, are cited before the name of the collection.

British Library, London
    Additional manuscripts
City of Birmingham Public Library
    Boulton and Watt manuscripts
Bristol Record Office
    14581   Haynes manuscripts
    32835   Ashton Court manuscripts
Clwyd County Record Office, Hawarden
    D/E   Erddig manuscripts
County Library of South Glamorgan, Cardiff
    Miscellaneous Manuscript collections
City of Coventry Record Office
    Official Records, Diaries
    Private Accession 136
Cumbria County Record Office, Carlisle
    D/Ben   Benson manuscripts
    D/Cu   Curwen manuscripts
    D/Lec   Leconfield manuscripts (Kindly made available in the Record Office on loan from the Earl of Egremont at Cockermouth Castle)
    D/Lons   Lonsdale manuscripts
    D/Sen   Senhouse manuscripts
Derbyshire County Record Office, Derby
    1832Z   Heanor Colliery manuscripts
    517   Miller Mundy manuscripts
    2672   Pashley collection
    1000   Sitwell manuscripts
Durham County Record Office, Durham
    NCB First Deposit: NCB/I/JB Papers of John Buddle
                       NCB/I/X   Miscellaneous papers
                       NCB/I/SC Stella Coal Company papers
                       NCB/I/TH Thomas Young Hall papers
    D/Lo   Londonderry manuscripts
    D/St   Strathmore manuscripts

Gateshead Public Library
Cotesworth manuscripts
Ellison manuscripts
Gloucestershire County Record Office, Gloucester
D260   Register of Coroner's Inquests
John Rylands Library, University of Manchester
Earl of Crawford and Balcarres muniments
Kirkcaldy Museum, Fife
40/81   Rothes papers
Lambton Estate Archives, Lambton Castle, County Durham
Lambton Estate papers
Lancashire County Record Office, Preston
DDBa   Bankes of Winstanley papers
NCBw   Bridgewater Collieries Ltd. papers
DDM   Molyneux of Sefton papers
Leeds City Archives
Accession 1546
MC   Middleton Colliery manuscripts
National Library of Scotland, Edinburgh
5381   Cadell of Grange papers
              Dundas of Dundas papers
              Halkett of Pitfirrane papers
              Minto papers
227   National Union of Mineworkers, Scotland, Lanark Division, Records.
              Prestongrange Colliery (East Lothian) papers
National Library of Wales, Aberystwyth
Aberpergwm manuscripts
Badminton manuscripts
Chirk Castle manuscripts
Glynne of Hawarden manuscripts
John Lloyd manuscripts
Maybery manuscripts
Miscellaneous manuscripts
Neville, Druce & Co. (Llanelli) manuscripts
Picton Castle manuscripts
Wynnstay manuscripts
Collection 788C
North of England Institute of Mining and Mechanical Engineers, Newcastle-upon-Tyne
Bell collection
Brown collection
Buddle collection
Buddle Atkinson collection
Easton collection
Forster collection
Grand Allies collection

Johnson collection
Miscellaneous collections
Watson collection
Weeks collection
Northumberland County Records Office, Newcastle-upon-Tyne

725	Armstrong manuscripts
MBE	Benwell Manor manuscripts
ZBG	Brandling manuscripts
ZCE	Carr-Ellison manuscripts
ZDE	Delaval manuscripts
1765	Delaval (Additional) manuscripts
650	Delaval (Hastings) manuscripts
ZFO	Forster manuscripts
263	Joint Northumberland and Durham Coal Owners' Association manuscripts
QSO	Quarter Sessions manuscripts
ZRI	Ridley (Blagdon) manuscripts
ZAN	Society of Antiquaries manuscripts
ZWI	Wilson (Forest Hall) manuscripts

Collections numbered 602 and 962
Nottinghamshire County Record Office, Nottingham

DDE	Edge manuscripts
DD3–5P	Portland manuscripts

Nottingham University Library

Dr E	Drury-Lowe manuscripts
M4640–4820	Manvers manuscripts
Mi Ac	Middleton manuscripts

Scottish Record Office, Edinburgh

GD288	Balfour of Balbirnie muniments
GD224	Buccleuch muniments
GD65	Carlops and Abbotskerse muniments
GD18	Clerk of Penicuik muniments
CS96	Court of Session papers
FS	Records of the Assistant Registrar of Friendly Societies for Scotland
RH15/119	Hamilton of Pencaitland papers
GD172	Henderson of Fordell papers
GD26	Leven and Melville muniments
GD40	Lothian muniments
GD124	Mar and Kellie muniments
CB9	NCB Records (Scottish Division)
GD1/378	Waldie-Griffith muniments

Sheffield Central Library
Arundel Castle manuscripts
Local Studies Department collection
Oborne manuscripts
Newton, Chamber & Co. manuscripts

Spencer Stanhope manuscripts
Wharncliffe manuscripts
Shropshire County Record Office, Shrewsbury
1224   Lord Forester manuscripts
2280   Madeley Parish records
Somerset County Record Office, Taunton
DD/HY   Hylton manuscripts
DD/SA   Samborne manuscripts
Staffordshire County Record Office, Stafford
D603   Anglesey manuscripts
D593   Sutherland manuscripts
Tyne and Wear County Records Office, Newcastle-upon-Tyne
394   Tyne Keelmen manuscripts
Library of University College of North Wales, Bangor
(Bangor) Mostyn manuscripts
Plas Newydd manuscripts
Wakefield Metropolitan District Library, Wakefield
Goodchild loan manuscripts
Warwickshire County Record Office, Warwick
CR136   Newdigate of Arbury manuscripts
CR270 and   Newdigate (Additional) manuscripts
CR 764
CR153   Paul of Tamworth manuscripts
CR114a   Seymour of Ragley manuscripts
Wigan Record Office
CR   Coroner's Court Records for the Borough of Wigan
D/D Lei   Leigh papers

B. *Contemporary Printed Material*

ANON. (J. HOLLAND?), *The History and Description of Fossil Fuel. The Collieries and Coal Trade of Great Britain* (London, 1835).

ANON. (believed R. BALD), article on 'Mine', in *The Edinburgh Encyclopedia* (Edinburgh, 1830), Vol. 14.

ANON., *Tables and Facts relative to the Coal Duties* (London, 1819).

BAILEY, John, *General View of the Agriculture of the County of Durham* (London, 1810).

BALD, R., *A General View of the Coal Trade of Scotland* (Edinburgh, 1808).

BEAUMONT, C., *A Treatise on the Coal Trade* (London, 1789).

BUDDLE, J., *The First Report of a Society for preventing Accidents in Coal Mines, comprising a Letter to Sir Ralph Milbanke on Ventilation* (Newcastle-upon-Tyne, 1814).

COLLIERS OF THE UNITED ASSOCIATION OF DURHAM AND NORTHUM-BERLAND, *A Voice from the Coal Mines; or a Plain Statement of the Various Grievances of the Pitmen of the Tyne and Wear* (South Shields, 1825).

CURR, J., *An Account of an Improved Method of Drawing Coals and Extracting Ores, etc., from Mines* (Newcastle-upon-Tyne, 1789).

CURR, J., *The Coal Viewer and Engine Builder's Practical Companion* (Sheffield, 1797).

NINTH EARL OF DUNDONALD, *Description of the Estate, particularly of the Mineral and Coal Property . . . at Culross* (Edinburgh, 1793).

DUNN, M., *An Historical, Geological and Descriptive View of the Coal Trade of the North of England* (Newcastle-upon-Tyne, 1844).

DUNN, M., *Treatise on the Winning and Working of Collieries* (Newcastle-upon-Tyne, 1848).

EDINGTON, R., *A Treatise on the Coal Trade; with Strictures on its Abuses and Hints for Amelioration* (London, 1813).

FYNES, R., *The Miners of Northumberland and Durham: a History of their Social and Political Progress* (Blyth, 1873).

HAIR, T. H., *Sketches of the Coal Mines in Northumberland and Durham* (London, 1839).

HAIR, T. H. and ROSS, M., *A Series of Views of the Collieries in the Counties of Northumberland and Durham, with Descriptive Sketches and a Preliminary Essay on Coal and the Coal Trade* (London, 1844).

HODGSON, John, *An Account of the Explosion which killed Ninety-two Persons in Brandling Main Colliery at Felling, near Newcastle upon Tyne on May 25, 1812* (Newcastle-upon-Tyne, 1813).

HOLMES, J. H. H., *A Treatise on the Coal Mines of Durham and Northumberland with Information relative to Stratification and Accounts of Explosions from Fire-damp and Methods of Ventilation* (London, 1816).

J. C., *The Compleat Collier* (London, 1708).

JARS, Gabriel, *Voyages Métallurgiques ou Recherches et Observations sur les Mines . . . en Suède, Norvège, Angleterre et Ecosse* (3 vols., Lyons, 1774–81).

MORAND, J. F. C., *L'Art d'Exploiter les Mines de Charbon de Terre* (3 vols., no place of publication, 1768–74).

PORTER, G. R., *The Progress of the Nation* (London, 1847).

SYKES, J., *Explosions, Inundations, etc. which have taken Place in the Coal Mines of Northumberland and Durham* (Newcastle-upon-Tyne, 1830).

SYKES, J., *Local Records* (Newcastle-upon-Tyne, 1833).

C. Parliamentary Papers

Report of Committee appointed to Consider the Coal Trade, 1800 First series x.538.

Report of Select Committee on State of Coal Trade, 1800 First series x.640.

Report of Select Committee on Admeasurement of Sea Coals, 1806 (40) ii.135.

Report of Select Committee on Petitions of the Owners of Collieries in South Wales, 1810 (344) iv. 151.

Report of Select Committee on the Combination Laws, 1825 (417) iv. 409.

Report of Select Committee (of the House of Commons) on the State of the Coal Trade (in the Port of London), 1830 (663) viii. 1.

Report of Select Committee (of the House of Lords) on the State of the Coal Trade, 1830 (9) viii. 405.

Report of Select Committee on Accidents in Mines, 1835 (603) v. 1.

Report of the Select Committee on State of the Coal Trade, 1836 (522) xi. 169.
Report of Select Committee on Church Leases, 1837–8 (692) ix. 1.
Children's Employment Commission, 1842 (380) xv. 1; 1842 (381) xvi. 1.
Report of Royal Commission on Coal, 1871 (326) xxxvi. 1.

D. *Theses*

Theses the bulk of the contents of which have been published in book or article form are not included in this list. It therefore omits important theses such as those by Bulley (1952), Campbell (1977), Hopkinson (1958), Raybould (1966), Langton (1970), and Mee (1972). See Section E for the relevant published work.

ARDAYFIO, E. A., 'The development of canals in Warwickshire and their influence on the social and economic geography of the county' (Birmingham University Ph.D. 1974).
BUNKER, R. C., 'Some aspects of population growth and structure in the Warwickshire coalfield since 1800' (Birmingham University MA 1952).
COX, R. M., 'The development of the coal industry in South Yorkshire before 1830' (Sheffield University MA 1960).
CROMAR, P., 'Economic power and organisation: the development of the coal industry of Tyneside, 1700–1828' (Cambridge University Ph.D. 1976).
DAVIES, J., 'Glamorgan and the Bute Estate, 1766–1947' (University College, Swansea, Ph.D. 1969).
DAVIS, J. F., 'The Forest of Dean and Bristol-Somerset coalfields' (London University Ph.D. 1959).
ELLIS, J. M., 'A study of the business fortunes of William Cotesworth, *c.* 1668–1726' (Oxford University D.Phil. 1975).
FLETCHER, A., 'The development of management in the South Yorkshire coal mining industry, 1770–1835: a study of management at the Fitzwilliam and Norfolk collieries' (Sheffield University MA 1973).
FORSTER, R. A., 'The industrial development of the Seaton Sluice hinterland in the late 18th century' (Newcastle-upon-Tyne University MA 1948).
GOODWIN, K. W. G., 'Hammerman's Hill. The land, people and industry of the Titterstone Clee Hill area of Shropshire from the 16th to the 18th centuries' (Keele University Ph.D. 1978).
GRANT, E. G., 'The spatial development of the Warwickshire coalfield' (Birmingham University Ph.D. 1977).
GRIFFIN, A. R., 'The development of industrial relations in the Nottinghamshire coalfield' (Nottingham University Ph.D. 1963).
GRIFFIN, C. P., 'The economic and social development of the Leicestershire and South Derbyshire coalfield, 1550–1914' (Nottingham University Ph.D. 1969).
GRUFFYDD, 'The development of the coal industry in Flintshire to 1740' (University of Wales (Bangor) MA 1981).
HAIR, P. E. H., 'The social history of British coalminers, 1800–1845' (Oxford University D.Phil. 1955).
HEWITT, F. S., 'The papers of John Buddle, colliery viewer, in the Mining

Institute, Newcastle-on-Tyne. An annotated list and assessment of their value to the economic historian' (Durham University MA 1961).

HISKEY, C. E., 'John Buddle (1773–1843), agent and entrepreneur in the North-East coal trade' (Durham University M.Litt. 1978).

HUGHES, M., 'Lead, land and coal as sources of landlord income in Northumberland between 1700 and 1850' (Durham University Ph.D. 1963).

JONES, T. E., 'The industrial revolution in Monmouthshire' (University College of Wales, Cardiff, MA 1929).

KANEFSKY, J. W., 'The diffusion of power technology in British industry, 1760–1870' (Exeter University Ph.D. 1979).

KENWOOD, A. G., 'Capital investment in north-eastern England, 1800–1913' (London University Ph.D. 1962).

MILLER, S. T., 'The progressive improvement of Sunderland Harbour and the River Wear, 1717–1859' (Newcastle-upon-Tyne University MA 1978).

MOLLER, A. W. R., 'The history of English coal mining, 1500–1750' (Oxford University D.Phil. 1933).

ROBERTS, R. P., 'The history of coalmining in Gower from 1700 to 1832' (University College of Wales, Cardiff, MA 1953).

SCOTT, H., 'The History of the miners' bond in Northumberland and Durham, with special reference to its influence on industrial disputes' (Manchester University MA 1946).

SMITH, D. J., 'A study of the importance of working capital, and some of its sources, in the mining and metal industries, 1750–1830' (Sheffield University MA 1974).

SYKES, J., 'The vend of coal, 1700–1830' (Leeds University MA 1928).

THOMAS, J. D. H., 'Social and economic developments in the Upper Swansea Valley, with particular reference to the parish of Llangiwg, c.1770–c.1800' (University College of Wales, Swansea, MA 1974).

THOMSON, A. G., 'The Rothes pits, 1738–1753. A case study in the eighteenth century Scottish coal mining industry' (St. Andrews University MA 1981).

WALKER, E., 'The development of communications in Glamorgan, with special reference to the growth of industry between 1760 and 1840' (University College of Wales, Swansea, MA 1947).

WHITE, A. W. A., 'Sixty years of coalmining enterprise on the north Warwickshire estate of the Newdigates of Arbury, 1680–1740' (Birmingham University MA 1969).

WHITE, A. W. A., 'Economic growth in eighteenth century Warwickshire: a study of the rise of the Warwickshire coal industry with special reference to Sir Roger Newdigate of Arbury, estate owner and coal-master' (Birmingham University Ph.D. 1972).

WOOD, O., 'The development of the coal, iron and shipbuilding industries of West Cumberland, 1750–1914' (London University Ph.D. 1952).

E. Secondary printed works

This section includes all secondary works used in the preparation of this book and referred to only by author's name and date of publication in the notes. It

excludes detailed local works, many of which are referred to with full references
in the notes. It does not, therefore, aim to be comprehensive. For a comprehensive bibliography, see Benson, Neville, and Thompson 1981. For abbreviations
of journals, see pp. xvii–xviii.

ALLEN, J. S., 'The introduction of the Newcomen engine from 1710–1733',
 TNS 42 (1969–70); 43 (1970–1); 45 (1972–3).

ANDERSON, D., 'Blundell's collieries. The progress of the business', *THSL & C*
 116 (1965).

ANDERSON, D., 'Blundell's collieries: technical developments, 1766–1966',
 THSL & C 119 (1967).

ANDERSON, D., *The Orrell Coalfield, Lancashire, 1740–1850* (Buxton, 1975).

ANON., 'The Grand Allies', *Monthly Chronicle of North Country Lore and
 Legend* 4 (1890).

ARNOT, R. P., *A History of Scottish Miners from the Earliest Times* (London,
 1955).

ASHTON, T. S., 'The coal miners of the eighteenth century', *EH* 1 (1929).

ASHTON, T. S. and SYKES, J., *The Coal Industry of the Eighteenth Century*
 (Manchester, 1929).

ASPINALL, A. (ed.), *The Early English Trade Unions* (London, 1949).

ATKINSON, F., 'Some Northumberland collieries in 1724', *Transactions of the
 Architectural and Archaeological Society of Durham and Northumberland* 11
 (1958–65).

ATKINSON, F., *The Great Northern Coalfield, 1700–1900* (Barnard Castle,
 1966).

BANKS, A. G. and SCHOFIELD, R. B., *Brindley at Wet Earth Colliery: an
 Engineering Study* (Newton Abbot, 1968).

BARKER, T. C., 'Lancashire coal, Cheshire salt and the rise of Liverpool',
 THSL & C 103 (1951).

BARKER, T. C. and HARRIS, J. R., *A Merseyside Town in the Industrial
 Revolution: St. Helens, 1750–1900* (Liverpool, 1954).

BEASTALL, T. W., *A North Country Estate: the Lumleys and the Saundersons
 as Landowners, 1600–1900* (Chichester, 1975).

BECKETT, J. V., *Coal and Tobacco. The Lowthers and the Economic Development of West Cumberland, 1660–1760* (Cambridge, 1981).

BENSON, J., *British Coalminers in the Nineteenth Century: a Social History*
 (Dublin, 1980).

BENSON, J. and NEVILLE, R. G. (eds.), *Studies in the Yorkshire Coal Industry*
 (Manchester, 1976).

BENSON, J., NEVILLE, R. G., and THOMPSON, C. H., *Bibliography of the
 British Coal Industry* (Oxford, 1981).

BEVERIDGE, W., *Prices and Wages in England from the Twelfth to the Nineteenth Century*. Vol. I. Price Tables. Mercantile Era (London, 1939).

BLAND, F., 'John Curr, originator of iron tram roads', *TNS* 11 (1930–1).

BOYD, R. N., *Coal Pits and Pitmen: a Short History of the Coal Trade and the
 Legislation affecting it* (London, 1892).

BROWNLIE, D., 'The early history of the coal gas process', *TNS* 3 (1922–3).

BULLEY, J. A., ' "To Mendip for Coal"—a study of the Somerset coalfield before 1830', *Proceedings of the Somerset Archaeological and Natural History Society* 97 (1953); 98 (1955).

BUNNING, T. W., *An Account of the Duties on Coal and the London Coal and Wine Duties* (Newcastle, 1883).

BUXTON, N. K., *The Economic Development of the British Coal Industry* (London, 1978).

CAMPBELL, A. B., *The Lanarkshire Miners: a Social History of their Trade Unions, 1775-1874* (Edinburgh, 1979).

CAMPBELL, A. and REID, F., 'The independent collier in Scotland', in HARRISON, R. (ed.), *Independent Collier: the Coal Miner as Archetypal Proletarian Reconsidered* (Hassocks, Sussex, 1978).

CAMPBELL, R. H., *Carron Company* (Edinburgh, 1961).

CHALLINOR, R., *The Lancashire and Cheshire Miners* (Newcastle, 1972).

CHALONER, W. H., 'Salt in Cheshire, 1600-1870', *TL & CAS* 71 (1961).

CLEGG, H., 'The third Duke of Bridgewater's canal works in Manchester', *TL & CAS* 65 (1955).

CLOW, A. and N., *The Chemical Revolution* (London, 1952).

CORRIGAN, J. V., 'Strikes and the press in the north-east, 1815-44', *IRSH* 23 (1978).

COURT, W. H. B., *The Rise of the Midland Industries, 1600-1838* (Oxford, 1938).

CROMAR, P., 'The coal industry on Tyneside, 1771-1800: oligopoly and spatial change', *Economic Geography* 53 (1977).

CROMAR, P., 'The coal industry on Tyneside, 1715-50', *Northern History* 14 (1978).

CROMAR, P., 'Spatial change and economic organisation: the Tyneside coal industry (1751-1770)', *Geoforum* 10 (1979).

DANIELS, G. W. and ASHTON, T. S., 'The records of a Derbyshire colliery, 1763-1779', *EHR* 2 (1929).

DAVIES, J., *Cardiff and the Marquesses of Bute* (Cardiff, 1981).

DAVIS, R., *The Rise of the English Shipping Industry in the Seventeenth and Eighteenth Centuries* (London, 1962).

DENDY, F. S. (ed.), *The Company of Hostmen of Newcastle* (Surtees Society, Durham, Vol. 105, 1901).

DODD, A. H., *The Industrial Revolution in North Wales* (2nd edn. Cardiff, 1951).

DOUGHTY, M. W., 'Samborne Palmer's diary: technological innovation by a Somerset coal-mine owner', *IAR* 3 (1978).

DOUGLAS, R., 'Coal mining in Fife in the second half of the eighteenth century', in G. W. S. Barrow (ed.), *The Scottish Tradition* (Edinburgh, 1971).

DOWDING, W., *Durham Mines: Names and Dates of Coal Workings in County Durham* (Durham, 1972).

DUCKHAM, B. F., 'Life and labour in a Scottish colliery, 1698-1755', *Scottish Historical Review*, 47 (1968a).

DUCKHAM, B. F., 'Some eighteenth century Scottish coal mining methods: the 'Dissertation' of Sir John Clerk', *IA* 5 (1968b).

DUCKHAM, B. F., 'Early application of steam power at Scottish collieries: a note and query', *IA* 6 (1969a).

DUCKHAM, B. F., 'The emergence of the professional manager in the Scottish coal industry, 1760–1815', *Business History Review*, 43 (1969b).

DUCKHAM, B. F., 'Serfdom in eighteenth century Scotland', *History* 54 (1969c).

DUCKHAM, B. F., *A History of the Scottish Coal Industry, Vol. 1 1700–1815* (Newton Abbot, 1970).

DUCKHAM, B. F., 'English influences in the Scottish Coal industry, 1700–1815', in BUTT, J. and WARD, J. T. (eds.), *Scottish Themes* (Edinburgh, 1976).

DUCKHAM, H. and B., *Great Pit Disasters. Great Britain, 1700 to the Present Day* (Newton Abbot, 1973).

FEWSTER, J., 'The keelmen of Tyneside in the eighteenth century', *DUJ* n.s. 19 (1957).

FEWSTER, J., 'The last struggles of the Tyneside keelmen', *DUJ* n.s. 24 (1962).

FINCH, R., *Coal from Newcastle: the Story of the North East Coal Trade in the Days of Sail* (Lavenham, 1973).

FISHER, C., 'The Free Miners of the Forest of Dean, 1800–1841', in HARRISON, R. (ed.), *Independent Collier: the Coal Miner as Archetypal Proletarian Reconsidered* (Hassocks, Sussex, 1978).

FLETCHER, I., 'The archaeology of the West Cumberland coal trade', *TC & WAAS* 3 (1876–7).

FORD, P., 'Tobacco and coal: a note on the economic history of Whitehaven', *Economica* 9 (1929).

FORDYCE, W., *A History of Coal, Coke and Coal Fields and the Manufactures of Iron in the North of England* (Newcastle, 1860).

GALLOWAY, R., *A History of Coal Mining in Great Britain* (London, 1882; reprinted with Introduction by Duckham, B. F., Newton Abbot, 1969).

GALLOWAY, R., *Annals of Coal Mining and the Coal Trade* (London, 1898; reprinted with Introduction and bibliography by Duckham, B. F., Newton Abbot, 1971).

GAYER, A. D., ROSTOW, W. W., and SCHWARTZ, A. J., *The Growth and Fluctuations of the British Economy, 1790–1850* (2 vols., Oxford, 1953).

GEORGE, D. M., 'The London coal-heavers; attempts to regulate waterside labour in the eighteenth and nineteenth centuries', *EH* 1 (1926–9).

GOODCHILD, J., 'On the introduction of steam power into the West Riding', *South Yorkshire Journal of Economic and Social History* 3 (1971).

GOODCHILD, J., *The Lake Lock Rail Road* (Wakefield Metropolitan District Libraries Archives Publication No. 4 (1977)).

GOODCHILD, J., *The Coal Kings of Yorkshire* (Wakefield, 1978).

GREEN, H., 'The southern portion of the Nottinghamshire and Derbyshire coalfield and the development of transport before 1850', and 'The Nottinghamshire and Derbyshire coalfields before 1850', *Transactions of the Derbyshire Natural History and Archaeological Society*, n.s., 9–10 (1935–6).

GREEN, W., 'The chronicles and records of the northern coal trade in the counties of Durham and Northumberland', *TNEIME* 15 (1865–6).

GREENWELL, G. C., *A Glossary of Terms used in the Coal Trade of Northumberland and Durham* (Newcastle, 1849); 3rd edn. (ed. ROBERTSON, T., Newcastle, 1970).

GRIFFIN, A. R., 'Bell pits and soughs: some East Midlands examples', *IA* 6 (1969).

GRIFFIN, A. R., *Mining in the East Midlands, 1550-1947* (London, 1971).

GRIFFIN, A. R., 'The Monster subdued—the origins of the miners' safety lamp', *Colliery Guardian* 226 (1978).

GRIFFIN, A. R. and C. P., 'The role of the coal owners' associations in the East Midlands in the nineteenth century', *Renaissance and Modern Studies* 17 (1973).

GRIFFIN, C. P., 'Technological change in the Leicestershire and South Derbyshire coalfield before *c.*1850', *IAR* 3 (1978a).

GRIFFIN, C. P., 'Transport change and the development of the Leicestershire coalfield in the Canal Age: a reinterpretation', *Journal of Transport History* 4 (1978b).

HAIR, P. E. H., 'The binding of the pitmen of the North-East, 1800-1809', *DUJ* n.s. 27 (1965).

HAIR, P. E. H., 'Mortality from violence in British coal mines, 1800-50', *EHR* 2nd ser. 21 (1968).

HAIR, P. E. H., ' "*The Lancashire Collier Girl*", 1795', *THSL & C* 120 (1969).

HALL, J. W., 'Joshua Field's Diary of a Tour in 1821 through the Midlands, with introduction and notes', *TNS* 6 (1925-6).

HALL, T. Y., 'The rivers, ports and harbours of the Great Northern coal field', *TNEIME* 10 (1862).

HAMILTON, H., 'Combination in the West of Scotland coal trade, 1790-1817', *EH* 2 (1930-3).

HARDWICK, F. W. and O'SHEA, L. T., 'Notes on the history of the safety lamp', *TIME* 51 (1915-16).

HARDY, S. M., 'The development of coal mining in a North Derbyshire village, 1635-1860', *UBHJ* 5 (1955-6).

HARRIS, A., 'The Ingleton coalfield', *IA* 5 (1968).

HARRIS, J. R., 'The early steam engine on Merseyside', *THSL & C* 106 (1954).

HARRIS, J. R., 'The introduction of coal into iron smelting', *Edgar Allen News* 37 (1958).

HARRIS, J. R., 'The employment of steam power in the eighteenth century', *History* 52 (1967).

HARRIS, J. R., 'The rise of coal technology', *Scientific American* 231 (1974).

HARRIS, J. R., 'Skills, coal and British industry in the eighteenth century', *History* 61 (1976).

HART, C. E., *The Free Miners of the Royal Forest of Dean and Hundred of St Briavels* (Gloucester, 1953).

HART, C. E., *The Industrial History of Dean* (Newton Abbot, 1971).

HARTLEY, H., 'Sir Humphry Davy, Bt. FRS, 1778-1829', *Proceedings of the Royal Society of London*, Ser. A 255 (1960).

HARTLEY, H., *Humphry Davy* (London, 1966).

HASSAN, J. A., 'The supply of coal to Edinburgh, 1790-1850', *TH* 5 (1972).

HASSAN, J. A., 'The gas market and the coal industry in the Lothians in the nineteenth century', *IA* 12 (1977).

HASSAN, J. A., 'The landed estate, paternalism and the coal industry in Midlothian, 1800–80', *Scottish Historical Review* 59 (1980).

HATLEY, V. A., 'Locks, lords and coal: a study in eighteenth-century Northampton history', *Northamptonshire Past and Present* 6 (1980).

HAUSMAN, W. J., 'Size and profitability of English colliers in the eighteenth century', *Business History Review* 51 (1977a).

HAUSMAN, W. J., 'Public policy and the supply of coal to London, 1700–1770: a summary', *JEH* 37 (1977b).

HEESOM, A. J., 'Entrepreneurial paternalism: the Third Lord Londonderry (1778–1854) and the coal trade', *DUJ* n.s. 35 (1974).

HEWITT, F. S., 'An assessment of the value to the economic historian of the papers of John Buddle, colliery viewer, in the North of England Institute of Mining and Mechanical Engineers, Newcastle upon Tyne', *Mining Engineer* 25–36 (1962–3).

HILTON, G. W., *The Truck System* (Cambridge, 1960).

HINSLEY, F. B., 'The development of coal mine ventilation in Great Britain up to the end of the nineteenth century', *TNS* 42 (1969–70).

HOPKINSON, G. G., 'The development of the South Yorkshire and North Derbyshire coalfield, 1500–1775', *Transactions of the Hunter Archaeological Society* 7 (1957), reprinted in Benson and Neville 1976 (pagination from reprint).

HOPKINSON, G. G., 'The inland navigations of the Derbyshire and Nottinghamshire coalfield, 1777–1856', *Journal of the Derbyshire Archaeological and Natural History Society* 79 (1959).

HUGHES, E., *Studies in Administration and Finance, 1558–1825* (Manchester, 1934).

HUGHES, E., 'The first steam engines in the Durham coalfield', *AA* 4th ser. 27 (1949).

HUGHES, E., *North Country Life in the Eighteenth Century. Vol. 1 The North-East, 1700–50* (Oxford, 1952).

HUGHES, E., *North Country Life in the Eighteenth Century. Vol. 2 Cumberland and Westmorland, 1700–1830* (Oxford, 1965).

HUGHES, W. M., 'Economic development in the eighteenth and nineteenth centuries', in DEWDNEY, J. C. (ed.), *Durham County and City with Teesside* (British Association, Durham, 1970).

HUMBLE, A. F., 'An old Whitby collier', *The Mariner's Mirror* 61 (1975).

JACKMAN, W. T., *The Development of Transportation in Modern England* (2nd edn. London, 1962).

JACKSON, J. H., 'Notes on early mining in Staffordshire and Worcestershire', *TIME* 27 (1903–4).

JENKINS, R., 'Coke: a note on its production and use, 1587–1650', *TNS* 12 (1931–2).

JOHN, A. H., 'Iron and coal on a Glamorgan estate, 1700–1740', *EHR* 13 (1943).

JOHN, A. H., *The Industrial Development of South Wales* (Cardiff, 1950).

KANEFSKY, J. and ROBEY, J., 'Steam engines in 18th-century Britain: a quantitative assessment', *Technology and Culture* 21 (1980).

LANGTON, J., 'Coal output in south-west Lancashire, 1590-1799', *EHR* 2nd ser. 25 (1972).

LANGTON, J., *Geographical Change and Industrial Revolution. Coalmining in South West Lancashire, 1590-1799* (Cambridge, 1979).

LEBON, J. H. G., 'The development of the Ayrshire coalfield', *Scottish Geographical Magazine* 49 (1933).

LEE, C. E., 'The first steam railway. Brandling's colliery line between Leeds and Middleton', *Railway Magazine* 81 (1937).

LEE, C. E., 'The world's oldest railway. 300 years of coal conveyance to the Tyne staiths', *TNS* 25 (1945-7).

LEE, C. E., 'Tyneside tramroads of Northumberland', *TNS* 26 (1948-9).

LEE, C. E., 'The waggonways of Tyneside', *AA* 4th ser. 29 (1951).

LERRY, G. G., *The Collieries of Denbighshire—Past and Present* (Wrexham, 1946; 2nd edn. Wrexham, 1968).

LEWIS, E. D., *The Rhondda Valleys: a Study in Industrial Development, 1800 to the Present Day* (London, 1959).

LEWIS, M. J. T., *Early Wooden Railways* (London, 1970).

LONES, T. L., 'The south Staffordshire and north Worcester mining district and its relics of mining appliances', *TNS* 11 (1930-1).

LOUIS, H., 'The pitman's yearly bond', *TIME* 79 (1929-30).

LOUIS, H., 'Early steam engines in the North of England', *TIME* 82 (1931-2).

McCORD, N., 'Tyneside discontents and Peterloo', *Northern History* 2 (1967).

McCORD, N., 'The seamen's strike of 1815 in North-East England', *EHR* 2nd ser. 21 (1968).

McCORD, N., *North-East England. An Economic and Social History* (London, 1979).

MACFARLAN, J., 'George Dixon: discoverer of gas-light from coal', *TNS* 5 (1924-5).

MACHIN, F., *The Yorkshire Miners. A History*. Vol. 1 (Barnsley, 1958).

McKECHNIE, J. and MACGREGOR, N., *A Short History of the Scottish Coal Mining Industry* (Edinburgh, 1958).

MALET, H., *Bridgewater. The Canal Duke, 1736-1803* (Manchester, 1977).

MARTIN, J., 'Private enterprise versus manorial rights: mineral property disputes in eighteenth-century Glamorgan', *Welsh History Review* 9 (1978).

MEE, G., *Aristocratic Enterprise. The Fitzwilliam Industrial Undertakings, 1795-1857* (Glasgow and London, 1975).

MEE, G., 'Employer: employee relationships in the Industrial Revolution: the Fitzwilliam collieries', in POLLARD, S. and HOLMES, C. (eds.), *Essays in the Economic and Social History of South Yorkshire* (Sheffield, 1976).

METCALFE, W. S., 'The history of the keelmen and their strike of 1822', *AA* 4th ser. 14 (1937).

MILNE, M., 'Strikes and strike-breaking in north-east England, 1815-44: the attitude of the local press', *IRSH* 22 (1977).

MINING ASSOCIATION OF GREAT BRITAIN, *Historical Review of Coal Mining* (London, n.d. but probably 1926).

MITCHELL, B. R. and DEANE, P., *Abstract of British Historical Statistics* (Cambridge, 1962).

MITCHESON, J. C., 'The East Warwickshire coalfield', in THE BRITISH ASSOCIATION, *Birmingham and its Regional Setting. A Scientific Survey* (Birmingham, 1950).

MOORE, R. W., 'Historical sketch of the Whitehaven collieries', *TIME* 7 (1893–4).

MORGAN, J. R., 'The search for a safety lamp in mines', *Annals of Science* 1 (1936).

MOTT, R. A., 'The Newcastle coal trade', *Colliery Guardian* 204 (1962).

MOTT, R. A., 'The Newcomen engine in the eighteenth century', *TNS* 35 (1962-3).

MOTT, R. A., 'English waggonways of the eighteenth century', *TNS* 37 (1964-5).

MOTT, R. A., 'Tramroads of the eighteenth century and their originator, John Curr', *TNS* 42 (1969-70).

MULLINEUX, F., *The Duke of Bridgewater's Canal* (Eccles and District Local History Society, 1959).

MULLINEUX, F., 'The Duke of Bridgewater's underground canals at Worsley', *TL & CAS* 71 (1961).

MUSSON, A. E. and ROBINSON, E., 'The early growth of steam power', *EHR* 2nd ser. 11 (1959).

MUSSON, A. E. and ROBINSON, E., *Science and Technology in the Industrial Revolution* (Manchester, 1969).

NEF, J. U., *The Rise of the British Coal Industry* (2 vols. London, 1932).

OSBORNE, R. S., 'Common lands, mineral rights and industry: changing evaluations in an industrializing society', *Journal of Historical Geography* 4 (1978).

PAYNE, P. L., 'The Govan collieries, 1804–5', *Business History* 3 (1961).

PAYNE, P. L., 'The Halbeath colliery and salt works, 1785-1791', forthcoming.

PHILLIPS, M., 'Early mining records of the district', *Transactions of the Aberafan and Margam District Historical Society* 4 (1931-2).

POLLARD, S., 'A new estimate of British coal production, 1750-1850', *EHR* 2nd ser. 33 (1980).

PREVOST, W. A. J., ' "A trip to Whitehaven to visit the Coalworks there in 1739" by Sir John Clerk', *TC & WAAS* 65 (1965).

RAISTRICK, A., 'The steam engine on Tyneside, 1715-1778', *TNS* 17 (1936-7).

RAISTRICK, A., 'The development of the Tyne coal basin', *TIME* 113 (1953-4).

RAISTRICK, A. (ed.), *The Hatchett Diary: a Tour through the Counties of England and Scotland in 1796 visiting their Mines and Manufactories* (Truro, 1967).

RAWSON, R. R., 'The coal-mining industry of the Hawarden district on the eve of the Industrial Revolution', *Archaeologia Cambrensis* 96 (1941).

RAYBOULD, T. J., 'The development and organization of Lord Dudley's mineral estates', *EHR* 2nd ser. 21 (1968).

RAYBOULD, T. J., *The Economic Emergence of the Black Country* (Newton Abbot, 1973).

RHODES, J. N., 'Early steam engines in Flintshire', *TNS* 41 (1968-9).

RICHARDS, E., 'The industrial face of a great estate: Trentham and Lilleshall, 1780-1860', *EHR* 2nd ser. 27 (1974).

RIMMER, W. G., 'Middleton colliery, near Leeds (1770–1830)', *Yorkshire Bulletin of Economic and Social Research* 7 (1955).

ROBERTSON, T. (ed.), *A Pitman's Notebook: the Diary of Edward Smith, Houghton Colliery Viewer, 1749* (Newcastle, 1970).

ROGERS, E., 'The history of trade unionism in the coal mining industry of North Wales to 1914', *Denbighshire Historical Society Transactions* 12 (1963).

ROLT, L. T. C., *George and Robert Stephenson. The Railway Revolution* (London, 1960).

ROLT, L. T. C. and ALLEN, J. S., *The Steam Engine of Thomas Newcomen* (Hartington, 1977).

ROSEN, G., *The History of Miners' Diseases* (New York, 1943).

ROWE, D. J., 'The strikes of the Tyneside keelmen in 1809 and 1819', *IRSH* 13 (1968).

ROWE, D. J., 'The decline of the Tyneside keelmen in the nineteenth century', *Northern History* 4 (1969).

ROWLANDS, M. B., 'Stonier Parrott and the Newcomen engine', *TNS* 41 (1968–9).

SCHUMPETER, E. B., *English Overseas Trade Statistics, 1697–1808* (Oxford, 1960).

SILL, M., 'Landownership and the landscape: a study of the evolution of the colliery landscape of Hetton-le-Hole, Co. Durham', *Durham County Local History Society* 23 (1979).

SKEMPTON, A. W., 'William Chapman (1749–1832), civil engineer', *TNS* 46 (1973–4).

SLATCHER, W. N., 'The Barnsley Canal: its first twenty years', *Transport History* 1 (1968).

SMAILES, A. E., 'The development of the Northumberland and Durham coal field', *Scottish Geographical Magazine* 51 (1935).

SMITH, A., 'A brief history of coalmining in Warwickshire', *TIME* 34 (1908).

SMITH, Alan, 'Steam and the City: the Committee of Proprietors of the Invention for Raising Water by Fire, 1715–1735', *TNS* 49 (1977–8).

SMITH, R., *Sea Coal for London. History of the Coal Factors in the London Market* (London, 1961).

SMOUT, T. C., 'The Erskines of Mar and the development of Alloa, 1689–1825', *Scottish Studies* 7 (1963).

SORBY, E., 'Coal mining near Sheffield from 1773 to 1820', *TIME* 65 (1923).

STEPHENS, F., 'The activities of John Gorrell Barnes: evidence from the Barnes family papers', *Transactions of the Hunter Archaeological Society* 10 (1977).

STURGESS, R. W., *Aristocrat in Business. The Third Marquis of Londonderry as Coalowner and Portbuilder* (Durham County Local History Society, 1975).

SWEEZY, P. M., *Monopoly and Competition in the English Coal Trade, 1550–1850* (Cambridge, Mass., 1938).

SYMONS, M. V., *Coal-Mining in the Llanelli Area, Vol. I. 16th Century to 1829* (Llanelli, 1979).

TAYLOR, A. J., 'The sub-contract system in the British coal industry', in

PRESSNELL, L. S. (ed.), *Studies in the Industrial Revolution* (London, 1960).

THOMAS, Brinley, 'Towards an energy interpretation of the Industrial Revolution', *Atlantic Economic Journal* 8 (1980).

THOMAS, W. G., 'The coal mining industry in West Glamorgan', *Glamorgan Historian* 6 (1969).

TOMLINSON, W. W., *North Eastern Railway. Its Rise and Development* (Newcastle, 1914; 2nd edn. Newton Abbot, 1967).

TRINDER, B., *The Industrial Revolution in Shropshire* (Chichester, 1973).

TROTT, C. D. J., 'Coal mining in the Borough of Neath in the seventeenth and early eighteenth century', *Morgannwg* 13 (1969).

TUNZELMANN, G. N. von, *Steam Power and British Industrialization to 1860* (Oxford, 1978).

TURNER, E. R., 'The keelmen of Newcastle', *American Historical Review* 21 (1915–16).

TURNER, E. R., 'English coal industry in the seventeenth and eighteenth centuries', *American Historical Review* 27 (1921-2).

VICTORIA COUNTY HISTORIES of CUMBERLAND, DERBYSHIRE, DURHAM, GLOUCESTERSHIRE, LANCASHIRE, LEICESTERSHIRE, SOMERSET, STAFFORDSHIRE, WARWICKSHIRE, and WORCESTERSHIRE.

VILLE, S., 'James Kirton, Shipping agent', *The Mariner's Mirror* 67 (1981).

WADSWORTH, A. P., 'The history of coal mining in Rochdale district', *Transactions of the Rochdale Literary and Scientific Society* 23 (1949).

WEBB, S., *The Story of the Durham Miners (1622-1921)* (London, 1921).

WELBOURNE, E., *The Miners' Unions of Northumberland and Durham* (Cambridge, 1923).

WELFORD, R. and HODGSON, J. C., 'Biographies of contributors to the Society's literature: John Buddle, F.G.S.', *AA* 3rd ser. 10 (1913).

WESTERFIELD, R. B., *Middlemen in English Business, particularly between 1660 and 1760* (New Haven, Conn., 1915).

WESTWATER, R., 'History of the explosives industry in Scotland', *TIME* 124 (1965).

WHATLEY, C. A., 'The introduction of the Newcomen engine to Ayrshire', *IAR* 2 (1977).

WHITE, A. W. A., 'Early Newcomen engines on the Warwickshire coalfield, 1714-1736', *TNS* 41 (1968-9).

WHITE, A. W. A., 'The condition of mining labour on a Warwickshire estate before the Industrial Revolution', *Transactions of the Birmingham and Warwickshire Archaeological Society* 84 (1967-70).

WHITE, A. W. A., 'Warwickshire coal mining in the eighteenth century', *Mining Engineer* 129 (1969-70).

WHITE, A. W. A., 'A Warwickshire colliery during the Industrial Revolution', *Warwickshire History* 2 (1973).

WIGAN PUBLIC LIBRARIES, *Jubilee Exhibition of Early Mining Literature: An Annotated Catalogue* (Wigan, 1928).

WILKINS, C., *The South Wales Coal Trade and its Allied Industries from the Earliest Days to the Present Time* (Cardiff, 1888).

WILLAN, T. S., *The English Coasting Trade, 1600–1750* (Manchester, 1938).

WILLAN, T. S., *River Navigation in England, 1600–1750* (2nd edn. London, 1964).

WILLIAMS, D. T., 'The Port Books of Swansea and Neath, 1709–1719', *Archaeologia Cambrensis* 95 (1940).

WILLIAMS, J. H., *The Derbyshire Miners: A Study in Industrial and Social History* (London, 1962).

WILLIAMS, M., 'Early coal working in Clyne Valley', *Gower* 11 (1958).

WILSON, G., 'Day-level drainage in eighteenth century Fife coal mines', *Scottish Industrial History* 2 (1978).

WOOD, A. C., 'The history of trade and transport on the River Trent', *Transactions of the Thoroton Society* 44 (1950).

WOOD, N., 'Address on the two late eminent engineers, the Messrs. Stephenson, father and son', *TNEIME* 8 (1859–60).

WOOD, O., 'A Cumberland colliery during the Napoleonic War', *Economica* n.s. 21 (1954).

WOOD, O., 'The collieries of J. C. Curwen', *TC & WAAS* n.s. 71 (1971).

WOOD, O., 'A colliery payroll in 1802', *TC & WAAS* n.s. 72 (1972).

Index